Economic Commission for Europe

ECONOMIC SURVEY

OF EUROPE IN 1990-1991

Prepared by the

SECRETARIAT OF THE

ECONOMIC COMMISSION FOR EUROPE

GENEVA

UNITED NATIONS PUBLICATION

Sales No. E.91.II.E.1

ISBN 92-1-116508-3

ISSN 0070-8712

NEW YORK, 1991

NOTE

The designations employed and the presentation of the material in this publication do not imply the expression of any opinion whatsoever on the part of the Secretariat of the United Nations concerning the legal status of any country, territory, city or area, or of its authorities, or concerning the delimitation of its frontiers or boundaries.

UNITED NATIONS PUBLICATION
Sales No. E.91.II.E.1
ISBN 92-1-116508-3 ISSN 0070-8712

08000P

PREFACE

The present *Survey* is the forty-fourth in a series of reports prepared by the secretariat of the Economic Commission for Europe to serve the needs of the Commission and to help in reporting on world economic conditions.

The *Survey* is published on the responsibility of the secretariat, and the views expressed in it should not be attributed to the Commission or to its participating Governments.

The pre-publication text of this *Survey* was completed in early March 1991 as a document for the 46th session of the Economic Commission for Europe. The final text, incorporating minor changes, was completed on 19 April 1991.

EXPLANATORY NOTES

The following symbols have been used throughout this *Survey*:

A dash (-) indicates nil or negligible;

Two dots (..) indicate not available or not pertinent;

An asterisk (*) indicates an estimate by the secretariat of the Economic Commission for Europe;

A slash (/) indicates a crop year or financial year (e.g., 1990/91);

Use of a hyphen (-) between dates representing years, for example, 1989-1991, signifies the full period involved, including the beginning and end years.

Unless the contrary is stated, the standard unit of weight used throughout is the metric ton.

The term "billion" signifies a thousand million.

References to dollars ($) are to United States dollars unless otherwise stated.

The following abbreviations have been used:

CMEA	Council for Mutual Economic Assistance
ECE	Economic Commission for Europe
EEC	European Economic Community
FAO	Food and Agriculture Organization of the United Nations
GDP	Gross domestic product
GNP	Gross national product
GSP	Gross social product
IMF	International Monetary Fund
NMP	Net material product
OECD	Organization for Economic Co-operation and Development
OPEC	Organization of the Petroleum Exporting Countries
SDR	Special drawing rights

CONTENTS

CHAPTER 1

The transition economies in 1990-1991: an overview

CHAPTER 2

Macro-economic developments and outlook

CHAPTER 3

International economic relations

The hard road to the market economy: problems and policies

Explaining unemployment in the market economies: theories and evidence

Statistical appendices

LIST OF TABLES AND CHARTS

Chapter 3

Table

Chart

Chapter 4

Table

Chapter 5

Table

Chart

Statistical Appendices

Appendix A. Western Europe and North America

Appendix table

Appendix B. Eastern Europe and the Soviet Union

Appendix C. International trade and payments

EVALUATION QUESTIONNAIRE

In order to improve the quality and relevance of the work of the Economic Commission for Europe, it would be useful to receive the views of readers on this publication.

PUBLICATION TITLE: ECONOMIC SURVEY OF EUROPE IN 1990-1991

1. Name and address of respondent (optional):

   _____

   _____

2. In which country do you work? _____

3. Which of the following best describes your area of work?

Government	☐	Public enterprise	☐
Private enterprise	☐	Academic or research institution	☐
International organization	☐	Media	☐
Non-profit organization	☐	Other (specify) _____	

   _____

4. Is this publication:

Read by recipient only?	☐	Circulated among colleagues?	☐
Filed for reference	☐	Deposited in library?	☐
		Other (specify) _____	

   _____

5. What is your assessment of the contents of this publication?

Very Good	☐	Adequate	☐
Good	☐	Poor	☐

6. How useful is this publication to your work?

   Very useful ☐   Of some use ☐   Irrelevant ☐

7. What aspects of this publication do you find most useful?

   _____

   _____

   _____

   _____

   _____

../..

8. Please indicate what you would like to see changed as regards the content and the presentation of this publication:

_____

_____

_____

_____

_____

9. What is your substantive judgement of this publication relative to your professional occupation - governmental, research, business, teaching or other?

_____

_____

_____

_____

_____

_____

10. Would you like to continue to receive/buy this publication?

Yes [ ]   No [ ]

It would be greatly appreciated if you could complete this questionnaire and return it to:

Evaluation Officer
Administrative Unit
Office of the Executive Secretary
Economic Commission for Europe
Palais des Nations
CH-1211 Geneva

Chapter 1

THE TRANSITION ECONOMIES IN 1990-1991: AN OVERVIEW

Hard realities emerge ...

The euphoria which followed the revolutionary political changes in most of eastern Europe and the Soviet Union in 1989 has now given way to a more sober appreciation of the economic and political problems of these countries. The transformation of centrally planned into decentralized market economies is now seen more clearly as a task of enormous complexity which cannot be accomplished by a quick transfusion of technology and technicians from the west. In the past year a diversity of approaches has emerged in the reforming countries,[1] a reflection in part of the different initial circumstances of each country but also of a lack of consensus as to the most appropriate or optimal path of transformation.

This reappraisal has been especially marked in Germany where the problems and costs of unification have escalated steadily throughout the past year. It is now accepted that the restructuring of the economy of the former German Democratic Republic will take much longer than was envisaged in the period between the collapse of the Berlin wall and the formal acts of unification. The transformation of the eastern economy will be a major preoccupation of German economic policy for several years to come and, as such, the transition process will have an important influence on economic developments in the rest of Europe. The German experience has also been a salutary one for other reforming countries in eastern Europe: the former German Democratic Republic had for a long time been regarded as the one centrally planned economy which had been successful in combining relatively high standards of living with advanced levels of technical efficiency in production. Its rapid collapse in the face of market forces, despite massive levels of support from the Federal government, has led not only to a revision of previous

perceptions but also, in some countries, to greater caution about the possibilities of a "big bang" approach to economic restructuring.

Considerable progress towards the establishment of a market economy has already been made in Poland, Hungary and, to a lesser extent, in Czechoslovakia. But elsewhere, progress has been slow and, in some cases, blocked either by the lack of political consensus on the objectives or profile of reform or, more fundamentally, on the domain of central government authority.[2] Thus, in the Soviet Union and Yugoslavia, the political struggle over the distribution of power between the Federal government and the constituent republics of each country has not only prevented the implementation of coherent programmes of economic reform but has also blocked the adoption of effective measures to deal with acute stabilization problems. Unwilling to return to the *status quo ex ante*, unable to move decisively onto a path of coherent reform, and incapable of confronting growing macro-economic imbalances, these countries are drifting further into economic disarray and political instability. Disagreements over the extent of Federal government authority also exist in Czechoslovakia but, at least so far, they have not had the same disruptive consequences for the economy as in the two previously mentioned countries.

Slow-down in the west ...

When the eastern countries embarked on programmes of radical transformation of their economies, they did so in a context of sustained growth in the market economies of the west. Poland and Hungary were able to take advantage of this favourable climate to boost considerably their exports to the west in 1990. Although after eight years of uninterrupted growth some slow-down was inevitable, up to the middle of

---

1 For a discussion on reforms in individual countries, see chapter 4 below.

2 Progress − or the lack of it − in the transition process in 1990 is reviewed in detail in chapter 4 of this *Survey*.

last year most forecasts for western Europe were still pointing to only a slight deceleration in the rate of expansion. However, the Gulf crisis led to a sharp fall in business and consumer confidence in the latter half of 1990 and this undoubtedly intensified the downturn which accelerated sharply in the last quarter of the year.[3] Growth in the western market economies, and the world economy as a whole, is now expected to weaken further in 1991. In western Europe average GDP growth is likely to fall below 2 per cent for the first time since 1983. The German economy remains much stronger than the average but, nevertheless, is also expected to slow down. Most of the standard forecasts envisage a recovery in western Europe getting under way in the second half of this year and in the United States from mid-year. The speedy end to hostilities in the Gulf and the possibility of weak oil prices speak in favour of this outcome. But many special features of the current downturn, in particular the high levels of corporate and personal indebtedness in some countries and the prospect of highly cautious lending policies being followed by the commercial banks, suggest that the recovery could be slower than expected. Thus average growth in western Europe and North America this year could fall to around 1 per cent with a stronger upturn — of around 2½ per cent — being delayed until 1992.

Much of the deterioration in business and consumer confidence in the western economies is cyclical (and therefore "normal") in character, although it was clearly aggravated by the months of uncertainty which followed Iraq's invasion of Kuwait last August. Nevertheless, there is, at least in Europe, a vague uneasiness that the weakening of confidence may not be entirely due to these two factors. Within the European Community, an earlier consensus on plans for monetary union has weakened somewhat in the light of problems which have emerged in the last year or so, not least the increased economic divergence between Germany and the rest of the community: the objective remains but its achievement may now prove more difficult and take longer than was previously hoped. The Uruguay Round of trade negotiations was supposed to have been concluded in December 1990. In spite of fundamental differences in negotiating positions, a breakdown has so far been avoided. The negotiations should resume in the course of this year; however, major problems remain to be solved and the possibility of failure carries considerable risks for the longer run development of the world economy. Not only would failure send the "wrong signals" from the developed market economies to both the eastern economies in transition and the developing countries, it would also reinforce the tendency toward regional trading blocks and undermine attempts to restore the rule-based multilateralism that has been a major support of the post-war expansion in international trade. The prospect of trade conflicts and unilateral retaliatory action among the highly interdependent market economies of the west is unlikely to boost business confidence.

For all these reasons Europe now appears to be a much more difficult and complicated place than it did a year ago, and for the eastern economies there has been a clear deterioration in their external environment. However, although this might dampen confidence for a while, it could prove to be a positive development if it means that much of the facile optimism of late 1989 and early 1990 is replaced by carefully constructed policies designed to deal with the highly complex problems of transformation in the east.

... and deep recession in the east

The recession in eastern Europe and the Soviet Union, which was already under way in a number of countries towards the end of 1989, spread throughout the region and deepened considerably in 1990. Net material product (NMP) fell, on average, by 11 per cent in eastern Europe and by 4 per cent in the Soviet Union. In Yugoslavia gross material product declined by more than 7½ per cent.

The recession was general but its severity varied considerably from one country to another: the fall in output ranged from 3-5½ per cent in Czechoslovakia, Hungary and the Soviet Union, to more than 10 per cent in Bulgaria, Poland and Romania. In the former German Democratic Republic output declined by nearly 20 per cent.

Although its extent varied, the decline affected all sectors of the economy. In most of the eastern countries industrial production fell more than net material product, by 18 per cent on average in eastern Europe, although by only 1.2 per cent in the Soviet Union. The Soviet figure seems rather low in the light of the reduced availability of supplies and reports of widespread strikes and other disruptions in working time: given the problems with Soviet production figures, it is quite possible that the actual fall was larger than shown by the official statistics. However, there is also evidence of large increases in the inventories of enterprises and this could explain part of the discrepancy between the production figures and the availability of supplies.

Agricultural output also fell in all the eastern countries, by 3½ per cent in eastern Europe (excluding the former German Democratic Republic) and over 2 per cent in the Soviet Union.[4] In fact, 1990 was the worst year for agriculture in the last decade. There was also a general decline in construction activity, ranging from 2 per cent in Hungary to 28 per cent in Romania.

Reforms and stabilization hit eastern output ...

It was not to be expected that the transformation of the former centrally planned economies could be achieved without severe cuts in the levels of aggregate output. In the first place some of the eastern countries introduced severe stabilization measures to curtail accelerating inflation and burgeoning budget deficits, to

---

3   The western economies are discussed in section 2.1.

4   However, about a quarter of the Soviet grain harvest was lost because of inefficiencies in collection, transport and storage.

establish some measure of control over monetary aggregates and, in some cases, to reduce the excess purchasing power immanent in the monetary overhang. Stabilization is a necessary adjunct to the distinct process of setting up a market economy which requires radical changes in the institutions and rules which provide the framework for decentralized economic decision-making. This transformation process cannot be completed quickly and, therefore, is likely to intensify and prolong any recession arising from stabilization *per se*. After all, the point of structural change is to ensure that not all of what goes down comes up again and that defunct enterprises are replaced by new ones.

However not all the countries in the east are following a coherent programme of stabilization and transformation. Although the slump in east European output is general, an important distinction must be made between those countries, such as Poland, Hungary and Czechoslovakia, where a stabilization-cum-adjustment recession is occurring within a coherent framework of policies and targets, and those where the deterioration reflects a loss of central control and the absence of coherent alternatives. The Soviet Union, Bulgaria and Romania fall into the latter group, although considerable efforts were being made in Romania in the latter half of 1990 to develop a framework for radical reform. In Yugoslavia the Federal government had a clear programme for reform at the end of 1989 but its failure to maintain central control over monetary and fiscal policy in 1990 places the country in the second group.

The differences between these two groups is reflected in the development of domestic absorption in 1990. Poland and Hungary squeezed domestic demand and shifted resources into the external sector with a significant improvement in exports to the west. Czechoslovakia is following more or less the same course from January 1991. However, in Romania, the Soviet Union and Yugoslavia private consumption was sustained at the cost of a marked deterioration in external and internal imbalances, thereby making the task of stabilization in 1991 even more difficult.

Nevertheless, the fall in output last year was still much greater than expected. There are a number of reasons for this, the importance of which varied from country to country but some of which were common to all. First, the old command system of the centrally planned economy generally collapsed much faster than anticipated and certainly much faster than the new institutions and practices of a market economy could be put into place. This has led to considerable disruption in those countries where no coherent alternative to the central planning system was being implemented: in the Soviet Union, Bulgaria and Romania economic life fell between two régimes.

... but external factors made matters worse

A second major influence on eastern output levels in 1990 was the effective disintegration of the system of trade and payments among the European members of the CMEA. It was known from the start of 1990

that the traditional system of negotiated trade agreements and settlement in "transferable" roubles was coming to an end and by mid-year it had been decided that from January 1991 the mutual trade of CMEA countries would be based on free market relations and settlement at world market prices in convertible currency. However, it was left unclear as to how outstanding claims and liabilities in "transferable" roubles would be settled at the end of the year. All the eastern countries therefore had an incentive to minimize outstanding rouble balances and to achieve this there was widespread resort to direct controls on their mutual trade.

The decline in CMEA trade was also exacerbated by the unexpectedly fast pace of German unification, which led to a very large fall of imports into the former German Democratic Republic from eastern Europe, and by disruptions in Soviet energy supplies to the eastern countries.

Altogether trade among the east European countries fell by about 20 per cent in volume in 1990, while the volume of trade between eastern Europe and the Soviet Union, more than half of which consists of fuels, dropped by some 13-15 per cent.

It is significant that the three countries which were able to offset part of this collapse in intra-eastern trade by boosting exports to the west were those where stabilization and structural reforms have made most progress, namely, Poland, Hungary and, to a lesser extent, Czechoslovakia. Their exports of manufactures to the west were particularly dynamic. It is too early for a detailed analysis of this performance, but it is clear that, driven by the fall in domestic and CMEA demand, exporters were able and willing to take advantage of the decentralization of economic decision-making and the liberalization of foreign trade procedures. In contrast, exports to the west from Bulgaria, Romania and, to a lesser extent, the Soviet Union were held back by supply constraints. In Yugoslavia export growth was less than half its rate in 1989.

However, the disruption in energy supplies was an important constraint on eastern output growth in 1990 and is one which is unlikely to be overcome quickly. Coal is the principal source of indigenous primary energy in eastern Europe, but reductions in output and consumption are necessary for pressing environmental reasons. Under the CMEA, eastern Europe became highly dependent on the Soviet Union for oil and gas supplies but these were affected in 1990 not only by cuts in Soviet output but also by failures in transmission systems. Altogether Soviet energy supplies to eastern Europe in 1990 were more than 20 per cent less than agreed. Since the eastern infrastructure for the transmission of energy was originally set up as an intra-CMEA system, it is difficult for east European countries to switch rapidly to alternative sources of supply.

Imports of energy from the Soviet Union are now paid for in convertible currency at world market prices. Since the intra-CMEA price in "transferable" roubles in 1989 was reckoned to be equivalent to about $7 a barrel,[5] the switch amounts to a considerable oil price shock for the eastern countries − although it is now rather smaller than was feared last October. Nevertheless, the higher price of oil reduces the economically viable capital stock in eastern Europe, which is already being diminished by the introduction of market prices.[6]

Given the appallingly low levels of energy efficiency in eastern Europe, considerable savings are possible through energy conservation. However, insofar as energy inefficiency is built into the existing capital stock, energy conservation is closely linked to the recovery of fixed investment as well as to the broader programmes of reform designed to improve price signals and market incentives for energy saving. Significant gains in energy efficiency are likely to emerge only in the longer run: in the short term, economic developments in eastern Europe will continue to be at risk from reductions and irregularities in the supply of oil, gas and electricity from the Soviet Union.

Investment has fallen ...

Investment, in both fixed assets and in human capital, is the principal instrument of structural change and economic transformation. It has recently been defined[7] as the cost of changing economic arrangements, a useful and apposite definition for the "transition economies" of eastern Europe and the Soviet Union. However, there are, as yet, no signs of an upsurge in investment in the eastern countries. In 1990 there was a general decline in gross fixed investment: it fell on average by 14 per cent in eastern Europe and by some 4 per cent in the Soviet Union where a still larger decline of 14 per cent is anticipated in 1991. There was in fact a small increase in Czechoslovakia but elsewhere the falls were large, ranging from 7 per cent in Yugoslavia to 35 per cent in Romania.

Given the slump in fixed investment it is obviously premature to expect to find clear evidence of structural change in the eastern economies. Nevertheless some tentative indications may be noted from the evidence of which sectors have survived the shake-out of recession better than others. The shift of resources to the external sector in Hungary and Poland has already been noted, and especially the marked improvement in exports of manufactures to the west. How far this reflects special (once-for-all) factors rather than a better exploitation of comparative advantage and an improvement in underlying competitiveness is impossible to say at the present time. Nevertheless it is an encouraging development and refutes the popular view that eastern industry is incapable of producing any manufactured goods of a quality which can be sold on western markets.[8]

Changes in the detailed structure of national output in the east are difficult to observe with any precision because of data limitations. Nevertheless, it does appear that there was a significant shift to services in 1990, either because they continued to grow or because they fell less than NMP. Again it is too early to draw any firm conclusions from this: the relative growth performance of services and goods is roughly what one would expect during a recession. Nevertheless, the service sector is one where there has been a rapid expansion of private enterprise and this is known to be underestimated in the official statistics.

There is also scattered evidence of the growing role of the private sector in the production of goods. In Hungary, industrial output in small companies, which are mostly private, more than doubled in 1990. In Poland, gross value added in the private material sector increased by 17 per cent whereas in the socialized sector it fell by 21 per cent. Also in Poland, the average level of job vacancies increased in 1990 at the same time as unemployment rose dramatically: this may be evidence of increasing demand for labour in the private sector.

Although these are positive signs of structural change they should not be exaggerated. The collapse of investment, the surprisingly small number of bankruptcies, and the relatively small increases in unemployment, given the large falls in output, all suggest that the major restructuring effort is still to come.

... unemployment is rising ...

The "transition economies" are bound to experience high levels of unemployment for at least two reasons. First, the implementation of tough stabilization policies will lead to short-run falls in aggregate output and employment. Second, the transition from centrally planned to market economy will inevitably lead to the elimination of overmanning ("hidden" unemployment) in some sectors and the disappearance of enterprises which will not be viable in a situation of hard budget constraints and market determined prices.

Although there are many problems with the statistics,[9] there is no doubt that unemployment has risen sharply in the eastern countries. In December 1990 the total number of persons unemployed in eastern Europe was probably over 3½ million with a further 2 million in the Soviet Union. However with the exceptions of Poland, the former German Democratic Republic and Yugoslavia, unemployment rates were still below 2 per cent of the labour force. All the transition economies expect large increases in unemployment in 1991: excluding Yugoslavia, the number of unemployed in eastern Europe is likely to exceed 4 million with another 5.3 million in the Soviet Union. Unemployment

---

5   See United Nations Economic Commission for Europe, *Economic Bulletin for Europe*, vol.42/90, New York, 1991.

6   For an analysis of the effects of oil price shocks on output and the capital stock in western market economies, see United Nations Economic Commission for Europe, *Economic Survey of Europe in 1983*, New York, 1984 pp.55-69.

7   Maurice Fitzgerald Scott, *A New View of Economic Growth*, Clarendon Press: Oxford, 1989.

8   The export performance of these countries is discussed in chapter 3.

9   See section 2.2(iv) below and box 2.2.1.

rates would then range between some 4 per cent in Romania and the Soviet Union to 15 per cent in the former German Democratic Republic, where the shock of transition has been greatest. Eventually the recovery of output and investment will lower these high levels of unemployment, but given the alleged scale of over-employment in the eastern countries it is likely that the fall in unemployment will lag some way behind the recovery in output. Unemployment is therefore likely to be a serious problem for quite some time.

... and inflation is high

The actual timing of an economic recovery in the eastern countries will depend partly on the speed at which the most serious problems of stabilization are overcome. In the past year Czechoslovakia, Hungary and Poland have achieved some success in this domain, but in the other countries the situation has deteriorated further. The problem of inflation has generally worsened and it is unlikely that it can be solved quickly. Annual inflation rates in eastern Europe last year ranged from 10 per cent in Czechoslovakia to more than 580 per cent in Poland and Yugoslavia. In the Soviet Union the official index of retail prices rose 5.3 per cent but this has little economic meaning when there are endemic shortages. In Poland the inflation rate has fallen sharply from the hyperinflation levels of early 1990, although by less than targeted in the stabilization plan: the year-on-year rate of increase in prices fell from over 1,000 per cent in the first half of 1990 to 249 per cent in December and 95 per cent in January 1991. In the other eastern countries inflation got worse during the year (except in the former German Democratic Republic where prices actually fell) and by January 1991 the month-to-month rate was above 5 per cent in all of them.

In the area of government budget deficits, the existence of which only became known in 1989 and 1990, rather more progress has been made. In Czechoslovakia and Poland the 1989 deficits (not very large in the former) were turned into small surpluses in 1990 and there was a large reduction in the Hungarian deficit (from 3.1 per cent to 0.1 per cent of GDP). The reported deficit in the Soviet Union was smaller than in 1989 but was still nearly 6 per cent of GDP. In Bulgaria and Romania adequate data are not available but the situation has almost certainly deteriorated. The elimination of government deficits in the eastern countries is an essential component of anti-inflation strategies since, in the absence of government bond markets, the only way they can be financed is through monetization.

On the external side, there have been some improvements, somewhat unexpected, in current account deficits (in convertible currency). In Poland the squeeze on domestic demand and the improvement in export performance led to such a large external adjustment that the current account moved into surplus (by about $1 billion). Hungary also moved into slight sur-

plus. Both Poland and Hungary had access to agreed financing for deficits in 1990. In contrast, financing difficulties in Bulgaria and the Soviet Union led to a rundown of reserves and the imposition of import restrictions. The Soviet Union's deficit was nearly $4 billion and would have been larger had sufficient financing been available. A major feature of 1990 was the increasing difficulties of the eastern countries in obtaining new commercial credit from the west. Borrowing conditions tightened through 1990 as western private creditors' perceptions of the credit risk of eastern borrowers underwent a marked change. Eastern Europe is now beginning to absorb a major terms-of-trade shock as a result of the switch to world prices and convertible currency settlement in trade with the Soviet Union, but the financing of current account deficits in 1991 appears to be forthcoming mainly from official sources. However, the financing requirements of the Soviet Union may be more difficult to meet, in which case the current account constraint will tighten.

Western approaches ...

A year ago the secretariat compared the present economic situation in eastern Europe and the Soviet Union with that of western Europe in 1947 and discussed whether another Marshall Plan would be an appropriate response on the part of the west to the problems of the east.[10] The basic conclusion was that although western support for eastern reform would probably need to match the scale of the original Marshall Plan, its composition would need to be very different in view of the crucial differences between the two situations: in the initial stages of transition from a centrally planned to a decentralized market economy much greater emphasis would need to be given to technical assistance than was the case in the Marshall Plan. This was certainly *not* an argument for technical assistance *instead* of financial aid: the importance of the latter was stressed, especially in helping to break key bottlenecks (in transport and communications, for example), providing balance of payments support, currency stabilization loans and so on. The emphasis on technical assistance was a recognition of the need to build, in most cases from scratch, the legal, financial and institutional infrastructure (including management skills) of a competitive market system − without that infrastructure, efficient markets could not be established and the capacity to absorb financial aid in productive uses would be limited. Of course the capacity to absorb financial assistance varies from country to country and the differences have probably widened in the last year: this just means that the mix of technical and financial aid has to be determined in the light of each recipient's particular circumstances. It was also argued in last year's analysis that foreign private investment was unlikely to make a significant contribution to eastern development until the processes of reform and transformation were well established and the eastern economies could provide an internationally competitive rate of return on capital. In the meantime western financial support for the transformation process would

---

10 United Nations Economic Commission for Europe, "Economic Reform in the East: A Framework for Western Support", *Economic Survey of Europe in 1989-1990*, New York, 1990, pp.5-26.

have to come from official sources — national and international — and should consist mainly of grants in order to avoid increasing existing burdens of debt.

Actual developments in 1990 do not suggest that these conclusions need radical revision. The experience of the former German Democratic Republic is instructive because it fits quite closely into the framework described in last year's *Survey*. Considerable publicity has been given to the very large financial transfers from the Federal government to the eastern *Länder*; but less visible have been the enormous amounts of technical assistance flowing east from both the public and the private sectors. This assistance has been widely based but there has been strong emphasis on the basic institutions of a market system: the legal and banking systems, private property rights and, by no means least, the reconstruction of administrative and local government structures. Private investors from the west have shown great interest in the potential of the east but considerable hesitancy in actually investing there. This is not surprising since the task of constructing market institutions takes time and is still far from complete: for example, the slow pace at which the system of property rights is being clarified has been one of the major obstacles to investment in the former German Democratic Republic.

This hesitancy of western private investors towards the east can be seen in the data on east-west joint ventures. Between October 1989 and January 1991 the number of foreign investment registrations in eastern Europe[11] and the Soviet Union increased nearly sixfold, from 2,900 to 16,700.[12] However, the amounts of foreign capital involved are still very small: in January 1991 it averaged only $0.5 million per joint venture compared with about $1 million in October 1989. This clearly suggests that western companies are keeping a foot in the eastern door but are unwilling to commit large sums of capital until the reform process is more advanced. It also implies that, once the reforms have reached some critical mass there could be a sudden upsurge of foreign investment into eastern Europe, perhaps on the scale that occurred in Spain and Portugal after they joined the European Community.

The present reluctance of the western private sector to commit funds to the eastern countries is also reflected in the dramatic reduction of commercial bank lending to these countries. Lending by BIS reporting banks to eastern Europe (excluding Yugoslavia) and the Soviet Union fell by nearly $7 billion in the first nine months of 1990 — and the decline would have been even larger had there not been an accumulation of payments arrears in Poland, Bulgaria and the Soviet

Union.[13] The increased unwillingness of the western banks to lend to the east partly reflects the more realistic appreciation of the problems of transition, noted above, and the worsening economic situation in the east; but it also reflects the general deterioration in the balance sheets of western banks, the pressures on them to raise capital asset ratios and, hence, their more cautious attitude to lending in general.[14] The fears in the west of a "credit crunch" are thus already being realized in the east.

A significant contribution to easing the external financial burdens of the economies in transition has come from various forms of debt relief, although this was not always subject to prior agreement with the creditors. In 1990 the value of debt relief far exceeded grants from the Group of 24 and was of the same order of magnitude as new official credit to the east. Poland benefited by over $6 billion last year as a result of Paris Club rescheduling of its official debt, delayed payments of interest on commercial obligations, and the write-off of part of the German "jumbo credit". Bulgaria suspended repayments of principal and some interest on its private debt, thus saving more than $3 billion in payments abroad. The Soviet Union ran up arrears of at least $5 billion on western suppliers' credits. Even larger amounts of debt relief are likely in the future. Paris Club members have recently agreed to write off some 50 per cent of Poland's $31 billion of official debt and bank creditors, holding claims of nearly $11 billion, may eventually follow suit. Given the poor state of the Bulgarian economy, a formal rescheduling of debt is probably inevitable. The possibility of Germany writing down Soviet rouble obligations and rescheduling some convertible currency debt is to be raised in forthcoming talks between the two governments.[15]

The issue that now arises with some urgency is whether the developed market economies of the west are ready to increase their levels of financial and technical assistance on a scale which would provide solid support to the process of reform in the east. The increased need for balance of payments support arising from the "eastern" oil shock and the collapse in intra-CMEA trade appears to have been largely met, but needs have also risen to deal with urgent domestic issues such as the expected rapid rise in unemployment. The risk in the present situation is that everything that goes wrong, from domestic political failures to shocks from the Middle East, will be blamed on the reform programmes and that the intensification of short-run constraints will divert attention from the longer-run objectives. The momentum of the reform process, which is barely under way in some countries and not yet in others, could then be checked. The consequences

---

11   Including Yugoslavia but excluding the former German Democratic Republic.

12   ECE Database on Joint Ventures, January 1991. See also, United Nations Economic Commission for Europe, *East-West Joint Ventures News*, Geneva (quarterly).

13   Bank for International Settlements, *International Banking and Financial Market Developments*, Basle, February 1991. In 1989 lending to the east had risen by $9.3 billion.

14   See below, section 2.1(v).

15   *Financial Times*, 13 March 1991. At stake are some TR 10 billion in German claims on the eastern countries, of which the Soviet Union accounts for TR 6.4 billion and Poland TR 800 million.

of such a failure are incalculable and would not be confined to the economic sphere. *One* consequence is likely to be greatly increased pressures for emigration from the east. Warnings about these pressures have been made on many occasions in the last year by eastern officials. Although the basis of their estimates of the likely scale of the problem is unclear and have an obvious purpose in trying to secure more aid from the west, the experience of Germany before unification suggests that the problem is a potentially serious one.

A great deal has already been done to organize assistance for the eastern countries, both on a bilateral and multilateral basis, and the scale of operations has expanded rapidly in the past year.[16] However, the number and variety of programmes and the multiplicity of countries and organizations involved make it difficult to assess whether they all add up to a coherent and adequate response to eastern needs. Co-ordination in the field of balance of payments financing appears to be working well but in the wider field of technical assistance and development projects the situation is far from clear. A great strength of the Marshall Aid programme for post-war reconstruction in western Europe was its institutional structure, mainly embodied in the Organization for European Economic Co-operation, for co-ordinating assistance to the recipient countries. This structure provided a forum where the plans and experience of recipient countries could be discussed in a comprehensive manner for the benefit of all. Equally important, it encouraged a co-operative approach to the aid effort on the part of both donors and recipients and enabled the various national programmes to be placed in a regional perspective. This was a significant contribution to the development of international economic co-operation in post-war Europe.

The need for institutional mechanisms to improve the co-ordination of present assistance to the reforming economies is not simply based on narrow arguments of efficiency, important though they may be. Aid programmes need to be seen to be well co-ordinated, effective and fair in order for parliamentary and popular support to be gained and maintained for this particular use of public money. The American administrators of Marshall Aid paid considerable attention to maintaining Congressional support for the programme, and in this they were greatly helped by the structure and procedures of the OEEC. At a time when the western countries are facing recession and the prospect of rising unemployment, and when the demands for economic assistance from other parts of the world are considerable, the matter of public support for assistance to the east assumes great importance.

---

16 For a review of these activities see section 3.3(vi) below.

Chapter 2

MACRO-ECONOMIC DEVELOPMENTS AND OUTLOOK

This chapter provides an account of the principal macro-economic developments in the ECE region in 1990 and discusses the prospects for 1991. The first section, 2.1, covers the market economies of western Europe and North America and the second, 2.2, deals with the economies in transition of eastern Europe and the Soviet Union.

2.1 WESTERN EUROPE AND NORTH AMERICA

(i) Output and demand

Economic growth rates fell in 1990 ...

After eight years of uninterrupted economic growth, the forces underlying the current upswing of the industrial countries have been weakened in the course of 1990. In western Europe a general deceleration of economic growth was already under way in the second half of 1989. Despite a relatively strong performance in the first quarter of 1990 — largely due to favourable weather conditions which benefited construction activities — the slow-down affected more and more countries in the second half of 1990 and gathered momentum in the final quarter. Among the major economies, the United Kingdom and the United States had already passed the peak of their current cycle in the summer of 1988.

For the 20 industrial countries shown in table 2.1.1 the average growth rate of real GDP growth slowed down from 3.1 per cent in 1989 to 2.4 per cent in 1990. Within this aggregate the deceleration was less marked in western Europe, but there was a sharp fall in the rate of economic expansion in North America, which entered into recession during the course of the year.

... and there was increasing desynchronization of national growth cycles

A major feature of economic developments in 1990 was the emergence of sharp differences in the cyclical positions of individual countries. Among the seven major economies, three (Canada, the United Kingdom and the United States) moved into recession, two (Germany and Japan) experienced faster growth, while in France and Italy the pace of expansion slowed down.

A similar divergence of cyclical developments is apparent among the smaller economies, where a boom (Austria, Ireland and Turkey) or relatively strong growth (Belgium, the Netherlands, Spain, Portugal and Switzerland) contrasts with below average growth in the Nordic countries, and especially in Finland, Greece and and Sweden where there was a severe economic downturn in 1990.

Chart 2.1.1 illustrates the current growth cycle by measuring the relative deviations of real GDP from an exponential trend fitted to the relevant annual data for the period 1979-1990. While annual data do not allow for a precise identification of the various phases of a cycle, it is nevertheless apparent that for the real GDP of 20 industrial countries combined the peak of the current growth cycle was passed in 1989, although this mainly reflects the large weight of the United States in the total. Looking only at the aggregate of west European countries, it is found that the positive deviations from trend have been rising since 1988 — indicating that, on average, the peak of the growth cycle was not reached before 1990. But the shape of the curve suggests that also for western Europe a period of cyclical downswing is ahead.

In any case, the significant divergence between the growth cycles in the United States on the one hand and in Germany and Japan on the other is clearly evident since 1988, as is the fact that the United Kingdom is out of phase with western Europe since 1988.

Although there has been a general upward trend in economic activity over the past decade (table 2.1.1) it is interesting to measure the degree to which the various national growth cycles have been synchronized over the past decade. This can be done with the help of a so-called diffusion index, which takes into account not

---

Germany

As a result of the accession of the German Democratic Republic to the Federal Republic of Germany on 3 October 1990, the two German States are now united in one sovereign state, the Federal Republic of Germany, designated henceforth as "Germany". The new nomenclature is used in this Survey but, for practical reasons, statisticians and economists cannot avoid continuing to treat the two regions of Germany as separate units. Official Pan-German data are not yet available for most economic variables, including the national income accounts, and when they are eventually published analysis will still be hampered by a lack of comparability in the pre- and post-unification data. In addition, the levels of economic development and the underlying economic problems in the two regions are so radically different that analysts will in any case probably find it useful, if not unavoidable, to continue to treat the two regions separately for some time to come.

In this chapter, the data, and the discussion of recent developments and the outlook for Germany in section 2.1 refer only to the Federal Republic of Germany before unification. However, the analysis of changes in the current account in 1990 (section 2.1(iv)) pertains to the united Germany although data for previous years cover only the western part of Germany. Current developments in the former German Democratic Republic are reviewed in section 2.2.

---

only the direction but also the relative amplitude of changes in real GDP.[17] . The index is calculated on the basis of changes in annual growth rates of real GDP and its values ranges from -1 to +1. A value of +1 indicates that all countries have increasing growth rates, while a value of -1 would reflect uniformly declining rates. A value of zero indicates that the declining growth rates are just offset by the increasing ones.[18]

The calculated indexes are shown in table 2.1.2. They suggest that the overall degree of cyclical synchronization has been rather high for the seven major economies over the period 1983 to 1989 but that the seven national cycles moved significantly out of phase in 1990.

The unweighted index for the group of 17 west European countries shows a low degree of synchronization of national growth cycles for most of the years of the current upswing. However, the weighted index suggests a much higher degree of synchronization than the unweighted index in 1988, when the dominant feature was accelerating growth, and in 1989, when growth was beginning to slow down.

The fact that the growth cycles of the 17 west European countries have been much less synchronized than those of the seven major industrial economies suggests that the smaller economies tend to follow, with uneven lags, the economic cycle of the "major loco-motives" which set in motion the international transmission mechanism of economic shocks, be they positive or negative. These lagged relationships are also

shaped by the particular demand-supply relationships that have evolved in the international division of labour between the larger and smaller economies.

This general conclusion is unchanged when the diffusion index is calculated for the total of 20 countries: the degree of synchronization shown by the weighted index reflects the high uniformity of changes in the direction of economic growth in the seven major economies, which is largely offset in the unweighted index by the more divergent changes in the 13 smaller economies.

Finally, chart 2.1.2 illustrates the very close relationship between the degree to which national growth cycles are synchronized and the rate of as well as accelerations and decelerations in economic growth in the region as a whole.

There are a number of factors behind the slow-down ...

The main factor at work behind the slow-down in the overall pace of economic expansion in the last two years or so has been the tightening of monetary policy in order to dampen domestic demand and thereby check inflationary pressures. This was notably the case for those countries in western Europe where the upswing in domestic demand growth was much stronger than the average (Finland, Sweden and the United Kingdom) and where the associated inflationary and wage cost pressures had proved difficult to contain, leading to adverse effects on external competitiveness and the balance on current account.

---

17 See Bert G. Hickman and Stefan Schleicher, "The Interdependence of National Economies and the Synchronization of Economic Fluctuations: Evidence from the LINK Project", *Weltwirtschaftliches Archiv*, Bd.114, 1978, pp.672-673.

18 *Op.cit.*, pp.672-673. The index is defined as follows:

$$D = \frac{\sum Pos_i - \sum Neg_i}{\sum Pos_i + \sum Neg_i}$$

where Pos(i) and Neg(i) − the positive and negative amplitudes of the i-th country series are defined by the *change* in the annual growth of the series for country i. Pos(i) takes the value of the positive change or is zero; conversely, Neg(i) takes the absolute value of negative growth or is zero. The above equation is a simple amplitude weighted diffusion index, which does not take relative country size into account. The latter can be done by weighting the various changes with the country shares in 1985 constant dollar GDP for the country group concerned. If w(i) is the relative country weight, then the fully weighted diffusion index is defined as:

$$D_w = \frac{\sum w_i Pos_i - w_i Neg_i}{\sum w_i Pos_i + w_i Pos_i}$$

TABLE 2.1.1

Annual changes in real GDP in western Europe and North America, 1980-1990

(Percentage change over previous year)

	Trend 1980-1989 a	1989	1990
Western Europe.........................	**2.2**	**3.2**	**2.8**
4 major economies	2.2	3.1	2.9
France...........................	2.0	3.7	2.6
Germany.......................	1.8	3.3	4.7
Italy...............................	2.3	3.2	2.5
United Kingdom	2.6	2.1	0.5
13 smaller economies	2.4	3.5	3.0
Austria...........................	1.8	4.0	4.5
Belgium..........................	1.7	4.0	3.9
Denmark.........................	2.3	1.2	1.0
Finland...........................	3.3	5.2	0.3
Greece............................	1.5	2.8	1.2
Ireland............................	2.5	5.9	5.0
Netherlands	1.5	4.0	3.2
Norway...........................	3.1	1.2	1.8
Portugal..........................	2.3	5.4	3.9
Spain..............................	2.6	5.0	3.5
Sweden...........................	2.1	2.1	0.3
Switzerland......................	2.1	3.5	2.7
Turkey............................	4.9	1.6	9.0
North America	**3.0**	**2.5**	**1.0**
Canada...........................	3.2	3.0	1.1
United States.....................	3.0	2.5	0.9
Total above..........................	**2.7**	**2.8**	**1.8**
Memorandum item:			
Japan.............................	4.0	4.9	6.1
Total above including Japan..	**2.9**	**3.1**	**2.4**

Source: Appendix table A.1.

a Trend growth rates estimated by fitting an exponential time trend to GDP data for the period 1979-1989.

TABLE 2.1.2

Synchronization of national GDP growth cycles, 1981-1990

(Diffusion index)[a]

	Twenty countries [b]		Western Europe [b]		Seven major economies [c]	
	UW	W	UW	W	UW	W
1980	-0.71	-0.94	-0.66	-0.85	-1.00	-1.00
1981	-0.49	0.33	-0.64	-0.59	0.06	0.53
1982	-0.01	-0.76	0.49	0.47	-0.52	-0.83
1983	0.47	0.92	0.21	0.44	0.80	0.94
1984	0.83	0.97	0.77	0.81	0.92	0.97
1985	-0.12	-0.87	0.15	-0.02	-0.68	-0.92
1986	-0.37	-0.75	-0.22	0.17	-0.65	-0.84
1987	0.26	0.71	0.15	0.11	0.68	0.83
1988	0.42	0.89	0.37	0.77	1.00	1.00
1989	-0.28	-0.93	-0.08	-0.68	-1.00	-1.00
1990	-0.22	-0.49	-0.17	-0.21	-0.38	-0.51

Source: ECE secretariat calculation.

Note: UW = unweighted average; W = weighted average.

a For method of calculation see text.
b See table 2.1.
c Canada, France, Germany, Italy, Japan, the United Kingdom and the United States.

ceteris paribus the negative terms-of-trade effect of an increase in the price of oil.

... but German unification provides an offset

In contrast to the above factors which restrained overall economic activity in 1990, a major stimulus to demand in western Europe resulted from the economic and monetary union of the Federal Republic of Germany and the German Democratic Republic on 1 July 1990, which was followed by political unification on 3 October 1990. Unification was accompanied by a steep rise in deliveries of goods − notably consumer goods − from west to east Germany as well as booming retail sales in west Germany because of direct purchases by east German citizens in the western part of the country. This pent-up demand for "western" goods was largely supported by huge financial transfers from the German government budget, which has swung from a surplus in 1989 to a sizeable deficit in 1990.[19]

In economic terms these transfers were tantamount to a highly expansionary fiscal stimulus. The "exogenous" boost to demand benefited not only west German industry but also firms in other countries, either because demand was directly addressed to foreign goods or because the high degree of capacity utilization in west German industry led to a diversion of demand to foreign producers. To this should be added the derived effect of higher demand for intermediate goods. There have been hardly any direct imports of western goods to east Germany: most were imported by west German companies and then shipped on.

Two other factors strengthening growth forces in Germany have been the sizeable cut in income taxes at

Another factor making for a weakening of economic growth in the region has been the slow-down in world trade. This is partly a consequence of the tightening of monetary policies which has led to a weakening of domestic demand growth. The other important factor for west European firms has been the decline in their price competitiveness due to significant appreciation of their currencies against the US dollar.

There was also some offset to growth from the negative terms-of-trade effects of the rise in oil prices after the Iraqi invasion of Kuwait on 2 August 1990. However, this is unlikely to have had a significant impact on the outcome for 1990. In the first place, the appreciation of their currencies against the dollar provided western Europe with a partial offset to the steep rise in the dollar price of oil. Secondly, in the large majority of countries there has been a sizeable decline in the energy − and notably oil − intensity of production since the first and second oil price shocks in 1972/1973 and 1979 respectively, which has reduced

---

19 The financial funds made available to support the east German economy in 1990 amounted to DM 47.8 billion. They originated in the three supplementary Federal Government budgets adopted in the course of 1990 and the first tranche of the German unity fund. See United Nations Economic Commission for Europe, *Economic Bulletin for Europe*, vol.42/90, New York, 1990.

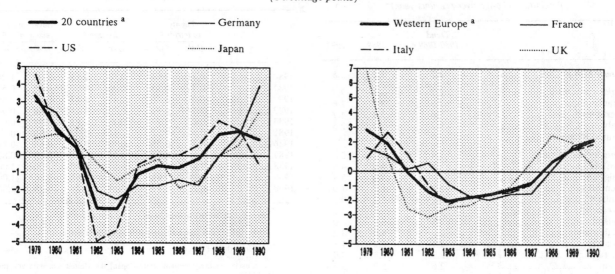

CHART 2.1.1

Real GDP 1979-1990: Relative deviation from trend
(*Percentage points*)

Source: ECE secretariat.

Note: Relative deviations from trend were computed as [(actual value of GDP/trend value of GDP) − 1].

[a] Western Europe, North America, Japan.

the beginning of 1990 and the continuing strong migration from eastern Europe and the Soviet Union.[20]

The demand impulses emanating from German unification have led to considerable increases in German imports from other countries, especially from the smaller west European countries, for which the German market takes an important share of their total exports (see below).

Domestic demand generally weaker ...

In general, the major factor behind the deceleration of economic growth in western Europe in 1989/1990 was the weakening pace of fixed investment and of foreign demand. Private consumption remained the mainstay of overall growth. As in 1989, the net foreign balance, in real terms, tended to subtract from overall growth. However, given that the slow-down of exports was accompanied by a similar slackening of imports, the size of the negative effect remained unchanged from 1989 (table 2.1.3).

In the United States, the growth of domestic demand came to a halt in the final quarter of 1990. For the year as a whole, small increases in private and public consumption were partly offset by changes in inventories. Private fixed capital formation neither supported nor subtracted from growth. Exports were

the main driving force of overall economic activity albeit with slightly less impact than in 1989. Given the slackening of imports, the net contribution of the foreign balance to output growth in 1990 was roughly the same as in 1989 (table 2.1.3).

... and a sharp fall in the growth of industrial production

Against the overall slow-down, the growth of industrial production was halved in western Europe in 1990 compared with 1989, although the modest average increase of 2 per cent masks considerable variation among individual countries (table 2.1.4). Total industrial output declined in Italy, Finland, Sweden and the United Kingdom, and the pace of expansion weakened considerably in a number of other countries (notably France and Spain). These developments contrast sharply with growth rates of 4.5 per cent and more in Austria, Belgium, Germany and Ireland. In the United States the growth of industrial production declined in the second half of 1990, largely because of weak demand for consumer goods. The output of firms producing business equipment was supported by strong export demand which was influenced by the substantial depreciation of the dollar since early 1990. For the year as a whole the increase in industrial output was only 1 per cent. In Canada, industrial production fell by 3 per cent, a major factor being the weak demand from the US market.

---

20 The total number of persons migrating to Germany was about 397,000 in 1990 following some 377,000 in 1989. These numbers, however, exclude persons who came from the German Democratic Republic, which in 1989 amounted to 344,000 and for January-June 1990 to 238,000. Migration from the former German Democratic Republic to the western part of Germany continued in the second half of 1990 but official data are no longer available.

CHART 2.1.2

Synchronization of national growth cycles, 1980-1990

——————— Weighted average   — — — Unweighted average

| 20 countries [a] | Western Europe |

Real GDP growth
(Percentage change over previous year)

Real GDP growth
(Percentage change over previous year)

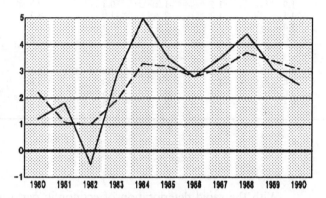
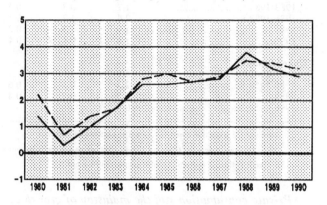

Change in annual growth rate
(Percentage points)

Change in annual growth rate
(Percentage points)

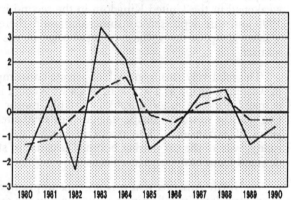
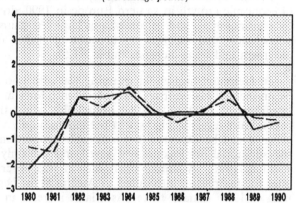

Diffusion index

Diffusion index

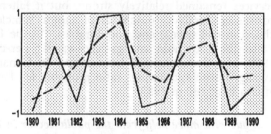
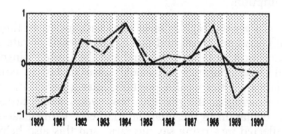

Source: ECE secretariat.

[a] Western Europe, North America, Japan.

TABLE 2.1.3

Contribution of demand components to real GDP growth in western Europe and North America, 1983-1990

(Percentage points)

	Domestic demand				Foreign balance			
	Private consumption	Fixed investment	Other	Total	Exports	Imports	Net	GDP
Western Europe								
1983-1985 [a]	1.2	0.3	0.4	1.9	1.5	-1.2	0.3	2.2
1986-1988 [a]	2.4	1.2	0.5	4.1	1.2	-2.2	-1.0	3.1
1989	1.9	1.3	0.2	3.4	2.5	-2.8	-0.3	3.2
1990	1.8	0.8	0.4	3.0	1.9	-2.7	-0.2	2.8
United States								
1983-1985 [a]	3.1	1.6	1.3	6.0	0.2	-1.5	-1.3	4.8
1986-1988 [a]	2.3	0.5	0.6	3.4	1.4	-1.0	0.3	3.6
1989	1.3	0.3	0.4	2.0	1.3	-0.7	0.5	2.5
1990	0.6	-	-	0.5	1.0	-0.6	0.4	0.9

Source: ECE secretariat based on national and international sources.

Note: Differences between totals and sum of components are due to rounding.

a Simple arithmetic average of annual growth contributions.

Private consumption still the mainstay of growth ...

Private consumption, as in 1989, was the backbone of economic growth in western Europe in 1990, driven by continuing — and in some cases large — gains in households' real incomes on account of higher employment and wage increases (table 2.1.5).

In Germany household spending was also boosted by an income tax reform[21] that entered into force at the beginning of 1990. Given that households adjust their expenditure levels to changes in net incomes only with a lag, it can be expected that a sizeable proportion of the additional net income was saved and will only be spent in 1991. A similar phenomenon was observed after the tax reform introduced in Austria at the beginning of 1989: initially there was a large increase in the savings ratio, but its subsequent fall in 1990 was a major factor behind the strong growth of real private consumption.

In general high interest rates have increased the cost of consumer credit and this has dampened private consumption, notably in Finland and the United Kingdom. In these countries households also started to consolidate their net wealth position, after a period of heavy borrowing in the previous few years made easier by deregulation in the financial markets. Consolidation is reflected in a rising savings ratio and this also helps to explain negative consumption growth in Sweden. In Denmark private consumption started to rise again after two years of consecutive declines. The mild recovery was supported by the abolition of a tax on consumer credit and, probably, by a fall in the savings ratio. There was also a strong turnround of private consumption growth in Norway, where real disposable incomes were supported by rising public sector transfer payments.

With the rapid deterioration of economic performance in the second half of 1990, and in particular with sharply rising unemployment, consumer confidence weakened in the United Kingdom in the second half of 1990 and this depressed consumer demand: there was a sharp drop in the volume of retail sales in the final quarter.

The relatively strong growth of private consumption in western Europe as a whole masks a weakening in the demand for consumer durables, notably motor cars. Car sales in western Europe stagnated in 1990 after five years of expansion. The major exception was Germany, where the car market boomed because of strong demand from east German citizens.[22]

In North America real private consumption weakened considerably, reflecting a slow-down in the growth of real disposable income which, in turn, was mainly due to weaker employment growth. The demand for services remained relatively strong, but it faltered for consumer durables (purchases of motor vehicles declined in real terms) and non-durables. In the United States the household savings ratio was 4.5 per cent in 1990, broadly unchanged from 1989. In Canada the average household savings ratio probably fell last year after a large rise in 1989.

... but with more help from the public sector in 1990

After relatively sluggish growth in 1989, *public sector consumption* picked up again in 1990. The average increase in the 17 west European countries was 2.1 per cent compared with only 0.8 per cent in 1989. In the United States real public consumption rose even more strongly, by 2.8 per cent in 1990. This acceleration raised the overall contribution of this component to total domestic demand growth from 0.2 to 0.4 percentage points in western Europe. In the United States it

---

21 In contrast, the introduction of the "poll" tax was a factor behind the weaker growth of consumer demand in the United Kingdom.

22 There was notably a very strong demand from east German citizens for second-hand cars which, in turn, encouraged west German households to accelerate their purchase of new cars.

contributed 0.6 percentage points to overall growth, the same proportion as for private consumption.

Fixed investment is slowing down in western Europe ...

After its rapid growth in the period 1987-1989, *real fixed capital formation* tended to slow down in western Europe in the course of 1990. Based on still preliminary data, the average increase in 1990 is calculated at 3.9 per cent, some 2.5 percentage points less than in 1989. These aggregate changes, however, mask considerable diversity in the performance of the individual countries (table 2.1.6).

The two major components of fixed capital formation, machinery and equipment and construction, both increased less in 1990 than in 1989, although partial data suggest that on average the deceleration was more pronounced for the former category. Manufacturing investment remained very strong only in Germany, France, Austria and Belgium, reflecting favourable profitability and/or high output growth (table 2.1.6). Another factor may have been the continuing efforts to improve competitiveness in anticipation of the European Community's internal market.

The general factors dampening investment growth in western Europe in 1990 were high interest rates, which particularly affected housing investment, and the deterioration of business profitability in a number of countries. An additional factor is that the strong demand for housing in recent years has driven up the price of land and real estate in many countries and this has also dampened demand. Investment plans may have also been reduced because of the slow-down in domestic and external demand which eased the pressures on existing capacities. With falling rates of capacity utilization the need for investment to increase capacity has been correspondingly reduced and this has led to a slow-down in the construction of new industrial buildings.

Investment expenditures were cut in Denmark, Finland, Sweden and the United Kingdom. There was also a conspicuous decline in Norway, although it should be noted that annual changes in Norway are heavily influenced by the large fluctuations of investment in the oil sector.[23]

The very weak performance in these last four countries stands in sharp contrast to the rest of western Europe, where aggregate investment growth has generally remained fairly strong.

... and remains weak in North America

Fixed investment remained quite weak in the United States, reflecting *inter alia* the depressed demand for housing, particularly for residential investment which was in absolute decline for the third consecutive year. Given weak domestic demand and the deterioration in business sector profitability, expenditure on

TABLE 2.1.4

Industrial production in western Europe and North America, 1989-1990
(Percentage change over previous year)

	Total		Manufacturing	
	1989	*1990* a	*1989*	*1990* a
Western Europe	**4.0**	**2.0**	**4.3**	**2.5**
4 major economies	3.5	2.0	4.5	2.0
France	4.2	1.5	4.5	1.5
Germany	4.9	5.5	5.2	5.5
Italy	3.9	-1.0	3.3	-1.0
United Kingdom	0.4	-0.5	4.2	-0.5
11 smaller economies	5.2	2.0	3.9	2.0
Austria	5.9	7.5	6.6	7.5
Belgium	3.5	4.5	4.2	4.5
Denmark	..	..	..	..
Finland	2.6	-1.5	2.8	-1.5
Greece	1.9	-2.0 b	2.3	-2.5 b
Ireland	12.4	4.5	12.6	4.5
Netherlands	5.1	2.5	3.7	3.5
Norway	16.3	3.5	1.0	1.0
Portugal	5.0	7.5 b	2.3	6.5 b
Spain	4.5	-	4.3	-
Sweden	2.8	-3.0	1.8	-3.0
Switzerland	1.8	3.5	3.6	3.5
Turkey	..	..	..	..
North America	**2.3**	**0.5**	**2.7**	**0.5**
Canada	0.1	-3.0	0.5	-4.0
United States	2.5	1.0	2.9	1.0
Total above	**3.0**	**1.5**	**3.6**	**4.5**
Memorandum item:				
Japan	6.1	4.5	6.2	4.5
Total above including Japan	**3.6**	**2.0**	**4.1**	**2.0**

Source: Appendix table A.8.

a Preliminary estimates rounded to nearest 0.5 percentage points.
b Based on January-September data.

business structures fell in 1990 and there was a considerable slow-down in the growth of spending on producers' durable equipment. Altogether, there was a slight decline in total private sector investment by 0.2 per cent. There was also a small decline in fixed investment in Canada (table 2.1.6).

Changes in stocks have not played a major role in the slow-down

The contribution of *stockbuilding* to the growth of GDP has generally been quite small in the last year or so. This reflects *inter alia* improved planning techniques aiming at "just-in-time production". The upward trend for interest rates in 1989/1990 created additional pressures for efficient inventory management, given the high opportunity cost of capital tied up in stocks. With the weakening of sales prospects in the second half of 1990, there is likely to have been some involuntary accumulation of inventories in manufacturing and distribution. Although the general feature has been a subdued role of stockbuilding in domestic demand growth, there are some exceptions. In the

---

23 These fluctuations reflect to some extent the accounting conventions applied in the system of national accounts. The construction of oil platforms takes several years but their total value as fixed investment is recorded in the national accounts only in the quarter or the year when they are towed out to the oil fields. See Statistisk Sentralbyra, "Economic Trends in Norway", *Okonomiske analyser*, No.9A, 1990, p.7.

TABLE 2.1.5

Real consumption expenditures in western Europe and North America, 1989-1990

(Percentage change over previous year)

	Private sector		Public sector	
	1989	1990	1989	1990
Western Europe..........................	**3.1**	**3.0**	**0.8**	**2.1**
4 major economies	3.0	2.8	0.4	2.1
France..................................	3.1	2.9	1.5	2.4
Germany...............................	1.7	4.4	-0.9	2.9
Italy......................................	3.8	2.7	0.5	1.0
United Kingdom..................	3.9	1.0	0.6	1.7
13 smaller economies	3.1	3.5	1.9	2.1
Austria..................................	3.2	4.3	0.6	1.0
Belgium.................................	3.8	4.0	-0.7	-
Denmark...............................	-0.8	0.7	-1.3	-0.3
Finland..................................	3.9	0.4	2.9	3.6
Greece...................................	3.9	2.1	5.1	1.6
Ireland..................................	5.2	3.0	-3.5	0.7
Netherlands	2.5	4.0	-	0.5
Norway..................................	-1.9	3.0	2.5	1.9
Portugal................................	3.1	4.5	2.0	2.2
Spain.....................................	5.9	3.7	5.6	4.2
Sweden..................................	1.1	-0.3	2.2	1.9
Switzerland...........................	2.1	2.0	2.4	2.0
Turkey...................................	3.7	11.0	2.8	11.9
North America	**2.1**	**1.0**	**2.3**	**2.8**
Canada..................................	3.8	1.4	2.6	1.7
United States........................	1.9	1.0	2.3	2.8
Total above..............................	**2.4**	**1.2**	**1.7**	**2.5**
Memorandum item:				
Japan.....................................	3.5	4.1	2.1	2.1
Total above including Japan..	**2.6**	**2.1**	**1.7**	**2.5**

Source: Appendix table A.2.

TABLE 2.1.6

Real gross fixed investment in western Europe and North America, 1989-1990

(Percentage change over previous year)

	Total economy		Manufacturing industry [a]	
	1989	1990	1989	1990 [b]
Western Europe......................	**6.3**	**3.7**	**8.0**	**4.0**
4 major economies	5.7	4.1	8.5	4.5
France..................................	5.9	4.7	8.4	9.0 [c]
Germany...............................	7.1	8.2	10.2	9.5
Italy......................................	5.1	3.8	9.2	-2.0
United Kingdom..................	4.0	-1.9	4.0	-3.0
13 smaller economies	7.4	3.3	..	..
Austria..................................	5.5	7.0	2.0 [d]	14.5 [d]
Belgium.................................	13.6	11.0	7.0	12.0
Denmark...............................	0.2	-0.8	7.7	4.0
Finland..................................	13.1	-1.9	30.2	-
Greece...................................	8.6	4.3	..	..
Ireland..................................	12.0	9.0	23.9	3.0
Netherlands	3.9	3.2	-2.7	3.0
Norway..................................	-4.8	-26.5	-21.4	-5.0
Portugal................................	7.5	9.0	..	..
Spain.....................................	13.2	8.6	..	..
Sweden..................................	10.9	-1.8	13.9 [c]	-4.0 [c]
Switzerland...........................	6.0	3.3	..	..
Turkey...................................	-0.8	8.6	..	..
North America	**1.9**	**-0.3**	**..**	**..**
Canada..................................	4.5	-0.6	..	..
United States........................	1.6 [e]	-0.2 [e]	7.3	4.0
Total above..............................	**4.0**	**1.7**	**..**	**..**
Memorandum item:				
Japan.....................................	10.9	10.7	..	..
Total above including Japan..	**5.7**	**4.0**	**..**	**..**

Source: Complied from national sources and from the Commission of the European Communities, *European Economy, Supplement B,* No.1 January 1991.

  a Excluding leased assets.
  b Preliminary estimates rounded to the nearest 0.5 percentage point.
  c Industry excluding construction.
  d Including mining.
  e Private sector only.

United Kingdom destocking subtracted considerably from overall growth, while strongly rising stocks in Finland, Ireland and Norway made a substantial positive contribution.[24] In the United States changes in total business inventories were a significant offset to overall growth (a negative growth contribution of 0.6 percentage points). Manufacturing inventories declined for the second consecutive year and destocking in automotive products was the major factor behind the sizeable decline in retail trade inventories.

Net foreign balances have weakened European growth ...

After exceptionally strong growth in 1989, there was a considerable slow-down in the volume growth of trade in goods and services in 1990 (table 2.1.7). Export growth slackened because of the weakening of economic activity in the majority of industrialized countries. This tendency was reinforced by the large depreciation of the US dollar against west European currencies over the last two years, which impaired European price competitiveness and led to losses in their world market shares. The weakening of foreign demand led to a substantial slow-down in export growth for France and Italy.

The continuing strength of export growth in Germany can be fully explained by the prevailing accounting conventions whereby 1990 shipments to the former German Democratic Republic are treated as exports rather than internal domestic trade. The same applies to direct purchases made by east German citizens in west Germany. All these data are based to large degree on estimates and, accordingly, should be treated with caution. Excluding "exports" to east Germany, the total volume of exports of goods and services rose by only some 3 per cent in 1990, a substantial deceleration compared with 1989. To a large degree this development reflects the slackening of economic activity in foreign markets and the appreciation of the Deutschmark against the US dollar. However, the effects of these adverse changes on total output growth were more than offset by the strong demand originating from east Germany and booming domestic demand in the western part of the country.

---

24 It should be recalled that the data on aggregate inventory investment reported in the national accounts are occasionally difficult to interpret because they include any discrepancy that arises between the expenditure and the output estimates of GDP. In recent years this discrepancy has sometimes been very large.

TABLE 2.1.7

Volume of trade in goods and services in western Europe and North America, 1989-1990

(Percentage change over previous year)

	Exports 1989	Exports 1990	Imports 1989	Imports 1990
Western Europe.....................	**7.8**	**5.8**	**8.3**	**6.0**
4 major economies.................	8.8	6.1	8.3	5.9
France.................................	10.9	4.5	8.3	6.3
Germany..............................	9.9	8.6	8.6	9.4
Italy...................................	10.1	5.0	9.6	5.5
United Kingdom..................	4.5	4.8	7.3	1.6
13 smaller economies............	6.4	5.4	8.3	6.2
Austria................................	10.5	9.9	9.4	9.3
Belgium..............................	7.6	7.0	8.7	7.8
Denmark.............................	6.0	4.6	4.2	2.1
Finland...............................	1.6	2.2	8.8	-1.7
Greece................................	2.0	4.4	9.8	7.5
Ireland................................	10.1	6.7	10.9	7.7
Netherlands.........................	5.5	5.2	6.0	6.0
Norway...............................	10.3	7.2	0.9	2.2
Portugal..............................	16.5	12.0	10.5	13.2
Spain..................................	5.2	3.8	16.0	9.0
Sweden...............................	2.4	1.2	7.1	0.5
Switzerland.........................	4.8	4.7	5.5	4.0
Turkey................................	7.5	-1.5	10.0	11.0
North America......................	**9.1**	**7.6**	**5.4**	**3.7**
Canada................................	0.7	4.3	5.1	1.4
United States.......................	11.4	8.4	5.5	4.2
Total above...........................	**8.2**	**6.4**	**7.3**	**5.1**
Memorandum item:				
Japan..................................	15.4	12.6	21.4	13.5
Total above including Japan..	**9.1**	**7.2**	**8.8**	**6.1**

Source: Appendix tables A.5 and A.6.

TABLE 2.1.8

Germany as a growth locomotive in 1990

Origin	Relative importance of German market [a]	German import growth in 1990 [b] Q-III	October	November
Austria...........................	34.7	14.9	14.5	24.5
Belgium..........................	19.3	12.1	30.9	32.5
Denmark.........................	16.5	23.3	34.1	39.3
France............................	16.2	15.2	11.8	19.5
Italy...............................	17.5	16.9	10.7	28.9
Netherlands	24.7	8.7	20.1	26.4
Portugal..........................	15.2	17.0	4.5	38.8
Spain..............................	11.9	29.9	32.5	36.8
Sweden...........................	12.4	5.5	-3.5	15.7
Switzerland	20.6	17.5	10.4	18.1
United Kingdom	11.8	7.1	9.5	20.1
CSFR	..	6.0	-1.6	12.0
Hungary..........................	..	22.8	9.3	26.6
Poland............................	..	57.0	60.0	66.7
USSR	..	3.3	-1.2	10.0

Source: United Nations COMTRADE data base and Deutsche Bundesbank.

a Average share of German market in the total exports of each country in 1988-1989.
b Percentage change over corresponding period of previous year. Imports valued at current prices in Deutschmarks (special trade).

Turkey). In striking contrast, the absolute fall in domestic demand in Denmark and Norway was more than offset by the changes in the real foreign balance, thus yielding positive growth of real GDP in 1990.

... but supported it in the United States

Export growth was the principal sources of support for overall economic growth in the United States in 1990, reflecting the effects of the depreciation of the dollar and efforts to rationalize production in manufacturing industry. Brisk export growth and the slow-down in import growth helped to reduce the deficit on the real foreign account from $54 billion in 1989 to $37.5 billion in 1990.[25] (These figures are based on trade measured in 1982 prices.) As in 1989, real net exports contributed some 0.5 percentage points to total GDP growth in 1990. However, whereas in 1989 this accounted for one fifth of the total growth in output, in 1990 the proportion rose to one half.

(ii) Costs and prices

Inflation accelerated, but less than expected ...

In 1990, inflation continued to rise, the annual rates of increase in consumer prices reaching 5.1 per cent in western Europe and 5.4 per cent in North America. In the south European countries rates remained higher and especially in Greece and Turkey. However, this price performance in the market economies of the ECE region was better than expected both at the beginning of the year and in the months following the start of the Gulf crisis in early August. On a 12-month basis, inflation rates appear to have peaked in October: in the

The expansion of demand associated with German unification spilled over to other countries and helped to support their export growth. This was notably the case for EC member countries and for Austria and Switzerland, but German imports from Hungary and also Poland increased substantially in the second half of 1990 (table 2.1.8). These developments help to explain the robust export growth in several of the smaller economies of western Europe in 1990 (table 2.1.7).

One direct consequence of the slow-down in domestic demand in western Europe has been a lower growth of imports. In fact, both export and import growth fell by about 2 percentage points compared with 1989 (table 2.1.7). Import growth was buoyant in Germany and in several of the smaller countries, but faltered under the impact of low domestic demand growth in the United Kingdom, Finland (where there was actually a fall) and Sweden.

On average the changes in the real foreign balances acted as a drag on domestic economic activity, subtracting on average some 0.3 percentage points from total GDP growth (table 2.1.3). This offset to domestic demand growth was much more pronounced in the south European countries (Greece, Portugal, Spain and

---

25 These figures include exports and imports of factor incomes. Excluding factor incomes − which is the foreign balance consistent with GDP rather than GNP − the deficit on the real foreign account declined from $84.3 billion in 1989 to $67.1 billion in 1990.

following two months a deceleration is evident in most of western Europe and North America both in terms of the overall consumer price index and in the underlying rate (i.e., consumer prices excluding food and energy).

For 1990 as a whole, the appreciation of most west European currencies against the US dollar, and an improvement in the terms of trade of some of the developed market economies, meant that import prices, in contrast to 1989, were not a significant source of pressure on domestic prices, except in the United Kingdom and a few smaller economies. In many west European countries, import prices even lowered domestic inflation rates. On the other hand, domestic cost pressures strengthened further in 1990. Unit labour costs, reflecting both a slow-down in productivity growth and higher wage and non-wage labour costs per employee, increased strongly. The rate of increase in unit profits and other non-labour costs generally slowed down in 1990. Thus, in the majority of the western market economies, the higher inflation rates of 1990 were largely due to domestic cost pressures, and in particular to unit labour costs.

... the price of oil increased ...

At the beginning of 1990 there was a sharp rise in energy and food prices due to an extremely cold winter and supply disruptions in North America. After January both sets of prices eased. Because of excess supply and weak seasonal demand, crude oil prices fell continuously to reach some $15 a barrel in mid-June (an 18-month low). Following Iraq's invasion of Kuwait at the beginning of August and the ensuing UN embargo on trade with these two countries, oil prices soared and reached $40 a barrel by the end of September. After fluctuating between $35 and $40 a barrel during October the oil prices eased considerably during the closing months of 1990. With the embargo, world markets had lost nearly 4.5 million bpd or some 7 per cent of the world supply. However, this reduction in supply was almost immediately and totally replaced by increased output in other OPEC countries, notably Saudi Arabia, the United Arab Emirates and Venezuela. Supply remained tight only for some oil products due to the loss of Kuwaiti and Iraqi refining capacities. The rise and subsequent fluctuations in the price of oil reflected changing expectations of possible future disruptions to supply rather than any actual shortage.[26]

The depreciation of the US dollar *vis-à-vis* the major European currencies dampened the effect of the rise in the oil price on the west European economies. Nevertheless, the oil shock affected all the ECE market economies although relatively less in western Europe than in the United States.

Measured by the HWWA[27] index, energy prices[28] in October were 105 per cent higher than in June in dollars and 86 per cent higher in ECUs. For 1990 as a whole, energy prices were 27 per cent higher than in 1989 in US dollar terms and 10 per cent in ECUs (chart 2.1.3).

... but other primary commodity prices remained weak

In contrast, non-energy (food and industrial raw materials) prices in 1990 were virtually unchanged in dollars and fell by 13.5 per cent in ECU terms. In fact, food prices fell rather strongly (nearly 10 per cent in dollars and 22 per cent in ECUs), reflecting a fall in grain prices due to a record US harvest and the near absence of China and the USSR from the market. Due to weak demand, and particularly a slow-down in fixed investment, industrial raw materials prices increased by 4 per cent in dollars but fell by 10 per cent in ECUs in 1990. Thus, except during the third quarter and to a much lesser extent in the fourth, world commodity prices did not contribute to domestic price inflation in western Europe in 1990. On the contrary, price changes for non-energy commodities pulled down the inflation rates in western Europe.

Compared with 1980, world energy prices (as measured by HWWA) in December 1990 were 19 per cent lower in dollar terms and 16 per cent lower in ECUs. During the same period consumer prices increased by three fifths in the United States and three fourths in western Europe. This suggests that during the 1980s energy prices rose much less than average consumer prices and hence had a dampening effect on the overall inflation rates of the developed market economies. In addition, the favourable effect of these large gains in the terms of trade on the costs of material inputs provided room for profit margins to increase without a squeeze on the real wages. In turn, this helped to stimulate growth in fixed investment and employment without disturbing the disinflationary process during the long period of expansion.

Consumer price inflation rose – but peaked in October

Consumer price inflation in 1990 accelerated to 5.1 per cent in western Europe[29] and 5.4 per cent in North America, as compared with 4.6 per cent and 4.8 per cent respectively in 1989 (Appendix table A.9). In the

---

26 From early August it was expected that the flow of oil would be disrupted in the event of a war in the Gulf, but to what extent and to what effect on prices was completely uncertain. In terms of traditional supply and demand analysis, buyers of oil expected a shift to the left of the supply curve and, given the relative inelasticity of the demand for oil, a sharp rise in price. This expectation, in turn, leads to a rightward shift in the demand curve and so the current price is driven up to reflect the expected future price. However, no one was sure of how far the supply curve would move or what the new market-clearing or equilibrium price would be. Expectations were thus highly sensitive to news and had a high variance among market participants.

27 Produced by the HWWA Institute for Economic Research, Hamburg, this index weights world market prices (in dollars) by the relevant commodity shares in total imports of the western industrialized countries in 1974-1976.

28 The weight of oil in the total energy component of the HWWA index is 91.3 per cent.

29 Weighted average of 13 developed market economies of western Europe – see Appendix table A.9 for the list.

CHART 2.1.3

World market prices of raw materials, in US dollars and ECUs, 1981-1990
(1980 = 100, semi-logarithmic scale)

——— US dollars   ----- ECUs

Energy	Raw materials excluding energy
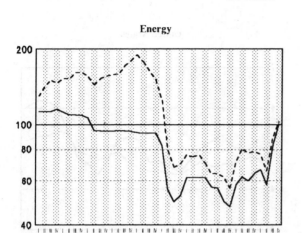	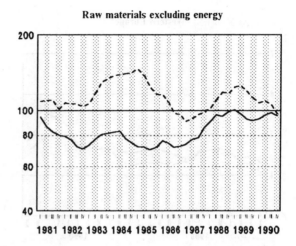

Source: The dollar index is published by HWWA (Hamburg) in *Inter-economics*. The conversion to ECUs was made by the ECE secretariat on the basis of the US dollar-ECU exchange rate published in IMF, *International Financial Statistics*, Washington, D.C.

south European countries[30] inflation rates averaged some 20 per cent, much the same as in 1989. However, among the individual countries not only have annual rates of inflation varied significantly but so have their trends. In 1989 inflation accelerated in all the market economies of the ECE region except Norway and Turkey. However, in 1990 consumer prices rose faster than in 1989 only in the United Kingdom (9.5 per cent, up from 7.8 per cent in 1989), the United States (5.4 per cent, up from 4.8 per cent) and in six smaller countries (Austria, the Netherlands, Switzerland, Sweden, Greece and Portugal). In the Federal Republic of Germany, Italy and Belgium, inflation rates remained fairly stable while in France, Canada and other smaller west and south European economies, they decelerated.

Much of the acceleration that did occur during the course of 1990 was concentrated in the third quarter (chart 2.1.4) and largely reflected the sharp increase in oil prices after Iraq's invasion of Kuwait in August. In fact, during the first half of 1990, thanks to significantly weaker world market prices for oil and most non-oil commodities, consumer price inflation in most of the market economies of the ECE region was less than expected at the beginning of the year. During the closing months of the year, inflation rates in most west Euro-

pean countries had fallen close to their pre-crisis levels and had more or less stabilized in North America.

... underlying inflation rates are now falling

As the prices of food and energy are relatively more sensitive to seasonal and other exceptional factors than remaining items in the consumer price index, a better indicator of the underlying rate of inflation is obtained by excluding these two items from the index. Chart 2.1.4 shows that this underlying rate moderated during the second half of 1989 both in western Europe[31] and North America. In the first quarter of 1990 the downtrend in the underlying rate stopped, and was then reversed in the following months until October, largely because of unit labour cost pressures (see below). In the US this tendency was amplified by the weaker dollar. In November the underlying rate eased but by much less than the overall consumer price index. The greatest deceleration was in the UK (from 11 per cent both in September and October to 9.8 per cent in November), where the average annual rate of increase in the underlying rate was 9.7 per cent in 1990 (up from 8.3 per cent in 1989) compared with 4.7 per cent for western Europe as a whole.

---

30 Weighted average of 4 market economies of southern Europe – see Appendix table A.9 for the list. Yugoslavia is excluded as its inflation rate (1,252 per cent in 1989 and nearly 800 per cent in 1990) distorts the regional average.

31 The west European weighted average in this chart excludes Finland and Sweden where data on food and energy in the consumer price index are not available separately. The south European countries are also excluded from this chart for the same reason.

CHART 2.1.4

Monthly changes in consumer prices, 1989-1990
(Percentage change over corresponding period of the preceding year)

——— Total   — — —- Excluding food and energy

Western Europe[a]   United States

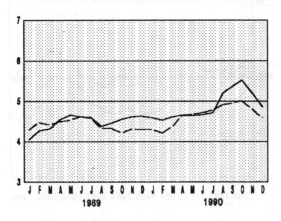

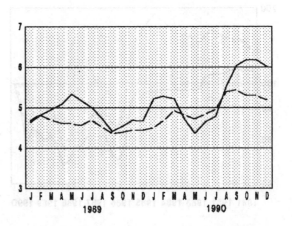

Source: National sources.

[a] Weighted average of 11 countries, excluding Finland and Sweden.

In western Europe, the average underlying rate of inflation in 1990 was higher than in 1989 in the United Kingdom, the Netherlands, Switzerland, and (probably) in Sweden. In the United States, the underlying rate was 5 per cent in 1990 compared with 4.5 per cent in 1989. In the United States both the rate and its acceleration were stronger than in western Europe on average, but in the United States the underlying rate started to decelerate from October. Among the developed market economies, the underlying rate of inflation was higher than the increase in the total consumer price index only in the United Kingdom and Denmark (and probably in Finland and Sweden): to a large extent, this reflects deterioration in the growth of productivity, except in Denmark where the underlying rate increased sharply in mid-1990 because of the half-yearly adjustment to rents.

Different price trends for manufactures and services

Between 1982 and 1989 consumer prices of services generally increased faster than those for manufactured goods (excluding food and drink). However, the gap narrowed significantly in 1989 because the rise in manufacturing prices accelerated due to higher energy prices, very high capacity utilization rates and a tighter labour market for skilled workers. During the first half

of 1990 in western Europe, the rate of increase in service prices continued on a high but stable trend (around 4.5 per cent) while that of manufacturing prices decelerated considerably (from 3.7 per cent in the last quarter of 1989 to 2.3 per cent in mid-1990).[32] In the second half of the year, however, the inflation of manufacturing prices resumed its uptrend (in some countries increasing even faster than service prices). This dissimilarity of manufacturing price trends between the first and the second halves of 1990 is largely due to the larger and more immediate impact of energy price changes on the production of manufactures. Changes in the prices of industrial raw materials amplified these differences further by falling in the first half and recovering during the second half of the year.

In North America, the prices of both services and manufacturing accelerated throughout most of the year and at rates higher than in western Europe in general. Most of this difference between North America and western Europe can be explained by the stronger rise in the unit labour costs in North America where the productivity gains were significantly weaker than in the majority of the west European economies.[33]

Both in western Europe and North America, manufacturing prices peaked in October whereas the change

---

[32] Weighted average of France, Germany, Italy, Belgium, Denmark, Norway, Switzerland.

[33] The major exceptions are the United Kingdom, Finland and Sweden which are not, in fact, included in this exercise due to lack of data.

CHART 2.1.5

Intermediate product prices and producer prices in manufacturing industry,[a] 1989-1990
(Percentage change over corresponding month of the preceding year)

——— Intermediate product prices   — — —- Final output prices

Western Europe[b]   United States

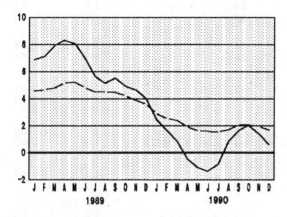
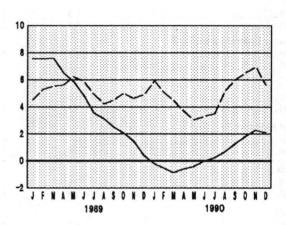

Source: ECE secretariat common data base, based on national sources.

[a] For definitions of indices, see United Nations Economic Commission for Europe, *Economic Survey of Europe in 1982*, New York, 1983, pp. 32-33.
[b] Unweighted average of 11 countries, excluding Italy and Norway.

in the prices of services gained some momentum during the last quarter of 1990 in western Europe.

The prices paid by manufacturers for their material inputs hardly changed in 1990

In western Europe,[34] intermediate goods prices continued their downtrend, which started in mid-1989, until August 1990 (chart 2.1.5). They actually fell between April and August, largely because of weaker import prices for oil and industrial raw materials. Despite their relatively strong rebound in the third quarter, intermediate goods prices in west European manufacturing industry increased at an average annual rate of only 0.6 per cent during January-October, compared with 6.7 per cent during the same period of 1989. At the same time, producer (or output) prices of manufactures in western Europe continued to decelerate during the first half of 1990. Although the downtrend was reversed in the third quarter, the annual average rate of increase during January-October was just above 2 per cent, less than half the rate in the same period of 1989. Thus, in western Europe in 1990 the pressure from material input prices weakened considerably in general and the rise in producer prices, which had strengthened in the previous two years, moderated considerably.

In the United States, material input costs, which were already decelerating much more rapidly than in western Europe between January and October 1989, fell in each successive month during the first half of 1990. As in western Europe, material input prices started to recover in the third quarter, although at a very modest rate. The increase in input costs during January-October 1990 was virtually zero for US manufacturing industry. On the other hand, producer prices in the US rose much faster than in western Europe, reaching 6.5 per cent in October, higher than in any west European economy and three times the west European average. In the United States, the average annual rate of increase between January and October was 4.7 per cent, compared with 5.2 per cent for the same period in 1989.

Unit labour costs were the main sources of inflationary pressure

Despite the fact that monetary policy has been tightened in western Europe, inflationary pressures arising from high rates of capacity utilization strengthened in most countries, especially during the first half of the year. In addition, while the economic growth has clearly lost momentum during the course of 1990, employment growth did not slow down in most, and then only late in the year in some economies of the region.

---

34 Unweighted average of 11 west European countries, excluding Italy and Norway.

TABLE 2.1.9

Contributions to the change in the GDP deflator, 1989-1990

(Annual percentage change)

	Change in the GDP deflator a	of which due to:				
		Unit labour costs			Unit profits c	Unit indirect taxes net of subsidies
		Total	Compensation per employee b	Labour productivity		
France						
1989	3.3	1.4	2.7	-1.3	1.5	0.4
1990	3.3	2.1	2.9	-0.7	1.0	0.2
Germany, Federal Republic of						
1989	2.6	0.6	1.6	-1.0	1.2	0.8
1990	3.5	1.5	2.4	-0.9	1.6	0.4
Italy						
1989	6.3	2.9	4.3	-1.3	2.6	0.9
1990	7.3	3.7	4.3	-0.6	2.5	1.1
United Kingdom d						
1989	6.7	4.9	4.2	0.6	1.2	0.6
1990	6.0	5.4	5.1	0.3	1.0	-0.3
Austria						
1989	2.9	1.3	2.7	-1.3	1.0	0.5
1990	3.4	1.4	2.8	-1.4	2.0	
Belgium						
1989	4.5	0.6	2.1	-1.4	3.1	0.7
1990	3.9	0.9	2.4	-1.5	3.0	
Denmark						
1989	4.3	0.9	1.9	-1.0	3.8	-0.3
1990	3.7	0.7	1.5	-0.8	3.0	
Finland						
1989	6.7	3.0	5.8	-2.7	2.9	0.8
1990	6.0	4.1	4.2	-0.1	0.5	1.4
Ireland						
1989	5.1	-0.5	2.7	-3.2	2.4	3.2
1990	2.3	1.0	2.1	-1.1	1.1	0.2
Netherlands						
1989	1.5	-0.9	0.3	-1.2	2.0	0.3
1990	2.9	1.6	2.4	-0.8	1.3	
Norway						
1989	6.4	-	2.5	-2.5	7.2	-0.8
1990	4.7	1.1	2.7	-1.6	3.8	-0.2
Sweden						
1989	8.0	5.7	6.0	-0.3	1.1	1.2
1990	9.9	6.5	6.4	0.1	2.1	1.4
Switzerland						
1989	4.3	1.9	3.4	-1.4	2.0	0.4
1990	4.7	2.6	3.1	-0.5	2.1	
Western Europe e						
1989	4.4	2.0	2.9	-0.9	1.8	0.6
1990	4.7	2.8	3.4	-0.6	1.9	
Canada d						
1989	4.9	3.2	3.8	-0.5	0.7	1.0
1990	3.2	3.6	4.0	-0.4	-0.9	0.5
United States						
1989	4.1	2.1	2.2	-0.1	1.5	0.5
1990	4.1	2.8	3.0	-0.1	0.7	0.5

Source: National accounts. Small discrepancies are due to rounding.

a   GDP at market prices.
b   Wage and non-wage costs per person employed.
c   Includes capital consumption.
d   Based on data for three quarters.
e   Weighted average of 13 countries.

Hence, *unit labour costs*, which were already putting pressure on prices in 1989, continued to accelerate in 1990, reflecting both the smaller gains in productivity in the majority of countries and a significantly faster growth of wage and non-wage labour costs in some. Unit labour costs increased on average by 5.3 per cent in western Europe and 4.9 per cent in North America in 1990, compared with 3.9 per cent and 3.7 per cent respectively in 1989. In both regions, these were the largest increases in the last eight years. In the United Kingdom and Sweden, where productivity actually fell, unit labour costs increased by some 10 per cent, and in Italy and Finland they rose by 8 per cent. In the rest of western Europe the increases were significantly less, although they were still considerably higher than in 1989. However, it is noteworthy that it was only in Austria, Belgium and the United States that the acceleration in unit labour costs was entirely due to a more rapid increase in compensation per employee.[35] Elsewhere the productivity slow-down was either totally (Italy, Finland, Ireland, Switzerland) or largely (France) responsible for the deterioration in the unit labour costs. Unit labour cost pressures in 1990 weakened only in Denmark thanks to smaller gains in compensation per employee.

In 1990, *the rate of change in the GDP deflator*, the broadest measure of inflation, accelerated in only a few countries: the former Federal Republic of Germany, Italy and four of the smaller west European countries (table 2.1.9). In the United States it stabilized at the 1989 rate and in Canada it decelerated strongly. Among the four south European countries, the rate of change in the GDP deflator accelerated in Greece and Spain, to reach 17.6 per cent and 7.4 per cent respectively.

Non-labour costs and particularly *unit profits* were the main reasons for the increase in the GDP deflator in 1989. In 1990, the rate of change in unit profits — except in the former Federal Republic, Italy, Sweden (and probably Austria, Spain and Turkey) — moderated considerably. Also in the US unit profits and their contribution to the overall inflation rate fell significantly (by half) whereas in Canada unit profits shrank and pulled down the inflation rate. In the western market economies of the ECE region in general, three fifths of the average increase in the GDP deflator in 1990 was due to unit labour costs, a reflection in general of lower productivity growth combined with rising compensation per employee.

Domestic inflation rates, as measured by the change in the domestic demand deflator,[36] accelerated only slightly in 1990, to 4.6 per cent in western Europe and 4.3 per cent in North America (table 2.1.10). The rate of acceleration was confined to just a few countries (Germany, Italy, the United States and four smaller countries). In most of the others it decelerated and in some rather strongly (Denmark, Ireland, Norway and Canada). In 1989, increases in the domestic demand deflator were generally higher than those in the GDP deflator, reflecting to a large extent a deterioration in the terms of trade. In 1990, however, the sharp decline in imported inflation reversed this pattern.

Import prices — as measured by the import deflator — increased by a mere 0.4 per cent in 1990 in western Europe compared with 6.2 per cent in 1989. In North America, in contrast, the rate accelerated from 0.6 per cent in 1989 to 2.0 per cent in 1990. In western Europe (except in the United Kingdom and to a much lesser extent in Italy, Ireland and Norway) this strong deceleration in import prices was due to a significant appreciation of exchange rates (5.3 per cent on average in effective exchange rate terms).[37] In the United States, however, a fall in overseas suppliers' prices for the year as a whole (4.5 per cent) offset a significant part of the effect of the weaker exchange rate on import prices. The fall in suppliers' prices in the United States, in turn, reflects a cut in exporters' profit margins as part of their attempt to maintain their market shares in the United States. Changes in the composition of US imports may have also had some influence. Altogether, the rise in domestic prices in 1990, both in western Europe and North America, would have been much larger without the moderating influence of weaker import prices.

(iii) Employment and unemployment

In 1990, despite the general easing in output growth, west European employment continued to grow for the seventh consecutive year, *and* with further momentum for the year as a whole: at 1.7 per cent (table 2.1.11), the increase was the largest in more than two decades.[38] This strong growth in the demand for labour was accompanied by a further decline in the rate of west European unemployment,[39] from 7.8 per cent in 1989 to 7.2 per cent in 1990, in spite of a relatively large increase in the labour supply (1 per cent compared with 0.6 per cent in 1989). The acceleration in labour force growth was mainly due to immigration into the western

---

35 The United States data are based on the January advance estimates of the Department of Commerce where annual real GNP growth in 1990 is estimated at 0.9 per cent. However, the Bureau emphasizes that "the fourth quarter estimates are based on preliminary and incomplete data". Hence, if the revised fourth quarter estimates result in lower GNP growth then the unit labour costs would be higher than in these calculations due to weaker productivity growth.

36 Inflation measured by the GDP deflator excludes, by definition, the effect of changes in import prices and includes the effect of changes in export prices. Hence, overall inflationary pressure in the domestic economy is better indicated by the change in the domestic demand deflator. The extent to which domestic inflation is home-made or imported can be seen by decomposing the change in the domestic demand deflator into the contribution coming from the change in the GDP deflator excluding exports and the change in the import deflator. However, this is essentially an accounting exercise and cannot itself say anything about the causes of inflation.

37 As measured by the IMF's Multilateral Exchange Rate Model (MERM).

38 Unless otherwise stated, employment data in this section are from labour force surveys and hence may differ from the national accounts data presented in Appendix table A.11.

39 Unless otherwise stated, unemployment data in this section are not adjusted for comparability across countries and hence may differ from the standardized rates presented in Appendix table A.12.

TABLE 2.1.10

Contribution to the change in the domestic demand deflator, 1989-1990

(Annual percentage change)

	Change in domestic demand deflator	Changes in GDP deflator excluding exports [a]	of which due to: Import prices Total	Exchange rates [b]	Export prices of suppliers [c]
France					
1989	3.5	2.1	1.4	0.5	0.9
1990	3.1	3.5	-0.4	-1.7	1.3
Germany, Federal Republic of					
1989	3.0	1.8	1.2	0.5	0.8
1990	3.6	3.6	-	-1.9	1.9
Italy					
1989	6.3	4.9	1.4	-	1.3
1990	6.8	6.7	0.1	-1.0	1.1
United Kingdom [d]					
1989	6.0	4.3	1.7	0.9	0.7
1990	5.7	4.9	0.8	0.6	0.2
Austria					
1989	3.1	1.8	1.3	1.0	0.3
1990	3.4	2.9	0.4	-3.1	3.5
Belgium					
1989	3.9	-0.7	4.6	1.1	3.5
1990	4.0	4.4	-0.5	-4.2	3.8
Denmark					
1989	4.7	2.7	2.0	1.2	0.8
1990	3.5	3.9	-0.4	-2.9	2.5
Finland					
1989	6.3	4.9	1.3	-0.5	1.9
1990	6.7	6.1	0.6	-1.3	1.9
Ireland					
1989	4.5	0.5	4.0	1.8	2.2
1990	3.6	6.5	-3.0	-4.6	1.6
Netherlands					
1989	1.5	-1.8	3.2	1.3	2.0
1990	2.5	3.5	-1.0	-3.2	2.2
Norway [d]					
1989	7.3	4.6	2.7	0.6	2.2
1990	4.9	4.6	0.3	-1.0	1.3
Sweden					
1989	7.4	5.5	1.9	0.3	1.6
1990	10.0	8.5	1.5	-0.3	1.8
Switzerland					
1989	4.6	1.4	3.2	2.7	0.5
1990	4.2	3.2	1.0	-3.1	4.1
Western Europe [e]					
1989	4.4	2.7	1.7	0.6	1.1
1990	4.6	4.5	0.1	-1.6	1.7
Canada [d]					
1989	4.3	4.3	0.1	-1.5	1.5
1990	3.7	3.6	0.2	0.2	-
United States					
1989	4.0	4.0	0.1	-0.5	0.5
1990	4.3	4.1	0.2	0.8	-0.5

Source: National accounts and IMF, *International Financial Statistics*, Washington, D.C. Small discrepancies are due to rounding.

a   Calculated as the residual of the change in the domestic demand deflator minus the contribution of the change in import prices.
b   Effective exchange rates (reciprocal of IMF MERM rates).
c   These are the prices of imports in terms of the national currency of the country of origin.
d   Based on data for three quarters.
e   Weighted average of 13 countries.

TABLE 2.1.11

Labour market developments, 1980-1990
(Percentages)

| | Annual average growth rates | | | |
	Labour force[a]	Employment[a]	Unemployment	Unemployment rates
Western Europe				
1980-1983	0.8	-0.2	16.5	7.2
1984-1988	0.9	1.0	0.2	9.1
1989.............	0.6	1.4	-8.9	7.8
1990.............	1.0	1.7	-6.9	7.2
Southern Europe [b]				
1980-1983	0.3	1.6	13.5	11.2
1984-1988	1.7	1.6	1.4	13.2
1989.............	2.1	1.3	-4.1	11.9
1990.............	1.2	1.0	-0.7	11.7
North America				
1980-1983	1.6	0.5	14.9	8.6
1984-1988	1.8	2.7	-8.6	7.0
1989.............	1.8	2.1	-2.4	5.5
1990.............	0.9	0.6	5.7	5.8

Source: OECD, *Labour Force Statistics*, Paris, various issues and national statistics.

a Civilian.
b Excludes Yugoslavia.

part of Germany which increased the population of working age. In contrast, in North America, with a stronger slow-down in output growth and a traditionally more elastic demand for labour, the rate of increase in employment fell sharply from 2.1 per cent in 1989 to 0.6 per cent in 1990. Also the growth in labour supply in North America, which was much stronger than in western Europe throughout the 1980s, decelerated considerably, from 1.8 per cent in 1989 to 0.9 per cent in 1990, mainly due to lower participation rates which reflect an increase in the number of discouraged workers. Nevertheless, the North American unemployment rate increased, for the first time since 1983, from 5.5 per cent in 1989 to 5.8 per cent in 1990. In southern Europe[40] also, contrary to western Europe, employment growth slowed down considerably in 1990, from 2.1 per cent in 1989 to 1.1 per cent, and the average rate of unemployment remained high at 11.7 per cent.

The above regional averages conceal the fact that, as in the case of output growth and inflation, 1990 was a year of increasingly divergent labour market changes, both among countries and from month to month. With the exception of Germany, and at much lower rates in Italy and a few smaller west European countries, the demand for labour slackened and rates of unemployment started to climb during the second half of the year. The deterioration was particularly fast in the United Kingdom during the fourth quarter.

The demand for labour remained strong in western Europe ...

Despite the slow-down in GDP growth, the upswing of employment which started in 1984 in western

Europe continued in 1990 with further momentum (by 1.7 per cent compared with 1.4 per cent in 1989, chart 2.1.6.). In 1990 more than 2 million new jobs were created in western Europe, more than one third of them in west Germany where employment rose by 2.5 per cent. After declining for more than a decade, manufacturing employment in western Europe recovered slightly in the last two years: nearly one sixth of all new jobs in 1990 were in manufacturing industries where employment (in national accounts terms) grew by 1 per cent as in 1989. This brought the total increase in new manufacturing jobs since the end of 1988 to nearly 600,000, more than four fifths of which was in the western part of Germany. Notwithstanding these gains, employment growth started to slow down after the first quarter, and industrial employment actually fell in some countries towards the end of the year, most notably in the United Kingdom and the Nordic countries. In Denmark and Norway, employment in the economy as a whole fell for the second consecutive year albeit at lower rates than in 1989. Employment continued to grow steadily throughout the year in the western part of Germany and, at much lower rates, in Italy, Austria, the Netherlands and Switzerland.

... but weakened considerably in North America

In North America, where the demand for labour is much more sensitive to changes in output than in most of western Europe, employment growth decelerated strongly to 0.6 per cent in 1990, compared with 2.1 per cent in 1989. This was the lowest rate of growth in employment since 1982. There was a net increase of less than 300,000 new jobs in North America in 1990 and they were all in the service sector. There were job losses in all other sectors of the economy, with manufacturing and construction being hardest hit. During the three months to February 1991, the growth of employment in service industries has also halted, most of the weakness being concentrated in business, transport and retail services.

In all four south European countries annual employment growth decelerated in 1990, although in Spain it still increased by some 2.5 per cent.

Growth in the labour supply: up in western Europe, down in North America

Since the beginning of the 1970s, and especially during the 1980s, both the demand for and supply of labour have been much more dynamic in North America than in western Europe. During the 1980s, labour supply in North America increased by 19 million (chart 2.1.7). During the same period 20 million new jobs were created and so there were 1 million fewer unemployed at the end of 1989 compared with 1980. In western Europe, in contrast, the labour force increased by 9 million during the 1980s, but only 5 million new jobs were created during the same period, and so there were 4 million more people without jobs in 1989 as compared with 1980.

---

40 Greece, Portugal, Spain and Turkey.

CHART 2.1.6

Output and employment changes, 1980-1990

(Annual percentage change)

———— GDP   — — — Employment

Western Europe   **North America**

A. Total economy

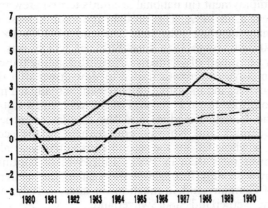

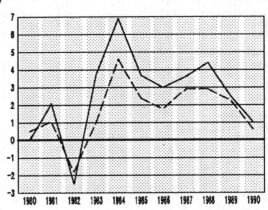

B. Manufacturing

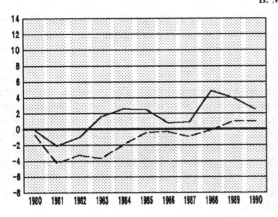

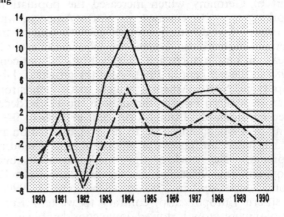

Source: National accounts.

In 1990 the number of new entrants into the work force was similar in western Europe and North America: 1.3 million and 1.2 million respectively. However, compared with 1989, in western Europe this was nearly twice as much whereas in North America it was less than half. Two fifths of the increase in the west European civilian labour force was in the western part of Germany, and was largely due to the influx of East Germans and ethnic Germans from east European countries. The rest of the increase was largely due to higher activity rates, since the growth of the west European population of working age continued to fall,

and with increased momentum in 1990. In contrast, the population of working age in North America in 1990 continued to grow as fast as in 1989, but labour force growth rate halved to 0.9 per cent, which implies a large increase in the number of discouraged workers.[41]

Unemployment began to rise during 1990

The rate of unemployment in western Europe in 1990 averaged 7.2 per cent, its lowest since 1981 and down from 7.8 per cent in 1989. However, this fall in

---

41 These are people who want work but have given up looking for it and hence are not counted as unemployed. According to the US Department of Labor's report to Congress, the number of discouraged workers rose to a two-year high of 941,000 in December 1990, and the women account for almost all the increase from 831,000 in the previous month *(International Herald Tribune*, 5-6 January 1991).

CHART 2.1.7

Labour market developments, 1980-1990
(Millions)

———Labour force[a]   — —Employment[a]   ▒▒▒ Unemployment

Western Europe

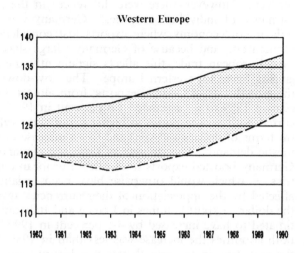

North America

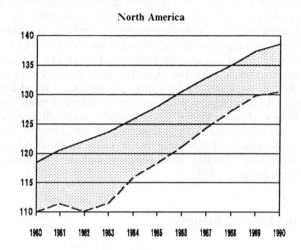

Source: OECD, *Labour Force Statistics, 1968-1988*, Paris, 1990; *Quarterly Labour Force Statistics*, Number 4, 1990, Paris; and national sources.

[a] Civilian.

the average conceals divergent changes among countries (Appendix table A.12) and during the year. As a result of the slackening employment growth, unemployment rates began to rise during the second quarter in the majority of countries for the first time since early 1983. This uptrend gained momentum during the second half of 1990 in all of western Europe except France (where the rate stabilized at 9 per cent over the year) and the western part of Germany (where the rate continued to fall, to 4.7 per cent in November 1990 compared with 5.5 per cent in November 1989).[42] After a large increase in 1989, the unemployment rate in Norway fell throughout 1990 after the first quarter. In the United Kingdom[43] the number of persons unemployed started to increase in April after falling continuously for the preceding 44 months. However, the rate of unemployment was stable at 5.7 per cent from January to July and started to increase slightly only in August reflecting the weaker growth of employment. However, during the closing months of the year the rate increased sharply to reach 6.5 per cent in December. At the end of the year the highest unemployment rate in western Europe was in Ireland, 14.8 per cent. Even though the Swedish rate of unemployment increased throughout the second half of the year, it was still the lowest in western Europe in December (1.9 per cent compared with 1.3 per cent in June). Among the four south European countries it was only in Spain that the rate of unemployment con-

tinued to fall during 1990, although it remained high (around 16 per cent).

In North America the unemployment rate increased in 1990: in the United States it jumped from 5.3 per cent in June to 6.1 per cent in December, and for the year as a whole the average rate increased for the first time since 1982, to 5.5 per cent compared with 5.3 per cent in 1989. Between June 1990 and January 1991, civilian job losses totalled more than 1 million. In January 1991 the rate of unemployment further increased to 6.2 per cent. However, this rate of unemployment is still very much lower than the rates recorded during the previous recession (nearly 11 per cent). It can be explained, apart from the difference in the depth of the two recessions, by the reduced population pressure, due to the lower birth rates of the early 1970s, and by smaller increases in female participation rates (a reflection of the fact that many women already have jobs). In Canada, the rate of unemployment increased from 7.1 per cent in March to 9.3 per cent in December, pushing the annual average to 8.1 per cent compared with 7.5 per cent in 1989.

Not only did unemployment start to increase in most countries during 1990, but its real extent became more ambiguous than usual. The average number of hours worked per week, one of the key measures of economic activity, fell in some countries, most notably

---

42   OECD standardized rates.

43   Seasonally adjusted unemployed as per cent of total labour force.

in the United States[44] and the United Kingdom,[45] as overtime work fell and short-time work increased. In contrast, in France, where the rate of unemployment was stable throughout the year despite a sharp slow-down in economic activity during the second half of 1990, there were few layoffs but many sectors of the economy (especially the durable goods industries) introduced part time unemployment, especially in the fourth quarter. In Switzerland early retirement schemes were developed in the chemical industry in order to cut employment without creating unemployment. In Italy, as in France, the car industry introduced temporary shut-downs, instead of laying off workers. In addition to all these schemes to save jobs and/or diminish job losses, there was the discouraged worker effect (especially in North America, as mentioned above) which kept registered unemployment rates artificially lower, particularly during the closing months of 1990 and the beginning of 1991.

(iv) External balances

In the western market economies, trade continued to grow at a higher rate than output in 1990. Export growth continued strongly in the United States but there was some decline in Japan and western Europe. With the exception of the United Kingdom, import growth remained buoyant in most of the west European economies. The trade and current account deficits in the United States fell for a third consecutive year, while the Japanese surpluses shrank sharply. The reduction in the US deficits was assisted by the depreciation of the dollar which boosted the competitiveness of US products. In the case of Japan, the impact of the real effective depreciation of the yen on exports was partly offset by sluggish demand in the United States. In western Europe, the reunification of Germany was a significant force behind the reduction in the German external surpluses. The increase in the oil bill negatively affected the external accounts of most European countries, especially France and Italy. The depreciation of the dollar, however, dampened the effect of higher oil prices. In the United Kingdom, lower domestic demand growth contributed to an improvement in the trade balance.

General slow-down in European export growth ...

As a consequence of lower output growth in most industrial countries, there was a slow-down in the vol-

ume growth of west European exports. For the group of 13 countries (excluding southern Europe), exports are estimated to have increased by 4.5 per cent in 1990, compared with 7.2 per cent in 1989. Exports to North America and Japan were hindered by the appreciation of the west European currencies against the dollar and the yen. However, there were differences in the performance of individual countries. Germany was the only major economy where exports lost considerable momentum, and because of Germany's large share in west European trade, this affects significantly the aggregate figure for western Europe. The slow-down in the growth rate of German exports, from almost 8 per cent in 1989 to an estimated 1.6 per cent in 1990, occurred both as a response to higher export unit values (in terms of dollars and yen) and to an increase in domestic demand. The strength of domestic demand in Germany boosted exports from other European countries — which would otherwise have been negatively affected by the appreciation of their currencies against the dollar. Export volumes in France and Italy are estimated to have increased by 4-5 per cent in 1990:[46] in both countries the increase was less than in 1989, but the reduction in the growth rate was less pronounced than in Germany. Export volumes in the United Kingdom, on the other hand, rose by 6.8 per cent in 1990, slightly more than in 1989 (table 2.1.12).

In the smaller European economies, export volume growth varied considerably, from 8 per cent and over in Austria and Norway[47] to around 1 per cent in Sweden. Among the south European countries, exports grew rapidly in Spain, by nearly 10 per cent during 1990, the strength of the peseta being offset by a reduction of export prices in local currency.[48] Exports rose over 12 per cent in Portugal, at around 7 per cent in Turkey and by 1.5 per cent in Greece.

... but intra-European trade remains strong

Intra-European exports in 1990 continued to be more dynamic than European exports to the rest of the world. This trend, in place since 1982, was reinforced by the appreciation of most west European currencies vis-à-vis the dollar and the yen and by the boost to demand arising from the unification of Germany. West European exports to the United States grew less rapidly than imports (an estimated 5 per cent compared with a 12 per cent increase in imports), a reflection of the recovery in the competitiveness of US exports. Trade between the European Community and EFTA contin-

---

44 In January 1991 the average number of hours worked per week fell by 0.5 hours to 34.1 hours.

45 "Overtime working by operatives in manufacturing industries in Great Britain fell to 11.83 million hours per week worked in November 1990. This is the lowest level since January 1987 (11.19 million hours per week) and some 0.89 million hours lower than the average for the previous six months. The number of hours lost through short-time working in manufacturing industries in Great Britain increased in November 1990 to 0.60 million hours per week compared with 0.30 million in November 1989. Except for the exceptional level recorded in September (0.92 million), short-time working is now at its highest level since October 1986." *Employment Gazette*, February 1991.

46 Due to a fall in export unit values, French exports increased by only 2.9 per cent in value.

47 Being an oil-exporting economy, Norway in general follows a different trade path than the other west European countries. The increase in oil prices during 1990 boosted export value, while the reduction of production in the Gulf area boosted oil exports in volume. Of the 9.3 per cent increase in the volume of exports, some 3.5 percentage points are accounted for by an increase in exports of refined oil products. Export volumes of non-oil goods were boosted by a fall in export prices. See: Norges Bank, *Economic Bulletin, 1990/4*, December 1990.

48 See: Instituto Nacional de Estadistica, *Boletin Trimestral de Coyuntura*, December 1990.

TABLE 2.1.12

Trade volumes, 1988-1990

(Percentage change over previous year)

	Export volumes			Import volumes		
	1988	1989	1990 a	1988	1989	1990 a
France	8.7	7.8	4.9	6.5	8.7	6.0
Germany	7.4	7.3	1.6	6.6	7.0	12.0
Italy	6.0	8.6	4.1	6.9	8.3	5.1
United Kingdom	1.1	6.6	6.8	13.6	8.8	1.3
Total 4 countries	6.0	7.5	3.9	8.3	8.1	6.7
Austria	12.1	13.6	8.5	8.2	10.9	9.9
Belgium	5.8	8.0	6.5	5.2	7.4	7.6
Denmark	5.9	6.5	5.8	-1.0	1.0	1.9
Finland	-1.0	1.9	3.3	-0.8	15.1	-4.2
Ireland	7.0	11.3	7.7	4.7	12.9	8.3
Netherlands	8.3	5.1	5.7	7.2	4.2	5.7
Norway	-1.9	14.7	9.3	-9.7	-5.9	5.0
Sweden	2.8	1.8	1.1	5.4	6.8	2.0
Switzerland	-2.9	5.2	4.5	7.9	5.3	2.7
Total 9 countries	4.3	6.7	5.6	4.3	5.9	4.8
Total 13 countries	5.4	7.2	4.5	6.8	7.3	6.0
Greece	-32.8	37.7	-20.6	-24.8	34.6	37.0
Portugal	10.2	20.7	12.3	22.1	10.6	9.5
Spain	7.0	7.4	9.6	18.1	18.4	9.0
Turkey	11.7	-0.3	7.0	0.3	8.3	7.2
Total 4 countries	4.7	10.8	8.6	7.1	17.8	9.2
Total 17 countries	5.4	7.4	4.5	6.8	7.2	6.2
Canada	9.7	0.8	5.2	15.1	4.8	-0.2
United States	18.0	12.5	8.8	3.8	6.4	3.7
North America	15.5	9.1	7.7	5.9	6.1	3.0
Total above	8.3	7.9	5.6	6.5	7.4	5.1
Japan	4.4	5.0	4.9	16.6	8.3	5.2
Total above	7.7	7.5	5.5	7.5	7.4	5.2

Sources: IMF, *International Financial Statistics*, February 1991; OECD, *Monthly Statistics of Foreign Trade*, Series A, Paris, January 1991; OECD, *Economic Outlook*, No.48, December 1990; national statistics and ECE estimates. Weights for aggregation are US dollars trade shares in 1985.

a Preliminary or estimates.

ued strongly, although German exports to the EFTA countries weakened.[49]

Export growth down but still buoyant in the United States and Japan

In the United States, export growth in 1990 was less than in 1989 but nevertheless remained strong, outperforming world exports and providing the main support to domestic output growth in an environment of sluggish domestic demand.[50] The volume of US exports expanded by some 70 per cent between 1987 and 1990. Canadian export growth recovered in 1990, to 5.2 per cent, after slightly less than 1 per cent in 1989. Intra-North-American trade expanded by some 5 per cent in spite of sluggish output growth in the two countries.

Japan maintained its share of world exports in 1990 despite a real depreciation of the yen during the year. Exports are estimated to have increased by some 5 per cent in 1990, the same rate as in 1989. Exports slackened during the first half of the year but recovered during the second.

For the market economies as a whole (i.e., western Europe, North America and Japan), export volumes increased by 5.5 per cent in 1990, less than in 1989. Exports of manufactured goods,[51] particularly capital goods and non-food consumer goods, were relatively dynamic in most countries but especially so in the United States, where they increased by well over 10 per cent. For the whole group the volume of imports increased by 5 per cent in 1990, compared with nearly 7½ per cent in 1989.

49 See: *Statistische Beihefte zu den Monatsberichten der Deutschen Bundesbank, Reihe 3, Zahlungsbilanzstatistik*, December 1990 and EUROSTAT, *External Trade Monthly Statistics*, December 1990.

50 Exports increased in volume by 8.3 per cent in the period January-October 1990 on a custom basis, compared with a 2.9 per cent increase in imports. On a balance of payments basis, exports rose by 9.0 per cent in the first three quarters of 1990, compared with 12.5 per cent in 1989. See: *United States Department of Commerce News*, 18 December 1990 and 27 November 1990.

51 According to the UN index, exports of manufactured goods by the developed economies increased by 5 per cent during the first three quarters of 1990. This increase was unevenly distributed: exports rose by 19 per cent in the United States, but by only 2.5 per cent in western Europe. See: United Nations, *Monthly Bulletin of Statistics*, December 1990.

Import growth slows in the United States and Japan ...

The slow-down of the economy, together with a depreciation of the dollar, are the main reasons behind the reduction in the growth of US import volumes. US imports increased by 3.7 per cent in 1990, down from 6.5 per cent in 1989. Despite very strong domestic demand, Japanese import growth slowed from 8.3 per cent in 1989 to an estimated 5.2 per cent in 1990, a consequence of the relative weakness of the yen.

... but remains strong in Europe

In western Europe, 1990 was another year of strong import growth. However, with the exception of Germany, import volumes increased less than in 1989, and import behaviour differed considerably between countries. Total west European imports rose by some 6.2 per cent in 1990. Among the larger economies, import growth strengthened in Germany, weakened slightly in France and Italy and decelerated considerably in the United Kingdom, a result of a sharp slow-down in economic activity. In Germany, the 12 per cent increase in the demand for imports in 1990 was triggered by the increase in domestic demand that resulted from the unification process.

In the smaller European economies, imports continued to expand at a fast pace, albeit lower than in 1989. There were large differences, however, among countries. While import growth was in the 7-10 per cent range in Austria, Belgium-Luxembourg, and Ireland, it barely reached 2 per cent in Denmark and Sweden. In Finland, the volume of imports fell.

In southern Europe, continued strong growth of domestic demand in Spain, Portugal and Turkey[52] led to larger increases in import volumes than in exports. Imports also increased faster than exports in Greece, although domestic demand weakened in the latter. The large increases in import volumes in southern Europe were also influenced by real currency appreciation. In Spain, Portugal and Greece, there was even a nominal appreciation *vis-à-vis* the US dollar and the yen, while in Turkey currency depreciation lagged well behind domestic inflation.

Terms of trade: up for Europe, down for North America and Japan

Although trade balances in 1990 continued to be largely determined by volume changes, changes in the terms of trade also had a significant effect on the direction of trade. The increase in the price of oil in the third quarter of 1990 led to a brief deterioration of the terms of trade of most industrial countries — with the exception of oil-exporting countries such as Canada, Norway and the United Kingdom. In western Europe this deterioration was partly offset by the lower value

TABLE 2.1.13

Terms of trade, [a] **1987-1990**
(Percentage change over previous year)

	1987	1988	1989	1990 [b]
France	0.7	0.7	-1.0	0.9
Germany	3.7	-0.3	-2.4	1.2
Italy	2.5	1.5	-1.2	4.6
United Kingdom	1.5	1.2	1.5	1.7
Total 4 countries	2.3	0.6	-0.9	1.9
Austria	1.8	1.1	-5.6	3.2
Belgium	0.7	-0.5	-0.2	1.5
Denmark	2.7	-0.7	-2.8	1.9
Finland	3.3	2.6	3.4	-2.4
Ireland	0.1	0.6	0.1	-2.1
Netherlands	-3.4	1.6	-2.2	2.0
Norway	-5.3	-7.0	-2.0	1.1
Sweden	-0.3	-0.5	3.4	2.1
Switzerland	7.8	-0.1	-0.6	1.7
Total 9 countries	0.4	-0.1	-0.8	1.5
Total 13 countries	1.7	0.3	-0.9	1.7
Canada	0.9	5.0	1.4	-2.2
United States	-5.1	2.1	-0.4	-2.3
North America	-3.9	2.8	-0.1	-2.3
Japan	1.7	3.2	-4.7	-5.5
Total above	0.1	1.4	-1.1	-0.4

Sources: Compiled from IMF, *International Financial Statistics*, February 1991; OECD, *Monthly Statistics of Foreign Trade*, Series A, January 1991; and national statistics.

a   Ratio of unit value index of exports to that of imports.
b   Preliminary or estimated.

of the dollar and by the fall in non-oil commodity prices. But for 1990 as a whole, the terms of trade improved for western Europe (table 2.1.13).

In the United States and Japan, higher oil prices together with currency depreciation led to a deterioration in the terms of trade. In Japan, they fell by over 5 per cent during 1990, with most of the deterioration taking place in the fourth quarter as a consequence of higher oil prices. In Canada, higher oil prices partly offset the fall in the terms of trade caused by lower prices of other commodities.

Changes in the terms of trade in 1990 largely reflected exchange rate movements (table 2.1.14), which tended to support the reduction of global imbalances.[53] The dollar depreciated by 6 per cent in nominal effective terms in 1990 and the yen by some 10.4 per cent (also in nominal effective terms) after a strong depreciation in 1989.[54] Interest rates in Japan increased significantly to halt the fall of the yen and the strong expansion in the money supply. In the United States, monetary policy was relaxed from mid-year, and even more in the autumn, as a response to low activity levels and problems in the financial sector. In western Europe, there were several increases in interest rates throughout the year. In some countries this reflected a

---

52   Although growth decelerated in the first two countries, it strengthened in the latter.

53   Due to short-run J-curve effects, the Japanese surplus fell.

54   According to the MERM developed by the IMF. See IMF, *International Financial Statistics*, February 1991. In real effective terms, the dollar depreciated by 9 per cent and the yen by some 12.5 per cent.

tightening of monetary policy in response to fears of renewed inflationary pressures, but a major influence was the increase in German interest rates which, via the ERM of the European Monetary System, either increased or prevented rates from falling in other EC countries.

Narrowing of global imbalances

The external imbalances of the United States and Japan were further reduced in 1990 but they remain large. In addition, the German trade surplus started to fall from its peak in 1989. The aggregate merchandise trade deficit of the developed market economies rose from $36 billion in 1989 to an estimated $53 billion in 1990.[55] This was due to the fall in the Japanese and German trade surpluses, which was not offset by the contraction in the US deficit. There was an increase in the aggregate current account deficit, to an estimated $80.2 billion in 1990, up from $62.5 billion in 1989.

In the United States, primarily due to strong exports, the trade deficit on a balance of payments basis narrowed from $114.9 billion in 1989 to $108.7 billion in 1990 (table 2.1.15).[56] Most of the fall in the deficit occurred in the first half of the year as exports, especially capital goods, soared. Although the deficit had started to increase before the Gulf crisis (due to a softening of exports), higher oil prices led to a nearly 30 per cent increase in petroleum imports and to an $11 billion deficit in October. In the last two months of 1990 the deficit fell again as oil prices declined. The bilateral deficit with Japan fell by 18 per cent in 1990, while trade with western Europe moved into a surplus for the United States, reversing the trend of previous years.

In Japan, the trade surplus on a balance of payments basis declined by some 17 per cent in 1990 to an estimated $63.9 billion, down from $76.9 billion in 1989. This fall, which occurred primarily during the first half of the year, was mainly due to the real effective depreciation of the yen during 1989 and the early months of 1990, which boosted the dollar value of imports during the first half of 1990 by 20 per cent; the value of exports fell by 1 per cent over the same period. Increased import liberalization and growing consumer taste for foreign products appear to have reduced the price elasticity of Japanese imports. In the second half

of the year, the trade surplus increased again despite the fact that imports were boosted by the increase in oil prices and exports suffered from lower economic growth in the United States.

In Germany, the trade surplus in 1990 fell[57] slightly in terms of dollars but in Deutschmarks (DM116 billion) it was some 20 per cent lower than in 1989.[58] For the second consecutive year, Germany's trade surplus exceeded that of Japan and was some 40 per cent larger in 1990. Germany remained in surplus with the other west European countries in 1990, but it was lower than in 1989 due to the trade effects of unification.

In the United Kingdom, the trade deficit fell slightly in 1990 mainly because of an 11.5 per cent increase in the value of exports, which in turn reflected a large increase in volume and an increase of nearly 6 per cent in unit values. Part of the latter was due to higher oil prices. Imports of manufactures increased by 3 per cent, compared with 14 per cent in 1989. The deficit with other EC countries fell by just over one third (to £10.8 billion), a result of particularly dynamic exports and sluggish import growth. However, the deficit with North America increased by two thirds (to £1.4 billion).

In France, the trade deficit increased to $14 billion on a balance of payments basis. On a customs basis, it was $9.26 billion (FF 50.1 billion) in 1990, 14 per cent higher than in 1989 in terms of French francs. The value of French exports increased by only 2.9 per cent, compared with 16 per cent in 1989. The deficit with the United States increased by more than a half, mainly because of the increased competitiveness of US exports, while the deficit with Germany fell by FF 16 billion, or 20 per cent.

In Italy, fast import growth in volume terms continued but, due to an improvement in the terms of trade, the trade deficit fell from $2 billion in 1989 to an estimated $1 billion in 1990 on a balance of payments basis. On a customs basis, the deficit reached L10.97 trillion ($11.6 billion) in 1990, down from $12.3 billion in 1989.[59] The deficit increased considerably in the first quarter of 1990 due to a strong increase in imports, but it fell in the next three quarters as a consequence of both higher exports and lower imports. The effects on the trade balance of the higher oil-import bill were more than offset by a large increase in the surplus in non-oil trade.

---

55 Estimation for the 24 member countries of OECD.

56 On a customs basis, the US trade deficit reached $100.4 billion in 1990, down from $109.4 billion in 1989. See United States Department of Commerce News, *U.S. Merchandise Trade*, Washington, D.C., 18 February 1991.

57 As a consequence of the appreciation of the Deutschmark, import prices fell by some 2 per cent. The appreciation of the Deutschmark against the dollar during 1990 approached some 11 per cent: the exchange rate of the Deutschmark *vis-à-vis* the dollar passed from 1.70 DM/US dollar at the end of 1989 to 1.51 DM/US dollar at the end of 1990. See: IMF, *International Financial Statistics*, February 1991.

58 This figure includes the former German Democratic Republic as from July 1990. The surplus of the pre-July 1990 Federal Republic alone fell considerably more. There was even a fall in terms of dollars, from $76.7 billion in 1989 to $57.1 billion in 1990. On a customs basis, the German trade surplus reached DM 107.3 billion in 1990 ($64.3 billion), down from DM 134.5 billion in 1989.

59 Due to the fact that the trade balance on a balance of payments basis considers both exports and imports at f.o.b. prices, the deficit sometimes appears substantially lower than if a customs basis is used, which values imports at c.i.f. prices. In the case of Italy, the difference between c.i.f.- and f.o.b.-valued imports amounts to as much as 7 per cent, or some $10 billion. A similar difference between customs-based and balance of payments figures exists in France and the United Kingdom.

TABLE 2.1.14

Nominal effective exchange rate indexes, [a] 1988-1990

(1985 = 100)

	1988	1989	1990	1990 QI	1990 QII	1990 QIII	1990 QIV
France	106.3	103.9	112.1	110.1	111.4	112.8	114.2
Germany	118.4	116.3	124.5	123.3	123.7	124.5	126.4
Italy	101.9	101.7	106.5	105.5	107.0	107.0	106.6
United Kingdom	97.7	94.3	94.8	91.1	91.9	98.0	98.0
Austria	120.0	117.0	126.6	124.9	125.6	126.0	129.2
Belgium	110.1	108.4	115.1	113.2	114.7	115.7	116.8
Denmark	115.7	111.1	121.9	119.5	121.3	122.3	124.4
Finland	107.5	109.8	116.0	114.3	115.3	117.0	117.2
Ireland	106.6	103.5	111.6	109.5	110.8	111.8	114.2
Netherlands	118.6	115.8	122.6	121.5	121.7	122.6	124.7
Norway	96.0	94.6	97.5	96.4	96.9	97.9	98.8
Sweden	102.2	101.3	103.4	101.8	102.5	102.6	102.5
Switzerland	119.8	111.6	122.6	116.4	121.3	126.0	126.8
Canada	95.2	101.0	99.3	99.5	100.5	99.9	97.4
United States	68.0	71.0	66.4	68.8	68.8	65.4	62.4
Japan	151.8	145.2	130.1	130.1	123.1	128.1	139.1

Sources: IMF, *International Financial Statistics,* February 1991, Washington, D.C.

a Based on weights derived from the IMF's Multilateral Exchange Rate Model.

Deterioration in south European trade deficit

Among the south European countries, trade deficits escalated in 1990. In Spain, continued strong growth was accompanied by an increase in the trade deficit, which is estimated to have reached nearly $30 billion in 1990 on a balance of payments basis,[60] some 20 per cent higher than in 1989. The slightly higher growth in the value of exports (6.5 per cent) than in imports (5.4 per cent) did not prevent the trade deficit, the third largest among the western economies, from increasing. Spain's trade deficit is now the second largest in western Europe, just behind that of the United Kingdom. The trade deficits of Greece, Portugal and Turkey also widened considerably during 1990, reaching nearly $28 billion for the three countries. The steepest increase was in Turkey, where the deficit doubled — partly as a consequence of strong domestic demand growth and partly because of the real appreciation of the Turkish lira. The trade deficit also increased substantially in Greece due to a sharp increase in imports in anticipation of a devaluation of the drachma.

Current account changes

In western Europe, the aggregate current account surplus of the 13 economies (table 2.1.15) fell from $17.7 billion in 1989 to an estimated $15.6 billion in 1990. For the four major European economies there was a small $1 billion surplus in 1990 after an $8.9 billion surplus in 1989. In Germany, the current account surplus fell by 20 per cent in 1990 to some $44 billion. The lower German surplus was partly due to increased interest payments abroad, triggered by higher interest rates. Only direct investment outflows remained dynamic, increasing by some 50 per cent in the

first three quarters of 1990 with respect to the same period of the previous year. Most of these investment flows were directed to other EC countries. Strong investment flows to the south European members of the Community continued. As regards the other major European economies, the United Kingdom's current account deficit declined, basically due to the improvement in the trade balance. In France and Italy, the current account deficits increased in 1990. In the case of France, this was primarily due to the increase in the trade deficit, while in the case of Italy it was caused by a deterioration in the balance of services and by an increase in the net outflow of investment income.

In Japan, the current account surplus fell sharply in 1990, to $35.8 billion, down from $57.0 billion in 1989. In 1990, the Japanese surplus was $52 billion or 59 per cent lower than in 1987. The reduction in the current account surplus reflected the lower trade surplus and a 50 per cent increase in the service deficit, which has been increasing rapidly in the past few years. Reflecting the lower current account surplus, Japan exported less capital in 1990 than in the previous years; the reduction of portfolio investment abroad was particularly strong.

In the United States, the current account deficit declined to some $95 billion in 1990, down from $110 billion in 1989. The reduction in the current account deficit was the net result of both a reduction in the trade deficit and of a small improvement in the service balance. As regards the capital account, the reduction in interest rate differentials with respect to other industrial countries discouraged long-run autonomous capital flows. Portfolio investment inflows declined and net foreign direct investment was negative. In contrast to previous years, the US current account deficit was mainly financed with short-term capital.

---

60 See Instituto Nacional de Estadistica, *Boletin Trimestral de Coyuntura,* Madrid, December 1990.

TABLE 2.1.15

Trade and current account balances, 1988-1990

(Billion US dollars)

	Trade balances			Current account		
	1988	*1989*	*1990* a	*1988*	*1989*	*1990* a
France	-8.5	-10.7	-14.1	-3.5	-3.8	-7.7
Germany	79.4	76.7	69.8 b	50.5	55.4	44.0 b
Italy	-1.4	-2.0	-1.0	-6.2	-10.6	-13.1
United Kingdom	-37.4	-39.2	-31.4	-27.3	-32.1	-22.0
Total 4 countries	32.1	24.8	23.3	13.5	8.9	1.2
Austria	-6.3	-6.6	-9.5	-0.5	0.1	0.3
Belgium	1.2	1.0	0.2	3.6	3.2	4.3
Denmark	1.9	2.4	4.9	-1.8	-1.4	0.5
Finland	1.1	-0.2	0.2	-2.8	-5.1	-6.7
Ireland	3.8	4.0	3.7	0.7	0.5	0.4
Netherlands	8.5	7.9	8.9	5.3	8.0	9.3
Norway	-0.1	3.8	6.8	-3.7	0.2	3.2
Sweden	4.7	4.1	3.9	-2.5	-5.2	-5.4
Switzerland	-4.6	-4.3	-3.5	8.8	8.5	8.5
Total 9 countries	10.2	12.1	15.6	7.1	8.8	14.4
Total 13 countries	42.3	36.9	38.9	20.6	17.7	15.6
Greece	-6.1	-7.4	-12.3	-1.0	-2.6	-3.6
Portugal	-5.1	-5.2	-6.3	-0.6	-0.6	-1.2
Spain	-18.0	-24.5	-29.7	-4.0	-10.9	-15.7
Turkey	-1.8	-4.2	-8.2	1.6	1.0	-2.4
Total 4 countries	-31.0	-41.3	-56.5	-4.0	-13.1	-22.9
Total 17 countries	11.3	-4.4	-17.7	16.6	4.6	-7.3
Canada	9.1	6.9	9.4	-8.2	-14.1	-13.7
United States	-127.0	-114.9	-108.7	-129.0	-110.0	-95.0
North America	-117.9	-108.0	-99.3	-137.2	-124.1	-108.7
Total above	-106.6	-114.8	-113.3	-120.6	-119.5	-116.0
Japan	95.0	76.9	63.9	79.6	57.0	35.8
Total above	-11.6	-35.5	-53.0	-41.0	-62.5	-80.2

Sources: IMF, *International Financial Statistics*, February 1991; OECD, *Monthly Statistics of Foreign Trade*, Series A, Paris, February 1991; OECD, *Economic Outlook*, No.48, December 1990; national statistics and ECE estimates. Weights for aggregation are US dollars trade shares in 1985.

a Preliminary or estimates.
b Including the former German Democratic Republic.

In southern Europe, the current account deficit soared to $22.9 billion, roughly double the level of 1989. The increase was primarily due to a much larger deficit in Spain — $15.7 billion, compared with $10.9 billion in 1989 — triggered by a reduction in tourism receipts and by higher interest payments. In Greece and Portugal, there was a slight increase in the deficit, while in Turkey the current account balances moved from a surplus in 1989 to a deficit in 1990. In both cases, the deterioration in the current account was caused by an increase in the trade deficit.

(v) The short-term outlook

Before the Gulf crisis erupted last summer most forecasts for western Europe pointed to continued GDP growth in 1991 of around 3 per cent. In the United States it was believed that the worst of the slow-down was over, that recession would be avoided and that a moderate recovery would be under way from mid-1990. Although the price of oil rose in August and fluctuated sharply in subsequent months, by October the forecasting consensus was that world supplies of oil would not be seriously disrupted and that the price, after remaining firm in the latter half of 1990 and in the early months of 1991, would decline through the rest of the year. Thus, the IMF assumed an average price of $26 a barrel for the remainder of 1990 which would then fall to reach the new OPEC reference price of $21 by the last quarter of 1991. In western Europe the average price for 1991 assumed in most government and independent forecasts was typically about $25, slightly above the IMF's annual average of $23.[61]

This assumed increase in the price of oil led to a lowering of forecasts of output growth, although not by very much. On the basis of current government forecasts, which were for the most part made in October-November last year and which provide the macro-economic framework behind the various national budget proposals for 1991, west European growth this year would average some 2.3 per cent compared with just under 3 per cent in 1990. Within this aggregate, national growth rates would continue to

61 IMF, *World Economic Outlook*, Washington, D.C., October 1990, pp.vii and 1.

vary considerably, from 3.5 per cent in Germany (GDP) to practically zero in Sweden and the United Kingdom (and even a fall in Finland). Similarly, the impact on inflation rates was also quite small. Some acceleration was expected in the last quarter of 1990[62] but this would be short-lived: fiscal and monetary policies were already tight in western Europe and there was little chance that governments would relax them until the risk of second-round effects of higher oil prices on inflation was judged to be negligible. Moreover, except in Sweden and the United Kingdom, the increase in wage costs continued to moderate and non-oil commodity prices (in terms of dollars) were stagnant or falling. Thus, although some acceleration in annual rates of (consumer price) inflation was forecast in France, Italy and Germany, the average inflation rate in western Europe was expected to fall slightly.

Compared with the shocks of the 1970s, this relatively sanguine assessment of the "third oil shock" reflects a number of factors. First, of course, is that the increase in the oil price last year was much less than in 1973 or 1979. Secondly, the cyclical position of the market economies is very different from that in the first two shocks: in 1990 output was much less close to capacity limits and growth was already beginning to slow down. Also, as shown above (section 2.1(i)), the cyclical position of the major economies in 1990 was much less synchronized than in the 1970s. Third, the previous shocks were preceded by rapidly rising commodity prices and accelerating rates of domestic inflation in the market economies: consequently there was a severe tightening of macro-economic policies which was largely responsible for the depth of the recession in the early 1980s. In 1990, monetary policy was already tight and any further reaction to the oil shock, if necessary, was expected to be moderate. Finally, the structural changes of the 1980s have not only led to a considerable reduction (some 30 per cent or more) in the amount of oil consumed per unit of output but also to generally increased flexibility in the market economies and, hence, to a greater ability to absorb external shocks.

Following the outbreak of war in the Gulf in mid-January the price of oil fell sharply. Although there has since been some recovery, at under $20 a barrel it is still well below the levels assumed in current forecasts. The fall reflected the removal of any risk of disruption to oil supplies from Saudi Arabia as a result of military action[63] as well as expectations of further declines in prices once hostilities ended. The lower price of oil, together with associated reductions in interest rates and inflation, is a major reason why many forecasters expect the current recession to be relatively short and a resumption or strengthening of growth to occur in the second half of 1991. In the United States, these factors, together with strong support from net export growth are the principal forces behind the official forecasts[64] of recovery from mid-year with output rising by just under 1 per cent between the fourth quarters of 1990 and 1991.

In western Europe, forecasts of growth in 1991 have been generally lowered since last autumn and it now seems increasingly likely that west European growth this year will average less than 2 per cent for the first time since 1983. There are also serious downside risks to the official outlook for the United States: if these were to materialize and, at best, postpone the recovery, annual growth might be close to zero. In that case, growth in the market economies of western Europe and North America could dip below one per cent.

Why this apparently paradoxical sequel to the unwinding of the third oil shock? It should be noted, first of all, that the typical forecasting model incorporated the effects of higher oil prices on output, inflation etc. on the assumption of no change in business and consumer confidence — and most forecasters were explicit about this in presenting their post-shock forecasts. However, as is clear from the survey data in chart 2.1.8, business and consumer confidence fell sharply in the second half of 1990 and particularly so in the last quarter. Moreover, it is also clear that confidence was already falling before the Gulf crisis broke in early August. The picture is broadly similar in the United States: output expectations in manufacturing industry had been falling since the third quarter of 1988; there was an acceleration in the decline in the first two quarters of 1990 and then a massive drop in the third.[65] The University of Michigan's index of consumer expectations was also falling before the Gulf crisis, but the rate of decline accelerated sharply from August and the index reached a record low in January 1991.[66] As the secretariat pointed out last October,[67] the prolonged period of uncertainty following the August crisis — uncertainty regarding the level of oil prices, the probability of war and the future stability of supply — risked severely affecting business expectations by strengthening "wait-and-see" attitudes and, thereby, leading to the postponement of decisions to invest, take on new employees etc.

As can be seen in chart 2.1.8, European output expectations were declining and excess capacity was rising before the Gulf crisis and, as a result, some weakening of investment was probable anyway. The Gulf crisis

---

62 Which did occur: see section 2.1(ii) above.

63 In the forecasts referred to above, the assumption that oil supplies would not be seriously disrupted was essentially a working or "technical" assumption rather than a calculated probability. The fear that supplies might be interrupted with large but unknowable effects on prices was a major source of the uncertainty which affected the oil and financial markets in the five and a half months from the Iraqi invasion of Kuwait.

64 See, *Economic Report of the President*, Washington, D.C., February 1991, and the testimony of the Federal Reserve Chairman to Congress on 20 February 1991.

65 See OECD, *Indicators of Economic Activity*, Paris, 1990/4, p.87.

66 US Department of Commerce News, *Composite Indexes of Leading, Coincident and Lagging Indicators*, Washington, D.C., monthly.

67 United Nations Economic Commission for Europe, *Economic Bulletin for Europe*, New York, vol.42/90, 1990, p.12.

therefore appears to have given an extra push in the direction in which the underlying trends were already moving. In this situation, business reactions to the Gulf crisis — and especially to the threats of higher inflation and lower output growth — were probably much faster than if the underlying economic trends were strengthening rather than weakening. Certainly the speed of the downturn in output and employment in the latter months of 1990 seems to have taken forecasters and policy makers by surprise. Also, the survey data, as well as later revisions to statistical data, (for example, the mid-year revisions to the US national accounts), suggest that the western economies were not as strong as expected when last summer's forecasts were being made.[68]

It is too early to say whether the outbreak of war in mid-January led to a further significant fall in business confidence. In some sectors — notably airlines, travel, hotels and advertising — sales fell sharply and this will have had multiplier effects elsewhere; airline companies, already suffering from recession, quickly postponed or cancelled investment in new aircraft. In any event, many of the consequences of the Gulf crisis were already being borne before the outbreak of war: the higher oil price in the second half of 1990, the loss of trade with Iraq and Kuwait, and the general effects on confidence of the prolonged period of uncertainty from August to January. Many observers therefore think that the outbreak of military conflict could have marked an improvement in confidence: this was based, not on the absurdity that war was good for the world economy, but on the fact that the threat to oil supplies was perceived to have been removed and on the assumption that the conflict would be short-lived. The rapid conclusion of hostilities would therefore seem to justify this view which appears to be reflected in the recent upturn in the principal stock markets. However, post-war surveys of business and consumer confidence are not yet available. The unexpectedly short duration of the war will ensure that its impact on government expenditures in the market economies will be negligible and, given that the reduction in military stocks is unlikely to be replaced in full, the effects on both inflation and growth are likely to be small.

It was widely thought that the end of the war might be followed by a large fall in the price of crude oil: once the threat to supplies was removed, falling demand and the reduction of precautionary stock levels would exert strong downward pressure on prices. However, this has not happened partly because of a temporary boost to demand in western Europe as a result of cold weather in February; but, more fundamentally, because the principal Gulf producers and their western allies in the Gulf war would now appear to have closer mutual interest in avoiding either a collapse or a renewed upsurge in the price of oil. Nevertheless, short-run fluctuations

in price will continue to be greatly influenced by the ability of OPEC members to adjust production levels to changes in demand. If the price of oil is sustained at around $20 a barrel, inflation rates in 1991 would still be about a percentage point lower than forecast toward the end of 1990 and this will help to lower interest rates in western Europe and hasten their decline in the United States. Still larger declines in the post-war oil price would reinforce these tendencies.

This optimistic scenario implicitly assumes either that the decline in confidence is due only to the Gulf crisis, which is clearly mistaken, or that the pre-crisis reasons for the decline will cease to be significant once the Gulf-related causes are removed. This is not necessarily implausible: the lower oil price, followed by falling inflation and interest rates, will boost the real incomes of households and lower the costs of enterprises. Falling interest rates will ease the burdens on heavily indebted companies, especially in the United States but also in the United Kingdom, which in turn will help to improve bank balance sheets and encourage a recovery in lending. However, the market economies are now faced with a number of problems which, if not entirely blocking the recovery process described above, may at least slow it down.

Forecasts of a prompt recovery in the second half of 1991 imply a projection of the average post-war cycle: for example, forecasts of a mid-year upturn in the United States fit precisely the average duration of post-war recessions of eleven months. But all cycles differ from one another in many respects, as is indicated by the range of 6 to 16 months in the length of recessions in the United States, and there are several features of the present situation which mark it out from previous downturns. Not the least of these is the concern, unprecedented since the 1930s, at the high levels of corporate and personal debt in the United States and, to a lesser degree, in the United Kingdom, some of the Scandinavian countries, and Japan. High debt burdens and falling asset values put strong pressures on banks and other financial institutions to reduce their lending, and on households and enterprises to lower their debt and to reduce their spending on consumption and fixed investment. In these circumstances, the initial gains in real income from lower inflation and interest rates are likely to be used to rebuild household and corporate balance sheets rather than to support a swift recovery in spending.[69] Moreover, the adjustment will tend to be prolonged if inflation falls faster than interest rates because in that case the burden of debt actually increases. Real interest rates in western Europe are already fairly high (typically in the range of 4.5 to 6.25 per cent) and could increase in the face of falling inflation and the pressure on interest rates deriving from German unification via the ERM (see below). The need to lower interest rates at a faster rate is one of the

---

68 This is in marked contrast to the situation in 1987/1988 when the negative effects of the stock market crash were swept aside by the underlying strength of the market economies. Business confidence and output expectations were actually rising strongly in 1987 and monetary policy was loosened although real growth was much stronger than realized at the time. See United Nations Economic Commission for Europe, *Economic Survey of Europe in 1988-1989*, New York, 1989, pp.4-9. During 1990, monetary policy generally remained tight — or was tightened — while, as noted above, the underlying economic developments may have been weaker than realized.

69 There have been large falls in personal wealth in the United Kingdom and the United States in 1990, the first since 1974 and 1961 respectively. See American Express Bank, *Amex Bank Review*, London, January 1990.

CHART 2.1.8

Survey data for the European Community, 1987-1990
(Balances, percentages)

(a) Business (BC) and Consumer Confidence (CC)

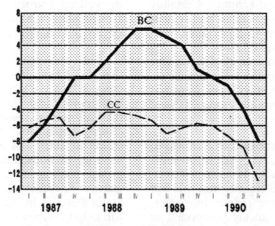

(b) Output expectations

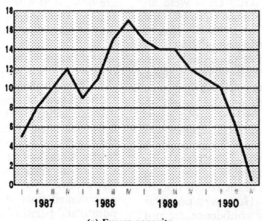

(c) Excess capacity

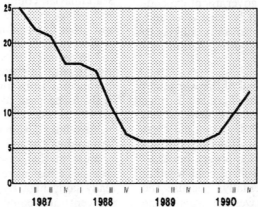

Source: Commission of the European Community, *European Economy, supplement B*, various issues.

Note: The indicators are the net balances (differences) between the percentages of respondents giving positive and negative replies respectively. Business and consumer confidence are averages of replies to several specific questions. For details of the questions, see any edition of the source. Business confidence, output expectations and excess capacity refer to manufacturing industry. The last refers to the balance of respondents expecting capacity to be more than sufficient in relation to output expectations. Data for the last quarter of 1990 refer only to October and November.

reasons for the more active loosening of monetary policy in the United States since November.

Some degree of balance sheet reconstruction takes place in every downturn, but it is the exceptionally high levels of corporate indebtedness which are giving cause for concern in some countries, especially the United States. The reasons for this situation are less important here than the possible consequences, but it might be noted that a combination of financial deregulation and the very length of the 1980s upswing may have encouraged borrowers (and lenders) to be less prudent about the risks of a downturn. Financial deregulation, particularly in the United States, has been associated with a considerable switch from equity to debt financing. The switch to debt financing effectively increases the rigidity of claims on corporate value added and enlarges the risk of either a more severe squeeze on fixed investment than would otherwise have been the case or of bankruptcy. Either outcome may aggravate the downturn and delay the recovery.[70]

The continuation of over-indebtedness and falling asset prices weakens the capital base of commercial banks and induces greater caution in their willingness to lend. This raises the prospect of a "credit crunch", which describes the point at which normally viable enterprises (or "good quality" borrowers) are unable to obtain loans. This would imply an upward shift in the supply of loanable funds and a degree of countervailing pressure to any lowering of interest rates by the central bank. Fears are widespread that such a situation has arisen – or may arise – in the United States, Japan and, to a lesser extent, in the United Kingdom. However, it is difficult to separate the effect of falling demand for credit from a shift in its supply. Falling demand is probably still the most important factor but, nevertheless, concern about the possibility of "debt deflation"[71] has been an important consideration behind the Federal Reserve's efforts to ease monetary policy since July and to reverse the sharp deceleration in the growth of the monetary aggregates.

In western Europe there are worries that the upward pressure on interest rates in Germany will deepen and prolong the downturn in the other economies of the EMS. The source of the problem is that the collapse of economic activity in the former German Democratic Republic has been very much greater than expected and this has led to massive government transfers from the western part of the economy to the east and these, in turn, have boosted consumption and capacity utilization in the west. The general government deficit has increased rapidly and is expected to reach some 4-5 per cent of GNP in 1991 (excluding borrowing by the *Treuhand*), while the Bundesbank, concerned at the increasing risks of higher inflation, has pushed up nominal interest rates. Insofar as nominal rates in other European countries differ from the German nominal rate by the difference between their inflation rates and

that in Germany, the former will be able to lower interest rates to some extent as their inflation rates fall. It will not be possible for real rates of interest in the rest of Europe to fall below the German real rate without risking a breach of the bilateral exchange rate limits. However, there is no reason why German real interest rates should be appropriate for the other European members of the EMS, especially when their economic cycles have become less synchronized. Thus, in the absence of an exchange rate realignment, the other member countries are likely to experience a prolonged period of high real interest rates. The German authorities have recognized that the German Government deficit is a source of pressure on monetary policy in the other ERM countries and have announced a package of tax increases to take effect on 1 July. These are unlikely to have a major impact on the deficit until 1992 and so the burden on monetary policy is unlikely to be eased significantly this year.

Although German interest rates are a problem for western Europe, the boom in domestic demand which has followed unification has clearly given a stimulus to exports from Germany's European trading partners. However, there are now signs that the post-unification boom is beginning to ease. Reconstruction in the east has proved a lot more difficult than envisaged last year and, so far, fixed investment, which should begin to support economic growth as the consumption boom weakens, has shown little sign of recovery. Uncertainties over property rights, the costs of repairing environmental damage, and grossly inadequate communications systems are among the major constraints on investment in the east. The German Government, in February 1991, adopted a package of measures designed to boost investment in the east, and, given the potential for increased activity in the new *Länder*, a sustained upturn could start to emerge some time in 1992. However, understanding of the complexities of the transition process is still very limited and policy makers are now unwilling to predict when a "take-off" is likely to occur in the eastern *Länder*. In the meantime, Germany will be increasingly affected by the slow-down in the rest of the world and by the depressive effects of the large tax increases announced in February.

It is of course possible that the swift conclusion of the Gulf crisis could lead to a rapid recovery of confidence which would ensure that the recession remains shallow and short. The considerations discussed here suggest that the likelihood of such an outcome, although highly desirable, is surrounded by considerable risks. The Gulf crisis clearly intensified the decline in business and consumer confidence and strengthened the forces making for recession. But the underlying trends – and the problems discussed above – were already in place before the crisis developed and it is by no means obvious that the end of the crisis will lead auto-

---

[70] A similar increase in the rigidity of claims on corporate income would occur if enterprises were pressured into maintaining unchanged dividend rates during the recession.

[71] "Debt deflation" is the process by which deflation increases the burden of debt, over-indebtedness leads to debt liquidation which, in turn, leads to a contraction in the money supply and further deflation. The process was first described by Irving Fisher in 1933 and is discussed in Gottfried Haberler, *Prosperity and Depression*, League of Nations, Geneva, 3rd edition, 1941, pp.113-116.

matically to their solution and to a rapid rebound in activity. Instead, the financial problems of households, enterprises and banks in some countries, as well as the costs of unification in Germany, and the associated pressures in the ERM, all suggest that the slow-down could intensify in the first half of 1991 and for the year as a whole growth is likely to slow quite sharply. In western Europe GDP will continue to rise on average, but by some 1.25 to 1.5 per cent compared with nearly 3 per cent in 1990. Within this aggregate, a year-on-year recession is forecast in the United Kingdom, Sweden and Finland while growth remains relatively strong in Germany at some 2.5 to 3 per cent. In the United States a slower recovery than expected by the Administration could leave growth between zero and a quarter of one per cent. Thus, for the market economies of western Europe and North America, growth in 1991 could be some 0.5 to 1 per cent. Outside the ECE region expansion is expected to slow in Japan but it would still be nearly 4 per cent.

A positive feature of the outlook for 1991 is that inflation rates are generally expected to fall (with the principal exception of Germany). Earlier fears about the impact of the Gulf war on oil prices have proved unfounded, while other commodity prices are expected to remain weak and domestic cost pressures to weaken. Lower inflation and a gradual easing of monetary policy, especially in the United States, will help to check the downturn and support a recovery in the latter half of the year. However, the upturn is likely to be slow and gradual while households and companies restore their financial positions and as banks go through a period of greater caution in their lending. For these reasons growth is likely to pick up more strongly in 1992, to around some 2.5 per cent, when an additional stimulus to the world economy is likely to arise from large-scale reconstruction in the Gulf states affected by the war.

2.2 EASTERN EUROPE AND THE SOVIET UNION

Economic activity in the eastern part of the ECE region was dominated in 1990 by the consequences of the political upheavals that had taken place in the course of 1989 and had accelerated at the year's close. Over the last 18 months, new governmental structures have arisen in all countries, including the Soviet Union, and in most of them the political régime of the ruling communist parties has come to an end. In all countries without exception, the once-guiding concept of the *centrally planned and administered economy* has been abandoned to be replaced by market-oriented economic models. If all countries of the region have that much in common, they differ widely, at the beginning of 1991, as regards the degree to which the new economic model to be aimed at has been defined, legislation to support such models and create the necessary institutions has been passed, and — perhaps most importantly — the path for the transition from one model to the other has been mapped out. In some countries, most of these tasks are resolved, if not fully implemented, while in others only the very first steps have been taken. The fact that new governments legitimized by regular elections took office only around the middle of 1990 in a number of countries explains part of the difference, but in many cases a lack of social consensus on how to deal with these issues is equally important. In the meantime, to varying extent, the existing, but discredited, old institutions continue to operate with decreasing effectiveness. As always when the shape of the future is uncertain, the anticipatory or precautionary actions of economic agents become important in determining the course of events, at times in a dysfunctional manner.

Domestic output and demand changes are examined in sections (i)-(ii), and sectoral developments and the energy situation in section (iii). Section (iv) reviews some issues of internal balance. The rise of unemployment is discussed in section (v), external balances in section (vi).

(i) Output and demand

In the last quarter of 1989, the economies of eastern Europe[72] and the Soviet Union were heading into a recession. In 1990 this deepened considerably. The downturn reflected a variety of factors, some of them inherited from the past and some linked with the rapid transformation of the former state-run economies into market-oriented systems. The impact of stabilization policies and economic reforms, coupled with the collapse of intra-CMEA trade, produced a severe recession, which is deeper than originally expected. Domestic output fell in all countries under consideration and in most of them this was accompanied by a worsening of internal and external imbalances.

Large declines in eastern output ...

Net material product declined by 11 per cent in *eastern Europe* in 1990 and by 4 per cent in the *Soviet Union* (table 2.2.1).[73] The fall in eastern Europe was general but its extent differed widely. The drop in output was some 3-6 per cent in Czechoslovakia and Hungary, almost 8 per cent in Yugoslavia, while in Bulgaria, Poland and Romania it was more than 10 per cent. In the former German Democratic Republic the adjustment recession was even more severe, with a 19 per cent drop in national output (table 2.2.2).

... great variance in external adjustment ...

Developments in *domestic absorption* reflected the different nature of domestic and external adjustment in individual countries. Although relevant data are not yet available from all countries, it appears that *NMP used domestically* has fallen less than total output in most or even has risen in the face of falling output in 1990 in some (table 2.2.3). The exceptions are Hungary, which squeezed imports but did not achieve an export take-off, and Poland, which achieved both. These countries, which aimed to stabilize their economies through severely restrictive domestic policies and improved export performance, recorded significant falls in NMP used.

---

72 The term "eastern Europe" as used in the text and the tables is employed for presentational convenience, to group together the former centrally planned economies of central and eastern Europe plus Yugoslavia, which also finds itself in transition from a "socialist" to a market economy. The statistical aggregates referred to under this term thus cover Bulgaria, Czechoslovakia, the former German Democratic Republic, Hungary, Poland, Romania and Yugoslavia in most instances. For the period after the accession of the GDR to the Federal Republic of Germany, the last quarter of 1990, data for the newly-formed east German *Länder* are used to extend the GDR-reported time series. It should be noted that in some instances this involved a change in measurement concept (e.g., from NMP to GDP).

Occasional utilization of the term "eastern Europe and the Soviet Union" should be understood along the same lines.

73 A number of countries now report "gross value added in the material sphere" (GMP) instead of the traditional NMP measure. All the eastern countries have started to transform their traditional system of macro-economic indicators, based on the material product system (MPS), to the system of national accounts (SNA) with GDP or GNP as the basic measure of production (this includes gross value added in both the material and non-material spheres), but measures on this definition reported for 1990 are in most cases rough approximations. Hungary has already completed the change; since 1968 parallel sets of estimates for main macro-economic indicators have been provided, and recently the statistical authorities have stopped publishing some indicators based on the MPS. The aggregate reported here for 1990 as "net material product" thus reflects a mixture of different indicators and some secretariat estimates (see notes to table 2.2.2).

TABLE 2.2.1

Eastern Europe and the Soviet Union: Basic economic indicators, 1976-1991
(Average annual and annual growth rates, in percentages)

Country or group, indicator	1976-1980	1981-1985	1986	1987	1988	1989	1990 Jan.-Sept.	1990 Full year	1991 Fore-casts a
Eastern Europe									
Net material product b	3.6	1.7	3.7	1.8	1.5	-0.7	..	-11.2	-1
Industrial output c	5.6	2.7	4.4	2.7	2.8	0.2	-16.5	-17.5	-2
Agricultural output c	1.9 d	1.0 d	1.8	-2.9	1.9	-	..	-3.5 e	..
Gross investment	2.7	-0.7	3.9	4.1	2.1	-1.5	..	-13.8	..
Exports	6.5	5.1	-1.2	1.4	3.7	-2.1	-11.1	-10.0	..
Imports	4.1	0.7	4.8	3.4	3.3	0.9	-3.6	-0.5	..
Soviet Union									
Net material product	4.3	3.2	2.3	1.6	4.4	2.4	-2.5	-4.0	-1 ½
Industrial output c	4.5	3.6	4.4	3.8	3.9	1.7	-0.9	-1.2	-2
Agricultural output c	1.7 d	1.1 d	5.3	-0.6	1.7	0.8	..	-2.3	5 ½
Gross investment	3.3	3.5	8.3	5.7	6.2	4.7	..	-4.3	-14
Exports	4.9	1.5	10.0	3.3	4.8	-	-6.3	-14.0	..
Imports	5.9	5.8	-6.0	-1.6	4.0	9.3	0.6	-5.0	..

Source: Secretariat of the United Nations Economic Commission for Europe, based on national statistical publications, plans and plan fulfilment reports.

a   Average of national forecasts, excluding the former German Democratic Republic.
b   Gross material product for Yugoslavia, and for Poland in 1990; gross domestic product (SNA) for the former GDR in 1990.
c   Gross output.
d   Annualized change in the five-year average production levels from the average of the preceding five years.
e   Excluding the former German Democratic Republic and Yugoslavia.

Other countries, such as Romania and the Soviet Union, protected consumption and living standards from falling and, since domestic output declined, this significantly worsened internal and external imbalances. Yugoslavia is a case in between these two models: its stabilization policies produced results for the first half of the year, but then broke down in the second half. The implementation of stabilization policies in these countries in 1991 will be more difficult.

Consumption appears to have generally held up better than *accumulation,* but high rates of growth of monetary incomes have been offset in most countries by a take-off in actual or concealed inflation and growing shortages, which encouraged stockbuilding by consumers through hoarding and anticipatory buying. In those countries which maintained comprehensive price controls (Bulgaria, Czechoslovakia, Romania, the Soviet Union) or where central distribution systems had not been replaced by functioning markets, accumulation was probably also swollen by a build-up of enterprise inventories in anticipation of supply disruptions.

... and a generalized fall of investment ...

Gross fixed investment in 1990 was considerably weaker than in 1989. It had already fallen in the earlier year in the five east European countries taken together; only Czechoslovakia and Hungary recorded increases but they were small and there was a noticeable deceleration in the Soviet Union. In 1990, investment in five of the six east European countries collapsed, falling by between 7 and 35 per cent; Czechoslovakia was the only country among the six to record any growth at all (table 2.2.4). This was accompanied by an un-

precedented decrease of 4 per cent in the Soviet Union. Investment changes generally paralleled but in some cases were rather smaller than declines in output (Czechoslovakia and Poland). Exceptions were the former GDR, where the recession following re-unification and full exposure to market conditions was much deeper than originally anticipated, and Romania, where the new government's rapid action to divert resources to consumption caused a one-third fall in investment — three times bigger than the output decline.

The first steps in privatization were taken in 1990, but concrete results were limited. Problems reported in settling ownership claims may have held back private capital commitments. Even so, private activity held up better than public sector investment in Hungary and Poland, the countries which have furthest advanced along the reform road.

Investment in most east European countries during the course of the 1980s had fallen to historically low levels under conditions of internal and external supply constraints. External constraints remain; indebtedness in all transition countries has risen fast in recent years and continued to do so in 1990. Internal constraints, notably the fall in output and consequent interruptions in supply, have even intensified but their nature is changing. Under actual or imminent market conditions, prudent enterprise managements in 1990 could not continue to accept poor quality investment goods produced domestically or the poor quality and high cost of output produced with them. Investment has been progressively decentralized and funds previously recycled by the central planning authorities are now left at the disposal of the investing enterprises. This could have accentuated the effects of uncertainties with regard

TABLE 2.2.2

Net material product (produced), 1981-1991
(Annual percentage change)

	1981-1985	1986-1990 Plan	1986-1990 Actual	1986	1987	1988	1989	1990	1991 [a] Projection
Bulgaria...	3.7	5.4	-0.5	5.3	5.1	2.4	-0.4	-13.6	-10.0
Czechoslovakia....................................	1.8	3.4	1.0	2.6	2.1	2.3	1.0	-3.1	-8.0
German Democratic Republic......................	4.5	4.6	-1.8	4.3	3.3	2.8	2.1	-19.5 [b]	-19.5 [b]
Hungary..	1.3	2.8-3.2	-0.5	0.9	4.1	-0.5	-1.1	-5.5*	-3.0*
Poland..	-0.8	3.0-3.5	-0.5	4.9	1.9	4.9	-0.2	-13 [c]	4.0
Romania...	3.0	10.3	-3.5	3.0	0.7	-2.0	-7.9	-10.5	2.8
Yugoslavia [c]..	0.7	..	-1.3	3.6	-1.1	-1.7	0.6	-7.6	..
Eastern Europe.....................................	1.7	5.2	-1.3	3.7	1.8	1.5	-0.7	-11.2	-1.0 [d]
Soviet Union..	3.2	4.3	1.3	2.3	1.6	4.4	2.4	-4	-1.5

Source: ECE secretariat Common Data Base, based on national statistics, plans and statistical reports and direct communication to the ECE secretariat. National data are aggregated by means of weights derived from CMEA studies.

a National forecasts.
b GDP (estimate, Deutsches Institut für Wirtschaftsforschung, Berlin).
c Gross material product (value added of the material sphere including depreciation).
d Excluding the former German Democratic Republic.

TABLE 2.2.3

NMP produced and NMP domestically used
(Annual percentage change)

Country and period	NMP produced (1)	NMP used [a] (2)	Consumption Total (3)	Consumption Personal [b] (4)	Consumption Social [c] (5)	Accumulation Total (6)	Net fixed capital formation (7)	Changes in stocks (8)	Retail trade turnover (9)	Real income per capita (10)	Gross invest-ment (11)
Bulgaria											
1989....................................	-0.4	-5.5	1.7	..	..	-26.9	..	..	0.4	-2.4	-7.7 [d]
1990....................................	-13.6	..	..	..	..	..	..	..	-9.3	..	-13.5
Czechoslovakia											
1989....................................	1.0	3.4	3.7	1.8	7.5	2.0	-12.1	82.7	2.3	1.8	1.6
1990....................................	-3.1	1.4	1.1	1.1	..	3.0	..	..	1.3	-1.3	5.7 [d]
German Democratic Republic											
1989....................................	2.1	1.6	2.8	3.5	2.1	-2.7	-2.8	-1.7	3.5	..	0.6
1990....................................	..	..	..	..	..	..	..	..	-2.0*	..	..
Hungary											
1989....................................	-1.1	-0.5	-0.5	-	-3.5	-8.5	-11.4	-2.5	-0.3	2.5	0.5
1990....................................	-5.5*	-7.5*	-4.5*	-4.5*	-4	..	..	..	-6	-4.5*	-7*
Poland											
1989....................................	-0.2	0.1	-1.7	0.8	-4.2	7.1	-7.4	36.7	-2.7	6.2	-2.4
1990....................................	-13	-17	..	-24	..	..	-9	..	-12.8	..	-8
Romania											
1989....................................	-7.9	-5.6 [d]	0.1 [d]	..	..	-26.2 [d]	..	..	-1.7	..	-1.6 [d]
1990....................................	-(10-11)	..	10	..	..	-15	..	..	13.2	..	-35.0 [d]
Yugoslavia											
1989....................................	0.6	2.1	..	1.0	-1.8	..	0.5	7.2	..	..	0.5
1990....................................	-7.6	-3.6	..	2.5	1.1	..	-7.0	-15.3	..	..	-7.0
Soviet Union											
1989....................................	2.4	3.2	7.7 [d]	8.0 [d]	6.2 [d]	-2.0 [d]	-10.7 [d]	10.2	8	..	4.7
1990....................................	-4	..	..	..	..	..	..	..	9.9	..	-4.3

Sources: National statistics and plan fulfilment reports.

a NMP used for domestic consumption and accumulation.
b Volume of consumer goods and material services supplied to the population.
c Consumption of material goods in institutions providing amenities and social welfare services.
d At current prices.

TABLE 2.2.4

Gross fixed investment, 1986-1991
(Annual percentage change)

	1986	*1987*	*1988*	*1989*	*1990*	*1991* a
Bulgaria	8.0	7.2	2.4	-7.7	-13.5	..
Czechoslovakia	1.4	4.4	4.1	1.6	3.0*	..
German Democratic Republic	5.3	8.0	7.3	0.9	-9.0*	..
Hungary	6.5	9.8	-9.1	0.5	-7.0*	-4.0
Poland	5.1	4.2	5.4	-2.4	-8.0	16.0
Romania	1.1	-1.4	-2.2	-1.6	-35.0	3.5
Yugoslavia	3.5	-5.1	-5.8	0.5	-7.0	..
Eastern Europe	3.9	4.1	2.1	-1.5	-14.0	..
Soviet Union	8.3	5.7	6.2	4.7	-4.3	-14.0

Source: ECE secretariat Common Data Base, based on national statistics, plans and plan fulfilment reports and direct communication to the ECE secretariat. National data are aggregated by means of weights derived from CMEA investigations.

a Projections.

to the future viability of existing enterprises, especially in those countries where price reform has not yet been carried through.

Investment performance in 1990 may thus for the first time have begun to reflect demand and confidence factors rather than the mainly physical supply-side constraints of the past. Tight money and in some countries high interest rates also began to play a role. Budgetary surpluses were posted in Czechoslovakia and in Poland. Bulgaria and Hungary both ran deficits but specifically attempted to cut back on centralized investment and other cash allocations to enterprises. Interest rates on enterprise credits in Hungary and Poland rose to very high nominal levels. Financial constraints appear to have played a smaller role in the Soviet Union where the budget deficit, though declining, remained very large. In that country, as in Bulgaria and Romania, the structures necessary to transmit interest rate and other macro-economic policy instruments are not yet in place.

Disruptions in the supply of investment goods worsened as a result of breakdowns in previously centralized trading networks. *Construction* output in 1990 declined in most east European countries and the Soviet Union, at rates ranging between 2-9 per cent and by as much as 28 per cent in Romania. In three of the four east European countries for which data are available, *engineering* output falls have exceeded the drop in investment (or, in Czechoslovakia, has not kept pace with its rise) – often by a considerable margin. In the Soviet Union, in contrast, engineering output rose. Supply disruptions may also have resulted from the collapse of intra-CMEA trading links but may have been partly offset by increased imports from western suppliers.

... with large inter-country differences

Although the recession in the east is general, there are important differences between countries both in its severity and in the forces which are shaping it. One group of countries consists of those where the decline in output reflects the impact of stabilization policies and determined efforts to speed up the pace of eco-

nomic transformation. Since most of them have been suffering from macro-economic instability for the last few years, severe controls on aggregate demand have been introduced in order to control inflationary pressures. These have led not only to falling output but also to reductions in domestic consumption and investment. Although there are differences among them in so far as the speed and scope of the reforms is concerned, Poland, Hungary, Czechoslovakia and the former German Democratic Republic can be placed in this group. In the second group (Bulgaria and Romania), in addition to country specific factors, the deteriorating situation reflects a collapse of central control while not putting into operation an effective programme of reform due to a lack of political and social consensus. In the Soviet Union this has been compounded by ethnic and social tensions as well as labour disputes, including strikes.

The problems of economic transformation in all the east European countries and the Soviet Union have been exacerbated by the collapse of intra-CMEA trade, the speed of German unification, the Gulf crisis and a major price shock stemming from the decision of the former CMEA members to switch to world prices and convertible currency settlement in their mutual trade.

Although the discontinuities of the transition period made any forecast for 1990 highly uncertain, it is clear, in retrospect, that policy makers' expectations for 1990 were much too optimistic. Since 1990 was the last year in the five-year planning period 1986-1990, actual developments over that span may be briefly compared with the original targets. These envisaged substantial average annual growth in all countries, but only two – Czechoslovakia and the Soviet Union – could claim production at all above the 1985 level five years later (table 2.2.2).

(ii) Review by country

Against the background of an unstable socio-political situation, weakened authority of the originally highly centralized economic management system and a lack of agreement on the legitimation of the government to undertake far-reaching reforms, the economy of *Bulgaria* was characterized in 1990 by large imbalances, collapsing markets and falling output.[74] In 1990, *NMP produced* fell by almost 14 per cent. The fall in *domestic absorption* (*NMP used*) must have also been significant — though smaller — since retail sales (a proxy for private consumption) declined by 9 per cent in volume and investment by 13½ per cent (table 2.2.3) while the external balance worsened in real (though not in nominal) terms (tables 2.2.15 and 2.2.19). The Bulgarian economy is now in a state of crisis for numerous reasons, many of them rooted in the past, and some arising from the revolutionary changes under way in the country. The declining authority of the centralized economic management system has not been compensated by a rise of market forces effectively backed by "hard budget constraints". It seems that the postponement of reforms, especially as regards the price system, has lead to much hoarding in anticipation of future price rises, thus disrupting supply linkages which, for consumer markets, were in any case under pressure in the wake of a very poor harvest. The high import dependence of the Bulgarian economy also made it very vulnerable to external shocks — the collapse of intra-CMEA trade, the Gulf crisis and cuts in imports from the west necessitated by the country's illiquidity, especially in the second half of the year (Bulgaria had to suspend the service of its external debt early in 1990).[75] Bulgaria has been highly dependent on the CMEA trade area (effectively, the Soviet Union) for its energy supplies and is one of European countries most affected by Soviet fuel export cutbacks as well as by the early impact of the Gulf crisis. Domestically, strikes and slackening labour discipline, together with the prolonged political crisis and continuing social frictions, also had a negative effect on production.

In 1990 *Czechoslovakia* abandoned the traditional system of central planning and began to introduce some market-oriented reforms. Given the better initial conditions of the country as regards internal and external balance, the fall in output was less than in the other countries of eastern Europe. NMP produced was some 3 per cent below its 1989 level. The fall in output was greatly influenced by the sharp drop in Czechoslovak exports to CMEA countries, by the conversion of the defence industry to civilian uses and by substantial cuts in deliveries of Soviet oil and raw materials. The disturbances of the transition process were reflected in material supplies difficulties, since the discipline of state plan has not been replaced by the workings of the market. Increased labour mobility and instability in the managerial apparatus added problems of their own to the above factors. Domestic absorption of resources increased, but as domestic output growth contracted, this was reflected in a deterioration in the external balance. The most dynamic component of NMP used was stockbuilding. The behaviour of economic agents has changed due to the introduction of some elements of reform and, mainly, in expectation of future systemic changes. Households have reduced their saving and enterprises have substantially increased hard currency imports and stocks in expectation of a devaluation of the koruna and of price rises.

In the former *German Democratic Republic* the decline of the economy continued in 1990. After the implementation of the economic, monetary and social union, enterprises in the east of Germany were suddenly exposed to competition from the Federal Republic and other western countries. The decline in domestic and foreign demand, due to the low competitiveness of domestic products, led to a sharp and accelerating fall in production (table 2.2.6). The rapidity of the move to unification and the collapse of central planning only accentuated the difficulties of adjustment. The developments in the east German economy are instructive because they demonstrate how feeble even a country which was considered the most developed of the former European centrally planned economies can be in the face of market forces.

Hungarian economic policies aimed at a slower pace of adjustment, and although stabilization and restructuring were pursued simultaneously, the recession was less severe than in most other east European countries. However, the decline in national output has continued for three consecutive years and in 1990 it accelerated sharply. The collapse of CMEA trade, the severe drought and substantially depressed domestic demand, coupled with the rising price of energy and ongoing restructuring led to a 4-5 per cent decline of gross domestic product in 1990.[76] However, industrial output in small companies, mostly private, more than doubled. On the utilization side, consumption and fixed investment both fell by some 5-6 per cent. On the positive side, there was a record surplus in convertible-currency trade, surpassing even the most optimistic forecasts.

In *Poland* tight fiscal and monetary policies, as well as systemic changes such as price liberalization and the introduction of internal convertibility of the currency, significantly affected developments in 1990. A severe squeeze on domestic demand led to a 13 per cent decline in gross material product (GMP) produced.[77] Strong private sector activity helped to soften the downturn: gross value added in the socialized material sector declined by 21 per cent while in the private sector it increased by 17 per cent. There was a large shift of resources into the external sector, the volume of exports increasing by 15 per cent and imports declining by a similar amount. Consequently domestic absorption (GMP utilized) contracted more strongly than output,

---

74 See section 4.5 below for a survey of reform and stabilization efforts in Bulgaria.

75 See section 3.3(v) for a discussion of Bulgaria's relations with western markets.

76 Given the growing share of services, the fall in NMP produced was even sharper.

77 Value added in the material sphere including depreciation. The statistical offices of Poland and Czechoslovakia have in recent years increasingly used this measure, rather than NMP (value added in the material sphere *net* of depreciation), as the basic indicator of national performance. The same indicator has been used by Yugoslavia since the 1950s. The broader measure of *gross domestic product* calculated according to SNA rules (GDP), including the non-material sphere, is now also estimated; on this indicator the decline was somewhat less — 12 per cent.

by 17 per cent: private consumption dropped by about 24 per cent and fixed investment by 9 per cent. The restoration of overall internal balance and the generation of a large trade surplus (and the first current-account surplus since 1971) are among the positive results of the Polish "shock treatment". Since the fall in domestic output was stronger in the first half of the year, it is possible that the recession has now bottomed out.

In *Romania,* where market-based reforms only began at the end of the year, external shocks and internal political and social tensions contributed to a 10 per cent fall in NMP in 1990. Government policies protected consumption, which rose by 10 per cent, but accumulation fell by more than 15 per cent, with a decline in gross investment of 35 per cent. Imports from the developed market economies increased dramatically. As a result, there was a substantial worsening of internal and external balance, shortages became widespread and the economy is in a critical state.

In *Yugoslavia,* a comprehensive reform package was adopted at the end of 1989, designed to introduce a fully-fledged market system and accompanied by measures to stabilize the economy. The main, indeed very ambitious, objective of the stabilization policy was to curb inflation to an average rate of 13 per cent in 1990, after it had accelerated to a rate of some 1,256 per cent in 1989. A core element of the package was the introduction of a new, convertible dinar pegged to the Deutschmark at a rate which, however, overvalued the currency from the outset. Other measures included a wage freeze for 6 months; a tightening of monetary policy, notably the end of monetary expansion to finance budgetary deficits at all levels; and a far-ranging price liberalization.

Although during the first half of the year the impact of the stabilization policy was considerable, notably as regards inflation, nearly all of the achievements were reversed in the second half of 1990. Wage controls were lifted by mid-year, and monetary and fiscal policies loosened. As a consequence, inflation accelerated again in the second half. Unemployment rose significantly, reaching 16 per cent of the labour force.[78]

After virtual stagnation in 1989, GMP (gross value added of the material sphere) fell by about 7½ per cent. Industrial output declined by more than 10 per cent as domestic demand contracted and export growth slowed to 2 per cent, probably in reflection of the overvaluation of the currency. Imports surged by 22 per cent by the same token. Private and public consumption supported economic activity, whereas investment slumped by 7 per cent and is now some 45 per cent below the 1979 level.

The rapid rise of imports (27½ per cent in current dollar terms) resulted in a substantial expansion of the trade deficit (from $1½ billion in 1989 to $4½ billion in 1990) and a $5 billion turnround in the current account, for the first deficit ($2½ billion) in eight years.

Despite some slow-down in the still very high inflation rate, the overall economic performance for the year has therefore been rather disappointing. The predicament of the country has worsened. There are several factors which help to explain the overall developments in 1990, but the most important is without any doubt the lack of political consensus on economic policy, notably as regards central macro-economic controls, which caused the stabilization effort to abort.

Production fell also in the *Soviet Union,* the rate of decline accelerating during the year. NMP produced fell by 2 per cent in the first half of 1990 and 4 per cent the whole year. Several factors contributed to the deterioration: the old centralized supply system collapsed and disrupted traditional links between enterprises; the conversion of the defence industry from military to civilian production has run into many difficulties and contributed significantly to the fall of industrial output; shortcomings in management, as well as increasing labour unrest and growing social tensions, exacerbated − and were exacerbated by − the above factors.

On the utilization side, gross fixed investment in the Soviet Union fell by 4 per cent, but consumption (including the stockbuilding of households) certainly increased. With a 10 per cent rise in the volume of retail sales this increase may have been substantial, and in that case NMP used may also have risen. Domestic demand was fuelled by a large increase in personal incomes (17 per cent in 1990) and a burgeoning state budget deficit which reached about 6 per cent of GDP in 1990. Given declining levels of national output, domestic absorption was supported by an increasing trade deficit. Thus, *perestroika* in the economic sphere has so far failed to arrest the country's decline into severe economic crisis.[79]

(iii) Sectoral developments

A big shift to services

The fall in output in the former centrally planned economies in 1990 was accompanied by some important structural changes. One of them is a large shift in favour of the *service sector.* At present this can be judged only indirectly from the difference between the changes in NMP produced and GDP calculated on the basis of the UN system of national accounts.[80]

---

78 See section 4.3 below for a discussion of the Yugoslav stabilization effort.

79 The resolution of the Congress of People's Deputies of the USSR "On the situation in the country and priority measures to overcome the critical socio-economic and political situation", 24 December 1990, speaks about the growing crisis in society, which affects all the aspects of the socio-economic, political and spiritual life in the country. Economic linkages among regions and enterprises are being disrupted and money-commodity relations upset. Inflation is growing, while the supply of consumer goods is deteriorating. See *Ecotass,* No.2, 14 January 1991, p.18.

80 The difference between NMP and GDP growth indicates indirectly only changes in the relative importance of non-material services, since transport and trade (producer services) are treated as belonging to the material sphere and, hence, are included in NMP.

TABLE 2.2.5

Gross social product (GSP) and sectoral gross output, [a] 1981-1990
(Annual percentage change)

	1981-1985 [b]	1986-1990 [b] Plan	Actual	1986	1987	1988	1989	1990
Bulgaria								
GSP total	4.0	..	0.1	4.5	5.2	3.2	1.0	-12.2*
Industry	4.3	4.9	-	4.0	4.2	5.1	2.2	-14.1
Agriculture	1.2	1.6-1.9	-0.7	11.7	-5.1	0.1	0.4	-8.8
Construction	3.9	..	0.8	0.3	4.0	2.4	1.5	-4.4
Czechoslovakia								
GSP total	1.7	..	0.9	2.8	1.9	2.3	0.4	-3.2
Industry	2.7	3.0	1.2	3.2	2.5	2.1	0.8	-3.7
Agriculture	1.9	1.3	0.6	0.6	0.9	2.9	1.8	-3.7
Construction	-0.4	1.9	-0.4	2.6	2.1	0.1	1.8	-6.6
German Democratic Republic								
GSP total	2.7	..	..	2.9	2.6	2.7	1.9	..
Industry	4.1	3.9	-5.1	3.7	3.1	3.2	2.3	-28.0
Agriculture	1.7	1.5	-8.7	-	-0.3	-2.1	1.6	..
Construction [c]	2.9	3.0	..	2.8	2.2	3.0	1.7	..
Hungary								
GSP total	2.0	..	-0.5	2.4	2.0	-0.2	-1.7*	-4.9*
Industry	2.0	2.7-3.0	-0.7	1.9	3.5	-0.3	-2.5	-5.0
Agriculture	2.2	1.4-1.9	-1.0	2.4	-2.0	4.3	-1.3	-7.0
Construction	-2.2	2.2-2.8	-0.4	0.7	3.8	-3.2	-1.1	-2 *
Poland								
GSP total	-	..	-1.0	4.9	2.6	4.6	0.1	-17.1*
Industry	0.4	3.0	-3.4	4.7	3.4	5.3	-0.5	-23.3
Agriculture	-0.5	2.0	1.0	5.0	-2.3	1.2	1.5	-1.4
Construction	-2.6	..	-5.1	3.6	3.2	2.5	-6.7	-9
Romania								
GSP total	4.4	..	-2.4	5.0	1.2	0.7	-2.5	-15
Industry	3.8	7.9	-2.9	7.3	2.4	3.1	-2.1	-19.8
Agriculture	1.8	6.1-6.7	-4.3	-5.5	-8.9	5.7	-5.1	-3.0
Construction	1.9	..	-5.1	5.2	2.7	-1.7	-3.5	-28
Yugoslavia [d]								
GMP total	0.7	..	-1.3	3.6	-1.1	-1.7	0.6	-7.6
Industry	2.7	..	-1.2	3.9	0.8	-0.7	0.9	-10.3
Agriculture	0.8	..	-	11.0	-4.4	-3.6	5.3	-7.0
Construction	-6.3	..	..	-1.4	-0.9	-6.5	-3.2	..
Soviet Union								
GSP total	3.3	..	1.9	3.3	2.6	3.5	2.2	-1.9
Industry	3.6	4.6	3.1	4.4	3.8	3.9	1.7	-1.2
Agriculture	1.1	2.7	1.2	5.3	-0.6	1.7	0.8	-2.3
Construction	1.9	..	2.3	7.8	5.2	4.3	1.0	-6.3

Source: ECE secretariat Common Data Base, based on national or CMEA statistics, plans and statistical reports and direct communication to the ECE secretariat.

a Both indicators include intermediate material costs.
b For agriculture, annualized changes between five-year totals of the period shown as compared with the previous five-year period.
c Building output in centrally and locally administrated construction industries.
d Data refer to gross material product (value added of the material sphere, including depreciation).

The available data indicate that the service sector continued to grow faster or decline less than the goods-producing sectors. Moreover, it can be assumed that due to the rapid expansion of private enterprise in the service sector, and the incomplete recording of private activities, the growth of services is underestimated. The contribution of producer and consumer services to GDP remains substantially smaller in eastern Europe than in the western market economies. Their share of GDP is close to 60 per cent in the latter but in Czechoslovakia, Hungary and the Soviet Union it is about one third or less.[81] This large discrepancy gives a rough idea of the structural lag relative to the market economies as well as of the potential for growth of services in eastern Europe in the years to come.

The growing role of services — both as a source of national output growth and in easing the process of transition to a market economy — is widely recognized by policy makers who have proclaimed their intentions to develop the service sector more rapidly. Transport, communications and banking facilities are considerably below the standards regarded as normal in the western market economies and constitute a major obstacle to the smooth and rapid flow of goods, services and information.

---

[81] See *Statistická rocenka CSFR 1990*, SNTL, Prague, 1990, p.148; *Statisztikai Évkönyv 1989*, Budapest, 1990, p.55, and a direct communication of the Soviet State Committee for Statistics to the ECE secretariat.

The assessment of developments in services is difficult since the information on production is missing in most countries, but 'brief indications are possible for five countries. *Czechoslovakia* was the only country in 1990 where the output of non-material services fell more than that of the material sphere. In *Hungary* the relatively faster growth of services has been apparent throughout the 1980s, although for 1990 data on NMP are not available. In *Poland*, GDP fell less than NMP. In *Romania* and the *Soviet Union* non-material services output continued to grow in 1990 despite large falls in NMP.

Since the statistics of the eastern countries are still mainly based on the MPS, sectoral developments for the most part can be identified only from the material sphere (table 2.2.5).

Industrial production slumps ...

The contraction of industrial output in most countries was steeper than of NMP produced. Gross industrial production declined by 17½ per cent in eastern Europe and by about 1 per cent in the Soviet Union (table 2.2.6). This was the worst industrial performance in the eastern countries since the post-war stabilization and far short of expectations for the year: Czechoslovakia and the Soviet Union had envisaged a rise in industrial output, Hungary had anticipated stagnation and Poland a fall of only 5 per cent. Except in Poland and Hungary, industrial production weakened as the year went on. Three external factors contributed to the deterioration after mid-year: the sharp downturn of industrial activity in the former German Democratic Republic and the negative impact of German unification on CMEA trade; cuts in fuel and energy supplies from the Soviet Union, which worsened substantially in the second half;[82] and the Gulf crisis which led to further cuts in oil supplies, higher oil prices and additional constraints on the foreign trade of eastern Europe.

Although there were a number of common factors behind the fall in east European industrial output in 1990, their relative importance varied from country to country – and, of course, there were additional country-specific reasons for the decline. Thus the disruption of energy supplies from the Soviet Union was general, but its greater dependence on CMEA trade meant that Bulgaria was much more affected by this factor than the other countries. Labour unrest was also a significant factor in Bulgaria and Romania, while the former German Democratic Republic was subject to the singular

shock of sudden unification with an advanced market economy.

A significant development in Hungary and Poland was the *expansion* of industrial production in private companies: their relative weight is still small, of course, but nevertheless their share of industrial sales in Poland has risen from 7.6 per cent in 1989 to 13.4 per cent in 1990.

The official figures for gross industrial production in the *Soviet Union* show a fall of only 1.2 per cent in 1990. However, this appears to be an underestimate and does not reflect the intense difficulties facing Soviet industry.[83] The collapse of central planning has led to widespread disruption and the breaking up of the traditional economic links between enterprises and also between the republics. Shortages have intensified. Attempts at conversion of the defence industry have led to falling output of military goods, which was responsible for one third of the decline in total industrial output. The expansion in civilian output was not sufficient to offset this.[84] Mounting national, ethnic and social tensions also contributed to the fall. Industrial performance continued to deteriorate throughout the year: in the last quarter of 1990 industrial output declined by 1.5 per cent and in December by 2.8 per cent. The recession is expected to deepen further in 1991.

... and agricultural output falls ...

Gross *agricultural output* in 1990 fell in all the east European countries and in the Soviet Union (table 2.2.8). It was the worst agricultural year of the last decade, with output falling in eastern Europe by 3.6 per cent and in the Soviet Union by 2.3 per cent.[85] The largest falls in output were in *Bulgaria* and *Hungary* (8.8 and 7 per cent, respectively) which suffered from drought: crop production fell by over 10 per cent in both countries.[86] However, while this led to widespread shortage of foodstuffs and rationing in Bulgaria, in Hungary supplies were maintained by cuts in exports and increased imports. In *Poland* agricultural output was affected by liberalization of food prices and the elimination of subsidies which resulted in reduced demand for foodstuffs and lower profitability in the agricultural sector. In *Romania* agricultural production fell for the fourth consecutive year, albeit at a lower rate. As a result of a state decree on the distribution of agricultural land, there has been a significant shift in favour of private farms. In the *Soviet Union,* gross agricultural production declined by 2.3 per cent. Due to widespread

---

82 Oil supplies from the Soviet Union to the countries of central and eastern Europe were generally more than 20 per cent below agreed deliveries. See *Financial Times,* London, 1 February 1991.

83 Taking the hidden inflation into account, the fall in industrial output in the biggest Soviet republic (RSFSR) is estimated to be at least 3.5-4 per cent in 1990. See *Ekonomika i zhizn,* No.1, January 1991.

84 According to estimates of the USSR State Committee for Statistics, the reduction of overall industrial output stemming from the conversion of defence industry was estimated to be approximately 0.4 percentage points. USSR Goskomstat, *O sotsialno-ekonomicheskom razvitii strany v 1990 godu i gody dvenadtsatoi pyatiletki* (Report on the Social-Economic Development of the Country in 1990 and the Years of the 12th Five-Year Plan), 17 January 1991, p.32.

85 Five east European countries, excluding the former GDR and Yugoslavia, for which data on gross agricultural output are not available. Value added in the agricultural sector fell by 28 per cent in the east German *Länder* and by 7 per cent in Yugoslavia (table 2.2.5), but this is a very different indicator. The decline in the former GDR reflected a sharp shift in consumer tastes away from the output basket of local producers.

86 Grain production in Bulgaria reached 8.0 million tons in 1990 as compared with 9.6 million tons in 1989. Tobacco, an important export item, production of which in 1985-1989 was on average 116,000 tons a year, in 1989 dropped to 81,000 tons and in 1990 to only 71,000 tons.

TABLE 2.2.6

Eastern Europe and the Soviet Union: Industrial output, 1986-1991
(Percentage change over same period of preceding year)

	1986	1987	1988	1989	1990 Jan.-March	1990 Jan.-June	1990 Jan.-Sept.	1990 Jan.-Dec.	1991 [a]
Bulgaria	4.0	4.2	5.1	2.2	-8.5	-10.8	-13.0	-14.1	-(15-17)
Czechoslovakia	3.2	2.5	2.1	0.8	-2.9	-3.0	-3.7	-3.7	-(8-11)
German Democratic Republic	3.7	3.1	3.2	2.3	-4.7	-7.3	-21.0	-28.1	..
Hungary	1.9	3.5	-0.3	-2.5	-6.3	-6.8	-6.6	-4.5	-5
Poland	4.7	3.4	5.3	-0.5	-27.8	-28.0	-25.0	-23.3	5 ½
Romania	7.3	2.4	3.1	-2.1	-18.4	-18.8	-20.6	-19.8	-
Yugoslavia	3.9	0.6	-0.7	0.9	-7.0	-11.0	-10.0	-10.3	..
Eastern Europe	4.4	2.7	2.8	0.2	-12.4	-14.1	-16.5	-17.5	-2 [b]
Soviet Union	4.4	3.8	3.9	1.7	-1.2	-0.7	-0.9	-1.2	-2

Sources: National statistical yearbooks and current reporting.

a National and ECE projections.
b Excluding the former German Democratic Republic.

TABLE 2.2.7

Gross industrial output by major branches, 1988-1990
(Annual percentage change)

	Fuel and energy	Metallurgy	Engineering and metal working	Chemicals	Construction materials	Wood and paper	Textiles	Other light industry	Food processing
Bulgaria									
1988	5.3	2.4	8.1	5.8	-0.5	3.4	4.5	6.1	1.7
1989	..	..	..	..	..	..	..	..	..
1990	-2.4	-26.6	-22.2	-25.5	-8.0	-7.7	5.0	-4.9	-7.1
Czechoslovakia									
1988	0.9	1.2	4.5	2.1	3.8	2.7	2.3	3.1	0.3
1989	-0.7	0.5	3.2	0.7	0.3	0.8	1.2	2.3	2.6
1990	-4.2	-2.6	-3.9	-9.1	-6.3	-2.1	-1.1	-0.2	-1.3
Hungary									
1988	-2.1	4.7	-1.2	1.3	0.5	2.9	1.2	2.0	-2.0
1989	-2.5	-2.0	-2.2	-3.1	-3.7	0.6	-4.5	-2.1	-0.3
1990 [a]	-11.0	-19.0	-13.7	-5.4	-5.0	-3	-10.2	..	-0.9
Poland									
1988	-	1.8	8.0	6.4	5.5	7.6	8.3	9.1	1.7
1989	-1.8	-4.9	0.6	2.6	5.0	6.5	4.3	3.0	-6.0
1990 [b]	-21.2	-19.7	-22.8	-24.7	-24.3 [c]	-24.0	-37.0 [d]		-25.7
Soviet Union									
1988	2.0	2.5	5.2	-	4.8	5.0	3.7	2.9	3.3
1989	-0.8	-	2.5	1.4	1.5	2.5	2.7	3.0	4.8
1990 [e]	-1.5	-3.0	2	-1	..		-0.2 [f]		-1.4

Source: ECE secretariat Common Data Base, derived from national statistics.

Note: The conversion of national classifications of industrial output by branches to the standardized classification above does not yield complete comparability of data. In Hungary fuel includes ore mining and fuel. In Poland fuel includes also the output of the oil and gas branches. Metallurgy in Bulgaria and the Soviet Union includes ferrous metallurgy only. There are also some slight differences in the coverage of "other light industry".

a Figures for companies with 50 or more employees.
b Industrial sales of socialized sector.
c Including glass and china.
d Textiles and other light industries combined.
e Gross industrial output of major industrial complexes.
f Wood and paper, textiles and other light industries combined.

TABLE 2.2.8

Gross agricultural production, 1981-1990
(Annual percentage change)

| | 1981-1985 [a] | 1986-1990 [a] | | 1986 | 1987 | 1988 | 1989 | 1990 |
		Plan	Actual					
Bulgaria								
Total	1.2	1.6-1.9	-0.7	11.7	-5.1	0.1	0.4	-8.8
Crop	0.2	..	-	22.7	-8.8	-0.3	4.1	-14.0
Animal	2.4	..	-1.0	3.7	-1.9	0.4	-2.6	-3.7
Czechoslovakia								
Total	1.9	1.3	0.6	0.6	0.9	2.9	1.8	-3.7
Crop	2.5	1.5-1.7	-0.1	-2.5	1.8	4.0	1.7	-5.2
Animal	1.4	1.0-1.2	1.1	2.9	0.3	2.1	2.0	-2.6
German Democratic Republic								
Total	1.7	1.5*	..	-	-0.3	-2.1	1.6	..
Crop	2.8	1.7 [b]	..	-3.7	-0.3	-6.6	1.4	..
Animal	1.1	..	..	2.2	-0.3	0.3	1.7	..
Hungary								
Total	2.2	1.4-1.9	-1.0	2.4	-2.0	4.3	-1.3	-6.5
Crop	2.1	1.3-1.4	-2.3	3.7	-5.5	7.5	0.1	-10.5
Animal	2.4	..	0.3	1.1	1.5	1.5	-2.7	-2.0
Poland								
Total	-0.5	2.3	1.0	5.0	-2.3	1.2	1.5	-1.4
Crop	1.2	2.1-2.5	1.6	6.3	-2.0	-0.3	2.7	-
Animal	-2.0	..	0.1	3.2	-2.7	3.2	-0.1	-3.2
Romania [c]								
Total	1.8	6.1-6.7	-4.3	-5.5	-8.9	5.7	-5.1	-3.0
Crop	2.4	..	..	-8.8	-14.0	8.4	-1.7	..
Animal	1.0	..	..	-1.4	-2.6	3.0	-8.9	..
Eastern Europe								
Total	1.0	2.7	-0.7 [d]	1.8	-2.9	1.9	-0.1	-3.6 [d]
Crop	1.9	..	..	1.4	-4.2	1.5	1.4	..
Animal	0.4	..	..	1.9	-1.4	2.1	-1.8	..
Soviet Union								
Total	1.1	2.7	1.2	5.3	-0.6	1.7	0.8	-2.3
Crop	0.6	..	-0.4	6.1	-2.7	-1.4	1.0	-4.3
Animal	1.4	..	2.7	4.7	1.2	4.1	1.6	-0.8

Source: ECE secretariat Common Data Base, based on national and CMEA statistics; national plan and statistical reports.

a   Average annualized percentage change as compared with average output in the previous five-year period.
b   Grain units.
c   Revised data.
d   Five east European countries (excluding the former German Democratic Republic).

inefficiencies in harvesting, transportation and storage, almost a quarter of the grain harvest was lost. The decline of Soviet agriculture is due to numerous factors: the lack of spare parts, difficulties on the side of agricultural equipment manufacturers, poor infrastructure, mismanagement and a general lack of motivation and incentives for producers. The prospects for Soviet agriculture in 1991 do not suggest there will be any marked improvement.[87]

... construction sector generally weak

Output in the *construction sector* fell steeply in most countries, although in Hungary and Poland by less than industrial output. This development resulted from a variety of factors, such as restrictive budgetary policies which froze some big investment projects already under construction and limited others, uncertain expectations on the part of enterprises and households coupled with a lack of domestic capital. The available data on construction activity which are still sketchy and not fully

comparable (for some countries only the data for state sector are available), indicate that the fall in construction output ranged from 2 per cent in Hungary to 28 per cent in Romania. In Poland construction output in the socialized sector declined by 18 per cent while in the private sector by only 2 per cent. Housing construction in most countries declined dramatically. The sector must be running well below capacity and short-term prospects remain bleak in most countries.

Some signs of structural change in industry ...

Among the failures of the centrally planned economies was an allocation of resources which resulted in distorted economic structures and low productive efficiency. This was, in part, reflected in a growing share of the energy sector and heavy industries in investment and output, permanent shortages of consumer goods on domestic markets and low levels of international competitiveness. Labour productivity growth decelerated (in 1990 it declined absolutely), capital productiv-

---

87   *Financial Times,* 15 February 1991, p.28.

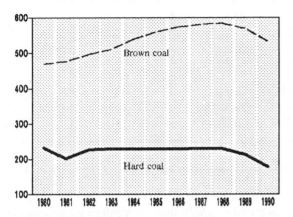

CHART 2.2.1

Coal production in eastern Europe, 1980-1990
(Million tons)

Source: ECE secretariat Common Data Base.

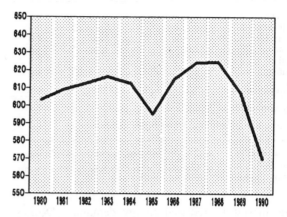

CHART 2.2.2

Oil production in the Soviet Union, 1980-1990
(Million tons)

Source: ECE secretariat Common Data Base.

ity fell and the consumption of materials and energy per unit of output is estimated to be at least twice as high as in the western countries.

A study of structural changes in industry in eastern Europe and the Soviet Union[88] indicated that a marked deceleration in the growth of industrial output and productivity in 1971-1985 was accompanied by a slow response in the structure of output to changes in the pattern of demand and input availabilities. This resulted in negligible transfers of labour and capital towards the more productive industrial branches. It can be assumed that in the second half of the 1980s this tendency continued and even intensified. The industrial structure of the east European countries was also distorted by CMEA trade, which was centrally administered and based on the exchange of Soviet raw materials for east European manufactured products. In 1990, the collapse of CMEA trade substantially affected the level and structure of east European industrial output.

In examining the changes in the structure of industrial output in 1990, three general observations can be made: *first,* structural change took place under conditions of falling output; *second,* a distinct break with the past pattern of industrial growth is clearly observable; and *third,* due to the interplay of so many factors, the differences between countries are very large, not only in respect of the changes in the relative importances of individual branches (see table 2.2.7), but also as far as the underlying factors is concerned. Thus, in countries

which have introduced important market-oriented reforms, such as Poland, east Germany and Hungary, demand factors have started to play a decisive role in structural change, while in Bulgaria, Romania and the Soviet Union supply shortages are still the main determinants.

The structural changes in 1990, particularly in those countries which have only started to implement economic reforms, are still a long way from being able to respond to the patterns of consumers' demand in a market environment. The changes have been somewhat erratic, subject to many influences, including severe input shortages. In those countries which have moved more rapidly to a market-oriented economy and which have implemented stabilization policies, the structural change was more abrupt and domestic shortages have been reduced. However, even in these countries, industrial restructuring in favour of high quality and competitive products has hardly started.

... but energy supply is a major constraint

In 1990, the overall energy situation in the region was an important constraint on NMP and industrial growth. Fuel and energy shortages appeared in most eastern countries, although to different degrees. The decline in east European domestic primary energy production was exacerbated by substantially reduced deliveries of Soviet fuel and energy.[89] However, the mild weather at the beginning of 1990 and the underlying

---

88 See United Nations Economic Commission for Europe, *Economic Survey of Europe in 1987-1988,* New York, 1988, pp.231-252.

89 For the six east European CMEA countries combined, deliveries of Soviet oil in the first nine months of 1990 declined by 21 per cent as compared with the same period of the previous year (Goskomstat SSSR, *Vneshneekonomicheskie svyazi SSSR, Ezhekvartalnyi statisticheskii byulleten',* No.5, 1990). The cuts

TABLE 2.2.9

Primary energy production, 1981-1990

(Annual percentage change)

	1981-1985	1986-1990	1986	1987	1988	1989	1990
Bulgaria	0.5	0.3	11.5	4.3	-5.0	-0.5	-7.8
Czechoslovakia	0.5	-2.8	0.6	0.8	-1.5	-4.1	-9.8
German Democratic Republic	4.0	-0.5	0.4	-0.6	0.5	-2.7	-
Hungary	1.4	-2.2	-3.6	1.4	-6.3	-2.2	-
Poland	0.6	-4.2	1.4	1.3	-	-7.0	-15.7
Romania	1.9	-5.2	-	-2.2	2.0	-4.6	-19.5
Eastern Europe	1.5	-3.1	0.9	0.3	-0.2	-4.8	-11.2
Soviet Union	2.5	1.4	4.5	3.2	2.7	-0.8	-2.4
Eastern Europe and the Soviet Union	2.3	0.6	3.9	2.7	2.2	-1.5	-3.9

Source: ECE secretariat Common Data Base, derived from national statistics.

Note: Data on primary energy production calculated by the ECE secretariat in standard coal equivalent (coefficients vary across countries). Figures for 1990 are based on national statistical reports and ECE estimates.

decline in output reduced energy demand. Domestic disturbances, such as strikes and transport difficulties, as well as growing environmental considerations also had a considerable impact on fuel and energy supplies in 1990.

For the seven countries combined, a slow-down in rates of growth of primary energy production in 1986-1988 turned into an absolute decline in 1989 and 1990 (table 2.2.9). Aggregate primary energy production in the six *east European CMEA countries* (i.e., excluding Yugoslavia), which had already fallen in 1989, decreased by 11 per cent in 1990 mainly because of large declines in Poland and Romania. In Czechoslovakia, east Germany, Hungary and Poland, demand shifts away from energy-intensive branches played an important role in the decline of fuel and energy output, but in Bulgaria, Romania and the Soviet Union the fall reflected enormous difficulties in production and distribution.

The decline in output affected all forms of primary energy (coal, natural gas, oil and primary electricity). Coal production, which accounts for 79 per cent of total primary energy production in the six east European countries, fell by 4.8 per cent in 1989 and by 11.6 per cent in 1990 (chart 2.2.1). The reduction of coal consumption was partly due to environmental considerations which are likely to play a growing role in the years to come. However, the question of replacing the polluting coal remains, since the oil imports will be limited and nuclear energy also raises environmental concerns.

The energy situation differed considerably from country to country. In *Bulgaria*, chronic fuel and energy shortages developed into a serious crisis in the winter of 1990-1991. There were frequent interruptions

in electricity supply due to insufficient generating capacity and breakdowns at some power stations. Petrol rationing was introduced in the wake of substantial cuts in imports of oil from the Soviet Union and Iraq.[90] Domestic production of electricity and coal declined by 1 and 8 per cent respectively. The energy crisis may be eased by the commissioning of the second 1,000-megawatt reactor at the Kozloduy nuclear power station, originally scheduled for the end of 1990, provided that improved security measures can be ensured.

In *Czechoslovakia*, the energy situation in 1990 was less dramatic, although there were serious cuts in deliveries of Soviet oil, particularly in the third quarter. For the whole year, total Soviet oil supplies were 13 million tons, a shortfall of 3½ million tons from the quantities contracted. Domestic output of coal declined by some 10 per cent and electricity production by 3 per cent. The ambitious nuclear energy programme has been downgraded and the dispute with Hungary over the hydropower station in Gabcikovo-Nagymaros has continued.

In *Hungary*, the energy situation was satisfactory, despite the stagnation of primary energy production and cuts in Soviet oil supplies. This was mainly due to declining demand for energy as output fell. According to first estimates, total energy consumption in 1990 dropped by 6 per cent and electricity by 3 per cent.[91] The shortfalls in Soviet oil supplies were concentrated mainly in the third and fourth quarters of the year. For the whole year, only 4.4 million tons were delivered instead of 6.5 million tons contracted (a 32 per cent shortfall).

In *Poland*, the output of hard and brown coal in 1990 was 17 and 6 per cent respectively, below the 1989 level. Electricity generation decreased by 6 per cent.

were probably steeper in the final quarter of the year. In Poland, where full-year data are available, oil imports from the rouble area were down 31 per cent in volume in the first nine months, but 41 per cent for the whole year. However, oil imports paid for in convertible currency increased by 150 per cent; part of this came from the Soviet Union.

90 In the first nine months of 1990 oil imports from the Soviet Union were reduced by 20 per cent against the same period in 1989 (from 8.5 to 6.8 million tons respectively). In December 1990 Bulgaria received 243,000 tons of Soviet oil instead of the usual monthly average of close to 1 million tons. In addition, Bulgaria expected to import 500,000 tons of oil directly from Iraq and approximately the same quantity through the Soviet Union. These deliveries were not realized.

91 See *Népszabadság*, 30 December 1990.

These developments were mainly due to falling energy demand in the major industrial branches. Moreover, increased fuel and energy prices encouraged energy savings. Deliveries of Soviet oil were cut by 16 per cent in the first nine months of 1990. It is likely that restricted investment in coal industry will result in further declines of output.

In *Romania*, the fall in energy output since the mid-1980s persisted and even worsened in 1990. Coal, oil and natural gas production fell by 38, 14 and 14 per cent respectively. Electricity production dropped by 15 per cent. Coupled with reduced energy imports, this caused serious difficulties in fuel and energy supplies.[92] In the harsh winter of 1990/1991 a serious energy crisis developed due to growing demand and further declines in output of electricity and gas.[93] It is likely that fuel and energy shortages will continue to impose a major constraint on industrial growth for some time. Except for the Cernavoda power plant, no other major power generation project is under way.

In 1990, *Soviet* primary energy production fell for the second consecutive year. Electricity and natural gas production increased by 0.3 and 2 per cent respectively, while oil and coal output decreased by 6 and 5 per cent. Oil production in 1990 (570 million tons) was at the level of 1978 and oil deliveries were 28 million tons short of the plan target. The development of Soviet oil production in the 1980s is shown in chart 2.2.2. Coal production in 1990 at 703 million tons, was 37 million tons less than in 1989 and 69 million tons less than in 1988. The growth of electricity and gas production slowed significantly. There were many reasons for the poor performance in the Soviet fuel and energy sector: shortages of material inputs and equipment, mismanagement and labour unrest, transport bottlenecks and a deplorable state of the infrastructure (including pipelines). These conditions, coupled with the absence of serious conservation measures, led to domestic energy shortages in the largest oil producing country in the world. Moreover, oil exports fell by 18 per cent in 1990. The decline in coal production was influenced by obsolete equipment, poor maintenance, strikes, transport shortages, and also by falling demand for low-calorific coal due to a delay in commissioning new capacities at thermal power stations. The situation in the Soviet fuel and energy sector was aggravated by the consequences of the Chernobyl accident: the nuclear

energy programme has been revised downward and some nuclear power stations have been closed. Prospects are bleak and the production of oil is expected to fall further.[94]

Efficiency gains in the use of energy have so far lagged substantially behind energy-saving targets. Developments in 1990 are difficult to assess since data on energy consumption are missing. In the Soviet Union the energy intensity of NMP in 1990 was virtually the same as in 1985.[95] Given the underestimation of inflation in the NMP statistics, this probably means that the energy intensity of national output increased in the second half of the 1980s. Thus, the transition to a less energy-intensive pattern of growth has not even started in some countries while in others it is only beginning. Given the extent of waste, the scope for energy saving is considerable.

Most countries have introduced or are preparing energy reforms as part of the transformation from centrally planned to market-based economies and in some of them substantial increases in energy prices have been introduced to reduce energy consumption. These reforms, among others, envisage greater energy efficiency, reduced pollution, enhanced nuclear safety and greater diversification of fuel and energy imports.[96]

CMEA trade resulted in a strong dependence of the east European countries on fuel and energy supplies from the Soviet Union. Due to the crisis in the Soviet energy sector and collapsing CMEA trade, these countries now face the need to reduce their dependence on Soviet energy supplies, at the same time as they increase energy efficiency. However, energy conservation is closely linked to the more comprehensive programmes of reform designed to establish market-driven economies and to changes in the behaviour of enterprises with respect to incentives for energy savings. The road to the market system (see chapter 4) involves industrial restructuring in favour of less energy-intensive branches and large investment in more advanced technology.[97]

Significant energy savings will only emerge over the longer term, however. In the short run, fuel and energy supplies will continue to be an important constraint on the economic development of eastern Europe. The bleak energy outlook will continue to be exacerbated by reduced and uncertain deliveries of Soviet oil.[98]

---

92 It should be noted that Romania was hit hard by reduced Soviet oil exports and the Gulf crisis. In the first nine months of 1990, Soviet oil deliveries were cut by 45 per cent against the corresponding period of 1989. Since Kuwait and Iraq were important oil suppliers for Romania, the Gulf crisis affected the country's energy balance severely.

93 See BBC, *Summary of World Broadcasts*, EE/0994, 12 February 1991, p.B/13.

94 See the article of Academician A. Sheindlin on the crisis in energy sector, *Izvestiya*, 4 February 1991. However, the Soviet government has decided to allocate an additional R25 billion to the ailing oil industry in 1991. This is to finance emergency technical re-equipment of the oil fields, and social measures to improve working conditions. See *Financial Times*, 21 February 1991, p.24.

95 USSR Goskomstat, *op.cit.*, 17 January 1991.

96 For details, see United Nations Economic Commission for Europe, *Energy reforms in central and eastern Europe − the first year*, ECE Energy Series, No.7 (pre-publication text), Geneva, January 1991. Doc. No. GE.91-30112.

97 Some estimates indicate huge investment requirements of the fuel and energy sector in eastern Europe and the Soviet Union. These cannot be met without western financial and technical assistance. See *Financial Times*, 30 April 1990, p.3.

98 The Czechoslovak Minister of Economics, V. Dlouhy, has indicated three possible supply scenarios, ranging from the "catastrophic" (cutting off the Soviet deliveries) to a plausible delivery of some 8-8.5 million tons of Soviet oil. See interview in *Hospodárské noviny*, 5 February 1991, p.7.

TABLE 2.2.10

Change in employment in the state and co-operative sectors, by branch, between 1989 Q-III and 1990 Q-III

(Per cent)

	Industry	Construction	Trade	Transport and communications	Total socialized sector
Czechoslovakia [a]	-3.2	-4.5	-2.1	..	-2.9
German Democratic Republic	-16.1	-22.6	-16.6	-10.8	-16.2 [b]
Hungary [c]	-9.5	-17.4	-11.8	-5.6	-10.7
Poland [d]	-11.7	-19.1	-27.7	-9.3	-15.0 [b]
Romania [e]	0	..	..	..	2.2
Yugoslavia	-2.8	-6.3	-4.3	-3.1	-3.8

Source: Monthly or quarterly statistical bulletins; estimate of the national conjunctural institute for Romania.

 a Industry figures cover centrally-directed industry only. Some state and co-operative enterprises are therefore excluded.
 b Sum of listed sectors only. State sector only.
 c All (not just state) enterprises with more than 50 employees are included. The total column includes all such enterprises for the material sphere only.
 d Change between 1989 Q-IV and 1990 Q-IV. In 1990 as a whole, total (not just state) employment fell by 3.2 per cent.
 e Estimates of change in 1990 compared to 1989. Excludes co-operatives.

Sectoral shifts in employment ...

In market economies, the continuous reallocation of labour from less to more efficient producers and to sectors producing goods and services for which there is a high demand is one of the most important means of improving economic performance and raising living standards. For the transition economies progress in this area is likely to be reflected in a relative shift of employment away from industry towards services, from heavy to light industry and from the state to the private sectors.

Unfortunately, the lack of comprehensive statistics makes it difficult to assess fully the direction and extent of recent changes in the overall structure of employment in any of the transition economies. Any regular monthly and quarterly estimates of employment are usually restricted to state or co-operative (or centrally controlled) enterprises and often exclude most of the service sector.

Despite national differences in the scale of adjustment, the available statistics do suggest a common pattern in the relative response of employment by branch (see table 2.2.10). Thus in each country, state sector employment in construction and in trade and distribution (except for Czechoslovakia) appears to have fallen the most rapidly, while job losses in industry have been less severe.

A more detailed breakdown of changes in industrial employment is only available for Poland, Hungary and Yugoslavia. In Poland and Yugoslavia, the fuel and power industries and the steel industry showed only small falls (or even some gains) in employment while the lighter industries such as textiles and clothing show larger than average falls. In Hungary, on the other hand, the largest losses of industrial employment have been in mining and the metals industry. In all three countries, the food, building materials and chemical industries show lower than average (for industry) falls in employment. Job losses in engineering were particularly severe in Yugoslavia but were approximately in line with the average for industry as a whole for Poland and Hungary.

If the changes in (mostly state) employment shown in the regular statistics are representative of the whole economy, then it would suggest that the desired shift of labour away from industry towards services and from heavy to light industry is not yet taking place.

... and the emergence of the private sector

In Poland, private sector employment has indeed grown strongly, rising by about 25 per cent in 1990 and offsetting nearly half of the job losses in the state sector. Private sector employment in distribution has grown particularly rapidly (more than tripling in 1990) so that the fall in overall employment in distribution was under 4 per cent last year, compared to a fall of over 16 per cent in the state and co-operative sectors alone. Figures for employment in the state sector may therefore be a particularly misleading indicator of overall shifts in the structure of employment in Poland.[99]

Survey evidence from Hungary indicates that employment in private sector enterprises accounted for 14 per cent of industrial employment and 38 per cent of employment in construction in July 1990, compared to figures of only 8 per cent and 23 per cent at the beginning of the year. In principle, the regular employment statistics do cover the private sector but, since they exclude enterprises with less than 50 employees, in practice the vast majority of new private sector businesses will not be included in the official statistics. It is likely therefore that the employment situation in Hungary is healthier than the regular figures would suggest.

In Czechoslovakia the number of private entrepreneurs has nearly quadrupled since 1989, but a large majority (70-80 per cent) also work full-time in another job.

99 However, latest figures suggest that the pattern of employment change across branches remains even when the private sector is included. As from January 1991, the regular Polish employment figures will cover all enterprises in the "main" sectors regardless of the form of ownership, with comparable figures currently available only for January 1990. These new figures show only small increases in private sector employment in the sectors covered, suggesting that the main growth in private sector employment in 1990 was in household and business services (which are still not included in the monthly statistics). In particular, private sector employment in distribution has remained low.

Figures for Yugoslavia show that the overall number of employees in the private sector is also growing rapidly (up 12 per cent in the year to the third quarter of 1990) but, as the Yugoslav private sector only accounts for about 3 per cent of dependent employment, the effects on the overall structure of employment are likely to be small (unfortunately, figures for the number of self-employed are not available).

(iv) Fiscal and monetary balance

Even a year ago, the imbalances in the domestic markets of the eastern countries were posing the most serious problems since the Second World War.[100] In the last 12 months the situation has deteriorated even further in Bulgaria, Romania and the Soviet Union. The governments of Czechoslovakia, Hungary and Poland have been more successful in reducing imbalances but there is little reason for satisfaction even in these countries.

The first part of this section outlines the causes of the current imbalances. The following section deals with consumer prices and the emergence of open inflation. The monetary overhang and the problem of shortages and the move to buyers' markets are reviewed thereafter. The final section takes a look at developments from the perspective of budget financing.

The principal cause of imbalances: the collapse of central control

Although the recent deterioration in the eastern countries is partly due to external shocks,[101] the primary cause of the underlying economic problem is the *erosion of central control over enterprise incomes and expenditures* and the lack of compensating discipline based on market forces. Over a period of one or two years, this has resulted in a sharp deterioration of monetary control, which has been reinforced by the household sector's loss of confidence in the domestic currency. Governments have been unable to check the resulting cycle of wage and price increases.[102]

In the past, the "levelling" characteristics of the system of enterprise taxation and finance under central planning meant that loss-making enterprises could be financed from the profits of profit makers, without requiring excessive credit creation.[103] However, this coordination system broke down as enterprises were given more autonomy and control over their own profits. The weakening (or in some countries the collapse) of central political authority finally removed the political leverage which governments had previously exercised over enterprises.

In countries plagued by widespread shortages, decision-makers have been squeezed from two sides. On the one hand, there was a need for immediate stabilization, but at the same time there were high expectations, both at home and abroad, of determined moves towards political liberalization and market-oriented reforms. Under these and other political pressures, the governments of Bulgaria, Romania and the Soviet Union have tried to cut through all the complications with a bold advance: price, wage and tax controls were abandoned − *de facto* at least − and private entrepreneurship was given incomparably more freedom than ever before. In Czechoslovakia, the former GDR and Hungary, where the central authorities were strong enough to prevent the collapse of consumer markets, price decontrol was implemented in a more orderly way.

Consumer prices and monetary expansion

In 1990, *Poland* and *Yugoslavia* launched programmes of macro-economic stabilization to deal with their inflationary problems and to solve the problem of shortages. Price liberalization is a bold jump into the dark, the precise effects of which are almost impossible to forecast. In Poland, the stabilization plan, launched on 1 January 1990, assumed that the monthly rate of inflation would decline from 45-50 per cent in January to 3-5 per cent in the second half of the year. This objective was not attained: with the exception of the August figure, the monthly rate was always above the target, although not by much (table 2.2.11).[104] In Yugoslavia, the authorities had fixed a target rate of 13 per cent for the year as a whole, which was very ambitious given the hyperinflation of 1989 (1,250 per cent on an annual basis). In both countries, inflation ran at an annualized rate of slightly above 70 per cent in the last five months of the year. As a result both countries still have a lot to do to get inflation under control.

In *Bulgaria*, prices have risen throughout the year. First, vegetable and fruit prices were liberalized, then in July petrol prices were increased by 80-100 per cent through an administrative decision. A preliminary estimate puts the year-over-year rate of inflation at about

100 See United Nations Economic Commission for Europe, *Economic Survey in 1989-1990*, New York, 1990, pp.134-139.

101 The collapse of the intra-regional trade in 1990 was, of course, a consequence of domestic disarray inside the CMEA countries and in the Soviet Union in particular, but for each of the eastern countries individually it constituted an external factor. Before the Gulf crisis, all countries had maintained intensive trade and financial relations with Iraq and Kuwait, which were then frozen. See United Nations Economic Commission of Europe, *Economic Bulletin for Europe*, vol.42/90, New York, 1991, pp.39-40, 40-47, 54 and 74.

102 The driving forces of this mechanism were eloquently portrayed in his letter of resignation of the Hungarian Minister of Finance: "If the unbearable local tensions, arising at various places and at various times throughout the economy, were not eased then the manifest syndromes of a general collapse would surface immediately, because economic and psychological forces would ensure that any manifestation of local disruptions (a stoppage in the railway system, the suspension of TV broadcasting, the closure of a large industrial company) would spread in an explosive manner". (*Heti Világgazdaság*, 22 December 1990).

103 For a theoretical analysis along these lines see R. Portes, "The Transition to Convertibility for Eastern Europe and the USSR", *Centre for Economic Policy Research Discussion Paper Series*, No.500, January 1991.

104 In the second half of 1990, the highest monthly rate (5.9 per cent) was recorded in December. The consumer price index of December 1990 had been projected to be 140 per cent above the December 1989 level, in reality the index stood at 250 per cent. These forecasts were made in statements of officials of the Ministry of Finance (*Trybuna Ludu*, 13 December 1989; *Zycie Warszawy*, 16-17 December 1989; *Rzeczpospolita*, 6-7 January 1990).

TABLE 2.2.11

Eastern Europe and the Soviet Union: Rate of inflation, 1989-1991

(Percentage change)

	Period over period of preceding year						Month over preceding month					
	Jan.-Dec. 1989	Jan.-March 1990	Jan.-June 1990	Jan.-Sept. 1990	Jan.-Dec. 1990	Jan.-Dec. 1991 a	Aug. 1990	Sept. 1990	Oct. 1990	Nov. 1990	Dec. 1990	Jan. 1991
Bulgaria	6.2	..	13.5	..	19.3*	..	10.9	4.5	4.1	4.9	10.4	13.6
Czechoslovakia	1.4	3.4	3.7	7.2 b	10.1	30	..	..	..	..	..	25.8
GDR	..	..	..	..	-2.5*	..	0.4	1.8	1.7	-0.1	1.0	7.4
Hungary	17.0	23.3	25.3	26.6	28.9	35-37	2.9	1.5	1.5	2.1	1.7	7.5
Poland	244.1	1 110.7	1 091.2	920.4	584.7	52	1.8	4.6	5.7	4.9	5.9	12.7
Romania	..	..	2.2	..	5.6	..	..	..	..	23.4	11.6	9.2
Yugoslavia	1 256	2 990	2 137	702	588	30-40	1.9	7.1	8.1	3.0	3.3	5.6
Soviet Union c	..	2.6	2.8	3.6	5.3	..	..	..	..	..	..	4-6

Sources: National statistics. Indices refer to cost-of-living index (Hungary), retail prices of goods and services (Bulgaria, Poland, Romania, the Soviet Union), or retail prices of the socialist sector (Bulgaria).

a National forecasts.
b The increase in July-September relative to the same period of 1989 was 14.1 per cent.
c Retail prices, goods and services. An overall measure of inflationary pressure, which reflects "unsatisfied demand", is officially put at 8 per cent for January-June, at more than 9 per cent for January-September, and at over 19 per cent for January-December.

20 per cent, but in the last five months it ran at an annualized rate in excess of 120 per cent.

In *Czechoslovakia*, the first push to retail prices was given in July, when subsidies to food prices were largely eliminated. This was a carefully prepared policy action, as it was known that the resulting 25 per cent rise of food prices would be the largest shock the population had to absorb since 1953. A few weeks later, however, the government was forced to increase petrol and diesel oil prices by almost 50 per cent from one day to the next because this seemed to be the only way to curb domestic demand in the wake of falling Soviet deliveries. All in all, the annual rate of inflation was only 10 per cent in 1990 − still among the lowest in eastern Europe.

In *Hungary* the level of consumer prices rose by 29 per cent as compared to the preceding year and reached a level about double that of five years before. The latest round of price rises affected low income strata strongly because because the price increases were much larger than average in the case of basic food products.

The *Romanian* government's price liberalization plan was only partially implemented in 1990 − two more steps are scheduled for 1991. State control was lifted on many prices in November 1990, while others remained frozen for the remaining part of the year. In the absence of official data, the year-over-year price rise has to be estimated; it is small because the impact of price liberalization affected only the last two months of the year.

The assessment of price developments in the *Soviet Union* is getting increasingly complicated with the proliferation of price measurement methods. The most aggregate figure quoted by the annual report of the

Soviet statistical office showed a 5.3 per cent annual rise of retail prices. This number reportedly comprises the turnover of goods in the state sector as well as in private, co-operative shops and on the *kolkhoz* markets. According to the same report, however, cost-of-living calculated on the basis of a "minimum basket" containing only basic necessities went up by 7 per cent in 1990. If allowance is made for "repressed inflation", the annual rate was put at 11.3 per cent, while a more complex method, which took into account the price changes on "black markets" yielded a 19 per cent rise in the cost-of-living.[105]

At the time of writing it is difficult to forecast the most likely course of *price developments in 1991*. In Poland the target for 1991 is for an annual inflation rate of 52 per cent, but the anti-inflationary incomes policy of the government was still under dispute in early 1991. In Yugoslavia the problems are more serious. Last year's stabilization programme was intended to support the central government's efforts to prevent the dismemberment of the country. At the beginning of 1991, Yugoslavia's political future is more uncertain than ever and this is paralysing decisions on economic policy. It is thus also uncertain whether the decisions on stabilization policy taken by the federal government can be implemented.

In *Hungary*, the most recent version of the government's medium-term policy document assumes that inflation will peak in 1991 at a rate of 35-37 per cent and then fall slowly to 21 per cent in 1992 and 13 per cent in 1993.[106] In *Czechoslovakia*, the reform and stabilization programme for 1991 assumed that inflation could be held to 30 per cent. This appears to be an ambitious objective. In *Romania,* a second round of price liberalization is scheduled for April 1991, with a "once-and-for-all" rise of food prices of some 200 per

105 USSR Goskomstat, *op.cit.*, 17 January 1991, pp.13-14.

106 *Magyar Hírlap*, 26 February 1991.

TABLE 2.2.12

Saving deposits of households, 1987-1990

	1987	1988	1989	1990
Panel A: Value at constant prices [a] (1980 = 100)				
Bulgaria.............................	150.4	158.3	154.5	..
Czechoslovakia.................	147.2	154.9	159.6	..
German Dem.Rep.	132.4	138.4	142.6	..
Hungary.............................	110.1	99.5	82.9	77.6
Poland................................	85.0	80.2	50.2	35.1
Romania	135.7	140.4	151.2	175.1
Soviet Union	156.4	170.0	189.9	203.1
Panel B: Savings ratio [b] (Percentage ratio)				
Bulgaria.............................	4.2	6.1	2.9	..
Czechoslovakia.................	3.8	3.0	2.5	..
German Dem.Rep.	6.1	6.0	4.8	3.0 [c]
Hungary.............................	-1.3	1.5	-0.3	4.7
Poland................................	7.9	7.8	9.9	..
Romania	..	..	3.7	8.3
Soviet Union	5.3	6.0	7.4	6.6

Source and Notes: See Appendix tables B.4, B.6. and B.19.

a Nominal value of saving deposits, deflated by the consumer price index.
b Ratio of increment in savings deposits to money incomes of the population.
c Savings as percentage of disposable income.

CHART 2.2.3

Ratio of saving deposits (stock) to annual retail sales turnover, 1985-1990
(Percentages)

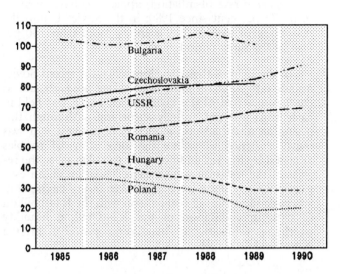

Source: ECE secretariat Common Data Base.

cent. No information is available on the pace at which prices are expected to rise in 1991 in *Bulgaria*.

In the *Soviet Union*, the authorities have prepared measures for implementing a radical price reform sometime in the course of 1991. The legislative documents are waiting for parliamentary approval and for presidential signature.[107] Some key questions, however, may still require political decisions. There are conflicting reports in the Soviet press about the estimated impact of the reform, and it seems that different government bodies are still working with different assumptions. The government itself reckons with a 60 per cent rise in retail prices;[108] the USSR State Committee for Labour and Social Affairs is working on a system of compensation payments, assuming that retail prices will double or treble.[109]

Alternative treatments of monetary overhang

There are several ways of measuring excess consumer demand represented by accumulated savings — the monetary overhang.[110] One of these indicators, depicted in chart 2.2.3, is the ratio of saving deposits to annual retail sales. This indicator measures the *poten-*

tial excess demand: how much of this will appear as extra spending depends on particular circumstances and, in particular, on consumers' expectations.

Excess demand in Czechoslovakia estimated in this way would appear to be larger than that in Poland, yet the removal of subsidies in Czechoslovakia in mid-1990 and the almost complete decontrol of prices in January 1991 have not let loose as large an adjustment shift as occurred in Poland at the turn of 1989/1990.

The same indicator for the former German Democratic Republic was similar to that in Czechoslovakia,[111] but when prices were liberalized and goods which had been in short supply became available, the release of pent-up demand did not lead to rampant inflation. After the currency conversion on 1 July 1990, private consumption in the eastern part of Germany was initially boosted by a fall in household savings and, more significantly, by large money transfers from the federal government. The rise in east German consumption led to increased output in the western part of the country and to higher imports. The increasing fear of unemployment in the east is likely to lead to an increase in the savings ratio, but as yet there are no data available to confirm this.

107 See a report on a meeting between members of the Soviet government and trade union officials, *Izvestiya*, 6 March 1991.

108 Report of Prime Minister V. Pavlov at the fifth session of the Supreme Soviet of the USSR, *Izvestiya*, 19 February 1991.

109 See the press conference of V. Shcherbakov (Chairman of Goskomtrud), as reported in *Izvestiya*, 15 February 1991.

110 The first systematic analysis of monetary overhang in the hands of the population in eastern economies came from Polish economists. For references and a more elaborate theoretical background, see United Nations Economic Commission for Europe, *Economic Survey of Europe in 1987-1988*, New York, 1988, pp.191-193.

111 Not included in chart 2.2.3, but see United Nations Economic Commission for Europe, *Economic Survey of Europe in 1989-1990*, New York, 1990, p.123 (chart 3.3.2).

In Hungary, Poland and Yugoslavia, the purchasing power of the monetary overhang has been gradually eroded by inflation (table 2.2.12). In contrast, the real value of household savings in Romania (adjusted for the *reported* rate of inflation) appears to have risen by some 75 per cent since 1980; in the Soviet Union the real stock of savings has risen by more than 100 per cent in the same period.

In the light of these developments, the recent Soviet initiative to *limit spending from saving accounts* and to *confiscate* a part of the saving stock which was held in cash form was not entirely surprising. Although this operation also had non-monetary objectives − it was partly designed to reduce the large sums of roubles amassed by foreign and domestic speculators − the results of the measure were meagre.[112] All in all, an estimated R8-10 billion have been taken out of circulation, a very modest sum in comparison with the R140 billion of cash in circulation or the R240 billion liquidity overhang ("unsatisfied purchasing power") in the household sector.[113]

Price liberalization

In the past, centrally planned economies were characterized by persistent shortages. This gave sellers a much stronger bargaining position in both goods and factor markets and buyers often had little alternative but to accept what they were offered. Although in a formal sense, goods and services were exchanged for money, the role of money in a shortage economy was limited. The obvious disadvantages of this situation were recognized long ago and the elimination of shortages and sellers' markets is one of the high priorities of each country's reform programme. Some reduction of shortages was always thought to be possible but few (if any) commentators believed that shortages could be eliminated quickly by means of administrative decisions *prior* to the abolition of state ownership.

Some countries − Czechoslovakia, Hungary or Yugoslavia − have followed a gradual approach and have tried to eliminate shortages in some consumer markets through a combination of price adjustments, administrative controls and targeted foreign trade measures.[114]

At the beginning of 1990, Poland and Yugoslavia attempted to cure the problem of shortages by freeing prices. Six months later, Czechoslovakia adopted similar policies[115] and in November 1990, Romania followed suit. Finally, Bulgaria liberalized prices in February 1991.

In *Poland*, the crucial part of the operation, was a complete liberalization of prices[116] coupled with a substantial devaluation of the zloty and the strengthening of monetary restraint. In *Yugoslavia*, the core element of the stabilization policy was the introduction of a new dinar (equivalent to 10,000 old dinars), which was declared internally convertible. Among the other measures announced for the first half of 1990 were a wage freeze at the levels prevailing in November 1989, a tightening of monetary policy and a price liberalization covering about 90 per cent of all goods and services.[117] After a few weeks, shortages of most consumer, investment and intermediate goods had disappeared.[118]

In the *German Democratic Republic*, unification with the Federal Republic of Germany meant that the strategy adopted was fundamentally different. As part of the currency union, nearly all prices were freed as from 1 July 1990,[119] and thus moved to reflect the existing west German price structure. This entailed substantial changes in *relative* prices with significant declines in prices for consumer durables[120] and increases in food prices. The overall price level rose by 7½ per cent between June and July, but in July was still 5½ per cent below the corresponding level of 1989.[121]

In the *Soviet Union* central price control has not been formally abolished, also the retail prices of certain "luxury goods" were freed in November 1990. A *de facto* freeing of prices also appears to have occurred as a result of the breakdown of the links between state-

---

112 Officially, the entire action was presented "not as a matter of confiscation but a matter of protection". According to Prime Minister V. Pavlov, a large influx of money threatened the Soviet Union, which was planned to be channelled into the country from abroad through various means, including buying up R50 and R100 denominations. (Interview in *Trud*, 12 February 1991.)

113 See also section 4.6(iv).

114 A good example of the Hungarian approach concerns the supply of imported lemons in winter. During winter, special funds were made available for imports, irrespective of the fluctuations in world prices. Domestic retail prices were fixed at relatively high, market-clearing levels. In springtime, when home-produced vegetables and fruits reappeared, the lemon imports were suspended. By contrast, developments in Yugoslavia were more erratic: years of abundant consumer supplies were followed by recurring periods of shortage.

115 The details of the Czechoslovak stabilization programme are described in section 4.4.

116 By the end of January 1990 only about 10 per cent of prices were subject to some sort of administrative controls, against some 50 per cent in 1989. Remaining official prices on food were abolished in the first half of 1990. In July 1990 coal and coke prices were partly liberalized (some ceilings being set) and three-year phasing-out of subsidies was announced for the user of natural gas.

117 Major exceptions were the prices freezes (at the December 1989 level) for some raw material inputs, electricity, petroleum products, railway and postal services.

118 For a more detailed analysis of the Polish and Yugoslav stabilization policy, see section 4.3.

119 Only rents for housing, energy and public transport remained frozen.

120 Prices for clothing and shoes fell by more than 40 per cent in July relative to their levels 30 days before.

121 It should be noted, however, that the representativeness of the consumer price index has become increasingly weak, given the strong shifts in consumption patterns and the difficulties that must exist in finding representative goods prices. Many products in the base year (1989) basket are simply no longer purchased or available.

owned production enterprises and the state-owned retail trade network.

High ranking Soviet officials have repeatedly stated, and there is no basis to question their assertions, that there was no "physical" deficit of goods in the country last year, and it seems that the food harvest in 1990 was comparable to that of previous years.[122] Reduced supplies were due to the collapse of the Soviet retail trade system and disarray in vital services, such as public transport and electricity generation.[123] The emerging private sector has been able to fill part of this shortfall, mainly in those areas where prices can be changed quickly to balance supply and demand. In areas such as public transport, electricity generation or heating, there is little possibility of substituting private sector for state provision. As the situation has gone from bad to worse, rationing in various forms, especially of food, has increased.[124]

Developments were similar in *Bulgaria* and *Romania*, although in these countries there has been more central control over price liberalization since March 1990. Some prices were liberalized in stages, but this in turn weakened control over the prices which were still centrally determined. In quantitative terms these liberalization steps had the same dramatic effect on prices as the "shock therapy" applied in other countries, but they lacked the persuasive power of a consistent economic strategy that could lead to a healthy change in expectations.

Many Romanian prices were freed on 1 November 1990, although prices of 55 basic goods, including crude oil and wine, were said to remain under government control. Prices of another 29 goods were frozen for the remaining part of 1990.[125] The population was partially compensated through wage and pension increments of 750 lei per month and 400 lei per month respectively.

In *Bulgaria*, shortages reached critical levels in the autumn of 1990. As from 1 February 1991, most consumer prices were freed, with prices increasing by some 400-500 per cent. However these increases do not appear to have had any immediate effect on shortages and many shops are still empty.

In *Hungary*, the switch from sellers' to buyers' markets has taken place gradually over the past decade, although the recent liberalization measures (see section 4.4) have given a major push to this process. As a re-

sult of the long process of reform, Hungarian shops already offer by far the widest choice of goods in eastern Europe. In *Czechoslovakia*, shortages increased in the last quarter of 1990 in anticipation of the price liberalization which took place in the new year. The first two months of free prices have reduced some of the imbalances on consumer markets. However, these improvements have not been as dramatic as was hoped, chiefly because suppliers have been reluctant (or unable) to react to the new situation.

Fiscal balances

In the system of central planning, where money on the whole had a passive role, government budgets were always in equilibrium. This followed from the logic of physical planning, where monetary flows were strictly subordinate to changes in the "real" sphere. Since the central authorities had − at least in theory − unlimited power to direct monetary flows, it was not difficult to generate sufficient government revenues to match expenditures.

However, as the countries of eastern Europe and the Soviet Union have gradually moved away from traditional forms of central planning, and to the extent that these economies have become more monetized, the achievement of fiscal balance acquired greater importance. If "money matters," then the government cannot arbitrarily deprive enterprises of their assets for the sake of keeping its own books in balance. In a similar way, once monetary incentives have really become a driving force of workers' behaviour − and this occurs soon after the abolition of most forms of rationing, when monetary purchasing power becomes the main avenue to individual welfare − the government is constrained in manipulating indirect taxes and other revenue sources.

In face of these difficulties some eastern governments took the line of least resistance: budget deficits were financed by money creation, but this transaction was included "above the line" among the revenue items of the budget. Thus, on paper the government budget remained in balance, although in reality this was not always the case. The existence of substantial state budget deficits became public knowledge for the first time in 1989 and 1990. In some countries new or revised data have been released for the most recent years (Soviet Union),[126] or detailed explanations have been given on how to "translate" the old, manipulated fig-

122 See e.g., the interview with V. Chernoivanonv, First Deputy Chairman of the USSR Council of Ministers State Commission for Food and Purchases, in *Izvestiya*, 14 December 1990.

123 The situation was further exacerbated by the conflict of interest among republics: traditional links were cut, not only because the enterprises concerned were − perhaps − not interested in maintaining them, but due to legislative orders issued by the respective republican governments. By the end of 1990, eight republics out of 15 had introduced formal export restrictions.

124 In August 1990, bread, almost the only item for which Muscovite had not been forced to queue, was added to the long list of scarce goods. "Bread fever" was reported from Leningrad, Tula, Kuybishev and other cities as well (*Pravda*, 8 September 1990). A plan to introduce a system of food coupons on 1 March 1991 for people living in the Moscow area (*Izvestiya*, 18 February 1991) does not seem to have been carried out.

125 *Heti Világgazdaság*, 10 November 1990.

126 For the two sets of figures see 1988 and the 1989 editions of *Narodnoe khozyaistvo SSSR* , pp.624 and 611 respectively.

TABLE 2.2.13

State budgets in eastern Europe and the Soviet Union, 1985-1991

(Percentage)

	1985	1988	1989	1990 budget	1990 actual	1991 budget
Ratio of budgetary expenditures to GDP						
Bulgaria	..	..	..	..	..	47.0
Czechoslovakia	..	59.0	56.3	..	41.0	..
German Democratic Republic	75.2	77.9	77.8 ‖	..	70.8	..
Hungary	58.9 ‖	38.2	34.5	29.9	31.5	36.7
Poland	39.0	33.8	28.5	..	26.6	27.7
Romania	34.5	33.5	36.1	..	..	..
Soviet Union	49.7	52.5	51.3	..	51.5 ‖	..
Size of fiscal deficit (+ surplus/-deficit) relative to GDP						
Bulgaria	..	..	..	..	-5.0	-5.0
Czechoslovakia	..	0.1	-0.9	..	0.8	..
German Democratic Republic	0.4	0.1	..	..	-8.0	-15.2
Hungary	-1.5	-1.4	-3.2	-0.5	-0.1	-3.1
Poland	-0.3	0.3	-3.0	..	0.3	-0.4
Romania	2.2	5.2	7.5	..	..	..
Soviet Union	-1.8	-9.2	-8.6	..	-5.9	..

Sources: National financial statistics, and for 1990 and 1991, national and secretariat estimates. The methodology applied in calculating fiscal revenues and expenditures differs significantly from country to country. In some countries, (Czechoslovakia, Hungary), different sets of figures are used by the statistical authorities, the finance ministries and the national banks.

Country notes: Bulgaria: Budgetary data for 1985 and 1988 are taken from CMEA publications. 1989-1990 GDP data estimates from *PlanEcon*, 28 December 1990. *Czechoslovakia:* Budget and actual figures for 1990 relate to 11 months. *German Democratic Republic:* Figures for 1990 in Deutschmark. *Hungary:* Budget figures reflect a narrow concept of public accounts, i.e., social security and other funds not included. *Soviet Union:* The officially announced 1990 budgetary expenditures (R510.1 billion) exclude outlays of R22.5 billion financed by supplementary loans from the State Bank. Budget figures for 1991 cover the activities of the union government only.

‖ Substantial discontinuity, due to changes in fiscal regulations.

ures into correct ones (Hungary).[127] Similar revisions are likely to appear in other countries in the future.[128]

In the context of domestic stabilization and market-oriented reforms supported by western financial assistance, sound financing has become a priority concern in all countries. There are two aspects of this task. The *short-term* objective is to reduce or eliminate fiscal deficits. Here, three countries − Czechoslovakia, Hungary and Poland − have made considerable progress. The governments of Czechoslovakia and Poland were able to post small surpluses in 1990, while in Hungary there was a major reduction in the deficit, both in absolute and relative terms. In Bulgaria and Romania the situation has almost certainly deteriorated, although reliable numbers are still not available. The preliminary Soviet numbers suggest some improvement − the reported deficit is smaller than a year ago. Nevertheless, its size is still high (almost 6 per cent of GDP).

Budgetary *plans for 1991* were drafted in most cases in the middle of the Gulf crisis, when governments had to prepare for the possibility of financing increased oil bills. At least in the case of Hungary and Poland it accounts for the expected deterioration of the fiscal balance (table 2.2.13).

A more daunting task in the *medium and long term* will be the restructuring the entire fiscal system of these countries along the lines of western market economies. Far-reaching budgetary reforms of both the revenue and the expenditure side of the budget are needed. Of critical importance is the elimination of subsidies to consumers and failing firms − a decision which will have to be accompanied by an overhaul of wholesale prices.

Last but not least, standard international practices will have to be applied to *financial statistics*, because the methods currently used vary from country to country and very often from year to year.[129] In relative terms, this domain is perhaps the weakest part of eastern statistics. Without a major overhaul of the statistical system it will be impossible to use market-based economic policy measures, because the true state of affairs remain obscured by behind the veil of confused statistics.

(v) Employment and unemployment

The transition to a market economy is likely to lead to substantial falls in the overall level of employment

---

[127] For references, see section 4.4(iv).

[128] The official Romanian statistics, for example, suggest that in 1989 the central government had a budgetary *surplus*, equivalent of 7.5 per cent of GDP. This cannot be easily reconciled with the existence of large imbalances in other parts of the economy. The relatively small Polish deficit for the year 1989, when inflation rose to 260 per cent, poses similar questions.

[129] In this respect one of the most important steps will be the incorporation of numerous extra-budgetary funds into the budget. In countries where federal structures have been recently reorganized (Czechoslovakia, the Soviet Union), fiscal statistics should provide adequate means to oversee the flows of expenditures and revenues between the central and the republican governments.

TABLE 2.2.14

Eastern Europe and the Soviet Union: Unemployment, 1989-1991
(Thousands and per cent of labour force, end-of-period)

	Unemployed (thousands)						Unemployment rate (per cent)					
	Dec. 1989	March 1990	June 1990	Sept. 1990	Dec. 1990	Jan. 1991	Dec. 1989	March 1990	June 1990	Sept. 1990	Dec. 1990	Jan. 1991
Bulgaria....................	..	..	22.4	..	72.2		..	..	0.6	..	1.8	..
Czechoslovakia.......	..	7.0	12.6	43.9	77.0	119.5	..	0.1	0.2	0.6	1.0	1.5
German Dem. Rep. a	..	38.3	142.1	444.8	642.2	757.2	..	0.4	1.5	4.9	7.3	8.6
Hungary.................	13.0	32.5	41.8	56.1	81.4	99.1	0.3	0.7	0.9	1.5	1.7	2.1
Poland...................	9.7	266.6	568.2	926.4	1 126.1	1 195.7	0.1	1.5	3.1	5.0	6.1	6.5
Romania.................	..	..	..	120.0	150.0	200.0	..	..	..	1.0	1.3	1.8
Yugoslavia..............	1 248.0	1 278.0	1 277.0	1 335.0	1 390.0*	..	12.2	12.5	12.5	12.7	13.2	..
Soviet Union..........	..	..	..	2 000.0 b	2 000.0 b	..	..	..	..	1.4	1.4	..

Sources: National statistics of "registered unemployed", except where otherwise noted.

a Excludes part-time unemployment (involuntary short-time working).
b "The number of people temporarily not working which according to the ILO methodology could be considered unemployed is estimated at about 2 million". Goskomstat January-September report, Izvestiya, 20 October 1990. This estimate is repeated in the report for the full year (Ekonomika i zhizn', 1991, No.5).

for two main reasons. Firstly, macro-economic stabilization requires the adoption of tighter credit and budgetary policies. While these policies should restrain inflation, the resulting fall in nominal demand is also likely to induce a domestic recession, leading to "cyclical" falls in real output and employment. Secondly, the shift from a centrally-planned to a market economy will mean substantial job-shedding in many sectors of the economy where overmanning has been rife. In the medium term, this excess labour will be absorbed by growth in new and previously underdeveloped branches of the economy but, in the short term, there is likely to be substantial "structural" unemployment.

In Yugoslavia, open unemployment has been high for many years but in all of the other countries open unemployment has not existed at all since just after the War. The emergence of open unemployment, even if at lower levels than now seem to be accepted in many western countries, is therefore likely to pose serious social problems.

Overall movements in employment and the emergence of unemployment

Figures for the overall level of employment in 1990 are available only for a few countries. In most of the transition economies, available within-year statistics only cover the socialized sector, and in some cases only the "productive" branches of the economy.

In Poland, where overall figures are available, total employment is estimated to have fallen by about 600,000 (about 3 per cent) last year. This fall is much lower than the fall in state employment — employment in the private sector has increased rapidly — but, even more strikingly, it is also much lower than the rise in registered unemployment (over a million in 1990). This discrepancy suggests that the original, relatively lax, benefit scheme may have exaggerated the level of unemployment.

In the Soviet Union, overall employment is estimated to have fallen by about 1 per cent in 1990. In all the other countries, only partial data is available. In Hungary, the former GDR and to a lesser extent Czechoslovakia, the available employment figures all show substantial falls in the first three quarters of 1990. Romania is a striking exception to this pattern of falling employment and non-agricultural employment there is reported to have risen in 1990, though this increase is due more to political than economic reasons (see table 2.2.10).

As only limited information is available on the employment situation in most countries, the newly-introduced unemployment statistics have to serve as the main indicator of labour market developments. However, quite apart from the ever-present difficulties in comparing unemployment rates across countries, there are also substantial transitional problems in evaluating the significance of short-term changes in unemployment (see box 2.2.1).

The countries experiencing the fastest rises in unemployment have been those who have opted for the most rapid reform programmes (Poland, east Germany), while those countries where the pace of reform has been slower have so far seen less dramatic increases in joblessness (table 2.2.14).

In eastern Germany, the registered unemployment rate rose from zero at the beginning of 1990 to 6½ per cent at the end of the year and has risen even further in the first two months of 1991. In addition, over 20 per cent of the workforce are now registered as working short-time and many of these are effectively unemployed (in November 1990 over 650,000 of these short-time workers were working less than 50 per cent of their normal hours). The stock of vacancies in eastern Germany fell dramatically over the course of 1990, ending the year at only 15 per cent of its level at the beginning of the year. However, as many workers in eastern Germany have opportunities for working in western Germany, the fall in registered vacancies probably exaggerates the deterioration in the eastern German labour market.

BOX 2.2.1

Problems in comparing unemployment statistics

Even in developed market economies with well-established systems of statistics, it is difficult to produce consistent comparisons of unemployment. The internationally accepted definition of unemployment — the ILO definition — counts as unemployed all those who are without work, are looking for work and are available to start work. The definitions used in national unemployment statistics usually cover only those people registered with labour offices as looking for work (the "registration" definition), or those receiving unemployment benefit ("claimant" definition). So far, all of the transition economies which are producing unemployment statistics have used the registration definition. Neither administrative definition can be assumed to have a stable relationship with "ILO" unemployment.

*In **Poland,** the original conditions for eligibility for unemployment benefit were weak and this may have encouraged entry to the labour force solely to claim benefit. In this case, the very fast rise in recorded unemployment in the spring and summer may have considerably overstated the increase in "ILO" unemployment. On the other hand, the tightening of the Polish benefit system in the autumn may have reduced the number of claimants eligible for benefit and this may account for some of the recent slowing in the rate of increase of measured unemployment.*

*In **Yugoslavia,** it appears that figures for those registered as seeking work include many workers already employed in the private sector or the underground economy who are looking for a job in the state sector, thus grossly overestimating the number of genuine unemployed (the 1987 OECD Survey of Yugoslavia estimated that genuine unemployment in 1986 was only 700,000, as compared to official figures of over one million registered job seekers).*

*On the other hand, it is likely that official unemployment figures in **Hungary** are underrecording the recent rise in unemployment. There is a substantial divergence between official statistics showing a large number of job losses in the material sector (over 300,000 in the first three quarters of 1990) and the relatively small increase (under 60,000 for the first eleven months of 1990) in registered unemployment. While employment growth elsewhere in the economy or the withdrawal from the labour force of discouraged workers may account for some of this discrepancy, it is still likely that there are substantial numbers of unrecorded unemployed.*

*When the benefit system does not yet exist, as in **Romania** or the **USSR,** or has only recently been set up, as in **Czechoslovakia,** there may be little incentive to register as unemployed, again leading to underestimation of unemployment.*

Only after regular household labour surveys (similar to the annual European Community Labour Force Survey) are established, will meaningful international comparisons of unemployment rates be possible. Eastern Germany and Poland are likely to carry out the first such surveys later this year and most of the other countries have plans for household surveys for 1992.

In the meantime, attention should be focused on changes over time in the level of registered unemployment, rather than on the levels themselves. While this approach still has considerable problems, particularly in the initial stages of the transition process (seasonal patterns are unknown and there may also be misleadingly high increases in measured unemployment as the newly-established labour offices catch up with the existing stock of unemployed), it should yield more reliable assessments of labour market trends.

Vacancy figures may eventually become a reliable indicator of changes in the demand for labour. However, they are currently probably being influenced as much by changes in recruitment patterns (employers in the emerging private sector may well use alternative methods of recruitment before turning to the state labour offices) as by changes in the underlying demand for labour. Dramatic falls in the number of available vacancies should therefore be interpreted cautiously.

Czechoslovakia and Hungary experienced relatively slow rises in unemployment in 1990, though the rate of increase appeared to quicken in the second half of the year. The number of registered vacancies in Hungary fell by over 50 per cent in the course of the year and this may indicate a more substantial fall in labour demand. However, despite recent increases, in both countries registered unemployment is currently only about 1-2 per cent of the active population.

In Poland, unemployment also rose dramatically, passing the million mark at the end of October and then continuing to rise, though at a slightly slower rate, to the end of the year. On the other hand, the level of vacancies increased over 1990 as a whole, albeit with substantial monthly variations, and this may be additional evidence for the gradual emergence of a demand for labour in the private sector.

In Yugoslavia, the number of registered job-seekers (which probably substantially overestimates the number of unemployed, see box 2.2.1) rose further last year from its already high level of over 10 per cent of the labour force. The level of vacancies in the first nine months of 1990 was slightly lower than in the same period of 1989, but is insignificant — 1 per cent of the labour force or 6 per cent of the number of unemployed.

Bulgaria, Romania and the Soviet Union all currently appear to have similar, low unemployment rates, though regular information is difficult to obtain for the latter two countries.

All of the transition economies expect unemployment to rise substantially in 1991. However, most of these countries' unemployment rates at the end of 1991 are still expected to be below typical western European levels. A sustained economic recovery will eventually reverse the trend of increased joblessness but, given the extent of overemployment, it is likely that there will be a substantial period when economic recovery will co-exist with rising unemployment. No early fall in unemployment is therefore to be expected.

In Bulgaria the Minister of Labour has quoted figures of 250-300,000 by the end of the year (around 6 per cent of the labour force).[130]

In Czechoslovakia predictions vary; the Ministry of Finance expects unemployment to reach between 4 and 6 per cent this year, while the economics minister has quoted figures of 700,000-800,000 (about 8-10 per cent) as being inevitable if economic reform is proceeding according to plan.[131] In Hungary, the Labour Ministry foresees joblessness rising to 200,000 (around 4 per cent) by the end of 1991.[132]

In Poland, where an economic recovery is hoped for later in the year, unemployment is expected to reach 2 million by the end of the year, about 10 per cent of the active population. In eastern Germany the end of state support for short-time working in June 1991 and the accelerating programme of enterprise restructuring are both expected to result in even sharper increases in unemployment in 1991, with unemployment expected to average 1.25 million (an unemployment rate of about 14 per cent) over 1991 as a whole and probably rising even higher by the end of the year.[133]

Romanian forecasts see unemployment rising to over 420,000 in 1991 – about 3.5 per cent of the workforce. In Yugoslavia, unemployment is likely to increase further, owing to the lack of effective macro-economic policies, but no forecasts are available.

In the Soviet Union, there are estimates that there will be 5.3 million claimants of the new unemployment benefit this year (if all these claimants were registered as unemployed at the same time, this would yield an unemployment rate of about 4.5 per cent).[134]

(vi) Foreign trade and external balance

The downturn in the foreign trade of the eastern countries observed in 1989 and the first half of 1990 accelerated in the second half of the year.[135] Exports, which had fallen slightly in 1989, plunged steeply in

volume. Imports, which had still grown in the preceding year, also contracted, but much less than exports. In consequence, trade balances generally worsened, but main imbalance developed within the region as the Soviet trade deficit with the countries of eastern Europe burgeoned.

Trade volumes

The contraction of output in the European CMEA countries was accompanied in most cases by a much steeper decline in *exports*. The volume of exports from eastern Europe and the Soviet Union probably fell by more than 12 per cent in 1990. *Imports* into the region also declined, by some 2½ per cent (table 2.2.15). The downturn accelerated in the second half of the year. As in 1989, this contrasts sharply with the continued expansion of world trade which rose some 7 per cent in volume in 1989 and, apparently, by a further 4 per cent in 1990 (see section 3.1 below).[136]

The larger part of this downturn reflected a steep downward spiral of trade *among the European CMEA countries*. This was caused by political and institutional developments in the region, including the impending dissolution of the special CMEA trade and payments arrangements, but also by the economic recession in these countries which acted on both supplies and demand.

Soviet exports to "socialist" economies declined by some 18 per cent in volume, in part reflecting the supply constraints mentioned above, especially in energy production. *Soviet imports from those economies* fell some 6 per cent (table 2.2.16). Owing to movements in intra-CMEA prices adverse to the Soviet Union, Soviet export revenues fell more sharply than volume while imports contracted less in value than in quantity (tables 2.2.16 and 2.2.19). A large increase in the Soviet trade deficit with eastern Europe was the consequence (table 2.2.18).

The trade of *the east European countries* with "socialist" economies (and, notably, among themselves) contracted even more sharply, by an estimated 18-21 per cent in volume, reflecting the greater severity of the recession in these countries, the first impact of the impending departure of the German Democratic Republic from the CMEA trading system, as well as the failure of the intra-group settlements arrangements.[137]

---

130 Statement by Emiliya Maslarova, Minister of Labour and Social Welfare on 21 January 1991. BBC, *Summary of World Broadcasts*, EE/0978.

131 *Financial Times*, 6 February 1991.

132 Statement by Head of Department in the Ministry of Labour on 7 January 1991. Reported in BBC, *Summary of World Broadcasts*, EE/0966.

133 There are signs that the short-time working scheme will be extended until December 1991. *Frankfurter Allgemeine Zeitung*, 7 February 1991.

134 Contained in speech to Soviet parliament by Nikolai Gritsenko, Chairman of the Parliamentary Commission for Labour, Prices and Social Policy. *Izvestiya*, 9 January 1991.

135 See United Nations Economic Commission for Europe, *Economic Bulletin for Europe*, vol.42/90, New York, 1991, chapter 2, for a more extensive review of trade developments through the first half of 1990.

136 Trade volume changes for the eastern economies are ECE secretariat estimates based on Hungarian and Polish price data for rouble area trade and international data for trade in convertible-currency markets.

137 These developments are reviewed in more detail in section 3.2 below.

TABLE 2.2.15

Eastern Europe and the Soviet Union: Volume of foreign trade, by country, 1988-1990

(Annual percentage change)

	Exports			Imports		
	1988	1989	1990 a	1988	1989	1990 a
Bulgaria	2.4	-3.4	-26.0*	5.3	-6.5	-20.0*
Czechoslovakia	3.2	-2.0	-13.0*	2.9	2.7	- *
German Democratic Republic	-0.2	0.5	-*	4.7	2.4	15.0*
Hungary	5.1	-	-4.3	-2.0	1.0	-3.4
Poland	9.1	0.2	14.9	9.4	1.5	-15.6
Romania	7.4*	-10.8*	-46.0*	-5.8*	3.7*	4.0*
Six countries above b	3.7	-2.1	-10.0	3.3	0.9	-0.5
Yugoslavia	-1.0	4.8	2.2	-8.6	13.1	21.9
Soviet Union	4.8	-	-14.0*	4.0	9.3	-5.0*

Source: Appendix table B.15.

a   Preliminary national data or ECE secretariat estimates.
b   CMEA countries only.

TABLE 2.2.16

Eastern Europe and the Soviet Union: Volume of foreign trade, by direction, 1988-1990

(Annual percentage change)

	Exports			Imports		
	1988	1989	1990 a	1988	1989	1990 a
Eastern Europe, b *to or from:*						
World	4	-2	-10	3	1	-1
Socialist economies	5	-2	-21	-	-2	-18
Market economies	2	-1	-	4	3	10
Soviet Union, *to or from:*						
World	5	-	-14	4	9	-5
Socialist economies	1	3	-18	1	3	-6
Market economies	6	-1	-7	9	19	-4

Source: ECE secretariat estimates. For explanation of country groups, see footnote (00).

a   Preliminary. Based on January-September data for eastern Europe.
b   CMEA countries only.

In trade with the *market economies,* Soviet exports decreased by about 7 per cent and east European exports stagnated in volume. There was an especially large fall in east European exports to *developing* countries. Soviet imports from the market economies contracted by some 4 per cent in volume (following growth by 19 per cent in 1989), but east European imports rose some 10 per cent.[138]

Except for Poland, whose exports increased by some 15 per cent in 1990, all east European countries registered stagnant or falling export volumes. The most striking falls were in Romania (46 per cent) and Bulgaria (26 per cent), reflecting primarily the steep decline of domestic production in these countries. However, output had also fallen sharply in Poland under the impact of that country's stabilization policy on domestic demand, and it is one of the first successes of the Polish transformation policies that this led to a determined search for outside markets by Polish enterprises.

Imports rose at a fast pace in the German Democratic Republic (data refer to the first nine months and include intra-German trade) and in Yugoslavia. The estimated 4 per cent rise in the volume of imports into Romania stemmed entirely from the rapid rise of convertible-currency imports from the developed market economies (Romanian imports from the rouble area plunged). This increase in imports, in combination with a fall in exports, appears to have absorbed most of the country's foreign-currency reserves by the end of the third quarter, requiring emergency steps (a hasty devaluation and domestic price liberalization in November) to salvage the situation.

Imports into Czechoslovakia stagnated and those into other countries declined in volume, constrained by devaluation and deflationary fiscal policies (as in Poland, where the fall was about 16 per cent), by general domestic austerity policies (in Czechoslovakia and Hungary) or by more traditional, centrally-administered import controls in response to balance-of-payment dif-

---

138 Developments in trade with the *developed* market economies in 1990 are discussed in detail in section 3.3 below. There are some differences between the east-west trade data given here, based on *eastern* sources, and those in section 3.3 below, which are based on *western* sources.

TABLE 2.2.17

Eastern Europe and the Soviet Union: Foreign trade, by direction, 1988-1990
(Value in billion US dollars; growth rates in percentages) [a]

Country or country group [b]	Exports				Imports			
	Value	Growth rates			Value	Growth rates		
	1989	1988	1989	1990 [c]	1989	1988	1989	1990 [c]
Eastern Europe, [d] *to or from:*								
World	81.1	7.5	-3.5	-13.4	75.8	3.0	-2.7	-6.2
Socialist countries (TR terms) [e]	*45.3*	*5.0*	*-1.4*	*-9.2*	*41.5*	*-1.4*	*-2.3*	*-17.3*
Eastern Europe (TR terms) [e]	*14.2*	*5.8*	*-1.2*	*-12.8*	*14.2*	*0.3*	*0.5*	*-17.0*
Developed market economies	28.6	10.7	6.5	7.8	27.9	10.9	4.8	24.2
Developing countries	7.2	1.8	-12.5	-19.8	6.5	0.5	5.5	-15.1
Soviet Union, *to or from:*								
World	109.1	2.7	-1.3	-2.9	114.5	11.6	6.9	7.9
Socialist countries (TR terms) [e]	*67.0*	*-3.0*	*-1.5*	*-13.8*	*70.9*	*3.0*	*3.0*	*-0.9*
Eastern Europe (TR terms) [e]	*50.4*	*-4.6*	*-3.2*	*-17.3*	*56.8*	*2.6*	*1.7*	*-2.7*
Developed market economies	26.0	7.8	7.8	12.2	32.5	22.6	21.1	10.1
Developing countries	16.1	2.2	2.0	-4.0	11.1	17.4	26.0	18.3

Source: Secretariat of the United Nations Economic Commission for Europe, based on national statistical publications, plan fulfilment reports and (for 1990) in part on trade partner data.

a Both export and import values are expressed f.o.b., except for Hungarian imports which are shown c.i.f. in the national returns. Growth rates are calculated on values expressed in US dollars for total trade and trade with developed and developing market economies, and on values expressed in transferable roubles (TR) for trade with "socialist" countries, and therefore will differ from those shown in national statistics.
b "Eastern Europe" refers to the east European member countries of CMEA (Bulgaria, Czechoslovakia, German Democratic Republic, Hungary, Poland and Romania). The partner country grouping follows the practice until recently prevalent in the national statistical sources, which differs from the breakdown usually employed in United Nations publications. Thus, "socialist countries", in addition to the east European countries, the Soviet Union, and the Asian centrally planned economies, includes Yugoslavia and Cuba. "Developed market economies" differs from the aggregate used in chapter 4 below by the exclusion of Turkey and Yugoslavia and the inclusion of Australia, New Zealand and South Africa.
c January-September 1989 to January-September 1990. Data for eastern Europe include estimates for non-reporting countries. See table 2.2.19 for full-year data for the Soviet Union.
d Excluding Yugoslavia..
e Growth rates only.

TABLE 2.2.18

Eastern Europe and the Soviet Union: Trade balances, 1987-1990
(Billion US dollars or transferable roubles)

Country group	1987	1988	1989	January-September		1990
				1989	1990	
Eastern Europe [a]						
World	2.5	6.1	5.2	5.5	1.2	-0.8 [b]
Socialist countries (billion TR)	*0.4*	*4.4*	*4.9*	*4.0*	*6.8*	*9.4* [b]
Developed market economies	0.3	0.2	0.7	1.6	-1.4	-3.6 [b]
Developing countries	2.0	2.1	0.7	0.7	0.3	0.3 [b]
Soviet Union						
World	11.7	3.4	-5.4	-4.5	-13.2	-17.1
Socialist countries (billion TR)	*2.1*	*-0.5*	*-2.4*	*-2.2*	*-6.2*	*-9.5*
Eastern Europe (billion TR)	*0.1*	*-2.4*	*-4.1*	*-2.8*	*-6.1*	*-8.6* [b]
Developed market economies	0.5	-2.7	-6.5	-4.4	-4.5	-4.8
Developing countries	7.9	6.9	5.0	3.4	1.6	3.9

Source and country groups: As for table 2.2.17.

a Excludes Yugoslavia..
b Extrapolated by assuming a continuation of the January-September trends of exports and imports to the end of the year.

ficulties (notably in Bulgaria, where imports fell some 20 per cent).

The more rapid fall of intra-group trade brought about a pronounced shift in the *regional structure* of the eastern countries' foreign trade. Thus, in eastern Europe the share of European intra-CMEA trade, as measured in national statistics, has fallen below 50 per cent for the first time in the post-war period. It should perhaps be remembered, however, that while this is a sign of reorientation in external relations, it reflects "trade destruction" rather than "trade diversion".

External balances

There was a sharp deterioration in the external balance of the Soviet Union in the last two years (table 2.2.18). For the first time since the mid-1970s the country incurred an overall *trade deficit* in 1989, as the remaining surplus with the developing countries was no longer large enough to offset the rising deficits with the developed market economies and the countries of eastern Europe. In 1990 the overall deficit surpassed $17 billion, more than treble its level in 1989. This was

TABLE 2.2.19

Eastern Europe and the Soviet Union: Change in foreign trade value and trade balances by partner region, 1988-1990

(Growth rates in percentages; trade balances in billion US dollars or billion transferable roubles)

Country and trade partner groups [a]	Growth rates						Trade balance, in billion US dollars		
	Exports			Imports					
	1988	1989	1990 [b]	1988	1989	1990 [b]	1988	1989	1990 [b]
Bulgaria									
World	9.1	-6.2	-17.8	3.4	-9.2	-15.0	0.6	1.0	0.4
Socialist countries (in TR terms)....	*6.5*	*-3.6*	*-25.3*	*-5.4*	*-10.2*	*-17.4*	*1.1*	*1.6*	*0.6*
Developed market economies	3.3	17.2	-12.4	4.4	0.6	-26.7	-1.5	-1.3	-0.8
Developing countries	-3.5	-35.8	4.5	81.3	-8.7	-22.6	0.3	-0.2	0.2
Czechoslovakia									
World	9.2	-2.9	-16.7	5.8	-2.2	-6.6	0.3	0.2	-1.3
Socialist countries (in TR terms)....	*5.9*	*-4.7*	*-20.2*	*1.5*	*0.4*	*-8.9*	*0.6*	*-0.1*	*-1.6*
Developed market economies	13.6	10.9	13.4	9.8	-1.6	28.1	-0.4	0.1	-0.6
Developing countries	-2.5	0.1	-10.9	-	17.0	-11.9	0.4	0.2	0.2
German Democratic Republic [c]									
World	1.4	4.3	5.6*	4.2	2.1	16.3*	-0.8	-0.4	-2.4*
Socialist countries (in TR terms)....	*1.6*	*-0.2*	*0.7**	*-0.8*	*-3.3*	*-28.3**	*0.3*	*0.7*	*4.6**
Developed market economies	6.0	9.5	11.3*	11.7	6.7	54.3*	-1.2	-1.9	-5.2*
Developing countries	-26.8	-0.2	-5.2*	-19.2	5.3	-12.0*	0.2	0.2	0.2*
Hungary									
World	4.3	-3.3	-1.3	-4.9	-5.4	-2.7	0.6	0.8	0.9
Socialist countries (in TR terms)....	*7.9*	*-2.4*	*-13.6*	*0.2*	*-7.7*	*-11.1*	*0.9*	*1.4*	*1.0*
Developed market economies	14.9	5.6	20.6	0.4	7.7	3.8	-0.1	-0.2	0.5
Developing countries	11.8	-6.8	-0.2	7.5	-22.0	60.9	0.3	0.4	-
Poland									
World	13.3	-6.6	10.8	12.8	-7.3	-15.9	1.6	1.6	4.8
Socialist countries (in TR terms)....	*3.2*	*5.2*	*30.5*	*-3.9*	*1.7*	*11.7*	*1.3*	*1.8*	*4.8*
Developed market economies	18.5	5.3	40.0	30.1	7.1	-4.7	0.4	0.3	3.1
Developing countries	14.0	-3.6	3.2	12.9	-8.8	-17.1	0.5	0.5	0.7
Romania [c]									
World	8.6	-7.9	-49.2	-8.1	10.4	-3.4	3.7	2.0	-2.8
Socialist countries (in TR terms)....	*9.0*	*-8.0*	*-45.3* [d]	*0.3*	*5.4*	*-17.6* [d]	*0.3*	*-0.4*	*-1.7* [d]
Developed market economies	4.6	-3.9	-40.0 [e]	-12.6	1.7	210.8 [e]	3.0	2.9	-0.8 [e]
Developing countries	15.5	-15.2	-38.1 [e]	-23.4	29.0	-12.2 [e]	0.4	-0.4	-0.9 [e]
Six countries above									
World	7.5	-3.5	-13.4*	3.0	-2.7	-6.2*	6.1	5.2	-0.8*
Socialist countries (in TR terms)..	*5.0*	*-1.4*	*-9.2**	*-1.4*	*-2.3*	*-17.3**	*4.4*	*4.9*	*9.4**
of which: Six countries above	*5.8*	*-1.2*	*-12.8**	*4.8*	*-1.7*	*-17.0**	*-*	*-*	*1.3**
Soviet Union	*3.4*	*-2.2*	*-6.6**	*-6.6*	*-5.7*	*-17.1**	*3.6*	*4.7*	*7.6**
Developed market economies	10.7	6.5	7.8*	10.9	4.8	24.2*	0.2	0.7	-3.6*
Developing countries	1.8	-12.5	-19.8*	0.5	5.5	-15.1*	2.1	0.7	0.3*
Yugoslavia									
World	6.7	6.1	7.1	2.5	12.6	27.5	-0.7	-1.4	-4.6
Socialist countries	3.1	3.1	-8.6	..	..	5.4	..	0.1	-0.5
Developed market economies	13.0	10.4	19.6	..	..	42.9	..	-1.2	-3.4
Developing countries	5.7	-2.5	-4.2	..	..	11.2	..	-0.3	-0.6
Soviet Union									
World	2.7	-1.3	-5.1	11.6	6.9	5.4	3.4	-5.4	-17.1
Socialist countries (in TR terms)....	*-3.0*	*-1.5*	*-19.2*	*3.0*	*3.0*	*-2.4*	*-0.5*	*-2.4*	*-9.5*
Developed market economies	7.8	7.8	14.3	22.6	21.1	6.1	-2.7	-6.5	-4.8
Developing countries	2.2	2.0	-3.2	17.4	26.0	4.8	6.9	5.0	3.9

Source: Secretariat of the United Nations Economic Commission for Europe, based on national foreign trade statistics. Figures for 1990 are in some cases ECE secretariat estimates based on trade data for the first 9-11 months, supplemented by trade partner statistics and trend analysis; these may be subject to substantial error margins and should therefore be considered first approximations only.

Note: Growth rates and trade balances are based on trade values in terms of US dollars in the case of total trade and trade with the market economies, and on trade values in terms of transferable roubles (TR) in the case of trade among socialist countries; growth rates may therefore differ from those shown in national statistics. National data are converted to dollars at the conversion coefficients used for statistical purposes. In most—but not in all—cases these are time-weighted averages of the official "basic" exchange rate against the dollar, as announced by national banks or other authorities.

   a The partner country grouping follows the practice of the national statistical sources, which differs from the breakdown usually employed in United Nations publications. Thus, "socialist countries" includes Yugoslavia and Cuba, in addition to the east European countries, the Soviet Union, and the Asian centrally planned economies. "Eastern Europe" refers to the six east European country-members of the CMEA shown separately in the table.
   b Preliminary. All entries marked with an asterisk are based on January-September data.
   c Based on substantially revised national trade statistics for 1988-1989.
   d Rouble-denominated trade only.
   e Trade denominated in convertible currencies. The breakdown between the two country groups is an ECE estimate based on January-September data of OECD countries.

due, however, to the quadrupling of the rouble deficit. The Soviet trade deficit with market economies diminished to some $0.9 billion, *inter alia* as a result of import restraints and the rise in oil export prices in the last quarter of 1990.

In the case of eastern Europe, trade surpluses with the market economies turned into deficits in Romania and Czechoslovakia. In Romania, a large surplus ($2.5 billion in 1989) swung into a deficit of some $1.7 billion in 1990. On the basis of January-September trade flows, a large deficit would have opened for the German Democratic Republic, but most of this arose in intra-German trade which disappeared as "foreign trade" with German unification. However, the surplus in rouble trade, which had reached TR 3.7 billion in the first nine months, continued to surge after unification and may have risen to TR 6 billion for the year as a whole.[139] The Bulgarian deficit in trade with market economies diminished in 1990 as imports plunged in the wake of the country's payments difficulties. Hungary and Poland registered growing surpluses in convertible-currency trade ($3.8 billion in the latter country). The convertible-currency position of the countries of eastern Europe worsened in the second half of the year, as their terms of trade on the world market fell and the share of convertible-currency transactions in their trade with the Soviet Union increased, notably in the last quarter.

Rouble area surpluses rose steeply in Poland and the German Democratic Republic, and decreased in Bulgaria and Hungary. Only Czechoslovakia and Romania had rouble-area deficits in 1990, which were much higher than in 1989.

The *outlook* for the foreign trade of the eastern countries is generally for a further sharp fall in 1991. This emerges in the first instance from the bilateral discussions shaping the post-CMEA intra-group trade arrangements between the Soviet Union and the east European countries, but also among these countries. In all cases significant reductions in the level of trade are envisaged, generally in the 15-30 per cent range. While it is not always fully clear what the numbers mentioned in this context mean — especially in view of the shift to convertible-currency transactions, that is, to a new *numéraire* for trade measurement — or what the trade levels mentioned must be compared with (e.g., whether prior interstate protocols, or prior year actual transactions), a pronounced weakening of trade within the group is clearly in the making. This is not offset by increases in transactions with the rest of the world, either because of expected domestic supply difficulties for tradeables (this seems to be the case in the Soviet Union) or because countries envisage the introduction of very austere stabilization policies (notably Czechoslovakia), or finally, because of the uncertain outlook for exports in a world market which is slowing down.

---

[139] New trade statistics for the territories of the former GDR are still under preparation. Preliminary data indicate a 1990 surplus of DM 14.9 billion (as against DM 2.1 billion in 1989) in trade with the European "state trading countries" (*Wirtschaft und Statistik*, No.2, February 1991). At the conversion rate of DM 2.34 per rouble applied since the currency union in July 1990, this would amount to R6.4 billion. However, these data probably cover both rouble-denominated trade and trade settled in convertible currencies; hence the rouble trade surplus could be even larger.

Chapter 3

INTERNATIONAL ECONOMIC RELATIONS

3.1 WORLD TRADE AND PAYMENTS

The expansion of world trade slowed somewhat in 1990 due to weaker economic activity and there was some reduction of the external imbalances between industrial nations. Although non-oil commodity prices weakened, oil prices recovered in the second half of the year improving the terms of trade. International interest rates on the US dollar declined, but those on most other currencies have risen. The growth of world trade is expected to ease further in 1991.

(i) Overview

The growth in the volume of world merchandise trade slowed to a rate of 4 per cent in 1990. The principal factor behind the deceleration is the slow-down of world economic growth, especially in North America and the United Kingdom, but also in eastern Europe and the Soviet Union and in some developing countries. Prospects are for a further slowing of trade growth in 1991.

The correction of the major external imbalances between industrial nations continued during 1990. The US trade deficit continued to fall, and the Japanese and German trade surpluses declined. The trade and current account balances of the developing countries improved in 1990, primarily as a consequence of higher oil prices.

During 1990, the terms of trade of primary commodities continued to improve, *vis-à-vis* manufactured goods, but only because of higher oil prices. Non-oil primary commodity prices declined owing to weaker demand in the industrial countries. This trend is expected to continue in 1991.

Prospects for the growth of international trade were also dampened by the failure to reach an agreement regarding agricultural liberalization within the Uruguay Round. Consequently, no agreement was reached in any of the other areas in the Uruguay Round, and the talks were suspended last December. A decision was

taken in February 1991 to renew the negotiations which are expected to continue through most of the year.

(ii) World trade developments: trade volumes and external balances

In 1990, the growth of *world trade* slowed to 4 per cent in volume (table 3.1.1), about equal to the average annual growth rate between 1980 and 1987. A further easing in growth, is expected in 1991.

Strong export growth continued in *North America* where it was the main support to economic growth, counterbalancing the slack in domestic demand. In the *United States*, exports were particularly dynamic, increasing by some 9 per cent.[140] This growth was helped by a real depreciation of the US dollar during 1990, which raised demand for US exports, particularly in western Europe. The slow-down of the US economy was reflected in a slower 4 per cent expansion of *import* volumes.

Due to fast export growth − particularly agricultural products and capital goods − and despite a sharp increase in the value of petroleum imports,[141] the *US trade deficit* fell to $109 billion in 1990.[142] There were large reductions in the deficits with other industrial countries, with the newly industrialized Asian economies and, significantly, with Japan. The balance with western Europe moved from a deficit to a small surplus, while the country's surplus with *eastern Europe* and the

---

140 *US Department of Commerce News*, 18 December 1990, Washington, D.C., 1990.

141 There was a 29 per cent increase in petroleum imports in the third quarter of 1990. This was partly due to higher oil prices and partly to an increase in the volume imported. *US Department of Commerce News*, 27 November 1990.

142 On a balance of payments basis. The trade deficit − on a customs basis − for 1990 was $100.4 billion. *US Department of Commerce News*, 18 February 1991.

TABLE 3.1.1

World trade: Volume changes, 1988-1990

(Percentage change from previous year)

	1988	1989	1990 [a]
Exports			
Developed market economies	7.7	7.5	5.5
North America	15.5	9.1	7.6
Western Europe	5.4	7.2	4.5
Southern Europe	4.7	10.8	8.6
Japan	4.4	5.0	4.9
Developing countries	10.5	6.7	5.0 [b]
Oil exporters [c]	12.1	7.6	1.7 [b]
Non-oil exporters	10.0	6.4	6.1 [b]
Eastern Europe and the Soviet Union	4.3	-1.0	-12.0
Eastern Europe	3.7	-2.1	-10.0
Soviet Union	4.8	-	-14.0
Total above	8.0	6.6	3.9
Imports			
Developed market economies	7.5	7.4	5.2
North America	5.9	6.1	3.1
Western Europe	6.8	7.2	6.2
Southern Europe	7.1	17.8	9.2
Japan	16.6	8.3	5.2
Developing countries	10.6	8.6	4.1 [b]
Oil exporters [c]	6.1	5.4	6.5 [b]
Non-oil exporters	11.7	9.3	3.6 [b]
Eastern Europe and the Soviet Union	3.6	4.8	-2.5
Eastern Europe	3.3	0.9	-0.5
Soviet Union	4.0	9.3	-5.0
Total above	7.4	7.1	4.3

Sources: IMF, *International Financial Statistics*, February 1991; OECD, *Monthly Statistics of Foreign Trade*, Series A, February 1991; and ECE secretariat estimates for the developed market economies; IMF, *World Economic Outlook*, October 1990 for developing country groupings; ECE secretariat calculations, based on national sources for the European centrally planned economies. Weights for aggregation are US dollar trade shares in 1985.

a Preliminary or estimated.
b IMF estimates for full year.
c OPEC members, except Ecuador and Gabon, plus Oman.

Soviet Union fell. As a consequence of higher oil prices, the deficit with the oil-exporting developing countries increased.

Due to the lower trade deficit and to a moderate increase in service receipts, the *US current account deficit* contracted to $95 billion in 1990. Lower interest rates had a beneficial effect on the current account. However, together with the weakness of the dollar, the decline in interest rates caused net private capital inflows to fall from $112 billion in 1989 to only $20 billion in the first nine months of 1990.[143] A substantial part of the current account deficit was financed with short-term funds in 1990, reflecting the difficulty of at-

tracting funds with longer maturities. Due to higher interest rates and investment yields abroad, the United States is experiencing greater competition for long-term funds. At the same time, the country's income receipts should benefit from these differentials.

In *western Europe, export* volume growth slowed to some 5 per cent in 1990, with most of the increase due to intra-European trade. The slow-down is mainly due to Germany, where the Deutschmark appreciated strongly. Export growth decelerated only slightly in most other west European countries. Western Europe's *import* volumes continued to grow rapidly during 1990, but the 6 per cent growth rate was less than in 1989. The slow-down was most pronounced in the United Kingdom, where imports rose by 3 per cent. Only in Germany − where unification boosted domestic demand − did import growth accelerate, to 12 per cent. German imports from eastern Europe and the Soviet Union increased by some 11 per cent in volume terms.

The trade imbalances among the western European nations were somewhat reduced in 1990 due to the effects of the unification of Germany[144] and to a slow-down in economic activity in the United Kingdom. The combined trade and current account surplus of western Europe deteriorated (table 3.1.2) owing primarily to the reduction in German surpluses. German private long-term capital exports increased sharply during 1990, but net short-term capital outflows fell considerably as a result of high real interest rates in Germany.[145] Capital exports to the eastern economies totaled DM 9.3 billion in the first three quarters of 1990, and were 120 per cent higher than in the previous year.[146]

In the other major west European economies, large trade and current account deficits persisted (see section 2.1(iv)). While the current account improved slightly in the *United Kingdom,* it deteriorated sharply in *France* and *Italy*. All three countries experienced a deterioration in their invisible balances.

Japan's exports continued to expand at 5 per cent in 1990, about the same as the growth of imports. The country's trade surplus fell to $64 billion, primarily because of the lagged effects of the depreciation of the yen since the end of 1989. Higher world oil prices boosted the value of imports, while exports were negatively affected by the slow-down in economic growth in the United States. The Japanese current account surplus declined sharply to $36 billion in 1990. As a consequence, Japan's exports of capital contracted, with net long-term capital exports falling by one half to $44

---

143 This excludes the statistical discrepancy which, according to the US Department of Commerce, reached $47.7 billion in the first three quarters of 1990. Including this item, net capital inflows totaled $67.4 billion, still far below the levels of the previous years. *US Department of Commerce News,* 11 December 1990.

144 Germany's trade surplus, on a balance of payments basis (f.o.b.-f.o.b.), is estimated to have fallen to $69.8 billion in 1990, or $59.3 billion if the former German Democratic Republic is excluded.

145 Net capital exports totaled DM 71.2 billion in the first ten months of 1990, and were almost three times larger than in the same period of the previous year. *Statistische Beihefte zu den Monatsberichten der Deutschen Bundesbank,* December 1990.

146 See *Statistische Beihefte zu den Monatsberichten der Deutschen Bundesbank,* Reihe 3, Zahlungsbilanzstatistik, February 1991. This figure includes flows to the former German Democratic Republic until June and to China and Vietnam. Most of the outflow occurred in the third quarter and so is not greatly affected by the inclusion of the former German Democratic Republic.

TABLE 3.1.2

Trade and current account balances, 1988-1990

(Billion US dollars)

	Trade balances			Current account balances		
	1988	1989	1990	1988	1989	1990
Developed market economies....................	-11	-39	-53	-49	-80	-97
North America...	-118	-108	-99	-135	-124	-109
Western Europe	11	-4	-18	17	5	-7
Japan..	95	77	64	80	57	36
Australia and New Zealand....................	1	-3	-	-11	-18	-17
Developing countries...............................	43	47	57	-10	-16	-5
Oil exporters...	28	41	52	-15	-6	12
Non-oil exporters...................................	15	6	5	5	-10	-17
Eastern Europe and the Soviet Union [a] ...	7	-	-1	4	-6	-6
Eastern Europe [a]...................................	3	2	-	2	-2	-2
Soviet Union [a]......................................	4	-2	-1	1	-4	-4
Total above..	39	8	3	-55	-102	-108

Sources: IMF, *International Financial Statistics,* February 1991, Washington, D.C.; OECD, *Economic Outlook,* No.48, December 1990; national statistics and ECE secretariat estimates. Small discrepancies are due to rounding.

a With market economies.

billion.[147] This reduction stems partly from the increased foreign borrowing by Japanese enterprises.

As a consequence of the slow-down in world economic activity, the expansion of exports of the *developing countries* slowed to 5 per cent in 1990.[148] Export growth decelerated in nearly all areas of the developing world in 1990, that of the oil producers falling to 2 per cent in volume and that of other developing countries to about 6 per cent (table 3.1.1).

Developing countries' imports growth declined to some 4 per cent in 1990, mainly because of lower demand in the *non-oil* developing countries. Conversely, the imports of fuel exporters are estimated to have expanded more rapidly in 1990. The trade surplus of the developing countries is estimated to have reached some $57 billion in 1990. There was a redistribution of trade shares towards oil-producing countries, owing chiefly to the rise in oil prices. The aggregate current account deficit of developing countries fell to $5 billion in 1990.

The developing countries' *foreign debt* stabilized in 1990, totalling $1.2 trillion, or 32 per cent of their GDP.[149] The debt service/export ratio was the lowest since 1981, partly as a consequence − albeit still limited − of debt reduction schemes, and of an increase in exports. Although there was some relief from lower US interest rates, developing countries are still constrained by their high debt servicing, their imports remaining depressed.

In contrast to the growth in world trade, the foreign trade of *eastern Europe and the Soviet Union* has con-

tracted. In 1990, export volume plunged by 12 per cent, while imports fell by 3 per cent.[150] The decline was very pronounced in intra-group trade, which reflects primarily the disintegration of intra-CMEA trade and payments arrangements, but also supply problems. Exports to market economies fell by less than intra-group exports, while imports from market economies increased (see section 2.2(iv)).

In *eastern Europe,* export volume decreased by 10 per cent in 1990. Except for Poland, whose exports rose by 15 per cent in volume, all countries experienced declines in 1990. The exports of Romania and Bulgaria contracted particularly strongly, by 46 per cent and 26 per cent in volume terms respectively. Imports of the group contracted by nearly 1 per cent in 1990. Trade among the east European countries fell by 15-20 per cent − as did their trade with the Soviet Union. Falling domestic production, often due to an uncontrolled dissolution of the central planning system, contracting CMEA demand and the demise of the rouble-based trade and payments régime, explain much of the fall in exports. Exports to market economies remained unchanged in volume terms in 1990. There was a very large rise in imports from non-CMEA markets (47 per cent in volume) in Romania, partly offsetting the steep contraction of preceding years under the policy of breakneck repayment of foreign debt. In Poland, imports were down 16 per cent.

In the *Soviet Union,* exports contracted by some 14 per cent in volume in 1990, mainly because of supply

---

147 Japanese capital outflows are estimated to have reached over $120 billion in 1990, down from $192 billion in 1989. Between 1986 and 1989, capital outflows totaled $607 billion. Although in recent years Japanese investors have favoured portfolio investment, they are increasingly shifting towards direct investment. See OECD, *Economic Surveys: Japan,* Paris, December 1990.

148 IMF estimates for the whole year. IMF, *World Economic Outlook,* October 1990.

149 *IMF Survey,* 24 September 1990, p.277.

150 ECE estimates.

TABLE 3.1.3

Developed market economies: Real GDP ª and imports, 1990
(Percentage change over previous year)

	GDP	Imports of goods and services
France..	2.6	6.3
Germany	4.7	9.4
Italy..	2.5	5.5
United Kingdom...........................	0.5	1.6
Total 4 countries	2.9	5.9
Austria..	4.5	9.3
Belgium	3.9	7.8
Denmark	1.0	2.1
Finland..	0.3	-1.7
Ireland..	5.0	7.7
Netherlands...................................	3.2	6.0
Norway..	1.8	2.2
Sweden..	0.3	0.5
Switzerland...................................	2.7	4.0
Total 9 countries	2.5	5.1
Total 13 countries	3.0	5.8
Greece...	1.2	7.5
Portugal...	3.9	13.2
Spain...	3.5	9.0
Turkey...	9.0	11.0
Total 4 southern Europe................	4.4	9.7
Total Europe	2.8	6.0
United States.................................	0.9	4.2
Canada...	1.1	1.4
Total North America....................	1.0	3.7
Total above.................................	1.8	5.1
Japan...	6.1	13.5
Total above.................................	2.4	6.1

Sources: As for tables 2.1.1 and 2.1.7.

ª At market prices, except for United Kingdom − output at factor costs.

problems in the energy sector, and imports fell by some 5 per cent.

In 1991, differences in growth rates and currency realignments are likely to contribute to a further reduction of the *external imbalances* of the main industrial countries. All the same, imbalances are expected to remain large. A large increase in exports and a reduction in non-oil imports are expected to lead to a further reduction of the *US trade and current account* deficits. Financing these external imbalances may become more difficult if financial capital is attracted by the relatively higher real interest rates in other industrial countries. In *Germany* the external surplus could even disappear in 1991 due to increased imports as a consequence of unification and weaker demand for investment goods in Germany's main trade partners. High interest rates, however, should continue to attract capital into Germany. Among the other major *west European* countries, external deficits are expected to increase in France, Italy and Spain, but increased exports to Germany may be an offsetting factor. In the United Kingdom, the continued weakness of domestic demand should lead to a reduction of the external deficits. Affected by weaker exports and higher oil imports, the

Japanese current account surplus is expected to fall somewhat in 1991 compared to 1990.

(iii) Development of the western market

The countries of western Europe and North America constitute the largest market for eastern goods outside of the traditional CMEA trading area. The western market has gained additional importance as the eastern countries have sought to offset declining sales among themselves and to speed up their integration into the world economy. For these reasons, it is desirable to take a closer look at the development of western import demand.

In 1990, western demand for imports of goods and services weakened, its growth rate declining to some 6 per cent (table 3.1.3). This reflects a slow-down in import growth in most countries, including the United States, Italy and, especially, the United Kingdom. Imports of goods and services into Germany increased strongly (by over 9 per cent) as a result of unification. Among the smaller west European economies, imports grew strongly in Austria, Belgium and the Netherlands, but declined in Finland. Strong demand for imports continued in southern Europe.

The value of imports from eastern Europe and the Soviet Union grew faster than average in Germany, France, Belgium, the Netherlands, Denmark, Norway and Greece, and in the United States and Canada, but declined in Italy, the United Kingdom, the United States and Japan (table 3.1.4). Demand for east European imports was especially dynamic in Germany, where it expanded by over 30 per cent in 1990.

As economic growth slows down in the industrial countries in 1991, the expansion of international trade is expected to lose momentum. As a consequence of the depreciation of the dollar and of depressed domestic demand and low consumer confidence, import growth is expected to decline in the United States. Import growth is expected to weaken also in Japan and in most of western Europe due to weaker domestic demand. In Germany, the largest single market for eastern goods, imports are expected to continue growing in 1991 supported by the unification of Germany. Import growth in France, Italy and particularly the United Kingdom will be lower than in 1990. Among the smaller west European economies, purchases will continue to grow steadily in Austria, Belgium and the Netherlands, as well as in southern Europe. Later in 1991, import growth could receive a boost if oil prices remain at their current low level and improve industrial countries' terms of trade.

The imports of oil-producing countries, which constitute the largest market for eastern goods among the developing countries, are expected to grow faster than the world average, partly as a result of the reconstruction of the countries involved in the Gulf conflict. As regards the non-oil developing countries, their imports are expected to increase only moderately. This partly reflects the impact of stabilization programmes in several of the countries in this group.

TABLE 3.1.4

Developed market economies' trade with eastern countries, January-September 1990 [a]

(Percentage change; value in US dollars)

	Bulgaria	Czecho-slovakia	Hungary	Poland	Romania	Eastern Europe	Soviet Union
Western imports from:							
France	8	29	20	47	-22	15	19
Germany	43	25	41	58	-17	32	25
Italy	22	14	28	23	-52	-5	11
United Kingdom	-10	-5	1	10	-46	-5	-10
Austria	55	10	22	26	-29	17	32
Belgium-Luxembourg	14	15	14	99	-16	39	14
Denmark	19	10	44	55	-26	41	4
Finland	34	27	6	8	-26	12	1
Greece	103	26	41	8	27	37	127
Iceland	318	-19	49	22	13	13	27
Ireland	51	20	72	-1	-37	4	27
Netherlands	-5	18	36	49	-25	26	5
Norway	2 500	35	27	4	-64	17	49
Portugal	-24	7	-9	-25	-53	-16	-5
Spain	8	1	-	63	-15	11	2
Sweden	-12	10	18	22	-24	14	-15
Switzerland	-4	-3	5	14	-37	1	14
Turkey	8	-2	55	48	-10	13	10
Yugoslavia	-3	-1	22	13	-41	4	4
EC	27	19	32	45	-31	22	15
EFTA	79	11	18	18	-37	14	6
United States	-11	7	1	3	-28	-7	23
Canada	-15	-3	1	-9	-8	-6	18
North America	-12	3	1	1	-24	-7	22
Japan	-5	-3	-2	56	-60	-10	8
Developed market economies	22	14	25	36	-31	15	12
Western exports to:							
France	-21	13	12	-9	82	9	-14
Germany	-32	28	10	14	137	83	15
Italy	-15	32	39	70	104	41	13
United Kingdom	-43	12	6	2	131	6	17
Austria	-19	103	35	-27	108	29	-4
Belgium-Luxembourg	-29	12	-16	-11	148	-4	-12
Denmark	7	57	11	19	670	33	70
Finland	-58	3	-17	8	215	-8	-5
Greece	67	32	43	57	47	51	50
Iceland	3	-78	270	-91	-	-82	-16
Ireland	26	-14	-8	89	5 000	61	305
Netherlands	-11	16	6	14	41	12	-11
Norway	-6	15	31	-2	514	8	-5
Portugal	-15	74	-34	86	-51	-3	-11
Spain	-26	-33	37	28	686	15	9
Sweden	-58	34	-	9	75	6	9
Switzerland	-36	17	19	-11	222	4	41
Turkey	-89	51	34	3	32	4	13
Yugoslavia	13	38	-33	-54	45	-9	12
EC	-24	23	12	16	116	61	11
EFTA	-35	55	24	-13	132	15	-
United States	-84	26	15	-9	216	11	-16
Canada	-55	19	28	7	-47	27	91
North America	-72	25	16	-8	184	12	-4
Japan	-55	-17	28	31	22	5	-20
Developed market economies	-31	31	12	5	112	14	3

Source: As for table 3.1.1.

a Relative to same period in previous year.

(iv) Trade prices, terms of trade and interest rates ·

During 1990, *commodity prices* declined as a consequence of weaker growth in the industrial countries (table 3.1.5). The rise in oil prices triggered by the Gulf crisis did not significantly increase the prices of other commodities, as was the case following the previous oil

shocks. The UNCTAD index, which reflects the principal exports of developing countries, fell by 11 per cent in terms of SDRs and 6 per cent in terms of dollars during 1990.[151]

Prices of *food* fell by some 6 per cent in 1990. *Cereal* prices continued to fall, partly due to an increase in cereal crops during 1990. *Wheat* prices fell by

151 See UNCTAD, *Monthly Commodity Price Bulletin*, January 1991.

TABLE 3.1.5

International trade prices in US dollars and in SDRs

(Percentage change from previous year)

	1987	1988	1989	1990		
				Jan.-March	April-June	July-Sept.
Manufactures [a]						
In US dollar terms	13	6	-	6	9	13
In terms of SDR	2	2	-2	6	6	4
Fuels and related materials [b]						
In US dollar terms	7	-12	12	21	-3	19
In terms of SDR	-3	-15	15	21	-7	10
Non-oil commodities [c]						
In US dollar terms	3	26	-	-8	-5	-3
In terms of SDR	-7	21	5	-8	-10	-10

Source: United Nations, *Monthly Bulletin of Statistics,* December 1990 and UNCTAD, *Monthly Commodity Price Bulletin,* December 1990.

a Export unit value index for manufactures of developed market economies.
b Unit value of the developed market economies' imports of mineral fuels.
c UNCTAD index of market prices of principal commodity exports of developing countries, using weights proportional to the value, in terms of US dollars, of exports from developing countries in the years 1984-1986.

some 20 per cent in dollar terms, *maize* by 5 per cent and *rice* by 10 per cent. After bottoming out during the first quarter of 1990, the prices of *minerals* recovered, peaking in September. Overall, prices of minerals fell by 10 per cent in terms of dollars during 1990, reflecting the slow-down in economic activity in the industrial countries. The further easing of economic growth in the developed countries is expected to keep non-oil commodity prices low in 1991.

The United Nations' unit value index of *manufactured goods* exported by developed market-economy countries rose by 9.2 per cent in dollar terms in the first three quarters of 1990.[152] The rise reflects the 11 per cent increase in the unit value of west European exports — primarily due to the effect on prices of the depreciation of the US dollar. In the United States, the export unit values of manufactured goods rose by only 1 per cent.

Due to global oversupply during the first half of 1990, crude oil prices declined, falling to just $14.3 a barrel in June. In the third quarter of 1990, the Gulf crisis led to expectations of a future shortage of oil, sending prices to $37.85 per barrel (for North Sea Brent) at the end of September. As stocks were replenished and output increased, oil prices started to fall in the fourth quarter of 1990. By the end of 1990, prices for North Sea Brent had fallen to $27.80 a barrel, although that was still 25 per cent higher than at the end of 1989. The average price for 1990 was $22.1 a barrel, some 29 per cent higher than the average price in 1989. The price of crude fell below $17 a barrel in February 1991 but recovered to around $19 a barrel at the beginning of March.

Exchange rate movements during 1990 were marked by the depreciation of the US dollar, especially during the second half of the year. For the whole of 1990, the dollar depreciated by 15 per cent against the ECU and

by 9 per cent in real effective terms.[153] The reduction and eventual reversal of interest rate differentials against the other major currencies, as well as reduced confidence in the US economy, were the main causes behind the depreciation of the dollar. Due to fears of recession, US monetary policy was relaxed in 1990 and short-term interest rates fell. This brought down dollar-denominated international interest rates. The three-month LIBOR declined from 9.1 per cent at the beginning of 1990, to 8.4 per cent at the end of the year. As the US economy continued to weaken during the first months of 1991, the LIBOR on US dollars continued to decline, to 6.8 per cent at the beginning of February. Lower dollar interest rates alleviated the interest burden for countries with a large share of debt denominated in US dollars.

However, there was a steep increase in interest rates in Europe — in response to inflationary pressures — and in Japan — to stop the depreciation of the yen. Since the bulk of east European and Soviet debt is in non-dollar currencies, those countries experienced a small rise in their interest burdens in 1990.

As the threat of increased inflationary pressures stemming from higher oil prices seems to have now disappeared, a certain relaxation of monetary policy is expected in 1991, notably in those countries where growth has faltered and consumer debt is high: North America, the United Kingdom and the Scandinavian countries. In the *United States*, interest rates are expected to fall moderately in 1991. By contrast, monetary policy is expected to remain tight in *Germany* and *Japan*. In Germany, the increase in the budget deficit will also help to keep interest rates high, but they are unlikely to increase further. In *Japan*, restraint on the growth of the money supply is likely to prevent a significant fall in interest rates. Lower interest rates on some currencies and the maintenance of current levels

---

152 See United Nations, *Monthly Bulletin of Statistics,* December 1990 and UNCTAD, *Monthly Commodity Price Bulletin,* January 1991.

153 According to the IMF, the dollar depreciated by 6.5 per cent in nominal effective terms during 1990. See IMF, *International Financial Statistics,* February 1991.

in others should provide some relief to debtor countries and partly compensate for the expected slow-down in the industrial countries' demand for imports.

As a consequence of the increase in interest rates in other industrial countries, the US dollar's attractiveness as a refuge currency has been negatively affected. Furthermore, in the light of weak US economic performance, the dollar is unlikely to recover from the low levels reached in 1990 and early 1991 unless confidence in the economy is restored or interest rates are increased. The latter option seems implausible in the short run, since the US economy is in recession and the Federal Reserve is actually relaxing the monetary grip. The yen, on the other hand, will benefit from high real interest rates and from an increasing participation in international capital markets. The Deutschmark is likely to remain strong. High interest rates and an increase in government financing needs will maintain demand for the German currency.

3.2 INTRA-CMEA TRADE

A pronounced contraction of foreign trade was one economic sequel of the political developments in the eastern part of the ECE region since the end of 1989. The change of the CMEA trade régime at the beginning of 1991 is likely to bring a further decline. In section (i) the sharp decline of intra-eastern trade is reviewed. Section (ii) concentrates on the dissolution of the CMEA trading system, and sections (iii)-(iv) discuss the emerging new shape of trade arrangements and the impact of the change.[154]

(i) The collapse of intra-CMEA trade

The unprecedented fall in the *volume* of trade among the European CMEA countries, by an estimated 14-16 per cent in 1990, continued a decline that had begun already in 1989.

Trade *among the east European countries* contracted particularly sharply in 1990, by perhaps as much as one fifth in volume (the decline in *value* was somewhat smaller, since transferable rouble (TR) prices of the goods traded among the east European countries rose slightly). In trade *between eastern Europe and the Soviet Union,* Soviet exports, over one half of which are fuels, fell some 13-15 per cent in volume in 1990, with a steeper fall in the rouble value of transactions (rouble prices for fuels were lower than in 1989 because of the CMEA pricing formula which reflects past changes in the world oil price). Soviet imports also declined, by some 8-10 per cent in volume.

Data on recent changes in the *value* of intra-CMEA trade flows by country (in terms of transferable roubles) are shown in table 3.2.1.[155]

Among the east European countries, only the former German Democratic Republic registered any growth in the value of *exports* to the European CMEA countries.[156] Exports of all the other countries fell more or less steeply, with the sharpest drop (over 42 per cent) in those of Romania. *Imports* from the rouble area declined in all the east European countries, the largest

fall in rouble transactions (35 per cent) being registered in Poland.[157] Soviet imports from eastern Europe also declined, but much less, owing primarily to relatively strong imports from Poland.

As a result of these various trade flows, bilateral trade balances changed considerably. There was a large and growing trade deficit of the Soviet Union with eastern Europe (table 3.2.2), which reached about TR 6.1 billion in the first nine months of 1990,[158] and grew further in the last quarter. Romania is the only country with which the Soviet Union recorded a surplus in 1990. Surpluses were registered in Poland and the German Democratic Republic, with both the Soviet Union and eastern Europe.

A number of disparate but interacting factors were responsible for the recent downturn in intra-CMEA trade:

− the impending disappearance of the intra-CMEA trade and payments system based on the transferable rouble, special intra-group price arrangements, and bilateral intergovernmental trade protocols;

− the differences among the European CMEA countries in the pace of political and institutional change, structural adjustment and in the severity of stabilization policies, and therefore in their capacity to continue living with the specific arrangements of CMEA trade;

---

154 This review updates the presentation in United Nations Economic Commission for Europe, *Economic Bulletin for Europe,* vol.42/90, New York, 1991, chapter 2.

155 Value changes are presented here in rouble terms because the transferable rouble has in the past been the transaction currency for most intra-CMEA trade. However, some part has always been conducted in convertible currencies and at world market prices, and in 1990 − especially in the second half of the year − this rose substantially. Data distinguishing between trade with CMEA countries as such and that part transacted in rouble terms are available only for Hungary, Poland and Romania; these are shown separately in the tables below and generally indicate a stronger fall of "rouble trade" than of total trade in 1990.

156 The apparent strong rise in the value of *total* Polish exports to CMEA countries expressed in rouble terms shown in table 3.2.1 (while *rouble-denominated* transactions fell) is something of a statistical mirage. While there was a substantial rise of convertible-currency transactions in Polish trade with the eastern countries, its impact on trade value is exaggerated by the shift in the rouble/dollar cross rate employed in Poland (from R3/$ in 1989 to R4.5/$ in 1990). Apart from its rise, the level of this cross rate is much higher than those used in the statistics of Poland's trade partners, where it ranges from R2.2/$ (Hungary) to R0.6/$ (Bulgaria, Soviet Union), thus giving a much greater weight to the non-rouble trade in the Polish trade data than in the trade partner statistics. If aggregated at the Soviet cross rate, total Polish exports to the Soviet Union in 1990 would show an increase of 0.5 per cent (as against the 32 per cent in table 3.2.1), and Polish imports from the Soviet Union would register a 31 per cent decline in value (instead of the 28 per cent increase shown). For a discussion of the measurement problems stemming from these inconsistent rouble/dollar cross rates, see United Nations Economic Commission for Europe, *Economic Bulletin for Europe,* vol.42/90, New York, 1991, pp.29-31.

157 The rise in the overall value of Polish imports from the Soviet Union reflects an upsurge of oil imports paid in convertible currency in the last quarter.

158 According to Soviet trade returns. Discrepancies between the trade balances derived from data reported by exporters and importers have been quite substantial also in the intra-CMEA data, but were diminishing in 1990 (see table 3.2.2).

TABLE 3.2.1

Eastern Europe and the Soviet Union: Intra-group trade, 1988-1990
(Value in billion transferable roubles; growth rates in percentages)

| Reporting country | Exports | | | | Imports | | | |
| | Value | Growth rates | | | Value | Growth rates | | |
Partner country or group	1989	1988	1989	1990	1989	1988	1989	1990
Bulgaria								
Eastern Europe	1.80	1.1	-10.1	-32.5	1.84	1.9	-15.6	-21.5
Soviet Union	6.86	6.8	-1.4	-24.2	5.20	-7.5	-9.7	-15.2
Czechoslovakia								
Eastern Europe	5.03	5.8	0.7	-26.5	5.39	7.9	3.5	-2.7
Soviet Union	6.64	4.8	-7.0	-18.5	6.38	-6.3	-1.9	-19.4
German Democratic Republic								
Eastern Europe	5.43	4.4	-1.1	4.3 [a]	5.00	4.8	1.9	-28.5 [a]
Soviet Union	7.19	-1.9	0.2	11.5 [b]	6.84	-6.1	-7.4	-28.6 [b]
Hungary								
Rouble transactions	7.64	1.4	-4.4	-24.4	7.10	1.4	-9.2	-18.5
Eastern Europe [c]	3.20	15.0	-2.7	-24.6	3.18	6.0	-6.6	-8.6
Soviet Union [c]	5.08	-1.2	-5.0	-12.8	4.09	-6.1	-10.1	-7.6
Poland								
Rouble transactions	12.22	6.4	2.3	-7.0	10.11	-2.4	-6.5	-35.0
Eastern Europe [c]	5.03	5.8	4.3	23.5	4.49	3.2	-1.9	-27.1
Soviet Union [c]	7.48	6.5	2.0	31.9	5.80	-7.9	-7.2	28.3
Romania								
Rouble transactions	4.64	7.7	-7.3	-42.0	5.13	0.2	6.8	-14.7
Eastern Europe [c]	1.72	1.5	-8.2	-51.1 [a]	1.82	1.0	-1.0	12.8 [a]
Soviet Union [c]	2.45	7.8	-4.2	-36.8 [b]	2.74	-3.8	10.0	-22.3 [b]
Eastern Europe								
European CMEA	57.93	4.3	-1.8	-5.9	52.77	-2.3	-4.1	-12.3
Eastern Europe	22.22	5.8	-1.2	-9.8	21.72	4.8	-1.7	-14.8
Soviet Union	35.71	3.4	-2.2	-3.4	31.05	-6.6	-5.7	-10.5
Soviet Union								
Socialist countries [d]	42.23	-3.0	-1.5	-19.2	44.65	3.0	3.0	-2.4
Eastern Europe	31.73	-3.7	-4.1	..	35.80	2.6	1.7	..

Source: Secretariat of the United Nations Economic Commission for Europe, based on national statistical publications, plan fulfilment reports and (for 1990) in part on trade partner data.

a Trade with eastern Europe estimated on the base of trade partner data for the full year.
b Trade with the Soviet Union estimated from trends in January-September 1990 relative to January-September 1989 as shown in Soviet data for that period.
c Some part of the trade with eastern Europe and the Soviet Union was always transacted in convertible currencies. This assumed significant proportions in 1990; hence the divergence between the growth rates of "rouble trade" and total trade with the eastern partners. See footnote (156) in the text for an explanation of the more substantial divergence in the case of Poland.
d Includes Asian socialist countries, Cuba and Yugoslavia in addition to the European CMEA countries.

— reductions in Soviet fuel production and energy exports, one of the key flows in intra-CMEA exchanges; the importance of these was accentuated by the impact of the Gulf crisis on world energy markets in the closing months of 1990;

— shocks to intra-CMEA (especially intra-east European) trade arising from the unexpectedly rapid process of German unification and its modalities, including the currency union which became effective at the beginning of July 1990.

Of these factors, the first, and probably the most important, the dissolution of the CMEA trading system, is discussed in some detail in section 3.2(ii) below.[159] However, the anticipation of this event obviously affected trade policy and behaviour in the period under review and will therefore have to be treated

briefly here. It is closely linked with the second factor, the impact of different rates of transformation of planned economies into market systems.

Early in 1990 it became clear that this would be the last year of the traditional CMEA trade and payments mechanism with its transferable rouble settlements and a separate price régime. The CMEA countries had to negotiate the shape of a new, but still largely unspecified, market-oriented system in their economic relations, based on world market prices and convertible-currency settlements. Among the many uncertainties concerning the future system, the modalities for the conversion of outstanding transferable rouble claims and liabilities were some of the most contentious issues. This alone was probably enough to induce the eastern countries to try to adjust their trade flows already in 1990 so as to minimize bilateral transferable rouble balances that would have to be carried over at the end of the year. It also explains

---

159 For more detailed discussion of other factors, see United Nations Economic Commission for Europe, *Economic Bulletin for Europe*, vol.42/90, New York, 1991.

TABLE 3.2.2

Eastern Europe and the Soviet Union: Trade balances in intra-group trade, 1987-1990

(Billion transferable roubles)

Country and partner country or group	1987	1988	1989	January-September 1989	January-September 1990	1990
Bulgaria						
Eastern Europe	-0.15	-0.17	-0.04	-0.05	-0.27	-0.23
Soviet Union	0.29	1.19	1.65	1.20	0.55	0.78
Czechoslovakia						
Eastern Europe	-0.11	-0.21	-0.36	-0.23	-1.22	-1.53
Soviet Union	-0.12	0.64	0.26	0.24	0.36	0.27
German Democratic Republic						
Eastern Europe	0.58	0.59	0.43	0.68	1.24	2.09 [a]
Soviet Union	-0.55	-0.21	0.35	0.50	2.52	3.13 [b]
Hungary						
Rouble transactions	0.16	0.17	0.53	0.42	-0.28	-0.01
Eastern Europe	-0.35	-0.11	0.02	-0.05	-0.22	-0.49 [c]
Soviet Union	0.57	0.80	0.99	0.76	0.36	0.65 [c]
Poland						
Rouble transactions	0.14	1.12	2.11	0.93	3.20	4.79
Eastern Europe	0.13	0.24	0.54	0.11	2.12	2.94 [c]
Soviet Union	0.11	1.09	1.69	0.99	2.21	2.43 [c]
Romania						
Rouble transactions	-0.14	0.20	-0.48	-	-1.22	-1.68
Eastern Europe	0.02	0.03	-0.10	-0.03*	-0.69*	-1.21 [a,c]
Soviet Union	-0.21	0.07	-0.29	-0.23*	-0.46*	-0.58 [b,c]
Eastern Europe						
Eastern Europe	0.14	0.37	0.49	0.45	0.95	1.55
Soviet Union	0.08	3.58	4.66	3.55	5.53	6.69
Soviet Union						
Socialist countries [d]	2.01	-0.05	-2.43	-2.24	-6.18	-9.50
Eastern Europe	0.06	-2.10	-4.08	-2.82	-6.12	..

Source: As for table 3.2.1.

a Estimated from trade partner data for the full year.
b Estimated on the assumption of continuation of the January-September trends of exports and imports shown in Soviet data to the end of the year.
c See footnote *c* in table 3.2.1.
d See footnote *d* in table 3.2.1.

a good part of the problems encountered with the implementation of contracts in 1990. At the same time, countries tried to strengthen their individual positions in the negotiations on the future trade arrangements.

The most serious balancing problems appeared in east European trade with the Soviet Union and with the former German Democratic Republic.

Structural trade and current-account surpluses with the Soviet Union were registered by Hungary and Czechoslovakia. Other eastern countries used to be in a net debtor position *vis-à-vis* the Soviet Union, with the largest debt accumulated by Poland (almost TR 6 billion at the end of 1989).

In the trade of eastern Europe and the Soviet Union with the German Democratic Republic (and the east German *Länder* after German unification in October), the currency union with the Federal Republic of Germany in July 1990 had a strong impact. Its immediate result was a steep fall in German rouble imports. German rouble exports, which had been falling in the first half of 1990, rose distinctly in the second half of the

year and were up by an estimated 8 per cent for the year as a whole (table 3.2.1). This turnabout was due both to the collapse of the internal demand in the east German *Länder* and to the application of the exchange rate of 2.34 DM/TR for pre-existing export contracts. Hence German rouble surpluses with its CMEA partners surged.[160]

Another feature of 1990 was a rapid evolution of eastern countries' foreign trade systems towards a wider use of market instruments of trade regulation, both in general and with respect to the CMEA partners. However, this process was much more advanced in Hungary and Poland than in other economies of the east. The asymmetries between countries in the extent of demonopolization and decentralization of trade, in the transparency and accessibility of their markets, and in the relative role of administrative and market-related instruments of commercial policy, also contributed to the reduction of trade and to controversies about trade imbalances and the volume and commodity composition of bilateral flows. Under these circumstances, a mixture of trade policy measures were temporarily introduced in Hungary and Poland, as well as in other

---

160 According to the German Minister of Economy J. Möllemann, outstanding German rouble claims amount to some TR10 billion. The largest claim is against the Soviet Union (equivalent of some DM 15 billion), followed by Poland (DM 2 billion), Czechoslovakia (DM 1.6 billion), Hungary (DM 1.3 billion), Bulgaria and Romania (DM 1.2 billion each). *Neue Zürcher Zeitung,* 8 March 1991.

economies, *vis-à-vis* their eastern partners. There was recourse to import and export licensing and the use of differentiated exchange rates in relations with countries employing more centralized and regulated trade systems.

Developments in *fuels trade* played a key role in the overall downturn of intra-eastern trade. The fall in the value of Soviet exports to eastern Europe by over 17 per cent in 1990 (see table 2.2.17) was mostly due to the reduction of energy deliveries, caused mainly by internal factors.

The Soviet Union has long been the major energy supplier of the east European economies. In 1989 it exported 84 million tons of oil and petroleum products and 47 billion cu m of natural gas to eastern Europe as well as some 17 million tons of coal and almost 33 billion kWh of electricity. Soviet energy deliveries to eastern Europe totalled some 139 million tons of oil equivalent. Above one half of Soviet oil exports to eastern Europe was destined for the German Democratic Republic and Czechoslovakia.

The contraction of Soviet primary energy output (2½ per cent in fuel terms, see table 2.2.8) was deeper than the decline in Soviet gross industrial output (1.2 per cent) in 1990.[161] The energy problems grew worse in the second half of the year.

Exports of Soviet crude and petroleum products to east European CMEA countries decreased by 20 per cent in January-September 1990 (from 60 to 48 million tons), while total exports of oil from the Soviet Union diminished by a little over 6 per cent only. Soviet deliveries of natural gas to eastern Europe grew slightly (under 3 per cent in the first three quarters of 1990), with falls in exports to the German Democratic Republic and Romania. Exports of electricity to six east European countries fell by some 4 per cent in nine months of 1990. This reflected a fall in exports to Poland (by almost two thirds) and Bulgaria (by about 7 per cent), while Soviet electricity exports to other east European countries increased, despite disruptions in energy deliveries owing to transmission breakdowns.[162]

Internal economic and political transformations in the eastern countries also contributed to the contraction of trade. The falls in industrial production and fixed investment in all the eastern countries (although to a different extent) were both cause and effect of the trade collapse. The synchronization of the downturn in all countries accentuated the reduction in trade. The severity of supply-side export constraints and the excess demand in the USSR, as well as in Romania and Bulgaria, coincided with a drastic fall in demand for domestic and imported products in Poland, Hungary and the German Democratic Republic stemming from tight monetary and fiscal policies. At the same time, the downturn somewhat alleviated the economic repercussions of the trade collapse. However, the implications of external cuts in supply could be more serious for the importing countries in the longer run, if their production begins to recover.

The asymmetry of supply and demand constraints also cushioned somewhat the trade collapse. New trade opportunities appeared, notably with respect to food and agricultural exports to the Soviet Union. Complete or partial liberalization of food prices and the reduction of subsidies curbed consumer demand in some eastern economies, notably in Poland and eastern Germany after the currency union. Growing stocks and surpluses of foodstuffs could be cleared *inter alia* through exports. However, these trade opportunities were only partly utilized, because of the constraints of bilateral balancing, the CMEA trade pricing system and trade restrictions.

(ii) The demise of the CMEA trade system

The traditional trade and payments system as well as other mechanisms of the CMEA were subject to general criticism during the 45th Session of the organization in Sofia on 9-10 January 1990. At this meeting, Prime Minister Ryzhkov of the Soviet Union proposed that economic relations between the CMEA countries should be based on settlements in convertible currencies and at current world market prices as from the beginning of 1991.[163] Representatives of the east European countries, notably Czechoslovakia and Poland, asked for a period of 3-5 years to allow for a gradual phasing in of the new system and for a partial sharing of the costs of transition. They also asked for the opening of the Soviet market to allow direct business contacts between enterprises of the different member countries.

The Session approved, in principle, the postulate of a gradual transition to a market-based trading system within the CMEA. It was agreed that the shift towards world market prices and hard currency settlements would be implemented on the basis of bilateral agreements between interested countries and with use of policy measures ("shock-absorbers") which would help to prevent one-sided losses or benefits.[164]

A special committee was also established to consider the proposals of the member countries on the reconstruction of the CMEA.[165] Following conclusions reached by the committee in 1990 on transformation of the CMEA into an open, market-oriented organization, facilitating the fuller integration of its members

---

161 See section 2.2(ii) above.

162 *Vneshneekonomicheskie svyazi SSSR,* No.5, 1990, pp.24-25.

163 *Pravda,* 10 January 1990.

164 Statement of J. Osiatynski, Chairman of the Central Office of Planning of Poland, *Rzeczpospolita,* 14 September 1990.

165 This replaced an earlier committee appointed in 1987 and headed by Professor Oleg T. Bogomolov. It was first chaired by Ernö Kemenes, former Chairman of the Hungarian Planning Office, and then by Béla Kádár, Hungarian Minister of International Economic Relations.

with the European and world economy, representatives of the CMEA member countries prepared draft documents on the abolition of the CMEA and the establishment of a successor institution, to be named "Organization of International Economic Co-operation", for submission to the 46th CMEA session which was to be convoked to Budapest on 27-28 February 1991.[166] However, the meeting was postponed, apparently due to differences between the CMEA member countries on the need for and the shape of the future organization, as well as on modalities of the liquidation of CMEA structures and assets.

Notably, some differences of opinions arose with regard to the geographical coverage of the new organization — i.e., should it include the same member countries as the former CMEA, or should it rather be replaced by a sub-regional organization encompassing the European ex-CMEA countries and open for other neighbouring European economies, e.g., Finland, Austria, Yugoslavia and, perhaps, Germany.[167]

The most immediate consequence of the new approach to regional economic co-operation is the switch in the trade and payments régime as of January 1991. The "transferable rouble" régime, which had been unravelling for some time, was thus to be wound down, an operation which proved as difficult and contentious as any bankruptcy.

In the first half of 1990 the Soviet Union appeared to be bent on arranging various kinds of clearing schemes for convertible currency transactions, with the modalities ranging from periodic settlement in actual convertible currency to carrying over any imbalances (that is, allowing *ex ante* for substantial swings) until the deficit partner could raise its exports. However, with the growing economic and political difficulties in the Soviet Union and the sharply rising expectation that the country will be running substantial surpluses with eastern Europe unless they are contained by direct measures, Soviet preferences have shifted in the direction of immediate cash settlement for raw materials and fuels, and "standard" supplier credits for imports of manufactures from eastern Europe.

With the declining role of the central authorities and *de facto* economic decentralization in the Soviet Union, however, solutions for 1991 are not so clear-cut as envisaged in early 1990. In fact, it now appears that there are three-tier arrangements between the Soviet Union and the east European countries. The first tier involves the barter of key Soviet raw materials and fuels, oil and gas in particular, against "hard" exports from eastern Europe — in the first place foodstuffs and acceptable

consumer products; in some cases, even high-quality manufactures are considered "hard". The central authorities deliver necessary export or import licences for the implementation of contracts on trade in goods and services covered by so-called "indicative lists"established in the negotiations. They should also provide convertible currencies for resulting import payments (in the case of the Soviet Union from centralized foreign exchange funds). A second tier appears to include arrangements between Soviet union republics and individual east European countries or firms. These relations can be conducted on a barter, clearing, or cash basis; the modalities are likely to be more *ad hoc* than in accordance with standard international trade practices. Finally, inter-enterprise relations are also being developed — some on a pure barter basis and others on a regular "transaction" account (involving essentially convertible currency payments, in cash, for raw materials and fuels, and supplier credits for manufactures).

Some joint venture agreements between Soviet and east European firms are also under preparation. They are, *inter alia*, expected to allow for settlement of bilateral transactions in national currencies.

(iii) The emerging shape of the new trade and payments arrangements

At the end of June 1990 the Soviet Union notified its partners that it was going to withdraw from the system of settlements in transferable roubles with other CMEA countries after 31 December 1990 and would switch to exchanges denominated in dollars and at world market prices.[168]

On 24 July 1990, President Gorbachev issued a decree "on introducing changes into the Soviet Union's foreign economic relations", committing the government to bring about a transition in economic relations with other CMEA countries to settlements at world prices and in convertible currencies from 1 January 1991.[169] It should be noted that a pronounced shift to non-rouble transactions in Soviet trade with the CMEA countries, based on current world market prices, occurred already in 1990, especially in the second part of the year.

An agreement between the Soviet Union and *Bulgaria* was signed on 20 September 1990. It envisages that further contracts will be based on world market prices and settled in convertible currencies. A type of "commodity clearing" would seem to be involved, as the the two sides also agreed to use commodity lists to balance deliveries of those products most vital for their

166 BBC, *World Broadcasts,* EE/099, 8 February 1991.

167 For instance, the Polish Government stated that the CMEA should be replaced by some form of regional economic co-operation among the countries of eastern and central Europe. A possibility of including other countries of the region which had not been the members of the CMEA, through a system of consultations or co-operation, was also discussed. *Zycie Warszawy,* 27 February 1991.

168 According to the 1963 agreement, the system of settlements in transferable roubles could be abandoned only by a decision of at least two thirds of member countries, or by a unilateral withdrawal of a member, with notification of other members at least half a year before the withdrawal became effective. *Izvestiya,* 1 July 1990.

169 *Izvestiya,* 25 July 1990.

economies (Soviet deliveries of fuels and energy, metals, timber, cotton, cellulose and paper against Bulgarian consumer products). There was also agreement that Bulgaria would continue to participate in energy and raw materials investment projects in the USSR.

In agreements on payments and on economic links in 1991, signed in December 1991, Bulgaria and the Soviet Union envisaged a transition period during which both countries would gradually transfer to full settlements in convertible currency. Under the trade agreement Bulgaria will import 5 million tons of Soviet oil from central sources, to be paid for by counter-deliveries of goods, according to current international prices and on a clearing basis. Another 1.5 million tons of oil will be delivered within the framework of a secondary agreement between organizations of the two countries and in exchange for Bulgarian goods. Bulgaria will pay through clearing half of the price of the large turnkey projects delivered from the Soviet Union as well.[170]

At the beginning of September 1990, the Soviet Union and *Czechoslovakia* concluded an agreement on the new terms in their trade and economic relations with effect from 1991. In principle, all goods will be exchanged against convertible currency and at world prices. However, the agreement provides for a transition period in which a part of the mutual deliveries would be tied into packages based on "indicative lists" of products which both sides agree to supply.[171] These commodity barter lists, for a centrally regulated part of trade, were established in another bilateral agreement, on trade and economic relations in 1991, signed on 17 December 1990. Under this agreement, the Soviet Union is to supply 7.5 million tons of oil. At least 5.5 million tons are to be paid for in convertible currency, and up to 2 million tons are to be exchanged against counter-deliveries of goods for use by Soviet enterprises of the gas and oil industries. Additional oil purchases will be also possible on the basis of direct contracts with Soviet enterprises and republics.[172]

In a payments agreement of 28 December 1990, it was agreed that the Czechoslovak rouble claims against the Soviet Union would be converted into convertible currency at the rate of TR 1/$1, to be used for future import payments in 1991-1994.[173]

During 1989 and 1990, *Hungary* has accumulated claims of 1.6-1.7 billion roubles against the Soviet Union.[174] A payments agreement between the two countries stipulates that the claims generated in 1989 will be settled at a conversion rate of TR1/$0.92, and it is likely that the 1990 claims will be handled according to the same principle. The time span over which claims are to be used is still under negotiation.

The negotiations on a new trading and payments system between the Soviet Union and *Poland* continued through most of October 1990. Among the unsettled issues were problems concerning the conversion of the Polish rouble debt; the offset against this debt which Poland claimed on account of losses incurred in connection with its participation in construction projects in the USSR; the possibility of a transitional period of hard-currency clearing in financial settlements; the sharing of the costs of transition to the new system; the volume of future Soviet energy deliveries to Poland, etc. A new agreement was signed on 14 November 1990. It envisages a shift to convertible-currency settlement in all mutual economic relations from 1 January 1991. Other internationally accepted forms of settlement will also be admitted, with the explicit exception of the clearing system employed until now. All outstanding transferable rouble claims should be settled by the end of March 1991. In the bilateral trade protocol for 1991, signed in December, the Soviet Union agreed to delivery of 4.5 million tons of crude to Poland in 1991, of which 3 million tons are to be paid in cash and 1.4 million tons in barter for Polish exports of machinery and ships. According to Soviet negotiators, additional deliveries of oil could be obtainable only from individual republics. The Soviet Union agreed to supply 8.1 billion cu m of natural gas, of which 1 billion cu m in exchange for cisterns for transportation of liquid gas or oil. No exports of petroleum products were envisaged (against some 2.2 million tons annually in the past). Soviet deliveries of electricity were set at 6.6 billion kWh in 1991.[175] The modalities of regulating outstanding financial balances between both countries are still under negotiation.[176]

In the second half of 1990, the east European countries also concluded bilateral agreements between each other to arrange the winding down of the transferable rouble trade régime and the transition to trade on a new basis. Generally, these envisage a switch to convertible-currency settlement, world market prices and direct contracts between enterprises as from January 1991. Some transitional solutions (e.g., hard-currency clearing settlements) were also adopted to prevent a further collapse of trade. Hungary and Poland agreed to settle the 1990 Polish trade surplus

---

170 According to statements of Bulgarian Deputy Prime Minister A. Tomov, *BBC Summary of World Broadcasts*, EE/WO160 A/5, 4 January 1991, and EE/WO164 A/1, 31 January 1991.

171 *Hospodarske noviny*, 3 September 1990.

172 *Hospodarske noviny*, 15 January 1991.

173 *Ibid.*

174 This includes claims from merchandise trade in 1989 and 1990 of R510 million and R630 million respectively. The rest is service-related (tourism, stationing of Soviet troops, etc.).

175 *Rzeczpospolita*, 17 and 28 December 1990.

176 The Polish rouble debt to the Soviet Union was reported to have fallen to TR 4.7 billion in 1990. In addition, Poland's outstanding convertible currency debt to the Soviet Union amounted to $1.5 billion. However, by the end of 1990 Poland accumulated TR 6.8 billion of claims against the Soviet Union and sought to have them recognized as an offset to its debts on a TR1/$1 basis. *Rzeczpospolita*, 14 and 26 February 1991.

against Hungarian long-term rouble claims on Poland, with merchandise deliveries for the small remaining balance. The winding down of rouble trade between Hungary and Czechoslovakia was to be implemented in three steps. Deliveries under 1990 contracts were to be cleared through the transferable rouble system until the end of January 1991. The balance was to be settled with merchandise deliveries until May, and any remainder with payment in national currencies.

Direct economic contacts were also established between east European countries and some Soviet republics and regions in the second half of 1990, aimed at increasing imports of energy and raw materials in barter exchanges for deliveries of foodstuffs, cigarettes, motor vehicles, building machinery, etc. For example, Czechoslovakia signed a contract with representatives of the Tyumen region in the Russian republic on 11 October 1990 for delivery of 500,000 tons of oil in 1990, in exchange for trucks, buses, loaders, bulldozers, cranes and consumer goods.[177] Such regional agreements, however, are still a matter of controversy in the Soviet Union, especially where oil is concerned, as this is one of the export commodities supposed to remain under central authority.[178] Barter trade is permitted only under special licence from the central Soviet authorities.

Poland also tried to cushion the fall in Soviet fuel deliveries in 1990 and 1991 by non-conventional trade agreements and contracts with central, republican and regional authorities in the USSR in the final quarter of 1990. Extra-protocol food exports to the Soviet Union, agreed upon during the visit of Foreign Minister Skubiszewski to Moscow, Kiev and Minsk in October, included sugar, butter, meat, powdered milk and cigarettes worth some $120 million, delivered on short-term credit. In exchange 1.5 billion cu m of natural gas were to be delivered to Poland in the first quarter of 1991. Bilateral economic deals between Poland and the Russian federation, the Ukraine, Byelorussia, Kazakhstan and other republics were also signed or envisaged.[179]

First steps into post-CMEA trade

At the beginning of 1991 it became evident that the sudden switch to the new trading system is at least as hard for Soviet enterprises as for their east European counterparts, due to their limited possibilities of financing imports (meagre, as yet, export currency retention quotas; a difficult access to centralized currency funds; restrictions imposed on barter transactions by central Soviet authorities). The fall in world oil prices and deteriorating prospects for Soviet energy supplies also changed the outlook for the impact of the switchover upon the Soviet balance of trade with east European economies in 1991.

The limited information available on east European trade with the Soviet Union in the first months of 1991 indicates that Soviet deliveries of contracted oil and other raw materials to eastern Europe, paid in cash, were generally supplied as scheduled. East European exports to the Soviet Union under 1990 contracts, to be settled in transferable roubles, were also still flowing.

Problems were reported, however, with the conclusion of new contracts for east European deliveries to the Soviet Union to be paid in convertible currencies, even if the commodities in question had been included in the indicative lists for 1991.[180] In addition to Soviet liquidity problems at the beginning of the year, this undoubtedly reflects the cumbersome administrative procedures under which a newly-established centralized foreign currency fund is managed,[181] as well as the lack of experience in handling the new trade and payments system.

Inadequate financing and risk insurance arrangements in all the former centrally planned economies also hamper trade since the beginning of the year. In the past, intra-CMEA trade was conducted under an automatic payment guarantee. The exporter had no reason to be concerned about payment, because as soon as the goods left his country the domestic foreign trade bank immediately credited his account. With the switchover from rouble to dollar trade and the mutual suspension of state guarantees for deliveries and payments, new commercial institutions and interbank agreements are required to take over these functions.[182]

The result was an accumulation of Soviet hard currency surpluses and simultaneous rouble deficits in trade with some east European partners in early 1991, even though the modalities of payment settlements

---

177 BBC, *Summary of World Broadcasts*, EE/0894, 13 October 1990.

178 Under the "Basic Guidelines for the Stabilization of the National Economy and the Changeover to a Market Economy" voted by the Supreme Soviet on 19 October 1990, "Oil, gas, gold, diamonds, precious stones, specialized technology and possibly some other goods ... are to be considered all-Union export resources and are traded under a special règime." (*Pravda*, 18 October 1990, p.3).

179 For example, on 25 January 1991 Poland agreed with the Ukraine to provide construction services, light industrial and engineering products against metal ores, tractors and other machinery. The agreement provides for the settlement of accounts in convertible currency. BBC, *Summary of World Broadcasts*, EE/W0166 A/4, 14 February 1991.

180 It was reported that even the opening of a letter of credit for payment of supplies for Soviet troops stationed in Poland proved impossible, although Polish deliveries worth $50 million were envisaged in the interstate indicative list for 1991. *Rzeczpospolita*, 1 March 1991.

181 Decisions to spend for imports apparently are made at the level of the USSR Cabinet of Ministers. At a recent Supreme Soviet hearing on his price reform proposals, Premier V. Pavlov explained that the first decision to allocate foreign currency for raw material imports was taken at a cabinet meeting on 30 January 1991 because "there were signs that light industry is coming to a halt" for lack of material inputs; the decision was delayed because before that "there was no hard currency". BBC, *Summary of World Broadcasts*, SU/1006, 26 February 1990. p.C1/4. According to RSFSR Prime Minister I.S. Silayev, import contracts for raw materials and semi-finished products concluded by the USSR Ministry of Foreign Economic Relations for first-quarter delivery provide for *less than 1 per cent* of the 1990 first-quarter levels of imports, which explains "why mills and factories in the light industry are at a standstill". BBC, *Summary of World Broadcasts*, SU/1006, 26 February 1990. p.C2/4.

182 Because payment guarantees were lacking, goods worth almost $300 million destined for export to the Soviet Union were in inventories in Hungary at the end of February 1991. *Heti Világgazdaság*, 9 March 1991.

have not been yet definitely established (e.g., with Poland).[183]

The weakening of oil prices in the aftermath of the Gulf war, accompanied by the further tightening energy supplies in the Soviet Union expected for 1991, is likely to exacerbate the external liquidity problems of that country and to restrict imports from eastern Europe. However, ample potential for recovery of trade seems to exist, as evidenced by a large interest in promoting barter trade and various forms of co-operation on the part of enterprises and republics within the Soviet Union and producers from eastern Europe.[184] Some recent developments in the intra-east European trade as well as in trade with the Soviet Union also indicate that a possibility of the intra-regional trade creation might exist, if the proper economic and institutional environment is established.[185] In the short term, however, a further fall of trade should be expected, notably as regards trade in engineering and consumer goods and construction services. Among the causes are structural and temporary factors, including the widespread recession and liquidity problems on the side of both importers and exporters, exacerbated by an inadequate development of the financial sector.

The dismantling of the CMEA mechanisms of trade and payments thus creates additional adjustment problems, which are likely to contribute to a further fall of the intra-eastern trade in 1991. A countervailing force may come from proposals (as yet unoperational) for the establishment of bilateral free trade areas between some east European countries, or a project on financing food deliveries from Poland and other east European economies to the Soviet Union from the EC credits granted on food aid to the latter country.[186]

(iv) Impact of the switchover

In the course of 1990 and early 1991, the main lines of a new system of trade and payments among eastern countries have gradually emerged. But many of its elements are as yet undetermined, owing to problems arising during bilateral negotiations and because of uncertainties concerning the future evolution and progress of reforms in the Soviet Union and other economies of the east. Irrespective of special transitional solutions agreed bilaterally, the shift to world market prices and convertible currencies after 1990 seems to be taking place.

Under more favourable internal and external circumstances, and in the longer run, such a shift is likely to support and even accelerate the transformation towards more efficient, competitive economic structures in the economies of the east. However, under present circumstances, the change in the trading system could give rise to serious difficulties in the short and medium run to the vulnerable east European economies.

The immediate costs and benefits for individual economies resulting from the switchover to convertible currencies and world market prices will depend on a number of factors, such as current world energy developments; the commodity composition of trade; the elasticities of domestic output, import demand and export supply with respect to shifts in world market prices and other changes in the external environment; the conditions of access to alternative export markets or sources of supply; outstanding debts or credits in intra-eastern and total trade, and so on. The impact of the switch will therefore vary significantly among countries. However, the Soviet Union is likely to be an unequivocal gainer.

A deterioration of the east European net barter terms of trade *vis-à-vis* the Soviet Union is expected to result from the switchover as the rise in the prices of energy and raw materials is likely to outpace the change in prices of east European exports of manufactured products. The impact on the east European current accounts with the Soviet Union will be magnified by the expected cuts in the volume of Soviet imports of machinery and other manufactured products from eastern Europe. There are concerns in eastern Europe that − without adequate transitional arrangements − a large part of Soviet hard currency proceeds from energy exports to eastern Europe could be rapidly used to import manufactures from the west or from the Asian newly industrialized economies.

Additional adjustment costs in eastern Europe will result from the curtailment of Soviet oil and gas deliveries. The technical and economic problems of even a partial shift to alternative sources of supply are considerable. Large new investments and reconstruction works in the areas of transport infrastructure and oil and gas processing will be necessary if east European energy imports are to be diverted to other suppliers. In the case of natural gas imports, an immediate shift is hardly feasible given the existing pipeline infrastructure.

The potential indirect economic impacts of the switchover to the new trade and payment system are no less important. Higher costs of energy and raw materials will diminish the internal and external competitiveness of east European products and add to in-

---

[183] Under these circumstances, Hungary reportedly accumulated another rouble surplus with the Soviet Union in the first two months of 1991 of some TR 400-500 million. *Magyar Hirlap*, 7 March 1991. Polish short-term rouble claims against the Soviet Union increased further, exceeding TR 7 billion by late February 1991. The switch from regular monthly surpluses in Polish convertible currency trade in 1990 to a deficit of $255 million in January 1991 was largely due to convertible currency imports of 1 million tons of Soviet oil, while the Soviet Union was not yet ready to import Polish pharmaceuticals, coal, coke and sulphur, as envisaged in the interstate trade agreement. *Rzeczpospolita*, 26 February and 1 March 1991; *Gazeta Wyborcza*, 1 March 1991.

[184] This is confirmed, *inter alia*, by the success of the "Promexpo" trade fairs, organized for Polish firms in Minsk (Byelorussia) by a private firm, "Stofratex", from Gdansk in February 1991. *Rzeczpospolita*, 28 February 1991.

[185] For example, a contract worth $11.6 million was signed by the Polish computer company, "Mera-Elzab", with a Soviet importer on delivery of 48,000 monitors, to be assembled in Poland in co-operation with a Taiwan producer. *Trybuna*, 19 February 1991. Convertible currency contracts on exports of 3.7 million tons of Polish coal to Czechoslovakia signed early in 1991 set a record in trade relations between these two countries. *Rzeczpospolita*, 23-24 February 1991.

[186] *Zycie Warszawy*, 1 March 1991.

flationary pressures in the economies in transition. On the other hand, the expected collapse of Soviet import demand for their industrial goods is bound to hurt severely the obsolete branches and enterprises of east European industries which have long specialized on large-scale exports to the Soviet Union. These effects will compound the depressing effects of internal stabilization policies. Thus massive bankruptcies, a rapid rise

in unemployment and extra burdens on central and local budgets are likely to arise in the east European economies in the near future.[187] Altogether, the move towards competitive, world market conditions in intra-eastern trade is expected to accelerate the pace of structural adjustment in the economies of the east, but the economic and social costs of such adjustments are likely to be high.

---

[187] According to a Polish government analysis based on industry surveys, some 90 industrial enterprises specialized in exports to the transferable-rouble area could be seriously endangered after 1990. In 11 enterprises the share of these exports exceeded 75 per cent of total sales. *Rzeczpospolita*, 28 September 1990.

3.3 EAST-WEST TRADE AND FINANCE

This section reviews recent changes in east-west trade and financial relations. The total trade of the eastern countries with the west is treated first, followed by a review of trade by direction and commodity groups (section (ii)). The trade flows of the Soviet Union and eastern Europe are then reviewed separately, the latter followed by some observations on the export boom experienced by three of the east European countries. Eastern financial developments are reviewed in section (iii). The prospects for east-west trade and finance are discussed in section (iv) while section (v) offers detailed profiles of the eastern countries presented from the standpoint of their east-west economic relations and prospects. The review of east-west issues concludes with a survey of international support for eastern reforms in section (vi).

(i) Overview

Growth in east-west trade slowed sharply in 1990,[188] coming to a virtual standstill as the year progressed.[189] However, the exports of Poland, Hungary, and, to a lesser extent, Czechoslovakia performed well, fostered by the impact of domestic austerity measures, economic reforms, buoyant western markets and the improved access to western markets granted by the Group of 24. The growth of these three countries' western exports reduced the adverse effects on domestic budgets and employment of the collapsed eastern markets. However, not all eastern countries fared as well. Supply problems led to falls in industrial output in Bulgaria, Romania and, to a lesser degree, in the Soviet Union, and restricted these countries' exports.

In the final months of 1989, international banks became increasingly cautious about lending to the east as they tried to assess the implications for credit-worthiness of the dramatic economic and political changes. The emergence of payments difficulties in Bulgaria and the Soviet Union in the first part of 1990 appears to have precipitated a large-scale withdrawal of inter-bank loans; and in some eastern countries this withdrawal of credit continued throughout the year. The authorities addressed the ensuing liquidity crisis by drawing down foreign currency reserves − in general, eastern reserves are now inadequate − and, in the case of Bulgaria and the Soviet Union, imposing restrictions on imports. In Hungary, Poland and the Soviet Union international support was crucial in dealing with the financial problems but, for various reasons, Bulgaria and Romania, qualified only for emergency assistance from the west.

The payments positions of the east European countries will probably deteriorate in 1991 as a result of the strong terms-of-trade shock stemming from the demise of the CMEA trade and payments system. Al-

though the recent easing of world oil prices has reduced the scale of current-accounts deficits expected in eastern Europe this year, these countries will still need substantial external financing. Given the defensive posture of the commercial banks, the bulk of financing will have to be provided by the various official creditors. The official international support network for these countries has expanded greatly and now includes the EC-led PHARE programme, the Bretton Woods Organizations, other international institutions and various bilateral initiatives.

In contrast, the Soviet Union will have to rely chiefly on bilateral arrangements for support. The country's payments position is likely to remain fragile if domestic production problems cause the volume of its oil exports to fall steeply and oil prices remain at their current, low levels.

(ii) Recent development of east-west trade

Growth in east-west trade slowed sharply in the first three quarters of 1990, coming to a virtual halt towards the end of the period. The growth of *eastern exports* to the west dropped to a mere 1 per cent, well short of the 6 per cent rise of western total imports (section 3.1), while the growth of *eastern imports* ceased completely (see table 3.3.1 and chart 3.3.1). This reflects a rise in *eastern Europe's* trade with the west by 4 per cent, and some contraction in that of the *Soviet Union*.

Although the growth of total western imports slowed somewhat in 1990 to about 6 per cent, the eighth year of expansion of western imports provided favourable marketing opportunities to eastern exporters (tables 3.1.1 and 3.3.1). Most eastern countries also benefited from improved access to western markets, as a result of the trade liberalization measures included in

---

[188] The terms "west", "western", or "developed market economies" as used here refer to the countries of western Europe (including Turkey and Yugoslavia), North America and Japan. The term "eastern Europe" refers to Bulgaria, Czechoslovakia (the Czech and Slovak Federal Republic), Hungary, Poland, and Romania taken together, and now excludes the former German Democratic Republic. The term "east" or "eastern countries" refers to eastern Europe and the Soviet Union jointly.

[189] Unless otherwise noted, growth rates are for the first nine months of 1990 relative to the same period in 1989. Data on trade flows are based on western statistics. In certain cases the results differ from those derived from eastern sources.

TABLE 3.3.1

East-west trade: Value, volumes, prices, and terms of trade, 1986-1990

(Percentage change over the same period of previous year)

From/To:	Eastern exports					Eastern imports				
	1986	1987	1988	1989	1990 QI-III	1986	1987	1988	1989	1990 QI-III
Values (in US dollars)										
Eastern Europe and the Soviet Union	-3	11	1	12	14	3	1	14	14	7
of which:										
Eastern Europe	9	14	8	6	15	15	9	9	11	14
Soviet Union	-10	10	-4	17	13	-3	-3	18	16	3
Volumes										
Eastern Europe and the Soviet Union	8	4	4	7	1	-16	-6	7	13	-
of which:										
Eastern Europe	1	1	7	5	4	-3	-1	2	11	4
Soviet Union	21	7	2	9	-	-20	-9	9	15	-3
Prices (in US dollars)										
Eastern Europe and the Soviet Union	-11	7	-2	4	12	20	9	8	-	8
of which:										
Eastern Europe	9	13	2	-	11	20	11	7	-1	9
Soviet Union	-26	2	-6	8	13	20	7	8	-	7
Values and volumes										
Memorandum item:										
Total western imports/exports										
Values	12	19	14	8	12	16	18	14	7	12
Volumes	8	7	8	8	6	2	6	8	7	5

	Eastern terms of trade (1975 = 100)							
	1983	1984	1985	1986	1987	1988	1989	1990 QI-III
Eastern Europe and the Soviet Union	152	153	146	109	108	98	102	106
of which:								
Eastern Europe	115	114	111	101	103	98	100	101
Soviet Union	190	198	191	117	112	97	104	111

Sources: United Nations commodity trade data base (COMTRADE); OECD, *Statistics on Foreign Trade,* Series A, Paris; IMF, *Directions of Trade* and *International Financial Statistics,* Washington, D.C.; United Nations, *Monthly Bulletin of Statistics* (volume indices of total western exports to and imports from the world); national statistics; and ECE secretariat estimates based upon western data (table 3.1.1).

Note: Price and volume indices: for the methodology and derivation, see United Nations Economic Commission for Europe, *Economic Bulletin for Europe,* vol.31, No.1, New York, 1979.

These data reflect the trade of 23 western reporting countries (Appendix table C.6 contains a list of the countries included). The same data are used in chart 3.3.1.

the Group of 24 programme of support for eastern economic reform. The opportunities offered by these developments provided an important offset to the collapse of eastern markets in 1990.

(a) Eastern Europe

In the first three quarters of 1990, the rate of growth of *eastern Europe's exports* to the west eased to 4 per cent in volume terms (table 3.3.1 and chart 3.3.1). The group's *imports* grew at the same rate, but this represented a markedly sharper slow-down. Since its *terms of trade* improved only marginally, eastern Europe's $1 billion *trade surplus* with the west remained substantially unchanged (tables 3.3.2 and 3.3.3).

Even though eastern European exports again lagged behind western import growth in 1990, *eastern Europe's export* performance is still notable. Eastern European exports have now been growing relatively strongly for the last three years, the most sustained period of export growth since the 1970s. This dynamism stems mainly from the improved performances of *Poland, Hungary* and, to a lesser extent, *Czechoslovakia* (table 3.3.4). For Hungary and Poland, 1990 constitutes the fourth year running, and for Czechoslovakia the third year, of continuous export growth. In contrast, during the *first half* of the 1980s no east European country had been able to mount a sustained export drive.

All three countries were particularly successful in raising sales to the EC, with Hungarian and Polish exports to the Community increasing by 32 and 44 per cent respectively.[190] However, these three countries' export gains in other markets were uneven. Sales to North America rose only modestly in value and declined in volume. The two-thirds increase in the value of Polish exports to Japan in 1990 is also worthy of mention.

---

190 Trade between the individual eastern and western countries and partner areas is shown in table 3.1.4.

TABLE 3.3.2

East-west trade balances, east with western country groups, 1986-1990

(Billion US dollars, f.o.b.-f.o.b.)

	1986	1987	1988	1989	1989 Jan.-Sept.	1990 Jan.-Sept.	1990 a
				(A)	Western data		
Eastern Europe and the Soviet Union with:							
Developed market economies	-1.0	2.7	-2.2	-3.4	-1.1	1.0	-0.2
Western Europe	1.9	4.2	1.0	0.6	1.8	3.1	2.3
of which:							
EC	3.8	4.5	2.8	2.3	2.6	3.7	4.4
EFTA	-0.8	-0.2	-1.2	-1.1	-0.8	-0.6	-1.3
North America	-0.9	-0.7	-1.9	-3.5	-2.6	-2.5	-3.2
Japan	-2.0	-0.8	-1.3	-0.5	-0.3	0.4	0.6
Eastern Europe with:							
Developed market economies	0.9	1.7	1.8	1.1	1.1	1.3	0.9
Western Europe	0.3	0.9	0.9	0.5	0.7	1.1	0.7
of which:							
EC	0.4	0.8	1.1	0.4	0.6	0.9	0.6
EFTA	-0.2	-0.1	-0.2	-0.3	-0.2	-0.2	-0.6
North America	0.8	0.9	1.0	0.5	0.4	0.2	0.3
Japan	-0.3	0.1	-0.1	-	0.1	-	-
Soviet Union with:							
Developed market economies	-1.8	0.9	-4.0	-4.4	-2.1	-0.3	-1.1
Western Europe	1.5	3.2	0.1	0.2	1.2	1.9	1.7
of which:							
EC	3.4	3.7	1.7	2.0	2.0	2.8	3.8
EFTA	-0.7	-0.1	-1.0	-0.8	-0.6	-0.4	-0.7
North America	-1.7	-1.6	-2.9	-4.0	-3.0	-2.7	-3.4
Japan	-1.7	-0.7	-1.2	-0.5	-0.3	0.4	0.6
				(B)	Eastern data		
Eastern Europe and the Soviet Union with:							
Developed market economies	-3.9	2.5	-0.9	-3.8	-3.0	-3.4	-3.1
of which:							
Eastern Europe	0.5	1.5	1.8	2.7	1.9	1.7	2.0
Soviet Union	-4.4	1.0	-2.7	-6.4	-4.9	-5.1	-4.8

Sources: As for table 3.3.1.

Note: Section A is based on western data which have been adjusted to an f.o.b.-f.o.b. basis by the ECE secretariat; section B is based on eastern national sources.

a Extrapolated on the basis of January-September data for exports and imports.

TABLE 3.3.3

East-west trade balances, by eastern country, 1986-1990

(Billion US dollars, f.o.b-f.o.b)

	1986	1987	1988	1989	1989 Jan.-Sept.	1990 Jan.-Sept.	1990 a
Bulgaria	-1.5	-1.6	-1.7	-1.6	-1.2	-0.5	-0.7
Czechoslovakia	0.4	0.1	-	0.4	0.5	0.1	-0.3
Hungary	-0.6	-0.3	-	-0.2	-0.2	0.2	0.4
Poland	0.7	0.8	0.7	-0.1	-0.1	1.3	1.6
Romania	1.9	2.7	2.8	2.6	2.1	0.2	-0.1
Eastern Europe	0.9	1.7	1.8	1.1	1.1	1.3	0.9
Soviet Union	-1.8	0.9	-4.0	-4.4	-2.1	-0.3	-1.1
Eastern Europe and the Soviet Union	-1.0	2.7	-2.2	-3.4	-1.1	1.0	-0.2

Source: As for table 3.3.1. ECE secretariat estimates based upon western data.

a Extrapolated on the basis of January-September data for exports and imports.

CHART 3.3.1

International trade of eastern Europe and the Soviet Union with the west

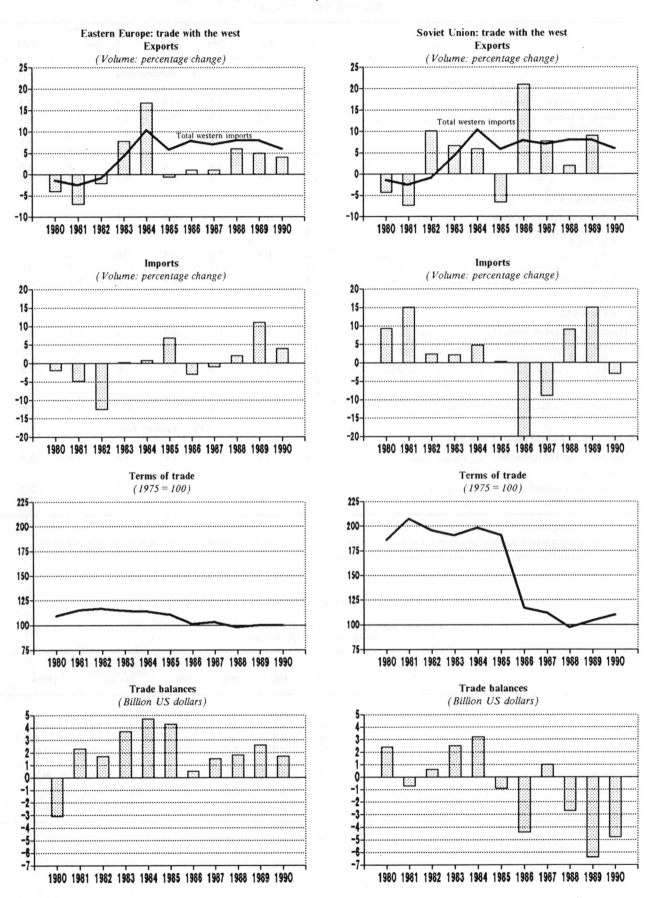

TABLE 3.3.4

East-west trade: Value and volume, by eastern country, 1986-1990

(Percentage change)

From/To:	Eastern exports					Eastern imports				
	1986	1987	1988	1989	1990 a	1986	1987	1988	1989	1990 a
	Value change (in US dollars)									
Bulgaria	3	3	-1	11	22	17	7	2	1	-31
Czechoslovakia	15	10	5	8	14	19	18	8	-1	31
Hungary	13	21	11	11	25	21	11	1	16	12
Poland	7	16	16	8	36	7	16	21	23	5
Romania	5	12	-	-5	-30	17	-24	-4	-1	112
Eastern Europe	9	14	8	6	15	15	9	9	11	14
Soviet Union	-10	10	-4	17	13	-3	-3	18	16	3
Eastern Europe and the Soviet Union	-3	11	1	12	14	3	1	14	14	7
Memorandum item:										
Total western imports/exports	12	19	13	8	14	16	18	14	8	14
	Volume change									
Bulgaria	-7	-9	4	10	10	-4	-4	-3	1	-37
Czechoslovakia	1	-2	3	8	4	-3	6	1	-	20
Hungary	-1	7	7	13	11	1	-1	-5	17	1
Poland	-6	8	9	8	24	-12	8	12	25	-2
Romania	7	-5	5	-8	-38	2	-30	-12	-	94
Eastern Europe	-	1	7	5	4	-3	-1	2	11	4
Soviet Union	21	7	2	9	-	-20	-9	9	15	-3
Eastern Europe and the Soviet Union	8	4	4	7	1	-16	-6	7	13	-
Memorandum item:										
Total western imports/exports	8	7	8	8	6	2	6	8	7	5

Source: As for table 3.3.1.

a   January-September.

Poland and Hungary have increased their shares of the dynamic western market in the last two years while Czechoslovakia has just managed to maintain its position. This, at least temporarily, reverses the long-established decline in these countries' market share and, while these shares are still minimal, recent achievements do point to some progress towards reintegration into the world economy.

Bulgaria and *Romania* did not share in these advances. The volumes of their exports to the west fell during the year as various distortions in industry caused sharp losses in output (see section (v) below).[191]

Czechoslovakia, Hungary and Poland managed to increase their exports of *manufactured goods* relatively rapidly in the *first half* of 1990 (table 3.3.6). Exports of *consumer goods* were particularly dynamic, increasing by 19-37 per cent in value, with sales of *engineering* products rising at slightly lower rates.[192] Exports of

semi-manufactures, which continue to be heavily represented in eastern Europe's export structure, rose roughly in line with overall exports. *Food* sales by Czechoslovakia and, especially, Poland also expanded comparatively quickly. Overall these incomplete results for 1990 point to some shift in the commodity structures of the three countries' western exports.[193] away from unprocessed goods, the share of which nevertheless remains high.

Romanian exports of all commodities declined sharply in value and even more in terms of volume. The country's sales of food and semi-manufactures posted the steepest falls, with food exports being diverted to the home market by the new government in order to improve domestic supplies.

Fuels — particularly petroleum products based upon Soviet crude — have traditionally been an important east European export. IEA data show that

---

191 Note that western data (table 3.3.4) indicate a further rise in Bulgaria's western sales in the first three quarters of 1990, although national data show a decline during the same period.

192 According to western reported commodity data (table 3.3.6), Bulgaria was also very successful in boosting its engineering and consumer goods exports (and those of food as well). However, in assessing this outcome, the disparity in western and national statistics (see preceding footnote) needs to be borne in mind.

193 In 1989 only Hungary achieved some success in this respect. United Nations Economic Commission for Europe, *Economic Bulletin for Europe*, vol.42/90, New York, 1991.

Although the shift in export structure toward more highly processed manufactured goods appears favourable, the economic gains to these countries are uncertain since new, more rational, net structures, which will serve as the basis for export profitability calculations, are only beginning to emerge.

TABLE 3.3.5

East-west trade: Value, by country group, 1986-1990
(Percentage change of value in US dollars)

	Eastern exports					Eastern imports				
	1986	1987	1988	1989	1990 a	1986	1987	1988	1989	1990 a
Eastern Europe and the Soviet Union with:										
Developed market economies	-3	11	1	12	14	3	1	14	14	7
Western Europe	-4	11	-	13	15	7	4	10	14	11
of which:										
EC	-4	12	-	12	17	10	11	8	16	14
EFTA	-9	13	-3	8	9	14	3	10	6	6
North America	-1	3	23	-9	4	-34	-3	61	28	-1
Japan	21	33	8	28	11	17	-17	22	-2	-16
Eastern Europe with:										
Developed market economies	9	14	8	6	15	15	9	9	11	14
Western Europe	11	14	7	8	17	16	10	8	11	15
of which:										
EC	14	17	8	8	20	19	13	5	16	17
EFTA	7	16	7	4	14	19	11	11	6	15
North America	-2	3	11	-16	-7	1	-6	12	19	12
Japan	10	52	34	11	-4	32	-8	21	-7	5
Soviet Union with:										
Developed market economies	-10	10	-4	17	13	-3	-3	18	16	3
Western Europe	-13	9	-6	16	12	2	-	11	16	8
of which:										
EC	-13	9	-5	16	15	2	10	11	16	11
EFTA	-16	11	-9	11	6	11	-1	9	6	-
North America	2	6	64	10	22	-41	-2	79	30	-4
Japan	24	28	3	33	15	15	-19	22	-2	-20

Source: As for table 3.3.1.

Note: Appendix tables C.6 and C.7 contain similar data for all western countries.

a   January-September.

western imports of these goods from the east European countries dropped dramatically during the year (table 3.3.7).[194] This is broadly consistent with the increasing tightness in the supply of energy in eastern Europe.

The modest overall expansion of *east European imports* in the first three quarters of 1990 reflects large inter-country differences (tables 3.3.1 and 3.3.4). *Czechoslovakia* and, especially, *Romania* sharply stepped up their purchases of western goods, with Romanian imports from the west nearly doubling in volume. The surge in Romanian imports reflects the new government's reversal of the previous autarkic policies when imports were drastically cut (by 1989 Romanian purchases of western goods had fallen to a mere $0.9 billion, compared to a figure of $4 billion in 1980). However, central control of imports remained in place. In contrast, the upturn in Czechoslovakia's imports reflected the liberalization of the import régime.

The growth of western imports into *Hungary* and *Poland* almost came to a halt in 1990. In both cases, low domestic demand, due in part to the implementation of stabilization policies, and, in Poland, to the strong devaluation of the currency, held imports down.

In *Bulgaria*, when confronted with severe financing constraints, the authorities sharply curtailed imports, particularly in the second half of the year.

Czechoslovakia's and Hungary's purchases from EFTA increased relatively rapidly in 1990.[195] EFTA was also the origin of most of Romania's additional imports, although the country's purchases from North America rose even faster. Polish importers showed a preference for Japanese and EC (especially Italian) goods while scaling back imports from EFTA and North America. Bulgaria reduced purchases from almost all trade partners.

Reflecting the changed priorities of the new governments, virtually all east European countries stepped up imports of western *consumer goods* in the *first half* of 1990 (table 3.3.6). Most countries needed to boost purchases of *fuels (coal, petroleum products, and electricity)* to compensate for supply shortfalls from traditional CMEA sources. Romania increased imports across the board, its expenditures on food rising eightfold. Bulgaria, however, was compelled to cut back purchases of nearly all commodities, in some cases with negative consequences for industrial production.

194 The drop in eastern Europe's exports of petroleum products reported by the IEA (table 3.3.7) is considerably steeper than shown in the COMTRADE commodity trade data in table 3.3.6.

195 Trade between the individual eastern and western countries and partner areas is presented in table 3.1.4.

TABLE 3.3.6

East-west trade, by commodity, first half 1990 [a]

(Increments in million US dollars; changes in per cent)

	Soviet Union		Eastern Europe		Bulgaria	Czecho-slovakia	Hungary	Poland	Romania
	Increment	Changes	Increment	Changes			Changes		
Eastern exports									
Total	632	6	1 082	14	11	14	20	31	-26
Primary	-322	-11	241	11	24	9	8	28	-62
Food	54	23	344	28	49	18	11	52	-63
Fuels	826	14	89	12	-55	9	37	29	-9
Manufactures	-13	-1	739	16	13	16	26	33	-21
Semi-manufactures	-90	-7	99	5	-10	14	16	28	-49
Engineering	68	15	244	24	50	17	29	33	-15
Consumer	9	5	396	21	39	19	32	37	-4
Eastern imports									
Total	560	4	505	7	-35	15	4	-4	159
Primary	157	4	11	1	-62	-23	-19	-15	361
Food	185	5	118	14	-71	-20	2	-12	919
Fuels	8	16	87	103	181	206	-64	177	103
Manufactures	74	1	354	6	-24	26	6	-4	82
Semi-manufactures	-667	-18	-89	-4	-23	9	-5	-27	118
Engineering	423	10	102	4	-28	34	5	-6	81
Consumer	318	33	341	38	-10	43	34	51	39

Source: United Nations Statistical Office, COMTRADE, Quarterly trade data, Series D.

Note: Increments may not add to the total because of incomplete reporting of commodities. Changes in total trade may not agree with data in table 3.3.4 because of differences in country coverage and period. These data reflect the developed market economies except Italy, Greece, Turkey and Austria.

[a] Relative to same period in 1989.

(a) The export upswing

The recent export upswing towards the west achieved by Poland, Hungary and, to a lesser extent, Czechoslovakia, merits special attention. These countries have managed to expand their exports to the west for the last three or four years, performances which stand in sharp relief to their former patterns of only intermittent export growth. Moreover, in 1990 they appear to have been successful in improving the commodity structure of their western exports, although it should be stressed that this assessment is based on incomplete trade returns.

There are several external factors which contributed to this improvement in export performance. Firstly, economic agents have managed to take advantage of the extended boom in western markets, particularly in Germany. They were also able to benefit from at least some of the trade concessions (GSP, larger quotas, etc.) granted by the G-24 countries.[196] Here, it should be borne in mind that to gain from greater market access, the exporter must be able to respond and increase supply.

However, even allowing for the favourable external environment, Poland's and Hungary's success in boosting the sales of manufactured goods, especially consumer goods, has been particularly impressive. In general, the quality of eastern manufactures has been thought to be of questionable quality so that, with the exception of various raw materials and semi-manufactures, only limited scope for shifting goods from eastern to western markets has been considered possible. While the degree of switching in the recent past still needs to be assessed, it would seem that the large increases in manufacturing exports in 1990 fly in the face of conventional wisdom, especially as it is unlikely that the physical characteristics of export goods could have been improved so quickly.

While a thorough analysis of these developments is beyond the scope of this section, it may be useful to explore some possible explanations. Firstly, it appears that enterprises sought out new outlets when confronted by collapsing demand in their traditional eastern markets. Tough domestic macro-economic policies, reinforced by falling exports to the CMEA, caused domestic demand to contract, particularly in Poland. As a result, industrial output fell but, at the same time released resources for export to the west.[197] The growth

---

[196] Hungarian economists have attributed some one third of the growth of exports to the EC in the first half of 1990 to the Communities' liberalization of trade. According to Mr. B. Kádár, Minister of Internal Economic Relations, in comments made at the ECE Symposium on *Reforms in Foreign Economic Relations of Eastern Europe and the Soviet Union*, Wildbad Kreuth, 29 August-2 September 1990.

[197] Output also fell in the other eastern countries, but it appears to have been due chiefly to supply-side factors – shortages of inputs and various dislocations in industry – which impaired export capacity. Some industrial disarray appears to have constrained output in Czechoslovakia, Hungary and Poland, but lack of demand was the predominant cause of output decline.

TABLE 3.3.7

Soviet and east European exports of fuels to the west, 1989-1990

(Billion US dollars and physical units)

	1989	January-September 1989	January-September 1990	1990 (Per cent)
Soviet Union: volumes				
Crude oil [a]	38.8	32.5	36.5	12.1
Oil products [a]	40.7	31.5	28.6	-9.1
Total [a]	79.5	64.0	65.1	1.7
Gas [b]	53.4	36.0	40.5	12.7
Soviet Union: values				
Crude oil	5.5	4.4	5.6	29.4
Oil products	6.0	3.8	3.8	-0.5
Total	11.5	8.2	9.5	15.4
Gas	3.4	2.1	3.2	52.7
Total above	14.9	10.2	12.7	24.5
OECD imports from the Soviet Union: volumes [a,c]				
Crude oil	40.6	30.2	33.8	12.0
Oil products	41.7	32.6	29.4	-9.8
Total	82.3	62.7	63.2	0.8
OECD imports from eastern Europe: volumes [a,c]				
Crude oil	0.1	0.1	-	-72.9
Oil products	18.4	14.1	8.7	-38.0
Total	18.5	14.1	8.7	-38.2

Source: IEA.

a Millions of tons.
b Billion cubic metres.
c Excludes Yugoslavia.

of exports to the west thus partially compensated for declining business activity in other markets.[198]

Secondly, in some cases exchange rate policies appear to have promoted foreign sales – at least temporarily.[199] In January 1990, Poland sharply devalued the zloty to the point where, according to several commentators, the zloty was significantly undervalued. Subsequently, its exports to the west – which had flagged for some months – turned up and accelerated throughout the year, despite the fact that the real effective exchange rate was continuously appreciating as domestic prices increased. In the last few months of the year, domestic inflation surged further and the real effective exchange rate now appears to have surpassed its level before the January devaluation.

Hungary did not pursue an active exchange rate policy in 1990. The forint was devalued by 11 per cent in November 1989 but the real effective exchange rate reattained its previous level after a few months. Continuing domestic inflation – industrial producer prices rose by 21 per cent in 1990 – pushed the real exchange rate up throughout the year, but without seeming to affect export growth.

The Czechoslovak koruna was devalued by almost 19 per cent against the US dollar at the beginning of 1990. However, the subsequent tendency for the nom-

inal value of the koruna to appreciate, together with a domestic inflation rate of at least 10 per cent, suggests that the depreciation in the real effective exchange rate and the overall impact on exports was small. The impact of the much larger 55 per cent depreciation of the koruna in mid-October on trade results in 1990 is probably small.

Thus – except in Poland in the first half of 1990 or so – adjustments in exchange rates do not appear to explain the growth of exports in these three countries. The exchange rate policies pursued by Czechoslovakia and Hungary do not appear to have actively promoted export growth but, at the same time, they did not seem to remove all incentives to export. Low demand in traditional markets does not by itself provide a full explanation either. In countries which are still in the process of shedding a centrally planned system, a lack of domestic demand will only be accompanied by increased efforts to export if enterprises are faced with market incentives and sanctions. Under the former system, enterprises were generally not motivated for foreign sales and, in any case, were simply compensated for any operating losses so that there was little incentive to replace domestic sales with exports. Thus, while the observed export response might well be taken for granted in well-functioning market economies, it would be unrealistic to assume that enterprises will behave in the same way in the transition economies.

These recent strong export performances therefore give the impression that economic reforms are starting to play a role in forcing economic agents in these countries to respond to market signals. Indeed it is tempting to draw attention to the perfect correlation between the progress of reforms in these countries and the strength of their export growth. In 1990, Poland was the most advanced in both respects, followed by Hungary; Czechoslovakia was still preparing to introduce a major reform package, although the authorities had previously implemented certain important measures. Several common features of their changing trade régimes may be pointed to:

– decentralization of economic decision making to enterprises, including the extension of foreign trade rights;

– involvement of dynamic middlemen in export-import activities;

– in Hungary and Poland, the increasing participation of private enterprises in trade, although their share of exports is still small;

– an easier access to foreign inputs with the liberalization of the import and payments régimes.

Another common reform-related feature has been the disciplined macro-economic policy stance adopted

---

198 Hungarian economists have estimated that the growth of Hungary's exports to the west in the first half of 1990 compensated for one third of the decline in the country's exports to the CMEA (B. Kádár, at the ECE Symposium mentioned in footnote 196).

199 Exchange rates have served as an economic function in only Hungary and Poland and, more recently, in Czechoslovakia.

by the three governments. National budget deficits were practically eliminated in all three countries, in part through the imposition of ceilings on, or even reductions of, subsidies to enterprises. Frequent public pronouncements concerning these restrictive policies were accompanied by warnings to enterprises that credits to cover losses could no longer be counted on. In these new circumstances, enterprise managers may have sought alternative markets to avert (or minimize) financial losses, the shedding of manpower and, in the future, possibly bankruptcy itself. If such behavioural changes have indeed taken place, they can be counted as one of the major successes to date of the reforms.

Recent export performance suggests that there is room for cautious optimism about the export prospects of these countries. In particular, they may point to an improvement in the various factors that determine international competitiveness, which is essential if these countries are to speed their integration into the world economy and obtain the full benefits from the recent and envisaged openings to western markets. Continued export growth will also be crucial if these countries are to avoid a permanent increase in their debt service burdens as their current accounts swing into deficit this year. During their present internal difficulties, the current lack of alternative marketing opportunities, above all in the east, underlines the importance of maintaining their access to western markets.

(c) Soviet Union

The *Soviet Union's* trade with the west developed unfavourably in 1990. In terms of volume, the growth of the country's *exports* ceased in the first three quarters of the year (table 3.3.1 and chart 3.3.1). Preliminary Soviet data for the fourth quarter of 1990 suggest that the volume of exports contracted, because of lower crude oil exports. However, export receipts rose, boosted by higher export prices. The boom in Soviet *imports* − the volume of the country's imports had risen by one quarter in 1988-1989 − continued at a slower pace through the first half of 1990. However, when faced with tightening constraints on external financing, the Soviet authorities curtailed purchases of western goods, leading to a small decline in the volume of imports over the whole nine-month period. These restraints were implemented at a time of mounting internal needs. As a result of the recent measures to curb imports, Soviet imports from the west have still not fully recovered from the 30 per cent cut in 1986-1987. The reduction was part of a draconian adjustment policy designed to avert a large increase in external indebtedness after the oil price collapse in early 1986.

Soviet *terms of trade* continued to improve last year. On the export side, the country benefited from higher fuel prices, although there was a decline in the purchasing power of the US dollar (fuel contracts are directly or indirectly denominated in US dollars). Price increases of the Soviet Union's imports were held down by falls in grain prices. Overall price movements reinforced the trends in export and import volumes so that, according to western data, the Soviet Union almost eliminated its trade deficit with the west in the first three quarters of 1990 (table 3.3.2 panel A and table 3.3.3). Preliminary Soviet data for the whole year indicate the persistence of a large ($5 billion) trade deficit (table 3.3.2, panel B). This is below the (record) $6.5 billion deficit recorded during the *first half* of 1990 and significantly smaller than the one expected earlier in the year when prospects for international oil prices were less favourable for the Soviet Union.

The Soviet Union achieved its most rapid growth of sales in the North American market (22 per cent), followed by exports to the EC and Japan (15 per cent, table 3.3.5). On the other hand, Soviet imports from the west increased only from the EC, those from North America and Japan falling.

Fuels accounted for most of the growth of Soviet export revenues in the first half of 1990 (table 3.3.6). Sales of *food* and *engineering goods* also rose comparatively rapidly but their share in the country's total western exports is small. On the other hand, Soviet exports of various *primary materials*, and *semi-manufactures* (including *chemicals and iron and steel*) faltered. Traditionally the Soviet Union has been able to boost deliveries of primary materials, especially non-ferrous metals, ores, and miscellaneous crude materials when pressed for additional revenues. However, in 1990 domestic supply conditions ruled out this course of action.

More disaggregated data on Soviet fuel exports during the first nine months of 1990 indicate that natural gas sales were particularly strong (table 3.3.7). The volume of gas deliveries rose by nearly 14 per cent, which in conjunction with a 34 per cent price rise,[200] boosted revenues from this commodity by over one half. Price increases were also responsible for the bulk of additional revenues from sales of crude oil and petroleum products. Soviet national statistics show an increase in deliveries to the west of 1 million tons in the first three quarters of 1990,[201] despite a steep decline in domestic oil production (Soviet oil production fell by 37 million tons during the full year). Since *total* Soviet exports of oil and oil products contracted by some 8 million tons in the first three quarters of 1990, the increased exports to the west were at the expense of the domestic economy and other traditional customers (see section 3.2). The need for convertible currency presumably motivated this shift, although, as the year progressed, the Soviet Union increasingly sold crude oil to its CMEA trade partners for convertible currency.

Preliminary IEA data for October and November indicate a dramatic drop in OECD imports of crude oil

---

200 Natural gas prices lag behind those of oil, which increased in 1989.

201 Data on Soviet crude oil and product exports compiled from the importer side by the IEA (see table 3.3.7) compare well with the Soviet national data (which also include Yugoslavia, in contrast to the IEA data) although there are some differences in statistical reporting conventions.

TABLE 3.3.8

Eastern Europe and the Soviet Union: Convertible currency current account of the balance of payments, 1985-1990
(Billion US dollars)

	Trade balances [a]		Net services plus transfers		Current account
	Total	of this: DME [b]	Total	Investment income	
Bulgaria					
1985	-0.4	-0.8	0.3	-	-0.1
1986	-0.8	-1.4	0.1	-0.1	-0.7
1987	-1.0	-1.4	0.2	-0.3	-0.8
1988	-1.0	-1.5	0.1	-0.4	-0.8
1989	-1.2	-1.3	-0.1	-0.6	-1.3
1990	-0.8	-0.7	-0.3	-0.7*	-1.1
Czechoslovakia					
1985	0.7	0.2	0.1	-0.2	0.7
1986	0.2	-0.1	0.2	-0.1	0.4
1987	-0.1	-0.4	0.2	-0.1	0.1
1988	-0.1	-0.4	0.2	-0.2	0.1
1989	0.4	0.2	-0.1	-0.1	0.3
1990*	-0.2	-0.6	-	-0.2	-0.2
Hungary					
1985	0.1	-0.5	-1.0	-0.8	-0.8
1986	-0.5	-0.7	-1.0	-1.0	-1.5
1987	-	-0.5	-0.9	-1.0	-0.9
1988	0.5	-	-1.3	-1.1	-0.8
1989	0.5	-0.1	-2.0	-1.4	-1.4
1990	0.3	0.8	-0.2	-1.4	0.1
Poland					
1985	1.2	0.7	-1.7	-2.4	-0.5
1986	1.1	0.5	-1.7	-2.6	-0.6
1987	1.0	0.9	-1.4	-2.8	-0.4
1988	0.9	0.6	-1.5	-2.8	-0.6
1989	0.1	0.4	-2.0	-3.1	-1.9
1990	2.2	3.2	-1.5	-3.3	0.7
Romania					
1985	1.4	2.3	-0.5	-0.6	0.9
1986	1.9	2.2	-0.4	-0.6	1.5
1987*	2.4	2.9	-0.2	-0.4	2.2
1988*	3.6	3.2	-0.2	-0.3	3.6
1989*	2.6	3.5	0.3	-	2.9
1990*	-1.6	-0.7	-0.1	0.2	-1.5
Eastern Europe					
1985	3.0	1.8	-2.8	-4.1	0.2
1986	1.9	0.5	-2.8	-4.4	-0.9
1987	2.4	1.5	-2.1	-4.6	0.3
1988	3.9	1.8	-2.4	-4.8	1.5
1989	2.5	2.7	-3.9	-5.1	-1.4
1990	-	2.0	-2.0	-5.5	-2.1
Soviet Union [c]					
1985	0.7	-0.9	-0.7	-1.9	0.1
1986	1.4	-4.4	-0.9	-2.1	0.4
1987	8.1	1.0	-1.0	-2.2	7.1
1988	3.5	-2.7	-1.2	-2.5	2.3
1989	-2.3	-6.4	-1.7	-3.0	-4.0
1990	-1.4	-4.8	-3.1	-4.4	-4.3
Eastern Europe and the Soviet Union					
1985	3.8	0.9	-3.5	-6.0	0.3
1986	3.3	-3.9	-3.7	-6.5	-0.4
1987	10.6	2.5	-3.2	-6.8	7.4
1988	7.4	-0.9	-3.6	-7.3	3.8
1989	0.2	-3.8	-5.6	-8.1	-5.4
1990	-1.5	-2.8	-5.1	-9.9	-6.4

Sources: National sources for Bulgaria, Czechoslovakia (1985-1989), Hungary and Poland; Romania; and ECE secretariat estimates.

a   Trade balance f.o.b.-f.o.b. except for Hungary's trade balance with the developed market economies which is reported f.o.b.-c.i.f.
b   Developed market economies (see definition in footnote (188) above). These data are on a customs basis.
c   The total trade balance reflects trade with all market economies. Estimates of investment income reflect only estimates of interest earned on assets held at BIS reporting banks.

and products from the Soviet Union.[202] This downturn may reflect the steepening decline in Soviet oil production, which in the fourth quarter of 1990 was some 9 per cent lower than in the same period a year earlier.[203] Press reports suggest that production was still falling at a similar rate in January 1991.[204]

In the *first half* of 1990, the *Soviet Union's* expenditures on western *machinery and equipment* and, in particular, *consumer goods* rose rapidly (table 3.3.6). There was also a small rise in *food* purchases,[205] but imports of *semi-manufactures*, required for production, declined steeply in both value and quantity terms.

(iii) Financial developments

(a) Eastern current account

Eastern Europe incurred a current account deficit of some $2 billion in 1990 (table 3.3.8), about the same as in the preceding year.[206] However, the positions of the individual countries shifted markedly. *Romania's* current account showed the greatest change (over $4 billion), from a large surplus to a deficit of nearly $2 billion. *Czechoslovakia's* current account also weakened, though the resulting deficit was small.

The positions of the other east European countries improved, in some cases counter to expectations. The *Polish* authorities intended to provide support for the reform programme through some loosening of the external constraint. Financing had become available which would have permitted an increase in the current account deficit to $3 billion in 1990. However, the austerity programme caused such a strong external adjustment that surpluses of $2 billion and $1 billion were achieved on the trade and current accounts respectively. *Hungary* also performed more favourably than anticipated with its current account moving into (a small) surplus. Originally Hungary's IMF programme for 1990 had incorporated a target current account deficit of $550 million. Contrary to preceding years, *Bulgaria* was constrained by a lack of financing in 1990. As a result, it was compelled to curtail its substantial current account deficit, chiefly by cutting its trade deficit.

Certain common factors influenced eastern current accounts in 1990. International interest rates rose marginally (see section 3.1), placing pressure on the *investment income* item. In the wake of the political changes, most countries appear to have benefited from the upswing in *tourism* from the west, although the flows in both directions increased last year. Several governments took special measures to improve net earnings from tourism, those taken by Hungary proving

TABLE 3.3.9

Soviet Union: Current account in convertible currencies, 1986-1990 [a]
(Billion US dollars)

	1986	1987	1988	1989	1990
ECE					
Trade balance.............	1.4	8.1	3.5	-2.3	-1.4
Current account	0.4	7.1	2.3	-4.0	-4.3
Houston Four Report					
Trade balance.............	4.1	8.3	4.8	-	-5.7 [b]
Current account	2.3	6.7	1.6	-3.8	-10.7 [b]

Source: ECE estimates and *Houston Four Report, op.cit.*

[a] Excluding gold sales.
[b] Preliminary estimates.

TABLE 3.3.10

Eastern Europe and the Soviet Union: Medium- and long-term funds raised on the international financial markets, 1988-1990
(Million US dollars)

	1988	1989	1990
Bulgaria...	194	580	
Czechoslovakia............................	330	334	377
Hungary...	1 016	1 708	989
Poland	-	163	-
Romania...	-	-	-
Eastern Europe.........................	1 540	2 785	1 366
Soviet Union.................................	2 679	1 858	3 250
CMEA Banks...............................	75	75	
Total above...............................	4 294	4 718	4 616
of which:			
Bank loans [a]	1 050	2 047	2 995
Foreign bank loans [b]	1 652	358	
Other [c]	232	75	-
Bonds....................................	1 360	2 239	1 621

Source: OECD, *Financial Statistics Monthly,* Part I, various issues.

[a] International bank loans in Eurocurrencies, excluding officially guaranteed loans and rescheduled of debt.
[b] In domestic currency of lending countries, excluding guaranteed loans.
[c] Other bank facilities, including bankers' acceptances.

particularly effective. All eastern countries incurred losses of exports of goods and services (especially of construction services) by joining the UN embargo of Iraq and Kuwait.

---

[202] IEA, *Monthly Oil and Gas Statistics, November 1990*, Paris, February 1991.

[203] IEA, *Oil Market Reports*, February 1991.

[204] *Financial Times*, 16 February 1991.

[205] Soviet national statistics show much stronger increases in the imports of both food and machinery and equipment.

[206] The current account data reflect all transactions in convertible currencies.

TABLE 3.3.11

Eastern Europe and the Soviet Union: Assets with BIS reporting banks and liquidity ratios, 1988-1990

(Levels, changes at constant exchange rates, in billion US dollars; ratio in per cent)

	1988	1989	1990-QIII
Bulgaria			
Assets (billion)	1.8	1.2	0.6
Changes (billion)	0.7	-0.6	-0.6
Liquidity ratio (per cent)	43.9	29.9	20.2
Czechoslovakia			
Assets (billion)	1.7	2.2	1.5
Changes (billion)	0.2	0.5	-0.7
Liquidity ratio (per cent)	28.5	37.5	22.3
Hungary			
Assets (billion)	1.4	1.2	1.5
Changes (billion)	-	-0.2	0.2
Liquidity ratio (per cent)	27.3	22.2	26.3
Poland			
Assets (billion)	3.6	3.9	8.1
Changes (billion)	0.8	0.2	3.9
Liquidity ratio (per cent)	52.6	54.1	125.6
Romania			
Assets (billion)	0.8	1.8	0.9
Changes (billion)	-0.6	1.0	-1.0
Liquidity ratio (per cent)	27.7	53.2	16.6
Eastern Europe			
Assets (billion)	9.3	10.3	12.6
Changes (billion)	1.1	1.0	1.8
Liquidity ratio (per cent)	37.4	40.0	46.3
Soviet Union			
Assets (billion)	15.3	14.7	7.8
Changes (billion)	1.8	-0.7	-7.2
Liquidity ratio (per cent)	39.0	30.9	16.9
Eastern Europe and the Soviet Union			
Assets (billion)	24.6	25.0	20.4
Changes (billion)	2.9	0.3	-5.4
Liquidity ratio (per cent)	38.5	34.1	27.8
Memo item: official reserves: [a]			
Czechoslovakia	1.6	2.2	1.1 [b]
Hungary	1.5	1.2	0.9
Poland	2.1	2.3	5.2 [b]
Romania	0.8	1.8	0.6 [c]

Sources: BIS *International Banking Developments – Quarterly Reports*, Basle. IMF, *International Financial Statistics;* National Statistics. ECE secretariat estimates.

Note: Asset positions and official foreign currency reserves refer to the end of the period; *changes* are from end-December of the previous year; *liquidity ratios* relate assets to annual merchandise imports from all developed and developing market economies.

a Foreign exchange only.
b December.
c August.

The progressive collapse of the traditional *CMEA trading and settlements system* also strained eastern Europe's convertible currency trade account in 1990 (section 3.2). These countries increased their purchases in world markets to compensate for shortfalls in Soviet deliveries, above all of crude oil and petroleum pro-

ducts. Moreover, some Soviet deliveries to eastern Europe were settled in convertible currencies, instead of in roubles as was originally expected. The adverse impact of these switches on convertible currency trade balances was concentrated in the last few months of the year.

The growing share of trade in the CMEA denominated in convertible currencies worked to the benefit of the *Soviet Union*. None the less its current account in convertible currencies remained in deficit in 1990, by over $4 billion (table 3.3.8).[207] The deficit would have been considerably higher if ample credits had been available to the Soviet Union. However, given the financing constraint, and confronted with a record trade deficit in the first half of the year, the Soviet Union was compelled to take stringent adjustment measures. As a result, its convertible currency trade deficit for 1990 as a whole turned out to be lower than in the previous year, but the invisibles deficit widened because of higher net interest payments. The Soviet Union's $4 billion current account deficit accounted for only a fraction of its total financing needs in 1990 (see section (v)).

(b) Financing

One of the salient features of the east's external financial situation in 1990 is the area's nearly total loss of access to new commercial credits. The scale of the problem has only become clear as financial data have gradually been released by both debtors and creditors.

By the end of 1989, international banks had already become far more cautious towards the eastern countries. Four reasons for the change were frequently cited at the time:

– a rapid increase in the indebtedness of some countries, particularly to commercial banks;

– poor economic performance and uncertain prospects in the light of accelerating reforms;

– the decentralization of borrowing, implying a possible loosening of the financial authorities' control over debt; and

– the movement towards democracy which raised questions about the authorities' capability to implement strong adjustment measures to control external imbalances.

The banks' concerns were reinforced when reports of substantial Soviet arrears in payments to western suppliers surfaced in March 1990 and the Bulgarian Foreign Trade Bank announced the suspension of repayments of principal. The deterioration of commercial creditors' perceptions of the eastern area is reflected in the various sets of commercial lending figures.

207 Attention is drawn to the fact that this discussion of the Soviet current account in convertible currencies is based on ECE secretariat estimates. Official estimates, compiled with the assistance of the IMF, have recently become available (see table 3.3.9). See International Monetary Fund, International Bank for Reconstruction and Development, Organization for Economic Co-operation and Development, and European Bank for Reconstruction and Development, *The Economy of the USSR: Summary and Recommendations,* December 1990 (hereafter *Houston Four Report*).

CHART 3.3.2

Claims of bank and non-bank creditors on eastern countries:
January-September 1990
(Changes, million US dollars)

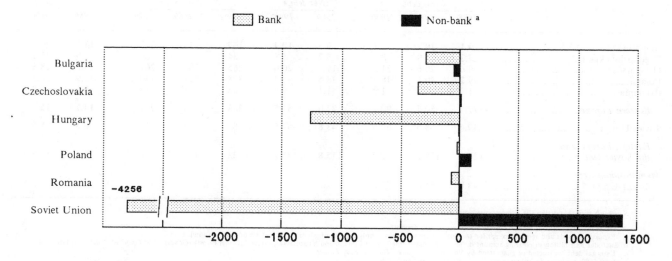

Sources: BIS, *International Banking Developments, Third Quarter,* Basle, February 1991 and *Maturity Distribution of International Bank Lending,* Basle, January 1991.
Note: Changes from end-December 1989, adjusted for exchange rate movements.
[a] First half 1990.

Eastern Europe raised only $1.4 billion in the *capital markets* in 1990, about one half of the volume registered in the preceding year (table 3.3.10). Only Czechoslovakia and Hungary retained access to this type of financing, in both cases via the DM Eurobond market.[208] Compared to previous years, their scope for acquiring syndicated credits was highly circumscribed. Bond flotations remained an option since bond holders have first claim on any interest payments made by debtors. The Soviet Union raised $3.3 billion in bank loans in 1990, considerably more than in most recent years. However, most of this reflects a DM 5 billion ($3 billion) credit, 90 per cent of which was guaranteed by the German government and thus did not reflect purely commercial considerations. Conditions on the limited number of new eastern credits continued to tighten for those who could borrow.[209]

The changes in commercial creditors' perceptions are seen even more dramatically in creditor *bank* expo-

sure *vis-à-vis* eastern countries (chart 3.3.2). In the second quarter of 1990 creditor banks not only scaled back the supply of fresh credits to the east but also ceased to renew maturing debt, particularly short-term inter-bank deposits.[210] As a result, most eastern countries experienced a severe liquidity squeeze which continued throughout the third quarter of the year and possibly longer. During this six-month period, international banks cut their exposure *vis-à-vis* the eastern countries by over $6 billion. The Soviet Union alone experienced net withdrawals of nearly $54 billion, concentrated in the second quarter of the year.

The Soviet Union was particularly vulnerable to a credit squeeze as the share of its bank debt maturing in one year or less had increased to a high level[211] while its ballooning current account deficit early in the year had sharply raised its financing needs. In the third quarter of the year a German bank credit of DM 5 billion ($3 billion), guaranteed by the German government, ap-

---

[208] It might be noted that the bond market became divided into three tiers in 1990: top quality borrowers, often supranationals; Japanese borrowers issuing equity-linked paper; and the others, often sovereign borrowers, paying high coupons. Sovereign borrowers in the latter group paid a high 11 per cent interest rate, but none the less found it increasingly difficult to launch bond issues. *Financial Times,* 18 September 1990 and *International Herald Tribune,* 11 October 1990.

[209] In the case of the Soviet Union, this is reflected in a recent $20 million credit arranged for the Soviet Bank for Foreign Economic Affairs and intended to finance the importation of IBM personal computers. The bulk of the 6½ year credit is backed by the United Kingdom's ECGD. The $3 million tranche borrowed on purely commercial terms carried a margin of 1½ points over the Libor Eurodollar rate, substantially above the ¼ margin at which the Soviet bank was able to borrow in 1989. *Financial Times,* 2 October 1990.

[210] BIS, *The Maturity and Sectoral Distribution of International Bank Lending,* First Half 1990, Basle, January 1991.

[211] At the end of 1989, nearly 50 per cent of the Soviet Union's debt *vis-à-vis* BIS reporting banks, or $21 billion, was slated to mature during 1990. BIS, *The Maturity Distribution of International Bank Lending,* Basle, July 1990.

TABLE 3.3.12

Eastern Europe and the Soviet Union: External debt and financial indicators, 1988-1990

(Billion US dollars, per cent)

	Gross debt			Net debt [a]		Net-debt/exports [b]			Net interest payments/exports [b]	
	1988	1989	1990	1989	1990*	1988	1989	1990	1989	1990
Bulgaria	9.1	10.7	11.1	9.5	10.4	167	234	327	13.7	20.5
Czechoslovakia	7.3	7.9	8.1	5.7	6.8	84	75	80	1.9	2.9
Hungary	19.6	20.6	21.3	19.4	20.0	265	255	267	18.2	18.8
Poland	39.2	40.8	48.5	38.5	43.4	398	413	340	32.9	26.3
Romania	1.9*	0.7*	1.2	-1.1	0.9	33	-18	18	-0.6	0.2
Eastern Europe	77.1	80.7	90.2	72.0	81.5	203	205	227	14.7	15.7
Soviet Union	49.4 [c]	58.5*	62.5	43.8	54.6	80	95	111	6.5	8.5
Eastern Europe and the Soviet Union	126.6	139.2	152.7	115.8	136.2	133	143	160	10.0	11.5
Memorandum item: Soviet Union [d]	43.0	54.0	52.2 [e]	..	..	..	..	..	..	..

Source: National statistics, ECE secretariat estimates and *Houston Four Report, op.cit.,* p.50.

a Gross debt less official foreign currency reserves or BIS deposits.
b Exports of goods and services except for the Soviet Union for which only exports of goods to market economies are used.
c Includes $3.2 billion in clearing account deficits, cumulated chiefly with Finland and Yugoslavia. *Pravitelstvennyi vestnik* (Government Gazette), No.19, September 1989.
d External debt contracted or guaranteed by Vneshekonombank. *Houston Four Report.*
e June 1990; excludes $5 billion in arrears on western supplier credits.

pears to have stemmed the decline in the overall exposure of international banks towards the Soviet Union. In general, the eastern countries met some of the forced repayment of loans by dipping into reserves (see below) and, in the case of the Soviet Union, incurring arrears on western supplier credits which at the end of 1990 totalled some $5 billion.[212]

Although faced with a reduction in bank credits, the east European countries did not compensate for this by stepping up their use of *non-bank financial instruments* (official bilateral credits, guaranteed supplier credits, etc.), at least not in the first half of 1990.[213] During this period, their level of non-bank obligations remained roughly constant (on an exchange rate adjusted basis – see chart 3.3.2).[214] In contrast, the Soviet Union's net borrowing using these facilities rose by $1.4 billion. This may represent a departure from recent practice, since the Soviet Union had been liquidating this type of obligation rapidly since the first half of the 1980s.

In 1990 and early 1991, western governments made available officially-backed credits to the eastern countries, generally with the intent of providing support for economic reform. Commitments to eastern Europe have been made chiefly within the framework of the PHARE programme, the membership of which now includes all countries of the region.

Separately, the G-24 and other governments in 1990 and early 1991 established credit facilities for the Soviet Union amounting to $22 billion, partially in recognition of the country's financial difficulties (see section 3.3(vi), table 3.3.16). The credit lines have been drawn on heavily, in part to make up arrears on credits extended by western suppliers, and, as a result, it is likely that not more than $15-17 billion will be available for 1991 and beyond.

Only Hungary and Poland had access to funding from the *multilateral financial institutions* in 1990 (see sections (v) and (vi)). Both countries arranged IMF standby credits and received loans from the World Bank, for the first time in the case of Poland.

The Soviet Union sold 234 tons of *gold* in 1990 worth 1.6 billion foreign currency roubles ($2.8 billion).[215] At various times during the year, the Soviet Union also swapped gold for credits (see section 3.3(v)). Other eastern countries sold small amounts of gold.

(c) Reserves

Given the severity of the credit squeeze experienced by the eastern countries, most of them were obliged to draw heavily on their foreign currency reserves (deposits with BIS banks)[216] to meet payments (table 3.3.11). In general, reserves were sharply reduced to below three

212 *Houston Four Report, op.cit.*

213 The bulk of the rise in Poland's non-bank obligations presumably reflects the capitalization of interest arrears, although there may also have been some drawing on the bilateral credit lines extended by the G-24 governments within the framework of the PHARE programme.

214 A constant level of these liabilities implies that new borrowing just offset repayments of maturing debt.

215 According to Prime Minister V. Pavlov, in a television interview reprinted in *Sovetskaya Rossia,* 23 February 1991. In the past official data on gold sales have not been available.

216 Data on official reserves are not yet available for all eastern countries (table 3.3.11). In lieu of this information, their deposits with BIS banks have traditionally been used as indicators of the level of available reserves. However as economic reforms have progressed, the BIS data increasingly reflect deposits other than official reserves. For example, Poland's $8 billion in BIS deposits significantly exceed the country's official reserves.

months' coverage of imports, the level often considered to be the prudent minimum. Hungary managed to partially reconstitute its foreign currency position in the second half of the year with the assistance of BIS and EC loans, from a level below $1 billion in April.

The fall in the Soviet Union's BIS bank deposits from $15 billion at the end of 1988 to $8 billion at the end of September 1990 (and possibly still lower by the end of the year) is another indicator of the country's grave financial situation.[217] Maintenance of an ample level of reserves (at least 4 months' import coverage) appears to have been a long-standing policy priority. Traditionally efforts were made to rebuild deposits after periods of exceptionally high use, but this did not prove possible in the last two years. The depletion of Soviet deposits and the reduction in the availability of commercial bank credits helps to explain the appearance of payments arrears early in 1990.

(d) External debt

Total eastern *gross debt* rose by some $15 billion, to $153 billion in 1990, as a result of the growing indebtedness of nearly all eastern countries (table 3.3.12). Much of this increase reflects the impact of the depreciation of the US dollar in the second half of the year. The remainder represents a "real" (i.e., exchange rate adjusted) rise in debt, due chiefly to the capitalization of Bulgaria's interest arrears, Poland's rescheduled interest obligations, and, in the case of the Soviet Union, the accumulation of arrears of principal on western supplier credits. The availability of some fresh credits from various official sources also contributed to the rise in debt.

Eastern gross indebtedness would have risen even more if international banks had not withdrawn inter-bank deposits.[218] As already noted, these actions reduced the east's bank debt by over $6 billion in the first three quarters of the year. Heavy recourse by most eastern countries to reserves resulted in the *net debt* of the area rising by more than the increase in gross debt.

Attention should be drawn to two points concerning eastern debt statistics. Firstly, there are some differences in Soviet external indebtedness in convertible currencies as reported at various times by the Soviet authorities and those cited in the *Houston Four Report* (table 3.3.12). The series presented in the latter comprises only debt contracted or guaranteed by the Vneshekonombank. Since it does not cover the financial debt of enterprises and supplier's credits, the $52.2 billion debt estimated for mid-1990 excludes the $5 billion in Soviet arrears. A larger debt figure of approximately R35 billion ($62-63 billion),[219] presumably

for the end of 1990, was cited by the Soviet authorities in January. In general, the Soviet data show higher debt than western estimates. This may reflect some differences in coverage − the official Soviet figures may include liabilities incurred in non-convertible currency transactions − and the methodology may differ, particularly as regarding the application of exchange rates.

Secondly, statistics on eastern debt and assets in convertible currencies will need to be adjusted once existing positions in roubles are transformed to convertible currencies, a process that was already under way in early 1991 (section 3.2). These modifications have not been introduced in table 3.3.12.

(iv) Prospects for east-west trade and payments

From the beginning of 1990, the trade and payments prospects of the *east European* countries for 1991 were a source of widespread concern, but recent developments indicate a more encouraging situation.

General factors shaping the trade and payments of the eastern countries are discussed in this section. More detailed information pertaining to the outlook for individual eastern countries is presented in the east-west trade country profiles in the next section. Although the discussion in principle encompasses all convertible-currency transactions of the eastern countries, in the area of trade it focuses on their interchanges with the west. Trade among the eastern countries, which from 1991 will also be conducted under a convertible-currency régime, is treated apart owing to the special circumstances of the changeover (section 3.2 above). Eastern Europe and the Soviet Union are discussed separately.

The new element transforming *eastern Europe's financial perspectives* was the decision taken in 1990 to replace the CMEA trade and payments régime with a system based on world market prices and convertible currencies as of January 1991. Eastern Europe's terms of trade were bound to decline markedly under the new system. The area's import prices would rise sharply when the Soviet Union raised the price of its fuel exports to world market levels, while the prices of east European manufactures would tend to decline. In consequence, eastern Europe's overall trade and payments position in convertible currencies was expected to deteriorate dramatically. Any assessment of the full terms-of-trade impact on east European trade balances was bound to be problematic owing to uncertainty about the proper valuation of rouble-based trade in terms of convertible currencies. For purposes of illustration, it can be noted that under the old system, the

---

[217] The *Houston Four Report* gives an estimate of $5.1 billion for the end of 1990. The Soviet Union is believed to hold considerable gold reserves − unofficially estimated in the range of 2,000-3,000 tons. The authors of the *Houston Four* study did not have access to the official statistics in the gold stocks.

[218] In Czechoslovakia's case, debt also declined because Czechoslovak foreign trade organizations reduced their use of short-term import (supplier) credits and enterprises increased their recourse to their own convertible currency funds, accumulated through the system of retention accounts. *Svet hospodarstvi*, 20 September 1990.

[219] According to Prime Minister V. Pavlov, *Izvestiya*, 16 January 1991. Calculated at the December 1990 official exchange rate of $1.795 per rouble.

Subsequently, Soviet Deputy Foreign Minister E. Obminski declared that the "state foreign debt was $60 billion or more than R40 billion at the beginning of March 1991". *Izvestiya*, 7 March 1991.

TABLE 3.3.13

Eastern Europe: Current account projections for 1991 and recent financial commitments
(Million US dollars)

	Bulgaria	Czechoslovakia	Hungary	Poland	Romania
Current account					
Initial...................................	-2 000	-2 500	-1 200	-1 000 *	-1 700
Revised..................................	..	..	-600	..	..
Recent financial commitments					
IMF a.....................................	634	1 783	2 563 b	2 000 b	1 000
World Bank..........................	300	500	300	600	200
Group-24..............................	800	1 000	1 000	-	1 000
EIB, ECSC............................	..	..	709	908	..
Bilateral...............................	200	..	2 505	2 700	500
Grants, other.......................	200	..	477	1 950	300

Source: National sources, IMF, press reports, United Nations Economic Commission for Europe, *Economic Bulletin for Europe,* vol.42/90, New York, 1991, table 3.20.

a Agreed or under negotiation. Includes contingency financing mechanism which can be accessed only if oil prices exceed those anticipated in country programmes.
b Includes a 3-year extended facility.

effective CMEA price of oil appears to have been in the range of $7-8 per barrel.[220] Thus a move toward the world market price, some $18 per barrel in the first half of 1990 (as well as in early 1991), would generate a large terms-of-trade loss for eastern Europe. In paying this higher price, the countries of eastern Europe (excluding the former German Democratic Republic) would experience an estimated $8 billion deterioration in their trade balances.[221]

With the onset of the Gulf conflict in mid-1990, the price of oil surged. Most analysts predicted a continuation of high prices well into 1991 (some scenarios constructed then incorporated oil price assumptions of up to $40 per barrel, the peak price reached in August 1990). Large current-account deficits together with additional requirements stemming from the need to refinance maturing debt and to rebuild inadequate reserves raised the spectre of severe financing shortages in 1991 that could endanger economic transition programmes.

Thus external payments issues moved to the top of the agenda for international support of eastern Europe, receiving the attention of G-24 governments and international financial institutions. Since late 1990, they have assembled assistance packages, tailored on a country-by-country basis, consisting of new arrangements with the IMF (including special mechanisms to provide for higher oil import bills), World Bank loans, and miscellaneous facilities established by the G-24 (table 3.3.13 and section 3.3(vi)). These initiatives have been critical in the light of declining eastern access to private capital markets.

Toward the end of 1990, all east European countries prepared trade and payments projections for 1991 within the context of their economic programmes.

Available official estimates of expected current-account deficits sum to over $8 billion (table 3.3.13), as compared to the $2 billion deficit registered in 1990. It appears that 1991 oil prices in the range of $25-30 per barrel have generally been assumed in these projections. In consequence of the various international initiatives, the new credit facilities committed or envisaged would appear to be adequate to meet eastern Europe's expected financing requirements. The key condition for the release of funds is, in each case, the country's commitment to an IMF-approved stabilization programme and to the implementation of profound economic reforms.

In the early months of 1991, the price of oil declined to some $17 per barrel. While some recovery is possible, oil prices are expected to remain below $20 per barrel in 1991 (see section 3.1). Since recent and prospective prices are considerably above the old CMEA price of $7-8 per barrel, the eastern countries will still experience a marked deterioration in their terms-of-trade. However, as oil prices are likely to remain *below* those underlying the east European countries' projections, their current-account deficits in 1991 should be *less* than initially forecast. In fact, some east European governments have recently revised downward estimates of their expected current-account deficits.[222] This has resulted in some optimism about their macro-economic prospects, including an easing of inflationary pressures.

Lower-than-expected current-account deficits would ease the pressure on financial resources. Maintenance of financial commitments by official creditors could increase the scope for building up foreign currency reserves. However this will also depend on the availability of private capital. Hungary and Czecho-

---

220 See "Foreign trade of the eastern countries", in United Nations Economic Commission for Europe *Economic Bulletin for Europe*, vol.42/90, New York, 1991, p.45.

221 United Nations Economic Commission for Europe *Economic Bulletin for Europe*, vol.42/90, New York, 1991, table 2.7. The estimate assumes no change in the 1989 volume of eastern trade.

222 For example, the Hungarian authorities had initially forecast a $1.2 billion current account deficit for 1991, but now expect half that amount under the new, lower price assumption for oil of $20 per barrel, according to Mr. G. Surányi, head of the National Bank of Hungary. *Financial Times*, 21 February 1991. Some of the expected improvement in the current account stems from the assumed strengthening of export growth.

slovakia have retained access to the international bond markets and their prospects for renewed borrowing from banks should improve with the completion of arrangements with the IMF and G-24 creditors.[223] The improved overall prospects could encourage joint venture formation and foreign direct investment inflows.

As in 1990, the volume of eastern Europe's *merchandise trade with the west* in 1991 is expected to be shaped by factors which will tend to foster export growth and hold down that of imports.

Firstly, prospects are for a further weakening of domestic demand in eastern markets, which should maintain the pressure on enterprises to find alternative outlets, above all in the developed market economies. Virtually all east European countries foresee additional falls in output and domestic demand, in part owing to the implementation of stabilization programmes. External demand from the CMEA areas will contract further in the wake of the abolition of the transferable rouble trade and payments régime. Trade returns from early 1991 indicate that the decline in trade will be much steeper than anticipated (section 3.2 above), in particular as regards east European exports to the Soviet Union.[224]

Secondly, with the exception of Poland, the east European countries all have devalued recently.[225] However, further devaluations may be necessary to maintain the profitability of exports, as inflation in general, has accelerated.

Thirdly, western import demand, which has provided large marketing opportunities for the eastern countries, is expected to expand further in 1991, although at a slower rate. According to the forecasts of western countries, many of the major markets for eastern goods – Austria, France, Italy and Germany – will be more buoyant than the average. The east European countries will also continue to benefit from improved access to western markets within the framework of the PHARE programme. Czechoslovakia has recently gained MFN status in the United States, joining Hungary and Poland in this regard. United States MFN for Bulgaria is pending. As eastern demand flags, the western countries now offer the main alternative outlet for east European goods. The recent experiences of Hungary and Poland show that the exports to the west can be an important stabilizing factor for the eastern economies and underline the importance of maintaining the access of these countries to western markets during the crucial early period of transition.

Fourthly, so far it seems that the reforms have had a favourable impact on exports in Poland, Hungary, and Czechoslovakia. A new and presumably more efficient pattern of export specialization should start to emerge, as enterprises are increasingly subject to relative prices reflecting world market patterns (price formation has now been largely freed), reductions in subsidies, more neutral tax codes, freer access to convertible currency, etc. However, full exploitation of the emerging possibilities will require that domestic and foreign enterprises make new investments. So far these have been inadequate, thus contributing to the slow pace of structural adjustment observed virtually everywhere in the east.

Expectations about export prospects of the individual east European countries are mixed. The Hungarian authorities are optimistic about entering a period of export-led growth. In Czechoslovakia, output results for early 1991 suggest that a strong contraction in consumer demand (due to a sharp drop in real incomes) has been partially offset by strong export growth, presumably to the west. The two recent devaluations should also play a role. Polish export prospects appeared gloomy at the beginning of the year, partly because of the increasing overvaluation of the zloty. The Romanian authorities foresee a further decline in exports, despite their expectation of an upturn in industrial production. Given their recent performance, Bulgarian exports may also remain weak. Stabilization programmes in Bulgaria and Romania seek to revive industrial output and exports, down in both countries because of supply-related causes, but these are not expected to produce rapid results.

On the import side, by virtue of their more favourable payments outlook, most east European countries may have more room for manoeuvre than expected at the end of 1990. Attention may be drawn to the boom in their consumer goods imports in 1990, following policy changes by the new governments. While additional imports may be desirable to satisfy internal demand and to promote competition in domestic markets, it would be prudent to monitor them carefully, so that present consumption does not crowd out other needs and contribute excessively to debt growth.

Although the prospects for eastern Europe's external financial situation now appear encouraging, several major problems remain to be tackled, at least two of which were pushed into the background when the possibility of future balance-of-payments problems arose initially.

First, falling production and rapidly rising unemployment in these countries are creating parallel demands for the establishment and funding of large-scale social safety nets and/or increases in subsidies to enterprises. Such demands on government resources will push against the ceilings on domestic budget deficits included in these countries' IMF-agreed stabilization programmes. Although all east European countries are in various stages of discussing structural adjustment

---

[223] As regards the other countries, Romania has yet to re-establish firm relations with international commercial banks. Bulgaria will need a major restructuring of its debt, which is not likely to involve large new private credits. The Polish authorities appear to have focused on the issue of debt reduction rather than on obtaining new credit facilities.

[224] Some east European countries will experience large reductions in imports from the Soviet Union, traditionally the largest supplier of raw materials. Unless these can be easily replaced from other sources, the implications for the domestic economies would be unfavourable.

[225] In general governments are reluctant to devalue because of the inflationary impact.

loans with the World Bank, it is not clear whether international support programmes are fully prepared to deal with these large potential needs. Well-designed and adequately funded programmes, including support for the creation of small private enterprises, could contribute to social stability and ease pressures on the population to emigrate.

Second, the eastern countries have vast and urgent need in areas of technical assistance (including large investments in human capital), restoration of institutions, creation of a business infrastructure — all that is required to create efficient market-economies. The Group of 24, co-ordinated by the EC, and the international economic organizations have launched programmes to provide various types of training, re-establish the banking sector, promote privatization, introduce international accounting standards — to mention just a few. These programmes are consistent with the suggestion of the ECE secretariat last year for a "Marshall Aid"-type programme in which technical assistance — broadly conceived — would be predominant (also see chapter 1).[226] Given the enormity of the task at hand, the resources currently allocated or envisaged would appear inadequate.

The third problem worth mentioning is the eastern countries' shortage of capital required for the restructuring and modernization of industry. Current export revenues and borrowing from the international development banks are unlikely to meet these needs. For this reason, a high priority has been attached to fostering the inflow of foreign direct investments into eastern Europe. In general, however, the volume of investment has been disappointing despite numerous efforts to promote it.

Prospects for the *Soviet Union's* trade with the west appear to be bleak. In spite of the abolition of the transferable rouble trade and payments régime, and also the conversion of intra-CMEA trade to convertible currency settlement, total convertible currency earnings are expected to fall sharply in 1991. This reflects in the first instance sharp cutbacks in overall oil exports caused by the 37 million ton fall in production in 1990 and the further declines expected in 1991. Exports of crude oil under the competence of the central authorities are to be reduced to some 60 million tons, from roughly 120 million tons exported in 1990.[227] Moreover, the world market price of oil is currently less than $20 per barrel, significantly below the expectations of last year. Taken together, export cuts of this magnitude and the persistence of the current comparatively low price of oil imply worse trade and payments prospects than the gloomy "low scenario" (alternative scenario) elaborated by the *Houston Four* (see section 3.3(v)). The "low scenario" assumes an average oil price of $20 per

barrel in 1991 and a 25 per cent decline in the exports of crude oil and oil products (i.e., a decline of some 40 million tons in 1991).

Under the "low scenario," the Soviet Union would have a financing requirement of some $27 billion in 1991 (of which a $11 billion current account deficit — including gold sales — $11 billion in repayment of maturing debt[228] and $5 billion for the settlement of arrears). Despite the possible availability of some $15-17 billion in bilateral credits and full settlement by eastern Europe of its current convertible currency obligations to the Soviet Union (now virtually certain), in this scenario the Soviet Union experiences a substantial payments gap. Recourse to foreign currency reserves is not an option since these are already inadequate. In consequence, it appears that the Soviet Union will have to cut its imports by considerably more than the 7 per cent assumed in the "low scenario".

Recent statements by the Soviet authorities do indeed refer to severe shortages of convertible currency at the beginning of 1991. As a result, purchases of raw materials and various inputs of semi-finished goods have had to be postponed, bringing industries in certain regions to a standstill.[229] Several eastern countries also reported sharper-than-expected falls in their sales to the Soviet Union in early 1991, also implying a lack of funds.

(v) Country profiles — east-west trade

These country profiles are intended to provide information on the particular situation in each eastern country with regard to east-west trade and finance. They complement the more general discussion of recent developments found in section (iii) and the overview of short-term prospects in section (iv).

It should be noted that the changes in trade flows discussed in this section relate to convertible currency transactions (or when these data are lacking, to eastern trade with market economies) and are taken from national sources (table 3.3.14). Hence they differ from the trade data presented in tables 3.3.1-3.3.4 which are based upon western sources and relate only to eastern trade with the developed market economies.

(a) Bulgaria

Despite facing stagnating exports in the second half of the 1980s, *Bulgaria* pursued a comparatively liberal import policy which resulted in progressively widening convertible currency current account deficits. Apparently, financing these deficits, chiefly through bank

---

226 See also "Economic reform in the east: a framework for western support" in United Nations Economic Commission for Europe, *Economic Survey of Europe in 1989-1990*, New York, 1990, pp.5-34.

227 S. Sitarian, BBC, *Summary of World Broadcasts*, SU/0967, 11 January 1991, p.C1/4.

228 According to various Soviet sources, the country faces a particularly heavy repayments schedule this year. S. Sitarian, *ibid*, notes that the equivalent of TR 9 billion in freely convertible currencies will go to repay debt in 1991. Another source cites repayments obligations of TR 12.5 billion, of which TR 3.5 has been covered by new loan commitments. *Izvestiya*, 7 March 1991.

229 According to Prime Minister Pavlov, cited in BBC, *Summary of World Broadcasts*, SU/1006, 26 February 1991, p.C1/4.

TABLE 3.3.14

Eastern Europe and the Soviet Union: Convertible currency trade, 1989-1990
(Changes in per cent; balances in million US dollars)

	Exports [a]		Imports [a]		Trade balances	
	1989	1990	1989	1990	1989	1990
Bulgaria [b]	-14.3	-4.8	-2.5	-25.4	-1 445	-594
Czechoslovakia [b]	8.5	8.4	1.3	21.1	287	-368
Hungary	2.4	16.9	2.4	11.7	554	935
Poland	2.7	39.4	6.4	4.2	766	3 798
Romania	-4.2	-43.5	24.4	45.1	2 604	-1 661
Soviet Union [b]	5.5	7.6	22.3	5.8	-1 536	-854

Source: National statistics.

Note: All trade data are on a customs basis and may differ significantly from the country's convertible currency trade reported on a balance of payments basis (see table 3.3.8). Hungarian imports are c.i.f.

a Changes in US dollars.
b Trade with non-socialist countries.

credits, was not a problem until late 1989, despite the rapid and persistent deterioration of the country's debt indicators. Bulgaria is another example of a country which, with the support of western creditors, chose to borrow rather than to undertake fundamental economic reform.

In March 1990 the Bulgarian Foreign Trade Bank was forced to declare a moratorium on payments of principal coming due and, eventually, also on interest obligations.[230] Commercial creditors not only ceased to advance fresh credits, but also refused to roll over existing short-term loans. The country's worsening economic situation and prospects undoubtedly played a role in this decision: industrial production was declining, pulling down exports (convertible currency exports fell by 26 per cent in value in the first quarter of 1990), the convertible currency current account deficit looked set to exceed $1 billion again and over $3 billion in maturing medium- and long-term debt needed to be refinanced in the course of 1990.[231]

The Bulgarian authorities responded to the liquidity crisis with two measures. Steps were taken which reversed the decline in exports and caused a strong recovery of sales in the last quarter of the year. However, the tightening of the import régime, which led to a 33 per cent reduction in the second half of the year,[232] had a greater effect in correcting the trade imbalance.[233] For

the year as a whole, total imports fell by 25 per cent in value and (incomplete) data suggest that purchases of virtually all commodities were restricted. This is reported to have contributed to the marked decline in consumption and industrial output. In addition, oil processing fell by 42 per cent due to reduced supplies of crude from the Soviet Union and Iraq.[234]

As a result of the adjustment measures, the country's convertible currency trade deficit narrowed modestly to $800 million in 1990. However, because of the rise in interest payments, the convertible-currency current account deficit contracted less, to an estimated $1.1 billion. Financing of the deficit was mainly achieved by reducing foreign currency reserves – these were drawn down by $875 million[235] – and the build-up of interest arrears (as a result of the Foreign Trade Bank's action early in the year).[236] Some official bilateral credits were also made available to Bulgaria.[237] However, these resources were insufficient for the country to cover the $3 billion in medium- and long-term debt maturing in 1990. Postponement of Bulgarian payments was eventually agreed by the creditor banks. Although the authorities had hoped to reach agreement with the IMF by November 1990, this timetable was not achieved.[238]

The outlook for Bulgarian trade with the west remains unfavourable. Of all the east European countries, it has had the largest share of trade with the

---

230 See United Nations Economic Commission for Europe, *Economic Bulletin for Europe,* vol.42/90, New York, 1991.

231 According to B. Belchev, Bulgarian Minister of Finance, $3.4 billion of debt matured in 1990. Repayments scheduled for 1991 and 1992 amount to $1.8 billion and $800 million, respectively. Reported in BBC, *Summary of World Broadcasts,* EE/W0140 A/1, 9 April 1990 and *Financial Times,* 21 September 1990.

232 Relative to the same period of the previous year.

233 A trade surplus was achieved in the last quarter of the year.

234 BBC, *Summary of World Broadcasts,* EE/W0162 A/6, 17 January 1991.

235 Fragmentary reports indicate that foreign exchange reserves were essentially exhausted by year-end. Bulgarian deposits at BIS reporting banks fell from $1.2 billion at the end of 1989 to $594 million at end-September.

236 The withdrawal by international banks of some $300 interbank loans during the first nine months of the year also strained Bulgaria's finances.

237 West European governments committed at least $300 million in bilateral credits to Bulgaria in 1990.

238 *Financial Times,* 7 February 1991 and 22 November 1990. Agreement between Bulgaria and the IMF on a standby arrangement appears to have taken longer than originally expected since the accord was considered imminent already in November. The Bulgarian government presented its programme for accelerating economic reform to the parliament in October. Due to a political crisis, this programme was not adopted and the new government, led by Mr. D. Popov, prepared a new programme of economic reforms at the beginning of 1991.

CMEA, the within-group exchanges of which will continue to contract, and has been relatively hard hit by the Gulf crisis.[239] A further fall in industrial production in 1991 could again damage exports. Bulgaria's recent poor export performance in western markets raises questions about its potential for a strong supply response, even after the stabilization programme currently under preparation is put into place. The commodity structure of trade remains unfavourable and the continuing deterioration in its terms of trade would increase the current account deficit to an estimated $2 billion in 1991.[240]

In February 1991 Bulgaria reached agreement in principle with the IMF on a tough austerity programme which will be supported by financing totalling up to $634 million.[241] World Bank funds of $300 million should now become available and the Bulgarian authorities also hope that the IMF agreement will pave the way for a resumption of bank credits and new official bilateral credit facilities.[242] However, it would appear that fresh commercial credits would have to be arranged within the context of a formal rescheduling of Bulgarian debt. Given Bulgaria's highly strained financial position, the rescheduling arrangements are likely to cover interest arrears and the $1.8 billion in medium- and long-term debt which matured in 1991 as well as the obligations which came due in 1990.[243] Certain rouble debts converted by agreement to hard currency liabilities will also have to be dealt with.[244]

Bulgaria will benefit from the PHARE programme in 1991. Currently the G-24 are assembling a $800 million loan and are also apparently willing to consider additional support in the event that Bulgaria encounters difficulties financing oil imports (see section 3.3(vi)). Negotiations with the Soviet Union on the conversion of Bulgaria's cumulated rouble surplus into convertible currency are under way. This surplus was built up in bilateral trade in 1990 and has been reported to lie in the range of R300-470 million.[245]

(b) Czechoslovakia

In 1990 *Czechoslovakia's* sales to the convertible currency area increased for the fourth consecutive year, but the 8 per cent expansion was relatively modest. A somewhat stronger export performance toward the west (growth of 13 per cent) was offset by a sharp contraction of sales to the developing countries.[246] Exports of raw food materials, construction materials, consumer goods, live animals and chemicals to the convertible currency area as a whole were especially strong, suggesting that there was only slight progress in improving the commodity structure of trade. On the other hand, data reflecting the country's exports to the west alone (section 3.3(ii)) indicate more success in this respect.

In 1990 exports appear to have benefited from the first round of economic reforms. These resulted in a growing number of enterprises exercising their foreign trade rights, wider use of the convertible currency retention scheme (seen as a strong export incentive), and broader access to foreign exchange through the system of currency auctions.[247] In addition, the koruna was devalued at the beginning of 1990 by 18.6 per cent (from kcs14.29/$ to kcs 17/$).[248] The impact of this measure on export growth may well have been minimal as the real exchange rate fell only slightly.[249] Some production and exports are likely to have been lost due to internal disputes over the legitimacy of existing enterprise management and the problems associated with the replacement of numerous managers.

The boom in convertible currency imports — they increased by over 20 per cent in value throughout the year — reflects the more liberal import policy of the new government. Also enterprises brought forward their foreign purchases in anticipation of a further devaluation, initially set by the authorities for the beginning of 1991.[250] Consumer and engineering goods imports grew particularly rapidly. Partially as a conse-

---

239 Bulgaria is owed some $1.2 billion by Iraq, which was to have been paid off over the period 1990-1994 with deliveries of oil totalling some 4.8 million tons.

240 According to A. Paparizov, Minister of Foreign Economic Relations, BBC, *Summary of World Broadcasts*, EE/WO/64 A/1, 31 January 1991.

241 IMF, *Press Release*, No.91/15, 15 March 1991. The total includes a 12-month standby credit of $394 million, a Compensatory and Contingency Financing Facility of $131 million and a contingency financing mechanism of $109 million.

242 According to Todor Vulchev, Director of the Bulgarian National Bank. Bulgaria is also to seek credits from Germany. *Financial Times*, 13 February 1991.

243 In December 1990, commercial bank creditors agreed another 90 days rollover of interest and principal payments. *Financial Times*, 13 February 1990.

244 Bulgaria built up a rouble trade deficit of R700-800 million with Poland and the former German Democratic Republic during 1990, according to A. Paparizov, the Minister of Foreign Economic Relations. BBC, *Summary of World Broadcasts*, EE/W0163 A/1, 24 January 1991.

245 According to Minister Paparizov. BBC, *Summary of World Broadcasts*, EE/W0163 A/1, 24 January 1991 and BBC, *Summary of World Broadcasts*, EE/W0164 A/1, 31 January 1991.

246 The fall in Czechoslovak exports to the developing countries appears to reflect the suspension of arms sales and the ongoing policy to phase out exports to non-creditworthy countries. The latter action explains the comparatively weak performance in 1990 (a 7 per cent rise in value) of the country's overall sales of engineering goods to the convertible currency (non-socialist) area remarked in national trade statistics. However, data reported by western importers alone show a dynamic development of Czechoslovak engineering goods (in the first half of 1990), as noted.

247 The foreign exchange system was liberalized further when enterprises were given the right to purchase foreign exchange from commercial banks between auctions, at rates of exchange set at the preceding auction.

248 A special, more advantageous, tourist exchange rate was introduced to promote western tourism. It also applied to Czechoslovak citizens, for whom travel was liberalized.

249 Given the tendency for the nominal value of the koruna to rise against the US dollar during 1990 and domestic inflation of at least 10 per cent, the depreciation of the real exchange rate appears to have been small during the first half of the year.

250 Press conference of J. Tosovsky, President of the Czechoslovak State Bank, in *Svet hospodarstvi*, 20 September 1990.

quence of the widening trade deficit, the authorities brought forward the date of the devaluation to 15 October, depreciating the koruna by 54.5 per cent (the commercial and non-commercial exchange rates of the koruna were modified from kcs 15.53/$ to kcs 24/$).[251] However, this measure appears to have had little, if any, effect in stemming import growth during the remainder of the year. In this period, enterprises were liquidating their holdings of convertible currencies in advance of the abolition of retention accounts at the beginning of 1991.

As a result, the country ran small trade and current account deficits in 1990, the latter being financed chiefly through a draw-down of reserves. Czechoslovakia's foreign currency reserves fell from some $2.2 billion at the end of 1989 to $1.3 billion at the end of October 1990. Presumably reserves were also tapped to repay the $400 million in short-term debt which international banks failed to roll over.

A wide-ranging programme of economic reform combined with the implementation of a new IMF-backed stabilization programme — tight fiscal and monetary policies, implementation of a restrictive incomes policy, liberalization of prices, launching of the privatization programme — will shape trade developments in 1991. The commercial and tourist exchange rates have been unified at a new rate — the koruna was devalued again in January 1991 by 17 per cent to 28 kcs/$ — at what the authorities consider a competitive level.[252] The new rate is to be maintained to provide a nominal anchor for newly-freed domestic prices. The country has also liberalized the trade and foreign exchange systems, removing restrictions on the current account transactions of enterprises. On 1 January 1991 internal convertibility (limited to current transactions of enterprises) was introduced and the currency retention scheme was abandoned. The combination of a tariff schedule and a temporary 20 per cent surcharge on certain imports has replaced administrative measures as the primary instrument for the control of imports.[253] The government considers the import surcharge to be vital in maintaining internal and external balance in the face of deteriorating trade and payments conditions.

The restraints on internal demand and the cumulative impact of the October and January devaluations, should encourage enterprises to find new outlets in the west. Resolution of management issues in enterprises would also be desirable, as some Czechoslovak econo-

mists see these uncertainties as a continuing brake on exports. In early 1991 enterprises met much of their demand for foreign goods from the high stocks accumulated at the end of last year. This has put downward pressure on imports, with the consequence that the value of imports remained flat in the first two months of 1991.

The bulk of the financing for Czechoslovakia's target current account deficit of $2.5 billion is to be provided by the IMF. IMF assistance is also intended to support the second stage of the country's reform — including the introduction of internal convertibility at a stable new exchange rate — and to replenish foreign currency reserves. Under the arrangement approved by the IMF board on 8 January 1991,[254] Czechoslovakia is to receive two loans totalling SDR 1,250.8 million ($1,783 million), 187 per cent of its quota.[255] A traditional standby credit of SDR 619.5 million ($833 million) will be available over 14 months.

The second element of the support programme involves Czechoslovak access to the compensatory and contingency financing facility (CCFF). This scheme has two components. The main part of the facility, which is fully committed, is intended to finance excess oil import costs arising from the new CMEA trading and payment régime and from higher world oil prices between October 1990 and September 1991. This component amounts to some SDR 483.8 million ($690 million),[256] of which $448 million can be drawn immediately and $241 million later, after six months' data become available, provided the necessary conditions have been met. The other component of the facility is a $210 million external contingency mechanism which will be available only if oil and gas prices rise beyond levels envisaged in the programme.

The World Bank is to provide loans of $500-750 million[257] and it appears that the G-24 will be able to assemble the $1 billion credit requested by the Czechoslovak government to create a currency stabilization fund. The issue of a DM 1 billion credit from Germany is apparently still under discussion (see section (vi)). As regards commercial financing, Nomura Securities has been mandated by the Czechoslovak State Bank to raise up to $1 billion in bonds. The launching of the first bond issue (some $300 million) was expected in February.[258] As a result of this borrowing, the gross debt of the country is expected to rise

---

[251] At the same time there was a small devaluation of the tourist rate.

[252] This resulted in the revaluation of the tourist rate of the koruna by 12 per cent.

[253] On 17 December 1991, Czechoslovakia introduced a temporary restrictive measure on imports of consumer goods and foodstuffs under GATT Art.XII:2. GATT L/6812, 31 January 1991.

[254] IMF, *Press Release*, No.91/1.

[255] The credit was available on 15 January, is repayable over 5 years, with a 3-year grace period and the interest is to follow market rates. BBC, *Summary of World Broadcasts*, 17 January 1991.

[256] Czechoslovakia, like other east European countries, already experienced higher oil import costs in 1990 for reasons noted above.

[257] Statement by Moeen A. Qureshi, Senior Vice-President of the World Bank. Reported in BBC, *Summary of World Broadcasts*, EE/0904 A1/2, 25 October 1990.

[258] *East-West (Fortnightly Bulletin)*, 28 January 1991.

from nearly $8 billion at end-1990 to about $11 billion at the end of 1991.

Czechoslovakia and the Soviet Union have agreed on the conversion of some TR 2.4 billion in Czecho-slovak claims into convertible currency obligations at the rate of TR1/$. The Soviet Union has undertaken to repay these obligations in the form of goods over the period 1991-1994.[259] These claims will therefore not be a source of liquidity, contrary to initial reports.

(c) Hungary

Overall, Hungary's convertible currency trade and payments developed favourably in 1990. Domestic de-mand contracted further and this, together with a good harvest in 1989, set the stage for continued export growth. Export growth was helped by the improved access to western markets granted within the framework of the PHARE programme.[260] As a result, convertible currency exports rose by 17 per cent in value. A good export performance in the western market was crucial in the light of collapsing CMEA demand and is esti-mated to have compensated for one third of the decline in Hungary's exports to the eastern trade area.[261]

Convertible currency imports were stagnant for most of the year, despite the further liberalization of the import régime undertaken in January 1990.[262] However, convertible currency imports turned up sharply in the last quarter of the year as a result of additional pur-chases from oil producing countries, and, possibly also because of the appreciating exchange rate. Overall, the value of convertible currency imports rose by 12 per cent in 1990.

As a result of the strong export performance, the convertible currency trade surplus reached a record $945 million ($348 million on a balance of payments basis) in 1990, compared to $540 million in the previ-ous year. The Hungarian authorities have observed that the trade surplus could have been even higher, perhaps some $1.5 billion. The summer drought and the Gulf conflict are estimated to have deprived the

country of some $100 million and $50 million in re-venues respectively. Moreover, additional expenditure of $400 million in convertible currency was needed to compensate for the shortfalls in Soviet deliveries of crude oil.[263]

In contrast to recent years, no significant use was made of the exchange rate to improve the trade balance (see section 3.3(ii)) mainly because of the authorities' concern about inflation. The scaling down of the pop-ulation's entitlement to foreign currency in late 1989 and a higher number of visitors from the west restored Hungary's traditional tourism surplus in 1990 — net earnings of $345 million were recorded, compared to a deficit of $349 million during all of 1989.[264] Together, the trade and tourism items improved Hungary's current-account balance from a deficit of $1.4 billion in 1989 to a small surplus of $127 million in 1990. The outcome far exceeded both the government's original current account target (a deficit of $550 million) and the revised target (a deficit of $400 million). The original target was a crucial element of the stabilization pro-gramme agreed with the IMF early in the year.[265] The lower, revised, target was set following the favourable trade results posted in the first quarter of 1990.

Despite the positive trade outcome, Hungary's ex-ternal financial position came under strong pressure during the year. Unplanned repayments to the IMF in March[266] and the subsequent sudden withdrawal of short-term deposits by international banks threatened the country's liquidity position (see section 3.3(iii)). Of all the east European countries, Hungary was the most adversely affected with a net loss of $1.3 billion in inter-bank deposits in the first three quarters of the year (chart 3.3.2). Obligations were met by drawing upon foreign currency reserves, which fell below $1 billion in May. The government requested a 5-month, $500 million bridging loan from the BIS. A $280 million 3-month credit was granted by the BIS in June, for use until other funds became available. Although foreign currency reserves were partially replenished in the sec-ond half of the year, import coverage remained inade-quate[267] and gold reserves, valued at the national

---

259 *Hospodarske noviny*, 15 January 1991.

260 As noted above, Hungarian economists have estimated that some one third of Hungarian export growth to the west in 1990 could be attributed to western trade concessions. Kádár, *op.cit.*

261 *Ibid.*

262 The share of convertible currency imports subject to controls was reduced from 50 per cent to 30 per cent in January 1990.

263 According to B. Kádár, Minister of International Economic Relations; BBC, *Summary of World Broadcasts*, EE/W0163 A/2, 24 January 1991.

264 In November 1989 the authorities trimmed annual travel allowances to $75 per person to relieve pressure on the balance of payments.

265 The arrangement with the IMF involved a one-year SDR 159.21 million standby credit extending from 14 March 1990 to 13 March 1991. The principal condition for the release of IMF funds was a reduction in the state budget deficit from Ft 54 billion in 1989 to Ft 10 billion. Within the context of the sta-bilization programme, the government undertook to reduce sharply the convertible currency current account deficit, to the levels noted, and to eliminate the rouble trade surplus (some R1 billion in 1989). Completion of an accord with the IMF was a pre-condition for the release of various funds assembled by the Group of 24.

266 The SDR 150 million repayment was made under IMF rules governing faulty or false reporting, in which case the borrower is obliged to return credits ob-tained during the preceding two years. Repayment was a condition for access to a new standby credit. Statement by A. Cseres, an official of the National Bank of Hungary, in *Heti Világgazdaság*, 10 March 1990.

267 The precarious reserve situation contributed to international banker's cautious credit stance *vis-à-vis* Hungary in 1990. According to Mr. Czirják, an official of the National Bank of Hungary, *Népszabádság*, 22 August 1990,

The credit rating on Hungary's international bonds (some $2.9 billion are outstanding) has been downgraded by Moody's Investors Services from Baa2 to Baa1. The decision was said to be based upon the speed of political and economic change in the east and the area's increased payments difficulties. *East-West (Fortnightly Bulletin)* No.485, 30 July 1990.

valuation of $320/ounce, amounted to less than $100 million.

Various credit lines established by the G-24 under the PHARE programme enabled Hungary to meet heavy scheduled repayments of medium- and long-term debt amounting to some $2 billion in 1990. Notable among these is a loan of ECU 870 million from the EC. The first, ECU 350 million, tranche of this loan was disbursed in 1990.

The economic policies outlined for 1991 should foster the further growth of exports to the west. In fact, the Hungarian authorities have recently become optimistic about achieving a situation of export-led growth.[268] Domestic demand is expected to decline further in 1991[269] and the forint was devalued by 15 per cent at the beginning of 1991 to improve the price competitiveness of Hungarian exports and to attract foreign investment. These measures should ease the pressure on import demand, which was increasing at the end of 1990 and which may also have been boosted by the latest round of import liberalization (as from early January, the share of imports free of licensing requirements has increased to some 90 per cent).

Last summer's drought will curtail the export sales of the agricultural sector, which had contributed to the good trade performance in 1989 and the first half of 1990. Exports of a variety of goods are likely to be affected — the government has already cancelled planned exports of grain worth some $250 million[270] — while some cereals will have to be purchased abroad.[271]

Despite the relatively favourable outlook for the development of trade volumes, deterioration in the terms of trade is expected to push Hungary's current-account back into deficit in 1991. Assuming a relatively high oil price, the deficit was estimated at $1.2 billion.[272] But recent revisions, which assume a lower (about $20/barrel) oil price reduce this expected deficit by about half or even further.[273] However, some $2.2 billion in maturing medium- and long-term debt must be refinanced this year[274] and additional funds will be needed to boost reserves if the government is to move ahead with plans to increase the degree of forint convertibility.

The new Hungarian stabilization programme was approved by the IMF in February 1991.[275] The agreement involves a three-year extended financing facility (EFF) of SDR 1,114 million ($1,621 million) intended to support the government's economic reform programme. A further $436 million may be available under a contingency financing mechanism if specified external factors, including higher than projected oil prices, adversely affect the country's payments position.

In 1990, the Hungarian government had requested access to resources under the compensatory and contingency financing facility (CCFF) to help cover the increased cost of oil imports and to replenish oil stocks. In January 1991 the IMF approved the disbursal of $318 million to cover such higher expenditures incurred during the period November 1990-October 1991.[276] An additional amount equivalent to $171 million will be available later provided that the necessary conditions have been met. Assuming that all facilities are taken up, new IMF credits to Hungary amount to some $2,563 million in total.

The World Bank is to provide some $300-400 million,[277] and in February the EC approved the disbursal of the second, ECU 260 million, tranche of a structural adjustment loan. The third and final tranche is slated for release in the spring. Hungary intends to raise credits in the international capital markets — Austrian Schilling, DM and yen denominated bond issues have been specifically mentioned in this regard.[278] The agreement with the IMF and the better overall outlook for 1991 should facilitate these operations. Some official bilateral credits will also be available and the Hungarian authorities have requested $500 million in new support from the EC (see section (vi)).

These credits will raise Hungary's indebtedness, but if export receipts continue to grow strongly, the debt burden should decline.

Hungary and the Soviet Union have been unable to reach agreement on the timetable for the repayment of Soviet liabilities amounting to TR 1.7 billion (converted by agreement to $1.6 billion in convertible currency — see section 3.2).[279]

---

268 According to G. Surányi, Head of the National Bank of Hungary, *Financial Times*, 21 February 1991.

269 Prospects for overall economic activity, i.e., including the output of the parallel sector, may be more favourable. *Ibid.*

270 Hungarian Telegraph Agency (MTI) in English, as quoted in BBC, *Summary of World Broadcasts*, 4 October 1990.

271 Imports of maize and wheat will need to be boosted by an estimated over $25 million. MTI in English, as quoted in BBC, *Summary of World Broadcasts*, 2 September 1990. *Népsabadság*, 31 August 1990.

272 *Financial Times*, 23 October 1990.

273 G. Surányi, *op.cit.* and a more recent statement of Mr. Harshegyi (Deputy President of the National Bank of Hungary) in *Népszabádság*, 9 March 1991.

274 National Bank of Hungary, *Market Letter*, 7/1990.

275 IMF, *Press Release No.91/8*, 21 February 1991.

276 *Ibid.*

277 *East European Market*, 19 October 1991.

278 *Népszabádság*, 18 December 1990.

279 BBC, *Summary of World Broadcasts*, 10 January 1991.

(d) Poland

Since the beginning of 1990, the development of Poland's external trade has been shaped by radical economic reforms and the implementation of an IMF-approved stabilization programme. This programme has been supported by an aid package assembled by the Group of 24, which granted Poland greater access to western markets and loosened the country's external financial constraint. The arrangements gave Poland scope to incur a $3 billion current account deficit in convertible currencies in 1990 (compared to a deficit of $1.9 billion in 1989). Such measures were thought to be crucial during the initial phase of the transition since Poland's convertible currency exports had faltered toward the end of 1989 — a collapse of exports was considered a possibility at the time — and an import boom was considered likely and to some extent even desirable.[280]

In fact the array of policy measures taken early in 1990 stimulated an unexpected degree of external adjustment. The combination of restrictive monetary and fiscal policies (which caused a strong contraction of internal demand), a steep devaluation of the zloty (from zl 6000/$ to zl 9500/$), the imposition of an import surcharge on consumer goods and various liberalizing reforms[281] reversed the decline in convertible currency exports and, for most of the year, sharply reduced imports.

The rate of growth of Poland's convertible currency exports quickened throughout the year, reaching a rate of nearly 70 per cent in value during the last quarter of 1990. Over the whole year, exports grew at a record pace of 39 per cent, with the vast majority of this increase directed to western markets. Apparently the adverse impact on export growth of a strongly and steadily appreciating real exchange rate was offset by other factors (see section 3.3(ii)).[282]

Poland's convertible currency imports declined by some 24 per cent in the first three quarters of 1990 but then recovered strongly in the last months of the year, bringing the annual growth rate to 4 per cent.[283] The

upturn, due overwhelmingly to stepped-up purchases from the developed market economies, may have been a response to the appreciating exchange rate. Imports from the developing countries, (presumably oil) and oil imports from the Soviet Union (paid for in convertible currency) also surged at the end of the year.

As a result of its success in increasing exports, Poland achieved a $3.8 billion trade surplus in 1990, instead of the expected deficit.[284] The trade surplus would have been even higher save for Gulf-related losses and the costs of switching from Soviet supplies to world market sources.

Although the scale of the adjustment was impressive, the results were not unequivocally positive since imports failed to promote domestic competition and mitigate domestic price increases. In July the authorities temporarily reduced or suspended most import duties (notably on intermediate and investment goods) and lifted certain surcharges on imports in an attempt to encourage competition from imports.[285] The appreciation of the real exchange rate and some relaxation of domestic economic policy may also have contributed to faster import growth towards the end of the year.

The surge in the trade surplus and larger net transfers led to a current account surplus of some $668 million, the first such surplus since the early 1970s. On the capital account, Poland enjoyed a large inflow of finance. Most derives from the rescheduling of official and some commercial obligations,[286] delays in meeting interest payments on commercial debt and drawings upon various bilateral and multilateral credit facilities. The latter include a $720 million (SDR 545 million) IMF standby credit.[287]

Owing to these capital inflows, the country's gross debt rose to over $48 billion at the end of 1990. At the same time, however, these capital inflows and the small current account surplus enabled Poland to add to its foreign currency reserves. Official convertible currency reserves peaked at $5.3 billion in October, but then fell in the next two months. Deposits with BIS reporting banks, which include some official reserves, reached

---

280 Polish imports from the convertible currency area had been expected to rise by at least 13 per cent in 1990. *Rzeczpospolita*, 14 December 1989.

281 These measures included the introduction of internal currency convertibility for current account transactions; a new liberal tariff schedule; the extension of foreign trade rights to all enterprises and the abolition of administrative controls on most trade transactions. In consequence, the activity of private enterprises, many of which are engaged in export-import, has increased rapidly and perceptibly augmented trade flows.

282 Since the nominal exchange rate was maintained throughout the year, high domestic inflation (especially at the end of the year) caused a continuous appreciation of the real exchange rate.

283 Data for the first three quarters of the year concern only the purchases of the state sector. Data on the imports of private enterprises, which were very dynamic importers in 1990, are available solely for the latter part of the year.

284 On a balance of payments basis the surplus was $2.2 billion (see table 3.3.8).

285 Duties on agricultural machinery, pesticides and fodder had already been suspended in March.

286 The relevant component of the February 1990 accord with the Paris Club concerns the postponement of $6 billion in interest and principal falling due from the beginning of 1990 to end-March 1991 (i.e., some $5 billion in 1990 alone). *International Herald Tribune*, 17-18 February 1990. Prior to this, London Club creditors had agreed to reschedule or roll over into a revolving trade credit facility some $200 million of Poland's debt maturing in 1989-1990, but they were unwilling to postpone nearly $1 billion in interest obligations due in 1990. In 1990 Poland made $460 million in interest payments out of $3.9 billion incurred and amortized $306 million.

287 Poland's first, 13-month, arrangement with the IMF was approved in February 1990 and ran until March 1991. Three credit tranches were disbursed, one in each of the first three quarters of 1990. The first amounted to SDR 170 million and the next two to SDR 93.75 million each. However the last, $200 million, tranche, slated for release on 15 November 1990, was postponed because macro-economic targets agreed with the IMF had not been met. *Rzeczpospolita*, 11 September, 1990. New negotiations intended to lead to the disbursement of the last tranche are in progress, but might involve a modification of the government's current financial policy. M. Russo, director of the IMF European Department, as reported in *Trybuna*, 14 January 1991.

$8.1 billion at the end of September. As a result of Poland's improved payments position, the $1 billion stabilization fund, established by the G-24 countries to provide backing for the zloty, did not need to be touched.

After the recent resurgence of inflationary pressures, austerity measures are likely to be reinforced and this is likely to slow any worsening of external imbalances.[288] However, the continued maintenance of the current exchange rate (zl 9,500/$) in the face of accelerating prices has eroded the profitability of exports and has rendered imports more attractive.[289] This contributed to unfavourable export prospects early in 1991[290] and made a devaluation of the currency probable in the coming months. In addition, the continuing terms of trade shock (from the switch to hard currency settlement of CMEA trade) is bound to cause the value of convertible currency imports to increase faster than the value of exports, pushing the country back into current account deficit.

In February, Poland and the IMF signed a draft accord under which credits of some $2 billion will become available over the next three years.[291] The initiating of the agreement was preceded by the Polish Parliament's approval of the budget for 1991 (the cornerstone of the government's anti-inflationary programme) and the elaboration of plans for accelerating the privatization of state companies. Although the details were not immediately available, it appears that the structure of the IMF financial package is similar to that recently approved for Hungary: a three-year extended facility, an element designed to provide compensation for higher oil prices and an external contingency mechanism, to come into force if the oil price rises beyond the level set out in the agreement. Paris Club members have considered the successful conclusion of these talks as a key pre-condition for further progress on the issue of debt reduction.[292]

World Bank funds and bilateral credits assembled within the framework of the PHARE programme will also be available.[293] As in past years, some kind of debt relief will play a central role in Poland's balance of payments financing. For some time the Polish government has been seeking forgiveness of 80 per cent of its external debt[294] (Paris Club and commercial bank claims on Poland have risen to $31.2 billion and $10.7 billion respectively).[295] The authorities argue that only a reduction of this size would give the country's reform programme a real possibility of success. If the debt burden remains, the authorities fear that the balance of payments will be constantly under strain and that foreign investment will be discouraged.

In January 1991, it was reported that G-7 industrial nations had approved the writing off of one third of Poland's official debt, the same reduction as was granted by western governments to the poorest African countries under the Toronto Accord. The proposed relief was to have been conditional upon the successful conclusion of Poland's current talks with the IMF. However subsequent reports indicate a lack of consensus in the Paris Club. Certain members have been prepared to make more substantial write-offs, nearer to the amount requested by Poland,[296] while others favour a much smaller reduction, or in some cases, no reduction at all. Those holding the latter view would prefer to extend new loans to Poland on concessionary terms.

Although Poland's bank creditors may eventually follow the Paris Club's lead, the banks' steering committee was also divided on the Polish debt reduction proposal at its meeting in January.[297] Even those banks willing to consider debt forgiveness remain opposed to any formal discussion of this option until Poland has made up some of its interest arrears, which have

---

288 The trade account slipped into deficit at the end of the year, remaining there in January 1991.

289 A new customs tariff, perhaps somewhat more restrictive than the one in force at the end of 1990 and in early 1991, is to be introduced in the second half of the year. The current import régime (extended beyond the original expiration date of 1 January 1991), is considered by some to be the most liberal in Europe. The incidence of the tariff in the fourth quarter of 1990 has been estimated at only 3.9 per cent *ad valorem*. All the information is based on a statement of the President of the Customs Office, *Rzeczpospolita,* 21 December 1990 and 12 February 1991.

290 Thirty two per cent and 43 per cent of enterprises expect a drop in exports to the west and the east respectively in the first quarter of 1990. *Trybuna,* 28 January 1991. Polish economists also point to the fact that supply side adjustments have been disappointingly slow.

291 *International Herald Tribune,* 25 February 1991.

292 *Trybuna,* 14 January 1991.

293 Poland's access to the $1 billion currency stabilization fund has been extended for another year. The fund could be used at a later stage to finance development projects, at an interest rate of merely 3 per cent.

294 Poland has already benefited from some debt relief on the 1975 DM 1 billion "jumbo credit" of which Germany undertook to cancel DM 760 million ($512 million). A further DM 560 million is to be paid in zloty over a 10-year period into a co-operation fund intended to finance projects agreed by both sides (e.g., infrastructure, youth exchanges, protection of German historical monuments, etc.). *East European Markets,* 16 November 1990. The arrangement was originally proposed in 1989 as part of G-24 initiative.

295 According to D. Kosidlo of the Ministry of Finances, reported in *Trybuna,* 17 January 1991. The largest Paris Club creditors are Germany ($7.8 billion), France ($4.8 billion) and Austria ($3.7 billion).

296 For example, the United States is reported to favour a write-off of near the 80 per cent sought by Poland. The Congress had already authorized the complete liquidation of Poland's $3.5 billion liability to the United States. *Financial Times,* 19 January 1991.

297 One group of commercial banks is willing to accord Poland debt relief, arguing that the new régime should not have to pay the price of ill-judged borrowing during the prior 40 years. Another group, however, maintains that such a policy towards a nation with growth potential would be misguided. In the view of the latter group, a debt write-off could be a dangerous precedent, committing banks to forgive loans to large debtors such as Brazil and Mexico. Instead these banks would opt for further rescheduling of debt. *International Herald Tribune,* 17 January 1991.

climbed to nearly $1 billion since the country suspended payments in the last part of 1989.[298]

Any debt reduction scheme would have to be approved by all members of the Paris and London Clubs and would take time to implement. In addition, the specific terms of the Paris Club debts would have to be negotiated bilaterally.

Although no firm decisions have yet been taken by creditors, it may be of interest to assess the impact of a possible one-third debt write-off on Poland's financial position. The country's liabilities would fall from nearly $49 billion at the end of 1990 to some $32 billion.[299] Annual interest obligations would be reduced by some $1.3 billion, to $2.6 billion, although this amount would presumably have to be settled as a condition for debt relief. Poland's current account would improve, and, even if it remained in deficit, could probably be financed from available facilities.

The country's financial indicators would also improve — the net debt-export and interest payments ratios would fall to 230 and 17 per cent respectively — but Poland would remain in the ranks of heavily-indebted countries. This raises the issue of whether the country would be able to regain creditworthiness and access to the capital market under these conditions. A heavy repayments schedule of the remaining debt could require additional international support measures. However, further rapid export growth — although now an uncertain prospect — could transform the external financial picture in a few years time.

(e) Romania

Since the beginning of 1990, Romanian foreign trade has been in a critical state, characterized by the collapse of industrial output and exports. However, the new government has abandoned the draconian trade policy pursued by its predecessor during the previous decade. In late 1989, with a view to improving supply to domestic markets, the authorities sharply cut food exports and boosted imports of food, consumer goods and various inputs needed for agricultural production.

Exports to the convertible currency area fell by 45 per cent in value in 1990.[300] This was considerably more than the 20 per cent decline in industrial production, which, it might be noted, occurred despite more ample imported inputs from the west.[301] Supply constraints, apparently stemming from disarray in Romanian industry, are likely to account for the bulk of the contraction of exports. Lack of external demand for Romanian goods appears to have been of secondary importance, judging from the fact that a host of contracts with foreign partners were not fulfilled.[302]

Convertible currency *imports* boomed throughout 1990, increasing by 45 per cent in value terms. Romania boosted purchases from the developed market economies by 210 per cent while curtailing imports, mainly of crude oil, from the developing countries. In response to the rapidly deteriorating trade balance, in July the government announced measures to reduce the inflow of imports and curb the depletion of the country's foreign reserves.[303] These trade measures were slow to take effect and may have contributed to the government's decision to devalue the leu at the beginning of November.[304]

Romania posted a $1.7 billion convertible currency *trade* deficit in 1990, in contrast to the large surpluses achieved in previous years ($2.5 billion in 1989).[305] The estimated current account deficit was only slightly larger. In the first half of the year, the current account deficit was financed primarily by drawing down foreign currency reserves, which fell from $1.8 billion at the beginning of the year to only $600 million in December. Romania also obtained $700 million in short-term supplier credits and may have used some of the $300 million in official bilateral credits which was committed by western governments in 1990. Humanitarian aid from the G-24 totalled several hundred million dollars.

Despite expectations of an upturn in output in 1991, the Romanian authorities foresee a further contraction of trade in 1991. The value of exports is to fall by an additional 12 per cent and imports by 26 per cent leaving the trade deficit at $1.6-1.7 billion. Any recovery in the sales of manufactures is extremely uncertain owing to continuing disarray in enterprises. The share of petrochemicals exports is to fall, reflecting the planned down-scaling of the petrochemicals industry. It is to receive fewer imported supplies of crude oil and natural gas as part of a more general contraction of purchases of industrial inputs from its eastern trade partners. Overall, finance will be required to cover another current account deficit of some $1.7 billion in 1991 and $1.4 billion in repayments of maturing short-term trade

---

298 *Financial Times*, 27 February 1991.

299 This of course depends on which countries would agree to reduce debt. Poland has requested relief from all creditor countries, including the Soviet Union.

300 Commission Nationale de la Prèvision du Plan et de la Conjuncture Economique (de la Roumanie), *Variante de Programme Economiqe pour 1991*, January 1991 and 1 February 1991 (the February revision is in Romanian). Hereafter, *Programme Economique*.

301 However, imports from the Soviet Union, chiefly of fuels, and the Middle East declined.

302 The Romanian authorities have estimated that contracts worth $669 million and R1.344 billion were not implemented in 1990 as scheduled. BBC, *Summary of World Broadcasts*. EE/W0160 A/5, 3 January 1991.

303 According to Prime Minister P. Roman, as quoted in *East European Markets*, 27 July 1990.

304 Beginning in February 1990, a single rate for the leu — initially L21/$ — was used, with weekly fixings by the central bank. However, by mid-September the official rate was L19.88/$, which implies a 5 per cent *appreciation* of the currency, opposite of the change needed to curb the growth of the trade deficit. Thus, the role of the exchange rate in economic decision-making at that time is uncertain.

305 *Programme Economique, op.cit.*

credits.[306] These latter obligations financed imports in 1990, and comprise some $700 million borrowed in convertible currencies and an equivalent amount in non-convertible currency, converted to US dollars by agreement.[307]

According to Romanian officials, the country has received backing from the IMF for its economic stabilization and reform programmes.[308] The agreement, which is expected to be announced shortly, includes IMF credits of over $1 billion. Other balance of payments financing is to come from the World Bank ($200 million), official bilateral facilities ($500 million) and various loans amounting to $1,700 million. The latter include credits to finance imports of crude oil in the last quarter of 1991.[309] The governments' financial plan does not appear to provide for much rebuilding of the country's foreign exchange reserves, though the $1 billion credit being assembled by the G-24 may provide some scope for this. Humanitarian aid has been prolonged into 1991.

Romania's trade is likely to be shaped principally by the development of industrial production. Recent reform measures could help to improve trade performance. In the first phase of a two-stage price reform, some internal prices were realigned on 1 November 1990 with, in particular, increases in the prices of energy, raw materials and consumer goods. After consultations with the IMF, the second stage of the price reform is to be moved forward to 1 April 1991 (as opposed to the 1 June date originally foreseen).

The commercial rate for the leu was devalued on the 1 November 1990 from L21/$ to L35/$. A separate non-commercial rate applying to tourist transactions was maintained. From the beginning of 1991 the two rates have been unified at L35/$ (although a parallel market exists where the value of the leu is several times lower). Internal and external prices have been linked to some extent, with the consequence that the devaluation has spurred domestic inflation.

From 1 November 1990 enterprises have been entitled to retain a maximum of 30 per cent of convertible currency receipts from exports of goods and services for the purpose of importing and settling certain other foreign business transactions. The ceiling was raised to 50 per cent in January 1991. An amendment to the law governing the retention accounts is envisaged, to curtail

enterprises' use of foreign exchange for the importation of consumer durables. The National Bank of Romania is to commence convertible currency auctions for commercial banks, including branches of foreign banks (enterprises will be entitled to buy currency directly from the banks). This implies the emergence of a second (market) exchange rate, in addition to the official rate.

Romania has instituted an automatic import licencing system, which applies to enterprises using their own convertible currency funds to import. A licence is now only required if a centralized credit allocation is sought. Export licences will be required for certain goods in order to ensure domestic supply. Since February 1990, industrial centres (production associations) and co-operatives have been given the right to conduct foreign trade and a new more liberal foreign investment law has also been adopted.

(f) Soviet Union

During the course of 1990, the Soviet Union's trade account came under intense strain and its external financial position deteriorated drastically. Although export receipts were buoyed by the rise in fuel prices in the second half of the year, imports of western goods had to be scaled back, despite mounting internal needs.

For most of the 1980s the Soviet Union pursued a conservative policy in trade and payments with the west. This was reflected in a nearly flat level of net indebtedness[310] and a reputation for prompt payments. More recently, the deterioration of the Soviet economy, with domestic shortages increasing, has prompted a more expansionary policy toward imports and indebtedness. At the same time, enterprises have been exercising their foreign trade and borrowing rights to a greater extent, making the country's overall foreign borrowing more difficult to control.

According to national statistics, the value of Soviet imports increased by some 46 per cent in 1988-1989 which, accompanied by flagging exports, led to a trade deficit with the west of over $6 billion in 1989. As a result, the net debt of the Soviet Union *vis-à-vis* western financial institutions increased by some $12-13 billion during 1988-1989,[311] mainly in the form of non-guaranteed commercial bank credits.

---

306 *Programme Economique, op.cit.* Romania will also incur penalties in convertible currencies if it does not make up large arrears in honouring contracts made previously on a clearing basis, especially those with eastern Europe and the Soviet Union. BBC, *Summary of World Broadcasts*, EE/0968 B/8, 11 January 1991.

307 The repayment concerns a trade credit, initially denominated in trade roubles, extended by eastern trade partners, principally the Soviet Union, to cover Romania's R1.6 billion trade deficit in 1990. By agreement it has been transformed into a convertible currency debt at the rate of TR1/$ roughly half of which is due in 1991 and the balance in 1992.

308 Direct communication to the ECE secretariat.

309 *Programme Economique, op.cit.* Apparently, the Romanian authorities will exercise caution regarding the raising of financial credits because of the "country's as yet unimproved political image abroad", uncertain economic prospects and the country's long absence from the credit market. Statement of M. Isarescu, Governor of the National Bank, published in *Adevarul* as reported by Rompres in English. BBC, *Summary of World Broadcasts*, EE/W0156 A/4, 29 November 1990.

310 On this point see United Nations Economic Commission for Europe, *Economic Bulletin for Europe*, vol.41, New York, 1989, p.45. Although the Soviet Union's net indebtedness, measured in US dollars, rose sharply in the mid-1980s, there was little change if exchange rate realignments are removed.

311 See United Nations Economic Commission for Europe, *Economic Survey of Europe in 1989-1990*, New York, 1990, p.211. These data are adjusted for exchange rate movements.

TABLE 3.3.15

USSR: Balance of payments in convertible currencies: scenarios for 1991
(Billion US dollars)

		Base scenario			Alternative scenario		
			of which:			of which:	
	1990 [a]	Total	Convertible currency area	CMEA area	Total	Convertible currency area	CMEA area
Trade balance	-5.7	5.4	-4.1	11.1	-3.6	-8.7	7.8
Service balance	-5.0	-7.2	-6.0	-1.2	-7.2	-6.0	-1.2
Current account balance (excluding gold)	-10.7	-1.8	-10.1	9.9	-10.9	-14.7	6.6
Current account balance (including gold)	-7.1	1.7	-6.5	9.9	-7.3	-11.1	6.6
Capital account net	-7.2	..	-11.0	..	..	-11.0	..
Overall balance	-14.3	..	-17.5	..	..	-22.1	..
Arrears	-	-5.0	-5.0	-	-5.0	-5.0	-
Financing requirements	..	..	22.5	..	..	27.1	..
of which:							
Identified financing	..	..	16.9	..	..	16.9	..

Source: Houston Four Report, op.cit.

Note: The balance of payments is broken down by the traditional convertible currency area, CMEA area (excluding the former German Democratic Republic) and countries with which the USSR had bilateral payments agreements in 1990 (which is not shown separately), although a large part of trade with the latter two areas will also be conducted in convertible currencies in 1991.

a Projections.

These trends continued in the first half of 1990. The value of exports stagnated, but imports, led by consumer and engineering goods, rose by 19 per cent. As a result, the Soviet Union posted a record half-year trade deficit with the west of over $6 billion. However, there was a dramatic improvement in the second half of the year, thanks mainly to the upturn in export revenues. Deliveries of petroleum products recovered, those of natural gas continued at a rapid pace and international oil prices shot up. However, persistent financing difficulties prompted the authorities to reduce imports from the west by $1-2 billion in the last six months of the year. As a consequence, the trade account with the west swung into surplus — a convertible currency surplus of $4 billion was achieved in the second half of 1990 — and the overall convertible currency trade deficit for the year as a whole was restricted to about $1 billion.

None the less these financial tensions had at least two major lasting consequences; firstly, reports of widespread delays in Soviet repayment of short-term supplier credits began to surface in March 1990,[312] although Vneshekonombank continued to service its obligations punctually. The Soviet authorities took several steps to clear the arrears: efforts were made to boost exports to the convertible currency area; newly-granted western government credits were drawn on (some were specifically extended by western governments to facilitate repayments to their own companies)[313]; a credit of $1 billion was raised against future deliveries of diamonds[314] and gold was sold and swapped for short-term credits. In spite of all these measures and higher oil revenues in the second half of the year, payments arrears still amounted to some $5 billion at the end of 1990.[315]

Another consequence was that western banks have become concerned about the creditworthiness of the Soviet Union; this led to a withdrawal of inter-bank deposits (short-term credits). BIS data show that international banks reduced their exposure *vis-à-vis* the Soviet Union by nearly $5 billion in the second quarter of 1990 (see section 3.3(iii)).[316] This liquidity squeeze undoubtedly exacerbated the arrears problem.

Bankers are now pointing to the Soviet Union's bleak economic prospects, the (perceived) uncertain direction of economic and political reform and the ap-

---

312 One explanation for this lapse in Soviet financial practices centres on economic reforms. In the ensuing decentralization of foreign borrowing, individual enterprises and ministries managed to obtain loans, but lacked the guarantee of Vneshekonombank. Many western suppliers were willing to extend non-guaranteed credits to Soviet enterprises because of the country's previous excellent payments record. In mid-summer, the then Deputy Prime Minister, S. Sitarian, Chairman of the State Commission for Foreign Economic Relations, warned western creditors to evaluate risks of lending to Soviet enterprises more carefully, however difficult that might be under present accounting practices, prices, etc. The stereotype of the Soviet organization, backed in all cases by the government, was no longer valid and western firms would have to build up the same kind of financial relations with Soviet enterprises as prevailed among themselves. *Izvestiya,* 22 May 1990. Beyond these technical problems, it should be noted that the Soviet Union's overall financial situation came under increasing strain since the government had increasingly resorted to large scale imports to meet pressing internal needs.

313 For example, the Soviet Union is reported to have immediately drawn down the DM 5 billion loan extended in June in order to settle payments arrears to German suppliers. *Financial Times,* 13 September 1990.

314 DeBeers Centenary and Glavalmazzoloto, the Soviet precious metal and diamond sale agency, reached agreement on a $1 billion 5-year credit to the Soviet Union which carries commercial rates of interest. DeBeers accepted uncut diamonds as collateral for the loan. Repayments will be in diamonds and were slated to begin in November 1990. As a part of the deal, which may be worth some $5 billion, the Soviet Union has agreed to sell its rough diamonds through DeBeers Central Selling Organization for a period of five years with hopes of obtaining higher prices for its diamonds. *International Herald Tribune,* 27 July 1990; *East-West (Fortnightly Bulletin),* 31 July 1990, p.7.

315 *Houston Four Report, op.cit.*

316 The *Houston Four Report, op.cit.* gives a higher, $7 billion, estimate of net withdrawals by international banks.

parent lack of a clear plan for making constructive use of western funds[317] as factors which deter them from further lending to the Soviet Union. As a result, banks have been prepared to make loans to the Soviet Union only if these loans are guaranteed by western governments. Recognizing the severe financing constraints facing the Soviet Union, western and other governments backed some $17 billion in new credit lines in 1990.

In 1990, the Soviet Union's financing requirement in convertible currencies is likely to have exceeded $11 billion, which reflects a $7 billion current account deficit vis-à-vis the developed market economies[318] and settlement of nearly $5 billion in withdrawn inter-bank credits. Financing comprised gold sales of some $3 billion, payments arrears of $5 billion, various credits bearing western government guarantees, and swap arrangements.

Despite its difficult financial situation, the Soviet Union is estimated to have extended some R10 billion in new credits to support its exports of goods and various services.[319] This will further raise its claims on partner countries (these amounted to R85.8 billion on 1 November 1989 − $143.3 billion at the official exchange rate of $1.67 per rouble).[320] Given the situation of the debtor countries, few of these resources appear to be recoverable in the foreseeable future. This assessment appears to be supported by the minimal debt service inflows − R500 million in cash and R1 billion in goods − expected by the Soviet authorities in 1991.[321]

In the light of the precarious condition of the Soviet economy (see section 2.2), the prospects for trade and payments are necessarily highly uncertain. In these circumstances, it may be more useful to examine the scenarios for Soviet trade and payments which were elaborated by the Houston Four in collaboration with the Soviet authorities, and then comment on them in the light of recent developments.

The two scenarios for 1991, set out in table 3.3.15, both reflect the switch to world market pricing and convertible currency settlements. Soviet transactions with the traditional convertible currency area and CMEA countries are treated separately. The two scenarios differ chiefly in the underlying assumptions concerning oil prices and the volume of Soviet oil exports.

Assumptions common to both scenarios are (with the secretariat's comments in brackets):

− a fall in Soviet manufactured goods exports, particularly to the CMEA area;

− a 7 per cent decline in the volume of Soviet imports (This assumes continuing foreign exchange constraints and a drop in purchases of machinery and equipment, in line with the expected contraction of domestic investment; however, some growth of imports of food and consumer durables is foreseen.);

− no further drop in inter-bank deposits and official foreign exchange reserves (Soviet reserves, reported by the Houston Four to be down to $5 billion at the end of 1990, are already inadequate.);

− gold sales of some $3.6 billion (This corresponds to sales of some 300 tons during the year, in line with recent practice. Although the Soviet Union is believed to have large gold stocks, accelerated disposal might drive down the world price, already at a four-month low of $365 per ounce in February.);

− repayment of $5 billion in arrears;

− amortization of medium- and long-term debt amounting to $11-12 billion;

− availability of $16.9 billion in identified financing, comprising chiefly of western government-backed credits.

The base scenario assumes an average oil price of $26 per barrel in 1991 and a 17 per cent decline in the exports of crude oil and petroleum products compared with 1990. (The latter implies a fall in oil and petroleum products exports of some 29 million tons in 1991.) Under this scenario, a financing gap vis-à-vis the traditional convertible currency area of nearly $5.6 billion would arise (i.e., a financing requirement of $22.5 billion less identified financing of $16.9 billion).[322] However, this could be more than filled by the prospective surplus vis-à-vis the CMEA of $9.9 billion, provided that these countries in turn can obtain the necessary financing.

---

[317] See, for example, the comments of Hilmar Kopper, chief executive of Deutsche Bank. The bank envisages no new loans to the Soviet Union unless 100 per cent backed by the German government. Financial Times, 15 January 1991. See also A. Lebahn, Financial Times, 28 November 1990.

[318] It should be noted that the $4 billion current account deficit estimated for the Soviet Union (table 3.3.8) incorporates a $4 billion trade surplus with the developing countries. However, since a share of Soviet exports to that area is financed by long-term trade credits, and, in consequence, yields little immediate cash, the trade surplus cannot be used to offset deficits elsewhere. The Soviet Union's $7 billion current account deficit with the developed market economies, reflecting a trade deficit with these countries of $5 billion, is subject to immediate settlement. It might be noted that the Soviet Union's trade with the market economies, the secretariat's proxy measure for convertible currency transactions, understates the country's actual convertible currency earnings since it does not reflect the socialist countries' payment of hard currency to the Soviet Union for their oil imports.

[319] Ekonomika i zhizn', No.29, July 1990; Izvestiya, 3 December 1990. The Soviet Union intends to provide a further R8 billion in new credits in 1991.

[320] Izvestiya, 1 March 1990, p.3.

[321] Ekonomika i zhizn', No.29 July 1990 and Izvestiya, 3 December 1990.

[322] ECE estimates of bilateral credit commitments made to the Soviet Union since early 1990 total over $22 billion, but it is likely that only $15-17 billion of this will be available for use in 1991 and beyond (see section 3.3(vi)).

The low export scenario assumes an average oil price of $20 per barrel in 1991 and a 25 per cent decline in the exports of crude oil and oil products (i.e., a decline of some 43 million tons in 1991). Under this scenario, the financing gap *vis-à-vis* the traditional convertible currency area nearly doubles to $10.2 billion (a financing requirement of $27.1 billion less identified financing of $16.9 billion). This, however, exceeds the expected $6.6 billion surplus *vis-à-vis* the CMEA countries which leaves the Soviet Union with an overall financing deficit.

Currently, the world market price of oil is some $18 per barrel and the outlook is for the price to remain below $20 per barrel (see section 3.1) before recovery begins towards a higher long-term equilibrium price. Soviet oil export appears set to contract very sharply in 1991 as the fall in oil output has quickened recently. It is estimated that exports of crude oil under the competence of the central authorities are to be reduced to some 60 million tons, from the roughly 120 million tons exported in 1990 (see section 3.3(iv). Reacting to the critical situation in the oil industry, in February the Soviet government agreed on emergency measures to stem any further contraction of production, the centrepiece being the provision of R25 billion of additional investment funds.[323] However, given the multitude of problems besetting the industry, it is unclear how long it will take to see real results.

On the financial side, questions have recently been posed about the firmness of the bilateral credit pledges to the Soviet Union.[324] As discussed elsewhere (see section 3.3(vi)), this issue has resurfaced because of questions in the west about the direction of political events and economic policy in the Soviet Union. These same concerns have been voiced by the business and financial communities, which could further endanger both the rolling over of short-term interbank deposits and the willingness to invest in the Soviet Union. More positively, it now appears that the east European countries will have access to sufficient financing to cover their current account deficits, including the component arising from exchanges with the Soviet Union. Thus the Soviet Union will benefit indirectly from IMF and other western financial assistance to eastern Europe.

In summary, given current world oil prices and output trends in the oil industry, the outlook for Soviet trade and payments would appear to be consistent with (or even worse than) the gloomy *low exports scenario*. If this is the case, imports will have to be cut by considerably more than the assumed 7 per cent. As noted in section 3.2, several eastern countries have reported sharper-than-expected falls in their sales to the Soviet Union in early 1991. It is not clear whether this is due to the teething troubles of the new trade and payments system (including of the new Joint Union-Republican Fund)[325] or whether it reflects an overall shortage of convertible currency in the Soviet Union.

(vi) Western support for eastern transformation

In 1990, financial support for eastern transformation, notably as for the solution of eastern balance of payments problems, emerged as one of the key tasks for international economic co-operation.[326] It will remain an important issue with respect to most eastern countries in 1991. In this section, the responses of the the Group of 24 (G-24)[327] and the international financial organizations to actual and prospective financing gaps are discussed separately for eastern Europe and the Soviet Union.

(a) Eastern Europe

In 1990 the focus of international assistance for eastern Europe shifted to meeting the area's prospective needs for balance of payments financing. However, other aid initiatives moved forward.

− The action plan of the G-24,[328] originally conceived in July 1989 to provide backing for economic reforms in Hungary and Poland, was extended to all east European countries in 1990. At that time, actions in favour of Romania were temporarily suspended. In January 1991 Romania qualified for G-24 assistance:

− within the framework of the western support, the east European countries were given greater access to most G-24 members' markets where they now generally benefit from GSP and larger quotas; improved market access provided real benefits to Hungary and Poland in 1990, and was particularly important as their traditional eastern markets collapsed (see section 3.3(ii));

---

323 Details of the emergency package, decided by the Cabinet of Ministers, were revealed in an interview with V. Kuramin, deputy chairman of the Bureau for the Fuel and Energy Complex. *Financial Times*, 21 February 1991. As an incentive, oil production associations will be able to retain up to 70 per cent of the export earnings from any oil they produce above the level of state orders.

324 For example, see *Financial Times*, 31 January 1991.

325 The Joint Union-Republican Fund was established by a recent presidential decree to provide a basis for the management of the portion of foreign exchange surrendered by exporters. Among other things, the fund is intended to service outstanding and future debts of the Soviet Union. In 1991, 40 per cent of export earnings proceeds are to be used in this manner.

326 This section updates and complements the section entitled "Western support for eastern transition" in United Nations Economic Commission for Europe, *Economic Bulletin for Europe*, vol.42/90, New York, 1991 and "International initiative in support of eastern reforms", in *Economic Survey of Europe in 1989-1990*, New York, 1990.

327 The Group of 24 are the G-7, the other members of the EC, the EFTA countries, plus Turkey, New Zealand and Australia.

328 The action plan of the G-24 includes PHARE, the contribution of the European Community. PHARE stands for "Pologne/Hongrie: Assistance à la restructuration économique".

− numerous G-24 programmes supplying a broad range of technical assistance to the eastern participants have gathered pace. In general, they have been funded by grants, among which are the EC's ECU 500 million commitment for 1990 (of which 40 per cent has been paid out) and ECU 820 million for 1991;[329]

− humanitarian assistance has been provided, initially only to Poland, but more recently to Bulgaria and Romania as well. In a new initiative, the EC is preparing an ECU 100 million package of food and medical aid,[330] in accordance with the decision reached in principle by the Rome II Summit in December 1990. An allocation of 60-40 in favour of Romania and Bulgaria, respectively, is under consideration;[331]

− in 1990, the G-24 and the international financial institutions met the pressing balance of payments needs of Hungary and Poland with new official credits. In the case of Poland, the rescheduling of obligations provided crucial relief from a heavy debt service burden;

− negotiations between EC and Czechoslovakia, Hungary and Poland opened on the new "European Agreements". The objectives of these negotiations are very broad, aiming at establishing an industrial free trade system, harmonizing legislation, developing economic, financial, and cultural co-operation, including through the establishment of institutions of co-operation. The agreements, the contents of which are likely to vary between countries, also envisage regular political dialogue.[332] All parties have agreed to continue negotiations as quickly as possible so that the agreements can be put into force on 1 January 1992.[333] The co-operation agreement between EC and Romania, the last of the "second generation" accords to be completed, was ratified in March 1991.[334] Also in the area of bilateral relations, the United States signed trade agreements with Bulgaria and Czechoslovakia, which in conjunction with changes in Czechoslovakia's legislation on emigration set the stage for the restoration of MFN treatment.

While balance of payments financing for the reforming countries has been a key element PHARE programme from its incipiency, it acquired special prominence during the course of 1990. As a conse-quence of the decision to replace the CMEA trade and payments régime with a system based on world market pricing and convertible currencies in 1991 (compounded by the repercussions of the Gulf crisis) the east European countries were expected to suffer large current account deficits in 1991 (section 3.3(v)). Studies undertaken last year suggested that the financial resources which were likely to be available to the east European countries in 1991 would fall significantly short of requirements.[335]

Subsequent steps taken by the Bretton Woods organizations, the G-24 and various bilateral creditors appear to have ensured sufficient financial resources for eastern Europe.

Given their great need for financial assistance, it has been fortunate that all east European countries have become members of the IMF. Bulgaria and Czechoslovakia joined only in September 1990. Accordingly, they were entitled to standby or extended fund facilities, once their stabilization and reform programmes were approved by the Fund. Moreover, with a view to providing additional support for member countries seriously affected by the Gulf crisis, in November 1990 the IMF introduced two important extentions of the compensatory and contingency financing facility (CCFF).

Firstly, a temporary oil import element to be in effect through end-1991 is intended to cover the increased costs of imported crude oil, petroleum products and natural gas. Access is up to 82 per cent of quota. Benefiting members are required to undertake satisfactory energy policy actions, implementation of which partially determines the disbursement of funds.

Secondly, expansion of coverage of the facility to shortfalls in receipts from various services (e.g., pipelines, canals, shipping, transportation, construction, and insurance). Initially only losses in workers' remittances and tourist revenues were compensated under this facility.

Agreements concluded by Bulgaria, Czechoslovakia, Hungary, and Poland since the beginning of 1991 incorporate both elements, in part applied retroactively, to compensate for higher oil prices incurred in 1990 (see table 3.3.13 and section 3.3(v)). It may be noted that the recent accords are still based upon existing quotas − the new, 50 per cent-higher quotas still need to be ratified by member governments.

The World Bank has committed project loans for the current year and is in the process of discussing

---

[329] *Europe*, 31 January 1991.

[330] *Europe*, 9 February 1991.

[331] *Europe*, 6 February 1991.

[332] See EC, *Association Agreements with the Countries of Central and Eastern Europe: A General Outline*, Brussels, September 1990.

[333] *Europe*, 29 December 1990.

[334] *Europe*, 9 February 1991.

[335] For example, see United Nations Economic Commission for Europe, *Economic Bulletin for Europe*, vol.42/90, New York, 1991, chapter 3. EC, *External Financing Requirements of the Countries of Central and Eastern Europe and the Potential Need for Complementary Financial Support*, Brussels, 15 October 1990.

structural adjustment loans with all eastern countries. Announced credits amount to over $2 billion.

Separately, the east European countries have requested financial support for their reform programmes from the G-24, generally for the build-up of foreign currency reserves. Assembly of the $1 billion requested by Czechoslovakia is the furthest advanced. In addition to the $500 million contributed by the EC, Japan is to provide $200 million. Arab oil producing countries also intend to participate in this action. Loans of $1 billion for Romania and $800 million for Bulgaria are in the preparatory stage,[336] and a $500 million loan requested by Hungary to cushion oil shocks is being acted upon.[337] In each case, EC participation is one-half of the target figure. In order to prevent oil supply shortages in Bulgaria and Romania, the EC has examined the possibility of intervening with additional funds.[338]

As an independent action, the EC has extended a $1 billion (ECU 870 million) medium-term loan to Hungary, of which ECU 350 million was made available in 1990. The second, ECU 260 million, tranche was disbursed in the first quarter of 1991 to help Hungary meet a high concentration of obligations. The third and final tranche is to be released in the spring when repayments are to continue at a high level.

EC finance ministers have approved extension of European Investment Bank (EIB) financing to Bulgaria, Czechoslovakia and Romania.[339] Up to ECU 700 million in loans will be available for a period of two years. The loans are to be guaranteed from the EC budget, as has also been the case with similar facilities established earlier for Hungary and Poland.[340]

Acting individually, western governments have opened new bilateral credit lines for east European countries.

In addition to providing needed financial resources for 1991, the international financial organizations and G-24 members have provided valuable technical expertise toward the design of stabilization and reform programmes. Moreover, the whole process of reform has received impetus from the fact that IMF approval of the national programmes is a condition for the disbursement of virtually all assistance funds. Given the

sacrifices which populations are asked to make during the implementation of the programmes, such an incentive is often decisive. However, the strict application of conditionality has meant that Bulgaria and Romania – which have had difficulties in formulating their programmes – have until recently been eligible only for humanitarian aid.

(b) Soviet Union

In 1990 international assistance to the Soviet Union was motivated by the emergence of severe financial difficulties (section 3.3(v)) and domestic shortages, particularly of foodstuffs. The country's financial options have been very limited since it is not a member of international financial institutions[341] and is not included in PHARE. Unable to tap private credit sources since at least the middle of 1990, it has relied entirely on official bilateral arrangements.

In general, western countries have sought to support the economic and political reforms in the Soviet Union. During 1990 the international response to the Soviet Union's predicament was threefold. The Houston Summit of seven leading industrial countries (G-7) charged four organizations with preparing a study on the Soviet economy.[342] This approach was motivated in part by some evidence that local food shortages were often due to distribution and transportion problems rather than to global shortages and, thus, that large-scale aid might not be efficiently absorbed. The study was to identify basic problems and make proposals for lasting solutions. In the meantime interested countries would provide emergency food and financial assistance to the Soviet Union on an individual basis.

In response to requests by the Soviet authorities, several countries and the EC offered emergency food and other assistance, in the form of either foodstuffs or credits.[343] Germany provided the largest amount, $338 million worth of food. As of 1 January 1991, the Soviet Union received some 26,000 tons of humanitarian aid, including 14,000 tons of foodstuffs, 522 tons of medicine, 72 tons of medical equipment and 211 tons of clothes.[344] In a further action in support of economic reforms in the Soviet Union, the EC decided at the Rome II Summit in December 1990 to adopt guidelines

---

336 *Europe*, 30 January 1991.

337 *Europe*, 1 February 1991.

338 *Europe*, 26 January 1991.

339 *Financial Times*, 26 February 1991.

340 *Financial Times*, 8 February 1991. The two-year limit for loans has been set to prevent overlap with the activities of the EBRD, by which time the EBRD will be fully operational.

341 The Soviet Union is a founding member of the European Bank for Reconstruction and Development, but its scope for borrowing will be limited to its contributions to the bank's capital.

342 Soviet participation in the study was one of the pre-conditions for the possible extension large-scale international assistance. See *Houston Four Report, op.cit.* The four participating organizations conclude that in the near term three types of aid for the Soviet Union would be justified: food aid, technical assistance, and limited project assistance (particularly in the energy area).

343 For example, in anticipation of a harsh winter, the Soviet authorities provided to western nations a list of urgently needed food, drugs and medical equipment worth some R2.2 billion. The list was given by Mr. Y. Kvitsinsky, Deputy Foreign Minister, to Mr. J. Delors on 3 December 1990. *Izvestiya*, 7 December 1990.

344 Report of USSR Goskomstat, *Ekonomika i Zhizh'*, No.5, January 1990.

concerning food aid worth up to ECU 750 million ($1 billion). Of this, ECU 250 million is in the form of gifts under the 1990 farm budget and ECU 500 million in medium-term loan guarantees. The conditions attached to the aid are that it actually reaches those for whom it is intended and does not jeopardize the advance toward the provision of supplies in accordance with market rules.

During the second half of 1990 and early 1991 various countries announced some $22 billion in *bilateral credits* and other financial assistance for the Soviet Union (table 3.3.16). These are chiefly government to government loans or, since purely commercial bank financing was no longer available to the country, bank loans carrying government guarantees. They constitute a mixture of traditional bilateral trade credits (including finance for food purchases), loans to enable the Soviet Union to repay arrears to the creditor country's enterprises, as well as untied credits available for balance of payments support. It is likely that not more than $15-17 billion remain available for use in 1991 and beyond. Some of the loans were drawn down almost immediately after disbursement last year to make up payments arrears (e.g., the DM 5 billion German credit extended in June). Use of other credits is often constrained by creditors to the purchase of certain types of goods or spread over several years. Creditors have not made disbursement of bilateral credits to the Soviet Union conditional upon implementation of a specific stabilization programme or economic reforms, as has been their policy toward eastern Europe.

In keeping with the recommendations of the *Houston Four Report*, the EC decided at the Rome II Summit to provide technical assistance worth some ECU 400 million in 1991 to help the Soviet Union mobilize its own resources to overcome pressing internal problems. Assistance is to be advanced in the fields of public and private management, financial services, energy, transport and foodstuffs distribution. The EC's level of support in 1992 remains to be determined.

Limited but important progress was achieved in the development of the Soviet Union's international institutional relations. This reflects the growing interest of the Soviet Union in adhering to the international economic organizations, its stated intentions to move toward a market system and currency convertibility,[345] and the overall improvement in the international political climate.

The Soviet Union obtained observer status in the GATT in May 1990.[346] More recently it has been proposed that it be granted a special associate status in the IMF and the World Bank.[347] While this scheme would not give the Soviet Union immediate access to their credit facilities, the country could benefit from various services provided by these organizations: a broad range of technical assistance, co-ordination of technical and financial assistance currently available to the Soviet Union, annual reviews of the Soviet economy and the establishment of permanent offices in Moscow.

On a bilateral level, the Soviet Union and the United States concluded a new trade agreement in 1990. The Soviet Union will gain permanent access to MFN benefits provided it changes its laws on the transborder movement of individuals.[348] Given the low level and commodity structure of United States imports from the Soviet Union, the impact of MFN would be small. However, the normalization of trade relations which MFN status signifies would be of great political significance. Separately, the US authorities have empowered the Commodity Credit Corporation and the Export-Import Bank to guarantee credits to the Soviet Union.[349] At the Rome II Summit, the EC decided to explore the idea of a major agreement with the Soviet Union, comprising *inter alia* political dialogue and covering all aspects of greater economic co-operation.[350] A first exchange of views was initially set for end-January, within the EEC-USSR joint committee which manages the co-operation agreement currently in force.

In the past few months there has been some interruption in the development of these relations. Following the events in the Baltic Republics and questions about the future of economic reform in the Soviet Union, certain initiatives have been put on hold. At the the G-7 meeting in January, there was an indication that the question of granting special associate status for the Soviet Union in the IMF and the IBRD had been suspended, as had all discussions between the Soviet Union and the World Bank concerning technical assistance. As regards relations with the EC, the already-scheduled session of the EEC-USSR joint committee on prospects for an enlarged global agreement was postponed[351] and the EC decided to slow down its planned technical assistance programme. Preparation of the food and food credit action was halted, although it has since been relaunched. Also the firmness of the bilateral financial commitments to the

---

345 For example, see "USSR ready to join IMF and World Bank", *ECOTASS*, 28 January 1991.

346 Observer status gives the Soviet Union only limited access to GATT activities. It will have the right to be present and speak (but not to vote) at meetings of the GATT Council and Contracting Parties, but it can attend meetings of other GATT standing bodies only by invitation. It cannot participate in the current Uruguay Round of trade negotiations.

347 The United States has proposed a special associate membership status which could be later upgraded to full membership.

348 US withdrew the Soviet Union's MFN privileges in 1951.

349 President G. Bush announced that he would propose a temporary waiver of the Jackson/Vanik Amendment, which would pave the way for US financial assistance.

350 The Rome II Summit defined four major areas for co-operation: a global co-operation agreement technical assistance, provision of agricultural products, and credit guarantees for agricultural exports.

351 *Europe*, 9 February 1991.

TABLE 3.3.16

Bilateral credit commitments to the Soviet Union

Date announced	Creditor	Amount in local currency	Amount in million US dollars	Comments
In progress	EC	ECU 500 million	$680	Credit guarantees to finance purchases of foodstuffs
January 1991	Kuwait	–	$1,000	Seven-year credit from Kuwait Foreign Trading Company to Vneshekonobank
December 1990	South Korea	–	$3,000	Credits and guarantees over three years; part of credit is earmarked for exports of Korean consumer goods and equipment
	Gulf Co-operation Council	–	$4,000	Soft loans for restructuring the Soviet economy and emergency relief. Assistance will be negotiated bilaterally with the members, Bahrain, Saudi Arabia, Kuwait, Oman, Qatar and United Arab Emirates
	Australia	A$525 million	$410	Revolving credit for wool and other commodities, guaranteed by EFIC. Total includes A$125 for purchase of Australian wheat
	Canada	C$500 million	$430	To be granted via Export Development Corporation for purchase of Canadian equipment
	Austria	SCH4 billion	$370	Medium-term guaranteed credit for purchase of Austrian food, consumer goods and raw materials
	United States	$1 billion	$1,000	Credit guarantees through the Commodity Credit Corporation for purchases of American agricultural products. Part of the facility will be used by the USSR to meet its obligations for previous grain purchases
	United States	$300 million	$300	Export-import bank is to provide insurance and loan guarantees for US corporations
	Japan	-	$100	To finance the export of Japanese goods
November	France	FF5 billion	$1,000	Part will go to settle arrears to French companies, the remainder to finance exports of agricultural products and chemicals
	Spain	-	$1,500	Guaranteed credit to finance sales of Spanish equipment and consumer goods
October	Turkey	-	$350	Credit to finance Turkish construction projects in the Soviet Union
	Germany	DM3 billion	$1,975	Loan stipulated in Treaty.a The first, DM2 billion, tranche was released in October 1990; The second DM 1 billion tranche is to be disbursed in October 1991.
	Italy	L3,200	$2,880	$880 million is to settle arrears to Italian companies; $1 billion is for export credit guarantees and $880 million is for export insurance
July	Germany	DM5 billion	$3,00	Deutsche Bank; 12-year credit, 90 per cent guaranteed by the German Government. Most was drawn immediately, to settle arrears to German suppliers
Uncertain	Japan	Y52 billion	$390	Through export-import bank to finance the purchase of Japanese foodstuffs (in discussion phase)
	Portugal	E10 billion	$75	To finance Portuguese exports
		Total	$22,380	

Source: Press Reports; Business International, *Business Eastern Europe,* 28 January 1991 and previous issues.

a See *Abkommen Zwischen der Regierung der Bundesrepublik Deutschland und der Regierung der Union der Sozialistischen Sowjetrepubliken über einige überleitende Massnahmen,* Press- und Informationsamt der Bundesregierung, *Bulletin,* No.123/S.1281, 17 October 1990, Bonn. The agreement also calls for Germany to provide DM 12 billion in subsistence to the Soviet Union, including a grant of DM 3 billion, to be distributed through 1994 during the repatriation of Soviet troops from the former German Democratic Republic. This assistance is not reflected above.

Soviet Union has been questioned (table 3.3.16).[352] However, it might be noted that these credits have been extended by market economies, at least in part, for domestic considerations. As the growth of the western economies slows down, the authorities will come under greater pressure to promote exports, including through the extension of credits.

The Soviet Union remains entirely dependant upon official or officially-backed credits. Despite the present high level of international commitments, it appears that the country will experience a significant financing gap this year (see section 3.3(v)). It is uncertain whether additional facilities will be forthcoming, as the announcements of new large credits appear to have slowed down since the beginning of 1991. Among other issues, there is the question of the scale of the foreign resources required − the Soviet Union's current needs seem to be very large − as well as that of the capacity of the country to absorb these resources efficiently.

---

352 For example, see *Financial Times*, 10 January 1991.

Chapter 4

THE HARD ROAD TO THE MARKET ECONOMY: PROBLEMS AND POLICIES

This chapter offers first a framework for viewing the reform processes as a whole (sections 4.1-4.2). The four subsequent sections survey the status of reforms in the various countries of the region within this framework.[353]

4.1 CONDITIONS FOR ECONOMIC TRANSITION

In the last eighteen months, the countries of eastern Europe and the Soviet Union have passed through an unprecedented wave of political and institutional changes. Perhaps the most fundamental "revolution" in these countries has been the rapid erosion of the dominant role of the Communist Party. Of course, the dominance of the Communist Party was not confined solely to the political process or economic management, but extended throughout society into the life of virtually every citizen. As Kornai has so passionately stressed,[354] the economies in transition face unusual circumstances at the outset of their transformation efforts. For decades the sovereignty of the individual, respect for the rule of law and political, intellectual and business freedoms were all subordinated to the needs of the ruling party. The wider social effects of over forty years of such single party rule will not disappear overnight. This means that, even in a study restricted to the economics of transition to a market economy, it is impossible to limit the enquiry solely to the economic analysis. Political, ethical and emotional questions are inextricably intertwined with purely economic issues.

The ever increasing flow of western advice to reformers in eastern Europe and the Soviet Union has tended to gloss over the political difficulties of agreeing on an agenda for rapid social change. Even in societies with well established democratic institutions, agreeing on proposals for relatively minor changes can be a tortuous process. In countries where pluralistic political structures have only just been re-established and there

are demands for radical change across the whole of society, it will be even more difficult to attain a reasonable degree of social consensus.

The first part of this chapter (4.1) therefore examines the political and social background to transition in eastern Europe and the Soviet Union and stresses the need to build a social consensus in favour of the shift to the market economy. Without such broad support, the prospects for any sustained change are slight. The second part of the chapter (4.2) outlines the necessary and sufficient conditions for quickly establishing the basis of a market economy and discusses the scope of the most urgent economic reforms (sections (i)-(iv)). In conclusion it sets outs a possible sequence for reform (section (v)). The last four parts (4.3-4.6) detail the experiences and immediate prospects for reform in the different countries.

The transition to the market economy will inevitably involve painful changes. Any foreseeable level of foreign assistance will only be able to reduce this burden slightly, so that the costs of the transition will mainly have to be absorbed by the peoples themselves.

What is more, there is no guarantee that the reforms will succeed. This uncertainty applies particularly strongly to any estimates of the social costs of the transition and reinforces the need for wide social backing for the reform programme. Otherwise, unforeseen setbacks could quickly lead to calls for the whole market economy policy to be reversed.

---

353 For earlier treatment of the economic reforms in ECE publications see United Nations Economic Commission for Europe, *Economic Survey of Europe in 1986-1987*, New York, 1987, pp.226-227; *Economic Survey of Europe in 1987-1988*, New York, 1988, pp.268-278; *Economic Survey of Europe in 1989-1990*, New York, 1990, pp.233-269; and *Economic Reforms in the European Centrally Planned Economies*, New York, 1989.

354 See János Kornai, *The road to a free economy − shifting from a socialist system: the example of Hungary* (New York: W.W. Norton & Company, 1990), and *The affinity between ownership and co-ordination mechanisms − the common experience of reform in socialist countries* (Helsinki, World Institute for Development Economics Research, 1990).

The bearing of the argument in 4.2 below is that there can be only differences of degree between the various countries in their concrete policies for moving to a market economy. Where the various countries do differ greatly is in the current level and depth of support for such policies. The following sections discuss these political questions in terms of three main components: (i) the degree of political consensus on the need for economic transition, (ii) the extent of any social consensus on the magnitude and distribution of the costs of adjustment and on the speed at which this burden can be absorbed, and (iii) the degree of agreement among policy makers on the broad components of the desired market economy.

(i) Political consensus

Without unambiguous political agreement on decision-making by consensus, a credible reform programme is all but impossible. This is particularly relevant to those countries, such as Albania and the Soviet Union, where the old political structures have lost popular legitimacy but new mechanisms of decision-making by consensus are not yet in place. This question may also be relevant for countries where the democratic process has been established but may still be vulnerable to possible economic set-backs.

Indeed, in some countries (including Czechoslovakia, the Soviet Union and Yugoslavia) there are deeply-rooted tensions between nationalities and regions that must be sorted out before any credible agreement on country-wide economic reform is possible. The key question here is the degree to which political agreement on reform will obtain wider popular support. Popular support may be easier to maintain in countries where policy makers have a popular mandate, endorsed by democratic elections, than in countries where they are not directly accountable and may be attempting to impose economic change from above.

Even if the project of moving to a market economy receives political backing and wide popular support, circumstances may force policy-makers to pursue other goals which may conflict with a rapid move towards a full market economy. Thus, a commitment to avoid rescheduling foreign debt obligations at almost any cost, as in Hungary, or the need to increase domestic food supplies, as in Romania and the Soviet Union, will tend to conflict with the rapid setting up of a market economy. While such decisions about relative priorities are intrinsically political, economists drawing up suggested blueprints for reform should be aware of the difficult political choices which their proposals may involve.

Commitments to international organizations may also restrict decision-makers' freedom of manoeuvre. For example, obligations under the GATT impose limits on the character of trade and foreign-exchange liberalization and IMF, World Bank and EBRD financed adjustment programmes often impose conditions on domestic economic policies.

The commitment to move towards democracy and the shift to a market-based economy has attracted significant financial and institutional support from abroad, both from a variety of regional and international organizations and from individual governments. This support should be organized so that it gives the maximum impetus possible to the reform effort in as transparent a way as possible. This is obviously desirable from the point of view of the transition countries themselves, but is also applicable to other agents: clear evidence that external aid is being used effectively will encourage continuing popular support for the reform process both in donor countries and in developing countries having a potential claim on scarce development assistance. The key question that arises here is the way in which outside assistance should be co-ordinated. This is not solely a matter for those in charge of the transformation in eastern Europe and the Soviet Union. It is also a question which has yet to be resolved by the donor countries and their designated agents.

(ii) Social consensus

Once most of the political difficulties of economic transition have been overcome, a broad social consensus needs to be reached on the steps to be taken. Even if such social agreement is attained initially, there is no guarantee that such a consensus can be maintained once the costs of the adjustment begin to emerge.

A market economy is expected to yield considerable benefits to the population. It is very important that reformers make clear the magnitudes of potential benefits and the likely time scale for their emergence in order to obtain the widest possible support for the transformation process. Qualitative benefits from the move to a market economy which are likely to appear quickly (such as more individual freedom, increased choice, and the disappearance of queuing) should be stressed. Similarly, the prospects for increased independence through the secure, individual ownership of wealth may be important for constructing and maintaining a social consensus behind the reform programme.

Even in the oldest democracy, where the rules of decision-making by the majority are widely accepted, there is still considerable uncertainty about the socially acceptable limits of changes in policy. Indeed, increases in inflation or unemployment, or substantial cut-backs in subsidies or government services have frequently led to changes in governments. There is no reason to believe that the new eastern democracies will find it easier to deal with such (hopefully short-run) economic problems, whatever the longer-term benefits of the market economy may turn out to be.

A particularly important question here is whether it is true that economic chaos leads to a social consensus in favour of "shock therapy" or "big bang" adjustment policies, as adopted in Poland in 1990 and Yugoslavia in 1989,[355] in contrast to the more gradualist approach taken by Hungary for over two decades. However, even if such a consensus in favour of shock therapy exists, whether implicitly or explicitly, there is no guarantee that this support can be sustained as the costs of the transition increase. There may, therefore, be apparent reversals in reform policies that are perfectly logical, given the social and political context.

On the other hand, if a gradual process is adopted, central planning may collapse with no replacement in sight at all. Informal co-ordination mechanisms, such as black markets, will tend to emerge instead of the expected gradual transition to the open market. Increasing inequality, open inflation and rapid increases in unemployment (even if this is not reflected in official figures) may lead to disenchantment with the incomplete reform process and result in the adoption of a policy of shock therapy. Whether this will help in reaching the necessary social and political consensus remains to be seen.

(iii) Market-economy consensus

All eastern countries have now committed themselves to some type of market-oriented reform. The Soviet Union, however, has still not decided, even at the political level, whether or not it wants to move to the fully-fledged market system.

In fact, the Soviet Union presents a *sui generis* case, and for that reason section 4.6 will be devoted solely to the vagaries of *perestroïka*. But the ongoing debates there have much in common with the fluid state of affairs in Bulgaria, Romania and especially Albania.

Once the political leadership has firm popular support for moving ahead with the transformation process, the next problem is the formulation of a clear-cut blueprint for the introduction of a full market system.

Some of these countries have already had experience with reforms which have some features of economic decentralization and market orientation. Some experience, however confined, of price liberalization, the use of surrogate exchange rates to link world and domestic prices or of restructuring the banking sector into at least two tiers may well help to ease the transition and would also make the adoption of "shock therapy" or "bigbang reform" easier.

---

[355] It should be noted that the measures introduced in late 1989 and early 1990 were *not* pure shock therapy as counselled by many outside advisors or even by participants in the policy debates on reforms in some economies in transition.

4.2 A FRAMEWORK FOR THE TRANSITION

A framework for the transition to a market economy must cover the comprehensiveness of the reform ("how much to change"), the speed with which the various reforms can be implemented ("how quickly can it be changed") and the sequencing of the various reforms ("what to change first"). Any attempt to do everything at once would simply lead to chaos and the probable abandonment of the reform process.

(i) Comprehensiveness, speed and sequencing

The questions of "speed", "comprehensiveness" and "sequencing" cover all the main aspects of the design of the reform strategy (sometimes "social safety net", "credibility" and "transparency" are also added but here they are incorporated in the concept of "comprehensiveness" or follow from the — assumed — degree of social consensus).

Both comprehensiveness and speed are vitally important but, pushed to extremes, they are also mutually incompatible; a sensible sequencing is needed to reconcile them and achieve the best trade-off between speed and comprehensiveness.

Two key constraints on speed and comprehensiveness must be taken into account. The first is the degree of social consensus on the tolerable burden of the costs of the transition and how quickly and how equitably these should be absorbed. The second constraint is the need not to overload the existing, often inexperienced, administrative structures with too many reforms at once. At the very least, this suggests that the design of the reform process needs to be tailored to the specific initial conditions in each country.

However, the scope for choice of differing approaches to this kind of drastic economic reform should not be exaggerated. Indeed, there may be no choice at all about the initial steps of the reform if the country is sinking into hyperinflation: in this situation macro-economic stabilization has to take priority. Moreover, some policies may be dependent for their success on the successful prior implementation (or at least a firm commitment) to other measures. The chosen sequencing should take this into account, laying particular stress on the need to maintain the credibility of the whole programme: the changes in household and enterprise behaviour which are basic to the success of the transition will only take place if governments are believed to be serious about the whole programme of reform. As mistakes are bound to be made, the sequencing of policy should be "robust" so that unavoidable errors and reverses do not endanger the whole programme.

On comprehensiveness, the minimum requirements that need to be put in place urgently would seem to be:

- the unambiguous anchoring of property rights;

- macro-economic stabilization;

- price liberalization;

- corporatization and enterprise reform;

- creation of a social safety net and labour market reform;

- the establishment of a commercial banking infrastructure; and

- trade and foreign exchange liberalization.

These priority requirements are dealt with in more detail in section (ii), while section (iii) deals with reforms which it will be desirable to start quickly but which are of slightly lower priority. The next section (iv) deals with longer-term changes. The reforms discussed in these three sections may be regarded as setting up the irreducible core or "necessary conditions" of structures and institutions for the operation of a market economy.

Section (v) summarizes the other changes which will help to maintain and establish more firmly the new economic system. Together with the earlier reforms, these can be viewed as "sufficient conditions" for ensuring the survival of a market economy.

Table 3.2.1 indicates the present status of a selection of these "building blocks" of systemic change in the transition economies.

Many of the suggested reforms involve building new institutions or drastically modifying existing structures. Here there is a choice to be made between slowly building the new structures from scratch, as occurred in Poland last year, or "borrowing" suitable structures from abroad — eastern Germany provides a particularly striking example of this, adopting the entire West German legal and institutional framework. Of course, such complete adoption of foreign systems is not open to the other transition economies. However, given the need to move rapidly, it might be worthwhile adapting such institutions as civil and commercial codes, financial regulations and competition law from existing foreign models.

(ii) Priority components of creating markets

The reforms listed in this section all need to be carried out as quickly as possible. Some may emerge through "shock therapy" while others may require a more comprehensive programme of structural adjustments. However, all these priority components need to be put in place quickly if the move towards the market is not to falter. Half-way measures are prone to yield unsatisfactory results that may lead to pressure to reversing the reforms.

(a) Property rights

Clearly defined property rights are central to the operation of any market economy. By laying down clear rules for the distribution of economic returns from property, they establish incentives for property owners to put their assets to the most productive use. Conversely, where clear property rights do not exist, uncertainty as to the ultimate ownership of assets and their returns will tend to discourage investment whether by emerging domestic entrepreneurs or by foreign companies. The question of property rights is here treated separately from that of privatization (which is dealt with in section (iii) below).

Although property-rights reform is a vital component of establishing market incentives in the former centrally planned economies, there is no unanimity among the reformers about how some property rights should be assigned. This debate concerns both the philosophy of how society is to be organized in future and also involves disagreements on the nature of the original process of nationalization.

This uncertainty is present not only in the Soviet Union, where the debate on property rights and privatization is still at an early stage, but it has still not been cleared up in eastern Europe. Although most countries of eastern Europe have decided to progress rapidly with the assignment of property rights to newly-formed capital and, in some cases, to most state-owned assets as well, nearly all of the countries have been unable to resolve the question of the ownership of state-owned land. Additional uncertainty arises from the moral commitment of some of the new leaderships of eastern Europe to provide some compensation to the original owners of property which had been nationalized by the previous régime.

There are two key aspects to property rights reform. Firstly, property rights should be clearly demarcated and be enforceable through a neutral judicial system and a modern system of commercial law. Changes in property rights must be entrusted to institutions that themselves neither exercise property rights nor enforce them. This should be linked to constitutional arrangements guaranteeing private property and committing the authorities to provide fair compensation for any assets that may have to be nationalized in future. While nationalization may not be desirable in general, there

are still likely to be cases where government will have to overrule individual's rights for the sake of the common good. Commitment to fair compensation should help to ensure that such powers are not abused.

Secondly, from a more strictly economic point of view, property rights should be vested in agents with purely economic responsibilities. This should encourage the more efficient use of scarce assets and, given a regulatory framework encouraging competition, should lead to an improvement of economic performance.

In the economies of eastern Europe and the Soviet Union, where much of the capital stock will remain in state ownership for many years to come, achieving this second condition will require the distancing of the state as ultimate owner from the operation of individual enterprises. The managers of state-owned enterprises should therefore be set only economic or financial objectives and given appropriate incentives to encourage them to behave in an economically sensible way. As the private sector takes on larger-scale investments, this problem of reconciling the interests of the ultimate owners of assets with those of the managers entrusted with the control of the assets will appear in the private sector too. A well functioning capital market will eventually be required to fill this role — see section (iv).

In some cases (including in Czechoslovakia since 1988, Hungary since the mid-1980s, Poland since the early 1980s and Yugoslavia since the creation of labour-managed firms), efforts to improve economic performance through devolution of control to individual enterprises have resulted in uncertainty as to the ultimate ownership of the assets of the enterprise: does the capital of the enterprise belong to the state or to the workers in the enterprise?[356] To remove this type of ambiguity, it may be necessary to renationalize all state-owned assets. If this course of action is adopted, it will be vital to make clear that this is a temporary measure designed solely to re-establish clear property rights. Even so, there may be serious political obstacles to such a revision in the "acquired" property rights of enterprise and worker councils.

(b) Macro-economic stabilization

In countries where macro-economic imbalance threatens the whole economy, absolute priority should be accorded to stabilization. This involves dealing with both any historical *stock* problems (usually involving the existence of a monetary overhang) and also current *flow* imbalances (usually the result of unrestricted credit creation, often caused by monetary financing of large government deficits). Correcting the stock problem without tackling *at the same time* the imbalances in monetary and fiscal affairs will merely postpone inflationary problems.

To come to grips with the instability in the *stock* sense, epitomized by the "monetary overhang", part of the money in circulation (not just currency but also deposits of various maturities) will need to be sterilized.

---

356 This has given rise to so-called "spontaneous" privatization, a derisory term referring to the alienation of state-owned property by management and functionaries in place. Notably in Hungary and Poland this process has complicated divestment programmes and needlessly delayed enterprise restructuring.

TABLE 4.2.1

Building blocks of systemic change in the transition economies

	Bulgaria	Czechoslovakia	German Democratic Republic	Hungary
Political consensus				
Free parliamentary elections	10 and 17 June 1990	8-9 June 1990 (two chambers)	18 March, 2 December 1990 (after unification)	25 March, 8 April 1990
Nationwide referendum	Not planned	Under preparation	Not planned	26 November 1989, 29 July 1990
Form of government	Three-party coalition and non-affiliated experts	Three-party coalition and non-affiliated experts	Coalition	Three party coalition and non-affiliated experts
Presidential election	3 April, 1 August 1990 (by parliament)	5 July 1990 (by parliament)		8 March 1990 (by parliament)
Local elections	Planned for first half 1991	23-24 November 1990	6 May 1990	30 September, 14 October 1990
Prior experience with economic reforms	None	Short-lived attempt in 1968	None	Several wave-like attempts since 1968
Clarification of property rights				
Restitution	Before parliament	Laws passed: October 1990, February 1991	Regulated by unification treaty amended in March 1991	Before parliament
Ownership of agricultural land	Approved by parliament	Before parliament	Privatization in progress	Before parliament
Corporatization of SOEs				
Petty privatization	Before parliament	Started in January 1991	Very advanced	Started in December 1990
Privatization of large SOEs	Under preparation	Starting in April 1991	In progress	In progress
Supervising government agency	Under preparation	Federal Fund of National Property, equivalent bodies in the 2 Republics	Trust-fund set up in March 1990	State Property Agency operational since March 1990
Stock market	..	Planned	In place in West Germany	In place since June 1990
Changes in price system				
Wholesale prices	Liberalization in February 1991	Liberalization in January 1991	Liberalization in July 1990	Gradual reforms since 1968
Retail prices	Liberalization in February 1991	Liberalization in January 1991	Liberalization in July 1990	Gradual reforms since 1968
Overhaul of safety net				
Unemployment benefits as percentage of last pay	100% first month tapering off to 50% by 6 months	60% first 6 months, 50% next 6 months	About 65-70%	70% first 12 months, 50% later
Minimum wage as percentage of average gross wages	Under discussion	60%	..	45%
Wage indexation	With a coefficient of 0.7 to inflation	State sector: annually re-negotiated on a tripartite basis	Not allowed by currency law	State sector: annually re-negotiated on a tripartite basis
Overhaul of fiscal system				
VAT	Under preparation	Planned from 1993	Complete takeover of west German fiscal system as from 1 July 1990	In place since 1988
Personal income tax	Under preparation	In place since 1991	..	In place since 1988
Property tax	Under preparation	Planned from 1993	..	In place since 1991
Expenditure reform	Under preparation	In progress since 1990		Planned from 1992
Overhaul of banking				
Two-tier system	In place since 1991	In place since 1990	In place since July 1990	In place since 1987
Independent central bank	Law in preparation	Law in preparation	In place since July 1990	Law in preparation
Foreign trade arrangements				
Liberalization of trading rights	Under preparation	In place since 1990	Since 1 July 1990	Gradual since 1968
Unified exchange rate	Under preparation	Since 1991	Since 1 July 1990	Since 1981
Domestic convertibility	Under preparation	Since 1991	Since 1 July 1990	Since 1990
Abolition of QRs	..	..		Accelerated since 1987
Co-operation with multilateral organizations				
EEC	Co-operation agreement	Co-operation agreement, negotiations on association	Membership since 3 October 1990 because of unification	Co-operation agreement, negotiations on association
IMF/IBRD	Membership 25 September 1990	Membership 20 September 1990	See EEC	Membership 6 May 1982
GATT	Under negotiation	Member since 1948	See EEC	Member since 1973
Foreign direct investment				
Protection of investors	..	Act on Economic Relations with foreign countries, 1988	Same as for domestic investors	Act on Investments of Foreigners, 1988
Estimated value at the end of 1990	$0.1 billion	$0.8 billion	..	$1.2 billion

TABLE 4.2.1 (continued)

Building blocks of systemic change in the transition economies

	Poland	Romania	Soviet Union	Yugoslavia
Political consensus				
Free parliamentary elections	Planned for 1991	20 May 1990	26 March 1989	Apr.-Dec. 1990: republican level
Nationwide referendum	Not planned	Not planned	17 March 1991	Not planned at federal level
Form of government	Government of experts	National Salvation Front	One party government	Federal Executive Council
Presidential election	25 November, 9 December 1990	20 May 1990	14 March 1990 (by parliament)	..
Local elections	27 May 1990	Not yet planned	March-October 1990	Various years from 1991
Prior experience with economic reforms	Wave-like attempts since 1956, 1981, radical reform 1989	None	NEP (1920s), Kosygin reform (1965)	Wave-like attempts since 1949
Clarification of property rights				
Restitution	Under discussion	Law passed (land)	Not planned	Considered in some republics
Ownership of agricultural land	Possibility of privatization state farms	Law passed	RSFSR decided 3 December 1990	..
Corporatization of SOEs				
Petty privatization	In progress since late 1988	In progress	Before parliament	In progress
Privatization of large SOEs	In progress since July 1990	Before parliament	Not planned	Legislation in place
Supervising government agency	Ministry of Property Transformation	Before parliament	State Assets Fund (Presidential decree 10 August 1990)	Regulated at republican levels
Stock market	Planned for 1991	Planned	Planned	Active since Spring 1990
Changes in price system				
Wholesale prices	Essentially liberalized) in 1989-1990	In three stages, November) 1989, April, June 1991)	New prices 1 January 1991	Progressively liberalized) since mid-1988)
Retail prices			1 April 1991	
Overhaul of safety net				
Unemployment benefits as percentage of last pay	110-125% minimum wage first 6 months, 95% later on	50-60% depending service, lowest 60% minimum wage	50%, no less than minimum wage	Differently regulated at republican level
Minimum wage as percentage of average gross wages	Set periodically in response to inflation	..	..	Only in some republics, regulations vary
Wage indexation	Coefficient of 0.6 to inflation	Indexed to prices of basic goods since November 1989	Increased wages since 1 April 1991	Non-existent
Overhaul of fiscal system				
VAT	Planned from 1992	Planned	..	Envisaged in medium term
Personal income tax	Planned from 1992	Since January 1991	Since July 1990	Applied in all republics
Property tax	Under preparation	Planned	..	In some republics
Expenditure reform	..	..	..	In progress
Overhaul of banking				
Two-tier system	In place since 1987-1988	In place since 1987-1988	Adopted in December 1990	Beginning 1960s
Independent central bank	In place since 1988	In place since 1988	Adopted in December 1990	End-1989, enlarged automomy since mid-1989
Foreign trade arrangements				
Liberalization of trading rights	Complete since 1990	..	..	Gradual since 1965
Unified exchange rate	Since 1990	Dual (official auction) rates	Planned	Since July 1965
Domestic convertibility	Since 1990	Planned from April 1991	..	December 1989-December 1990
Abolition of QRs	..	Some remain	..	..
Co-operation with multilateral organizations				
EEC	Co-operation agreement, negotiations on association	Co-operation agreement, ratified 3 March 1991	Trade and co-operation agreement in force	Special agreements since 1970
IMF/IBRD	Member: 12 June 1986	Member: 15 December 1972	Under negotiation	Founding member in 1945
GATT	Member since 1967 (re-negotiation)	Member since 1971	Observer	Member since 1965
Foreign direct investment				
Protection of investors	Bilateral agreements with 14 western countries	Laws passed March 1990	Bilateral agreements	Guaranteed by federal legislation
Estimated value at the end of 1990	$0.4 billion	$0.8 billion	$4.6 billion	$1.4 billion

It should be noted that the "monetary overhang" is a somewhat elusive phenomenon. Presumably it designates the changes in demand that are likely to occur with any relaxation of price controls. If so, the monetary overhang includes not only the amount of "hot money" that households and enterprises may be keeping but it also includes any spending which is the result of "forced substitution". Once prices are freed and most shortages are eliminated, spending patterns may change drastically from the current, "quantity-rationed" pattern. Hence, stabilization in the stock sense may entail far more than simply getting rid of the apparent currency overhang.

There are various ways of sterilizing the pure excess money in circulation. The means available include confiscation *de jure* through monetary reform or *de facto* through inflation; the sale of foreign goods at prices that reflect the exchange rate observed in the black or parallel markets; the sale of state-owned property; the freezing of bank deposits with withdrawals being permitted only when the supply situation has improved; the creation of new financial assets bearing credible interest rates (which may not necessarily be above the expected rate of inflation) and fostering private capital formation.

Apart from the confiscation route, all the elements of this stabilization package require the creation of new, market-oriented institutions and the introduction of new laws. These cannot be set up quickly even under the most favourable circumstances so that even putting in place the fundamentals of economic stabilization may call for structural reforms. Stabilization certainly requires more than the simple confiscation of a part of the bills in circulation such as was carried out in the Soviet Union in January 1991.

Stability in the *flow* sense requires the balanced financing of state expenditure and introduction of measures to control the growth in the money supply. Initially, these new monetary and fiscal policies are likely to be fairly elementary but the objective should be to ensure a tight macro-economic stance.

The *fiscal* contribution to stabilization could be regarded as a simple matter of reducing the budget deficit, coupled with moves to finance any remaining deficit in a less inflationary way. However, the shift to a market economy requires far more fundamental changes in the role of the government than this. After the transition, the state will lose its power to control the economy directly and, instead, it will have to work through the indirect tools of fiscal and monetary policies.

Fiscal stabilization is therefore likely to involve substantial structural change, with the introduction of systems of income, expenditure and corporate taxation and sharp reduction of subsidies to firms and households. Any desired redistribution (which will obviously vary substantially between countries) should, if possible, be carried out directly through transfer payments rather than through subsidizing selected goods.

The shift to a market economy will also force radical changes in the role of *money and credit*. Money will now have to perform an active role in guiding the allocation of resources instead of the mostly passive role it has played up to now. An effective monetary policy will be a key tool in ensuring an adequate supply of money and credit, maintaining the stability of the exchange rate and helping to move towards sustainable currency convertibility.

There are various systems of monetary control but the delegation of control of the money supply to a relatively independent agent seems to work well in mature western economies. At the very least, a *genuine central bank* will be needed to manage monetary policy, to act as lender of last resort and to regulate the commercial banking sector (and perhaps later on other kinds of financial institutions). Policy tools such as reserve requirements, discount rates (perhaps differentiated across assets) and ceilings on loanable funds will need to be put in place quickly and adjusted in the light of current indicators such as the rate of credit growth and, later on, the level of the exchange rate.

At the same time, the provision of credit to the rest of the economy should be devolved to the emerging commercial banking sector. These *commercial banks* should not subsidize borrowers but should finance economic endeavours at their own risk. It will be necessary to clean out the loan portfolio of the existing universal bank and recapitalize existing commercial banks in a way that will not hinder these financial institutions from quickly performing their intermediating functions on a strictly commercial basis.[357]

In some countries, including Bulgaria, Romania and the Soviet Union, measures to combat aggregate imbalances have yet to be taken. Czechoslovakia and Hungary have taken some initial steps towards stabilization in the flow sense, though budgetary discipline appears to be stricter in Czechoslovakia than in Hungary. The ex-GDR, Poland and Yugoslavia have moved furthest in the direction of stabilization. Of course, German unification has provided the background for stabilization in the former German Democratic Republic but this does not mean that progress has been easy. Poland and Yugoslavia attempted to come to grips with their imbalances at the beginning of 1990. Some progress has been made in getting inflation under control but much remains to be done. Indeed some indicators suggest that macro-economic policy in Yugoslavia has been relaxed again recently.

(c) Price liberalization

For brevity's sake, prices are here viewed as summarizing the terms at which alternative products, services or production factors are traded. The concept therefore includes domestic wholesale and retail prices,

---

357 For an interesting analysis and suggestion of how this could be accomplished, see L. Brainard, "Strategies for economic transformation in Eastern Europe – the role of financial market reform", in Hans Blommestein and Michael Marrese (eds.), *Selected issues and strategies in the transformation of planned economies* (Paris: OECD, forthcoming 1991).

wage rates, interest rates and also the exchange rate to some degree.

Since the heart of the market economy is the co-ordination of economic decisions via the price mechanism and one of the main problems of the planned economy was distorted prices, price liberalization is fundamental to the transition to the market economy. There is little disagreement among reformers on the importance of early price liberalization. However, whether the liberalization should be decreed all at once through shock therapy or be phased in more gradually (perhaps by first freeing up wholesale prices and interest rates, next consumer prices, then trade prices and the exchange rate, and finally nominal wage rates) is still a controversial question.

Price liberalization provokes at least two main worries. The first is how prices will behave in the absence of a properly competitive environment. The other is concern that price liberalization will set off inflation. In this connection, a fundamental question is whether price liberalization should be carried out before or after enacting measures to increase domestic competition. A related question is whether competition should be fostered primarily by exposing the economy to foreign competition or by encouraging the emergence of new domestic agents through private capital formation, demonopolization and the break up of conglomerates.

The standard advice offered to the reforming countries is to foster trade and foreign-exchange liberalization as quickly as possible. This provides both an adequate system of relative prices for traded goods and injects some competition to reduce the scope for monopolistic price increases for domestic suppliers. Whether this can be accomplished in an orderly fashion depends critically on the initial gap between domestic and world relative prices. If domestic prices are extremely distorted, as is likely to be the case in economies where central planning was not decentralized at all, the adjustment cost (in terms of bankruptcies, unemployment and inflation) of moving quickly towards scarcity pricing are likely to be very large indeed.

The need to avoid a wage-price spiral has led to the adoption, in several countries, of tax-based income policies, thus restricting the extent of wage liberalization. Increases of nominal wages above a norm (usually set substantially lower than the increase in prices) are subject to penal levels of taxation. While such policies are likely to be effective in reducing inflation, the resulting cuts in real wages may push lower-paid households into poverty. In these circumstances, the construction of a social safety net becomes even more urgent (see section (ii)(e) below).

To the extent that trade liberalization may be an important instrument in fostering competition and in providing a set of relative prices for traded goods, the gradual phasing of price liberalization is not possible. An alternative procedure is for the central authorities to provide "guidance" to simultaneous price and trade liberalization by first resetting the relative prices of key inputs (say, fuels and basic ores) and then, with minimal delay, letting markets set the levels of other prices.

Poland and Yugoslavia have already gone quite some way to reducing trade restrictions, at least for relations with convertible-currency partners. At the same time, legitimate traders' access to foreign exchange has been measurably eased. Czechoslovakia followed suit in January 1991. Since the mid-1980s Hungary has been gradually liberalizing its trading régime so that about 90 per cent of trade in convertible currency is now free of foreign-exchange or import constraints. In the other countries, some measures have been taken to ease the trade and foreign-exchange régimes but these have remained largely in the areas of easing administrative rules.

(d) Corporatization and enterprise reform

The active pursuit of enterprise reform is an essential complement to sound macro-economic policies and the setting of clear property rights in promoting competition and providing meaningful incentives.

Under central planning, enterprises tended to be organized in a highly monopolistic fashion. Big conglomerates were preferred because integrating them into the overall plan was considerably easier than was dealing with smaller firms. Protection against foreign competition, the absence of any possibility of bankruptcy (or of hostile takeover) further reduced the incentives for efficient production. Any losses were almost invariably made good through subsidies, either directly from the central budget or indirectly through the banking system.

Policy during the transition should aim at reducing the scope for these distortions and introducing as much of a market environment as possible. Thus access to credit should be granted solely on commercial terms and commercial accounting rules should be introduced quickly so that potentially profitable enterprises may be identified more easily. Subsidies should be cut back as quickly as the social consensus allows to reduce the scope for haggling between enterprises and the government. Slow reduction of subsidies could endanger the credibility of the reform programme so there should perhaps be a commitment to phase out all subsidies by a set target date. In any case chronic loss-makers should not be supported (a suitable criterion could be whether firms can cover their short-run variable costs). Changing managerial attitudes in the state sector is likely to take time, but installing an incentive system designed to make managers more concerned about profitability and the net value of the assets under their control will help to encourage change.

Although both Hungary (for several years now) and Poland and Yugoslavia have tried to introduce enterprise reforms, progress so far has been slow. Managers of state-owned firms still have insufficient incentives to pursue actions which are in the interest of the ultimate owners, the state. Only slight progress has been made with encouraging private capital formation outside the service sectors. Even in the most radically reforming economies, domestic capitalists and foreign investors find business opportunities restricted by all kinds of bureaucratic impediments and difficulties in obtaining elementary public services (such as telecommunication connections).

(e) Labour market reform and social safety net

Under socialist central planning, every able-bodied person was constitutionally ensured remunerative employment, in practice with almost absolute job security. Wage differentials were very narrow and were unrelated to skill or productivity. This situation not only ossified labour behaviour, it also fostered shirking, cynicism and apathy. Where labour rewards are automatic and no longer tied to effort or productivity, productivity is likely to remain low.

Effectively functioning labour markets must therefore be created as quickly as possible, where wages are tailored to effort and results and job security is more related to economic factors. Some kind of *modus vivendi* among effectively functioning labour unions, management and government needs to be created to ensure that labour rights are protected but also not abused by sectional interests. In this context, the prospect of workers directly benefiting from the economic transformation through profit sharing or employee share-ownership programmes, once the divestment process gets under way, will help to improve the attitudes of workers to change (although in all these discussions, the interests of "outsiders", especially the unemployed, should not be forgotten).

The restructuring of enterprises along commercial lines and the collapse of existing recruitment patterns will lead to considerable unemployment. In addition, the effects of inflation on pensioners and of likely cuts in real wages on the low-paid may lead to the emergence of poverty.

In these circumstances, it would be helpful to have in place a reserve mechanism to ensure that the burden of the transition will not be borne solely by the weakest members of society. While the countries under examination have provided a minimal level of universal social security for many years, this system will need to be improved considerably to cope with the stress of the transition to a market economy.

The social safety net should reflect the social consensus on the adjustment burden society will be willing to absorb and how equitably the burdens should be distributed. However, it would be utterly false to claim to be able to protect nearly everyone against this burden. In fact, the limits of feasible support are likely to be reached once the more vulnerable layers of society (notably the elderly, handicapped and unemployed) have been taken care of; more ambitious measures may well lead to budgetary problems.

As far as *unemployment* is concerned, the system of unemployment benefit should encourage the unemployed to remain in the labour force and to return to work as quickly as possible. Benefits should be available to all those who can show they are looking for work (not just those who have recently lost their jobs) and the unemployed should be helped with retraining and advice on available vacancies. Labour mobility should be encouraged and, to forestall the emergence of long-term unemployment, job guarantees for the unemployed may be required. In other words, the package should combine strict limits on the duration and magnitude of unemployment benefits with considerable expenditures on active labour policy measures.[358]

Although reformers have seen the need for a safety net for a long time, only slow progress has been made so far. Systems of unemployment insurance for employees have been set up or are planned in several countries but these may well be insufficient if unemployment proves more than a short-term problem or if there is substantial youth unemployment. Measures to help the unemployed back into work have so far received a relatively low priority and this situation may deteriorate further if, as expected, unemployment rises quickly.

(f) Commercial banking infrastructure

In addition to markets for goods, services and labour, a market economy also requires a means of allocating assets, that is a capital market. This will have to be created from scratch and is likely to be difficult, given the considerable political and ideological overtones of this feature of the "capitalist" economy. Needless to say, lengthy debates on such issues will merely delay the necessary improvements in the productive use of public and private savings. Despite the advocacy by a number of western advisers of the early establishment of sophisticated capital markets, there is little doubt that the commercial banking sector will provide the main link between savers and investors for the foreseeable future. In particular, an effective commercial banking sector is needed to set private capital formation on the right track. This may require a comprehensive restructuring of the existing weak two-tier banking structure created in some countries (including Bulgaria, Hungary and Poland) in the mid-1980s.

Questions of the precise future role of the emerging banking sector (the extent to which they will be active investors and participate in enterprise management) can probably be left for now. Instead, rather than aiming right away at creating a very complex commercial banking system, it would be useful to bear in mind that the most elementary functions of banks in a money economy have to be firmly established. These include not only acting as intermediaries between savers and investors through the taking of deposits and the on-lending of money, but also the provision of an effective clearing system. This latter feature is often overlooked, but if account holders encounter serious obstacles in transferring funds there will be only slow progress with decentralization and the formation of efficient markets.

---

358 For a review of the benefits that some market economies have obtained through such a comprehensive approach, see chapter 5 ("Explaining unemployment in the market economies: theories and evidence") of this publication.

(g) Trade and foreign-exchange liberalization

As the economies in transition wish to integrate themselves quickly and as fully as possible with the international economy, special attention must be devoted to the reconstruction of the trade and foreign-exchange sectors of these economies. As mentioned in the section on price liberalization, openness to the world economy will help to provide a system of relative prices and much needed competition for domestic producers.

In the former economic set-up, there was pervasive protection against imports. This took various forms of export and import quotas, foreign exchange licensing, often through bilateral trade agreements, and other even less transparent methods. Virtually all of these barriers to trade will have to be replaced by conventional commercial-policy instruments, mainly tariffs and exchange-rate policies.

Some commentators have suggested that very early on in the transition all these non-tariff protection measures should be converted into explicit *ad valorem* tariffs and that this should be effected at a rather high level, perhaps even maintaining the existing degree of non-tariff protection.[359] This new tariff would be structured into several — perhaps half a dozen — cascading tariff categories, with a commitment to reduce the level and dispersion of rates over a set time period. The objective would be to avoid an early collapse of large segments of industry (especially the so-called "value-subtracting" or "negative value-added" enterprises) that could create a downward momentum from which policy makers might have great difficulty extricating themselves.

Although some measures to protect existing economic structures may be necessary, it would appear to be counter-productive to seek to insulate the reforming countries from foreign competition. In view of the weak central actors in the economies in transition, any commitment to such a phasing-out of customs duties, even if a waiver under the GATT rules could be secured,[360] would not be widely believed and would also postpone the urgently needed benefits of a sensible structure of relative prices and an increase in competition.[361]

Rather than aggravate price distortions and introduce levies that may be hard to repeal later, the economies in transition could maintain a comparatively uniform and low tariff, but permit income transfers on a strictly temporary basis to threatened sectors. This would prevent widespread early bankruptcies and might help to preserve viable assets which might otherwise be shut down (of course, there is little hope that policy makers will be able to neatly separate the potentially profitable firms from those that should be fundamentally restructured or eliminated altogether). Perhaps the transfer could be based on the level of subsidies prior to the introduction of the transformation and some estimate of the impact of the devaluation of the exchange rate. Enterprise-specific income transfers, like price subsidies, should, however, be avoided.

The former exchange rate system with its perplexing multiplicity of rates tailored to segmented transactions will need to be replaced with one based on a single exchange rate. Given the many adjustments that will have to take place in the economies in transition, it would not be advisable to cling to an absolutely fixed exchange rate, for this might plunge the country into an unnecessarily deep depression. On the other hand, there is little to be said in favour of a fully-flexible exchange rate policy. A crawling-peg policy may well offer the most desirable choice for the exchange régime.

The key questions to be addressed in transforming the foreign-exchange régime will therefore revolve around the kind of crawling peg to be chosen, how the exchange rate should be adjusted without affecting the credibility of policy and the precise initial devaluation that should be carried out. Substantial undervaluation will foster exports and allow competitiveness to be maintained at the given exchange rate even after a period of "corrective inflation". On the other hand it will lead to a sharp drop in the real value of wages and incomes and this may itself increase inflationary pressures.

In practice, the majority of the countries in transition appear to be opting for undervaluing the exchange rate (as compared with a rate that would generate current-account balance) without an explicit commitment to a crawling peg policy. Thus Poland has used the exchange rate, together with restrictions on nominal wage increases, as the nominal anchor to the entire transformation process. The initial exchange rate (9,500 zloty to the dollar) has been kept unchanged for much longer than was initially expected (at the time of writing it is still at that level). This is in spite of very large differences in the movements of domestic and trade prices, which suggests that the initial devaluation was too large (see section 4.3 for a more detailed discussion).

These changes in the foreign-exchange régime will help the economy to move towards current-account convertibility. However, a rapid move towards convertibility is likely to be useful only in two cases. Countries that have utterly lost control over their

---

359 The champion of this position is Ronald I. McKinnon (see his "Liberalizing foreign trade in a socialist economy: the problem of negative value-added", in John Williamson (ed.), *Convertibility in Eastern Europe* (Washington, D.C, Institute for International Economics, 1991, forthcoming). John Williamson has come out for such an approach as well (see his "Convertibility, trade policy and the payments constraint", paper prepared for the conference on "The transition to a market economy in Central and Eastern Europe" organized by the OECD Centre for Co-operation with the European Economies in Transition and the World Bank, Paris, 28-30 November 1990).

360 In eastern Europe only Bulgaria is not yet a full Contracting Party, although it has been seeking this status since 1986. The Soviet Union has been an observer in the GATT only since early 1990. Not all countries entered the GATT with a full tariff in place, however. But by the time the transformation began, all had some customs tariff in place, although it had been structured more for administrative convenience and foreign policy-making (such as granting GSP and MFN) than for effectively linking domestic with foreign transactions.

361 It would probably also be an insuperable task to make explicit the degree of protection which segments of the planned economy have traditionally enjoyed.

economies and where households no longer have faith in the leadership may make current-account convertibility one component of the "shock therapy" – convertibility will provide vital credibility for the reform programme in this case. Early current-account convertibility may also be desirable for countries where domestic prices have already been freed substantially and restrictions on foreign trade and foreign exchange have been relaxed somewhat.

On the other hand, countries that enter the transition with substantial imbalances or price distortions may well elect to postpone current-account convertibility, as distinct from liberalizing foreign-exchange allocation mechanisms, until the most important adjustments have been completed (see section (iii)(d)).

With the collapse of the CMEA system of transferable-rouble clearing and its peculiar price arrangements, it is important that the economies in transition avoid falling into the trap of trying to balance their mutual transactions on a bilateral basis. A rebilateralization of the trade among the former CMEA members, let alone the resort to *ad hoc* bilateral arrangements which in some cases go down to the enterprise level (i.e., pure barter) now observable, can pose new barriers to the introduction of markets in these economies.

The price of transformation

There is probably little chance of undertaking this initial phase of priority reforms without suffering a fall in output. For one thing, a contraction in output attributable to the elimination of the worst loss-making activities may even be desirable.[362] Likewise, the emerging market environment will cut out some of the wasteful demand typical of centrally planned economies (such as overconsumption of fuels, raw materials and transportation). The depth of such a recession, which will depend to a considerable extent on the responsiveness of the supply side of the economy, cannot be known in advance. However, it is likely that countries that lack even a rudimentary market tradition will suffer the largest falls in living standards and national income.

(iii) Desirable speedy actions

Some of the measures outlined above as the high-priority components of the transition will need to be fine-tuned in line with experience. Putting in place the necessary institutions and legal frameworks cannot be accomplished overnight. However, modifications of the first wave of measures should not be an excuse for delaying the next round of measures.

Matters that deserve speedy attention during the next phase of the transition fall essentially into five categories: (1) competition, (2) the legal infrastructure of markets, (3) privatization, (4) current-account convertibility and (5) encouraging foreign capital inflows.

(a) Competition

Competitive markets are useful conveyors of knowledge and information. However, to function well, markets need the back-up of anti-trust legislation and regulation to guard against monopolistic behaviour and rent-seeking. Fostering a competitive environment will be particularly difficult for the transition economies. These economies are all dominated by multi-product and multi-plant conglomerates with special relationships with the government bureaucracy and little or no foreign competition. To promote a competitive environment, these conglomerates will need to be broken up (though there is a delicate trade-off here between encouraging competition and taking advantage of economies of scale).

Particular emphasis must be placed on the importance of fostering private capital formation. Special measures may be needed to provide potential entrepreneurs with access to credit, perhaps at favourable interest rates on a non-discriminatory basis. However, such a policy will initially conflict with the need of stabilization policy to restrict credit growth through high nominal, or even high real, interest rates and to keep down government expenditure. Once the threat of inflation is lower and monetary policy can be relaxed somewhat, such a public-support programme for loans at easy interest rates could be particularly effective in increasing the number of small firms. The emergence of "new" agents, possibly by legalizing the second economy, is of critical importance in encouraging competition.

Reaching a state of reasonably competitive behaviour on the part of producers and consumers is by no means an easy task.

Households will have to modify their behaviour from the attitudes inculcated during the post-war period. These include patterns induced by the shortage-economy syndrome. Others stem from habituation to the considerable state protectionism (on basic incomes, values and jobs). These will need to change if citizens are to come to terms with the less secure, riskier market environment that, however, promises in time to reward this insecurity with a higher standard of living than they could possibly count on under central planning.

As noted earlier, it should be possible to organize labour markets in such a way that workers are protected, but not to such an extent as to block reform efforts of enterprises. Transparency in such formerly non-existing markets will be of the utmost importance in making the transition bearable and recording rapid and orderly progress with its introduction.

On the producer side, however, the monopolistic behaviour of state-owned enterprises, even if corporatized, should be curtailed, perhaps initially through foreign competition and the rapid build-up of private capital. Even when turned over to private

---

362 This point should not, of course, be exaggerated. A sharp downward trend in the macro-economic aggregates of the countries in transition may, but will not necessarily and certainly not over the whole spectrum, be indicative of loss-making activities being weeded out.

owners, there will eventually be a need to adopt a fully-fledged regulatory environment.

Even more important is the transformation of enterprises in such a way that their management will be induced to follow the precepts of competitive behaviour. For that a sufficiently flexible and comprehensive system of managerial incentives needs to be established, so that management of state-owned enterprises, like their corporate counterparts in market economies, will by and large formulate their entrepreneurial decisions with a view to maximizing net asset values. This can work only if the state as such is removed from its erstwhile roles of commercial decision-maker and supplier of unregulated loans to state-owned firms. The creation of commercial corporations of some kind placed under the authority of a "privatization agency" or "state asset management authority" that owes full accountability to parliamentary organs would seem to be indispensable. At the same time, a substantive infusion of managerial skills appropriate to the market economy will be required; this is one area where a "technology transfer" from existing market economies would be particularly valuable.

Issues of regulation of natural monopolies, while important, are not as pressing at the initial stage of the transformation and can be dealt with later (see section (iv)).

(b) Legal instruments of the market

Modern markets with their far-reaching division of labour and highly complex co-ordination tasks cannot function properly in the absence of a clear legal environment and institutions for the adjudication and enforcement of legal claims. This is obvious when it comes to ensuring property rights, for example, but wider civil and commercial legal codes will be required to ensure that all agents, whether firms or private individuals, have enforceable rights.

The necessary areas for legislation include company, anti-monopoly, contract, bankruptcy and foreign-investment laws as well as financial-sector legislation. Consistency across laws needs to be ensured and any new institutions need to be set up as quickly as possible. This area is one where taking advantage of foreign experience by adapting legislation which has worked well abroad can be particularly useful. The resources saved by this type of short-cut could then be used for setting up institutions and training the individuals who will be entrusted with applying and interpreting the new laws.

(c) Privatization

Some confusion has been caused by the different meanings attached to the term "privatization". Privatization can be seen as a process that takes the state (political bodies as well as government administration and the *nomenklatura*) out of the decision making over the allocation of the returns from state-owned assets. In this sense of the word, privatization should be an urgent priority for all the economies in transition.

However, the term "privatization" is often implicitly restricted to the sale of state-owned enterprise assets. Privatization under this definition can come relatively late in the transition sequence. Even in the case of so-called small or petty privatization, the process need not get under way immediately, although in this respect it would be desirable to proceed with minimal delay.

The term "privatization" is here utilized in its wider sense, namely the withdrawal of the state from directly influencing the allocation of capital resources. The agents who take on the powers may be private, but they could also be co-operatives or family undertakings, or even lower-level organs of government, such as municipalities. Privatization in this sense encompasses "corporatization" − the enterprise reform which alters the legal status of firms from state agents to corporations or joint-stock companies supervised by a state asset-management agency, and the notionally separate "commercialization" − the subjection of their management to the task of maximizing the value of assets subject to a hard budget constraint. The sale of state assets can then be regarded as the final stage in this process.

Asset sale in the economies in transition is generally separated into "small" (or "petty") privatization and "big" (or "real") privatization. There is no hard and fast dividing line between them but petty privatization is essentially concerned with the sale to the general public (whether residents, nationals, or foreigners) of capital assets that should never have fallen under state control in the first instance − such as housing, shops, restaurants and small workshops whose service yield under centralized state management has been notoriously deficient. On the other hand, big privatization usually refers to the sale of the property rights to the large and monopolistic state-owned enterprises.

Both types of privatization will be made far more complicated if there is a socio-political consensus on restoring nationalized property to its original owners. While *restitution* may well be justified on moral grounds and would demonstrate a renewed commitment to the rule of law, the resulting legal arguments are likely to complicate greatly the transition process and to impede the restructuring and the economic recovery of these countries. A commitment on the part of the state to offer *compensation* to those whose assets had earlier been confiscated poses fewer problems in that respect, although it creates other complications, notably in putting pressure on government budgets during the stabilization phase. Perhaps a moral commitment to compensate former owners from the sale of capital assets would provide some remedy without imposing too many obstacles to the process of privatization.

Privatization may be pursued to serve several different objectives, and the precise method of privatization chosen will reflect these. In addition to the objectives commonly invoked in privatization in market economies (improving productive and allocative efficiency and raising government revenues), in the economies in transition there are other objectives which are equally or more important.

The first is the need to reduce the power of the existing managers of state-owned assets. These managers were often selected because they were ready to follow the instructions of the Party rather than because they were individuals with demonstrated management ability. In this connection, the outright sale of state-owned assets may be an effective way of breaking with the old power structure if the new, democratic structures have not had time to become established. However, once the new political structures are firmly in place, any abuses of the power of the existing *nomenklatura* management can be dealt with through the political and legal process and do not necessarily require outright divestment. Indeed, some of the managerial skills needed for the transition to the market economy may well emerge from within the existing management once the appropriate incentives are in place; the previous inefficiencies may also reflect the distorted incentives provided by central planning rather than a lack of management ability *per se*.

The second main objective of privatization is to help the consolidation of democracy by establishing a critical minimum level of private property as soon as possible. If the available level of savings in these countries is limited, achieving this objective may involve imaginative schemes of privatization rather than conventional cash sales. Such schemes include the giving away of a certain proportion of shares to the population, perhaps in the form of a stake in mutual funds yet to be created, allowing workers to buy a stake in their enterprises at a preferential price, or devolving ownership to local authorities.[363]

On the other hand, any need to maximize the revenue from asset sales would lead to a policy of selling assets to the highest bidder, which would obviously conflict with other, more political objectives. In practice, more than one objective will be important and a trade-off will have to be made between conflicting requirements. This makes it unlikely that universal, quick and cost-free privatization will be adopted, as this would imply the complete dominance of political over economic and revenue considerations.

The large-scale sale of state assets is therefore likely to be delayed until later in the reform process, with only petty privatization proceeding quickly. In most cases, the divestment of small assets is being organized on the basis of competitive auctions, initially open exclusively to resident nationals and only at a later stage to foreigners and non-residents. However, in some countries, notably Czechoslovakia, this process has run into severe problems as a result of the commitment to restore property to the original owners.

In general, the scale of divestment as a result of "petty privatization" has so far been small, though several countries are planning to move more quickly with such sales in the course of 1991.

(d) Current-account convertibility

The importance of starting the move towards current-account convertibility, at least for merchandise transactions, has already been emphasized as one of the high-priority items of the transition process (see section 4.2(ii) above). However, except for the two cases mentioned there, it does not seem to be desirable to move directly to full current-account convertibility, and a more gradual process of convergence between domestic and world prices is to be preferred.

Convertibility and a functioning market for foreign exchange are essential ingredients of mature market economies. However, in countries where structural changes are to take place rapidly, it is usually counterproductive to immediately declare that currency is available for any transaction. It may be useful here to distinguish between domestic convertibility, current-account and capital-account convertibility.

Domestic convertibility is somewhat of a misnomer. It simply means that duly registered resident economic agents can obtain foreign exchange at the prevailing exchange rate for merchandise and related transactions. In turn, all agents without exception must surrender all foreign-exchange earnings to the proper authorities, usually the central bank, at the prevailing exchange rate. This rate may be fixed or floating, but the point is that virtually the entire supply of foreign exchange is available for transaction purposes at a rate that the monetary authorities manage. At least in Poland, the needs of the remaining demand for foreign exchange are being met through the parallel market, where the exchange rate fluctuates more than in the official market.

Making progress towards domestic convertibility can be based on expanding the role of foreign-exchange allocation mechanisms. For merchandise and related transactions, retention quotas might be useful if only administrative mechanisms are available. Otherwise, open auction markets in which the bulk of foreign-exchange earnings are allocated are preferable. By gradually increasing the share of export revenues transacted in these markets to 100 per cent, policy makers will eventually be in a position to achieve domestic convertibility.

Current-account convertibility encompasses a range of other transactions, including many of those undertaken by private individuals (all but capital transactions). To inhibit the circumvention of foreign-exchange controls on capital transactions, which is desirable at the earlier stages of the transition, it may be useful to create a formal parallel market for these other current transactions. The exchange rate in that market would also be determined by demand and supply, but it would be affected by different forces from those setting the merchandise rate.

Eventually, however, moving as far and fast as possible towards the régime stipulated in article VIII of the

363 For a review of various forms of privatization, see Farid Dhanji and Branko Milanovic (World Bank), "Privatization in east and central Europe: objectives, constraints, and models of divestiture", paper prepared for the conference on "The transition to a market economy in Central and Eastern Europe" organized by the OECD Centre for Co-operation with the European Economies in Transition and the World Bank, Paris, 28-30 November 1990.

Articles of Agreement of the International Monetary Fund (convertibility for current transactions, which include, in addition to current-account transactions, the repayment of moderate sums on capital account for the amortization of loans or the depreciation of foreign direct investment, and moderate family expenses) would be highly desirable to ease current transactions and to attract foreign direct investment.

Full convertibility on current and capital account requires that foreign exchange is available without restrictions to whoever is able to pay the going price. It is not necessary to move very quickly towards capital-account convertibility as foreign direct investment can be attracted through other channels, as discussed in the next section. By keeping capital movements under control, the managers of the transition will avoid a premature upward pressure on the exchange rate which may be undesirable.

(e) Fostering foreign investment

All the countries in transition are chronically short of capital. They are, therefore, hoping to attract foreign direct investment through joint ventures, the sale of state-owned enterprises and new capital formation. Not only do policy makers hope that such transfers will provide financial resources but direct capital inflows are also expected to help the economies in transition gain access to modern technology and managerial skills.

Although the countries in transition are hoping to attract substantial foreign capital, this process poses several problems, which have parallels in the worries about the role of transnational corporations in developing countries and the cautious approach in western Europe to liberalizing capital movements after the Second World War. The main problem here is the issue of property rights and whether these should be acquired by foreigners.[364]

There is nothing inherently wrong with selling society's assets to foreigners, provided such sales can be conducted in an economically warranted manner and society is willing to accept the resulting dilution of its economic sovereignty. However, in countries whose scope for autonomy was so restricted for so long by Soviet-type development precepts, questions of sovereignty are likely to be particularly sensitive.

Once the decision has been taken to seek foreign direct investment, the questions to be looked into are probably less whether to sell assets to foreign owners than questions of the precise areas where foreigners will be allowed to buy assets and of how foreign ownership

will be regulated. A particular problem here is the possible undervaluing of the capital stock during the initial phases of the transition. A sharply depreciated exchange rate may give foreign capital the opportunity to indulge in rent-seeking or monopolistic activities which are unlikely to be of much economic benefit to the host country.

To attract foreign capital, the countries of eastern Europe and the Soviet Union have already developed a wide-ranging regulatory framework over the years, beginning with the first Hungarian joint-venture law in 1972. Some of these legal provisions have been modified as problems have emerged (notably in Hungary throughout the 1980s and also in the Soviet Union after its first joint-venture law was passed in 1986). It is an open question whether the current legal structures are suitable for the radically different situation of transition to a market economy.

So far, although foreign capital has shown considerable interest in investing in the transition economies, only small sums have actually been committed. Despite the considerable, and in some cases even excessive, incentives offered to foreign investors, Hungary and Poland have succeeded in attracting a total of perhaps $1.5 billion; it is probably even less in the Soviet Union.[365] One of the main reasons for this caution is a profound uncertainty over how long it is likely to take to establish solid market economies.

Some commentators stress the role of current-account convertibility in attracting foreign capital; some even recommend that these countries also adopt capital-account convertibility.[366] While achieving current-account convertibility may be an important element for building confidence, individual investors tend to be more concerned with the ability to repatriate profits than with general currency convertibility. Repatriation of profits is part of the current account and can thus be gradually liberalized in the same way as merchandise and related transactions.

(iv) Longer-term actions

There are some reforms which do not need to or cannot be put in place quite as quickly. These include: (1) creating an adequate regulatory environment, (2) starting the process of "large privatization" through the outright sale of state-owned enterprises, (3) creating some components of capital markets other than central and commercial banking, (4) ensuring reliable statistics and a more reliable flow of information more generally,

---

364 In Czechoslovakia, for example, land cannot constitutionally be owned by foreigners. This is an impediment to asset sale, although the countries may study the experience of market economies, such as Finland, that similarly prohibit the alienation of land or other assets.

365 Goskomstat reports 3,000 joint ventures, some 2,400 of them involving partners from developed market economies, with statutory capital of R6 billion, of which one third is the foreign contribution (*Ekonomika i zhizn'*, No.5, 1991, p.9). At the end-year commercial exchange rate this would amount to $3.6 billion. The ECE Database on Joint Ventures lists some 2,000 JVs registered in the Soviet Union by end-1990 with a foreign share in the statutory capital of some R2 billion, or some $3 billion at the commercial exchange rate (*ECE East-West Joint Ventures News*, No.7, March 1991). However, very little is known about how the valuation of the foreign share is obtained, and hence what convertible currency equivalent it represents, as well as what proportion of these amounts is actually paid in.

366 Notably Herbert Giersch – see his "Lessons from West Germany", paper prepared for the conference on "The transition to a market economy in Central and Eastern Europe" organized by the OECD Centre for Co-operation with the European Economies in Transition and the World Bank, Paris, 28-30 November 1990.

(5) setting up an independent pension system and (6) instituting new accounting rules.

(a) Regulatory environment

However averse current policy makers in the countries in transition may be towards intervention in the market, a considerable corpus of anti-trust legislation and regulatory laws will need to be written or adapted from abroad to cope with problems of market failure. The emerging financial sector will need to be effectively regulated by the central bank, disclosure laws for corporations will be required and the government may need to regulate natural monopolies.

(b) Sale of state-owned enterprises

The outright sale of state-owned assets in large enterprises can be conducted through auctions or other, more discretionary channels. If auctions are chosen, the ability and willingness of households to invest in these assets may be limited by lack of savings and general uncertainty.

To mitigate the lack of funds and to entice individuals into adopting a share-holding culture, state assets could be sold off through debt-financed auctions. Financial resources could be made available on a non-discriminatory basis to those willing to acquire state assets who seem able to manage them profitably. In essence, the state as lender would become a rentier, while the private sector would become debtors and capitalists, hopefully without foreign capital access distorting the process (debt-financed buy-outs).

Several countries have already committed themselves to allowing workers and existing management to obtain a share in the sale of large enterprises at a favourable price. Some are even envisaging endowing mutual funds with part of these assets to foster a new culture of private investment.

Although in principle it would be possible to conduct auctions with a clear reservation price, in practice the general atmosphere of uncertainty probably rules this out. Reservation prices may be more feasible in a discretionary divestment programme and could be based on plausible estimates of asset values. Of course the agents drawing up such estimates (outside accounting firms, the state asset management agency or parliamentary bodies) should not be allowed to acquire any ownership rights to avoid conflicts of interest.

(c) The creation of capital markets

Many policy makers have stressed the importance of erecting a capital market as soon as possible and some have already taken steps in this direction. All the reforming countries have expressed the desire to create a stock market quickly, though, so far, only Hungary has a more or less functioning stock market.[367]

Two observations are worth bearing in mind. The first is that capital markets contain a wide variety of institutions and instruments, of which the most basic is having a two-tier banking system with strong and competitive commercial banks. Indeed, the creation of a strong banking sector is one of the priorities of the transition (see section 4.2(ii) above). Secondly, stock markets in mature market economies trade mostly in secondary capital. Primary or venture capital is normally raised privately or elsewhere in another, specialized part of the capital market.

Eventually, of course, financial intermediation in these economies in transition will have to be extended beyond the commercial banking sector. For one thing, the government will have to develop instruments of government debt so that deficits can be financed without printing money. Markets in such instruments should be set up relatively quickly, although at first the marketing can be left in the hands of commercial banks.

Insurance companies will need to be set up to help spread the costs of uncertainty while the desire to reduce risk through asset diversification will lead to the creation of mutual funds. Private pension funds may eventually be created which would invest in the stock market or other available assets.

(d) Statistics and dissemination of information

Both government and firms in a market economy require timely and accurate statistics if sensible policies are to be adopted. They will require a far wider range of more reliable economic statistics than was previously available under central planning. Accurate statistics will also help donor countries to evaluate the effectiveness of aid programmes.

More generally, the transparency of economic relations needs to be greatly improved. This requires not only adequate and accurate statistical information but also the dissemination of a whole range of economic and commercial information that was simply irrelevant to the planned economies. Eventually, as in mature market economies, some of these activities will be undertaken by private enterprises or by sectoral bodies, such as industry organizations. However, during the early stages of the transition, international organizations can play a considerable role in helping national governments to improve the flow of information.

(e) Pension system

In the short run there can be little doubt that the elderly will have to be taken care of by the state. Some loss in security of the elderly is probably unavoidable, whatever their work history or contribution to society. Over a longer period, old age pensions should be based on insurance systems with entitlements depending on contributions.

Once again, a number of mature market economies have developed this type of insurance-based pension

---

367 Only some 30 shares are traded and the volume of transactions has remained small since the market's inception in 1990. See footnote (469) below.

system and it would be simplest for the economies in transition to copy from a properly functioning system abroad. Households may also wish to have available alternatives to the state social-security system and this may lead to the establishment of private pension funds.

(f) Accounting rules

A serious impediment to economic decision-making in all the transition economies is the lack of open, standardized accounting systems. Indeed, many details of enterprise accounts were kept secret either for political reasons or to protect the existing management. Without a standardized accounting system that can stand international scrutiny, a modern economy cannot function; real profitability is difficult to assess, public finance cannot function properly and the valuation (and hence the sale) of assets is made more difficult.

As with many institutional features of the market economy, there are several foreign accounting systems which the economies in transition could adapt for their own use. Once a system of accounts is adopted, it should be made mandatory for all economic agents.

(v) The sufficient conditions for the stability of the market economy

The overall framework required for a stable market economy able to adapt flexibly to unexpected changes includes all of the institutions listed in the previous three sections (the "necessary" conditions for setting up a market economy in the first place). These institutions must be well-rooted and able to change organically in the face of unexpected developments.

This flexibility in the basic structures of a market economy will take time to emerge in each of the reforming countries. Efficient markets do not simply spring to life on the retreat of central planners and bureaucratic controls. They require all the institutional changes set out in this chapter but, more fundamentally, they also require substantial changes in individual attitudes. All agents in these societies, be they producers or consumers, workers or owners, households or firms will have to change their behaviour radically if the shift to the market is to succeed and not to collapse in the face of unexpected setbacks.

(vi) On the sequencing of market-oriented reform

Having described the key requirements for the creation of a functioning market economy, we can now set out a suggested sequencing for reform.

As the structure of this chapter suggests, the order in which the various reform components are introduced is not a random matter at all. Some features of a desirable sequencing are already implicit in the analysis earlier in this section. The sequencing suggested here consists of four stages, the precise time needed for each stage obviously depending on the precise circumstances in the country concerned.

The *first phase* should aim at eliminating any chronic imbalances inherited from the past. To do so, the pent-up demand should be diverted either to new goods made available to the domestic market or it should be invested in new financial instruments; full-scale monetary reform may be necessary in some cases. At the same time monetary and fiscal policies will have to be tightened. State assets transferred to enterprise councils or "social ownership" may have to be re-nationalized to establish the principle of clear property rights, which will eventually encourage the emergence of new property structures from gross state, corporate, and private savings. To help absorb excess money balances, a start should be made with the divestment or sale of small-scale undertakings (such as retail and catering outlets or small-scale production units) and housing. The authorities should ensure that any bidding is open to the whole population and some variant of a give-away may be preferred for non-economic reasons. As far as land reform is concerned, farmers should be given definite rights to any residual profit resulting from their efforts to maintain and improve the land.

The *next phase* of the reform programme should emphasize macro-economic balance in current monetary and fiscal policies.

Initially, policy should aim at regaining domestic equilibrium but resources must gradually move to regain external balance as well. For this, a tight monetary policy and fiscal reforms will be needed to ensure that money supply remains adequate and that any government deficit does not become a chronic source of inflation. Big monopolies should be broken up into meaningful autonomous units while any remaining petty assets should be sold quickly in open auctions. If inflation has destroyed household's liquid wealth, generous state financing at a realistic interest rate may be desirable to ensure that private ownership takes root effectively. Initially, prices are likely to be volatile and experimentation and publicity may be required to overcome popular scepticism. Finally all state-owned enterprises (excepting perhaps those providing strategic goods and public utilities) should be converted into joint-stock companies. Monitoring of the management of these companies could initially be executed under the supervision of an impartial, professional body that owes responsibility to parliamentary oversight. At the same time, capital formation from private sources should be fostered to strengthen competition.

The *third stage* of this progression consists of enforcing competitive behaviour by creating a regulatory environment and managerial incentive schemes which reduce the principal-agent problem in state-owned corporations. Gradually, such state assets should be opened up to competitive bidding, for example, for leases or management contracts. The supervisory authority would be charged with maximizing the net return on assets and seeing to it that sufficient schemes are in place to minimize abuses. At the same time, the government should continue macro-economic stabilization, carry out further fiscal and monetary reforms, act to reduce the power of monopolies and replace the material-technical supply system with genuine whole-sale trading. It should also introduce market-type pricing, perhaps by first anchoring key input prices to world prices, using a realistic exchange rate. The system of job-security needs to be sharply relaxed and a social safety net put in place. Lastly, the economy should be opened to foreign competition through trade liberalization and perhaps current-account convertibility for merchandise transactions. Foreign direct investment and joint ventures will need to be encouraged.

Finally, once the former state-owned enterprises are behaving like competitive firms, the most urgent structural adjustments have been completed, domestic monetary and fiscal stability reigns and competition is well ingrained, divestment of most state-owned corporations through outright sale should get under way. This should take the form of feeding the budding domestic stock market or other parts of the growing capital market. Participation in such programmes should be open to both domestic and foreign economic agents.

4.3 SHOCK TREATMENT: EAST GERMANY, POLAND, YUGOSLAVIA

(i) Introduction

The policy measures designed to introduce a market economy system in the former German Democratic Republic, Poland and Yugoslavia have been characterized as a "big-bang" or "shock treatment". What happened in these countries can be described as a sudden and comprehensive liberalization of all domestic markets for goods, services and production factors, a liberalization which also extended to foreign trade. In Poland and Yugoslavia this radical change was accompanied by draconian measures to combat hyperinflation at the end of 1989. Indeed, stabilizing the economy has been an integral part of the reform process itself.

Although there cannot be a unique model for the transition process, it is nevertheless interesting to compare the various countries involved, because the major problems to be tackled are similar.

The three countries dealt with in this section had followed markedly different policies in the past. Economic decision-making had already been decentralized to a large degree in Poland and Yugoslavia, although this had not led to the creation of real markets. In the former German Democratic Republic central planning continued until the end to provide a firm guide to the producing sectors. There were also sizeable differences with regard to the relative importance of private sector economic activity. In Poland and Yugoslavia the private sector accounted for some 19 and 14 per cent, respectively, of total economy output in 1989, though the bulk of this was accounted for by agriculture. In contrast, in the German Democratic Republic this share was only about 4 per cent.

Any assessment of relative economic strength at the end of 1989 would have certainly put the German Democratic Republic ahead of the other east European countries and of the three countries considered here Poland would be at the bottom of the scale. At the beginning of 1991 all three economies are in serious economic crisis, and not much remains of the apparent economic strength of the former German Democratic Republic, where the downturn in activity has been much deeper than in the other countries.

Despite facing similar problems, however, the former German Democratic Republic constitutes a unique case in that a centrally planned economy was suddenly united with the highly advanced market economy of west Germany. This meant that *uno actu* the complete institutional and legal framework of a market economy system was adopted and the task of creating competitive market structures in the eastern part of the country is transformed into a regional development problem for the united Germany.

In contrast, the other countries of eastern Europe have to create the legal and institutional framework for the new system largely from scratch, although this does not exclude, of course, the possibility of adopting some of the institutions that have proved their worth in other market economies. But a complete and sudden takeover as in the case of east Germany is neither a realistic nor necessarily a desirable option.

(ii) The consensus on reforms

It is evident that such far-reaching reforms cannot be embarked upon without the existence of a broad political and social consensus in favour of creating a market economy. At the same time it is important to emphasize the close relationship between targets and means. Often a consensus on a desired objective may fall apart because an agreement as to the required means cannot be achieved or maintained over time. The latter is a risk that cannot be avoided, of course, but agreement on the reform process in Yugoslavia broke down already a few months after its inception.

In *Poland* the round-table negotiations held between the government and Solidarity in spring 1989 resulted in a broad consensus on future political and economic reforms. The elections that followed in June revealed the lack of any widespread support for the Polish communist Party (PUWP), which subsequently broke up into different factions in January 1990.

The new consensus on political and economic reforms was represented in the new government formed by Mr. T. Mazowiecki in September 1989. Important measures to stabilize the economy had already been taken in the final months of 1989 and the basic blueprint of reform[368] and the many laws related to it were prepared and passed by parliament in a very short time.

The government had made it clear in the reform outline that the new policies would be painful, and lead to declines in output and real incomes, bankruptcies and rising unemployment; but at the same time it was

---

[368] See "*Poland's Economic Programme*", Outline, Warsaw, October 1989, (submitted by the Polish delegation to the thirty-eighth session of the ECE Committee on the Development of Trade, Geneva, 4-8 December 1989). Published in Polish in *Rzeczpospolita*, 12 October 1989.

optimistic that a turning point would occur relatively quickly.[369]

The hard consequences of the draconian stabilization package launched at the beginning of 1990 did not shake the consensus on the reforms but new social and political tensions did emerge in the course of the year.

The surprising performance of a hitherto unknown candidate (Tyminski) in the presidential elections in autumn 1990 suggests that there is a risk that populist policies could quickly erode the social consensus should the costs of reform and stabilization rise much more.

As in the western democracies, a political business cycle appears to be emerging in Poland. The first completely free parliamentary elections are to be held in the autumn of 1991.

Not surprisingly there has been increasing pressure on the new government to adopt a more expansionary policy stance. Trade unions are pushing for a relaxation of the stringent wage controls and various sectors are demanding financial support to cushion the costs of adjustment. For the time being the new government under Prime Minister Bielecki has been able to check these demands and in parliament a clear majority voted at the end of February 1991 in favour of a restrictive government budget.

In the former *German Democratic Republic* a political revolution swept away the established political forces, which were stubbornly refusing any political reforms, only a few weeks after the 40th anniversary of the German Democratic Republic.[370] After the opening of borders on 9 November 1989 it quickly became clear that further developments would be dominated by the striving for unification. The increasing disintegration of the German Democratic Republic economy and society, and massive migration to the Federal Republic led the west German government to propose on 7 February 1990 the creation of an economic, monetary and social union, with the Deutschmark as sole legal tender. This proposal amounted to the complete adoption by the German Democratic Republic of the institutional and legal framework of the market economy system of the Federal Republic and aborted any attempts for a "third way". Thereafter events moved rapidly: the state treaty on the modalities of the economic and monetary union was signed by the two governments on 18 May and it came into effect on 1 July 1990; political unification followed on 3 October 1990.

While there is a firm political and social consensus in Poland and the former German Democratic Republic for the transition to a market economy, this is currently not the case in *Yugoslavia*. In fact, the country is in disarray, beset by political and nationalist rivalries, which have led to a collapse of the economic reform programme adopted in December 1989.

Yugoslavia has long been distinct from the other countries of eastern Europe with its own specific economic system, purporting to combine market forces with workers' self-management.[371] Previous attempts to introduce a kind of market economy during the mid-1960s and 1970s[372] foundered, largely because of a lack of consensus between the republics and the federal government on the role and functions of the latter. In 1988 the League of Communists of Yugoslavia (LCY) — the only party at that time — was separated from the state apparatus and a multi-party system was introduced in 1990, although Yugoslavia is not yet a pluralistic society.

The new federal government, which took over in spring 1989, drew up plans to consolidate and radically reform the ailing economy after a decade of failed attempts at restoring macro-economic balance. The package, designed at the same time to introduce a fully-fledged market economy in the medium term, was passed by the federal parliament in December 1989. But the apparent consensus on the reforms was not real and fell apart in the course of 1990, when the republics again challenged the right of the federal government to exert any macro-economic control over, let alone to reform, the economy. Another reform package presented by the federal government in December 1990 appears to be in a state of suspension.

The discussion on economic reforms has now taken second place to the controversy over the future constitutional arrangements of the country.

(iii) Macro-economic stabilization: policies and effects

Stabilizing the economy was given first priority in the programmes implemented in Poland and Yugoslavia, where hyperinflation had emerged in the second half of 1989.

In *Poland* the new government, which took office in September 1989, immediately tightened budget controls, restrained the growth of the money supply, and applied more strictly the wage indexation formula that had been introduced in April 1989.[373] As a result real

---

[369] *Loc.cit.*, p.6.

[370] This hard line against reforms was at the same time a refusal of the need for *perestroika* and *glasnost* in the German Democratic Republic, which provoked the widely-quoted remark by Mr. Gorbachev that " ... history has its own regularities, its own tempo and rhythm. ... To ignore this is to invite further problems". See "Address by Mikhail Gorbachev at the Meeting to Mark the 40th Anniversary of the German Democratic Republic". Berlin, 6 October 1989. Novosti Press Agency.

[371] The Yugoslav economic system has also been labelled "socialist market economy" and "market socialism".

[372] The constitution of 1974 introduced the so-called "system of associated labour", a form of decentralization that split enterprises into smaller autonomous units.

[373] The wage indexation agreed in April 1989 aimed at offsetting the impact of inflation on purchasing power but, in fact, the allowances granted by firms led to a rapid rise in real wages between April and August of 1989. This overshooting of nominal wage growth in turn accelerated inflation, thus creating a wage-price spiral.

wages fell sharply and to maintain consumption households had to draw on their accumulated reserves of foreign exchange, leading to an appreciation of the zloty in the parallel market, which had been legalized in March 1989. These measures eliminated a sizeable part of the accumulated monetary overhang by the end of 1989 and substantially reduced the existing distortions in the structure of prices.[374] At the same time the authorities devalued successively the official exchange rate of the zloty against the US dollar and by the end of 1989 the gap between the official rate and that in the parallel market had narrowed considerably.

The stage was then set for the Polish "shock" therapy aimed at curbing inflation and eliminating the government budget deficit. On 1 January 1990 a package of draconian stabilization measures was launched: fiscal and monetary policies were tightened further and punitive wage controls were applied which kept nominal wage growth significantly below the inflation rate. The introduction of these measures were accompanied by comprehensive price liberalization, the cutting of subsidies, and drastic increases in a few remaining controlled prices, notably energy products. At the same time the official exchange rate was fixed at 9,500 zloty per US dollar, which compared to the rate prevailing at the end of December 1989 amounted to a devaluation of 46 per cent.[375] These measures were complemented by the decision to completely free foreign trade, the reduction of import tariffs and the introduction of internal convertibility.[376]

This programme allowed for a certain amount of "corrective inflation" to siphon off the remaining monetary overhang and an adjustment in the relative prices of tradeable goods to those prevailing in the world market. Consequently, in January 1990 there was a considerable surge in inflation to a monthly rate of 79.6 per cent compared with 17.7 per cent in December 1989. Thereafter, inflationary pressures subsided under the impact of restrictive policies. Budgetary balance was also quickly achieved by cutting expenditures, mainly on subsidies and tax exemptions. In fact, the budget moved into balance early in 1990 and for the year as whole recorded a small surplus.

The stabilization package has achieved a number of objectives. It has restored confidence in the domestic currency, which had lost its function as a store of value and medium of exchange. The shortage economy has given way to more balanced markets and, in some cases, to a situation of excess supply. Hoarding of goods and queues in front of shops have disappeared,

and inflation has been substantially reduced. There was dynamic export growth and a significant improvement in the foreign accounts. Of considerable importance was the ability to maintain a stable dollar exchange rate after the initial large devaluation, as this provided a nominal anchor for the adjustment of tradeable goods prices.

On the other hand, the costs of the austerity policy have been high. There have been large declines in real incomes, industrial output and employment, and consequently unemployment is on the rise.[377]

However, the question arises as to what extent the deterioration in output and the labour market can actually be attributed to the austerity measures. Hidden unemployment is still very high, firms need to restructure to survive in the new competitive environment and many will have to be closed down. Many of these structural adjustments have started to occur at the same time as restrictive policies curbed real demand. Thus part of the decline in output is "systemic" reflecting adjustments to the changing supply-demand relationships, without necessarily reducing the welfare of the private household sector.[378]

Nevertheless, while acknowledging that the available statistics are imperfect, it is difficult to dispute that real standards of living have fallen, possibly significantly. In fact, in 1990 the fall appears to have been much deeper than expected by the government. The steep fall in real wages may partly reflect a too restrictive wage policy in view of the erosion of forced savings by hyperinflation in the final quarter of 1989.[379]

In the second half of 1990 policy priorities shifted slightly as the monthly inflation rate in June and July fell 3 to 4 per cent (corresponding to an annual rate of 40 to 60 per cent). Monetary policy was eased and the wage policy was slightly relaxed. Real wages started to rise in the second half of 1990 but inflation accelerated to an annual rate of 80 to 100 per cent in the final quarter of 1990, partly because of higher oil prices and the shift to convertible currency and world market prices in trade with the Soviet Union.

In January 1991 large increases in rents and energy prices and intra-CMEA air transport tariffs pushed the monthly inflation rate to 12.7 per cent (corresponding to an annual rate of 320 per cent).[380] Although there are exceptional factors at work, it is clear that high inflation remains a matter of great concern. According to a recent industrial survey by the CUP (Central Office of

---

[374] An alternative way of reducing the excessive monetary overhang would have been a monetary reform, but for various reasons this option was not chosen.

[375] To defend the new exchange rate a stabilization loan of $1 billion was made available by a group of industrialized countries and there was a standby agreement with the IMF.

[376] For the precise meaning of internal convertibility see section 4.2 above.

[377] See section 2.3 above.

[378] Thus demand will decline insofar as there is no longer any need for hoarding; the hard budget constraint will eliminate the waste of resources and reduce the demand for intermediate and capital goods etc. See Jan Winiecki, "Post-Soviet-type Economies in Transition: What Have We Learned from the Polish Transition Programme in its First Year?", *Weltwirtschaftliches Archiv*, vol.126, 1990, No.4, p.782.

[379] See J. Winiecki, *loc.cit.*, p.779.

[380] The upward trend of consumer prices may have been reinforced by the pass-through of producer cost increases in preceding months.

Planning), some 80 per cent of enterprises plan to raise their prices by 30 per cent or more in the first quarter of 1991, which could trigger a new wage-price spiral. The target for 1991, which may be very difficult to achieve, is to reduce the annual inflation rate to 52 per cent, compared with an actual rate of 585 per cent in 1990.[381]

Given the fixed nominal exchange rate against the dollar and the high rate of domestic inflation, there has been a significant appreciation of the real exchange rate since the beginning of 1990 and this has increasingly reduced the profit margins of exporters and affected price competitiveness.[382] In the final months of 1990 the surplus in convertible currency trade fell. Export prospects for 1991 have also deteriorated substantially given the likely further decline of intra-CMEA trade. Enterprise managers expect a considerable weakening of exports to both the CMEA and western countries in the first quarter of 1991.[383]

The fixed nominal exchange rate together with the liberalization of imports helped to bring down the inflation rate in 1990 but the costs associated with the current exchange rate policy could become too high in 1991. The targets for inflation and nominal wage growth, as agreed in the letter of intent to the IMF for the second half of 1990 were surpassed by a relatively large margin and the next tranche of the standby credit has been suspended.[384] Negotiations for a new three-year programme are underway.

The overall economic situation in Poland will remain very difficult in the foreseeable future. Opinion polls suggest that the optimistic mood prevailing at the end of 1990 has been deteriorating. It is thus important to provide an adequate social safety net and to raise expectations of increases in standards of living in the not too distant future.

The overall economic situation in *Yugoslavia* at the end of 1989 was basically similar to that in Poland. After nearly a decade of economic decline marked by lax monetary and fiscal policy, excessive foreign debt and uncontrolled wage growth, the country was beset by hyperinflation. Several previous attempts at stabilization and reform had foundered but at the end of 1989 the new federal parliament adopted a comprehensive package of reform and stabilization measures. The main objective of the austerity measures was to reduce the annual inflation rate from 1,250 per cent in 1989 to a 13 per cent in 1990.

A key element in the economic strategy was the introduction of a new dinar[385] as from 1 January 1990, which was declared internally convertible. At the same time the dinar was pegged to the Deutschmark at a rate of 7 dinar/1 DM until the end of June 1990.[386] As in Poland, Yugoslavia used the nominal exchange rate as an anchor for domestic stabilization, but in contrast to Poland, the Yugoslav authorities did not devalue but tried a rate that was overvalued.

Among the other measures, similar to those adopted in Poland, in the first half of 1990 were:

  − a wage freeze at the level prevailing in November 1989;

  − a tightening of monetary policy, notably to end the monetization of federal and republican budget deficits;

  − price liberalization covering about 90 per cent of all goods and services.

Under the combined impact of an overvalued currency, increasing import competition, wage restriction and tight fiscal and monetary policies, inflationary pressures eased considerably in the first half of the year: between May and June there was even a decline in the aggregate price index. But thereafter the already weak consensus concerning the stabilization policy broke down in the face of strong centrifugal political forces. Wage controls were largely lifted and monetary and fiscal policy was loosened. The discount rate which had been 23.4 per cent in the first six months of 1990 − this was the target rate for the whole year − was reduced to 14 per cent in July, possibly in the belief that the battle against inflation had been won and that an excessive tightening should be avoided.[387] However, in the final quarter inflation accelerated and monetary policy was again tightened: the discount rate was raised to 25 per cent and then to 30 per cent in November.

For the year as a whole the inflation rate was 590 per cent, way off the target of 13 per cent, but still somewhat less than half the rate in 1989. It should also be noted that the statistical "overhang" from December 1989 alone would have entailed a year-on-year inflation rate of 280 per cent. Comparing December 1989 with December 1990, monthly inflation − expressed at an annual rate − declined from 275 per cent to 50 per cent.

---

381 There is a already a sizeable statistical carry-over effect of about 28 per cent from the end of December 1989.

382 The squeeze on profits was considerably attenuated by the fact that companies built up large inventories of imported raw materials and intermediate goods at an overvalued exchange rate and favourable conditions for credit in 1989. This will shift the adjustment burden to 1991. On this point see also J. Winiecki, *loc.cit.*, p.774.

383 *Trybuna*, 28 January 1991.

384 See *Zycie gospodarcze*, 20 January 1991.

385 One new dinar is the equivalent of 10,000 old dinars.

386 This amounted to an exchange rate of 1:1 with regard to the Austrian Schilling, which is also pegged to the DM and indicates the overvaluation of the Yugoslav currency. Effectively, this pegging of the exchange rate to the DM was sustained much longer than expected, namely until the end of 1990, when the authorities had to opt for a devaluation. As from 1 January 1991 the new exchange rate is 9:1.

387 See National Bank of Yugoslavia, *The Economic Scene of Yugoslavia in December 1990*. Belgrade, February 1991.

Certainly some discipline has been exerted by the hard exchange rate policy. This can be seen in the fact that industrial producer prices rose much less (by 434 per cent) than the consumer price index, the difference reflecting the considerably higher inflation rate for services.

Against a background of inconsistent and unco-ordinated policies, the overall economic situation in Yugoslavia therefore took a further turn for the worse in 1990. Real gross social product (the value added originating in the so-called material sphere) fell by about 7.5 per cent in 1990 and total employment fell by 3.5 per cent, the unemployment rate rising to 13.6 per cent in December 1990 compared with 12.3 per cent in the same period of 1989.

After virtual stagnation between 1987 and 1989, industrial production fell in 1990 by more than 10 per cent. Exports were hampered by the overvalued dinar and domestic sales were also squeezed by increased competition, a result of import liberalization and the high exchange rates. To some extent lower demand is not yet reflected in the output data since firms increased their inventories. Liquidity shortages have become widespread, leaving many firms with unpaid bills and this in turn added to the forces that made for a decline in output. As a response to the downward slide in industrial output, the authorities devalued the dinar against the DM by 29 per cent as from 1 January 1991. But even at the new exchange rate of 9:1, the dinar appears to be still strongly overvalued.

In conclusion, after an initial success the stabilization package launched by the federal government was undermined by centrifugal political forces. Public spending by the republics and wage growth exceeded all targets and were accommodated by monetary policy. Also real interest rates became negative again after having been positive for some months around summer. The recent upgrading of the authority of the central bank was undermined by illegal money creation in some of the republics and the non-monetization of government deficits was not adhered to.

The financing of federal government expenditure was also undermined by some republics not transferring to the federal government the revenues that had been agreed upon.[388]

At the beginning of 1991 Yugoslavia is at a crossroads. The overriding issue is whether a political consensus will emerge between the republics, which is a necessary condition not only for conducting a coherent macro-economic stabilization policy but also for the continuation of the reforms.[389]

In contrast to Poland and Yugoslavia, inflation in the former *German Democratic Republic* had been repressed until spring 1990. The persistent excess demand was reflected in forced savings. Inflation was also concealed by enormous subsidies designed to maintain low and stable prices,[390] and many goods that entered the official price index were not available in the shops. There was a huge pent-up demand for durable consumer goods, notably motor cars. According to the official statistics the authorities had maintained the public sector budget in broad balance, at least until 1988.

The economic and monetary union that started on 1 July completely changed the fundamental parameters of the economy: prices were liberalized, international trade was no longer subject to restrictions and economic agents (firms and households) disposed of a fully convertible currency.

This is in principle akin to the measures introduced in Poland and Yugoslavia. The introduction of the Deutschmark is tantamount to the pegging of the domestic currency to a reserve currency but in the case of east Germany the exchange rate has been irrevocably fixed.

Fears that the high conversion rate of the GDR mark for the DM[391] would lead to a surge in the German inflation rate have not materialized. The monetary overhang was apparently not very high[392] and the pent-up demand for western goods was absorbed by increased output in west Germany and by imports from other western countries. Retail sales boomed in the west, but plunged in the east.[393]

The liberalization of prices and the cutting of subsidies has led to sizeable changes in relative prices in east Germany. Prices of tradeable goods quickly adjusted to west German levels. The official price index for east Germany, however, remained below its average value in 1989. But the meaning of this index is dubious given the large shifts in the pattern of consumption: many products in the underlying "representative" basket, which was fixed in 1989, are no longer purchased or produced.

---

388 See Federal Executive Council, *Basic Facts of the Reform*, loc.cit. "... in September last year the republics and provinces started to pay in lower amounts of revenues in relation to those regulated by .... the Law on the Financing of the Federation".

389 According to opinion polls the economic reform programme launched by the federal government does not appear to lack popular support, though the government may for the moment derive only cold comfort from these statistics. In fact, about 66 per cent of all respondents stated to be in agreement with the direction of federal government economic policies and about the same proportion held the view that the success of reforms was most threatened by local and regional conflicts. See *Yugoslav Survey*, Vol.XXXI, 1990, No.3, pp.9-10.

390 In 1989 some 20 per cent of total government expenditures were accounted for by food subsidies.

391 The basic rate was 2:1; but effectively the conversion rate varied with the age of individuals. The average conversion rate was 1.5:1. For a detailed presentation see United Nations Economic Commission for Europe, *Economic Bulletin for Europe*, vol.42/90, New York, 1991, chapter 4: "The unification of Germany".

392 See United Nations Economic Commission for Europe, *Economic Survey of Europe in 1989-1990*, New York, 1990, p.31.

393 See section 2.1 above.

The sudden and comprehensive exposure to international competition led to a collapse of the east German industrial sector and a drastic deterioration in the labour market, although this was partly masked by an increase in short-time working arrangements. It became rapidly evident in the months following the economic union that assessments of the ability of the east German economy to cope *in the short run* with the abrupt and enormous change in economic parameters were far too optimistic.

There are many reasons for the current crisis but three can be singled out. First is the overall poor state of the capital stock — much worse than anticipated — and the low quality of products. Second, the adjustment shock was intensified by the introduction of the Deutschmark as sole legal tender. No market-determined exchange rate between the DM and the GDR Mark was available in the past, but given the existing production apparatus in the east, the introduction of the DM amounted effectively to a huge appreciation of the GDR Mark, viz. to an enormous overvaluation.

These two factors have been compounded by the steep rise in labour costs. In an integrated labour and capital market pressures for factor price equalization must quickly emerge. In theory, capital will flow to the area where labour is still cheap and the higher demand will eventually raise the price of labour; at the same time some labour will move to the region where wages are higher thus exerting downward wage pressure there. Both tendencies will tend to bring about labour cost equalization.

Although migration from east to west is continuing, this process is regarded as undesirable given that skilled workers and the young will tend to move first. Moreover, German trade unions clearly want to avoid downward wage pressure in the west on account of migration. The overriding objective of the unions has therefore been to initiate a catch-up process for wages in the east, without wage restraint in the west.

On average, wages in the east may have risen some 30-40 per cent in 1990 compared with 1989, bringing them to about half the levels in the west. The current wage round will bring a further narrowing of wage differences. In fact, in a recent agreement between the trade unions and employers, metal workers in the eastern part of the country will obtain the same basic wage as in the west by 1994. Similar projections are likely to emerge in wage agreements in other sectors.

These wage increases are completely disconnected from changes in productivity in the east. More importantly, the changes in labour costs are not accompanied by corresponding flows of capital that embody the technology which would be "compatible" with these higher wage levels.

Against this background an even larger part of the east German capital stock has been rendered obsolete. The threat of bankruptcy will have become even more acute for many firms, and incentives to migrate to the west have probably risen. Given these developments, the only strategy for survival for east German firms is to scrap the existing capital stock and move immediately to the technological frontier.[394] However, it is clear that a rapid and comprehensive improvement of the east German infrastructure is necessary in order to attract private investment. In any case, considerable investment incentives will be needed to bring about the flows of private capital required to keep unemployment within acceptable bounds. The authorities might also consider the introduction of wage subsidies or direct subsidy schemes which would lower production costs, but lead to a substantial narrowing of the real income gap between the two parts of the country.[395] Such schemes could be phased out with the closing of the productivity gap.[396]

(iv) Systemic reform

At the core of the transition process from centrally planned to market economies is the creation of the legal institutions which support the market economy system. However, a much more difficult problem is to create the micro-economic foundations for systemic change. Decentralization of decision-making, privatization, price liberalization, the creation of a two-tier banking system, the liberalization of foreign trade are some of the priority elements.

In *east Germany* the complete legal and institutional framework of a market economy was put in place, virtually overnight, with the start of the economic union on 1 July 1990. This saved enormous amounts of time and resources, but the costs are also high. The legal framework that has evolved over the last 40 years in west Germany is suited to the very specific problems of a highly complex social, political and economic system and it may only imperfectly suit the specific needs of an economy in transition. Also, for the system to work smoothly and provide a firm basis for decision-making, it requires human resources which are familiar with the rules and exceptions incorporated in the various legal provisions. This is certainly not the case in east Germany and has become a serious obstacle for the smooth functioning of the civil administration and legal services. Substantial technical assistance has been provided by the western part of the country. Thus, to illustrate, many west German local authorities have "adopted" a local authority in the east and are helping to establish a functioning administration.

Progress in creating the new legal foundations for a market economy has been quite fast in *Poland* where

---

394 Evidently, the sharp decline in east German exports to the markets of eastern Europe and the Soviet Union expected in 1991 is much more a reflection of the lack of competitiveness entailed by the above-mentioned developments than a consequence of the stabilization-cum-adjustment recession in these countries.

395 Given that prices of non-tradeables are lower in east Germany, a complete equalization of nominal incomes will not be required to close the real income gap.

396 See United Nations Economic Commission for Europe, *Economic Bulletin for Europe*, vol.42/90, New York, 1991, chapter 4, p.100.

the large majority of fundamental new laws has been passed or prepared since autumn 1989.[397] The need for speed at this stage, however, may suppress many diverging opinions among policy-makers on details, which will have to be settled at a later stage. In fact, the new Prime Minister has said that the government sees the need for some 7,000 new legislative proposals to settle problems in various areas, such as foreign investment, housing, environmental protection and social security.[398] Whether or not the figure is precise, it indicates the amount of work that is still to be completed. The Polish authorities have been looking out for suitable legal and other institutions abroad which they could use as basic models for their own legislation and they are employing foreign consultants to help them in this. Thus the securities exchange to be opened in Warsaw in 1991 will be closely modelled on the exchange in Lyon.

In *Yugoslavia* some of the basic institutions of a market economy already exist in rudimentary form — such as a two-tier banking system[399] — but any substantial progress in building new institutions has been impeded by the lack of political consensus among the republics on the economic system.

(a) Price liberalization

A common element in the reforms in the three countries has been the virtually complete liberalization of consumer and producer prices. The major exceptions to liberalization have been rents and energy for household use and some public services such as transport and communication. Such controls have also been a pervasive feature of post-war western Europe.

In *Poland* the remnants of the rationing system for private consumers had already been abolished in 1989 and subsidies on consumer goods were reduced. As from the beginning of August 1989 most consumer prices were liberalized, a step which led to an acceleration of the open inflation. Since the beginning of 1990 there has been a substantial reduction in subsidies on fuel and energy, which has resulted in a temporary resurgence of inflation. About 10 per cent of all prices are currently still subject to some sort of administrative control — partly to regulate the behaviour of monopolistic state companies — as compared with some 50 per cent in 1989. These so-called official prices were increased several times in 1990 as subsidies were cut on natural gas, coal and coke, telecommunications, and public transport.

In *east Germany* all prices were liberalized as from 1 July except rents, energy, transport and communications. These exceptions helped to contain inflation at very low levels in the course of 1990 but the support schemes will be partly phased out in 1991 leading to considerable price increases in some cases. For these reasons the average inflation rate in east Germany will be much higher than in west Germany during 1991.

Also in *Yugoslavia*, the large majority of prices are free from control, although a number of public sector and major raw material prices (electricity, coal and coke, petroleum products, public transport and postal services) have been frozen since the end of December 1989.

(b) Foreign trade and exchange liberalization

In *Poland* some limited steps towards the liberalization of foreign trade had already been introduced in the 1980s, especially with regard to trade with convertible-currency countries. This was reflected in a large increase in the number of firms holding permits allowing them to make independent arrangements with foreign partners. As noted above, the authorities completely liberalized foreign trade for registered firms at the beginning of 1990. Customs duties and the exchange rate have replaced administrative regulations as the major regulators of external commercial relations. The few exceptions to free trade concern radioactive and nuclear materials, weapons and arms, as well as selected services, such as franchising. Restrictions were also imposed on trade in alcoholic beverages and tobacco in 1990. A major feature of the reforms has been the cutting of import tariffs on many goods in order to increase competitive pressure from abroad. Many customs duties, especially on intermediate goods, were suspended in the course of 1990, a suspension which is supposed to be prolonged during the first half of 1991. Export quotas were strictly limited during 1990 and applied mainly to areas where free trade may have led to serious domestic supply shortages (e.g., of coal).

Since 1982 the Polish authorities had followed a policy of flexible adjustment of the zloty to the US dollar to ensure the profitability of the bulk of exports. A system of retention quotas was introduced that permitted firms to keep for themselves a sizeable part of their foreign exchange earnings from exports and use them for import of inputs. As from 1 January 1990 the exchange rate was fixed at 9,500 zloty per US dollar, which compares with a rate of 6,500 zloty per dollar at the end of December 1989 — a nominal devaluation of 46 per cent.

At the same time internal (or resident) convertibility was introduced. The former system of retention quotas has accordingly been abolished. Also foreign currency cannot be legally used in domestic settlements.[400] Internal convertibility entails that registered firms can freely convert domestic currency into other currencies for most foreign transactions but at the same time they have to surrender their foreign exchange holdings to the

---

[397] See "Warunki zdrowej gospodarki," *Rzeczpospolita*, 8 January 1991.

[398] *Trybuna*, 29 January 1991.

[399] However, in 1989 the national bank was still engaged in many commercial transactions.

[400] In special shops where Polish citizens could purchase foreign goods against foreign exchange, sales against foreign currency are no longer allowed since the beginning of 1991.

central bank. In contrast, non-resident firms are still restricted in this respect.

The demand for foreign exchange for non-trade purposes (e.g., tourism) is met in the open parallel market. It is noteworthy that this market rate has remained stable and close to the official uniform rate since early 1990. It is also noteworthy that since the sizeable devaluation at the beginning of 1990 there has been no pressure on the exchange rate; indeed, the stabilization loan of $1 billion made available by a group of western countries to defend the exchange rate has not been drawn on so far.

To stimulate foreign direct investment it is planned to provide for free transfer of profits abroad in the course of 1991, once the necessary changes in the existing joint-ventures law have been passed. This will be a further step towards current account convertibility.

The *Yugoslav* foreign trade régime in the past was characterized by comprehensive import restrictions, a reflection of a development strategy based on import-substitution. In 1987 only some 12 per cent of all convertible currency imports were "free", the remainder being subject to various restrictions such as quotas, licences or to the condition of being non-competitive with Yugoslav goods. Imports have been successively liberalized since 1989 and currently about 90 per cent of all merchandise imports are free from control. Imports of equipment used in joint ventures are duty free and the level of tariff protection has been reduced, although non-tariff barriers may still be very important.

The Yugoslav authorities introduced internal convertibility of the dinar as from the beginning of 1990, but with the deteriorating economic performance in the second half of 1990 and increasing speculation the national bank restricted sales of foreign exchange. Withdrawals from foreign exchange accounts are currently only possible if exchanged into dinars. This applies to foreigners as well.[401]

In *east Germany*, foreign trade since 1 July 1990 has in principle been subject to the same rules that govern trade in west Germany. Some transitory provisions exist for contracts with CMEA countries which were concluded before that date.[402] With the introduction of the Deutschmark east German firms and households have had access to a fully convertible currency since last July.

(c) Property rights and privatization

Privatization of state-owned assets, notably enterprises, is probably *the* key element of the economic reform programme. After more than 40 years of central planning the notions of restructuring the economy and privatization have become almost synonymous in the transition economies.[403]

The objectives of privatization in the transition countries are manifold; but at their centre is a radical reduction of the role of the state. At the same time the process of privatization often requires that companies be re-structured or consolidated to prepare them for the new competitive environment, but in many cases it will not be possible to avoid the closing down of firms. Given the overall weak competitiveness of the producing sectors, this raises more general questions about the relationship between consolidation and privatization, and notably the sequence in which they should occur. Thus, in Germany, the Council of Economic Advisers has argued that privatization should be the vehicle for restructuring and consolidation and not vice versa.[404] This, however, is still a matter of controversy. In Poland the authorities intend in principle to restructure potentially viable companies before attempting to privatize them. These companies will be under the authority of the "Industrial Restructuring Agency", but the details of the arrangements are not yet available.[405]

The corporatization of state owned enterprises as a first step to privatization requires the creation of an institution that represents the state as owner. In Poland this role has been mainly designated to the newly created Ministry for Property Transformations. In the former German Democratic Republic, a special trust body *(Treuhandanstalt)* was created and has formally owned all state assets since 1 March 1990.

The establishment of pluralistic forms of ownership of the means of production was part of the reform package launched in *Yugoslavia* at the end of 1989. However, the process appears to have faltered in the initial stage mainly because of the vagueness of property rights over enterprises in the "public domain".

According to the Yugoslav constitution of 1974, these enterprises do not belong to the state but are viewed as "social *(drustvena)* property", for which rights of disposal are unclear. Under these circumstances a way out might be a temporary re-nationalization of these assets, but it is not clear

---

401 See "Jugoslawien mit Leistungsbilanzproblemen," *Neue Zürcher Zeitung*, 9/10 March 1991; and "Finanzsystem Jugoslawiens vor dem Zusammenbruch", *Frankfurter Allgemeine Zeitung*, 5 March 1991.

402 See General Agreement on Tariffs and Trade, "European Communities – Transitional measures to take account of the external economic impact of German unification", L/6792, 14 December 1990.

403 This is illustrated by the very broad objectives defined for the Polish privatization programme, which include the shift to a market economy system, increased efficiency of firms, the fostering of private initiative, a reduction in the size of the public sector, a wider distribution of private wealth, the development of entrepreneurial and managerial skills, the breaking up of existing monopolies and the generation of funds to finance the restructuring of potentially viable firms. See "Summary of the Work Plan for the Privatization Programme", Government of Poland, Ministry of Ownership Change. Warsaw, 22 September 1990.

404 See "Jahresgutachten 1990/91 des Sachverständigenrates zur Begutachtung der gesamtwirtschaftlichen Entwicklung", Deutscher Bundestag, Drucksache 11/8472, pp.229-231.

405 See "Summary of the Work Plan ...", *loc.cit.*

whether this is permitted under the current constitution.[406]

The problem is further complicated by the fact that in practice control of "social property" is vested in the republics, viz. in local groups of officials, republican bank managers and company managers. Also, it is only at the republican level that agencies for the transformation of property have been established. Evidently, the ambiguities surrounding current property and ownership rights extend also to companies controlled jointly by foreign and domestic management and workers' councils.

Although the Yugoslav federal government believes that private property should have a substantial role in the future Yugoslav economy, this view is not shared by all the republics. These differences will have to be settled before the technical and legal aspects of changes in ownership can be discussed. At present, the question of privatization in Yugoslavia has, like many other fundamental economic problems, been put aside because of the lack of consensus on the economic and political system.

The change of legal status, the so-called commercialization, is a second step to privatization.[407] In east Germany after 1 July all state-owned enterprises were transformed into joint stock or limited liability companies. In Poland, such a change in legal status is only envisaged once the authorities have actually decided that a company should be privatized. A complication in the privatization process may arise in Poland from the strong participation of workers' in the management of firms: this may have blurred actual property rights and eventually could pose an obstacle to privatization. The privatization law stipulates that the authorities can commercialize a state-owned firm on their own initiative only after workers and management have been consulted. Given the strength of the trade unions this may give rise to protracted bargaining processes which may not always be conducive to successful and speedy privatization.

It is clear, in all countries concerned, that privatization will take considerable time and that the majority of firms will need to be restructured or closed down. This leads to the question as to what extent the authorities will be prepared to enforce a hard budget constraint on loss-making firms if the unemployment consequences may be severe and/or if this threatens to undermine the social and political consensus.

Thus the trust fund has been providing substantial liquidity support to many companies and favourable

export subsidy and export credit guarantee schemes have been introduced. Moreover, the German authorities have set up a generous short-time working benefit system for eastern Germany, which allows employees to receive (probably until the end of 1991) up to 90 per cent of their last net income, even if the company where they work is unlikely to survive.[408] This allows many firms to continue producing at a low level of capacity utilization and avoids immediate closure.

Before privatization can actually start it is necessary to clarify the issue of the rights of the former owners of assets which were expropriated or nationalized. In theory, two basic principles can be distinguished, restitution *versus* compensation. In east Germany the basic principle applied is that restitution will be given priority over compensation. In Poland no clear view has as yet emerged.

In an early response to warnings that restitution might become a hindrance to investment the *German* authorities have weakened this principle and allowed for compensation in cases where an urgent investment project designed to preserve or create employment may be blocked. This has led to a situation which many now regard as a cul de sac. More than one million claims for restitution have been submitted by former private owners of nationalized assets, including the former owners of about 12,000 small and medium-sized firms nationalized in 1972. In addition there are a further 16,000 claims by local authorities requesting the transfer of property rights over a diversity of assets such as bakeries, cinemas, land, and dwellings.[409]

It goes without saying that the east German civil and legal administration has been overwhelmed by this avalanche of claims. Apart from the sheer number of claims, which would test the capacities of any administration, the burden on local administrations in east Germany is especially heavy because of their lack of familiarity with the west German legal codes and a shortage of qualified staff.[410] It also appears that often the legal records concerning private property were not kept in an orderly fashion in the former German Democratic Republic. Against this background, the priority of the restitution principle has been in general difficult to apply in practice. There are many cases for which decisions are pending but over which hangs the threat of legal recourse by former owners.

The ensuing blockage of investment projects has given rise to an animated debate as to how the situation can be remedied. The federal government has drafted a law that is intended to facilitate the application of the compensation principle in the case of planned invest-

---

[406] In fact, part III, article 4 of the Constitution, contains the provision that nobody has the right of property over the social means of production and correspondingly the right to dispose of them. This sounds like a catch-22 because then the state would not have the right to "re-nationalize".

[407] This does not pertain to so-called petty privatization, notably of retail shops, restaurants, etc.

[408] In west Germany short-time working benefits are only granted in case of a temporary − often seasonal − interruption of the production process and the benefits are less generous.

[409] See Werner Moeschel, "Entschädigung vor Rückgabe," *Frankfurter Allgemeine Zeitung,* 7 March 1991; Edgard Meister, "Eigentumsverhältnisse schneller klären", *loc.cit.*, 8 February 1991.

[410] There is hardly any incentive for a west German civil servant to move to the eastern part of the country, given the sizeable income differences.

ment projects.[411] But there are many who argue that this may not be effective and that instead the authorities should completely reverse the present situation and make compensation the rule rather than the exception. The rationale would be to subordinate private interests in restitution to the common interest in a rapid strengthening of economic growth in the east.[412]

In *Poland* the legal provisions concerning private property rights are gradually being put into place. As a first step the Civil Code of 1934 has been updated and parts that were eliminated during the early 1950s have been restored. The clear-cut determination of property-rights will in practice also involve the elimination of different forms of workers' participation in economic decision-making, which became a regular feature of earlier attempts at reform and decentralization. Illegal expropriations of small property (land, retail shops, housing etc.) will be dealt with either by restoring the rights of former owners or by paying compensation. Pressure has recently risen to reconsider the post-war laws concerning the nationalization of private property and a draft law on re-privatization is being prepared. Given the complex practical problems involved, and especially the negative repercussions of unclear property rights on investment projects, the government has been reluctant to support the restitution principle. But the direction which policies may take is not yet clear.

As mentioned above, the privatization of state-owned assets in *East Germany* is the task of a trust body *(Treuhandanstalt)*. The trust fund has formally taken over the ownership of more than 8,000 companies and about 4 million hectares of agricultural and forestry land, an area which corresponds to some 40 per cent of the whole of east Germany. The 8,000 companies have all been transformed into joint stock companies.

Although privatization started in the second half of 1990, progress has been slower than expected. One reason for this is the complexity of the issue of property rights. Among other factors are the general lack of attractiveness of many east German firms and the still very poor state of the infrastructure.[413]

In its privatization strategy the trust fund has so far concentrated on the sale of assets to private investors, rather than the transfer of management rights to private economic agents in a state-owned firm. The techniques of privatization applied have been diverse ranging from the public offering (the rule) to direct "private" negotiations with private companies expressing an interest in individual firms. Management or employee buy-outs have occurred but they are rare exceptions. There are

no plans to issue free or relatively cheap certificates that can at a later time be converted into company shares, a proposal which is being discussed in Poland and the Czechoslovakia.

In contrast to the other east European countries, the privatization process in east Germany has been preceded by the introduction of a capital market by virtue of the economic and monetary union, which should, in principle, considerably ease the task of selling assets. Also, there is no problem of a small domestic savings base in the united German market. In fact, given the openness of the German economy, the psychological resistance to high levels of foreign direct investment in east Germany is likely to be much smaller than in eastern Europe. In any case, there are no longer any formal barriers to foreign investment.

At the end of February 1991 the trust fund had privatized 700 companies, yielding revenues of DM 4 billion. This is, however, more than offset by interest payments on old company debt, financial outlays for consolidation, the support of exports to eastern Europe, and so on. In 1991 the trust fund expects privatization revenues of DM 14 billion, but total expenditures of DM 35 billion will produce a net loss of DM 21 billion.[414]

Small-scale privatization in the sectors of retail trade and restaurants has already made considerable advances: out of 11,000 properties in this sector more than 70 per cent have been sold and the general expectation is that the rest will be sold by the end of 1991.

In *Poland* the process of privatization of large state-owned enterprises started only at the end of 1990. The overall objective is interlocked with intricate questions concerning *inter alia* the viability of companies, the breaking up of monopolies, the distribution of wealth, the lack of a domestic capital market, small domestic savings relative to the value of assets to be sold, a lack of qualified business managers and the large number of state-owned companies.

First and foremost is the question of how many profitable firms there are and what to do with the remainder. According to official estimates, out of the 500 largest state-owned enterprises roughly one third have a good profitability record, while about 25-30 per cent show a poor or very poor performance, with an intermediate group recording satisfactory profitability (about 40-45 per cent).[415]

The general approach to privatization is to transform a state-owned enterprise into a joint stock company, with all shares initially held by the authorities

---

411 See "Bonn will Eigentumsfragen schnell geklärt wissen", *Frankfurter Allgemeine Zeitung*, 1 February 1991; and "Bonn baut Investitionshürden ab", *Süddeutsche Zeitung*, 7 February 1991.

412 See section 4.2 above and W. Moeschel, *loc.cit.*

413 There has been no rush of west German companies to invest in the east, recalling the plain fact that in a market economy national sentiments are not an argument in the investment function.

414 See "Treuhand erwartet 21-Milliarden-Defizit", *Frankfurter Allgemeine Zeitung*, 8 March 1991.

415 See "Summary of the Work Plan ... " *op.cit.*

(Ministry of Property Transformation).[416] The strategy is to identify profitable companies that can survive in a market environment and will be attractive to private investors. Chronic loss-makers will be closed down rapidly and the remaining firms will be subject to restructuring and consolidation, which will be done under the auspices of an Industrial Restructuring Agency.

The law on privatization adopted in July 1990 stipulates *inter alia* that:

- foreign investors can acquire more than 10 per cent of the nominal shares of a company only with the consent of the authorities;

- a feasibility study must be carried out to determine the value of a company and the required organizational and technical changes before issuing stock;

- employees of the company concerned have priority in buying up to 20 per cent of the nominal stocks of the company concerned at half the issue price.

Progress in privatizing state-owned enterprises in Poland has so far been slow, but for petty privatization the record is much better. Thus, about 12,000 retail shops have been sold to the private sector, a process that was at the same time designed to break up existing monopolies in the retail sector.[417]

After a pilot project in December 1990 resulted in the privatization of five highly profitable companies, it is now planned to transform some 300 large enterprises into joint-stock companies in 1991 with the state as temporary sole shareholder – the so-called commercialization approach. It is hoped to privatize about 100 of these in the course of 1991 and about 250-300 large state enterprises by 1994. The total number of state-owned companies (excluding retail shops etc.) is about 8,000.[418]

A major feature of the Polish privatization programme is to create a broad distribution of property against the background of a small domestic savings base. Various schemes to accelerate privatization are being considered: for example, the government intends to distribute 10 per cent of nominal shares in a company to its employees free of charge. A further 30 per cent will be freely distributed to the public in the form of privatization bonds which later can be exchanged against shares,[419] 20 per cent to the social security fund and the remaining 10 per cent to commercial banks.

The government is to retain 30 per cent of the total shares, which will be placed in a mutual investment fund (to be established), in which shares can be sold to the private sector later on.

The new government hopes to speed up the process, of "small privatization" by setting up regional privatization offices in 1991. One priority is the breaking up of monopolies in the food-processing sector by means of privatization. A serious bottleneck to privatization is seen in the lack of managers with experience in a market environment.

Asset sales is but one way of creating a private economic sector. It can be complemented by incentive schemes to encourage the creation of new small and medium-sized enterprises. This is sometimes referred to as privatization from below, in contrast to privatization from above by means of asset sales.[420]

Privatization from below is encouraged by the German authorities with attractive credit and guarantee facilities. In 1990 the number of new small firms created in east Germany was nearly 281,000: in the same period about 12,000 closed down. In Poland the overall institutional support for privatization (banking services, easy credit facilities etc.) appears to be much less favourable.[421]

Notwithstanding the inadequate financial environment and the constraints deriving from the restrictive stance of policies, the number of small private firms in the area of trade, handicraft and services rose in 1990 by 362,000 to 1.14 million. Some 516,000 new firms were created, but 119,000 were liquidated.[422]

(d) Banking system and capital markets

An important component of systemic economic change is the reform of the monetary system. A two-tier banking system needs to be created as well as markets for the efficient allocation of financial capital.

In *east Germany* that problem was solved with the beginning of the economic and monetary union: the Bundesbank controls the money supply and there is no such thing as a regional capital market within a country. The existing banks and other financial institutions in the western part of the country are also serving the east German economy, most of them having created branch offices there.

Some progress in this direction had been made in *Poland* with the creation of an independent banking system in 1987. Thus when the radical reforms were

---

416 See Law on Privatization of State-Owned Enterprises of 13 July 1990.

417 See "Summary of the Work Plan ... " *loc.cit.,* section V.

418 See "Summary of the Work Plan ...," *loc.cit.*

419 The plan is to grant privatization bonds worth at least one million zloty to every member of the population, which corresponds to about 50 per cent of the current average monthly wage.

420 See J. Winiecki, *loc.cit.,* p.784.

421 *Ibid.*

422 GUS, "Komunikat o sytuacji społeczno-gospodarczej kraju w 1990 r.", No.2, 2 February 1991, in *Rzeczpospolita,* 2-3 February 1991.

launched at the beginning of 1990, a rudimentary two-tier banking system was already in place. The National Bank is now concentrating on the functions of a central bank and its other functions have been transferred to nine state-owned commercial banks, which were separated from the National Bank in 1988. These banks are included in the privatization programme, but no concrete plans have as yet been developed. The banking law, as amended in December 1989, provides the legal foundations for the creation of a universal banking system[423] in Poland. The total number of banks has been increasing quite rapidly over the last year or so: at the end of 1990 there were 63 banks registered, including three joint ventures with western participation. For the time being commercial banks and insurance companies are the only financial institutions in Poland. It is hoped that mutual funds and more private insurance companies (including private old-age insurance) will emerge in the near future, partly as a response to progress in privatization.

Not surprisingly, the state-owned banks are still dominant, accounting for some 80 per cent of total domestic credit provided. The commercial banking sector is still in a weak structural position. Often the capital base is inadequate and there is an acute shortage of skilled employees and bank managers. Subsidiaries set up by western banks will help to transfer the corresponding know-how.

Part of a functioning efficient capital market is a stock exchange, where companies can attract the capital needed for investment by issuing shares and obligations. An official stock exchange in Warsaw, modeled on the stock exchange of Lyon, is scheduled to start operating in mid-1991. The Polish national bank has been issuing short-term bonds to the public at weekly auctions since July 1990.

With the successive marketing of the shares of state-owned enterprises and the issuance of privatization bonds, the process of privatization should also stimulate the growth of a capital market but at the moment the small size of the latter is actually a hindrance to the more rapid sale of state assets.

In *Yugoslavia* a reform of the banking sector was started at the beginning of 1989. The basic thrust of the reform was to make banks more independent from enterprises and to increase the role of profitability in lending policy. In order to broaden their equity base the authorities decided that all banks had to transform their legal status into shareholding companies. Although private individual investors are in principle entitled to purchase bank shares, they have no voting rights. Part of the reform package of 1989 was to give the national bank the power to impose stringent solvency ratios on banks.

Many structural weaknesses in the banking sector remain to be solved. In the past enterprises were often founding members of banks and this led to considerable distortions in banks' lending policy. As full or partial

owners of a bank, enterprises extended credit to themselves in order to finance their loss-making activities. Given that many firms have not been able to pay back loans and meet interest payments, the banks are now recording huge losses and many are probably on the brink of bankruptcy.

The rehabilitation of the banking sector is therefore a major task for the authorities as it is intimately linked to the consolidation of the enterprise sector. Complications could arise from the fragmented banking structure, which is dominated by small, local or regional banks exposed to pressures from local authorities and enterprise managers. The federal government intends to examine the whole banking sector with a view to deciding which banks can be restructured and which to close down. The necessary financial resources for this are supposed to come from the federal budget, from the enterprise sector and from abroad.

The national bank has been increasingly concentrating on the functions of central bank by reducing its commercial activities. During the first half of 1989 it was given increased power, at least in principle, to better control the money supply. It was also decided to end credit subsidies to loss-making enterprises, which instead will have to be supported, if at all, directly from the federal budget.

(e) Labour markets and the social safety net

An important part of systemic reform is the creation of a labour market, where employees (or autonomous trade unions) negotiate the conditions of work with employers (or employers' associations). A wage reform which would allow for a greater differentiation of wages according to relative skills and shortages is a high priority.

Pending privatization, the larger part of employment, by far, is still in state-owned enterprises. Wage negotiations in *Poland* therefore take place directly between the trade unions (especially Solidarity and OPZZ) and enterprise managers, which are not independent from employees, or with government representatives. A true countervailing power to the trade unions has therefore not yet emerged. Wage policy in Poland is still largely dominated by the restrictive policies designed to curb inflation. A minimum wage has been fixed, which is also binding for the private sector. It is not clear to what extent wage negotiations in 1991 will focus on the need for stronger wage differentiation. In principle a hard budget constraint has been imposed on all state-owned companies so that wage increases negotiated with the trade unions have to be fully financed from business revenue.

In *eastern Germany* all the labour market institutions of western Germany have been adopted. The former state-dependent trade union has been dissolved and west German trade unions are now negotiating wage agreements in the east with west German employers' associations. As noted above, their primary

---

423 Broadly speaking, the term universal banking system means that commercial banks can extend their business beyond the realm of traditional credit activities to areas such as portfolio administration, insurance, and real estate.

focus is on the rapid closing of the wage gap between the two parts of the country. In the course of 1991 the wage differentials prevailing in the collective wage agreements in for west Germany will be applied to the east. In practice this means that each job in east Germany has to be allocated to a particular skill category.

In *Yugoslavia* there is still a lack of clearly distinct social partners to negotiate the terms of employment. The basic pattern, that employees essentially negotiate wage increases with themselves, continues to prevail. The attempt to introduce a greater independence of managers from workers' councils has been difficult to realize so far. Companies that negotiate wages incompatible with business profitability continue to be bailed out by the state.

In *Poland*, an unemployment benefit system, financed by contributions from the employers and government transfers, was introduced on the eve of the stabilization programme. Not surprisingly the number of employment offices, which are to organize the labour exchange, is still insufficient and the creation of an efficient administration is hindered by a shortage of qualified staff. The general rule is that only persons who were employed for at least six months during the year preceding their unemployment are eligible for these benefits which, as a general rule, cannot exceed 95 per cent of the minimum wage. The expenditures and revenues related to other parts of the social security system are administrated in separate funds mainly financed by employer's contributions.

To combat unemployment the Polish government has been designing support schemes for the restructuring of small private firms. It is hoped that small and medium-sized firms will provide a substantial offset to the expected large fall of employment in large enterprises. Measures designed to encourage labour mobility and retraining, as well as the re-structuring of firms, are not only running against the financial constraints of a tight budget, but have proved inadequate because of the much larger than expected rise in unemployment. For 1990 unemployment was expected to number 400,000, but in the event it was about 1.1 million. In the 1991 budget, funds allocated to unemployment benefits, retraining and other labour market measures amount to $2 billion.[424] One incentive for labour to shift to the private sector has been the recent abolition of the tight wage controls for employees in private firms: this has led to much higher real wage growth than in state-owned enterprises. There is now considerable pressure to ease wage controls in the other sectors as well. In a more general way, however, labour mobility is restricted by an acute shortage of housing especially in the more industrialized regions of Poland.

In *east Germany* the established legislation and institutions of the west German social security system have been adopted *de facto*. Labour offices had already been created in the former German Democratic Republic at the beginning of 1990, i.e., at the onset of the economic crisis. These have now been absorbed into the established west German institutions. Branch offices of the Federal Labour Office have been created to attend to the needs of unemployed persons.

East German workers qualify for west German unemployment and other social security benefits according to the same rules prevailing in the west.[425] The major exception is a generous scheme for the payment of short-time working benefits. This was designed to avoid an explosion in the number of unemployed persons in the east and will probably be extended until the end of 1991.[426]

Several official programmes have been designed to create incentives for east German workers to follow retraining and job qualification courses. Overall the response to these measures has been weak. This probably reflects a host of factors, *inter alia* insufficient knowledge about the existence of the schemes and a persistent illusion of job security in the state-owned enterprises awaiting restructuring.[427]

(f) Fiscal reform

The *Polish* government intends to launch a major reform of the fiscal system with a shift to a value added tax and the introduction of a uniform, progressive income tax from the beginning of 1992. The basic thrust of the income tax reform will be to increase transparency by replacing various existing categories of taxes on earnings and to differentiate the tax burden more in line with the greater spread in incomes.

In a move to eliminate tax discrimination between different economic sectors or activities, and especially to abolish discrimination against the private sector, the government harmonized the turnover tax for all sales in mid-1990. During the first half of that year some other taxes were also changed with a view to eliminating the preferential treatment of some sectors.[428]

In *Yugoslavia* a radical reform of the fiscal system to make it compatible with a market economy system was part of the medium-term reform strategy. An important element of any reform is the elimination of disparities in tax rates between republics on the one

---

[424] *Zycie gospodarcze*, 13 January 1991.

[425] A sizeable imbalance between the unemployment contributions received and the benefits paid out to east German workers is projected for 1991. The deficit is estimated at some DM 24 billion, which is, however, nearly offset by a surplus for west Germany of some DM 20 billion, partly on account of the rise in unemployment contributions in the course of this year. This increase is intended to alleviate the German budget because any deficit in the unemployment system has to compensated by government transfers. See DIW, *Wochenbericht*, 8/1991, 21 February 1991.

[426] Originally this scheme was planned to be phased out at the end of June 1991.

[427] This reflects partly a distortion in the incentive system. Persons working short-time in a non-viable company (and often doing nothing) receive up to 90 per cent of their last net income, but when they register as unemployed in order to follow training courses the share drops to 65-73 per cent.

[428] *Rzeczpospolita*, 20 April 1990.

hand and industrial sectors on the other hand. There were also plans for the introduction of a progressive incomes tax and a value added tax.

In principle *east Germany* switched overnight to the west German tax system, although some elements (notably the income tax) were phased in only gradually. A major problem is the establishment of a functioning internal revenue system in the east.

(v) Conclusions

East Germany, Poland and Yugoslavia have been implementing economic policies in 1990 which have often been characterized as "shock treatment" or as a "big bang". The above overview reveals that when a distinction is made between stabilization policy and reform policy a more differentiated view appears appropriate.

Thus Yugoslavia pursued a draconian stabilization policy for about six months, after which it foundered. Virtually no progress was made as regards the transition to a market economy system in 1990 given the lack of consensus not only on the economic system but also on the functioning of the federal state as a whole.

This is in marked contrast to Poland where a harsh stabilization policy and far-reaching reform measures were closely connected and, in fact, were set up in such a way as to be mutually reinforcing.

East Germany, without any doubt, experienced a "big bang". However, despite the similar nature of its problems, it is a special case, because of the way these problems can be dealt with in a united Germany.

The overview has shown that progress in setting up the legal framework of a market economy can be achieved rather quickly, In the case of east Germany,

it was even done "overnight", but progress has also been quite fast in this respect in Poland.

The next step will generally be much more difficult, namely, to move quickly ahead in creating the institutions of a market economy: this refers notably to privatization and the creation of competitive markets. But it also involves the creation of an efficient public service.

A central problem in all the transition economies is that, because of the many obstacles to rapid privatization, the state sector will continue for quite some time to control the bulk of fixed assets in the economy and to account for the larger share of employment. This could have undesirable implications because privatization is a major element in the creation of competitive markets. It is therefore important to enforce a hard budget constraint on those firms and to make it clear to employees and managers that there is no alternative to privatization. These implications are somewhat different in the case of east Germany. Here the enterprise sector has to integrate with the already existing competitive structures in the much larger west German economy and accordingly this will induce different behaviour on the part of managers in companies yet to be privatized. Similar pressure can emanate in the other countries mainly from exposure to foreign competition, hence the importance of free international trade. Viewed in this perspective the creation of an environment which will encourage the creation of new enterprises ("privatization from below") becomes also very important.

It is clear that much still needs to be done to create a true market economy system in the three countries reviewed here. Evidently, progress has been greatest in east Germany, but it has been substantial also in Poland, though in the latter country the point of no return may not have been reached yet.

4.4 REFORM-IN-THE-MAKING: CZECHOSLOVAKIA, HUNGARY

(i) Introduction

Czechoslovakia and Hungary share two features which justify their joint treatment in this section. First, to the extent that anything can be certain about the future, it is likely that in these two countries the political and institutional transformations that occurred in late 1989 are *irreversible*. There will be no return to one-party rule, to unconditional alliance with the Soviet Union or to central economic control based on the collective ownership of the means of production. Second, although it was perhaps not evident during the twenty years prior to 1989, in retrospect it is clear that the two countries were fortunate in preserving *functioning economic mechanisms* until the arrival of Soviet *perestroika* and its well-known consequences for international relations. This may increase the chances of successful systemic change, as decision-makers are less exposed to pressures to launch ill-timed and inadequately prepared stabilization initiatives to arrest economic disarray.

(ii) The emergence of consensus

(a) Political consensus

For more than two decades Hungary had been in the vanguard of economic reform among the centrally planned economies, while in Czechoslovakia the traditional system remained almost intact until 1989. Interestingly, at the time of the basic Hungarian reform initiatives in 1968, the two countries had much in common. With the end of the *Prague Spring*, the hope of economic reform vanished for a long period in Czechoslovakia, but the reform drive in Hungary also suffered a setback. Cardinal issues, such as the development of a pluralist political system, relations with the Soviet Union and property rights were not even touched upon. Nevertheless, from the perspective of a transition towards a market economy, the Hungarian reforms were not in vain. Important building blocks of a fully-fledged market system have gradually emerged.[429]

By 1988, Hungarian history had taken another twist. During its 16 months in office (November 1988-May 1990), the government of Prime Minister Miklós Németh achieved a remarkable record in facilitating a smooth alteration of the political and economic systems.[430] Fundamental constitutional changes set up the conditions for a multi-party democracy and a western-type market economy.[431] These amendments and the legislation regulating election procedures were all negotiated outside Parliament throughout the second half of 1989 by various opposition political movements, the communist party[432] and six pro-communist organizations (trade unions, youth organizations, etc.).

After the June 1990 parliamentary elections, a centre-right coalition consisting of three parties — the Hungarian Democratic Forum (MDF), the Independent Smallholders', Farmworkers' and Citizens' Party and the Christian Democratic People's Party — was formed by Prime Minister József Antall (MDF). This coalition has a solid parliamentary majority and is able to rely on votes of more than 60 per cent of legislators. Árpád Göncz, a prominent, though not leading figure of the largest opposition party, the Alliance of Free Democrats, was elevated to the relatively powerful post of State President.

The political transition in Czechoslovakia occurred through the "velvet revolution" of November 1989. Within weeks, a broadly based political consensus led to the creation of a Government of National Understanding (10 December), which also included the communists. The Federal Assembly (Parliament) was reconstructed and Václav Havel, as candidate of the

---

[429] For a recent assessment of these achievements, see "Economic Reform in Hungary", in United Nations Economic Commission for Europe, *Economic Survey of Europe in 1989-1990*, New York, 1990, pp. 244-252.

[430] Victims of the political oppression which had occurred between 1945-1987 were legally and politically rehabilitated, and even financially compensated, albeit on a modest scale. New laws were passed on travel, emigration and immigration and several international agreements on human rights were enacted into the Hungarian law. The barbed wire was removed at Hungary's western frontier. The 1950 Concordat regulating the role and the rights of the Catholic church was terminated. In March-April 1990, agreements were signed with the Soviet Union on the complete withdrawal of Soviet troops by 30 June 1991 at the latest and on the transition to convertible-currency trade in bilateral relations from 1991. A 12-month standby agreement was reached with the IMF (14 March 1990), which was a pre-condition for all other western financial assistance. This agreement was based on the annual budget for 1990, which remained in force after the change of government. Diplomatic ties were established or re-established with countries like South Korea, South Africa, Israel, the Vatican and Chile. In view of the country's desire to join the EC, numerous political, trade and credit agreements were signed with the Commission of the European Communities.

[431] These changes were symbolically reflected in a decision to change the country's official name to the *Republic of Hungary* from the *Hungarian People's Republic*.

[432] After October 1956, the communist party's official name was the Hungarian Socialist Workers' Party (MSZMP). During its October 1989 congress, the party dissolved itself and a new party was formed under name of Hungarian Socialist Party (MSZP). In the parliamentary election of June 1990, the MSZP secured more than 11 per cent of the vote and became the fourth largest party in the legislature.

Civic Forum (*Obcanské fórum,* hereafter termed the OF), was unanimously elected President of the Republic by the Federal Assembly. The new government took a number of decisive steps in the political, economic and other fields to accelerate the transition of Czechoslovakia into a pluralistic democratic system. In the first months of 1990, laws securing basic human rights (free elections, the right of assembly and of petition and a free press) were passed, and important constitutional and foreign policy changes were adopted. A constitutional bill changed the name of the country to the Czech and Slovak Federal Republic.[433]

The June 1990 elections produced clear victory for the OF and its Slovak ally, the Public Against Violence, which together won 46 per cent of the vote.[434] The reorganized communist party gained more than 13 per cent and became the second strongest party. The Christian Democratic Union, combining the People's Party and the Czech and Slovak Christian Democrats, took third place. The OF could have formed a government but lacked the three-fifths majority needed in the two chambers to implement constitutional changes. Finally, a coalition government was formed, bringing together the OF, its Slovak ally and the Christian Democratic Movement. Prime Minister Marian Calfa, who had served in this post since December 1989, remained in office.

In Czechoslovakia, the process of political consensus building is complicated by the existence of *two constituent republics* and national frictions. Economically Slovakia is still at a lower level than the Czech Republic and will probably be much harder hit by structural changes involving the decline of heavy industry in general and arms production in particular. In August 1990, the Slovak government proposed the abolition of most of the Federal government's executive powers with regard initially to communications, transport, foreign trade, fuel, energy and metallurgy. In November 1990, an accord was reached between the three governments envisaging a shift of power in favour of the republics. Foreign affairs, foreign trade, the central bank, taxation and price policies will remain under Federal control, but three separate budgets will be presented. It was agreed that the Czechoslovak economy should be a unified market with a single currency and that there will be no restriction on the free movement of people, goods and capital between the republics. On 12 December 1990 the Federal Assembly finally agreed on legislation dividing powers between

the Federal, Czech and Slovak governments (*Law on Competence*).[435]

The time dimension of the transformation effort in the two countries is circumscribed by the fact that the Czechoslovak Federal Assembly and President Havel were given a mandate for *two* years only, while their Hungarian colleagues were elected for *four* years. From a socio-political point of view the preference for a shorter mandate is understandable. In 1990 voters of both countries were asked to choose between more or less unknown political groupings and, hence, the desire for an opportunity to make known any subsequent "second thoughts" was logical. However, the four-year mandate can be an advantage for meaningful economic change in Hungary as it may extend the government's freedom to implement measures likely to be unpopular during early stages of the transformation process.

(b) Social consensus

For the majority of the population, the introduction of truly *democratic institutions* represents an immense political and ethical achievement. This is very important for maintaining social consensus throughout the transition period to counterbalance the negative social impacts of economic adjustment.[436] The *satisfaction of consumers* — chiefly in terms of comparison with their own country's current and past situation and the problems seen in other transition economies — is also an important ingredient of social consensus. So far both countries have fared reasonably well on this score, and their people appear to be well aware of this.

A few months after the parliamentary elections, when the newly-emerging political parties had become better known to the public, voters of both countries once again went to the polls. In Hungary, the local elections brought surprising results. In municipalities with less than 10,000 inhabitants, 83 per cent of the mayors elected were independent candidates. A good portion of these "new" mayors, were in fact re-elected, as the population seemed to have been satisfied with their performance under the *ancien régime*. Similar tendencies were reflected in the compulsory elections of directors of all state-owned enterprises (SOEs) by their staff: most were easily re-elected. The main lessons of the municipal elections were painful to all political parties. Low participation rates[437] and the overwhelming support for non-affiliated candidates showed that voters view all parties with mistrust. In relative terms the Alliance of Free Democrats strength-

---

[433] Foreign policy initiatives included an agreement on the withdrawal of Soviet troops by 30 June 1991 and the establishment or re-establishment of diplomatic ties with the same countries mentioned in the Hungarian case.

[434] The OF was originally an umbrella organization of various opposition movements and proto-parties in the Czech Republic. Its counterpart in Slovakia adopted the name "Public Against Violence". The OF led the revolution and ran the country in the pre-election period. At the beginning of 1991, disagreements among the wide spectrum of political forces within the OF caused its split into two currents. One is a more sharply defined "liberal-conservative" political party and the second a looser "social-liberal" grouping. These two forces have formed a coalition until the next parliamentary election.

[435] More recently, President Havel has raised the possibility that Moravia — presently part of the Czech Republic — could become the *third* republic of the federation. See President Havel's interview on Prague radio on 3 February 1991, as quoted in BBC, *Summary of World Broadcasts*, 6 February 1991.

[436] Thus, in a broad sense, it appears sensible to assign democratization the first place in the sequence of systemic transformation. See section 4.1 above, and also G. Roland, *The Political Economy of Sequencing Tactics in the Transition Period*, Discussion paper, No.9008, Université Libre de Bruxelles, 1990.

[437] During the four major elections of the past 12 months (two rounds of general elections and two rounds of local elections), successive participation rates were 65, 45, 40 and 33 per cent (*Heti Világgazdaság*, 22 December 1990).

ened its position as the second strongest political party and as the main force of the opposition.

By contrast, the Czechoslovak municipal elections confirmed the existing distribution of power among the main political forces. However, participation rates also declined and losses were registered by the OF in the Czech Republic, while the People's Party and independent candidates made gains. The Christian Democratic Movement strengthened its position in the Slovak Republic.

It seems that since late 1989, the social consensus has been eroded somewhat in both countries. This is indicated not only by declining electoral participation rates but also by public opinion surveys.[438] Voter apathy and public opinion at large are both a cause and a consequence of the fact that political changes in 1989 were swift and orderly. This is a paradox. On the one hand there had been no public pressure to destroy and remove the state apparatus of the *ancien régime,* which then guaranteed a reasonable functioning of the state machinery before and after the elections. This meant that many officials of the previous régime − members of the *nomenklatura,* enterprise managers, media personalities, etc. − remained in their positions. On the other hand, this situation has created a certain uneasiness and anger in the population − particularly in Hungary − as people saw no evidence of systemic change in their own immediate environment.[439] Some discontent has built up in both countries, especially in Czechoslovakia, from the fact that, after a swift crisis-free political turnround, popular expectations on the possibility of a smooth, painless economic transition as well were high. During the months-long electoral campaigns politicians had little motivation to moderate these high expectations.

(c) Market-economy consensus

In Czechoslovakia, the reform blueprint is contained in an official document entitled the *Scenario of Economic Reform.*[440] The actions of the Hungarian government, however, do not derive directly from a single, comprehensive document for reasons discussed below. None the less, it is beyond question that both countries have now committed themselves to pursue market-oriented reform − a direction which is unquestioned by any major political force represented in the two parliaments. The aim is to reduce the share of state ownership from an initial 90-95 per cent to 40-50 per cent within the next 3-4 years. Within this consensus, however, there are certain differences in accent and priorities between the two countries.

The main objective of the Hungarian government programme[441] is to establish a strong *social market economy,* in which private property is to dominate but where the poor and other vulnerable groups are entitled to the protection of a social safety net. The Czechoslovak *Scenario,* a more comprehensive programme with precise sequencing and deadlines over a 3-4 year period, reflects a more determined approach: "it is of paramount importance to place emphasis on the market economy as our true goal, *market economy with all its positive and negative aspects,* a goal that we seek to accomplish at the earliest possible date".[442] This radical approach was approved in its essentials by Parliament, although five academic and research bodies commissioned by legislators presented their views on the government's proposal and offered alternatives. The idea of a "social market economy" has found some echo in Czechoslovakia as well. Professor Ota Sik, the spiritual father of the 1968 economic reforms, and Richard Wágner, then the economic adviser of President Havel, have publicly argued for a slower transition with more active state involvement to minimize inflation and unemployment.[443]

Since the very beginning, decision-making has been seriously hampered in both countries by outspoken debates between various key personalities in the new administration. In Czechoslovakia, most of this occurred prior to the June 1990 election. A debate over the pace and direction of the reform culminated in an open dispute between Valtr Komárek, then first Deputy Prime Minister in charge of economic reform, and Václav Klaus, Minister of Finance.[444] The radical reforms proposed by Klaus (full liberalization of prices from January 1991, internal convertibility of the crown, large-scale sale of state assets) were refused by Komárek as too risky, on the grounds that internal and external imbalances and the monopolistic position of many enterprises could lead to high rates of inflation, recession, unemployment and a rise in foreign indebtedness, as in Poland. Komárek proposed a regulated market economy. During the transition period, market principles would be applied together with the attainment of macro-economic balance, decentralization and demonopolization. State economic policies were to be selective, restrictive in relation to heavy industries and designed to stimulate supply for the internal and ex-

---

[438] According to a *Gallup poll* conducted in December 1990, 84 per cent of Hungarians expected that 1991 would be a worse year than 1990. The relevant 1990 figure for Czechoslovakia was almost as high (78 per cent). In this competition of pessimism both countries were far ahead of their neighbours in Bulgaria (49 per cent), Poland (17 per cent), USSR (64 per cent) and Yugoslavia (21 per cent). *Népszabadság,* 2 January 1991.

[439] J. Kis, "On the law of conservation of the elite", *Beszélő,* 9 February 1991.

[440] Published in the supplement to *Hospodárské noviny,* 4 September 1990.

[441] The *Programme of National Renewal* was published in *Népszabadság,* 26 May 1990. (For an extensive summary in English see *National Bank of Hungary Market Letter,* No.5. 1990.) This relatively short political document was elaborated on the basis of the programmes of the three coalition parties. Studies by independent expert groups such as *Batelle Europe,* the *Bridge Group* and the *Blue Ribbon Committee* were also used as inputs.

[442] Supplement to *Hospodárské noviny, op.cit,* p.1.

[443] See, e.g., Sik's article "The third road and economic discussion" (*Hospodárské noviny,* 24 January 1991) and an interview with Wágner (*Rudé právo,* 27 November 1990).

[444] See, e.g., *Mladá fronta,* 20 June 1990, *Hospodárské noviny,* 20 and 27 June 1990.

ternal markets. After some hesitation, influenced by a pre-election split in the government in mid-May, the government opted for the radical path. In September this option was confirmed by parliamentary approval of the *Scenario* and the success of Klaus in his contest for the chairmanship of the OF in January 1991.

In Hungary, disputes at two different levels have been apparent since late 1989. Unlike Czechoslovakia, the government has a strong liberal opposition which takes every opportunity to criticize the slow pace of transition. At the same time, there has been a political debate both within the government and in the key decision-making centres of the state apparatus. Originally, the disputes turned on questions of timing and sequencing. During the second half of 1990 the participants' stance changed several times, but these issues were subsequently overtaken by events. After the Gulf crisis and the resistance of the Soviet Union to share the costs of switching from rouble to dollar trade, it became evident that the "big bang" would start on 1 January 1991, whether the government wanted it or not. As a consequence of these internal disputes − during which Finance Minister Ferenc Rabár offered his resignation after four months of service[445] − all the economic programmes published so far were rather short-lived. In retrospect, specific commitments and targets have lost their importance but, for the sake of completeness, it is worth placing them on record:

− in July 1990, Finance Minister Rabár launched an *emergency programme* to stabilize the budget. Since this programme triggered strong criticism everywhere, Rabár went ahead without seeking parliamentary approval;

− in September the government published a *White Book*,[446] containing an up-date and an elaboration of the programme which was approved by parliament in May. The book-size document (220 pages) covered all aspect of social, economic and political developments (albeit with few quantified objectives or deadlines) and set guidelines for 1991-1993. In contrast to the *Scenario*, this document was not discussed in parliament;

− in early December 1990, Rabár's team presented the government's budget proposals which were subsequently passed by parliament. This document was reportedly based on the Ministry's own three-year programme, of which only a few details were made public.[447] Mihály Kupa, the incoming Finance Minister, then took responsibility for the implementation of the 1991 budget. At the same time, however, he promised to elaborate a four-year work programme by late February 1991.

After the first attack on the political institutions of the one-party state, the governments of both countries have started to *dismantle the remnants of central planning*. In Czechoslovakia, a decree putting an end to annual plans was published as early as June 1989 but entered into force only after the Revolution. Enterprise associations, which constituted the link in the chain of command between the ministries and enterprises, have been dismantled.[448] In July 1990 the five-year plan 1986-1990 was abandoned and the State Planning Commission was abolished. Economic decision-making at the federal level has been put in the hands of the Ministry of Finance and the newly created super-ministry, the Ministry of Economics. Due to its longer experience with economic reforms, there was much less to dismantle in Hungary. Annual planning had had a rather indicative character for some time and in 1988 even this was abandoned. Five-year planning was essentially a political ritual, with rapidly diminishing relevance after the first year of its implementation. Perhaps this is why parliament has "forgotten" to annul the relevant legislation: on paper the 1986-1990 plan never ceased to exist. At the time of writing, the two most important economic ministries are the Ministry of Finance (amalgamated with the former National Planning Office) and the Ministry of International Economic Relations. These ministries are currently headed by independent experts, rather than party politicians.

(iii) Clearing up property rights

In theory, there is agreement in both countries that unambiguous property rights are the pre-condition for individual, collective and social stability, domestic capital formation and the influx of foreign capital. But it is easier to agree on this objective than to accomplish it. The problems of federalism in the CSFR − already mentioned in section (ii) above − are relevant from this point of view as well. Before property rights are cleared up, political decisions are required to designate the proper state bodies who will then oversee the process.

(a) Restitution

The newly-elected governments of both countries felt a moral obligation to restore property rights that had existed before the communist takeover. Thus the *restitution of confiscated property* in general, and the future of agricultural *land* in particular have dominated the political debate on property right reforms. At the time of writing, these issues are still under discussion in the parliaments of both countries.

---

445 Rabár gave his resignation in early October, but it was not accepted until mid-December.

446 *The Programme of National Renewal (The first three years of the republic)*, Budapest, 1990. For an extensive summary in English see *National Bank of Hungary Market Letter*, No.8-9, 1990.

447 *Figyelö*, 6 and 13 December 1990.

448 See H. Matejka, "Czechoslovakia: The Reform Accelerates", Manuscript, The Graduate Institute of International Studies, Geneva, August 1990.

The future of land ownership is a particularly sensitive issue in Hungary, which is still very much an agrarian country and where agricultural policy has succeeded in maintaining food supplies and generating an export surplus over the past two decades. The crux of the problem is that the minor partner in the coalition, the Smallholders' Party, fought a single-issue electoral campaign. They wanted at least a minimum programme of *de jure* restoration of the land ownership rights existing in 1947 – i.e., before collectivization. This was a very effective campaign weapon, but numerous legal, moral, economic and technical objections seriously call into question its feasibility. Following a request from the Government, the Constitutional Court also examined the question. Its ruling issued on 2 October 1990 declared the proposed land reform measures unconstitutional as they amounted to unlawful discrimination between citizens. The process of reprivatization, the Court said, cannot be selective according to the type of property in question. Land is no different from any other type of fixed asset. Moreover, the process of reprivatization should not become a new source of injustice. Hence, land cannot be confiscated from the existing agricultural co-operatives, as the government had envisaged, without adequate compensation.[449] In this battle, the Minister of Agriculture was dismissed and replaced by another member of the Smallholders' Party in January 1991. Currently, the government's latest self-imposed deadline for a new draft law on land is March 1991.

The problem of land ownership, however, cannot be avoided. It has also crept back in the context of restitution, which was an important pre-election commitment of the MDF. The government believes that assets worth some Ft 60 billion may be involved in such restitution deals (land: Ft 40 billion, housing stock: Ft 15 billion, industrial assets: Ft 6 billion) to compensate for nationalization and the confiscations which occurred after 8 June 1949.[450] Physical persons, the original owners or their direct heirs, should receive compensation in the form of tradeable interest-bearing *restitution certificates*. These certificates, denominated in forints, would represent vouchers for the purchase of state assets. Restitution would be on a sliding scale with an upper limit of Ft 5 million per person. (This sum buys a good house in any village or a medium-size apartment in towns.) In the case of land, the lawmakers envisage positive discrimination so that claimants permanently residing in agricultural areas can stake a claim on their previously-owned agricultural land and use their vouchers to buy it back from the local co-operative or state farm.

The bill is not acceptable in its present form to anybody outside the MDF. The Smallholders' Party is not willing to accept the proposed limitations on land restitution, the opposition parties and independent experts are worried about a possible flood of lawsuits and the accompanying legal uncertainties, as well as about the inflationary impact of the newly created purchasing power. It is also clear that in the final instance these restitution certificates will constitute claims on the already heavily indebted Treasury, and it is difficult to see how the Treasury can afford to pay realistic interest (30-35 per cent) on such a liability. Currently, law makers are proposing a 9 per cent interest rate.

Public discussion on land reform has only just began in Czechoslovakia and it centres around the same questions as in Hungary. However, draft laws on property restitution have already been tabled at the Federal Assembly. In October 1990, together with the law on small privatization (see below), a bill on *small restitution* was adopted which did justice to those whose homes, shops, etc. had been confiscated between 1955-1959. These assets are to be restored to their original owners or their heirs. In February 1991, a second restitution bill was passed (*Law on Out-of-Court Rehabilitation*) which regulates the compensation of those proprietors whose assets were nationalized between 25 February 1948 (the day of communist takeover) and 1 January 1990.[451] The new law does not cover big industries and land which were nationalized immediately after 1945, or property which was legally nationalized before and after 1948. But even so, owners of property worth an estimated Kcs 300 billion (8 per cent of total national wealth) will have their assets returned or will be financially compensated by vouchers in a move aimed at both correcting an historic injustice and at re-creating a property-owning middle class. The future of legally nationalized properties, land, as well as the properties formerly owned by the churches, will be decided later.[452]

(b) Property of labour-managed firms

Re-establishing clear property rights for those state assets which for all practical purposes belonged in the past to the state by virtue of the post-1945 nationalizations is not a simple operation either. The creation of *labour-managed firms* in Hungary and Czechoslovakia, in 1984 and 1988 respectively, was an attempt to break the chain of the administrative command system. This process (which did bring some efficiency gains)[453] led to the *de jure* privatization of many state enterprises. This problem can be clearly seen from the example of Hungary, where self-management companies had been created earlier and more vigorously. The 1977 *Law on Enterprises* already granted almost unlimited legal independence from the ministerial apparatus to the SOEs. Later, in the course of the half-hearted reform wave in 1984-1985, 70 per cent of enterprises were transformed into self-management units, with an elected managerial

---

[449] *Népszabadság*, 3 October 1990.

[450] This date was the first working day of the Hungarian parliament in which only communist-supported MPs could have a seat.

[451] *Lidové noviny*, 23 February 1991.

[452] *Financial Times*, 22 February 1991.

[453] This was certainly the case in Hungary. In Czechoslovakia the time was too short to produce results.

body on the top. Finally, the 1989 *Conversion Law*[454] opened a legal way for the enterprise councils to turn the firm into a corporation and then to sell it entirely or in part to any domestic or foreign buyer.

Six months after the Conversion Act came into effect, an important and potentially valuable part of the state sector was already partly or fully in the hand of foreign companies and private Hungarian citizens. This process was particularly rapid in the activities related to tourism and the media (newspapers, publishing houses). A temporary re-nationalization by administrative *fiat* of state assets transferred to enterprise councils may now seem justifiable from an institutional point of view in order to start with a clean sheet, but this could run against the principle of legality.

(c) Local government property

Finally, there is a further obstacle to the "clean sheet" approach in property rights. In both countries, albeit for somewhat different reasons, there is a political commitment to decentralize political life by reinvigorating local authorities. This requires saleable and/or taxable resources to be left with them, especially at a time when central governments are in no position to help. Land, much of the urban housing stock, the retail trade network and many service-related activities are already under local government control and the central governments cannot instruct these self-government units to follow central guidelines just for the sake of uniformity or macro-economic rationality. Sorting out these problems will certainly take time and willingness to compromise between conflicting interests.

(iv) Slightly different concepts of stabilization

Economic decision-makers in both countries agree with the prevailing western view that, due to the existing macro-economic instability, absolute priority should be accorded to *stabilization*. However, the meaning of stabilization is understood differently in the two countries. The *Scenario of the Economic Reform* notes that "Blocking the inflation process is indeed the macro-economic priority function of the process of transformation and it is to this priority that all other fundamental macro-economic goals – economic growth, employment and sound balance of payments – must, in a rational measure, be subordinated".[455] In

the Hungarian view, stabilization chiefly means structural adjustment in the production sphere, permitting a gradual acceleration of economic growth without an accompanying rise in foreign indebtedness or the internal fiscal deficit and without endangering the level of equilibrium already achieved on the consumer goods market.[456] Though the fight against inflation is often mentioned, it is clearly not the first priority. In Czechoslovakia, the effort to block inflation seems to be aimed at maintaining the country's relatively favourable position in this respect. In the past, long-term open inflation did not exceed 2 per cent annually and even hidden inflation was no more than 3 per cent a year. Thus the tolerance for higher than targeted price increases is much less in Czechoslovakia than in Hungary, where the inflationary process has been pronounced since the early 1970s.[457] Moreover, the external position of the latter country does not permit the subordination of all other objectives to a stricter control of inflation.

As it is often claimed that a low inflationary record is one of Czechoslovakia's main advantages in comparison with other reforming economies,[458] it is worth noting that long-term experience may prove of little importance in assessing *future* expectations at a time when inflation has jumped from 1.5 per cent in 1989 to 10 per cent in 1990.

(a) Overall balance in the domestic market

Maintaining or restoring equilibrium on the producer and consumer goods markets is indisputably one of the key elements of stabilization policy. But in Hungary, where economists have been strongly influenced by the views of their compatriot, Professor J. Kornai, this has become a top priority since the second half of the 1970s.[459] His reasoning is based on the conviction that rational market behaviour cannot be expected from enterprises if perennial shortages prevent them from concentrating on product innovation and cost efficiency. Moreover, workers and employees cannot be effectively motivated through monetary incentives in a world of empty shelves. In the consumer sphere, pent-up demand (the monetary overhang) constitute a major threat which has been attacked on several fronts in the past couple of years:

– the value of accumulated households' savings has been substantially eroded by planned and centrally determined price rises. This also helped to remove extreme anomalies from price

---

[454] The full title of the act is the *Law XIII 1989 On the Conversion of Economic Organizations and Economic Associations.*

[455] *Op.cit.*, p.1.

[456] Since 1987 there have been several ill-fated attempts to put in place a medium-term stabilization programme in this sense. These intentions, however, always remained behind the pace of political change and brought only temporary results. Among these programmes, the most comprehensive initiative was the three-year *Work Programme of the Council of Ministers*, announced by Prime Minister K. Grósz on 16 September 1987, for the period 1988-1990. Subsequently, as the Grósz programme became outdated, the annual plans for 1989 and 1990 were conceived and presented as short-term stabilization programmes. On 21 November 1989, the Németh government also presented a programme for 1990-1992, but this was not accepted by parliament due to the lack of convincing proposals on housing related questions.

[457] See Appendix table B.6.

[458] See e.g. K. Kouba, "Systemic changes in the Czechoslovak Economy" (Manuscript), Prague, October 1990.

[459] For an English edition of his most important work, see J. Kornai, *The Economics of Shortage*, 2 volumes, North Holland, Amsterdam, 1980.

TABLE 4.4.1

Hungary: Factors hindering continuous production
(Percentages) [a]

	1987	1988	1989			1990			
	June	March	March	September	December	March	June	September	December
Nothing	10.3	10.7	10.8	12.7	13.6	10.8	8.7	6.9	8.9
Lack of orders	27.4	28.0	38.0	40.4	51.2	51.3	56.1	50.9	54.5
Labour shortage	23.7	15.7	21.5	22.0	13.5	12.2	13.9	10.3	4.3
Shortage of domestic components	42.3	50.1	37.7	27.5	21.5	13.9	13.0	15.4	11.4
Shortages of imports denominated in roubles	46.8 [b]	16.7	14.4	10.4	8.0	5.8	3.4	4.6	3.2
Shortages of imports denominated in dollars	46.8 [b]	32.9	18.0	8.9	6.3	3.9	2.2	5.2	3.7
Capital shortage	24.3	32.8	49.6	46.9	49.4	57.8	45.3	51.9	48.7
Insufficient capacity	6.7	6.4	4.8	5.3	7.0	3.6	3.4	2.5	2.7
Lack of incentives	28.5	24.9	24.0	24.7	21.2	16.5	16.0	17.3	20.4
Domestic uncertainties in general	43.0	45.4	46.7	42.6	54.6	50.9	47.3	54.1	54.7

Source: The result of the KOPINT-DATORG, Industrial Business Surveys.

a The questionnaire allows for multiple choice, thus answers do not add up to 100 vertically.
b In 1987 the questionaire asked for difficulties in imports in general.

and wage relatives and to bring them closer to equilibrium;

— a good part of savings has been channelled into illiquid forms (small-scale productive investments, real estates, works of art, jewellery). Since 1982, alternative saving facilities (bonds, treasury bills, shares, convertible currency accounts) have also been available;

— although the real rate of return on forint saving deposits was mostly negative in the past decade, the shortfall was not large. In addition, from 1 January 1991 the central bank abolished compulsory "interest ceiling" regulation and commercial banks have been free to determine their interest rate policies;

— finally, the policy of import liberalization (including private imports) helped to pacify consumers.

Indeed, this persistent concern for market equilibrium has brought results. There is a wide consensus that Hungarian shops offer a range of goods similar to western countries. A feeling "you never had it so good" prevails. More importantly, similar positive developments can also be documented in the production sphere (table 4.4.1). Since 1987, KOPINT-DATORG, a Hungarian research institute, has prepared quarterly surveys on the views of industrial enterprise directors on the factors currently determining production. These surveys indicate that in the third quarter of 1989 the views of managers clearly changed. There are fewer complaints about shortages of production inputs, the main preoccupation now being to obtain more orders.

This is in marked contrast to recent Czechoslovak experience, where consumer behaviour has suddenly changed in anticipation of price rises. The propensity to save has diminished and a buying spree occurred in the last months of 1990. This led to growing shortages. However, significant price rises on 1 January 1991 weakened demand and markets calmed down. The first part of this process is well documented. Consumer surveys carried out among the managers of retail trade outlets (table 4.4.2) in the second and third quarters of 1990 suggest that shortages were on the rise. The consumer satisfaction index confirms this: in 1990 consumers were less satisfied with supplies than two years before. Since September 1990, the growth of purchases has been characterized as a shopping panic by some observers.[460] Comparable data on the behaviour of production enterprises are unavailable, but it seems that material input supply difficulties persisted throughout 1990.

(b) Fiscal policies

Both countries conducted prudent *fiscal policies* in 1990. In Czechoslovakia, budgetary deficits have traditionally been low — below 1 per cent of NMP — and a small surplus was attained last year. Restrictive fiscal policies are also reflected in the 1991 budget, which again makes provision for a moderate surplus. The Hungarian situation is less sound in this respect. First, there is a problem of accumulated state indebtedness. To a great extent this reflects the combined impact of actual foreign indebtedness *plus* its nominal increase because of the continual depreciation of the forint. There is also a flow problem. In the past, excessive deficits — occasionally concealed by statistical distortions — were tolerated by Hungarian planners.[461] Provisional figures for 1990 suggest an almost perfect

---

460 K. Janácek et al., *Social Feasibility of Czechoslovakia's Economic Reform* (Analysis of 1990 and short-term outlook), Ekonomicky ústav CSAV, Prague, November 1990, p.17.

461 In 1975, for example, the deficit was Ft 46 billion (almost 10 per cent of GDP), but only Ft 2.9 billion was publicly acknowledged. In the following two years the corresponding figures were Ft 35 billion and Ft 2.5 billion, Ft 45 billion and Ft 3.5 billion. According to figures recently revealed by the National Bank of Hungary, these huge discrepancies ended only in 1984. (E. Bakó, "Honesty about concealed figures", *Figyelő*, 22 November 1990.)

match of expenditures and receipts, but for 1991 a deficit of more than Ft 78 billion (3 per cent of GDP) was approved by parliament.

(c) Monetary policy

Tight *monetary policy* was pursued in both countries throughout 1990 and no relaxation is envisaged in the foreseeable future. According to figures for the first 9 months, both country's money supply growth has remained within the targeted range, entailing a slight decline in the nominal value of the money stock in Czechoslovakia and a 7 per cent real decline in Hungary. However, tight monetary policy has aggravated an old and well-known problem of the centrally planned economies: large number of companies cannot meet their payments obligations on time. The Hungarian terminology speaks of "queuing" enterprises, while in Czechoslovakia the problem is known as "excessive inter-firm crediting". This problem is difficult to resolve, because the same companies are both culprits and victims. A consistent implementation of existing (or planned) bankruptcy procedures would probably cause more harm than good, as it would lead to a chain reaction throughout the economy.[462] Some Hungarian experts find solace in the fact that, after the first year of monetary austerity, the number of illiquid enterprises and the volume of outstanding arrears (about 10 per cent of GDP) have remained unchanged. This may be so, but on the other hand there remain serious uncertainties concerning the measurement of queuing and widely different estimates are used by different authorities and experts. In Czechoslovakia, the liquidity crisis worsened considerably at the beginning of January 1991[463] and the question arises of how long a rigorous monetary and fiscal policy can last without causing great damage to inter-enterprise relations. At the end of 1990, the value of payment arrears was estimated at 7 per cent of GDP, but it jumped to about 10 per cent at the end of January 1991.

(v) Core elements of the reform

In Czechoslovakia, following some important steps already taken in 1990, a new phase of reform was launched on 1 January 1991 with a major liberalization of prices, external trade and an extensive programme of de-nationalization of state enterprises.

(a) Price liberalization

Liberalization of virtually all wholesale and retail prices as from 1 January 1991 is officially regarded as the single most important step in the Czechoslovak reform *Scenario*. In fact, the process had been launched

TABLE 4.4.2

Czechoslovakia: Tests of consumer demand satisfaction

Period	Trade conjuncture test (saldo)	Period	Consumer satisfaction test (index)
1987	-8.7	1987	92.2
1988	-15.5	1988	76.1
1989	-14.7	1989	80.9
1990 I	-13.6	1990 Spring	75.9
1990 II	-18.3	1990 Summer [a]	80.0
1990 III	-22.1	1990 Autumn [a]	50.8

Source: Materials of the Trade Research Institute, Prague reproduced in K.Janacek et alia, *Social feasibility of Czechoslovakia's economic reform* (Analysis of 1990 and short-term outlook), Prague, November 1990.

Note: The trade conjuncture test is based on opinion polls among salesmen as to the degree of demand satisfaction. The balance can vary from -100 to +100, negative values indicating a negative evaluation (shortage). Positive values would indicate a surplus of supply over demand, zero value equilibrium. The consumer satisfaction test is based on opinion polls among consumers. These polls concern satisfaction with their living standards, price developments and the market supply. If the number of positive answers exceeds the number of negative ones, the index exceeds 100, and vice versa. A decrease in the index signalizes a worsening of the economic public opinion.

[a] Owing to changed methods of gathering data, full comparability with previous periods is not guaranteed.

a few months earlier with the abolition of direct subsidies (negative turnover taxes) on the retail prices of foodstuffs and energy products and a sharp increase in the retail prices of petroleum products. The higher costs of imports, following the October 1990 devaluation were reflected in domestic prices, too.

The recently adopted *Law on prices* lays down the methods and forms of price regulation which are to be used under the prevailing monopolistic conditions. Several regulatory tools are to be applied (administratively fixed prices, mainly in the form of upper limits on prices, regulation of the timing of price changes and price moratoria) which are to be used only exceptionally. The law lays down that prices should be determined on the basis of agreements between producers and consumers. The separate treatment of prices (wholesale, purchaser, commercial and retail prices) is to be abandoned.[464] The total coverage of goods initially affected by the price regulations will amount to only 15 per cent of total output.

Preliminary calculations, highly tentative even under normal circumstances let alone in a period of volatile international energy prices, suggested that the combined effect of price liberalization and the introduction of a realistic exchange rate for the crown would push up the rate of inflation from 10 per cent in 1990 to 30 per cent in 1991.[465] This is similar to the Hungarian target rate for 1991 (35-37 per cent, up from 29 per cent in 1990). Hungarian planners have been experimenting for some time to find a middle way between price liberalization, allowing price relativities to find equilibrium and taking

---

462 This is not a question of legislation – the Hungarian bankruptcy law was passed in September 1986 – but rather a question of choosing among unfavourable alternatives. In the Hungarian case, for instance, a series of enterprise closures and writing off illiquid assets by the banking sector, where the state is still the dominant owner, would deteriorate the central government's budget, both in terms of tax and profit revenues.

463 See *Hospodárské noviny*, 12 February 1991.

464 See *Hospodárské noviny*, 23 November 1990.

465 This figure is taken from the projection of the Ministry of Finance (*Hospodárské noviny*, 2 January 1991).

prudent anti-inflationary measures to preserve the purchasing power of the national currency. Price control had been largely eliminated in the production sphere even before 1989 and little central control was left with respect to agricultural production and certain consumer services after 1 January 1991. Put differently, Hungarian officials assume that the combined impact of external price effects (oil prices, the switch from rouble to dollar trade) and the liberalization of a relatively small segment of domestic prices, will provoke a *greater* inflationary push than the same external impacts *plus* a large-scale domestic price liberalization which was introduced in Czechoslovakia. This is particularly relevant in view of the first statistical accounts of price liberalization in the latter country. According to the January 1991 figures, the consumer price index rose by 45 per cent (as compared with January 1990) and it is known that further liberalization is still in the pipeline. Critics of the current reform strategy now assume that the annual rate of inflation in Czechoslovakia will be in the range of 50-60 per cent.[466]

(b) Corporatization and restructuring of state-owned enterprises

In the Czechoslovak *Scenario,* the initial legislative step leading to *corporatization and restructuring of state-owned enterprises* was the adoption of the law on "big privatization".[467] This law defined the basic types and content of ownership — private, co-operative, state, federal, republican and municipal. It was originally planned that a substantial number of SOEs should be commercialized — i.e., turned into joint stock companies — before the end of 1990, but this process was delayed as the law was adopted only in late February 1991. According to the law, a large part of equities of enterprises will be reserved for distribution to the population by means of vouchers. All Czechoslovaks over 18 will be offered non-saleable bonds worth 1,000 points for 2,000 crowns. The bonds can be traded for shares in the companies on offer. Bids from buyers for the remaining equity will be entertained. In this second step foreigners are also allowed to participate. Additional one-point bonds will cost 50 crowns each.[468] The technical details of the voucher system will be worked out in three months' time.

According to the authors of the *Scenario* "the one and only possibility of involving the broadest section of the population in the process of major privatization within a relatively brief period of time is to offer below-cost shares to the population by means of 'investment coupons' (vouchers)". Nevertheless, the idea of privatization by vouchers had been criticized by various academic and political circles for failing to create a genuine capital market. New flotations would be made practically impossible, it was argued, with a market awash with shares given out practically free of charge and with excessive dispersion of ownership. The voucher system could also block foreign share holdings and contribute to inflationary pressures.

In Hungary, there will be four major avenues for changing the ownership of state enterprises and encouraging private participation in traditionally state-run activities:

— the Government will organize the sale of *larger* SOEs through the stock exchange and by other means.[469] Packages of shares will be placed on the market several times per year. At the moment five packages are in the process of implementation or preparation. *Smaller* units will be denationalized through auctions (pre-privatization);

— private individuals, firms or groups of individuals can bid to purchase existing state enterprise. The conditions of purchase are to be regulated on a case-by-case basis and preferential credits made available to facilitate the transaction (third-party privatization);

— state enterprises and co-operatives have the right to work out their own privatization programme and/or to look for foreign partners (spontaneous or self-privatization);

— private companies (domestic and foreign) will have the right to compete for contracts to operate telecommunication networks, highways, mines, etc. — i.e., areas where in the past the principle of strict state monopoly prevailed. The relevant legislation (*Law on Concessions*) is under preparation.

In Czechoslovakia there is strong opposition to "spontaneous privatization". This recalls the initial attitude of the Hungarian government (and the MDF in particular). This stance is both anti-communist and anti-capitalist, but certainly not irrational. The two governments are concerned that the managers of these enterprises, as well as top government officials, may unjustly benefit from their membership of the "old régime" from this type of uncontrolled privatization. The problem with this approach is twofold, as the Hungarian experiences clearly suggest.

---

466 See V. Komárek, *Rudé právo*, 12 February 1991, p.3.

467 Officially, *Law on the Conditions of Transformation of State Property*. For the full text, see *Hospodárské noviny*, 28 February 1991.

468 *The Wall Street Journal*, 25 February 1991.

469 The Budapest Stock Exchange was formally (re-)opened in June 1990. It has five trading sessions per week, using an open outcry system for the less active and a continuous trading system for the more active stocks. It has two tiers, one for the (9) listed and another one for the (20-25) non-listed but registered securities. In 1990 almost 400 corporate bonds were also traded, but in 1991 this practice was discontinued. After a trial period of few months, dealers of 44 authorized firms were required to pass an examination and those who failed were suspended. Currently there are 300 qualified brokers in the country. Six months after the market's inception, the volume of transactions has remained small and prices fluctuated widely. See L. Bokros, "Privatization in Hungary", paper presented at the IMF Institute seminar on "Centrally Planned Economies in Transition" 9-19 July 1990; *Heti Világgazdaság*, 9 and 16 February 1991. The Budapest Commodity Exchange, launched also in 1990, is currently limited to transactions in wheat and corn, but in the future trade in various types of meat is also planned (*Magyar Hírlap*, 1 March 1991).

In Hungary the process of denationalization was entrusted to the *State Property Agency* (SPA). Unlike in Czechoslovakia, where the equivalent structures are to be created at the federal level and in the two republics, the SPA is a relatively small, centralized unit (30-35 professionals) which directly reports to government.[470] One of the difficulties stems from the fact that the legal mandate of the SPA covers three conflicting functions and the government has not yet made up its mind on priorities. Firstly, the SPA has a certain "police" function — to oversee the legal aspects of asset transfers and make sure that officials involved in the privatization process do not abuse their position. At the same time, the SPA must play the role of a bureaucratic authority, and attempt to co-ordinate the process of privatization taking due account of the consequences of other policy decisions. Thirdly, the SPA has a commercial function — i.e., to oversee the management of SOEs and to maximize state revenues as the ultimate owner of, or shareholder in, these firms. These are conflicting objectives and there is now mounting pressure on the SPA to drop the second and the third objectives, and to function solely as a technical privatization agency and leave the protection of state interests to the Ministry of Finance.

The second problem with both governments' opposition to spontaneous privatization is that there are few people available with sufficient technical and commercial competence who can do the job better than the existing management. This is not a question of property rights. The competent people are usually insiders, especially in relatively small countries like Hungary or Czechoslovakia. Independent experts can, of course, be invited from abroad, but this is not a cheap solution. Moreover, it is sometimes questionable whether the increase in objectivity they bring is great enough to outweigh their lack of detailed knowledge. Under such circumstances a centrally-supervised process of denationalization can easily degenerate into a purely bureaucratic exercise. It is not obvious that this is a justified price in reducing the danger of profiteering inevitably involved in such unprecedented operations. In addition, spontaneous privatization is appropriate only for labour-managed firms and it requires the agreement of the staff. If managers are able to rally this support, the government is put in a difficult position in arguing for the moral superiority of a centrally-administered privatization process.

In Hungary, where privatization of large SOEs is already underway, two SPA programmes have been launched so far. The first was targeted at 20 industrial firms with a total asset value of Ft 33 billion.[471] As a first step, some 250 domestic and foreign consulting firms competed for the right to work out and execute this first privatization programme.[472] The second programme (still in its initial phase) was targeted at auctioning thousands of small units engaged in retailing, catering and consumer services. This is very similar to the Czechoslovak programme of small privatization through auctions which started in January 1991. In this latter country, it is expected that the sales of these small enterprises will be completed by the end of 1991. There is no such deadline in Hungary. Another common element is the exclusion of foreigners from the competition.

A third SPA programme was announced in December with the intention of privatizing another 23 industrial SOEs. Participation in this programme is voluntary — i.e., SOEs have to register if they are interested.[473]

Parallel to these measures, self-privatization (or spontaneous privatization) is also on course. In the period March-December 1990, SPA authorization was accorded to 130 transactions of this kind. Altogether, an inflow of some $300 million from abroad was recorded by the SPA arising from the privatization process.[474]

In the meantime the process of restructuring existing enterprises has continued in both countries. It is noteworthy that the possibilities opened by the Hungarian *Transformation Act* as well as the spontaneous emergence of new ventures have resulted in a near doubling in the total number of firms (table 4.4.3). This process is less pronounced in Czechoslovakia but the number of firms is nevertheless growing and their average size is becoming smaller (table 4.4.4).

While both countries are eager to speed up the process of dismantling state ownership, it is accepted that it cannot be done overnight. Hence, the question arises of how to run the existing SOEs in the next three to four years. Analogies with state-owned western companies are certainly misleading. Running a few major companies in a long established market environment, where state ownership represents only a minor share of economic activity, is a vastly different proposition from overseeing dozens or hundreds of such companies (representing 70-80 per cent of output) in a still developing market environment. The earlier calls in both countries for economic independence and for financial discipline (or the hard budget constraint) to be imposed on state enterprises through administrative fiat have not proved successful.[475] It is certain that legal action to transform these enterprises into shareholding

---

470 When first created, the Németh government put the SPA under parliamentary supervision. A return to this practice is still strongly demanded by the opposition.

471 *Heti Világgazdaság*, 22 December 1990.

472 *Figyelő*, 6 December 1990.

473 *Magyar Nemzet*, 4 December 1990.

474 *Heti Világgazdaság*, 22 December 1990, *Magyar Hírlap*, 23 January 1991.

475 A few years ago, officials in Czechoslovakia spoke of "full *khozraschet*". It was assumed that after introduction of the State Enterprise Act of 1988 all enterprises would behave like firms in market economy textbooks. See for instance Frantisek Valenta, "Framework of economic reform", in United Nations Eco-

TABLE 4.4.3

Hungary: Number of economic production units
(End of period)

	1988	1989	1990
Total............................	10 811	15 169	29 470
of which:			
Joint stock companies .	116	307	646
Limited companies.......	451	4 485	18 317

Source: KSH, *Statisztikai Havi Közlemények*, various issues.

TABLE 4.4.4

Czechoslovakia: Number and average size of state-owned enterprises
(End of period)

	Total	Industry	Construction
1989			
Number of units..........	2 586	814	231
Average number of employees................	2 019	3 453	2 267
1990 Q-III			
Number of units..........	3 567	1 373	428
Average number of employees................	1 141	1 947	1 107

Source: Federal Statistical Office, *Quarterly Statistical Bulletin*, December 1990.

companies will not be sufficient to alter this situation. So far neither Czechoslovakia nor Hungary have come out with clear responses to this issue.

(c) Social safety net

As a result of restructuring, human resources will be reallocated from the state to the private sector, from large to small and medium-sized enterprises and from industry to services. This, however, cannot happen without a significant overhaul of the existing *social safety net*. This raises paradoxes for both countries. The institutions and measures traditionally in place are vast and excessively generous in many respects. This creates acute budgetary problems. At the same time, the existing framework is inadequate to meet the new challenges. Substantial additional resources are needed. The essence of reform will be the transformation of the "big networks" (as they are termed in Hungary — that is, the system of pensions, education, housing, health, culture, etc.). Currently these networks are heavily involved in income redistribution.[476] All changes therefore are likely to be painful, even if their net fiscal impact is neutral nationwide.

The need for active labour market policies is one obvious addition to the list of tasks. An *unemployment benefit* system and a *labour exchange network* are in the making in both countries, although in Hungary a provisional scheme was put in place as early as January 1989. Both governments have decided to set up autonomous funds to finance unemployment, retraining and other related activities. In Czechoslovakia financing is divided equally between employers and the state, while the recently approved Hungarian scheme prescribes a 70:22:8 division between the state, employers and employees. From 1 June 1991, employees will have to pay 0.5 per cent of their wages into the fund, employers contributing 1.5 per cent of the wage bill. The estimated total financing requirement for 1991 was put at Ft 31 billion, assuming a continuous rise in unemployment up to 200-260,000 (4.2-5.4 per cent of the labour force).[477]

In Czechoslovakia, the release of labour from energy-intensive industries and armaments, together with the entry onto the labour market of school-leavers, are expected to raise the number of unemployed to some 700-800,000 or 8-10 per cent of the labour force in 1991.[478] Unemployment benefit has been set at 60 per cent of previous earnings for the first six months and 50 per cent for the following six months. According to the recently adopted Hungarian *Employment Act*, the corresponding figures are 70 and 50 per cent. Benefit must exceed the minimum wage, but cannot exceed it by more than three times.

(d) Banking system

The establishment of a two-tier *banking system* is conceived as a major step toward the creation of a fully-fledged capital market in both countries. This will probably be followed by a gradual dismantling of the monopoly position of the central bank in foreign exchange transactions in favour of the commercial banks. In Hungary, this process started already in 1987, but further progress will certainly be very cautious in view of the country's high level of indebtedness. An additional barrier to the rapid evolution of the capital market is the under-capitalization of the commercial banks. It will take several years to overcome this obstacle, especially since there is also a shortage of qualified experts. One possible remedy envisaged by recent legislation is the establishment of partly- or fully-owned foreign banks in both countries. Some 20 banks in foreign and mixed ownership are currently operating in Hungary and in 1991 this door has also been opened in Czechoslovakia. But both governments are aware of the risks of allowing strong and aggressive competitors to sweep away the recently created network of commercial banks, let alone of selling these banks directly to foreigners. In Hungary, such reservations were explicitly

---

nomic Commission for Europe, *Economic Reforms in the European Centrally Planned Economies* (proceedings of an international symposium held in November 1988 in Vienna), New York, 1989, pp.20-27.

[476] In Hungary the share of earned money incomes in total incomes was only 53.1 per cent in 1989. The corresponding Czechoslovak figure for 1988 was only slightly higher, 56.8 per cent.

[477] *Népszabadság*, 11 February 1991.

[478] Statement of the Federal Minister of Economic Affairs Vladimir Dlouhy at the annual World Economic Forum in Davos. Finance Minister V. Klaus, however, declared his continued adherence to the government's earlier estimate of 4-6 per cent unemployment in 1991 (*Financial Times*, 6 February 1991).

formulated in the *1991 state property policy guidelines*, which state that the five major commercial banks would not be privatized in the foreseeable future.

(e) Foreign trade liberalization and convertibility

After price liberalization, the second cornerstone of the Czechoslovak reform proposals is the immediate establishment of *internal convertibility* of the crown from 1 January 1991. This implies the compulsory sale of foreign exchange to banks and the possibility of free purchase of currencies for the purpose of imports. At first, such access to foreign currencies is to be reserved for companies only (including joint ventures). Unlike in Poland or Yugoslavia, private citizens, state-financed bodies and non-profit organizations continue to be controlled and limited.[479] This concept of internal convertibility thus goes no further than in Hungary after the introduction of its *New Economic Mechanism* in 1968. The difference is essentially semantic: at that time the Hungarian regulation and academic literature preferred the term "import competition". More recently, the same proposition is called "import liberalization". In practice there is no difference between these various formulations. The real question, and this is where the Hungarian initiative failed after a year or so, is whether this commitment of the Czechoslovak authorities to convertibility is sustainable over a prolonged period.

One decisive issue connected with the establishment of internal convertibility concerns the determination of a sustainable exchange rate policy. If a fixed nominal exchange rate policy is chosen, as in Poland and Yugoslavia, misvaluations cannot be easily corrected without risking loss of confidence. Being one year behind Poland and Yugoslavia in this respect, the Czechoslovak authorities paid great attention to assessing the possible consequences of over- or undershooting. They have finally opted for a relatively large initial devaluation and set the exchange rate at 28 crowns to the dollar,[480] somewhat below the estimated marginal cost of producing 1 dollar's worth of exports. The tourist rate was abolished, and the foreign exchange auction, last held on 12 December, was discontinued.[481]

After the failure of initial moves to convertibility, the issue of liberalizing imports in Hungary (more precisely: convertible currency imports) was put aside for almost two decades. At the end of the 1980s, however, the issue recurred by default, as the question of profit repatriation became an important issue with the rise of foreign joint ventures. Hence in 1988 a gradual liberalization of imports and a relaxation of profit repatriation limitations were launched at the same time. As a result of further measures introduced in January 1991, the forint has now become almost fully convertible for the purposes of imports[482] and profit repatriation. The National Bank of Hungary appears to be following a policy of cautious floating, allowing the forint to devalue to maintain competitiveness, but at the same time it wants to maintain the disciplinary role of the exchange rate.[483]

Changes in corporate structures also mean that a growing number of agents can perform foreign trade activities besides the traditional foreign trade organizations. In Hungary this process started in 1968, while in Czechoslovakia the decisive step was taken only in April 1990. The changes in legislation allowed foreign trade to be carried out by any economic agent irrespective of the type of ownership (co-operative or private) and irrespective of the agent's nationality (domestic or foreign) on the basis of simple registration with the authorities.[484] A decisive push has been given to this process by the termination of the intra-CMEA trading and payment agreements from 1 January 1991. In the past, reform efforts in both countries ran aground at this point. The lack of competition on the CMEA markets and the dominance of bilateral trade relations meant that it was impossible to give real commercial independence to firms with significant trading relationships with CMEA partners. In both countries a complicated system was required to link domestic producers with their CMEA partners and an almost completely different mechanism was needed to link them with the western market economies. But since January 1991 all this has become obsolete, opening the way to a unified foreign trade system based on appropriate exchange rates and market conformity regulations.

Nevertheless, some temporary administrative measures are still maintained or have been recently introduced by both countries to prevent a rapid rise of consumer goods imports. Hungary, for example, ever since its accession to the GATT, has been operating a quota system for this purpose. According to the 1991 guidelines, the quota for the aggregate of non-liberalized consumer goods is set at $630 million, which is actually

479 J. Zahradnik, *Czechoslovakia's Approach to Currency Convertibility Issues*, Paper presented at a conference in the Austrian National Bank, January 1991.

480 At the beginning of 1990, the official exchange rate − used mainly for statistical purposes only − was 14.29 Kcs/$. After the October devaluation, the end-1990 exchange rate rose to 24 Kcs/$.

481 According to a seemingly authentic account (Zahradnik, *op.cit.*), three options were thought through in banking circles. Purchasing power parity calculations implied a 8-10 Kcs/$ rate, the average cost estimates varied around 16 Kcs/$, while the marginal export price was put at 30-35 Kcs/$. It is interesting to note that in 1968 the Hungarian planners followed the identical line of thought but finally opted for a rate below average costs. This was certainly one of the reasons for their failure to achieve internal convertibility.

482 Some 8 per cent of imports (chiefly consumer goods) are still subject to licensing.

483 National Bank of Hungary, *Annual Report 1989*, p.72.

484 Recent developments in this area were discussed at greater length in M. Hrncir, "The Institutional Framework of Foreign Economic Relations in Czechoslovakia", United Nations Economic Commission for Europe, *Reforms in Foreign Economic Relations of Eastern Europe and the Soviet Union*, New York, 1991, pp.7-14. and K. Mizsei, "The Institutional Framework of Foreign Trade Reforms in Hungary", *ibid.*, pp.15-20.

three times the 1990 figure.[485] To achieve the same objective, Czechoslovakia has recently introduced a temporary restrictive measure in the form of a 20 per cent surcharge (for more details see section 3.3) on consumer goods imports.

(vi) Concluding remarks

Since the introduction of political changes in late 1989 and 1990 there has been little time in either Hungary or Czechoslovakia to implement fundamental economic changes. Indeed, as noted above, there has been no real economic need for urgency, let alone for hasty action in either country. Thus the main burden of adjustment will be felt only in 1991 and perhaps in 1992. This will certainly adversely affect living standards and less resources will be available for capital formation. This could lead to conflicts within the governing coalitions and to a further erosion of the public consensus. This, in turn, could paralyse decision-makers at a very sensitive time, when the old system has already been dismantled but the new one is not yet in place. The increasing risk of inflation getting out of control suggests that this may already be happening. Unfortunately, the international economic environment is unfavourable for both countries. Any unexpected deterioration in this respect will certainly hit Hungary proportionally harder, since it has built its external strategy on a commitment to servicing hard currency debt for which purpose it has only the minimum of reserves.

---

[485] This is explained by the switchover from rouble to dollar trade (*Heti Világgazdaság*, 2 February 1991).

4.5 LATE STARTERS: BULGARIA, ROMANIA

(i) Introduction

Both Bulgaria and Romania have had more difficulty than the other eastern European countries in definitively breaking with the communist past. Political disagreements and continuing question marks over the democratic legitimacy of the governments in power have hampered reform efforts in both countries. Meanwhile in both countries the economic situation deteriorated steadily as the old system of central planning collapsed without being replaced by any market-based system of co-ordination.

The formation of a coalition government in Bulgaria in December 1990 should provide a more secure foundation for restarting the process of economic reform, which was virtually paralyzed in 1990. In Romania, the National Salvation Front government is making progress with the framework of its radical reform programme but, given the weakness of support for the government's policies, there is a substantial risk that the programme will run out of steam as it runs into popular opposition. Although governments may try to impose the framework of a market economy from above, without popular support for the changes, the new legislative framework will remain an empty shell unable to deliver the hoped for improvements.

(ii) The emergence of political consensus?

In *Romania* the political situation has been plagued by the continuing uncertainties about the precise roles played by the army, secret police and the communist party in the overthrow of the Ceausescu régime in December 1989. The elections held in May 1990 gave the National Salvation Front (NSF) a large majority in the new parliament, despite allegations that the NSF was merely becoming a vehicle for former communists. The NSF won the elections on its reputation acquired during the December revolution and on a promise to introduce a market economy gradually, protecting those most vulnerable to change. Opposition parties, who generally favoured a faster move to a market economy, claimed that the elections were not fair and kept their distance from the NSF. Their distrust of the NSF increased in June 1990 when students, demonstrating in Bucharest against the government, were attacked by miners, allegedly brought in from outside by the NSF.

These tensions have led to a sharp polarization of political views so that economic reform proposals are often judged on the political affiliation of their creator rather than on their actual content.

The political atmosphere in *Bulgaria* has been similarly tense. In the June elections the Bulgarian Socialist Party (the BSP — formerly the Bulgarian Communist Party) gained the majority of seats in the new Grand National Assembly, with the Union of Democratic Forces (UDF, broadly in favour of a faster shift to a market economy) as the principal opposition movement. However the elections did not resolve the political tensions in the country. The BSP only managed to form a government at the end of September — nearly three months after the elections — and disputes over the government's economic reform plans led to a further political crisis. The BSP government eventually fell at the end of November and was replaced by a coalition government involving both the BSP and the UDF. It is to be hoped that the new government will be more successful in mobilizing a consensus behind its policies of genuine market reform.

(iii) Social support for a market economy

In *Bulgaria*, the new coalition government has negotiated an agreement on preserving "social peace" with the trade unions. This agreement calls for a period of 200 days to be kept free from strikes to ease the introduction of market reforms in return for improvements to the social safety net. However, given the deteriorating economic situation and the likely initial adverse effects of the economic reforms (prices are expected to rise by some 90 per cent after they are liberalized in February 1991 and unemployment is expected to quadruple in 1991), it is likely that social tensions will grow. Thus, the maintenance of the current degree of social consensus may prove difficult.

In *Romania*, the lack of social consensus already appears to be a problem. The first phase of price liberalization in November 1990 led to large price rises and demonstrations against the government. Strikes have been widespread and while some strikers have merely demanded pay rises and improved working conditions, others also demanded a quickening in the pace of reforms. There thus seems to be little chance of an early emergence of a wide social consensus in Romania.

However, the government seems determined to press ahead with its chosen, radical reform programme, despite the lack of a broad social consensus and strains such a policy is likely to put on the unity of the NSF itself. The NSF leadership now seems to be committed to a process of radical economic reform, although it appeared to support a more gradual transition during the election campaign. As much of the popular support for the NSF comes from workers in heavy industry, whose positions would be endangered if the radical policies now being advocated by the NSF government were actually adopted, the government seems to be acting against the interests of the NSF's natural supporters. There is therefore a continuing risk of a split within the ruling party. Although the opposition parties claim to be in favour of more rapid economic reform, in the current atmosphere of political distrust they are unlikely to support the NSF leadership in pushing through reforms if the current government were to run into problems with its natural supporters. Some political realignment therefore seems necessary in Romania if the planned reforms are to prove durable within a democratic system.

(iv) Evolution of programmes for reform

In *Bulgaria*, the successive programmes of economic reforms have become steadily more radical as the country's economic situation has worsened and as the BSP has lost its dominant political position.

The first economic programme, presented before the elections in March 1990, reflected a gradualist approach to reform.[486] Thus, ownership of economic assets was to be gradually broadened and enterprises given more freedom with the aim of fostering a *mixed* economy, some important prices were to be liberalized and a uniform exchange rate régime set up, the government's budget position was to be improved and a social safety net was to be established. However, only some of the measures in this programme were actually carried out.

In October 1990, four months after the elections, the new BSP government presented a revised and more comprehensive programme. This programme was more radical and was intended to quicken the pace of reform. The plan was formulated in three stages: the first stage included emergency measures, such as improvements in the supply of fuels and foodstuffs, designed to help the economy through the winter. This would be followed by macro-economic stabilization measures (price liberalization and tighter wage, fiscal and monetary policies). The wider reforms of the economic system such as privatization, liberalization of foreign trade, tax reform and the setting up of a new banking system were to be left to the final stage. However, because of the lack of political consensus, this programme was not approved by parliament.

The new coalition government is drawing up another, more radical, reform programme in consultation

with the IMF and the World Bank and the first emergency measures of this programme are now being implemented.[487] However, the paralysis caused by political disagreements has meant that the process of economic reform has only just started, with the economy in a far worse position than it was a year ago.

In *Romania*, reforms before the elections were restricted to *ad hoc* measures reversing some of the unpopular policies of the previous régime, such as reducing the export of foodstuffs which were in short supply on the domestic market, reversing the policy of "systematization" – the elimination of rural villages – and the granting of land to individual farmers. The working week was also reduced to five days, which contributed to a considerable fall in production. The first detailed economic reform proposals were presented by the newly-elected NSF government in August-September 1990,[488] and since then the government has repeatedly emphasized the importance of accelerating the programme of economic reform.[489] The goverment's programme sets out six successive stages of reform from September 1990 until June 1992. While the document seems to be comprehensive and to set out a sensible timetable for reform, the lack of domestic consensus for such policies brings into question the practical feasibility of the programme.

(v) Progress in particular areas

(a) *Property rights and the status of the private sector*

Both Bulgaria and Romania have now officially recognized an equality of status between the private and public sectors. However, the old administrative apparatus still appears to be restricting the development of the private sector and entrepreneurs are finding it difficult to obtain finance from the state banking system, trading licences or premises. In addition, the Romanian government also appears to be cracking down on black market and unofficial trade, and this is likely to further slow the growth of the private sector.[490] Thus, although the private sector does seem to be growing, it is not likely to have a significant effect on the economic situation in either country in the near future.

Given the size of the agricultural sector in both economies, clearing up property rights to land (and the associated problem of the future status of the co-operative farms) is particularly urgent. A land law was approved by the Bulgarian parliament only in February 1991,[491] while the Romanian land law was discussed in

---

486 See the speech of the Bulgarian Prime Minister A. Lukanov in BBC, *Summary of World Broadcasts*, EE/0728, 2 April 1990.

487 The government's programme of reforms was set out to parliament by Prime Minister D. Popov on 23 January 1991. See BBC, *Summary of World Broadcasts*, EE/0980, 26 January 1991.

488 The reform policies were set out in the *Programme of working out and co-ordinating reform projects*, The Council for Reform, Public Relations and Information, Bucharest, Augst-September 1990.

489 See Petre Roman's speech to parliament "On the state of implementation of the economic reform and the demand to step up its pace" on 18 October 1990 and, most recently, his "state of the nation" report to parliament of 26 February 1991 excerpted in *Romania libera*, 27 February 1991. For a translation, see BBC, *Summary of World Broadcasts*, EE/1013, 6 March 1991, pp.B/10-13, and EE/1016, 9 March 1991, pp.B/9-14.

490 See BBC, *Summary of World Broadcasts*, EE/0929, 23 November 1990.

491 The law was passed on 22 February 1991. See BBC, *Summary of World Broadcasts*, EE/1006, 26 February 1991 for details.

parliament in December 1990 and January 1991.[492] Both laws lay down the right of individuals or companies (but not foreigners) to own land and transfer it to others, provided agricultural land is still cultivated and individual holdings do not exceed certain limits — 30 hectares in Bulgaria, 100 hectares in Romania (the Romanian law also confirms the distribution of land to individuals carried out in January 1990).[493] Co-operative farmers may become individual farmers of their own land or may continue to work in "joint associations" with other farmers. There are also provisions for property to be restored to those whose land was confiscated under the former régime.

(b) Commercialization of the state sector and privatization

Progress in enterprise reform and privatization in *Bulgaria* has been particularly affected by the political disagreements. Each economic reform plan has stressed the importance of early moves towards making the state sector more commercially minded and proposed schemes for privatizing state assets. Despite the obvious collapse of central planning, very little progress has so far been made in these areas. The new coalition government's reform programme intends that the process of privatization should begin in the second quarter of 1991[494] and subsidies to enterprises from the state budget will be cut sharply.

In *Romania*, progress with changing the legal status of enterprises has been more rapid, though it is not clear if these legal changes have yet had much effect on enterprise performance. Law 15/1990,[495] which was passed in the autumn of last year and is the centrepiece of the government's economic reforms so far, sets out the new status of state-owned industry. A limited number of state enterprises in strategic industries such as energy, railways and armaments, will be designated as "autonomous units" and will not be privatized. However, most state-owned firms will be organized as joint stock or limited liability companies, with their capital initially held by the state. These firms will be independent of central control (though subject to restrictions on monopolistic behaviour) and will be expected to act on a commercial basis. Their subsidies will steadily be reduced to zero over a 4-year period.[496]

A draft law on privatization was published on 20 December 1990 and sets out a variety of methods of disposing of state assets. Small enterprises will be sold directly to the private sector while larger firms may have their shares sold by auction or public offering; up to 10 per cent of an enterprise's shares may be sold, on preferential terms, to its employees; finally each Romanian citizen will be given claims on the "common ownership fund" which will hold shares in all privatized enterprises. These claims will be tradeable and inheritable. The common ownership fund is thus a mutual fund which, presumably, is intended to exert some external discipline on the newly-privatized enterprises.

(c) Foreign trade régime

Reform of the trade régime is particularly urgent in *Romania* as a collapse in exports in 1990 (due to much reduced domestic production and the diversion of exportables to home use) meant that the country ran down much of its foreign exchange reserves in paying for imports. Many enterprises have obtained licences to trade directly with foreign firms and the role of the trade ministry has been reduced, though the ministry still has the power to limit certain imports and exports.[497] The 60 per cent devaluation of the official exchange rate in the autumn (to a rate of 35 leu to the dollar) was designed to discourage imports. Foreign currency auctions have been introduced as a first step towards convertibility (the government's reform programme aims for full convertibility of the leu in 1992), with the exchange rate set in the auctions operating in parallel with the official rate until convertibility is achieved.[498]

Bulgaria, which has a heavy burden of foreign debt, stopped interest and principal payments on its debt in 1990 because of a sharp fall in exports. Despite this, the government has recently moved towards import liberalization and has kept the export of commodities in short supply on domestic markets under strict control.[499] There are plans to establish a floating exchange rate for the leva against convertible currencies.

Both countries have plans to liberalize foreign investment and have now started negotiations with the IMF and the World Bank (these talks were delayed by scepticism amongst western governments about both Bulgaria's and Romania's commitment to economic and political reform). Substantial IMF and other foreign help is likely to be required to reschedule Bulgaria's debts and to prevent balance of payments problems in both countries aborting the reform process

---

492 See BBC, *Summary of World Broadcasts*, EE/0954, 22 December 1990 for details of Prime Minister Petre Roman's speech to the Senate presenting the land bill.

493 " ... what was granted on the basis of the decree-law in January — within the limits of 5,000 square metres — must be considered as granted for good". Excerpt from P. Roman's speech presenting the land law to the Senate, *loc.cit.*

494 See *Duma*, 30 December 1990.

495 The official title is "Law No.15/1990 concerning restructuring of state economic units as self-sufficient administrations and trading companies".

496 However, the same article (43) which lays down that subsidies will be withdrawn also states that the state can still help these companies through "economic levers such as special interest rates, credits, state orders, subsidies, taxes and duties".

497 BBC, *Summary of World Broadcasts*, EE/0968, 12 January 1991.

498 BBC, *Summary of World Broadcasts*, EE/W0168, 28 February 1991. The first auction set a rate of 200 leu to the dollar and it is not clear how the coexistence of two such divergent exchange rates will be managed. More recently, the government has agreed with the IMF further to liberalize trade in foreign currency from April 1991. See *Neue Zürcher Zeitung*, 11 March 1991.

499 BBC, *Summary of World Broadcasts*, EE/W0167, 21 February 1991.

(see section 3.3(vi) for more details of western aid to Bulgaria and Romania).

(d) Banking reform

Both Romania and Bulgaria plan to introduce a western style two-tier banking system with the central bank withdrawing from direct provision of credit and the setting up of a network of competing commercial banks.

(vi) Stabilization policies supporting reforms

(a) Price reform and policies

Price reform has a high priority in both countries' reform programmes. In *Bulgaria*, the successive schemes for price reform set out in 1990 have been abandoned and the new government has opted for a "big bang" approach. On 1 February 1991, most prices were freed (the exceptions were bread, meat and some dairy products, which were kept under central control) and prices rose sharply − some products increasing more than 20-fold. To prevent the price rises setting off an inflationary spiral, the government and trade unions have agreed that wages are to be only partially indexed.

In *Romania*, the situation is more complicated. The first round of price rises took place on 1 November 1990 and the second was scheduled for January 1991. The regulations covering the November price reform gave the government considerable powers to control excessive "monopolistic" price rises but left energy prices and rents unchanged. It is therefore not clear how far the November price increases were the result of freeing prices from central control and how much it was due to increases in centrally administered prices. Despite the official compensation scheme, which attempted to compensate workers and pensioners for the increase in the price of basic foodstuffs, there were widespread popular protests after the price rises and the government initially postponed the second round of price increases to June 1991.[500] On the wage side, the government has plans to allow wages to be negotiated collectively, with excessive wage increases subject to penal taxation (this is similar in many respects to the Polish scheme; the main difference seems to be that wages will seemingly be more fully indexed to price rises in Romania).

(b) Budgetary and monetary policies

While price increases may go some way towards improving internal balance, budgetary and monetary policies need to be brought under tighter control if inflation is not to get out of hand. In both countries, the monetary overhang worsened in 1990 as production collapsed and wages were allowed to increase. Government budget projections for 1991 show a deficit of about 2 per cent of GDP in Romania and of about 5 per cent of GDP in Bulgaria (the Bulgarian figure being the highest that would be permitted by the IMF). These deficits will only be attainable if subsidies to enterprises and consumers are cut drastically. While tighter government budget policy should reduce one source of credit growth, a much tighter monetary policy is also required to encourage newly autonomous enterprises not to borrow excessively from the fledgling banking system (or from each other). To this end, interest rates in Bulgaria were tripled to 45 per cent on 1st February 1991, again in line with IMF recommendations. In Romania interest rates for private depositors are set to double in 1991.[501]

Over the longer term, reforms of the tax system are planned. The Romanian government has presented a draft law establishing a progressive personal income tax,[502] and intends to set up a system of VAT from January 1992, together with a corporate profits tax. In Bulgaria, the turnover tax was drastically simplified in February 1991 as a first step towards the introduction of a VAT (the previous 43 tax bands have been replaced by two with tax rates set at 10 per cent and 20 per cent) and there are plans to introduce income and profits taxes.

(vii) Creation of a social safety net

Bulgaria's first system of unemployment benefits was introduced in December 1989 and is due to be replaced as part of the new package of economic reforms. The existing system entitles redundant workers and unemployed school-leavers to unemployment benefit[503] for six months, followed by assistance payments at the level of the minimum wage for another three months. The Romanian unemployment benefit system is still under discussion but current proposals envisage that payment will last for a maximum of 6 months and vary between 60 per cent of the minimum wage and 60 per cent of earnings in the last job with entitlements increasing with the length of employment record and, for school-leavers, with the level of education.[504] Both countries seem to be setting up training schemes to help the unemployed to return to work, though it is hard to find specific details.

---

[500] Prime Minister P. Roman announced in his "state of the nation" speech that food prices would be freed in April 1991, though there would still be upper limits on increases for some basic products. *Neue Zürcher Zeitung*, 27 February 1991.

[501] BBC, *Summary of World Broadcasts*, EE/W0154, 15 November 1990.

[502] *Neue Zürcher Zeitung*, 28 January 1991.

[503] The amount of benefit payable declines steadily from an initial entitlement of 100 per cent of the worker's former earnings to 50 per cent after six months.

[504] BBC, *Summary of World Broadcasts*, EE/0983, 30 January 1991.

They are also introducing other measures to protect the weaker members of society. Bulgaria plans to introduce new social security and public health bills

while, in Romania, transfers to pensioners and workers have been increased to cushion the effect on them of price increases.

4.6   THE CASE OF THE SOVIET UNION

(i) Introduction — the run-up to transition

The year 1990 saw a substantial increase in the number of legislative acts, including presidential decrees, designed to put in place the new institutional framework for transition to a market economy in the Soviet Union. This has been made possible by a restructuring of the system of political representation which opened the way for wide-ranging public political and economic debate on a scale not experienced since the 1920s.

On 14 March 1990, Article VI of the constitution guaranteeing the "leading role" of the Communist Party of the Soviet Union was struck out by a vote of the 3rd Congress of People's Deputies of the USSR.[505] The right to form political parties was granted by the Law on public associations of 9 October 1990.[506] Legislative power is vested in the Union Congress of People's Deputies. Its 2,250-strong membership was elected for five years in March 1989. The Congress elects about 540 of its members by secret ballot to the Supreme Soviet, half of which sit in the Union Chamber and half in the Chamber of Nationalities. The Plenary session of the Supreme Soviet, consisting of both of these Chambers in joint session, is the organ responsible for day-to-day parliamentary business including discussion, review and adoption of new legislation.[507]

Not all deputies to the Congress are mandated by popular suffrage, one third of them (750) being elected by institutional constituencies, including the Communist Party, the Young Communist League *(Komsomol)*, the trade unions, the USSR Academy of Sciences, women's organizations, etc. Some 85 per cent of these are reckoned to be party members or supporters. The Congress is replicated at republican level at which, in contrast, all deputies are directly elected. This is also the case for city and other lower echelon local authority councils. The Union and republican presidents are elected by the respective Councils of People's Deputies.

In a law passed by the 3rd Congress of People's Deputies in March 1990[508] a new body, the Federation Council, was set up "to consider questions concerning the Union Treaty; to work out measures for the implementation of the national policies of the Soviet state; to make recommendations to resolve disputes and to regulate conflict situations and inter-ethnic relations; to co-ordinate the activity of the Union-republics and ensure their participation in resolving questions of all-Union significance ...". The Council consists of the highest republican state office holders. Their equivalents in the autonomous regions can also participate in its meetings. In the economic sphere, the Council has played a significant role in debating and designing basic aspects of economic development strategies at the Union level. The Council works under the chairmanship of the USSR President and reaches decisions on the basis of a minimum two-thirds majority.

Although at the Union level the Congress of People's Deputies and the Supreme Soviet contain a disproportionate number of institutional representatives whose often conservative voice may not always coincide with public opinion, the contrast with the former highly-restricted system of popular representation is clear. The new electoral system has opened the way for genuine public debate on an unrestricted range of topics.[509] These new arrangements have provided a forum for the discussion and passage of policy measures in areas of domestic and external economic affairs. They illustrate an approach to economic policy-making different in kind to anything which has gone before. Even so, the new departures do not yet add up to a consistent or coherent programme. Some backtracking and failure to act at all in several key areas have reinforced the considerable uncertainties still holding back popular and indeed international confidence in the transition. Without them, the grass roots initiatives needed to replace state centralized planning in the conduct of economic affairs and the co-operation desirable with other countries are unlikely to develop at the speed required.

There is still uncertainty about the final objectives of transition to a market economy. This might appear surprising given that clear indications of President Gorbachev's personal commitment to *radical* reform of economic management were given as long as five

---

505 *Vedomosti Verkhovnogo Soveta SSSR* (List of Acts of the USSR Supreme Soviet), No.12, 21 March 1990.

506 *Pravda*, 16 October 1990.

507 Law on the election of USSR national deputies of 1 December 1988, published in *Pravda*, 4 December 1988.

508 Law on the institutions of the post of President of the USSR and additions to the Constitution, 14 March 1990.

509 According to an opinion poll organized jointly by the Japanese Kyodo and the Soviet TASS news agencies, some 27 per cent of Soviet respondents supported the Communist Party, 33 per cent parties other than communists while 40 per cent remained uncommitted. About 31 per cent of the sample supported national independence movements, 24 per cent considered that the Union should remain intact while 35 per cent favoured a looser federal system. President Gorbachev was supported by 38 per cent of the sample. See BBC, *Summary of World Broadcasts*, SU/0931, 26 November 1990, p.B/5.

years ago.[510] The first blueprint advocating a comprehensive dismantling of the previous system of economic management was offered by Deputy Prime Minister Academician L.I. Abalkin in November 1989. This fairly radical programme was one of the sources used in the more cautious draft offered by the then Prime Minister N.I. Ryzhkov to the Second Congress of People's Deputies in December 1989 and in revised and more radical form to the Supreme Soviet in May of the following year. This did not meet the approval of the Supreme Soviet. A more detailed variant of his own November programme was completed by Deputy Prime Minister Abalkin in August 1990 embodying the concept of a "regulated market economy". However, this was superseded by a joint inter-republican working group under the direction of Academician S.S. Shatalin which produced what became known as the "500 Days" programme in the same month. This also failed to muster general support. Both of these were used in the drafting of a compromise programme by a team chaired by Academician Aganbegyan very shortly afterwards.[511] The Prime Minister's first attempt to put together a transition programme, considered too modest by many commentators inside and outside the Soviet Union, already indicated the need for the large-scale and rapid creation of new institutions as well as the development of policy instruments and legal innovations to underpin and extend the first institutional reforms made during the course of 1987-1989.[512] But no final programme was approved by the USSR Supreme Soviet until the autumn of 1990.

(ii) The transition blueprints

(a) The Union programme of October 1990

The basic policy document for the transition to a market economy now in force is the "Main Guidelines for Economic Stabilization and Transition to the Market", adopted for implementation with immediate effect by the USSR Supreme Soviet on 19 October 1990.[513] The "Guidelines" cover a period lasting 18 months to two years and divided into four stages. At the outset of the *first* phase a series of legislative acts enshrining the basic principles and directions of economic reform were to be promulgated, together with a system of special measures to stabilize the economy — the latter being considered as the main problem at this stage. The immediate objectives were to improve government finances and control the money supply, restructure the banking system, regulate enterprise sector finances and raise interest rates to protect savings. Steps were to be taken to balance consumer incomes and expenditures including the provision of incentives for consumer

goods production. This would help to avert price rises and begin the saturation of the market. A start would be made on the denationalization *(razgosudarstvlenie)* of state enterprises and dismantling of monopolies. Finally, measures would be introduced to stabilize foreign economic relations.

The *second* phase was to be dominated by a gradual transition to market prices for a broad range of technical and consumer goods, continued control of price rises by tough financial and credit policies and the maintenance of state prices for at least one third of all goods (fuel, raw materials and semi-finished goods), the monitoring and regulation of retail prices of consumer necessities, privatization of small enterprises and reallocation of investment toward consumer goods production. The first results of the extraordinary measures taken in the first phase should at this point begin to yield marked improvements on the consumer markets, considered a necessary condition for further progress. Special measures to protect vulnerable groups of the population will be necessary, including indexation of incomes and price freezes. A new state contract and distribution system is to maintain production and ties with suppliers. The system is essentially a new framework for the placing of state orders and will contain provision for price regulation.

The prime objective during the *third* phase is full stabilization of the market for both consumer and producer goods on the basis of market forces and increased supplies. The creation of a housing market will help to mop up excess consumer demand. The wage system will be reformed; minimum wage provisions will be included but the new system will also be designed to reward hard work. The restructuring of mutual relations between enterprises and local authorities and price liberalization are to be carried further against the background of equilibrium prices, balanced government budgets and markets for goods and services, a modern banking system and a currency market. Trade unions will be strengthened to enable them to defend workers' interests and employer associations will be created. Labour relations are to be based on mutual agreements between them, subject to public supervision of incomes and prices. Changes in tax legislation and relaxation of financial and credit restrictions will help revive business activity.

The *final* phase of the stabilization period is expected to be the consolidation of gains in economic and financial equilibrium, continued improvements in consumer markets and, especially, in the growth of competition. Considerable progress is expected in denationalization, privatization and in the dismantling of monopolies. Market prices should predominate at

---

510 M.S. Gorbachev, speech to the XXVII Congress of the CPSU, *Pravda*, 26 February 1986.

511 For a comprehensive account of these developments see Commission of the European Communities, *European Economy*, No.45, December 1990, entitled "Stabilization, liberalization and devolution: Assessment of the economic situation and reform process in the Soviet Union", pp.83-98.

512 These included a first Law on the Enterprise (Association) in June 1987 (superseded by the Law on Enterprises of June 1990 — see below), the Law on Co-operatives of May 1988 (amended in October 1989 to impose upper limits on prices of goods and services and their monitoring by the state) and the Law on Leasing of 23 November 1989 which provided possibilities for private individuals to engage in productive activity on land or industrial plant leased from state enterprises or farming co-operatives.

513 See *Pravda*, 18 October 1990 (for the text); *Izvestiya*, 20 October 1990 (for the Supreme Soviet resolution on its adoption).

this stage. This would provide a basis for internal convertibility of the rouble, give all firms the opportunity to buy and sell foreign currencies as needed and set the scene for an inflow of foreign investment. The latter is considered to be "an important pre-condition for ensuring that the market mechanism runs on full power".

This document, which took up many of the elements of the Shatalin programme, was considered by many Soviet commentators — including Academician Shatalin himself — as inadequate, especially given the swift deterioration in the economy which occurred in the second half of 1990. It is clear that the programme leaves only limited room for the market in the early stages of economic stabilization. Problems are to be approached largely on the basis of administrative direct action along the lines used under central planning — though the immediate objectives, notably the priority accorded to the consumption sector, are different from before.

With regard to the longer-term objectives following stabilization, the first paragraph of the "Guidelines" begins with the words "There is no alternative to switching to a market". This is "dictated solely by people's interests and aims to create a socially oriented economy, gear all production to consumer needs, overcome the shortages and the disgraceful queues, ensure citizens' real economic freedom and establish conditions for encouraging hard work, initiative and high productivity". This is held not to "contradict our people's socialist choice" and suggests that non-market (central or perhaps local government) intervention is expected even in the longer term to ensure that the priorities included in the term "socialist" are maintained. The key question is the extent of such non-market intervention and especially its impact on the institutional arrangements now being created in anticipation of transition to the market.

(b) The "500 Days" programme

The most radical of the transition blueprints yet offered is that generally known as the "500 Days" programme, prepared under the joint responsibility of Presidents Gorbachev of the USSR and Yel'tsin of the RSFSR.[514] This programme was already approved by the RSFSR Supreme Soviet on 11 September 1990 — that is, prior to the passage of the "Guidelines" through the Supreme Soviet of the USSR the following month. None the less, the Russian Parliament confirmed its decision on 31 October and the "500 Days" programme came into effect on the territory of the RSFSR on 1 November 1990. The draft programme was also agreed by the "plenipotentiary" (*polnomochnie*) representatives of almost all the other republics (excluding only Estonia), which discussed it in a working group in preparation for the debate in the USSR Supreme Soviet at which the "Guidelines" were adopted in its stead. The main provisions of the programme are discussed in the following paragraphs.

The general objective of the "500 Days" programme was stated to be the implementation of measures in a short time to lay the foundations of a new economic system *which, without extraordinary efforts on the part of the state* will orient production towards the satisfaction of private and social needs, create effective stimuli for work and entrepreneurship, guarantee the saturation of the market with all kinds of goods at stable prices and ensure prosperity for the country and its people of all nationalities.

This programme also made provision for four phases of transition. As the passage highlighted above indicates, a central feature and one which distinguishes it from the "Guidelines" was its considerable reliance on the progressive incorporation of market forces rather than government action to guide the direction of change and its whole-hearted commitment to the market as the final goal. The programme gave precise targets for the various stages along the path of transition and set a final goal of privatizing some 70 per cent of industrial enterprises and 90 per cent of those in other service-related sectors.

The *first* stage of the programme (the first 100 days, roughly the beginning of October 1990 to the beginning of 1991) specified the passage of a set of laws, if necessary by presidential decree in the event that they could not be agreed in the USSR or republican Supreme Soviets, and the drafting of others to provide the institutional basis for a market economy within that period. Shares in 50-60 large state enterprises and other state assets, including housing and small enterprises, should be sold or leased immediately to private individuals. The republics were to decide on their own principles of land reform but state and collective farmers should be permitted to cultivate land made available to them by the farms to which they belong. The programme also made detailed recommendations for reductions in government spending, including an early halt to subsidies paid to enterprises except in certain special cases, which were omitted from the "Guidelines". Efforts to control the growth of the money supply were not to preclude assistance from the beginning of 1991 to potentially viable firms in difficulties due to tight credit, but 100-200 particularly inefficient enterprises were to be closed down. Existing supply linkages between enterprises were initially to be obligatorily maintained and mutual deliveries held at the levels of the recent past, with the support of parallel inter-republican agreements and severe sanctions for enterprises which did not comply. But these expedients were expressly ruled out after July 1991. Enterprise taxation was to be introduced from 1 January 1991. These measures, together with the development and use of credit instruments and a simplification of foreign exchange rates and procedures, were to play an important initial confidence-building role and add credibility to the transition process. Arrangements to protect vulnerable groups from price rises were to begin with the indexation of wages towards the end of this phase.

---

514 *Perekhod k rynku, kontseptsiya i programma* (Transition to the Market, Design and Programme), Working Group set up jointly by decision of M.S Gorbachev and B.N. Yel'tsin, Archangel'skoe, Moscow, August 1990.

Price liberalization and notably the withdrawal of the price-setting powers of the government were foreseen during the *second* phase of the programme (day 100 to day 250), combined with a further tightening of financial discipline. The main task during this phase was to consolidate the gains already made, facilitate the ongoing transition and prepare the way for a "full-blooded" (*polnokrovnyi*) market economy. State controls on the price of producer goods were to be eased. The extraordinary measures previously taken would moderate price rises and thus the effects of wage indexation introduced at the end of the first half of 1991. Higher interest rates and new taxes might at this stage squeeze enterprise finances but would also force them to adjust output in line with demand, especially in those branches which had no monopoly. At a later stage, subsidies to vulnerable groups or assistance by wage indexation or temporary price freezes were to be determined by republican authorities. Meanwhile denationalization was to be pursued, the number of joint stock companies rising to 1,000-1,500 by the end of the period, and superfluous administrative structures broken up.

The *third* phase (from the 250th to the 400th day) was to be devoted to market liberalization for both consumer and producer goods. The attainment of internal convertibility at the end of this stage would permit the full market operation of domestic firms and attract foreign investment, thereby opening the way for comprehensive restructuring of output potential: some 70-80 per cent of prices would be free, leaving only fuel, some metals and a restricted list of basic necessities under state control while about 30-40 per cent of productive capacity in industry, half of construction and 60 per cent of trade, public catering and services were to be privatized. Price pressures during this phase were to be reduced by the break-up of monopolies, sharper competition and more economical use of inputs, which would ease shortages of producer goods. Signs of crisis due to the collapse of the former command-administrative system, unstable prices and falling output were to be viewed as a necessary pre-condition of structural change and the disappearance of inefficient enterprises. Potentially efficient enterprises in difficulty would be identified and helped. The burden of unemployment on the social safety net put in place in the first stage might, however, rise. Inflation could take off and feed wage claims if competition were not stimulated but pressure on prices could be absorbed in part by increased sale of housing. Enterprise finances would be eased by limiting wage rises in line with changes in the cost of a subsistence budget and freeing firms from the task of providing social welfare and housing.

The *fourth and final* phase of the programme (the 400th to the 500th days) was to see the beginning of an upturn in the economy, the stabilization of the market and of finances and the introduction of competitive measures on the scale necessary to ensure fully functioning market mechanisms and self-regulation. The central element would be significant further progress in denationalization, demonopolization and privatization together with the activation of a structural change-oriented investment policy favouring especially consumer supplies, agriculture and services. By the end of the period at least 70 per cent of industrial enterprises should have been converted into joint stock companies or leased, rising to 90 per cent in the case of construction, road transport, wholesale and retail trade, public catering and domestic services.

(c) Major differences

The two programmes show some important differences in approach. With regard to institutional factors, perhaps the most important is the setting of specific objectives and a tight timetable for the removal of state controls on prices and for privatization in the "500 Days" programme. Also the "Guidelines" appear to advocate a more limited aspect of privatization, stressing the distribution of shares to workers in state enterprises. The "Guidelines" are also considerably more circumspect than the "500 Days" programme with regard to the privatization of land, advocating the distribution of *land use* rights rather than outright sale of land as proposed in the latter. On the other hand, while neither programme goes into the detail of relationships between the Union and the constituent republics, the "500 Days" noted that the reform laws already adopted in the republics and the Union were not mutually consistent while a range of legislative acts required for the rapid implementation of transition either did not exist or were unworkable. About 20 draft laws and regulations to deal with this were attached to the report. The "Guidelines" specify provisions, notably in taxation, which imply expanded revenue-raising and expenditure rights for both the republics and certain of the autonomous republics within them.[515]

Other contrasts concern specific aspects of policy during successive phases of reform. The "500 Days" programme provided for emergency measures to achieve the virtual elimination of the budgetary deficit by the fourth quarter of 1990 while the "Guidelines" foresee its being maintained well into 1991 and for the year as a whole. This is clearly connected with the greater reliance of the former on market forces; according to the "500 Days" programme, subsidies to enterprises were to cease from 1 January 1991 and bankruptcies, as noted above, were expected even during its first phase. This programme also contrasts with the "Guidelines" and subsequent legislation in its summary rejection of administrative actions and penalties to maintain inter-enterprise delivery obligations beyond July 1991. Even in its early stages it stresses instead the role of free inter-enterprise trade on a contractual basis to preserve the momentum of the transition process. The "500 Days" programme also specifically rejected administered producer prices in 1991 (actually introduced at the beginning of 1991), advocating instead an extension of the new freedom to conclude free and contract pricing in inter-enterprise exchanges apart from those involving fuel, energy and certain raw materials.

---

515 Some of the points made in this paragraph are based on an interview with Academician A. Aganbegyan in the Polish newspaper *Zycie Gospodarcze*, No.44, 4 November 1990.

A final contrast is the progressive dismantling during 1991 of state-administered retail prices, except for basic necessities, foreseen in the "500 Days" programme.

However, one of the main weaknesses of both programmes is their treatment of the price problem. The "500 Days" programme does not directly discuss either the likelihood, the extent or the control of the inflationary pressures which have built up and are still rising in the Soviet economy. It makes the implicit assumption that the problem will be dealt with by a combination of increasing competition and cost reductions as enterprises raise their efficiency and cut their previously excessive use of materials. As discussed below, the "Guidelines" do implicitly accept the need for higher prices though actual price policy, based on the programme, relies on administered rather than market prices. Price reform is taken up again in section (v)(c) below.

(d) Slow movement to a market economy

Notwithstanding repeated declarations in favour of a market economy in both programmes, perhaps the most serious weakness of policy to date has been failure to clarify final reform objectives. While there is broad recognition that the previous system has proved inadequate, there is still no consensus on what should replace it. The prevailing option in early 1991 seems to be a "third way" which seeks to fuse a market system with a high degree of protection of the population from the full rigours of the market and to preserve to a considerable if not precisely defined extent the principles of communal ownership of productive resources and state choice of economic priorities. Echoes of this can be found not only among those politicians generally considered most strongly in favour of a cautious approach. Boris Yel'tsin, for example, has gone on record with his opposition to retail price rises without full cost-of-living compensation through wages.[516] I.S. Silayev, Chairman of the Council of Ministers of the RSFSR, has also spoken of the need for "constitutional guarantees of the right to work" within the framework of a "regulated market economy."[517] (The latter phrase was also used in the presidential decree of 9 August 1990 setting up a state property fund.)

The transition process from a system handicapped by the diseconomies and imbalances resulting from decades of unrestrained central planning is likely to prove particularly painful in the Soviet Union. Preoccupation with this is inhibiting the speed of the transition and also threatens important departures from the required path. Successful transition requires both institutional reform and, on that basis, the pursuit of appropriate policies. Institutional reform has so far been limited. The measures enacted so far are not only few

in number (box 4.6.1) but their detailed provisions reveal the ambivalence which underlies the search for a "third way" already mentioned. Moreover some of them restrict or even reverse legislation previously enacted to prepare the transition to a market economy.

(iii) Relations between the Union and the republics

The transition programme approved by the Supreme Soviet in October 1990, and also previous drafts, are all based on the assumption of a single market and common or at least mutually compatible fiscal, financial and monetary policies throughout the territory of the Soviet Union. The implementation and further development of policy has, however, been hampered by disagreement on the division of responsibilities between Union and republican legislative and executive organs. It also leaves uncertainties as to the legality and hence the permanence of actions carried out by the republics when the republican laws on which such actions are based conflict with Union law. This has led to a number of frictions between the Union and republican authorities in cases where the latter have attempted to move faster than the Union authorities wished.

All the republics have adopted legislation to guarantee the primacy of republican over Union Laws. The Laws on sovereignty of the RSFSR and several other republics simply assert that the relevant Union laws must also be ratified by the republican Supreme Soviets.[518] The RSFSR Law on economic sovereignty claimed the republic's full ownership of all mineral rights including, inter alia, oil and precious metals.[519] This was voided by a presidential decree of 23 August 1990.

Decrees countermanding initiatives by other republics have also been issued. Moreover, the full range of republican managerial and administrative structures are in any case not yet in place. This constitutes a strong barrier to fully independent republican initiatives. Towards the end of 1990, the chairman of the RSFSR Council of Ministers, for example, pointed out that banking activity in the republic was still "in the monopoly possession of the USSR State Bank". A previous attempt by the RSFSR authorities to take control of USSR State Bank branch offices on Russian territory on 13 July 1990 was countermanded by a presidential decree of 29 July, which stated that existing arrangements for bank loans and settlements should remain in force until the conclusion of a new Union treaty. Premier Silayev also pointed out that the distribution of material resources in the republic was still determined by the fact that state orders and the territorial supply organizations which ensure the delivery of the necessary

---

516 *Sovetskaya Rossiya*, 23 February 1991. See also BBC, *Summary of World Broadcasts*, SU/1002, 21 February 1991, p.B4.

517 Speech to the RSFSR Supreme Soviet, 4 December 1990. See *Sovetskaya Rossiya*, 5 December 1990.

518 See for example the declaration of sovereignty adopted by resolution of the Byelorussian Supreme Soviet, *Argumenty i fakty*, No.31, August 1990, and that of Moldavia, *Molodezh Moldavii*, 3 July 1990.

519 See *Sovetskaya Rossiya*, 2 November 1990.

BOX 4.6.1

Main enactments of economic institutional change at the Union level, 1990-Spring 1991

1990

Basic legislation on land (28 February);
Law on property (6 March);
Law on economic relations between the Union and republics (10 April);
Law on income tax (23 April);
Law on pension rights (15 May);
Law on the rights, duties and responsibilities of the state tax inspectorate (21 May);
Law on enterprises (4 June);
Amendments to the Law on co-operatives (6 June);
Draft Law governing the regulation of labour disputes and the rights of citizens (8 June);
Law on enterprise taxation (14 June);
Presidential decree on external economic practice (24 July);
Presidential decree setting up a state property fund (9 August);
Law on additional measures to stabilize economic and political life in the country (24 September);
Presidential decree on first-priority measures on transition to a market economy (4 October);
Resolution of the USSR Supreme Soviet on economic stabilization and transition to a market economy (19 October);
Presidential decree to encourage savings in the USSR savings bank (25 October);
Presidential decree to introduce a commercial rate for the rouble and to create a foreign exchange market (26 October);
Presidential decree on foreign investments in the USSR (26 October);
Presidential decree on special procedures for using foreign currency resources in 1991 (2 November);
Resolution of the USSR Supreme Soviet on the situation in the country after the introduction of free market contract prices on certain consumer goods on 15 November (23 November);
Law on trades union (10 December);
Law on investment activity in the USSR (10 December);
Law on the USSR State Bank (11 December);
Law on banks and banking activity (11 December);
Resolution of the USSR Supreme Soviet for a referendum on private ownership of land (24 December);
Resolution of the Congress of People's Deputies of the USSR on the situation in the country and first-priority measures to overcome the socio-economic and political crisis (24 December);
Presidential decree introducing a sales tax (29 December);
Presidential decree creating extra-budgetary funds for economic stabilization (29 December);

1991

Presidential decree on the first-priority measures to implement land reform (7 January);
Law on the state budget for 1991 (11 January);
Basic Legislation on employment (15 January);
Presidential decree on banknotes (22 January);

---

input for their fulfillment continue to be managed exclusively by the Union authorities.[520]

Thus it has not proved possible in practical terms for the republican authorities to move at a significantly faster pace than specified in the "Guidelines". Some republics have not adopted important elements of the "500 Days" programme – the Ukrainian and Byelorussian Supreme Soviets, for instance, rejected the outright sale of land. This has not prevented the passage of laws differing from Union legislation. The Law on land adopted by the Supreme Soviet of the RSFSR on 3 December 1990,[521] for example, unlike its Union equivalent, permits the the outright sale of land, and this republic's Laws on property and on the enterprise also contain important divergences from the corresponding Union acts.[522] The second of the two defines

the object of entrepreneurship simply as "independent activity of citizens and their associations directed to making a profit". This a much clearer and less ambivalent definition than that given in the Union law (see box 4.6.2).

The greater freedom of economic decision-making at republican level contained in the "Guidelines" provides room to minimize some of these frictions. The precise distribution of responsibilities between the two tiers of government have still not been clarified, however. Several republics have made it clear that retail price formation and the extent of compensation to offset price rises should be a republican rather than a Union responsibility – a position rejected by the Union Prime Minister.[523]

---

520 I.S. Silayev, speech to the RSFSR Council of People's Deputies, *Sovetskaya Rossiya*, 5 December 1990.

521 *Sovetskaya Rossiya*, 4 December 1990.

522 The RSFSR acts, dated 24 and 25 December respectively, were published in *Ekonomika i zhizn'*, Nos.3 and 4 of January 1991.

523 Speech by V.S. Pavlov to the USSR Supreme Soviet, *Izvestiya*, 19 February 1991.

Frictions *between* republics have also become apparent. Continuing shortages due to delays in reforming retail prices to market clearing levels have led to widespread rationing of food and restriction of the distribution of coupons to residents only. Measures formally prohibiting exports of consumer goods have now been taken by eight republics since the first prohibition (by Lithuania) on 1 October 1990. Frictions have also occurred between rural and urban residents within the same republic. Controls on consumer goods purchases by non-residents were imposed in Moscow, Leningrad and other cities. But these measures excluded rural workers from city shops and resulted in a refusal by state and collective farmers to meet food procurement targets, adding to existing food shortages in the towns.

These were doubtless all important elements in the decisions taken by various republics to conclude independently economic accords with other republics, bypassing the Union authorities. Meetings to this end in fact began on 27 July in Latvia, attended by the chairmen of the Supreme Soviets of Latvia, the RSFSR, Estonia and Lithuania. Trade and co-operation treaties have been concluded by all of the 15 republics. By early 1991, the RSFSR had signed 11, the Ukraine 14 and Byelorussia 7 — altogether, about 40 such agreements out of a possible 105.

(iv) Short-term stabilization policy

Before proceeding with an assessment of the main institutional changes promulgated for the transition process, a brief examination of recent short-term economic policy offers some preliminary indications of how far the shift towards the market for longer-term objectives is influencing the conduct of day-to-day decisions. In fact, little progress has been made in addressing the immediate issue of economic stabilization, let alone in laying the foundations for the medium- and longer-term changes involved in transition towards a market economy. There is evidence that the implementation of the first stabilization phase of the "Guidelines" is behind schedule.

The principal problems towards the end of 1990 were crippling imbalances on consumer markets, falls in output, large government budgetary deficits and, as a consequence of these imbalances, both open and hidden inflation — or more precisely "stagflation" — accompanied by a worsening of the balance of payments. Measures to deal with these problems have followed the old tradition of administrative sanctions; there has been little evidence of increased reliance on market forces.

The imbalances on the consumer market have led to a rapid rise in inflationary pressures. Retail prices of certain "non-essential" goods (for instance furs, goods made of precious metals, etc., but also including furniture, consumer durables and other household goods, clothes made of natural materials, certain foods, wines and imported consumer goods) were freed in November 1990.[524] However, the only other noticeable retail price rises in 1990 occurred in the already relatively free collective farm markets (about 20 per cent). The recorded 5 per cent rise in the state retail price index over 1989 appears to have been due mainly to changes in the structure of demand, part of which was due to the introduction of so-called new products which can be priced higher than those which they replace. Limited price rises reflected the continuation of central retail price formation, which led to increasing imbalances between retail price levels and personal income growth, worsening shortages and rationing by queue and by coupon. In global terms, and taking into account the effects of administrative price controls, the underlying rate of inflation has been estimated at an unprecedented 19 per cent in 1990.[525]

These imbalances were reinforced by the high and only slowly declining government budgetary deficit, amounting in 1990 to R80.6 billion or 8.1 per cent of GNP (compared with 11 per cent in 1988 and 9.6 per cent in 1989).[526] Government expenditures grew by over 8 per cent. Continuation of price controls on food and other goods in state shops caused substantial rises in food and other consumer subsidies. Food subsidies alone in 1990 accounted for R119 billion (over a fifth of total budgetary expenditures) and rose by 18 per cent over 1989. This was over 50 per cent higher than the annual increases between 1985 and 1989. The transfer of enterprises to full cost-accounting has not yet resulted in the closure of loss-making firms which, as in the past, were kept afloat by subsidies. Declining output due to interruptions in the production process resulting from shortages of inputs and strikes has surely increased their number. This, and the lax discipline suggested by large wage increases when output and productivity were falling, suggest a rise in subsidies to enterprises also. The overall deficit was accompanied by higher interest payments on external debt and a further rise in the deficit on foreign trade.

Falling output in 1990 has, according to official data, been located mainly in the areas of producer goods and in the transport and distributive services. Contractual obligations were underfulfilled by about 2 per cent for industry as a whole.[527] State orders and other administrative controls to secure supplies remained widespread during the first phase of transition to a market economy. A presidential decree of 28 September 1990 lays down heavy fines for enterprises which fail to fulfil contracts. Producer price lists es-

---

[524] *Izvestiya*, 16 November 1990.

[525] Report of USSR Goskomstat, *Ekonomika i zhizn'*, No.5, January 1991.

[526] The officially announced 1990 deficit of R58.1 billion (5.8 per cent of GNP) excludes expenditures of R22.5 billion financed by supplementary loans from the State Bank. Direct communication to the ECE secretariat.

[527] Report of the USSR Goskomstat, *Ekonomika i zhizn'*, No.5, January 1991.

tablished by the central authorities were still in place throughout 1990 and the new prices introduced on 1 January 1991 are of the same kind.[528] They do, however, represent a first attempt to approximate world market prices. Energy, fuel and timber prices were doubled and those for metals and engineering goods were increased by 50 and 40 per cent. (The changes were expected to result in price increases for cars and consumer durables of around 40 per cent at retail level.)

Administrative centralized price setting in the state retail network (the latter is still responsible for about 90 per cent of sales to consumers) continued throughout 1990 and will be largely maintained in 1991. This is clear from the announcement of centrally-determined increases in state retail prices which will double or more the cost of some consumer goods. However, further increases in prices for a range of basic necessities will be controlled. Compensation in the form of wage, child allowance and pension supplements and income tax concessions will amount on average to some 85 per cent of the total increase in prices. For wage-earners this will amount to a minimum of R60 per month. Not all retail prices will be directly affected by this latest measure. About 30 per cent of goods in state shops are to be sold at contract prices.[529]

Continuation of administrative pricing could mean that the relationship between producer and retail prices, and between different products at either level, remain effectively as arbitrary as they always were. State retail prices have traditionally been uniform throughout the Soviet Union. Noting that the state retail price of tomatoes is the same in the area in which they are produced as in the arctic circle, the Soviet Prime Minister recommended that retail prices should henceforth be determined taking into account distribution costs.

Finally, direct administrative measures against speculation were incorporated in a Law to outlaw, *inter alia*, the resale of goods bought from state organizations at state retail prices.[530] Direct local administrative authority to control the price of food on the collective farm markets has always existed, though this appears to be breaking down under pressure from shortages. Two presidential decrees enlist the good offices of the security organs to deter speculation by granting them the right to inspect company records — including, apparently, companies established with foreign participation.[531]

Looking now to the future, budgetary policy for 1991 should be a litmus test of the transition to a market economy. The extent of progress would be revealed by a fall in the size of the budget as a whole because greater enterprise autonomy should result in a reduction of profit transfers to the centre, while government expenditures should fall as enterprise investment decision-making replaces state allocation of productive resources and subsidies to loss-making enterprises are reduced. The introduction of market mechanisms and the consequent reduction of consumer subsidies would also suggest smaller expenditures.

Food subsidies in 1990 were equal to some 60 per cent of the value of state retail sales of food. Price distortions of this size were a major cause of shortages as well as a heavy burden on the budget. But they also provided an important degree of social protection for low-paid workers and other low income groups. The February 1991 proposal to raise state retail prices will have an impact on the level of such protection but basic foodstuffs will continue to be subsidized. A sum of R34 billion was mentioned in the Union budget for 1991,[532] some 17 per cent of retail trade in food. However, the provisions of the 1991 Union budget cannot be compared with those for previous years, since no consolidated general government budget (i.e., including republican budgets) has been published. The only information available is that the Union budget includes a deficit of R27 billion for 1991. This equals about 2½ per cent of GNP and is in line with the objective mentioned in the "Guidelines" programme for the consolidated Union and republican budgets — provided that the republican budgets are themselves in balance.

This is an important question in so far as it affects the now central question of the money supply. The amount of money in circulation, which amounted to R132.7 billion at the beginning of 1991, grew by R28 billion in 1990 compared with R18 billion in 1989.[533]

The first and so far the only measure directly aimed at reducing the money supply was enshrined in a presidential decree (23 January 1991) to withdraw some R48 billion worth of 50- and 100-rouble banknotes and to replace them, provided that evidence of legal ownership could be proved, by new ones. Withdrawals from private saving accounts were restricted to R500 per month. The objective of the exercise was twofold: first, to confiscate the suspected large sums amassed by individuals from illegal speculative activities, and only secondarily to reduce by this means the excess supply of money and thereby damp down inflation. The exercise resulted in the surrender of R40 billion worth of notes out of R48 billion in circulation. Thus about R8 billion were not presented, including an estimated R0.5 billion held abroad. The legitimacy of a further

---

528 Presidential decree on priority measures for transition to a market economy dated 4 October 1990, *Izvestiya*, 5 October 1990. The prices concerned were put in place by Resolution 741 of the USSR Council of Ministers of 14 June 1988.

529 Speech by V.S. Pavlov to the USSR Supreme Soviet, *Izvestiya*, 19 February 1991.

530 USSR Law on increased penalties for speculation and illegal trade activities and for abuses in trade, dated 31 October 1990.

531 Decrees on measures to ensure the struggle against economic sabotage and other crimes in the economic sphere, dated 26 January 1991, and on measures to strengthen the struggle against the most dangerous crimes and their organizational forms, dated 4 February 1991.

532 *Izvestiya*, 15 January 1991.

533 Report of the USSR Gsokomstat, *Ekonomika i zhin'*, No.5, January 1991.

R3 billion was challenged and their exchange held up pending local review.[534] The R11 billion reduction of cash in circulation constitutes less than 5 per cent of the Goskomstat estimate of the monetary overhang at the end of 1990 (R238 billion).[535]

The principal channel for the rise in the money supply and the inflationary pressures to which it gave rise appears to have been the enterprise sector. No concrete events (bankruptcies) can be identified which suggest that state budgetary constraints have been tightened sufficiently to ensure the closure of loss-making firms or a reduction in subsidies. The large rise in the wage bill at a time of falling output and productivity can only be explained by lack of enterprise budget constraints. Compensation for reduced enterprise profits or rising losses may have risen at a time when the enterprise profits tax base is shrinking due to production declines, thereby giving a twofold impetus to the budgetary deficit.

The "Guidelines" do not specify the exact timing of any of its four phases. The first, stabilization, phase of the "500 Days" programme roughly covered the last quarter of 1990. Although this phase seems to extend over a rather longer period in the "Guidelines", there were signs towards the end of the first quarter of 1991 that the implementation of the necessary measures may be falling behind. It is not possible to assess how far the 1991 budget will contribute to the objective of attaining monetary equilibrium during the first phase. The withdrawal of high-denomination banknotes to restrain the growth of purchasing power is clearly inadequate on its own. The restructuring of the banking system has begun (section (v)(e) below), but there is no sign yet that the policy instruments of the central bank (interest rate policy, reserve requirements) have been made operational. At the same time, it is also clear that the breakdown in communications between enterprises and the organs of state supply and distribution contributed to the falls in output in the second half of 1990. The introduction of new mechanisms for inter-enterprise relations has not kept pace. Price pressures have continued to build up, but the problem is being solved by centrally administered price increases rather than market forces. This may jeopardize the financial position of enterprises which may be potentially competitive under market conditions while keeping in business those which are not − with adverse short- and longer-term consequences for the budget. Denationalization and, even less, the breakdown of monopoly have not yet begun.

(v) The creation of market economy institutions

The adoption of clear laws and safeguards for various ownership categories, changes in the behaviour of enterprises, the introduction and use of market mechanisms, instruments and infrastructures and, as a precondition for the efficient functioning of any of these, price reform are the basic elements of transition to a market system. The dismantling of central planning organs will clearly be an important earnest of intent as well as a logical step forward in the transition process. The following paragraphs review the legislative and other acts promulgated in each of these and related areas and their appropriateness at the present juncture. The underlying questions are whether, taken individually and as a whole, they add up to a market economy framework as generally understood, the time scale needed for the process to become self-sustaining and the gaps which remain. A general assessment of these questions is deferred to section (vi) below.

(a) Property

During the course of 1990 and early 1991, basic laws on property and land rights were adopted (box 4.6.1). The Law on property defines several forms of ownership right, which can be vested in individuals, collectives (leasing enterprises, enterprises sold to their workers, co-operatives, joint stock companies, joint associations of different types of enterprises engaged in economic activity and religious bodies) or the state (including republican and local governments). The rights extend to productive assets as well as amenities such as housing and can be exercised jointly between any of these categories of owners. The Law makes no provision for the sale of productive assets other than the compensation of participants in a collective enterprise for their share of the property in the event of their withdrawal. The recent or imminent setting-up of stock markets in Moscow and Leningrad indicates, as do several policy statements, that the sale of shares in companies is planned at a later stage.

The provisions of the Law on property refer only to ownership of equipment, buildings and stocks of goods (including farm animals) − not of land. This reflects the provisions of the Law on land. All land belongs to the state ("the people"); even collective farmers have no individual title to the land they work. Land use rights (i.e., for private housing or for agriculture or other productive purposes) may be allocated to any individual or collective. In agriculture, the new Law offers to the individual state or collective farmer, or to a co-operative formed by a group of them, the right of individual exploitation of land and equipment and the possibility of bequeathing such rights to heirs or passing them on to a family member on retirement. Land use rights are allocated by the collective or state farm or other source with the agreement of the local authorities concerned. Land may also be leased for agricultural purposes by any individual or collective. The size of plots, the length and conditions of leases are regulated by agreement subject to the approval of the local authorities. These arrangements are predominantly directed towards family operation rather than the

---

[534] *Izvestiya*, 31 January 1991.

[535] "Unsatisfied purchasing power" *(neudovletvorennyi platezhesposobnyi spros)* rose by R55 billion last year, from R183 billion in 1989 to R238 billion in 1990; it had been R60 billion in 1985. Report of USSR Goskomstat, 17 January 1991.

hiring of labour and there is no provision for outright ownership or sale of land.

With this exception, the above two laws set out, for the first time since the 1920s, a legal framework for private ownership, guarantees of rights, protection against interference by the state and procedures for settling disputes. There has already been a sharp rise in employment in private enterprises which were set up following the adoption of the Law on Co-operatives on 8 June 1988. Over 7 million workers – over 5 per cent of the labour force – were employed in co-operatives (other than collective farms but including the cultivation of private plots)[536] by the end of 1990. There were also some 700,000 individuals relying on professional earnings (1989 data).[537] In addition, about 41,000 independent farmers cultivated 700,000 hectares of agricultural land – perhaps around 50,000 workers at the current ratio of arable land per worker.[538]

These data apparently exclude individual agricultural and industrial workers who have leased land or productive equipment. Private activity could thus now account for up to about 7 per cent of employment, a substantial change compared with the situation two years ago. However, they work in mainly small-scale industrial operations, handicrafts, service activities and small peasant holdings. State enterprises still account for the overwhelming share of output and resource use.

(b) Commercialization of enterprises

The term "commercialization" here means the steps taken to induce enterprises, including state-owned but also private firms, to adjust their behaviour in response to market stimuli. As already noted, there has been little or no progress in the privatization of state-owned enterprises. The speed of adjustment of state-owned firms to market conditions is thus of great importance for economic stabilization. It will depend largely on when the government will cut subsidies to loss-making firms, thus stimulating those which are capable of improved performance to achieve it.

Recent policies towards the state sector have not included a time-scale for privatization or even a firm commitment to it or to the means by which it is to be carried out. An initial step was taken with the setting up of a State Property Fund by presidential decree on 9 August 1990, which is charged with the task of assessing the value of state property and the role of state enterprises and to set rules for the conversion of state firms into joint-stock companies, leasehold or other categories of private ownership.

In terms of the practical agenda of enterprise reform, the main legal instrument so far is the Law on Enterprises promulgated by the USSR Supreme Soviet on 12 June 1990. In comparison with the past, this Law provides considerable potential for enterprise independence from interference by the state in its day-to-day operations, lays down the right to and conditions for private ownership, provides remedies against local authorities which refuse registration without good reason and specifies the principles for purchase of inputs and disposal of products by means of contracts with other enterprises without discrimination between private and state-owned firms. It also makes provision for raising finance from private sources, bank credits or the issuance of shares to the public. However, a considerable number of articles in this Law could be used to constrain the purely commercial activity of an enterprise and the regulatory role of the market – in particular the stress placed on participation by representatives of the working collective in managerial questions and a certain ambivalence with regard to the "main task" of the enterprise, which is apparently only secondarily to make profits (box 4.6.2).

In practice, the provisions of the Law apply predominantly to state enterprises, given the lack of progress so far in privatizing them. In conformity with the Law on property, the presidential decree of 9 August 1990 instructed the State Property Fund to work out plans for the transformation of state enterprises into "joint stock companies (aktsionernye obshchestva) and enterprises based on other forms of property" but no concrete results of its work have yet been announced. Apart from the co-operatives, which now number some 260,000 and which are to a considerable extent based on industrial equipment and buildings leased from existing state enterprises, the private sector contains so far as is known no former state enterprise as such. More than 1,200 firms have been converted into joint stock companies by issuing shares to their workers.[539] These shares cannot be sold on the open market.

(c) Price reform

Arguably the single most important component of both short-term stabilization and long-term restructuring policy is price reform. Lack of progress on this front explains most of the current imbalances mentioned earlier – notably those on the consumer market. Price reform is also a pre-condition for rational decisions concerning the size and mix of output and inputs. The framing of Soviet policy in this area has been unclear and its implementation indecisive and half-hearted. An announcement of impending retail price rises in May 1990, for example, sparked panic buying, hoarding and the disappearance of many goods from the shops.

Reform of prices under present Soviet conditions has three aspects. First, market clearing prices are

536 Report of USSR Goskomstat, *Ekonomika i zhizn'*, No. 5, January 1991.

537 *Narodnoe khozyaistvo SSSR v 1989 g.*, Finansy i Statistika, Moscow 1990, p.275.

538 Report of USSR Goskomstat, *loc.cit.*, p.9. The presidential decree of 7 January 1991 also calls for the distribution of 3-5 million hectares of land for private purposes during the spring of 1991. The number of workers involved is not given but could represent around 200,000-350,000, including leaseholders, on the assumption of the same land/worker ratio.

539 Report of USSR Goskomstat, *loc.cit.*

BOX 4.6.2

The Law on enterprises

The Law on Enterprises was published on 12 June 1990 to come into force on 1 January 1991 (except for Chapter IV, on Management of the Enterprise, which took effect from the date of publication and Article 24.1, paragraph 2, giving freedom of choice with regard to contracts, which will not come into force until 1 January 1993). The "main task" of the enterprise is stated to be "to satisfy public needs for its products, work and services, and, with the profit received, to satisfy the economic and social interests of members of the work collective and the interests of the owner of the enterprise's property" (article 1). Elsewhere it is stated that "the administration of the enterprise ... shall be carried out on the basis of a combination of the principles of self-management of the work collective and the rights of the owner to economic use of his property". Profit itself is considered only as "the main generalizing indicator of the financial results of economic activity" (article 21.1). Moreover, although profit is said to be "completely at its (the enterprise's) disposal" the state may influence "the selection of uses for net profit ... through taxes, tax breaks and also economic sanctions" (article 21.2).

Managerial freedom may also be constrained by the powers reserved for the General Meeting of the Work Collective of the enterprise which include resolution of "questions related to the purchase of property by the enterprise" (article 16) and for the Enterprise Council. This second body is not apparently obligatory. Article 14.1 states that "the owner shall exercise his rights to manage the enterprise directly or through a body authorized by him. The owner or his authorized body may delegate their rights to an enterprise council (board) or other body envisioned by the charter which represents the interests of the owner and the work collective". But if an enterprise council is created, it must consist of an equal number of representatives appointed by the owner and by the work collective and is empowered by the Law to "determine the economic and social development of the enterprise; determine the procedure for distributing net profit; at the request of the manager..., make a decision to issue securities of the enterprise and also to purchase the securities of enterprises and organizations; resolve questions of creating subsidiary enterprises and creating and terminating the activity of other separate sub-divisions of the enterprise and the entry or withdrawal of the enterprise into associations; make decisions pertaining to the enterprise's foreign trade activity" etc. It is difficult to see how this list of powers in highly important areas can be consistent with the prohibition that "the council is not allowed to intervene in the operational and managerial activity of the administration" (article 18.4).

The Law also specifies that enterprises must sell their products at prices "established independently or on a contractual basis, and in cases envisaged by legislation of the USSR and union and autonomous republics, at state prices" (article 26.1). State regulation of prices is also envisaged in cases of monopoly. There is also provision for "inspections and reviews (which) should contribute to the effectiveness of management" (article 35.3).

---

needed to equilibrate the supply of goods with aggregate disposable incomes. Second, retail and wholesale prices must be brought into line, differences between them generally being confined to no more than normal distribution and retailing margins. Third, relative prices at all levels must reflect relative costs and scarcities.

The limited action on prices during 1990 left the way open for an intensification of inflationary pressure. Apart from the adjustments occurring spontaneously for food sold on the collective farm markets, the freeing of the retail prices of "non-essential" goods in November and a rise in the procurement prices paid to farms by the state for grain and meat, introduced from 1 October, the state prices at which the bulk of transactions were conducted were left unchanged. The new producer-price rises introduced from the beginning of 1991 and the higher retail prices proposed in mid-February 1991 could thus be important steps in the stabilization of the market in aggregate.

As noted earlier, the adjustments so far are based on administrative methods of price formation. Central price setting of this kind can exert a stabilizing effect on the market under certain conditions. If income growth is restrained, a rise in wholesale and retail prices can reduce the speculator's margin between illegal purchases of goods at official prices and their re-sale on the black market. But such price reforms do not necessarily take into account geographical differences in either production or distribution costs. Nor can they take into account the real costs of production (because these

are themselves based on input prices which are also administratively set) or the relative scarcities of different products in terms of the prices that consumers are prepared to pay for them.

There is still little sign that the Soviet government is prepared to use the market or market prices as a *means of solving current problems*, even though it has accepted the market as a desirable mechanism for optimal economic management in the unspecified longer term. Nevertheless, important elements of market behaviour are emerging which are, in fact, fed by the breakdown in the old command system before a market system is yet in place. The existence of relatively free markets for farm products and the activity of speculators both give indications of the size of shortages, real supply/demand imbalances and the prices which consumers are prepared to pay for certain types of goods. At present these phenomena are being suppressed by their criminalization on one hand and, on the other, by administrative action to tax away "excessive" profits deriving from the legitimate exercise of enterprises' rights to set an agreed "contract price" in place of the official wholesale prices for certain categories of goods.

These developments strongly suggest that it has not yet been appreciated that certain apparently negative phenomena associated with the introduction of a market economy may be inevitable in the short term but can provide important indications for the shaping of future economic policy. The accumulation of super-

normal profits can provide resources for private investment, recommended elsewhere as a so far untapped
source of economic expansion, which would help to
reduce the shortages of which they are a symptom. At
all events, failure to overcome political pressures to
preserve the traditional Soviet disapproval of unregulated profit creation could jeopardize domestic confidence in the whole restructuring programme.

(d) The dismantling of the command-administrative structure

Up to the first quarter of 1991 few concrete results
had been achieved in abolishing the institutions of central planning and management. However a start has
been made with personnel cuts in some central organs
including the State Planning Commission (*Gosplan*),[540]
the abolition of the monopolies of the sector- and
branch-specific Foreign Trade Organizations in foreign
trade decisions and in banking (see (f) below). But
most organs of the state have remained in place and
appear to be expected to play a considerable role in the
transition process as laid down in the "Guidelines".
This applies especially to the agricultural procurement
organizations and the material supply and purchasing
agency (*Gossnab*) which have traditionally been used
as a substitute for a wholesale trade network. The industrial branch ministries also continue to function.

In late February 1991, Union Prime Minister V.S.
Pavlov presented the first draft of a law to recast "the
structure and basic orientation of the activity of the
USSR Cabinet of Ministers".[541] His outline submitted
to the Supreme Soviet proposed the setting up of a state
Council for Economic Reform to ensure the "comprehensiveness *(kompleksnost')*, co-ordination and synchronization" of the transition process. This should
be chaired by the Prime Minister and his deputy should
be a presidential nominee. Most of the former industrial branch ministries will disappear and are to be replaced by consolidated industrial ministries for various
fields of Union economic activity where state ownership predominates. They include ministries for armaments, engineering, energy, atomic energy, transport
and the agro-industrial complex. Various technical
committees would also be set up to operate in the area
of inter-republican relations and relations between the
republics and the Union. One is to concern itself with
the breakdown of monopolies. Other organs are proposed to look after science and technology and environmental questions. They are intended to refrain from
interference in enterprise management.

The measure is the first concrete action to reorgan-
ize organs of centralized state management. But it has
been criticized on the grounds that it removes powers

in general and in the economic sphere, currently residing with the Supreme Soviet, to the cabinet of ministers.[542] According to the chairman of the Supreme
Soviet committee on legislation, it also does little to
promote the development of market relations or leasing
and still leaves in place 48 ministries and other authorities instead of abolishing the old structure
completely.[543] The draft law as originally announced in
fact proposed 55 new authorities compared with the 68
former industrial ministries. Modifications could follow
from the second reading of the draft law in March 1991.
It is too early to judge whether the proposals represent
any substantive transformation of the state administrative apparatus in directions consistent with the requirements of transition to a market system.

(e) Domestic banking and finance

The two laws on domestic banking adopted with
immediate effect at the end of 1990 provide first for the
transformation of the State Bank into a central bank
with counterparts at republican level which will constitute the Union reserve system. The banking laws also
provide for the transformation of existing specialized
banks (the savings, industry/construction and the foreign economy banks) into commercial banks. Some
previous specialized functions will be retained by them
and some of the assets of these banks may be transferred to other owners under the republican authorities.
New banks may also be set up including those under
foreign ownership. At the end of 1990 as many as 1,400
commercial and co-operative banks had already been
set up and had extended some 7.2 per cent of the new
credits granted in the country during that year.[544]

There is no sign that credit and interest rate policies
are yet playing a significant role in economic policy-
making or that the commercial banks have the practical
know-how or an unambiguous mandate to transmit the
financial authorities' intentions. No enterprise bankruptcies have been announced, suggesting that loss-
making firms are still receiving financial coverage.
Important mechanisms, such as the use of short-term
government debt to influence the financial climate, are
in any case not yet in place. Interest rates on savings
deposits were raised by a presidential decree of 26 October 1992, but the maximum rate payable on 10-year
deposits was 9 per cent and as little as 5 per cent for
1-year deposits – rates which are unlikely to encourage
savings or preserve their value under present conditions.
Rates charged on commercial credits and loans are not
known. In any case, interest rate policy will not markedly affect enterprise behaviour until real pressures for
financial discipline have been imposed. State budgetary
subsidies to enterprises have apparently not yet been
cut back severely enough for this to have occurred.

---

540 *Izvestiya*, 30 January 1991, reported a drop in *Gosplan* personnel from 3,600 to 2,200 in the last two years. Reports of similar 30 per cent cuts have also been
reported from the republics. *Izvestiya*, 24 January 1991.

541 *Izvestiya*, 21 February 1991.

542 *Izvestiya*, 22 February 1991.

543 *Izvestiya*, 25 and 26 February 1991.

544 See *Ekonomika i zhizn'*, No.5, January 1991, p.9.

(f) Foreign economic relations

Changes introduced in this area include the abolition of the monopolies of the sector- and branch-specific Foreign Trade Organizations and of the Foreign Economy Bank (*Vneshekonombank*) in foreign financial transactions and the transfer of some of the latter's responsibilities in this area to republican institutions, exchange rate policy, the abolition of the separate arrangements for trade with other CMEA member-countries and new regulations to encourage direct and other types of foreign investment.

Since 1987, certain classes of Soviet enterprise have been permitted to conclude import or export deals with foreign organizations independently and without the mediation of the Foreign Trade Organizations.[545] By end-1990, some 26,000 enterprises were registered to participate in foreign trade,[546] but the volume of transactions generated by this expansion of trading rights remained very small (just over 1 per cent of trade turnover in 1988-1990) and the expected improvement in the structure of trade had not materialized. This has been attributed to the inadequate strength of the incentive to enterprises, which was to have been their right to retain a share of the foreign currency earnings for their own import needs — in 1990 on average some 30 per cent.[547] Opportunities to import on this basis only accrued to firms which had earned foreign currency. Other firms wishing to acquire foreign exchange for imports could do so by attending auctions organized by *Vneshekonombank* since November 1989. These were important innovations which created room for the individual firm rather than the central planning authorities, with some important exceptions (fuel exports, food and some other strategic imports), to decide whether they wished to import or export goods.[548]

These arrangements were changed in several respects by the Presidential decree of 2 November 1990 on "Special procedures for using foreign currency resources in 1991", which was motivated by the need to secure resources to finance a peaking of the debt service burden in that year.[549] The decree created a joint Union-republican foreign currency committee to administer a special fund, held at the *Vneshekonombank*, to which exporting enterprises must surrender 40 per cent of their foreign exchange earnings against payment in roubles at the commercial exchange rate. It first appeared that the retention norms in force in 1990 were

then to be applied to the remainder, thus effectively reducing the foreign currency funds at the disposal of enterprises by 40 per cent; this provoked complaints that the new arrangements could considerably diminish the attractiveness of sales for hard currency.[550] However, the resolution of the USSR Council of Ministers which implemented the decree, issued in December 1990,[551] appears to have revised these norms significantly and also to have extended the coverage of retention entitlements to additional commodity positions and to transactions conducted through intermediaries. One estimate indicates that this will increase foreign currency earnings retained at the disposal of enterprises by two and a half times — to R5 billion.[552] The new norms are designed to encourage the export of manufactures and other high value-added products, rising from a low 20 per cent in the case of gas, electrical energy and other mineral products, to 35 per cent for oil products, 40-55 per cent for coal, hides and leather, glass, ceramics and textiles and 70 per cent for engineering and other manufactures. The retention norm was set at 60 per cent for earnings from the 61 million tons of oil to be exported under the system of "state orders" and at 70 per cent for additional oil exports.

In November, an exchange rate reform reduced the number of official exchange rates and set new parities for those which remained. In particular the "exchange rate coefficients", different rates for the conversion of valuta rouble values into domestic rouble values depending on the type of product, were abolished. This still leaves a number of different rouble/foreign currency rates for different types of transaction: the "official" rate (0.6 roubles/dollar), used to convert external rouble-denominated claims; the "commercial" rate (1.8 roubles/dollar), used for exports and imports of goods; the "tourist" rate (5.6 roubles/dollar) and the rates deriving from the auction of hard currency for roubles already referred to. The auction rate of the commercial rouble moved from 21 roubles/dollar in November 1990 to 25 roubles/dollar in mid-January 1991. It is of interest that the black market rate around the latter date was about 30 roubles per dollar.[553]

One of the most important developments in foreign economic policy was the decision to eliminate the old CMEA system of trade in its entirety and to replace it from 1 January 1991 by a normal system based on world market prices and denominated in hard curren-

[545] Joint Resolution No.991 of the Central Committee of the CPSU and the USSR Council of Ministers on "Measures for perfecting the management of external economic relations", 19 August 1986.

[546] Report of USSR Goskomstat, *Ekonomika i zhizn'*, No.5, January 1991.

[547] Report of USSR Goskomstat, 17 January 1991, p.58.

[548] With regard to exports, the Soviet Union is still "the only country in the world which licences almost all of its exports ... more than 90 per cent of export commodity groups are licensed ... by 58 authorities which have no criteria for decision-making other than their own bright ideas". *Izvestiya*, March 2 1991.

[549] For the servicing (interest and repayments) of foreign debt, 9 billion valuta roubles are required in 1991 out of the expected convertible-currency earnings of R21-22 billion. This falls to R6½ billion in 1992. *Izvestiya*, 7 March 1991.

[550] *Moskovskie novosti*, No.46, 18 November 1990.

[551] Resolution 1253 of the USSR Council of Ministers, 8 December 1990 (*Ekonomika i zhizn'*, No.1, January 1991).

[552] Interview with I.D. Ivanov, Deputy Chairman of the State Commission for Foreign Economic Relations, *Ekonomika i zhizn'*, No.1, January 1991.

[553] *Kommersant*, No.5, January 1991, p.18.

cies.[554] Some transitional difficulties have resulted on the Soviet side with regard to payments for imports. The old system was based on payment guarantees to CMEA suppliers by the *Vneshekonombank*; although these modalities have now broken down, it appears that no alternative mechanism is yet in place and suppliers are finding it difficult to receive payment. Indeed, similar difficulties have also been reported by western suppliers.[555] Difficulties may well be compounded by the combination of a more restrictive hard currency régime mentioned already and the changeover to hard currency trading with former CMEA member countries.

Finally, there was a considerable relaxation in the regulations governing foreign investment in the Soviet Union in 1990.[556] In 1987, foreign investors were allowed to take a majority holding in joint ventures with a Soviet partner by legislation for the first time. This had resulted in the registration of some 3,000 joint enterprises with foreigners and domiciled in the Soviet Union by the end of 1990, of which about 2,400 involved partners from western countries.[557] But the average sums invested were rather small, the foreign contribution amounting in total about to 3.6 billion dollars.[558] This partly resulted from the fact that under previous regulations the only profits which could be repatriated were those resulting from hard currency export earnings as well as other restrictions.[559] The latest provisions enable foreign partners to set up wholly-owned subsidiaries and, in the spirit of the Law on enterprises, allow arrangements to be concluded between individuals as well as legal persons. They also permit the foreign investor to choose freely between re-investment and repatriation of profits. However, the attraction of these investments is considerably curtailed by the fact that while the initial hard currency investment must be converted at the commercial rate, rouble profits can only be converted into hard currency at the "free market" (i.e., the auction) rate. As noted above, the difference in the number of roubles per dollar between the two is at present about 1:15.

Progress so far in reforming foreign economic relations has been patchy. Although the steps taken are clearly in a market-oriented direction, the complete contrast with the past which this represents cannot disguise a number of basic divergences from normal market practices. These are continuing to inhibit the interest of domestic producers in production for export and in the choice of imports and the interest of overseas investors in the Soviet market. The practice of making often restrictive modifications to policy instruments — as may have occurred initially with regard to exporters' foreign currency retention rights described above — does not encourage confidence in the transition programme as a whole.

(g) Social safety net

The main new provision of the Soviet social security system designed to cope with the new phenomena associated with the introduction of a market economy is contained in the Basic Legislation on employment passed by the USSR Supreme Soviet on 15 January 1991. The Law entered in force on 1 January 1991 except for Chapter IV specifying unemployment benefits which is to come into force on 1 July. In addition, the protection of vulnerable groups of wage-earners is to be ensured by minimum wage policies to offset the rise in retail prices proposed for introduction in the spring of 1991. A new Law on pensions was also adopted on 15 May 1990; its provisions are also to be modified as circumstances require.

The Law on employment limits the categories of worker who can be classified as unemployed for the purpose of receiving benefit. Those qualified must have left their previous job no more than 11 days before registration, have worked for at least 36 weeks in the previous year, be looking for a job and be prepared to take any of those offered. The pay must be no less than 50 per cent of the worker's previous wage and must also exceed the minimum wage of R70 a month (the current average wage is about R270 a month). The unemployed may also be offered training. The Law also specifies redundancy procedures. Job losses must be announced at least three months in advance and workers affected must be paid salary for three months thereafter. New entrants to the labour force (notably school-leavers) appear to be ineligible for benefit.

The plan to increase retail prices includes provision to protect vulnerable groups (pensioners, low-paid workers and certain other categories) by increasing their emoluments through a form of indexation based on a basket of necessities. This option was also spelled out in the "Guidelines".

With regard to pensions, the Law is a new departure in that it is designed to cover public and private sector workers according to common principles — including individuals working on their own account. It sets no

---

554 See United Nations Economic Commission for Europe, *Economic Bulletin for Europe*, vol.42/90, New York, 1991, pp. 40-48.

555 See *Magyar Hirlap*, 26 February 1991, on the difficulties of Hungarian suppliers in getting paid. Arrears with western firms at the end of 1990 apparently amounted to some $500 million. See International Monetary Fund, International Bank for Reconstruction and Development, Organization for Economic Co-operation and Development and the Bank for European Reconstruction and Development, *The Economy of the USSR*, a study undertaken in response to a request by the Houston Summit, 19 December 1990, p.10.

556 Presidential decree dated 26 October 1990.

557 Report of USSR Goskomstat, *Ekonomika i zhizn'*, No.5, January 1991.

558 Based on a total statutory capitalization of R6 billion and the conversion of the one-third foreign contribution to this at the commercial exchange rate. Report of USSR Goskomstat, *Ekonomika i zhizn'*, No.5, January 1991, p.9. The UN/ECE Database lists 2,050 joint ventures which had reported statistics (i.e., were presumably operational) in the Soviet Union at the end of 1990. The foreign share in the statutory capital was R2 billion or about $3 billion at the commercial exchange rate. About 1,850 of these operations were concluded with western participants. See United Nations Economic Commission for Europe, *East-West Joint Ventures News*, No.7, March 1991.

559 For a full account of these see United Nations Economic Commission for Europe, *East-West Joint Ventures*, New York, 1988, pp.14-18.

level of pension though minima are established which are linked to the minimum wage. The pension funds, contributions to which are obligatory for employed persons, are to be set up and financed at republican level.

The dispositions made are not strikingly different from those in western Europe and other market-economy countries. But such schemes are expensive especially in the early stages before the financial backing of a contributory state insurance scheme has been established. Unemployment in the Soviet Union in the last quarter of 1990 was about 2 million workers. Assuming that unemployment peaks at about 13 million (10 per cent of the employed population) and that no worker's unemployment benefit exceeds the minimum wage, the total cost in a full year would be some R11 billion — equivalent to over one third of the Union budgetary deficit for 1991.

(vi) Prospects

The new legislation introduced in the last 18 months, policy statements and public debate indicate a powerful movement away from the command-administrative system of economic management which has prevailed in the Soviet Union during the last 70 years. Other measures are in the pipeline — including laws on entrepreneurial activity and on denationalization and privatization.[560] As argued in the first part of this section, there none the less remains considerable ambivalence as to the final goal of transition as well as the speed and timing of the transition path.

These two areas of uncertainty overlap but are not necessarily strongly linked. As noted by some western commentators, there may be a trade-off between the *speed* of transition and its *cost*. "A more radical reform programme might, for instance, give rise to even higher unemployment ...".[561] Thus, the slow pace of dismantling the institutions of central planning may be motivated by an ambition to avoid economic disruption and, under Soviet conditions in particular, the social unrest to which it could easily give rise. These are cases which belong to the domain of political rather than economic decision-making and should therefore not be judged exclusively by economic criteria.

Nevertheless, on numerous occasions — some of which have been pointed out in the foregoing sections

— both actions and terminology indicate that a good many conceptions rooted in a traditional collectivist world view still dictate the framework and, in particular, the tone of policy, while their consequences within a market economy have not been thought through. The low priority accorded to profits as an object of entrepreneurial activity (box 4.6.2) is a striking case in point. Could an enterprise be closed down at some stage if it were shown to have taken inadequate steps to "satisfy public needs for its products" — even if it is profitable? Who would decide, and according to what criteria? Again, positions are taken which disregard vital elements of a market structure — for instance the central failure to permit outright ownership of or a free market in land.

Some of these hesitations are also holding back short-term stabilization measures. They are thus adding the stigma of short-term economic collapse to the widespread uncertainties in any case inseparable from large-scale system reform, without providing a credible framework for longer-term remedies. The likely growing unpopularity of the transition effort under these conditions and the lack of credibility which inhibits the individual initiatives without which a market system cannot function are perhaps the greatest problems with which the Soviet leadership is now faced. These problems need to be confronted. The only other option is a return to administrative controls along the old lines of central planning — possible in theory, but hardly a viable alternative. Many of the institutions and especially the channels of communication through which that system functioned have now been dismantled. Their reinstatement would certainly prove a complex and likely an impossible task given the now widespread knowledge of the long-term systemic failure which has been the driving force of the partial but none the less drastic restructuring efforts of the last few years.

A combination of urgent stabilization policies and genuine market-oriented reform, tuned and timed where necessary to take account of the peculiarities of the system it is to replace, appears to be the only viable course for Soviet policy-makers. While it is inevitable that many difficulties will be encountered along this road, that is no reason for abandoning it. Quite the contrary, it is important for the credibility, as well as the success of short-term measures necessary to surmount current difficulties, that they should be elaborated within the framework of market solutions. At the same time, longer-term objectives should be clarified wherever they appear at present to be inadequately specified.

---

560 A draft of the latter was published in *Ekonomika i zhizn'*, No.7, February 1991.

561 See International Monetary Fund, International Bank for Reconstruction and Development, Organization for Economic Co-operation and Development and the Bank for European Reconstruction and Development, *op.cit.*, p.34. This study quotes an official estimate that unemployment could rise to between 1 and 6 million (about 1-5 per cent of total employment) in 1991.

Chapter 5

EXPLAINING UNEMPLOYMENT IN THE MARKET ECONOMIES: THEORIES AND EVIDENCE

Unemployment has re-emerged as a major problem in most of the developed market economies since the late 1970s. Using some of the theoretical approaches developed by economists in recent years, this chapter discusses the reasons for rising unemployment in western Europe, the United States and Japan. A selection of theoretical explanations is discussed in a non-technical manner and their ability to account for higher unemployment assessed. Although it is not intended to make detailed recommendations for reducing unemployment, a few broad conclusions are drawn from the empirical literature.

(i) Introduction

Unemployment has re-emerged as a major social and economic problem throughout most of the developed world during the past twenty years. The problem became particularly acute in the late 1970s and early 1980s. Although unemployment has fallen somewhat in the past five years, there were around 28 million people unemployed throughout the OECD by the end of the last decade. This is more than double the number unemployed prior to the first oil price shock of 1973-1974.

The general rise in unemployment is evident from table 5.1, which shows standardized unemployment rates for some of the major market economies. An examination of the table and also of chart 5.1 shows that the experience of unemployment has varied considerably. The rise in unemployment was most acute in the countries of the European Community which also show the most marked upward trend. The EFTA countries by contrast fared much better, while unemployment in the United States, although fairly high, exhibits a cyclical pattern with little noticeable upward trend. Finally, there are countries such as Sweden and Japan where unemployment has risen slightly over time but remains at very low levels.

This paper will discuss both the rise in unemployment and the differential experience of unemployment. It will do so by reference to the evolving theoretical perspectives of economists and related applied research. Much of the theory and research findings are to be found in highly technical papers; as a result they are often inaccessible to the non-specialist. A prime purpose of this paper is therefore to provide a non-technical account of the key features of current academic debate.[562]

(ii) Some basic facts on the structure of unemployment

Unemployment is a stock phenomenon, i.e., it measures the total number of people without work who want jobs at any point in time. The accuracy with which any particular country's unemployment statistics measure this stock is not discussed here. Official British statistics, for example, include only people claiming unemployment benefits of one kind or another and thus omit those who, for whatever reason, are not eligible for, or are not receiving, benefit (often in practice married women). Administrative procedures and other subtle factors therefore distort international comparisons although these problems can to some extent be resolved by cross-country surveys conducted on a comparable basis (such as the annual Labour Force Surveys conducted throughout most of the European Community). OECD figures, such as those already referred to, are "standardized rates", adjusted for national differences in definition. Although not always perfect, these figures none the less provide the best point of comparison between developed countries.

It is important to understand that the size of the stock of unemployment is determined by both the rate

---

562 Those interested in technical surveys and more detailed analysis are referred to Blanchard and Fischer (1989), Nickell (1990), Bean (1990), Carlin and Soskice (1990), Jackman, Layard and Nickell (1991).

185

TABLE 5.1

Standardized unemployment rates, selected countries

	Germany a	United Kingdom	France	Italy	Sweden	Japan	United States
1970	0.8	3.0	2.4	5.3	1.5	1.1	4.8
1971	0.9	3.7	2.6	5.3	2.5	1.2	5.8
1972	0.8	4.0	2.7	6.3	2.7	1.4	5.5
1973	0.8	3.0	2.6	6.2	2.5	1.3	4.8
1974	1.6	2.9	2.8	5.3	2.0	1.4	5.5
1975	3.6	4.3	4.0	5.8	1.6	1.9	8.3
1976	3.7	5.7	4.4	6.6	1.6	2.0	7.6
1977	3.6	6.1	4.9	7.0	1.8	2.0	6.9
1978	3.5	6.0	5.2	7.1	2.2	2.2	6.0
1979	3.2	5.1	5.9	7.6	2.1	2.1	5.8
1980	3.0	6.6	6.3	7.5	2.0	2.0	7.0
1981	4.4	9.8	7.3	7.8	2.5	2.2	7.5
1982	6.1	11.3	8.1	8.4	3.1	2.4	9.5
1983	8.0	12.4	8.3	9.3	3.5	2.6	9.5
1984	7.1	11.7	9.7	9.9	3.1	2.7	7.4
1985	7.2	11.2	10.2	10.1	2.8	2.6	7.1
1986	6.4	11.2	10.4	10.9	2.7	2.8	6.9
1987	6.2	10.2	10.5	11.8	1.9	2.8	6.1
1988	6.1	8.3	10.3	11.8	1.6	2.5	5.4
1989	5.7	6.6	9.5	11.3	1.3	2.3	5.2

Sources: OECD, *Quarterly Labour Force Statistics*, various issues.

Note: The Italian figures for 1986-1989 are the national rates, which are very close to the OECD standardized definition; the difference is that army conscripts are excluded from the Italian labour force definition, but included in the OECD.

a Data exclude the five new eastern *Länder*.

CHART 5.1

Unemployment rates:
International comparison, 1960-1990
(Per cent of total labour force)

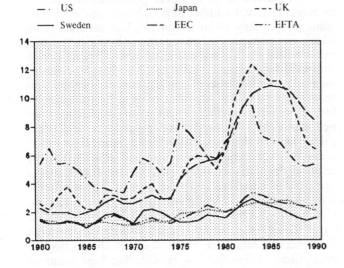

Source: OECD, *Quarterly Labour Force Statistics*, Paris.

of inflow into unemployment and the length of time people remain in the stock before flowing out (i.e., the duration of unemployment). The joint influence of the inflow and duration can best be appreciated by consid-

ering a "steady state", a position where the stock of unemployment remains unchanged. The size of the stock will be equal to the inflow multiplied by the average completed duration of unemployment. If the stock is one million and the inflow rate is 100,000 per month, the average duration of unemployment will thus be 10 months.

From this it should be clear that the precise nature of flows into and out of unemployment determine the duration structure of the stock. This will clearly influence the way in which the problem is perceived. If, for example, the outflow rate (i.e., the number of people leaving unemployment in a month as a proportion of the stock) is high and people who enter unemployment leave again quickly, the stock of unemployment will be composed largely of different individuals over time. If instead the outflow rate is low, there will be a slower turnover with some individuals experiencing long spells of unemployment.

Table 5.2, taken from Bean (1990), shows flows into and out of unemployment for a variety of OECD countries, in 1979 and 1988. Also shown is the share of long-term unemployment (those unemployed for more than a year) in total unemployment which gives some indication of the duration of unemployment in a number of OECD countries. Although there is considerable variation in the flow-duration relationship, countries can be divided into three broad groups with regard to the proportions of long-term unemployment (see also OECD 1988).

One group, the United States, Canada, Japan, Norway and Sweden, has very low proportions of long-term unemployment. A second group comprising

TABLE 5.2

The structure of unemployment
(Per cent)

| | | Percentage of source population [a] | | Long term unemployment [b] | |
		Inflows	*Outflows*	*Share of total unemployment*	*Share of prime age workers*
Belgium	(1979)	0.22	..	58.0	49 [c]
	(1988)	0.10	2.7	77.5	62
Denmark	(1979)	0.76	15.0	..	47 [c]
	(1988)	0.44	8.3	28.7	58
France	(1979)	0.27	6.6	30.3	46
	(1988)	0.33	5.7	44.8	61
Germany [d]	(1979)	0.18	19.6	19.9	49 [c]
	(1988)	0.26	6.3	46.7	47
Ireland	(1979)	0.72	-	31.8	46 [c]
	(1988)	0.37	3.2	66.0	49
Italy	(1979)	0.17	8.3	35.8	28 [c]
	(1988)	0.18	2.3	69.0	37
Netherlands	(1979)	0.29	..	27.1	50 [c]
	(1988)	0.23	..	50.0	61
Spain	(1979)	0.25	2.2	27.5	26
	(1988)	0.12	1.3	61.5	41
United Kingdom	(1979)	0.41	14.3	24.8	32 [c]
	(1988)	0.68	9.5	44.7	44
Australia	(1979)	0.84	19.3	18.1	29
	(1988)	0.92	18.2	28.4	41
Canada	(1979)	1.77	32.0	3.5	46
	(1988)	1.89	30.8	7.4	53
United States	(1979)	2.07	43.5	4.2	32
	(1988)	1.98	45.7	7.4	41
Japan	(1979)	0.31	19.1	16.5	50
	(1988)	0.37	17.2	20.6	34
Finland	(1979)	1.04	..	19.3	41
	(1988)	1.55	..	..	38
Norway	(1979)	0.55	41.7	3.8	..
	(1988)	0.79	30.3	6.3	..
Sweden	(1979)	0.58	34.5	6.8	28
	(1988)	0.40	30.4	8.2	28

Source: OECD, *Employment Outlook*, July 1990, after Bean (1990).

a Working-age population (15-64) less the unemployed for inflows; total unemployment for outflows. The inflow data are monthly averages. For details of the calculations, see OECD, *op.cit.*, p.13.
b Greater than 12 months.
c 1983 figures.
d Data exclude the five new eastern *Länder*.

Australia, France, Germany, Ireland and the United Kingdom have moderate proportions, while Belgium, Spain and the Netherlands have very high proportions. It would seem in general that European countries are characterized by small flows and long durations whereas in North America there are relatively large flows in and out of unemployment and correspondingly short durations of unemployment. The Nordic countries, Norway and Sweden, exhibit relatively high outflow rates.

Of particular interest in table 5.2 is the fact that outflow rates have fallen substantially in the European

Community in the 1980s. As Bean comments, this indicates that "the high levels of unemployment in the European Community are thus primarily associated with a reduction in the probability of finding a job, rather than an increased frequency of losing one". This, he continues, "suggests that high unemployment is associated with increased duration of unemployment with given mean duration".

The significance of this for understanding the rise and persistence of unemployment in the European Community will become clearer later in the paper. For the time being, however, it is sufficient to note from the final column of the table that long-term unemployment has been borne predominantly by prime age workers (those aged between 25 and 45) rather than the old and the young. Indeed this is true of total unemployment; although youth unemployment was clearly a major problem in the late 1970s and early 1980s, it is none the less "core" prime age groups which have borne the greatest burden of unemployment during the past decade. Other important features of the structure of unemployment are regional differences within countries and differences between males and females. This paper refrains from a detailed discussion of regional unemployment which would justify a paper of its own, although the problem is referred to from time to time in later sections. Differences in the experience of males and females as unemployment has risen are considered in section (iv), below.

(iii)   Analysing unemployment

In analysing unemployment, it is helpful to begin by distinguishing between an economy's underlying long-run or *equilibrium* rate of unemployment and the *actual* rate of unemployment observed at any particular time. All economies are subject to short-run fluctuations in unemployment but these are almost exclusively associated with cyclical fluctuations in economic activity. Equilibrium unemployment, by contrast, is determined by the structural characteristics of labour markets and it is to these that one must look in order to understand why some countries experience higher unemployment than others. As will be seen, the concept of equilibrium unemployment is a rather slippery one − not only is equilibrium subject to change but also cyclical fluctuations in unemployment may themselves influence the underlying equilibrium rate − but it none the less offers a useful starting point from which to consider the phenomenon.

What is meant by equilibrium unemployment? Throughout this paper several different concepts of equilibrium will be referred to. In the most simple abstract terms, however, it may be defined as the difference between the total labour force (i.e., all those people who are economically active) and total employment in a given country at whatever real wage equates supply and demand in the labour market. Put rather differently, it is the rate of unemployment at which there is neither excess demand for, nor supply of labour.

CHART 5.2

The relationship between unemployment (U) and vacancies (V).

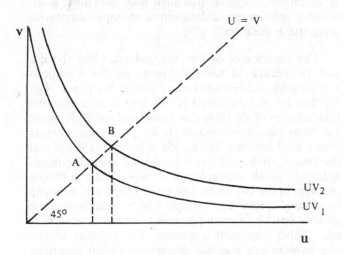

It must be emphasized that equilibrium, as defined here, may not correspond to "full employment" of labour resources because of a whole host of factors influencing the parameters of labour supply and demand. This possibility becomes easier to comprehend if the demand for labour at any time is seen as consisting of people in jobs plus those unemployed. Given this, if vacancies are equal to the number of people unemployed supply will equal demand and the labour market will be in equilibrium. Such a position of equilibrium is shown at point A in chart 5.2 which depicts the well-established relationship between unemployment and vacancies, known as the U/V (or Beveridge) curve.

Two central characteristics of the U/V relationship need clearly to be understood. First, as is visually apparent, the relationship is hyperbolic. Unemployment and vacancies are inversely related; as the level of demand for labour falls, vacancies fall and unemployment rises. Points *along* the U/V curve reflect different levels of demand, but at any time only one level of demand will be consistent with labour market equilibrium at A. Unemployment above A can thus be considered to be due to deficient demand. Secondly, as is also apparent from chart 5.2, the further the U/V curve is from the axis the higher the rate of unemployment at any given rate of vacancies and the higher the equilibrium rate (point B on U/V$_2$, for example, represents a higher unemployment equilibrium than point A on U/V$_1$).

What determines the number of people unemployed at any given level of vacancies − i.e., the *position* of the UV curve as opposed to *points* along the curve? There are two broad determinants.

The first determinant is what is commonly termed "frictional unemployment", consisting of people between jobs and looking for work. Frictional unemployment is a natural characteristic of labour markets,

which are dynamic entities subject to fairly rapid turnover. Following Phelps (1970), economists have sought to explain such friction by developing increasingly sophisticated theories and models of job search behaviour on the part of firms and individuals (see also Burda (1988)).

Given that firms set wages in competition for labour it is normal for a dispersion of wage rates to prevail in the market. Workers, therefore, spend time looking at work alternatives before accepting a job, with the result that vacancies are not filled immediately, the cost of search being earnings foregone. It is normally accepted that such "search unemployment" will be higher the less good is information about vacancies and the higher the ratio of unemployment and related benefits to earnings (the so-called "replacement ratio"). In principle, a higher replacement ratio lowers the cost of search and therefore prolongs it.

Employer search will also contribute to frictional unemployment. Given quality differences between potential employees, employers will seek out the best candidates. In doing so they will set the benefits of eventually gaining more productive employees against the cost in terms of lost output while job vacancies remain unfilled during the search period; these two factors will determine the length of that period and hence the employer search component of frictional unemployment. Similarly, larger numbers of vacancies will remain unfilled at any given level of unemployment the more choosey are employers about who they will employ. In this respect they may be influenced by employment protection laws which make it more difficult to dismiss workers once they have been taken on.

The second broad determinant of the position of the U/V curve is the degree of *structural* or "mismatch" unemployment due to the immobility of labour and capital. Structural change, for example, may result in regional concentrations of unemployment regardless of whether vacancies exist elsewhere in a country simply as a result of geographical immobility on the part of workers or firms. Similarly, mismatches may occur if workers made redundant from declining industries and sectors are unable or unwilling to gain skills or aptitudes necessary to move into expanding industries or sectors.

In principle, market forces, by operating through adjustments in regional and occupational wage differentials, should ensure such unemployment disappears. In practice, however, workers are often reluctant or unable to move from high unemployment regions or sectors because, for example, of failure in housing or training markets. By the same token, a whole variety of economic and social factors often deter firms from moving from low to high unemployment regions. Historically, "divergent development" has been a more common characteristic of market economies than regional convergence (see Armstrong and Taylor (1985) and (1988)). It is normal therefore for economies to exhibit some amount of structural unemployment.

In simple conceptual terms, unemployment may therefore either (a) rise or fall about a given equilibrium position because of fluctuations in demand or (b) rise or fall because of shifts in the UV curve. In practice, because economies are dynamic entities, both (a) and (b) may occur simultaneously, although in most countries there has been an outward shift of the UV curve since the 1960s (Jackman, Pissarides and Savouri (1990)).

In view of this dynamism it is far from easy either to determine the precise causes of equilibrium unemployment or to establish how far an economy's actual unemployment rate is from its equilibrium rate. To complicate matters still further, it is possible to conceive of unemployment as at times *a disequilibrium* phenomenon unrelated to deficient demand. Such a disequilibrium will occur if impediments exist which cause real wages to be above the level which equates supply and demand in the labour market or, put rather differently, prevent wages from adjusting when changes in demand or supply conditions require them to do so. As it will become clear later, wage adjustment is also crucial to the speed at which unemployment returns to equilibrium following sudden changes in supply or demand − commonly known as "shocks" to the economic system.

The broad consensus of opinion is that various supply-side shocks were crucial to the rise in unemployment in many market economies from the mid-1970s onwards. Principle amongst these were the oil price increases of 1973-1974 and 1979-1980 (OPEC-1 and OPEC-2), increases in commodity prices more generally, and a slow-down in productivity growth.

Few economists dispute that shocks such as these served to raise both inflationary pressure and unemployment while depressing growth in output, i.e., the phenomenon which has become known as "stagflation". Moreover, it is widely accepted that the response of labour market institutions and policy makers to the shocks was as important as the shocks themselves. None the less, there has been considerable debate about the precise mechanics of the rise in unemployment following the shocks and why the problem was more acute in some countries than in others. The rest of this paper offers a guide to the main features of that debate.

(iv) The accounting approach: examining labour supply and demand

Before proceeding to more detailed analysis, it is worthwhile pausing simply to acknowledge OPEC-1 as a watershed for the post-war economy. In simple accounting terms, Rowthorn and Glynn (1987) show that 1973 marked a major turning point in the economic fortunes of the OECD countries. Until that year, output had grown steadily in all the major sectors of all the OECD economies but since then the trend has been reversed. Virtually all experienced a rapid slow-down in the growth rate of industrial production. For the OECD countries as a whole, the annual growth rate of GDP halved from 5 per cent between 1960 and 1973 to

TABLE 5.3

Accounting for increased unemployment in OECD countries, 1973-1985 [a]

(Millions)

	Male	Female	Total
Unemployment			
1973	5.1	4.2	9.3
1985	15.8	11.9	27.7
Change in unemployment (1973-1985)			
Total	10.7	7.7	18.4
of which due to change in growth rate of: [b]			
Employment	13.2	-1.8	11.4
Participation	1.4	10.2	11.6
Population	-3.9	-2.3	-6.2
Residual	0.0	1.6	1.6

Source: Rowthorn and Glynn (1987).

[a] Australia, Austria, Belgium, Canada, Denmark, Finland, France, Germany, Ireland, Italy, Japan, Netherlands, New Zealand, Norway, Spain, Sweden, Switzerland, United Kingdom, United States.
[b] As compared to the period 1960-1973.

2.4 per cent between 1973 and 1985. The impact of this slow-down on employment growth was muted somewhat by a considerable reduction in the rate of growth of productivity, which more than halved. But despite this, industrial employment, having risen quite rapidly prior to 1973, began to fall in the following years throughout the industrial market economies.

Rowthorn and Glynn estimate that if industrial unemployment had continued to grow at the pre-1973 rate there would have been 129 million people employed in the industrial sector of the OECD countries by the mid-1980s. The actual figure for 1985 was 104 million, suggesting a loss of 25 million potential jobs. Employment growth as a whole slowed from 1.1 per cent per annum in the 13 years prior to 1973 to only 0.8 per cent per annum in the period 1973-1985. However, while employment growth in the former period proceeded at the same pace as growth in the labour force, in the latter period labour force growth accelerated slightly to 1.3 per cent per annum. The combination of reduced employment growth and higher labour force growth led to an increase of around 18 million in the number of people unemployed in the OECD countries. Around three fifths of this increase can be attributed to the slow-down in employment growth.

One should note that the increase in the labour force was not a result of demographic change but rather of higher participation (i.e., there was no increase in the size of the population of working age but more people decided to participate in the labour market). Demographic factors did not therefore play a role in the rise in unemployment, although, as Rowthorn and Glynn point out, the relative contributions to the rise in unemployment of slower employment growth and higher participation rates differ significantly between men and women. This is shown clearly in table 5.3. The main cause of male unemployment was the loss of industrial employment. Women, by contrast, were more able and more willing to slot into service employment (which was barely affected by the slow-down in growth and increased as a proportion of total employment), al-

TABLE 5.4

Labour force participation rates, by sex, 1975-1989

	Male					Female				
	1975	1979	1983	1986	1989	1975	1989	1983	1986	1989
France	84.3	82.8	78.3	76.5	75.1	51.0	54.1	54.4	55.0	55.4
Germany [a]	87.0	84.5	80.6	79.9	80.4*	49.6	49.6	49.7	51.2	52.0*
Italy	84.7	82.6	80.7	79.0	78.2	34.6	38.7	40.3	42.0	44.0
United Kingdom	92.1	90.5	87.6	87.9	87.0	55.1	58.0	57.1	61.1	63.7
United States	85.4	85.7	84.6	85.2	85.8	53.2	58.9	61.8	65.1	67.9
Japan	89.7	89.2	89.1	87.5	87.2	51.7	54.7	57.2	57.4	59.3
Sweden	89.2	87.9	85.9	84.2	85.1	67.6	72.8	76.6	78.3	80.9

Source: National statistics.

[a] Data exclude the five new eastern *Länder*.

though growth in this sector was unable to absorb the larger numbers of women wishing to participate in the labour market. One possibility, not discussed by Rowthorn and Glynn, is that the rise in unemployment may have been dampened to some extent by falling male participation. Some men, particularly older men, may have withdrawn from the labour market because they were "discouraged" about their prospects of finding work in traditional sectors of industrial employment. This possibility is not explored here but it is clearly true, as table 5.4 shows for a selection of countries, that there was a tendency for male participation rates to decline (except in the United States) between the mid-1970s and the mid-1980s at the same time as female participation rose.

(v) 'Keynesian' versus 'Classical' unemployment

The accounting approach illustrates the basic labour market movements that underlie the rise in unemployment. It does not, however, say a great deal about the precise nature of the rise in unemployment. For example, to what extent was the high employment experienced by many countries in the late 1970s and 1980s an equilibrium or a disequilibrium phenomenon? One approach to answering this question has involved attempts to determine to what extent the unemployment of the 1970s and 1980s was by nature "Classical" or "Keynesian" where these labels refer to the traditional schools of economic thought commonly associated with them.

Both "Classical" and Keynesian unemployment are forms of disequilibrium unemployment, but emerge for radically different reasons (see, for example, Malinvaud (1977)). "Classical" unemployment is said to occur when the real wage as determined in the labour market is higher than that consistent with market equilibrium. Such a disequilibrium is thought to be associated with rigidities in the labour market, such as the existence of trade unions, which cause real wages to be "excessive" (i.e., above the market clearing level). Keynesian unemployment, by contrast, results from deficient demand that causes people to be involuntarily unemployed because firms face constraints in product markets rather than in the labour market.

Each type of unemployment gives rise to a different solution: "Classical" unemployment is solved by removing labour market rigidities so as to ensure the labour market clears, whilst Keynesian unemployment requires a boost to demand.

Chart 5.3 shows how "Classical" unemployment may arise following a shock to the economic system, such as a rise in the oil price. Assume that the labour market is originally at full employment equilibrium, with an employment rate (unemployment/labour force) of N and a real wage of W/P. The oil price rise causes a fall in production and an inward shift of the labour demand curve from position D to D'. If the *ex ante* real wage remains unchanged, employment falls to N' and unemployment rises. In order to restore equilibrium, the real wage must therefore fall from W/P_f to W/P' (assuming that the supply of labour is completely inelastic in the short run). The amount by which the real wage must fall to re-establish equilibrium has come to be called the "real wage gap" (see, for example, Bruno and Sachs (1985)).

It is often contended that real wage rigidity in many OECD countries, especially those in western Europe, following the oil price shocks prevented the necessary reduction in real wages, thus giving rise to a period of "Classical" unemployment. The essential argument is that money wages adjusted too rapidly to rising prices, due to such factors as "real wage resistance" on the part of workers and indexation procedures (had money wages not increased, rising prices would have resulted in real wage reductions).

In addition, however, governments in most countries in the late 1970s and early 1980s were clearly worried about the impact of higher oil prices on inflation and in many cases were more concerned with this problem than that of rising unemployment. Therefore, it is argued, the use of deflationary fiscal and monetary policies resulted in firms being unable to sell as much as they wished at prevailing product prices; job losses were thus incurred for reasons other than real wages being too high. In terms of chart 5.3, this means that firms in aggregate were operating off their labour demand curve, at a point such as X. At point X firms − assuming they are profit maximizers − employ only N_{dd}. Unemployment of this kind is of course due to deficient demand and was described earlier as

TABLE 5.5

The real wage gap, 1965-1981
(1965-1969 average = zero)
(Per cent)

	1965	1969	1973	1975	1979	1981
United Kingdom	-1.5	1.1	3.1	9.9	14.1	19.3
United States	1.2	-	3.1	-10.0	6.1	8.1
OECD, Big Six, (average) [a]	0.4	-0.2	3.7	7.4	8.0	10.4

Source: Bruno and Sachs (1985, p.180).

[a] Canada, France, Germany, Japan, United Kingdom and the United States.

Keynesian. In the presence of the demand constraint, such unemployment is impervious to a cut in real wages.

Attempts to assess the relative importance of "Classical" and Keynesian unemployment include those of Bruno and Sachs (1985). Their concept of the "real wage gap" has already been mentioned. It is defined more formally as the difference between the prevailing real wage at any time and the marginal product of labour at full employment. Since the latter cannot be observed, Bruno and Sachs measure the wage gap as an index of the average product of labour at each peak of the economic cycle (between peaks it is assumed to grow at a constant proportional rate). The index is then subtracted from an index of the actual real wage to provide a "real wage gap index".

Table 5.5 shows the real wage gap for the United Kingdom, the United States and six major OECD countries combined. The wage gap was small in the 1960s and 1970s but increased in the 1970s during the period of rising unemployment following OPEC-1. Interestingly, while the wage gap closed in the United

States in the immediate aftermath of OPEC-1, it increased in the six-country group as a whole and remained higher than in the United States throughout the remainder of the decade. Later work by Bruno (1986), however, suggests that the wage gap began to fall almost everywhere after 1981 yet unemployment remained high and continued to rise.

On the basis of a decomposition of the rise in unemployment into real wage gap and demand components, Bruno concludes that although real wages played an important role in causing unemployment to rise through the 1970s, in the 1980s deflationary policy came to the fore. In other words, whereas unemployment in the 1970s was primarily "Classical", in the early 1980s Keynesian, demand deficient unemployment began to emerge. This seems consistent with the rather different policy response to OPEC-1 and OPEC-2. The immediate tendency of many governments after OPEC-1 was to attempt to maintain aggregate demand in order to protect output and jobs. But by the time of OPEC-2, most governments were engaged in the fight against inflation which clearly exacerbated unemployment.

As table 5.6 illustrates, however, the extent of disinflation was similar throughout the OECD yet, as already noted, unemployment rates varied quite substantially. The costs of reducing inflation thus appear to have differed considerably. These differences have usually been attributed to variations in the responsiveness of wages to unemployment. The hypothesis that wages are slow to adjust to macro-economic shocks has been the subject of a number of studies, most notably that of Coe (1985). He finds that various measures of wage rigidity differ across countries and also that they are correlated with the rise in unemployment – greater wage rigidity was associated with high unemployment. Hyclaek and Johnes (1989), in a study of regional labour markets in the United Kingdom, the United States and West Germany, also find wage rigidity to be an important determinant of regional differences in the response of labour markets to macro-economic shocks (see also Disney et al., 1991).

The conclusion of studies of this type is that wages are least responsive to unemployment in the European Community, rather more responsive in the United States and most responsive in countries such as Japan, Austria, Switzerland and Sweden, i.e., those with the

CHART 5.3

"Classical" versus "Keynesian" unemployment

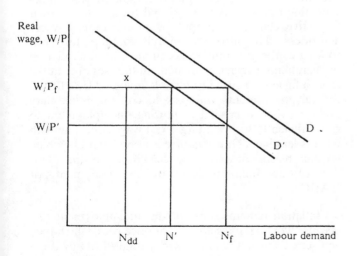

TABLE 5.6

Unemployment and inflation rates, 1960s to 1980s
(Per cent)

	EC (12)	EFTA	United States	Japan
Unemployment				
1960s.............................	2.3	1.3	4.7	1.3
1970s.............................	4.0	1.6	6.1	1.7
1980s.............................	9.6	2.8	7.2	2.5
Inflation				
1960s.............................	4.1	4.2	2.8	5.3
1970s.............................	10.4	7.9	7.0	8.0
1980s.............................	7.5	6.0	4.8	1.6

Source: Layard (1990c), taken from European Commission, *European Economy*, No.42, November 1989, Tables 3 and 23; except EFTA: OECD, *Economic Outlook*, No.47, June 1990.

lowest rates of unemployment. The possible reasons for this outcome are examined later. But before doing so it is important to look at one of the most influential current approaches to analysing unemployment. This is the so-called New Keynesian approach which has developed an analytical framework designed to provide a coherent and comprehensive explanation of the causes of unemployment throughout the developed world during the past decade.

(vi) New Keynesianism

The preceding section focused on the possible role of real wage rigidity in generating unemployment. As Solow (1986) argues, however, the explanation of unemployment in terms of "too high" or "excessive" real wages is incomplete because it is unable to isolate the exogenous factors responsible for the observed levels of real wages. Moreover, when looked at in the Keynesian tradition the explanation clearly leaves something to be desired since modern adherents to the broad Keynesian approach consider wages to be determined, together with prices, within the economic system; the suggestion that real wages are an exogenous variable that can be manipulated directly in order to reduce unemployment is therefore slightly erroneous.

It is this practical deficiency in the "wage gap" analysis that provides part of the impetus for "New Keynesianism". It is "new" primarily because its micro-economic foundations are rather different from those of traditional Keynesianism, with the real wage, employment and unemployment being determined jointly within the empirically more realistic setting of imperfectly competitive product and labour markets, with both firms and workers exerting some degree of market power.

New Keynesianism is exemplified by the work of Layard and Nickell (1985, 1986 and 1987), Bean, Layard and Nickell (1987), Blanchard and Kiyotaki (1987), Layard (1986 and 1990a, 1990b and 1990c) and Jackman, Layard and Nickell (1991). Emphasis is placed upon labour market institutions such as trade unions not as "rigidities", and hence, "causes" of dis-

equilibrium unemployment that can be removed in simple fashion, but rather upon the role of such institutions together with other factors (such as the level and availability of unemployment benefits, "mismatch" etc.) in determining an equilibrium rate of unemployment that is consistent with stable inflation.

Layard (1986 and 1990) offers the most easily accessible account of this approach (see also Johnson and Layard, 1986). His basic theoretical model is depicted in chart 5.4. At its root lies a struggle between employers and workers to increase their respective shares − in terms of profits and wages − of real per capita output (see also Rowthorn (1977) and Meade (1982)).

The employers' claim on output is shown by the horizontal line in chart 5.4. This is the "feasible real wage" (FRW) and has two main determinants viz. labour productivity and the size of the mark-up firms apply to prime cost. Prime cost may include raw materials, such as oil, but comprises mainly labour costs. The assumption is that since firms are not price takers they use their market power to maximize profits by setting prices relative to costs by some constant proportion. As against this feasible real wage there is a "target real wage" (TRW) to which workers will aspire at any given rate of unemployment. The target real wage will be higher the lower is unemployment, because workers will feel more able to extract wage increases from employers the tighter is the labour market.

Given the parameters of this relationship, there will only be one level of unemployment at which the target real wage is compatible with the feasible real wage: shown as U_n in chart 5.4. If actual unemployment were less than this, say at U_1, workers would push for a higher real wage. In order to do so they would seek a higher money wage but, on the assumption that firms maintain their mark-up over costs, if they succeed prices will increase. If unemployment were to remain at U_1 the result would be a wage price "spiral" with workers seeking still higher wages to compensate for higher prices, followed by firms raising prices once more.

In such a situation, the spiral reflects the conflict over the division of per capita output and results in accelerating inflation as workers and firms reiterate their respective claims on output by raising money wages and prices. This situation can only continue, however, so long as the government accommodates the inflation by maintaining aggregate demand in the economy at the level sufficient to sustain unemployment at U_1. But in general governments will seek to contain inflationary pressure when it arises by allowing unemployment to rise sufficiently to bring target real wages into line with what is feasible. This of course is at position U_n, which for this reason has come to be known as the Non-Accelerating Inflation Rate of Unemployment, or NAIRU.

Inflation remains stable at this unemployment rate because workers' *expectations* of price rises, which they will seek to match, will be exactly fulfilled. Only if expectations are not fulfilled, because of some shock to the system, will inflation rise or fall.

CHART 5.4

Real wage bargaining and the NAIRU.

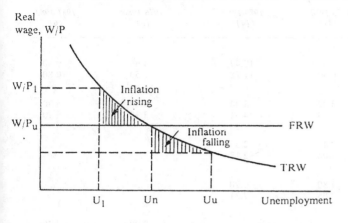

Note: Un = NAIRU, the Non-Accelerating Inflation Rate of Unemployment

Consider, once again, a fall in unemployment below the NAIRU and assume a rate of inflation at the NAIRU of 5 per cent. The target real wage lies above the feasible real wage and unions will therefore seek a money wage that will increase the real wage to W/P_1. Since, on the basis of the past rate of inflation (at the NAIRU), they expect inflation to rise by 5 per cent, they will seek a money wage rise higher than 5 per cent in order to take the real wage up to W/P_1. With money wages likely to rise by more than 5 per cent, firms will raise prices by more than 5 per cent with the result that a wage price spiral and accelerating inflation ensue. If, by contrast, unemployment is higher than the NAIRU, say at U_u, union bargaining power is weakened and unions are only able to negotiate a wage rise below 5 per cent. With wage costs rising only at this rate, firms find that they can raise prices by less than 5 per cent and still maintain their profit margins. Inflation thus decelerates.

This basic theoretical model of course represents only the most simple account of the determination of the NAIRU. A full account requires consideration of the claims of government and the overseas sector on an economy's real domestic per capita output. Government, for example, can exact a share of real output by means of taxation of profits or wages (where "taxes" may be taken to refer to taxation and social security contributions). From the point of view of employers these taxes either raise costs or lower profits, thus lowering the feasible real wage. Similarly, taxes lower workers' take home pay and cause them to push for a higher real wage in "compensation". The "tax wedge" which the government drives between employers and workers therefore tends to raise the NAIRU, other things being equal. By the same token, higher import prices represent a claim by those overseas on an economy's domestic real output and by driving another

wedge between the claims of firms and workers result in a higher NAIRU.

Without elaborating further on this theory, it should be clear that, when viewed empirically, a rise in unemployment can occur either as a result of demand factors that drive unemployment above the NAIRU (and hence reduce inflationary pressure) or because of an increase in the NAIRU itself, perhaps as a result of shocks to the system that alter either the feasible real wage or the target real wage. Attempts to estimate the NAIRU for a number of OECD countries and to decompose changes in actual unemployment into those associated with demand induced movements about the NAIRU and movements in the NAIRU itself are examined below. Before doing so, however, it is important to clarify the important distinction between the NAIRU and the concept of the "natural rate of unemployment" (or NRU) as applied by monetarist and so-called New "Classical" economists.

The natural rate of unemployment is also an equilibrium concept and is said to correspond to an economy's equilibrium or natural level of output. The term gained widespread currency in the 1970s — following Friedman's (1968) seminal work on accelerating inflation — as many economists retreated from the notion of a long-run trade-off between unemployment and inflation. The trade-off was implied by the "Phillips curve" — a hyperbolic relationship between the rate of change of money wages and unemployment — and gave rise to the notion that policy makers could "choose" any preferred level of unemployment at the cost of some known and stable rate of inflation.

Friedman's diagnosis was that this notion was flawed since efforts to sustain unemployment at a rate below the NRU would lead to accelerating inflation. At first sight this resembles the conclusion derived by the New Keynesians. On closer examination, however, the approaches are very different. The NRU is determined within a labour market assumed to consist of atomistic agents supplying and demanding labour, with market forces, operating through the real wage, adjusting when necessary to ensure that equilibrium is maintained. This is in sharp contrast to the New Keynesian assumption of imperfect competition with both unions and firms exhibiting some form of market power, a contrast which also gives rise to a different account of the manner in which accelerating inflation is generated.

The New Keynesians, as shown above, view accelerating inflation as the consequence of any impulse to aggregate demand which causes unemployment to fall below the NAIRU and is then accommodated by monetary growth. According to monetarist exponents of the NRU hypothesis, however, only a monetary impulse can initiate inflation. Whatever the real wage that equates supply and demand in the labour market at the NRU, a rise in the money supply, by pushing up prices and money wages, fools workers and employers into thinking that real wages and real demand for goods and services have risen. Workers thus supply more labour and firms expand output, thereby allowing unemployment to fall below the NRU, but eventually all parties realize that they have been victims of this

TABLE 5.7

Actual and estimated equilibrium unemployment rates

(Per cent)

	1957-1966 (1)	1967-1974 (2)	1975-1978 (3)	1979-1982 (4)	1976-1980 (5)	1981-1983 (6)
United Kingdom						
Natural rate................	2.03	4.25	7.53	10.47	4.60	9.50
Actual rate.................	2.03	3.78	6.80	11.28	5.50	10.80
Germany [a]						
Natural rate................	2.03	1.06	3.82	3.34	3.70	5.30
Actual rate.................	1.38	1.12	3.89	4.51	3.70	6.70
Japan						
Natural rate................	1.56	1.89	2.47	2.37	..	..
Actual rate.................	1.56	1.25	2.04	2.18	..	..
United States						
Natural rate................	5.18	4.71	7.80	6.20	..	..
Actual rate.................	5.18	4.35	7.05	7.31	..	..
Italy						
Natural rate................	..	..	..	..	8.90	7.70
Actual rate.................	..	..	..	..	7.10	9.40
France						
Natural rate................	..	..	..	..	5.30	6.90
Actual rate.................	..	..	..	..	5.30	7.30
EC						
Natural rate................	..	..	..	..	5.30	7.30
Actual rate.................	..	..	..	..	5.40	8.80

Sources: (1) to (4) Layard and Nickell (1985), (5) and (6) Layard et al. (1986).

[a] Data exclude the five new eastern *Länder*.

"money illusion" and both supply and demand will return to the levels consistent with the natural rate of unemployment, albeit at a higher level of money wages and prices.

In principle, this would be a higher stable level of prices but, it is argued, governments — particularly in the 1960s and 1970s — sought continually to fool workers and firms by administering successive injections of monetary demand into economies. The aim was to sustain high rates of output and low rates of unemployment but it became increasingly clear that this could not be achieved, as the Phillips relationship had suggested, at the cost of higher stable inflation. Instead, the cost was *accelerating* inflation since ever higher prices and money wages were given so that firms and workers would each year incorporate the previous year's inflation rate into their expectations about the course of real wages.

Moreover, whereas Friedman and early exponents of this hypothesis at least considered it possible for governments to generate short-run deviations of unemployment from the NRU, later exponents believe that the increased sophistication of market agents rule out even this possibility since firms and workers will fully anticipate future inflation when making decisions about supplying and demanding labour. This view has come to be known as the Rational Expectations Hypothesis and is closely associated with the New "Classical" school of economics. Put simply, the idea is that labour market agents form expectations of future inflation on a highly rational basis, taking into account money supply data and other information relevant to price setting as supplied by public agencies. These are

incorporated into labour market decisions based upon real rather than monetary values with the result that changes in monetary growth will simply result in either accelerating or decelerating inflation at the NRU.

Whether these latter assertions are justified is a matter of keen debate, the substance of which is discussed in some detail by Davies (1986). All that needs to be understood for present purposes are the differences between monetarists/New Classicals and New Keynesians with regard to the determination of equilibrium unemployment. The treatment of one factor, unemployment benefits, provides a good example of these differences. For NRU adherents, the importance of unemployment benefits lays primarily in their impact upon the level of search unemployment (see, for example, Minford (1983) and (1990)). The New Keynesians, however, stress in addition the impact of benefits on the target real wage; if benefits are low or not available, employed workers will be less keen to push for higher wages since they know that they will sustain a heavy loss of income if they lose their jobs and that those people already unemployed will be more than willing to step into their shoes.

(vii) Estimating causes of the rise in unemployment

The NAIRU cannot be directly observed but must be estimated econometrically. Considerable effort has been put into such estimation (see, for example, Layard and Nickell (1985) and Layard et al. (1987)). The normal procedure is to estimate a series of labour demand, real wage and price formation equations the joint solution of which is a rate of unemployment at which price expectations are fulfilled from one period to the next (i.e., inflation, in terms of the earlier theoretical account of the NAIRU, remains stable). Table 5.7 contains NAIRU estimates using this method for a number of countries covering the period from the late 1950s until the early 1980s. In all the countries shown there is a jump in the NAIRU from the middle of the 1970s. How does one account for this?

The major, and most widely accepted, explanation is a reduction in the feasible real wage following, in particular, OPEC-1 (although the effects of other commodity price rises should also be included). Put in simple terms, the effect of the oil price shock was to reduce the feasible real wage since the attendant cost increases led to higher prices for goods and services. In terms of chart 5.5, this implied a downward shift in the FRW curve and required an equivalent shift in the feasible real wage if the NAIRU were not to rise. In the event, as was noted earlier, many workers resisted the fall in real wages that OPEC-1 necessitated and pushed for higher money wages in order to compensate for price increases, thus causing the NAIRU to rise.

In this regard, the experience of European countries, which exhibited a marked degree of real wage resistance, is in marked contrast to that of Japan. Immediately following OPEC-1, the rate of inflation in Japan rose to 20 per cent, but this was halved in 1975 and fell to 5 per cent in 1978 at relatively little cost in terms of higher unemployment. This is rather surprising given that Japan is more oil dependent than most other major industrial nations. A feature of the Japanese economy, however, is profit-related pay. It is often suggested that, as a result of this, wages fell in line with profits following the oil induced recession, thereby ensuring that wage pressure was quickly muted.

Another explanation of the rise in western unemployment is the general slow-down in productivity growth in the market economies during the 1970s (see section (v) above). The precise causes of the slow-down are not clear but their impact was to reduce the feasible real wage (or at least its rate of growth) again requiring a compensating reduction in the target real wage. Grubb, Jackman and Layard (1982) attribute around two percentage points of the rise in total OECD unemployment between 1960-1972 and 1973-1980 to this factor. This is roughly similar to the role they attribute to the rise in oil and commodity prices although it should be noted that later work by Layard and Nickell (1986) finds no such "productivity effect" once a broader range of factors affecting the NAIRU are accounted for.

Such differences in results have led to more concerted empirical work, involving more detailed cross country comparisons. Bean, Layard and Nickell (1986) report findings for the OECD economies drawn from a conference which has come to be known as Chelwood Gate I. The starting point for the conference was the broad New Keynesian framework of analysis, the aim being to apply a common modelling procedure to data for a variety of countries in the hope that such an approach would offer a useful means of isolating the key

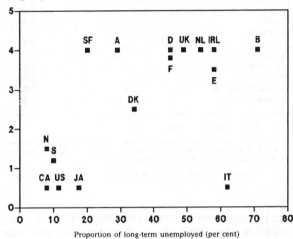

CHART 5.5

The duration of benefits
and the duration of unemployment, 1989

Source: Layard and Philpott (1991).
Note: Indefinite benefits have been treated as equivalent to 4 years duration.

factors in the story of rising unemployment. The quantitative results for a selection of countries are shown in table 5.8.

The table provides a breakdown of the change in unemployment between the periods 1955-1966 and 1980-1983 for a number of countries. The change is accounted for by change in aggregate demand and a number of supply side factors. The supply side factors require some comment. "Taxes" refer to those on incomes and profits, including employment taxes and social security payments. Together with import prices these provide the total "wedge" between the claims upon real output of firms and workers. "Search" is used in a rather loose (and somewhat confusing) way in this context since it refers to a variable included to account for shifts in the U/V curve.

As was argued above, while this shift can be attributed to increased (employee or employer) search unemployment it may also convey the effect of broader changes in the labour market, for example, of increased "mismatch". As Bean et al. are careful to point out, the "search" variable may therefore reflect a number of factors entirely unrelated to the search intensity of the unemployed. They stress the search element, however, since the broad consensus of opinion amongst economists is that mismatch and structural change in general has made little contribution to the rise in unemployment.

This latter conclusion often comes as a surprise since unemployment is commonly perceived as a consequence of changes in the structure of demand and/or

Breakdown of the change in unemployment, 1956-1966 to 1980-1983

(Percentage points)

	Taxes	Import prices	Search	Demand	Total	Actual
Australia	2.56	-0.03	2.44	-0.28	4.69	4.98
Belgium	1.41	-0.04	5.28	2.53	9.15	8.93
Canada	1.34	0.02	-	4.59	5.95	4.56
Denmark	-	-	-	5.40	5.40	7.56
France	0.46	-0.04	3.27	2.39	6.08	5.98
Germany [a]	-	-	3.68	-0.03	3.65	4.02
Netherlands	2.93	-1.38	-3.41	9.68	7.84	8.77
Sweden	1.70	0.12	-0.47	-0.49	0.85	1.04
United Kingdom	2.06	-0.05	2.25	5.33	9.60	8.33
United States	1.30	0.19	-	0.48	1.97	3.35

Source: Bean *et al.* (1986).

Note: Dashes indicate that restrictions were imposed on the estimated results for certain countries because of implausible coefficient signs in the unconstrained equations. For full details of this procedure see Bean, *op. cit.*. Obviously in trying to impose one empirical model across a host of OECD countries there will be many difficulties, so the results should be treated in a very tentative way.

a Data exclude the five new eastern *Länder*.

the introduction of new technology, which, it is argued, explains why unemployment is concentrated amongst the unskilled and in regions of traditional heavy industry. There is continuing controversy as to the importance of technological unemployment (see Driver (1987)) but while some economists (for example, Lilien (1982)) have argued that sectoral shifts have contributed strongly to higher unemployment since the 1970s, detailed econometric analysis has been unable to identify any such effect.

Layard and Nickell (1986), for example, estimate that structural change contributed less than one percentage point to the rise in unemployment in Britain between the late 1960s and the early 1980s. Similarly, a multi-country study by Jackman and Roper (1987) finds no evidence of an increase in the second half of the 1970s and the early 1980s. These findings should not, of course, be interpreted as indicating that mismatch or structural unemployment is not a serious problem which need not be confronted by policy makers. It simply means that the degree of mismatch does not appear to have worsened and thus cannot explain the *rise* in unemployment.

The results of Chelwood Gate I, in general, confirm the importance of demand influences on the rise in unemployment, especially in the European Community. In most countries, however, there is also a significant contribution from reduced search intensity and the higher tax burden. Import prices play a relatively small role overall although Bean et al. note that they had a significant impact in the immediate aftermath of OPEC-1 and OPEC-2 and the commodity price booms of the 1970s. On the basis of Chelwood Gate they answer the question "was the rise in unemployment in the OECD countries between the late 1960s and the early 1980s the result of supply or demand factors?" by stating that *"Our answer is that it is six of one and half a dozen of the other"*.

Significantly, the conference also concluded that by 1985 actual unemployment and NAIRU's were in most cases congruent, which was consistent with the relative

stability of inflation rates in many OECD countries. Thus, even though demand factors were found to be an important cause of the rise in unemployment, reflation was not considered a viable option for reducing unemployment. The broad policy thrust of Chelwood Gate I was thus in favour of supply side measures to act directly upon the NAIRU.

(viii) The role of labour market institutions

In view of the fact that bargaining over the real wage underpins the New Keynesian approach to analysing unemployment it is perhaps surprising that institutional factors do not figure in table 5.8. As it turns out, the main reason for this is a practical one: lack of appropriate data made the construction of a straightforward multi-country institutional variable difficult. The contribution for Britain by Layard and Nickell, however, did attempt to estimate the impact of union power or "industrial militancy" on wage pressure, and hence the NAIRU.

Layard and Nickell's estimates are based on changes in the union "mark-up" i.e., the percentage difference between the wages of unionized and non-unionized workers. From the mid-1950s to the mid-1960s the mark-up was fairly stable but rose steadily between 1968 and 1972. The impulse seems to have been the wave of political unrest and industrial militancy that swept several (mostly west European) countries following the Paris riots of 1968 (see also Bruno and Sachs (1986)). The mark-up was then stable until the mid-1970s before rising again in the early 1980s. Increases in the mark-up can be taken to reflect autonomous surges of wage pressure, with workers seeking to secure higher real wages at any given level of aggregate demand and unemployment. In terms of the earlier diagram (chart 5.4) this amounts to a rightward shift of the "target real wage" curve and thus a higher NAIRU, other things being equal.

Layard and Nickell find that union power did make a significant contribution to higher unemployment in

Britain but attribute to it only 2 percentage points of the total 10 percentage point increase in unemployment between 1967-1974 and 1980-1983. There are no comparable estimates available for other countries although the broad consensus of Chelwood Gate I was that institutional factors in general were an important influence on countries' experience of unemployment. In particular, wages seem to be more responsive to labour market disequilibrium and less responsive to tax and import price shocks in the economies that are more "corporatist" or where wage bargaining is more centralized or "co-ordinated": in general such economies appear more able to adjust quickly to change.

This idea emerges strongly from the work of Bruno and Sachs (1985) who combine it with the "wage gap" methodology as part of their comparative analysis of "stagflation". Bruno and Sachs define corporatism as "a mode of social organization in which functional groups rather than discrete individuals wield power and transact affairs". Various criteria may be used to classify the degree of corporatism in a country, ranging from the level of bargaining to the degree of influence national labour organizations wield over their memberships and the extent of organization of employers' associations. Defined in this way, non-EC western Europe and the Scandinavian countries tend to be corporatist while the United States is at the other extreme, with virtually no organized labour movement. Most of the European Community economies fall between the extremes, as does Japan. On this basis, Bruno and Sachs construct a ranking measure of corporatism and find it strongly related to change in what they call the "misery index" (the sum of the inflation and the unemployment rates) between 1965-1973 and 1973-1979.

Critics of this approach point to the qualitative and "judgmental" nature of variables of this kind, and point to a degree of circularity in definition (see Bean (1990)). For example, countries that co-ordinate bargaining successfully tend to be classified as corporatist while those that fail are not. In order to avoid this, Calmfors and Driffil (1988) focus on the formal structure of wage setting in various countries in order to determine their own ranking measure of "corporatism". They find a weaker link between their measure of corporatism and macro-economic performance than Bruno and Sachs and also suggest that the relationship between changes in unemployment and the institutional structure of the labour market is hump-shaped. Countries at either extreme of the corporatism ranking appear to perform better in terms of unemployment than countries in the middle.

Jackman (1990) in a study of the Nordic countries considers whether a key element of corporatism, co-ordinated wage bargaining, is an important reason for the lower unemployment rates of these countries compared with those of the European Community. He discovered some association between unemployment rates and the degree of co-ordinated bargaining but it is not clear that co-ordination is the key factor since differences between the labour markets of the Nordic countries and those of the European Community extend well beyond the characteristics of wage bargaining. For

TABLE 5.9

Regression to explain unemployment, 1983-1999
(Twenty countries)

	Regression coefficient		Standardized regression coefficient
Coverage................................	2.45	(2.4)	0.30
Union co-ordination..........................	-1.42	(2.0)	-0.22
Employer co-ordination......................	-4.28	(7.0)	-0.82
Benefit duration................................	0.92	(2.9)	0.31
Replacement ratio	0.17	(7.1)	0.68
Active labour market spending............	-0.13	(2.3)	-0.21
Change in inflation (1982-1988)...........	-0.35	(2.8)	-0.28
Constant...	0.24	(0.1)	..
Bar - R².	0.91	..	..
Standard error..................................	1.41	..	..
Mean of dependent variable...............	7.87	..	..
Standard error of dependent variable...	4.63	..	..

Source: Layard (1990b).

Note: T-statistics in brackets. Where benefits last indefinitely, the value of four years was assigned. In the equation with standardized regression coefficients, all variables are divided by their standard deviations.

example, although benefits are relatively generous in the Scandinavian countries they are available for only a relatively short period of time. Moreover, there is rather more widespread use of active supply side labour market policies in these countries (Jackman singles out in particular the substantial use of public sector employment programmes in Sweden).

An interesting recent study by Layard (1990a) attempts to explain variations in unemployment rates across 20 OECD countries (taking the average rate for the period 1983-1988) by reference to a variety of factors, including labour market institutions. The estimated regression equation to explain unemployment is shown in table 5.9, with the relevant data presented in table 5.10. Each of the variables is related to unemployment via its impact upon wage pressure, with the change in inflation also included in the regression since disinflation requires higher unemployment.

The institutional variables, coverage, union co-ordination and employer co-ordination, refer, respectively, to the fraction of workers in each country covered by collective bargaining, ranging from 1 (under 25 per cent) to 3 (over 75 per cent), and the degree to which unions and employers co-ordinate wage claims and offers ranging from 1 (decentralized) to 3 (centralized).

Greater union coverage tends to raise unemployment by making unions more powerful, but greater union co-ordination has the opposite effect. If, for example, unions adopt a single national claim for wage increases they will be more aware of the impact of claims upon the prices they will subsequently have to pay in the shops and this will instil a sense of moderation in wage aspirations. If, by contrast, union claims are unco-ordinated and decentralized, workers will be less aware of the wider consequences of the bargains they seek to strike. As Layard puts it — quoting former British Prime Minister Harold Wilson — under a decentralized system "*One* man's wage increase will be *another* man's price increase, and that will not cause him much loss of sleep."

TABLE 5.10

Unemployment, the treatment of the unemployed and collective bargaining in different countries

	Unemployment rate, 1983-1988 (per cent) (1)	Duration of benefit 1985 a (years) (2)	Replacement ratio 1985 b (per cent) (3)	"Active" Labour market policy c (per cent) (4)	Union coverage d (rank) (5)	Union co-ordination e (rank) (6)	Employer co-ordination f (rank) (7)	Change in inflation 1983-1988 (per cent) (8)
Belgium	11.3	*	60	7.4	3	2	2	-3.60
Denmark	9.0	2.5	90	7.9	3	3	3	-3.00
France	9.9	3.75	57	3.9	3	2	2	-6.50
Germany g	6.7	*	63	10.4	3	2	3	-1.70
Ireland	16.4	*	50	5.0	3	1	1	-7.60
Italy	7.0	0.5	2	0.8	3	2	1	-8.90
Netherlands	10.6	*	70	2.7	3	2	2	-0.10
Portugal	7.7	0.5	60	7.4	3	2	2	-12.70
Spain	19.8	3.5	80	2.1	3	2	1	-5.80
United Kingdom	10.7	*	36	4.6	3	1	1	1.40
Australia	8.4	*	39	2.8	3	2	1	1.10
New Zealand	4.6	*	38	13.1	3	2	1	1.40
Canada	9.9	0.5	60	4.3	2	1	1	-1.80
United States	7.1	0.5	50	2.4	1	1	1	-0.50
Japan	2.7	0.5	60	5.6	2	2	2	-0.30
Austria	3.6	*	60	11.3	3	3	3	-1.90
Finland	5.1	*	75	12.9	3	3	3	-1.60
Norway	2.7	0.5	65	9.8	3	3	3	-3.50
Sweden	2.2	1.2	80	34.6	3	3	3	-3.80
Switzerland	2.4	1.0	70	3.7	2	1	3	-0.30

Sources: Col (1): OECD standardized rates as available in OECD, *Quarterly Labour Force Statistics*, Paris, otherwise unstandardized, except for Italy (US Bureau of Labour Statistics figure) and Switzerland (registered unemployment x 3). Cols (2) and (3): Mainly US Department of Health and Human Services — Social Security Administration: *Social Security Programs Throughout the World 1985* (Research Report No.60). See also OECD, *Employment Outlook*, September 1988, tables 4.3 and 4.4. Col (4): OECD, *Employment Outlook*, September 1988, Table 3.1. Cols (5), (6), (7) and (8): Layard (1990c).

a   An asterisk (*) denotes that benefits are paid indefinitely.
b   The replacement ratios are those that apply during the period that insurance-based unemployment benefit is payable. The exact period varies according to the administrative rules of each country.
c   Expenditure on "active" labour market programmes in 1987 per person unemployed as a percentage of output per person.
d   Proportion of workers covered by collective bargaining arrangements, ranging from 1 (under 25 per cent), through 2 (25-75 per cent) to 3 (over 75 per cent).
e   Degree to which unions co-ordinate wage claims, both formally and informally, ranging from 1 (decentralized) to 3 (centralized).
f   Degree to which employers co-ordinate wage offers, formally and informally, ranging from 1 (decentralized) to 3 (centralized). Co-ordination here refers only to pay bargaining. In nearly all countries, employers can voluntarily pay more than the level of the highest bargain.
g   Data exclude the five new eastern *Länder*.

Similarly, if employers do not co-ordinate their wage offers and pursue only their individual self-interest, each will continually seek to "leapfrog" others to gain a competitive advantage in the effort to recruit and retain workers. If they act together, however, they recognize they cannot all improve their wages relative to one another and that competitive bidding-up of wages becomes pointless. By working against a build-up of wage pressure, this too serves to reduce the amount of unemployment necessary to contain inflation.

The next three variables in table 5.10 are the replacement ratio, the duration of benefits and active labour market policy. The replacement ratio was mentioned in section (iii) above where it was suggested that a higher replacement ratio would increase the amount of search unemployment, other things being equal. The average replacement ratio has risen in most countries since the late 1960s (see Burda (1988)) although in some, notably the United Kingdom, it has fallen in recent years. UK studies find an elasticity of unemployment with respect to benefit ranging from 0.7 (Layard and Nickell (1986)) to 4 (Minford (1983)), although the latter estimate is generally considered to be rather high. In addition to the replacement ratio, however, the duration of benefits is also important, since this will undoubtedly affect the level of job search activity of the unemployed.

Improvements in the replacement ratio and the duration of benefits can both be considered possible causes of the secular outward shift of the UV curve that was noted above for many countries. But their importance extends beyond this since they influence wage pressure. As mentioned earlier, benefits affect the perceptions of wage bargainers as to the risks associated with job losses that might result from their wage claims. Similarly, if benefits reduce search activity by the unemployed they will effectively serve to reduce the number of potential "competitors" for the jobs of those in work.

The final variable in the table, active labour market policy, refers to spending (per unemployed person as a percentage of output per head) on measures such as effective job placement and counselling, training, recruitment subsidies and direct job creation measures. Put simply, it can be viewed as a means of counteracting the shift in the UV curve and thereby reducing wage pressure (for more detailed evidence on this, see Jackman et al. (1990)).

As table 5.9 shows, Layard finds each of these variables to be statistically significant and together they account for 90 per cent of the variation in unemployment across the countries considered. A key feature is the relative importance of co-ordinated bargaining, especially employer co-ordination. The results are interesting when applied to the data for each country since they offer some (albeit rough) indication of the joint contribution of different factors to a country's unemployment experience which has often tended to be ignored by studies looking at factors, such as the degree of "corporatism", in isolation.

Sweden, for example, exhibits a high level of unionization and a high replacement ratio which in many other countries would suggest a tendency toward relatively high unemployment. Its co-ordinated and "solidary" bargaining institutions (albeit now under considerable strain) counteract this tendency, however, as does its adoption of the so-called "employment principle" i.e., strict limits on the duration of benefit coupled with very high expenditure on active labour market policy measures.

The United States, by contrast, spends little on active labour market policy and exhibits a highly decentralized system of wage bargaining. The reason why it has moderate rather than high unemployment almost certainly reflects very low union coverage, a relatively low replacement ratio and the fact that unemployment benefits normally last for no longer than six months.

The duration of benefits are also limited in Japan, where a moderate degree of unionization coexists with a moderate degree of wage co-ordination. In the case of Japan, however, the *degree* of co-ordination may be less significant than the *nature* of that co-ordination. Wage settlements are synchronized in April each year as part of the bargaining "ritual" known as the *Shunto*. This in itself tends to reduce any tendency toward "leapfrogging" in pay, but, in addition, the *Shunto* is preceded by an open and public discussion on the part of wage bargainers about the average level of wage increases that the economy can sustain (see Dore, (1987)). This process has operated since the 1950s and some commentators consider it crucial to the achievement of low unemployment in Japan (see for example, Robinson (1990) who argues that this is far more important than other features of the Japanese system, such as profit-related pay referred to earlier, in enabling that country to maintain unemployment at very low levels).

Most of the countries of the European Community exhibit the worst of all worlds: high levels of union coverage but (with the exception of Denmark) at best only modest levels of employer and union co-ordination. In most cases benefit lasts for a reasonably long time (in several cases indefinitely) and, with the exception of Germany, expenditure on active labour market policy is minimal. Non-EC European countries, by contrast, tend to spend more on such measures but significantly, although their benefit systems appear similar to those of EC countries, wage bargaining is conducted on a highly co-ordinated level. One should note, however, that two of the non-EC European countries, Switzerland and Austria, have to some extent "cheated" with regard to unemployment (see Rowthorn and Glynn (1987)).

Switzerland, for example, had one of the lowest rates of growth of GDP following OPEC-1 (0.3 per cent per annum between 1973 and 1985) and the proportion of its adult population in employment declined from 77 to 71 per cent. The reason why unemployment did not rise was that many of the workers who lost their jobs were foreign "guest workers" with temporary residence permits. Bargaining agreements stipulate that these are the first to be made redundant when labour market conditions deteriorate and the last to be hired when conditions improve. Moreover, on being fired they must leave the country if unable to find a new job quickly. The Swiss were thus able to "export" some of their unemployed. In addition, strong social pressures have caused many married women to "return to the home". Switzerland is the only major industrial country where there has not been a rise in female participation in the labour force since OPEC-1, and this has also acted against the rise in measured unemployment. Austria has also seen poor employment growth. Unemployment has remained low because of slow labour-force growth and Swiss-style "export of guest workers", although its highly centralized "corporatist" approach to economic management has clearly been important.

Results derived from statistical analysis of this kind are, of course, largely illustrative. They do not reveal the wider social, political and economic processes that give rise to a particular institutional context and, although this is a rather more controversial point, neither should they be taken to imply that a high unemployment country could simply "import" institutions and policies conducive to low unemployment. Attempts, for example, to instil features of the so-called "flexible" United States' labour market into countries of the European Community confront traditional industrial relations and social welfare institutions with which they rest uneasily. The experience of the United Kingdom in the 1980s indicates the very strong social and political tensions that can arise when such attempts are made, even though certain elements of the "flexibility experiment" (such as efforts to counter aspects of union power) have proved worthwhile.

These reservations aside, comparative analysis of the type just described none the less provides statistical backing for the views of those (such as Therborn (1986)) who locate the causes of international differences in unemployment in the mixture of attitudes and institutions which are either favourable or antipathetic to "full employment" as an attainable target.

(ix) 'Hysteresis' and the persistence of unemployment

In view of the earlier discussion, the fact that unemployment persisted at a high level in many countries throughout the first half of the 1990s could be attributed to the actions of governments to sustain unemployment below the NAIRU in an effort to reduce inflation. It is certainly true, for example, that the near doubling of unemployment in the European Community between 1980 and 1984 was accompanied by marked reductions in the rate of wage and price rises. However, the longer unemployment persisted the less did wages decrease and by the end of the 1980s, with average unemployment in the EC still at 10 per cent, inflation was rising once more. The story is broadly similar for the OECD countries as a whole.

This suggests that the rate of unemployment consistent with stable inflation increased in the 1980s and, indeed, estimates of the NAIRU show it to have increased in many countries along with actual unemployment throughout most of the decade. One possibility is that some or all of the underlying supply side determinants of the NAIRU were such as to cause it to increase. This seems rather implausible, however. Union power, for example, as measured by strike activity and union density has, as table 5.11 indicates, tended to decline in most OECD countries in the 1980s. Similarly, while factors such as higher oil prices following OPEC-1 and OPEC-2 undoubtedly contributed to rising unemployment, their impact soon began to wane and indeed by the mid-1980s oil prices were falling, which if anything should have served to reduce the NAIRU.

An alternative, and much discussed possibility, however, is that changes in aggregate demand do not simply cause unemployment to fluctuate around the NAIRU but instead induce changes in the NAIRU itself. This notion of equilibrium unemployment following or "tracking" actual unemployment has come to be termed "hysteresis" and, if accepted, has profound implications for the view one takes not only of the causes of unemployment but also solutions. The term became fashionable following the work of Blanchard and Summers (1986) and Lindbeck and Snower (1989), the former focusing particularly on the causes of persistent unemployment in the European Community. The central hypothesis of hysteresis was an important focal point for the Chelwood Gate II conference (see Blanchard (1988), also Blanchard and Diamond (1990)).

Two competing views of hysteresis are normally presented. The first, known as the "pure hysteresis" view, implies that there is no unique NAIRU at all; changes in aggregate demand cause actual unemployment to change and, after a time, the equilibrium rate consistent with stable inflation as well. The second view retains the notion of a long-run NAIRU but concludes that economic processes associated with changes in aggregate demand may cause the economy to settle temporarily at a short- or medium-run NAIRU before adjusting gradually (or being helped to adjust) toward long-run equilibrium.

The essential implication of pure hysteresis is that demand management can, with a time lag, be used to secure any level of equilibrium unemployment that is desired. This is in sharp contrast to both the monetarist/New Classical view of the relative impotence of government with regard to its affect upon the "natural rate of unemployment" and the rather cautious, standard New Keynesian view (such as emerged from Chelwood Gate I) that governments should use supply side measures to reduce unemployment unless it is obvious that the actual rate is above the NAIRU. Not surprisingly, debate (mostly at an academic level) as to the validity of the pure hysteresis

TABLE 5.11

Strikes and union membership in four west European countries

(a) Strikes

(Working days lost per annum per 100 employees in industry)

	1967-1971	1977-1980	1981-1983
France	350	25	19
Germany [a]	8	10	..
Italy	161	165	147
United Kingdom	60	132	37

(b) Union membership

(Percentage of non-agricultural wage and salaried employees)

	1970	1979	1984-1985
France	22	28	28
Germany [a]	37	42	42
Italy	39	51	45
United Kingdom	51	58	52

Source: Carlin and Soskice (1990).

[a] Data excludes the five new eastern *Länder*.

view is intense. A sense of the debate is conveyed by Blanchard (1988) and Cross (1987).

The details of the debate are not reviewed here, although it can be said that many economists hold the view that at least some form of partial hysteresis underlies the persistence of unemployment in the 1980s, especially in Europe. Even those who accept this, however, differ as to the actual mechanisms at work. There are three commonly presented (although by no means mutually exclusive) accounts of the cause of hysteresis and unemployment persistence.

The first is the so-called "insider-outsider" theory, discussed by Blanchard and Summers (1987) and in some depth by Lindbeck and Snower (1989). The theory is most commonly associated with the "pure hysteresis" view. "Insiders" are those existing employees with firm-specific skills and therefore non-comparable with unemployed "outsiders". Firms are not willing to lay off insiders since outsiders will be of little use to them until they have been trained, which is of course costly to the firm. Similarly, firms will be eager to retain insiders in order to ensure that they reap a reward for previous investment in training (the basic notion here is akin to that of the seminal work of Oi (1962) and Becker (1964)). This offers insiders a degree of power over employers.

The "insider-outsider effect" is said to arise because, when bargaining over their real wage, insiders will seek to exact from employers the highest wage they can without placing their jobs at risk and will not moderate claims so as to create more jobs for outsiders. The significance of this is that, when unemployment rises, although it has some initial impact upon wage claims, the effect will diminish once the rise in unemployment tails off at a new, higher level because those insiders who retain their jobs will not moderate their bargaining behaviour simply in order to encourage employers to hire unemployed people. In the absence of any further change, the higher level of unemployment thus has no subsequent effect upon wage setting and the economy settles at a higher equilibrium rate of unemployment.

A second account of hysteresis concentrates (in the terminology of the preceding paragraphs) not on the insiders but on those outsiders who are long-term unemployed. The argument here, presented strongly by Layard and Nickell (1987) and Jackman et al. (1991) is that the long-term unemployed exert little influence upon wage bargaining (see also Philpott, 1990). Several factors are normally cited.

First, the intensity with which unemployed people search for work tends to diminish the longer they are unemployed (see Hughes and McCormick (1989)). They are not therefore likely to be "beating at the gates of factories" looking for work and those in employment will not consider them competitors for their jobs. Secondly, so-called "duration dependence" effects mean that the long-term unemployed will in effect drop out of the active labour market even if formally "unemployed". They may develop psychological problems and/or suffer loss of previous skills and competences. Moreover, employers may believe that the long-term unemployed will prove inferior simply because of the negative signal which a long period without work conveys (see Metcalf and Meager (1987) for British evidence). In general, it appears that the probability of being hired diminishes the longer a person has been unemployed because employers will prefer to hire people who have only recently entered unemployment. The usual metaphor is of blooms in the flower shop: on their first day in the shop, new blooms are most attractive to customers, but, if they remain on the shelf unsold, they will be less attractive than the next day's bloom and thus less likely to be bought.

For all these reasons, those in employment will be unlikely to moderate wage claims simply because there exists a large pool of long-term unemployed. As one leading British economist has commented, it is almost as though Britain's long-term unemployed had been transported to Australia as far as wage bargainers are concerned (Davies (1986)). Layard and Nickell (1986 and 1987) provide econometric evidence to suggest that wage pressure increases the higher the proportion of long-term unemployment, concluding that although there is a relationship between unemployment, wage pressure and price inflation it is only *short-term* unemployment that is relevant to this.

According to this account, the steep rise in long-term unemployment that occurred in the 1980s, particularly in European Community countries, may therefore explain why inflation eventually became less responsive to unemployment and equilibrium unemployment appeared to rise. Layard (1986 and 1990), Clark and Layard (1989) and Layard and Philpott (1990) attribute this rise in long-term unemployment in large measure to the benefit systems prevailing in most

EC countries. That a strong association exists is clear from chart 5.5.

As noted earlier in section (viii), it is common in European Community countries for financial assistance to be provided indefinitely to unemployed people after any insurance-based unemployment benefit has been exhausted. Moreover, especially in the early 1980s, relatively little effort was made by public unemployment agencies to ensure that recipients of benefit were actively seeking work. As a result a "culture of unemployment" was able to develop in the wake of the shock-induced rise in unemployment of the late 1970s and early 1980s, with the result that long-term unemployment soared.

Layard cites the "culture of unemployment" as a major cause of the outward shift of the U/V curve (see also Budd, Levine and Smith (1988)), and contrasts the experience of EC countries with that of Sweden where no such shift was observed. As we have seen, the Swedes place strict limits on the availability of benefits and ensure that training and employment placements are guaranteed as of right to those unemployed for more than a year. It should be noted, however, that several EC countries have made more strenuous efforts in recent years to raise the job search activity of the long-term unemployed (OECD 1988 and 1990, PACEC 1990). A good example has been Britain's Restart programme which was a major contributory factor to the sharp fall in unemployment in Britain between 1986 and 1989 and helps to explain the inward shift in that country's U/V curve since 1986 (see Philpott (1990a and 1990b)).

Finally, and perhaps rather more intuitively, hysteresis may be due to reductions in productive capacity and hence increased capacity utilization induced by reductions in aggregate demand. Such reductions will tend to lead to lower investment and an eventual rundown of the capital stock and raise capital utilization even at relatively low levels of economic activity. Since there is greater pressure to increase prices when firms are operating at close to capacity, any deflationary effect associated with high unemployment of labour resources will diminish as capacity utilization increases. The level of unemployment associated with stable inflation will thus be seen to rise.

(x) Conclusion

This paper has reviewed various competing explanations of the rise in unemployment since the mid-1970s in the developed market economies. Few economists would disagree with the assertions that factors affecting both labour demand and supply have been important, and that the precise impact of these factors has depended crucially on the structure of labour markets and labour market institutions in different countries.

There is of course disagreement on the precise role and relative importance of specific factors and, as has been shown, economists in recent years have questioned the degree to which a notion of equilibrium unemployment should influence the approach of policy makers to the problem.

The purpose of this paper has not been to offer detailed policy recommendations for combating unemployment. It would, however, seem reasonable to draw three broad policy conclusions.

First, governments should seek to encourage employers and unions to develop co-ordinated wage bargaining procedures (which, as is clear from countries where such procedures exist, *does not* require governments to implement an "incomes policy").

Secondly, the state should ensure that systems of providing financial benefits to unemployed people do not encourage the growth of long-term unemployment.

Thirdly, they should place ever greater emphasis upon active labour market policy measures, notably the provision of high quality placement services and training.

The OECD (1990) has recently recommended the second and third of these policies. The Organization recognizes that a shift toward active labour market policy would place no additional financial burden on the public sector so long as active support measures were used as an alternative to long-run financial support for the unemployed.

In combination, the three policies outlined above would make a substantial contribution to the attainment of full employment throughout the market economies during the 1990s.

References

H. Armstrong and J. Taylor, *Regional Economics and Policy*, Philip Allan, London (1985).

_____, *Regional Policy and the North-South Divide*, Employment Institute: London (1988).

C. Bean, R. Layard and S. Nickell, *The Rise in Unemployment*, Basil Blackwell: Oxford (1986).

C. Bean, *European Unemployment: A Survey*, Centre for Economic Performance, London School of Economics, Working Paper No.35, August 1990.

G. Becker, *Human Capital*, NBER: New York (1964), second edition 1975.

O. Blanchard, *Getting the Questions Right − and Some of the Answers*, Massachusets Institute of Technology, mimeograph (1988).

O. Blanchard and L. Summers, *Hysteresis and the European Unemployment Problem*, R. Cross (ed.) (1987).

O. Blanchard and N. Kiyotaki, "Monopolistic competition and the effects of aggregate demand", *American Economic Review*, vol.77, (1987), pp.647-666.

O. Blanchard and S. Fischer, *Lectures on Macroeconomics*, MIT Press: Cambridge Mass (1987).

O. Blanchard and P. Diamond, *Unemployment and Wages: What have we Learned from the European Experience*, Employment Institute: London (1990).

M. Bruno and J. Sachs, *The Economics of Worldwide Stagflation*, Basil Blackwell: Oxford (1985).

M. Bruno, *Aggregate Supply and Demand Factors in OECD Unemployment: An Update*, Bean et al. (1986).

A. Budd, P. Levine and P. Smith, "Unemployment, Vacancies and the Long-Term Unemployed", *Economic Journal*, Vol.98, No.393 (1988).

M. Burda, "Wait Unemployment in Europe", *Economic Policy*, October 1988, pp.391-426.

W. Carlin and D. Soskice, *Macro-economics and the Wage Bargain*, Oxford University Press: Oxford (1990).

L. Calmfors and J. Driffil, "Bargaining Structure, Corporatism and Macro-economic Performance", *Economic Policy*, April 1988, pp.64-80.

D. Coe, "Nominal Wages, the NAIRU and Wages Flexibility", *OECD Economic Studies*, (1985), vol.5, pp.87-126.

R. Cross (ed.), *Unemployment, Hysteresis and the Natural Rate of Hypothesis*, Basil Blackwell: Oxford (1987).

G. Davies, *Government's Can Affect Unemployment*, Employment Institute: London (1986).

R. Disney, L Bellman, A. Carruth, W. Franz, R. Jackman, R. Layard, H. Lehman, J. Philpott, *Helping the Unemployed: Active Labour Market Policy in Britain and Germany*, Anglo-German Foundation (1991), forthcoming.

R. Dore, *Taking Japan Seriously*, Stanford University Press: New York (1987).

C. Driver, *Towards Full Employment*, Routledge and Kegan Paul: London (1987).

M. Friedman, "The Role of Monetary Policy", *American Economic Review 58*, (1968), pp.1-17.

D. Grubb, R. Jackman and R. Layard, "Causes of the Current Stagflation", *Review of Economic Studies*, (1982), vol.49, No.5, pp.707-730.

G. Hughes and B. McCormick, *Hidden Unemployment and Suppressed Labour Monopoly in the British Labour Market*, University of Southampton, mimeograph, (1989).

F. Hyclaek and G. Johnes, "Real Wage Rigidity in Regional Labour Markets in the United Kingdom, the United States and West Germany", *Journal of Regional Science*, Vol.29, (1989), pp.423-432.

R. Jackman, "Wage Formation in the Nordic Countries Viewed from the International Perspective", L. Calmfors (ed.), *Wage Formation in the Nordic Countries* (1990). SNS: Stockholm.

R. Jackman, R. Layard and S. Nickell, *Unemployment*. (forthcoming 1991, publisher undecided).

R. Jackman and S. Roper, "Structural Unemployment", *Oxford Bulletin of Economics and Statistics*, Special Issue on Wage Determination and Labour Market Flexibility (1987).

R. Jackman, C. Pissarides and S. Savouri, *Labour Market Policies and Unemployment in the OECD*, Centre for Economic Performance, London School of Economics (1990), Working Paper No.1210.

G. Johnson and R. Layard, "The Natural Rate of Unemployment: Explanation and Policy", O. Ashenfelter and R. Layard (eds.), *Handbook of Labour Economics* (1986), vol.2, North Holland: Amsterdam.

R. Layard, *How to Beat Unemployment*, Oxford University Press: Oxford (1986).

_____, *Wage Bargaining and Incomes Policy: Possible Lessons for Eastern Europe*, Centre for Economic Performance, London School of Economics (1990a), Discussion Paper No.2.

_____, *Understanding Unemployment*, Centre for Economic Performance, London School of Economics (1990b), Discussion Paper No.4.

_____, *Problems of European Labour Markets*, Centre for Economic Performance, London School of Economics (1990c), Working Paper No.45.

R. Layard and A. Clark, *UK Unemployment*, Heinemann Educational: London (1989).

R. Layard and J. Philpott, *Full Employment*, Center for Economic Performance and Employment Institute, mimeograph (1990).

R. Layard and S. Nickell, *The Causes of British Unemployment*, National Institute of Economic and Social Research (1985). NIESR: London.

_____, "Unemployment in Britain", Bean et al. (1986).

_____, "The Labour Market", R. Dornbusch and R. Layard, *The Performance of the British Economy*. Clarendon Press: Oxford (1987).

R. Layard, G. Basevi, O. Blanchard, W. Buiter and R. Dornbusch, "Europe: the Case for Unsustainable Growth", R. Layard (ed.), *Restoring Europe's Prosperity*. MIT Press, Cambridge: Mass (1989).

D. Lilien, "Sectoral Shifts and Cyclical Unemployment", *Journal of Political Economy* (1982), vol.90, pp.777-793.

A. Lindbeck and D. Snower, "The Insider-Outsider Theory", MIT Press, Cambridge: Mass (1989).

E. Malinvaud, *The Theory of Unemployment Reconsidered*, Basil Blackwell: Oxford (1977).

J. Meade, *Stagflation: vol.1, Wage-Fixing*, George Allen and Unwin: London (1982).

N. Meager and M. Metcalf, *Recruitment of the Long-Term Unemployed*, Institute of Manpower Studies, University of Sussex, Report 138, September 1987.

P. Minford, *Unemployment: Cause and Cure*, Basil Blackwell: Oxford (1983).

_____, "Corporatism, the Natural Rate and Productivity", J. Philpott (ed.) *Trade Unions in the Economy: Into the 1990s*. Employment Institute: London (1989).

S. Nickell, "Unemployment: A Survey", *Economic Journal 100*, June 1990, pp.391-329.

OECD, *Measures to Assist the Long-Term Unemployed*, Paris (1988).

____, *Labour Market Policies for the 1990s*, Paris (1990).

W. Oi, "Labour as a Quasi Fixed Factor", *Journal of Political Economy*, (1962), vol.70, pp.538-555.

PACEC, *Measures in Favour of the Long-Term Unemployed in the European Community*, PA Cambridge Economic Consultants for Commission for the European Communities, ERGO Programme (1990).

E. Phelps, "Money-Wage Dynamics and Labour Market Disequilibrium", E. Phelps (ed.) *Micro-economic Foundations of Employment and Inflation Theory*. W.W. Norton: New York (1970).

J. Philpott, *The Effects of Labour Policies to Assist the Adult Unemployed: An Appraisal of British Evidence*, Employment Institute, mimeograph (1990a).

_____, *A Solution to Long-Term Unemployment: the Job Guarantee*, Employment Institute: London (1990b).

P. Robinson, *Full Employment in the 1990s*, Gower: Avebury (1990).

R. Rowthorn, "Conflict, Inflation and Money", *Cambridge Journal of Economics*, (1977), vol I, pp.215-239.

R. Rowthorn and A. Glynn, *The Diversity of Unemployment Experience since 1973*, University of Oxford, Applied Economics Discussion Paper No.40, November 1987.

R. Solow, "Unemployment: Getting the Questions Right", Bean et al. (1986).

G. Therborn, *Why Some Peoples are More Unemployed than Others*, Verso Books: London (1986).

STATISTICAL APPENDICES

INTRODUCTORY NOTE

For the user's convenience, as well as to lighten the text, the *Economic Survey of Europe* includes a set of appendix tables showing annual changes in main economic indicators over a longer period (1970-1990). The data are presented in three sections, following the structure of the text: *Appendix A* provides macro-economic indicators for the market economies of western Europe and North America, *Appendix B* does the same for the east European transition economies and the Soviet Union, and *Appendix C* collates time series on world trade and the development of foreign trade of the ECE economies.

Except where otherwise stated, time series reflect levels or changes in *real* terms, i.e., at constant prices in case of series measured in value terms.

Data were compiled from international (United Nations, OECD, CMEA) or national statistical sources, as indicated in the notes to individual tables.

Regional aggregations are ECE secretariat calculations, based on 1985 US dollar weights in the case of the market economies and on CMEA estimates of relative per capita levels in the case of the CMEA economies.

All figures for 1990 are preliminary estimates, based on data available in the first weeks of March 1991.

Appendix A. Western Europe and North America

Data for this section were compiled from national and international [1] statistical sources, as indicated in the notes to individual tables. Volume figures underlying the data in tables A.1-A.6 reflect data at constant prices of the following years: Greece (1970), Yugoslavia (1972), Denmark, France, Germany, Italy, Netherlands, Norway, Spain, Switzerland (1980); Turkey, United States (1982); Austria (1983), Belgium, Finland, Ireland, Portugal, Sweden, United Kingdom (1985); Canada (1986). Regional data in tables A.1-A.6, A.8 were aggregated from index series at 1985 US dollar exchange rates. Country data in tables A.9-A.10 reflect percentage changes expressed in national currencies.

---

[1]   UN, OECD, EUROSTAT, IMF.

APPENDIX TABLE A.1

Gross domestic product

(Annual percentage change)

	1970	1971	1972	1973	1974	1975	1976	1977	1978	1979	1980	1981	1982	1983	1984	1985	1986	1987	1988	1989	1990
France	5.7	4.8	4.4	5.4	3.1	-0.3	4.2	3.2	3.4	3.2	1.6	1.2	2.5	0.7	1.3	1.9	2.5	2.2	3.9	3.7	2.6
Germany, Fed. Rep. of	5.1	2.9	4.2	4.7	0.3	-1.6	5.4	3.0	2.9	4.2	1.4	0.2	-0.6	1.5	2.8	2.0	2.3	1.7	3.7	3.3	4.7
Italy	5.3	1.6	2.7	7.1	5.4	-2.7	6.6	3.4	3.7	6.0	4.2	1.0	0.3	1.1	3.0	2.6	2.5	3.0	4.2	3.2	2.5
United Kingdom [a]	1.8	1.4	3.0	5.9	-1.5	-1.9	2.0	2.8	3.4	3.0	-2.9	-1.0	2.0	3.3	2.8	3.4	3.2	4.3	4.3	2.2	0.9
Total 4 countries	4.6	2.8	3.7	5.7	1.7	-1.5	4.6	3.1	3.3	4.0	1.1	0.3	1.0	1.6	2.5	2.4	2.6	2.7	4.0	3.1	2.8
Austria	7.1	5.1	6.2	4.9	3.9	-0.4	4.6	4.5	0.1	4.7	2.9	-0.3	1.1	2.0	1.4	2.5	1.2	2.0	3.9	4.0	4.5
Belgium	6.4	3.7	5.4	6.0	4.2	-1.4	5.7	0.6	2.9	2.2	4.2	-0.9	1.5	0.4	2.0	0.8	1.6	2.3	4.6	4.0	3.9
Denmark	2.0	2.7	5.3	3.6	-0.9	-0.7	6.5	1.6	1.5	3.5	-0.4	-0.9	3.0	2.5	4.4	4.3	3.6	0.3	0.5	1.2	1.0
Finland	7.5	2.1	7.6	6.7	3.0	1.2	0.3	0.1	2.2	7.3	5.3	1.6	3.6	3.0	3.1	3.3	2.1	4.0	5.4	5.2	0.3
Ireland	3.5	3.4	6.4	4.7	4.3	3.7	1.4	8.2	7.2	3.1	3.1	3.3	2.3	-0.2	4.4	2.5	-0.4	4.4	3.9	5.9	4.7
Netherlands	5.7	4.2	3.3	4.7	4.0	-0.1	5.1	3.6	2.5	2.4	0.9	-0.7	-1.4	1.4	3.1	2.7	0.8	0.8	2.7	4.0	3.2
Norway	2.0	4.6	5.2	4.1	5.2	4.2	6.8	3.6	4.5	5.1	4.2	0.9	0.3	4.6	5.7	5.4	4.2	2.0	0.1	1.2	1.8
Sweden	6.5	0.9	2.3	4.0	3.2	2.6	1.1	-1.6	1.8	3.8	1.7	-	1.1	1.8	4.0	2.2	2.2	2.8	2.3	2.1	1.1
Switzerland	6.4	4.1	3.2	3.0	1.5	-7.3	-1.4	2.4	0.4	2.5	4.6	1.5	-0.9	1.0	1.8	3.7	2.9	2.0	2.9	3.5	2.7
Total 9 countries	5.6	3.4	4.3	4.5	3.0	-0.6	3.3	1.7	2.0	3.5	2.7	0.1	0.7	1.8	3.1	2.9	2.3	2.0	2.9	3.3	2.5
Total western Europe	4.8	2.9	3.8	5.4	2.0	-1.3	4.3	2.7	3.0	3.9	1.5	0.3	0.9	1.7	2.6	2.5	2.5	2.5	3.7	3.2	2.8
Greece	8.0	7.1	8.9	7.3	-3.6	6.1	6.4	3.4	6.7	3.7	1.8	0.1	0.4	0.4	2.8	3.1	0.8	-0.1	4.1	2.8	1.2
Portugal	9.1	6.6	8.0	11.2	1.1	-4.3	6.9	5.6	2.8	5.6	4.6	1.6	2.1	-0.2	-1.9	2.8	4.1	5.3	3.9	5.4	3.9
Spain	4.1	5.0	8.1	7.9	5.7	1.1	3.0	3.3	1.8	0.2	1.5	-0.2	1.2	1.8	1.8	2.3	3.3	5.5	5.2	5.0	3.5
Turkey	4.9	9.1	6.4	4.4	8.5	7.5	8.7	4.3	2.8	-0.9	-0.7	4.4	5.0	3.7	5.7	5.1	8.3	7.4	3.6	1.6	9.0
Yugoslavia [b]	5.6	8.1	4.2	5.0	8.5	3.6	3.9	8.0	6.9	7.0	2.2	1.5	0.7	-1.2	2.0	0.5	3.6	-1.1	-1.7	0.6	-7.6
Total southern Europe	5.1	6.2	7.5	7.2	5.1	2.4	4.5	4.2	3.2	1.7	1.5	0.8	1.7	1.4	2.3	2.6	4.0	4.4	3.8	3.6	3.0
Total Europe	4.9	3.3	4.2	5.6	2.3	-0.9	4.3	2.9	3.0	3.7	1.5	0.3	1.0	1.6	2.6	2.6	2.7	2.7	3.7	3.2	2.8
United States	-0.3	2.7	4.9	4.9	-0.7	-1.0	4.8	4.6	5.2	2.1	-0.2	2.0	-2.5	3.7	7.0	3.6	2.9	3.6	4.4	2.5	0.9
Canada	2.6	5.8	5.7	7.7	4.4	2.6	6.2	3.6	4.6	3.9	1.5	3.7	-3.2	3.2	6.3	4.8	3.3	4.0	4.4	3.0	1.1
North America	-0.1	2.9	5.0	5.1	-0.3	-0.8	4.9	4.5	5.1	2.2	-	2.1	-2.5	3.7	6.9	3.7	3.0	3.6	4.4	2.5	1.0
Total above	1.9	3.1	4.7	5.3	0.8	-0.8	4.7	3.8	4.3	2.8	0.6	1.4	-1.1	2.8	5.2	3.2	2.9	3.3	4.1	2.8	1.7

Sources: National statistics.

[a] Output measure at factor cost.
[b] Gross material product.

APPENDIX TABLE A.2

Private consumption
(*Annual percentage change*)

	1970	1971	1972	1973	1974	1975	1976	1977	1978	1979	1980	1981	1982	1983	1984	1985	1986	1987	1988	1989	1990
France	4.3	4.9	4.9	5.3	1.2	2.8	4.9	2.7	3.7	3.0	1.2	2.1	3.5	0.9	1.1	2.4	3.9	2.7	3.2	3.1	2.9
Germany, Fed.Rep. of	7.6	5.2	4.5	3.1	0.7	3.2	3.7	4.3	3.8	3.6	1.2	-0.5	-1.3	1.7	1.5	1.4	3.4	3.3	2.7	1.7	4.4
Italy	8.4	3.5	3.7	6.9	3.7	0.3	5.2	4.1	3.4	7.3	5.6	1.4	1.3	0.6	2.1	3.1	3.8	4.2	4.1	3.8	2.7
United Kingdom	2.8	3.1	6.1	5.1	-1.5	-0.5	0.3	-0.5	5.6	4.2	-	1.1	1.0	4.6	1.6	3.5	6.3	5.2	6.9	3.9	2.5
Total 4 countries	5.6	4.3	4.8	4.9	0.9	1.6	3.5	2.7	4.1	4.3	1.9	0.9	1.0	1.9	1.6	2.5	4.3	3.8	4.1	3.0	3.2
Austria	4.2	6.7	6.1	5.4	3.0	3.2	4.5	5.4	-1.5	4.4	1.5	0.3	1.2	5.0	-0.1	2.4	1.8	2.9	3.1	3.2	4.3
Belgium	4.4	4.7	6.2	7.8	2.7	0.6	4.9	2.4	2.5	4.8	1.9	-0.9	1.4	-1.6	1.1	2.0	2.6	3.1	2.8	3.8	4.0
Denmark	3.5	-0.8	1.7	4.8	-2.9	3.7	7.9	1.1	0.7	1.4	-3.7	-2.3	1.4	2.6	3.4	5.0	5.7	-1.5	-0.8	-0.8	0.7
Finland	7.6	1.7	8.4	5.9	1.8	3.1	0.9	-1.2	2.5	5.5	2.0	1.2	4.7	2.6	2.7	3.2	4.1	5.7	5.0	3.9	0.4
Ireland	2.9	3.2	5.1	7.2	1.6	-2.7	2.8	6.8	9.1	4.4	0.4	1.7	-7.1	0.9	2.0	3.5	2.0	2.2	2.4	5.2	3.2
Netherlands	7.4	3.3	3.5	4.0	3.7	3.3	5.3	4.6	4.3	3.0	-	-2.5	-1.2	0.9	0.9	2.5	2.7	3.5	1.3	5.2	4.0
Norway	-	4.6	2.9	2.9	3.9	5.1	6.1	6.9	-1.6	3.2	2.3	1.1	1.8	1.5	2.7	10.4	5.6	-1.0	-2.5	-1.9	3.1
Sweden	3.5	0.1	3.4	2.6	3.4	2.8	4.2	-1.0	-0.7	2.4	-0.8	-0.5	0.7	-2.2	1.7	2.8	5.2	4.6	2.5	1.1	0.6
Switzerland	5.4	4.8	5.4	2.8	-0.5	-2.9	1.1	3.0	2.2	1.3	2.6	0.4	-	1.7	1.6	1.4	2.8	2.1	2.1	2.1	2.0
Total 9 countries	4.8	3.1	4.6	4.5	2.0	1.8	4.2	2.7	1.7	3.1	0.7	-0.6	0.5	0.9	1.5	3.2	3.5	2.7	1.9	2.1	2.6
Total western Europe	5.4	4.0	4.8	4.8	1.1	1.7	3.7	2.7	3.5	4.0	1.6	0.6	0.9	1.7	1.6	2.7	4.1	3.5	3.6	2.8	3.0
Greece	8.8	5.6	7.0	7.6	0.7	5.5	5.3	4.6	5.7	2.6	0.2	2.0	3.9	0.3	1.7	3.9	0.3	0.9	3.4	3.9	2.1
Portugal	2.6	12.7	4.0	12.0	9.7	-0.9	3.5	0.6	-2.0	-	3.7	2.9	2.4	-1.4	-2.9	0.7	5.6	5.4	6.6	3.1	4.5
Spain	4.2	4.9	8.3	8.0	5.2	2.4	4.7	2.5	1.3	1.2	1.3	-0.6	0.2	0.3	-0.4	2.4	3.6	5.4	5.5	5.9	3.7
Turkey	2.2	13.5	6.4	0.2	9.0	7.7	10.1	6.7	-3.9	-3.1	-5.2	0.6	4.2	5.0	6.8	1.3	11.5	6.5	2.6	3.7	11.0
Yugoslavia	14.6	8.3	4.6	2.7	7.3	3.4	4.4	7.0	7.0	5.6	0.7	-1.0	-0.1	-1.7	-1.0	-	4.5	0.3	-1.3	1.0	2.5
Total southern Europe	5.2	7.4	7.1	6.3	5.9	3.5	5.6	3.8	1.1	0.9	0.1	0.1	1.4	0.8	0.9	2.0	5.0	4.6	4.1	4.6	5.0
Total Europe	5.4	4.3	5.0	5.0	1.7	1.9	3.9	2.9	3.2	3.7	1.4	0.5	1.0	1.6	1.5	2.6	4.2	3.7	3.7	3.0	3.3
United States	2.4	3.1	5.4	4.2	-0.9	2.3	5.4	4.4	4.1	2.2	-0.2	1.2	1.3	4.6	4.8	4.7	3.9	2.8	3.6	1.9	1.0
Canada	2.0	5.9	7.5	7.5	5.8	4.7	6.5	3.2	3.4	2.9	2.2	2.3	-2.6	3.4	4.6	5.2	4.4	4.5	4.3	3.8	1.4
North America	2.4	3.3	5.5	4.4	-0.5	2.4	5.5	4.3	4.0	2.3	-	1.3	1.0	4.6	4.8	4.7	3.9	3.0	3.7	2.1	1.0
Total above	3.6	3.7	5.3	4.6	0.4	2.2	4.8	3.7	3.7	2.8	0.6	1.0	1.0	3.3	3.5	3.9	4.0	3.2	3.7	2.4	1.9

Sources: National statistics.

APPENDIX TABLE A.3

Public consumption

(Annual percentage change)

	1970	1971	1972	1973	1974	1975	1976	1977	1978	1979	1980	1981	1982	1983	1984	1985	1986	1987	1988	1989	1990
France	4.2	3.9	3.5	3.4	1.2	4.4	4.2	2.4	5.2	3.0	2.5	3.1	3.8	2.1	1.2	2.3	1.7	2.8	2.9	1.5	2.4
Germany, Fed.Rep, of	4.4	5.1	4.2	5.0	4.0	3.7	1.5	1.4	3.8	3.4	2.6	1.8	-0.8	0.2	2.4	2.1	2.6	1.6	2.3	-0.9	2.9
Italy	4.4	5.2	5.1	2.6	2.5	2.5	2.3	2.8	3.5	3.0	2.1	2.7	2.9	2.9	2.5	3.5	2.9	3.7	2.8	0.5	1.0
United Kingdom	1.7	2.9	4.2	4.3	1.9	5.6	1.2	-1.7	2.3	2.2	1.6	0.2	0.8	2.0	0.9	-	1.8	1.3	0.5	0.7	1.5
Total 4 countries	3.6	4.3	4.2	4.0	2.5	4.2	2.2	1.0	3.7	2.9	2.2	1.9	1.4	1.6	1.7	1.9	2.2	2.2	2.1	0.4	2.1
Austria	3.3	3.3	4.1	3.0	5.7	4.0	4.3	3.3	3.3	3.0	2.7	2.2	2.3	2.2	0.2	1.9	1.7	0.4	0.3	0.6	1.0
Belgium	3.3	5.9	5.9	5.3	3.8	4.7	4.0	2.7	5.9	2.7	1.6	0.3	-1.6	-	0.1	2.4	1.8	0.8	-0.4	-0.7	-
Denmark	6.9	5.5	5.7	4.0	3.5	2.0	4.5	2.4	6.2	5.9	4.3	2.6	3.1	3.7	-0.4	2.5	0.5	2.5	0.2	-1.3	-0.3
Finland	5.4	5.8	7.8	5.6	4.5	6.9	5.7	4.2	4.1	3.8	4.2	4.3	3.5	-0.4	2.8	5.2	3.1	4.5	2.4	2.9	3.6
Ireland	7.5	8.7	7.5	6.7	7.6	6.5	2.6	2.1	7.9	4.6	7.1	0.3	3.2	1.2	-0.7	1.8	2.5	-4.9	-4.2	-3.5	1.0
Netherlands	6.0	4.4	0.8	0.8	2.2	4.1	4.1	3.4	3.9	2.8	0.6	2.0	0.7	4.6	-0.7	1.4	2.0	2.4	0.4	-	0.5
Norway	6.3	6.0	4.5	5.5	4.0	6.4	7.4	4.9	5.3	3.5	5.4	6.1	3.9	0.8	2.4	3.4	2.2	4.0	0.5	2.5	1.9
Sweden	8.1	2.2	2.4	2.6	3.1	4.7	3.5	3.0	3.3	4.7	2.2	2.3	1.0	0.8	2.3	2.4	1.4	1.0	0.6	2.2	1.7
Switzerland	4.8	5.8	2.9	2.4	1.6	0.7	2.7	0.5	2.0	1.1	0.9	2.5	1.1	3.9	1.2	3.3	3.7	1.8	4.3	2.4	2.0
Total 9 countries	5.9	4.5	3.7	3.3	3.4	4.1	4.2	2.9	4.2	3.6	2.5	2.4	1.5	1.6	0.9	2.6	1.9	1.8	0.8	0.9	1.3
Total western Europe	4.1	4.3	4.1	3.8	2.7	4.1	2.7	1.5	3.8	3.1	2.3	2.0	1.4	1.6	1.5	2.1	2.2	2.1	1.8	0.5	1.9
Greece	5.9	4.9	5.7	6.8	12.1	11.9	5.1	6.5	3.5	5.8	0.2	6.8	2.3	2.7	3.0	3.2	-0.6	1.8	6.4	5.1	1.6
Portugal	7.0	6.4	8.6	7.8	17.3	6.6	7.0	11.8	3.3	6.5	7.9	5.2	3.6	3.7	0.1	0.1	7.2	4.9	5.3	2.0	2.2
Spain	5.2	4.7	5.5	6.7	8.2	5.3	5.3	4.1	5.5	4.2	4.4	1.9	4.9	3.9	2.9	4.6	5.7	9.0	4.1	5.6	4.2
Turkey	3.6	6.1	7.3	10.3	9.9	13.4	10.8	3.2	9.9	1.7	8.8	0.9	2.0	1.7	2.1	3.1	6.5	5.0	3.0	2.8	11.9
Yugoslavia	9.3	-0.1	5.1	4.1	7.3	9.3	9.5	7.4	6.5	4.5	-1.0	-4.8	-0.7	-5.1	-0.2	1.9	4.6	-1.5	0.1	-1.8	1.1
Total southern Europe	5.8	4.4	5.8	6.8	9.5	7.7	6.4	5.3	5.6	4.4	3.8	2.1	3.4	2.6	2.3	3.6	4.8	6.2	4.1	4.4	4.2
Total Europe	4.2	4.3	4.2	4.0	3.1	4.4	2.9	1.7	3.9	3.2	2.4	2.0	1.5	1.7	1.6	2.2	2.3	2.4	2.0	0.8	2.1
United States	-3.1	-1.1	0.7	-0.9	1.4	1.3	-0.1	1.5	2.5	0.8	1.9	1.5	1.9	1.1	4.4	7.9	4.2	2.3	0.2	2.3	2.8
Canada	9.4	4.4	2.7	5.8	5.6	6.5	2.0	4.6	1.7	0.6	2.8	2.5	2.4	1.4	1.2	3.2	1.6	1.8	2.8	2.6	1.7
North America	-2.4	-0.7	0.9	-0.5	1.7	1.7	0.1	1.8	2.5	0.8	2.0	1.6	1.9	1.2	4.2	7.5	4.0	2.3	0.4	2.3	2.8
Total above	-0.2	1.0	2.1	1.2	2.2	2.7	1.2	1.8	3.1	1.7	2.1	1.8	1.8	1.4	3.1	5.4	3.3	2.3	1.0	1.7	2.5

Sources: National statistics.

APPENDIX TABLE A.4

Gross domestic fixed capital formation

(Annual percentage change)

	1970	1971	1972	1973	1974	1975	1976	1977	1978	1979	1980	1981	1982	1983	1984	1985	1986	1987	1988	1989	1990
France	4.6	7.3	6.0	8.5	1.3	-6.4	3.3	-1.8	2.1	3.1	2.6	-1.9	-1.4	-3.6	-2.6	3.2	4.5	4.1	8.6	5.9	4.7
Germany, Fed.Rep. of	9.4	6.1	2.7	-0.3	-9.6	-5.3	3.6	3.6	4.7	7.2	2.8	-4.8	-5.3	3.2	0.8	0.1	3.3	2.2	5.1	7.1	8.2
Italy	3.0	0.2	1.3	8.8	2.0	-7.3	-	1.8	0.6	5.7	8.7	-3.2	-5.2	-0.9	4.5	1.4	1.6	5.8	6.7	5.1	3.8
United Kingdom	2.5	1.8	-0.2	6.5	-2.4	-2.0	1.7	-1.8	3.0	2.8	-5.4	-9.6	5.4	5.0	8.5	4.0	1.9	9.5	14.8	4.2	-1.5
Total 4 countries	5.4	4.2	2.7	5.2	-2.8	-5.5	2.3	0.6	2.8	4.9	2.5	-4.5	-2.4	0.7	2.1	2.0	2.9	4.9	8.4	5.7	4.2
Austria	9.8	13.8	12.1	0.3	4.0	-5.0	3.8	5.1	-4.1	3.5	3.0	-1.4	-8.2	-0.6	2.1	5.0	3.7	2.8	6.0	5.5	7.0
Belgium	8.8	-2.0	2.9	7.0	7.4	-1.8	3.8	0.1	2.6	-2.6	4.6	-15.9	-2.0	-4.5	1.8	0.7	4.5	5.8	13.4	13.6	11.0
Denmark	2.2	1.9	9.3	3.5	-8.9	-12.4	17.1	-2.4	1.1	-0.4	-12.6	-19.2	7.1	1.9	12.9	12.6	17.1	-3.8	-6.6	0.2	-0.8
Finland	12.5	3.8	6.5	8.5	3.5	5.9	-8.8	-3.5	-6.9	3.0	10.4	2.2	4.4	4.1	-2.1	2.9	-	5.4	10.5	13.1	-1.9
Ireland	0.3	8.8	7.4	16.2	-11.6	-2.6	13.6	4.1	18.9	13.6	-3.2	7.3	-3.3	-9.0	-2.7	-7.4	-1.3	-3.7	2.6	12.0	9.0
Netherlands	7.5	1.5	-2.3	4.2	-4.0	-4.4	-2.2	9.7	2.5	-1.7	-0.9	-10.4	-4.1	2.1	5.2	7.0	7.4	1.1	9.2	3.9	3.2
Norway	14.9	18.8	-4.1	13.6	5.1	11.9	10.1	3.6	-11.2	-5.0	-1.5	17.9	-11.0	5.8	10.9	-21.0	23.9	-2.1	0.7	-4.8	-26.5
Sweden	3.3	-0.6	4.2	2.7	-3.0	3.1	1.9	-2.9	-6.8	4.5	3.5	-5.8	-0.3	1.9	6.0	7.3	0.7	7.6	6.0	10.9	1.8
Switzerland	8.9	9.9	5.0	2.9	-4.3	-13.6	-10.5	1.6	6.1	5.1	9.9	2.4	-2.5	4.1	4.1	5.3	7.9	7.4	6.9	6.0	3.3
Total 9 countries	7.7	5.1	3.6	5.0	-1.0	-2.7	1.1	2.1	-1.2	1.1	2.0	-3.6	-2.9	1.6	4.7	2.1	7.2	3.1	6.2	6.3	0.9
Total western Europe	6.0	4.4	2.9	5.1	-2.3	-4.8	2.0	1.0	1.7	3.9	2.4	-4.3	-2.5	0.9	2.8	2.0	4.0	4.5	7.8	5.9	3.4
Greece	-1.4	14.0	15.4	7.7	-25.6	0.2	6.8	7.8	6.0	8.8	-6.5	-7.5	-1.9	-1.3	-5.7	5.2	-6.2	-7.8	8.8	8.6	4.3
Portugal	11.5	9.8	13.5	9.5	-7.0	-11.3	0.8	12.0	6.2	-1.3	8.5	5.5	2.3	-7.1	-17.4	-3.5	10.9	15.1	15.0	7.5	9.0
Spain	3.0	-2.9	15.8	14.3	6.6	-3.9	-2.0	-0.2	-2.3	-4.5	1.3	-3.3	0.5	-2.5	-5.8	4.1	10.0	14.6	14.2	13.2	8.6
Turkey	13.5	-4.9	14.8	13.2	10.7	24.7	17.7	3.9	-10.0	-3.6	-10.0	1.7	3.5	3.0	0.5	16.7	11.0	5.6	-1.2	-0.8	8.6
Yugoslavia	12.8	4.6	1.8	4.2	9.1	9.7	8.1	9.5	10.5	6.4	-5.9	-9.8	-5.5	-9.7	-9.6	-3.7	3.5	-5.1	-5.8	0.5	-7.0
Total southern Europe	5.6	1.0	13.1	11.4	2.4	1.1	3.3	3.6	0.3	-0.6	-2.1	-3.7	-0.4	-3.4	-6.6	4.3	7.6	8.1	8.6	8.7	6.7
Total Europe	5.9	4.1	3.9	5.8	-1.8	-4.1	2.2	1.3	1.5	3.4	1.8	-4.2	-2.3	0.4	1.7	2.2	4.4	4.9	7.9	6.2	3.8
United States	-3.1	7.1	11.0	8.4	-6.8	-11.6	8.9	14.1	9.8	3.7	-7.9	1.1	-9.6	8.2	16.8	5.3	1.0	1.9	5.6	1.6	-0.2
Canada	0.3	7.9	4.3	9.9	6.6	5.8	4.6	2.1	3.1	8.5	10.1	11.8	-11.0	-0.7	2.1	9.5	6.2	10.3	10.2	4.5	-0.6
North America	-2.8	7.1	10.4	8.5	-5.7	-10.0	8.5	12.9	9.1	4.1	-6.2	2.2	-9.7	7.2	15.2	5.7	1.5	2.8	6.1	1.9	-0.3
Total above	1.8	5.5	6.9	7.1	-3.7	-6.9	5.0	6.7	5.3	3.8	-2.3	-1.0	-6.1	3.7	8.5	4.1	2.8	3.7	6.9	4.0	1.7

Sources: National statistics.

APPENDIX TABLE A.5

Volume of exports of goods and services
(Annual percentage change)

	1970	1971	1972	1973	1974	1975	1976	1977	1978	1979	1980	1981	1982	1983	1984	1985	1986	1987	1988	1989	1990
France	16.1	9.2	12.0	10.8	8.8	-1.7	8.2	7.4	5.9	7.5	2.7	3.7	-1.7	3.7	7.0	1.9	-1.4	3.1	8.3	10.9	4.5
Germany, Fed.Rep. of	5.8	6.3	7.1	10.6	12.3	-6.8	9.7	3.9	3.2	4.3	5.1	7.7	3.4	-0.8	8.0	7.0	-0.5	0.4	5.5	9.9	8.6
Italy	-2.5	6.8	9.3	4.1	7.0	1.6	10.5	9.9	9.0	8.5	-8.7	7.6	-1.1	2.4	7.3	3.9	3.8	3.3	4.8	10.1	5.0
United Kingdom	5.2	7.0	1.1	11.9	7.3	-2.8	9.1	6.9	1.9	3.8	0.2	-0.8	0.8	2.0	6.6	5.9	4.6	5.7	0.2	4.4	4.4
Total 4 countries	6.2	7.2	6.8	9.9	9.4	-3.3	9.3	6.4	4.4	5.6	0.8	4.6	0.8	1.4	7.3	5.0	1.2	2.8	4.6	8.8	6.0
Austria	16.4	5.9	9.2	2.2	10.7	-2.4	11.1	4.2	7.3	11.7	5.2	4.9	2.7	3.2	6.1	6.9	-2.7	2.4	9.5	10.5	9.9
Belgium	10.0	6.3	10.0	14.4	6.8	-8.9	11.7	12.7	3.4	7.1	3.3	3.1	2.1	3.2	5.7	1.3	5.4	7.1	9.0	7.6	7.0
Denmark	5.6	5.6	5.6	7.8	3.5	-1.8	4.1	4.1	1.2	8.4	5.2	8.2	2.5	4.9	3.5	5.0	0.0	5.1	7.3	6.0	4.6
Finland	8.7	-1.3	14.5	7.3	-0.6	-14.0	12.8	15.7	8.9	8.8	8.4	4.9	-1.1	2.5	5.4	1.2	1.3	2.6	3.7	1.6	2.2
Ireland	4.4	4.1	3.6	10.9	0.7	7.2	8.1	14.0	12.3	6.5	6.4	2.0	5.5	10.5	16.6	6.6	2.9	13.4	8.7	10.1	5.0
Netherlands	11.9	10.7	10.0	12.1	2.6	-3.1	9.9	-1.8	3.3	7.4	1.5	1.5	-	3.5	7.3	5.5	2.9	3.5	7.8	5.5	5.2
Norway	0.1	1.1	14.1	8.3	0.7	3.1	11.3	3.6	8.4	2.6	2.1	1.4	-0.1	7.6	8.2	10.7	1.6	1.2	5.4	10.3	7.2
Sweden	8.6	4.8	5.9	13.7	5.3	-9.3	4.3	1.5	7.8	6.1	-0.6	2.0	5.7	9.9	6.9	1.4	3.2	3.9	3.0	2.4	0.7
Switzerland	6.8	3.9	6.4	7.9	1.0	-6.6	9.3	9.7	3.7	2.5	5.1	4.6	-2.9	1.1	6.3	8.3	0.4	1.7	5.8	4.8	4.7
Total 9 countries	8.9	6.0	9.0	10.6	3.8	-5.1	9.3	5.1	5.0	6.6	3.1	3.2	1.2	4.4	6.7	4.8	2.2	4.2	7.0	6.3	5.4
Total western Europe	7.2	6.7	7.6	10.2	7.3	-4.0	9.3	6.0	4.6	6.0	1.7	4.1	0.9	2.5	7.1	5.0	1.6	3.3	5.5	7.9	5.8
Greece	12.4	11.9	22.9	23.4	0.1	10.6	16.4	1.8	16.4	6.7	6.9	-5.9	-7.2	8.0	16.9	1.3	14.0	16.0	9.1	2.0	4.4
Portugal	-1.6	9.9	18.5	4.2	-15.7	-15.6	0.0	5.9	9.1	33.0	2.2	-4.4	4.7	13.6	11.6	6.7	6.8	8.6	10.2	16.5	12.0
Spain	17.5	13.0	12.2	9.0	0.8	-1.4	10.1	8.5	10.7	6.4	0.6	8.4	4.8	10.1	11.7	2.7	1.3	5.9	7.5	5.2	3.8
Turkey	14.3	15.5	14.6	26.2	-11.0	-1.1	37.5	-21.8	12.9	-12.3	7.4	62.2	36.9	14.6	20.4	11.3	-0.6	26.0	16.5	7.5	-1.5
Yugoslavia	3.3	3.7	17.6	6.8	1.0	-1.3	9.3	-3.1	-2.4	14.9	7.5	12.0	-18.5	-4.4	6.4	7.9	-2.6	0.5	4.9	4.8	2.2
Total southern Europe	10.7	10.7	15.2	10.4	-2.4	-1.8	11.8	2.2	8.9	8.9	3.2	9.4	2.1	8.6	12.7	4.9	2.3	9.6	9.2	6.4	3.7
Total Europe	7.4	7.0	8.1	10.2	6.6	-3.8	9.5	5.7	4.9	6.2	1.8	4.4	1.0	2.9	7.5	5.0	1.6	3.8	5.8	7.7	5.6
United States	9.3	0.0	8.5	21.6	9.9	-0.7	5.0	1.5	9.3	8.3	10.1	-0.4	-8.8	-2.7	6.1	2.9	11.9	15.3	18.3	11.4	8.4
Canada	8.7	5.2	7.8	10.6	-2.0	-6.8	10.6	8.9	13.6	5.0	2.7	4.4	-2.2	6.4	17.7	6.0	4.5	3.0	8.9	0.7	4.3
North America	9.2	1.2	8.3	19.0	7.3	-1.9	6.0	3.0	10.2	7.6	8.5	0.6	-7.4	-0.7	8.8	3.7	10.0	12.3	16.1	9.1	7.6
Total above	7.9	5.3	8.2	12.7	6.8	-3.2	8.4	4.9	6.5	6.6	3.9	3.2	-1.6	1.9	7.9	4.6	4.1	6.4	9.1	8.2	6.3

Sources: National statistics.

APPENDIX TABLE A.6

Volume of imports of goods and services

(Annual percentage change)

	1970	1971	1972	1973	1974	1975	1976	1977	1978	1979	1980	1981	1982	1983	1984	1985	1986	1987	1988	1989	1990
France	6.3	6.3	13.2	14.2	1.9	-9.7	17.4	0.1	3.0	10.1	2.5	-2.1	2.6	-2.7	2.7	4.5	7.1	7.7	8.6	8.3	6.3
Germany, Fed.Rep. of	14.9	10.5	6.0	4.3	1.4	0.3	11.1	2.9	6.3	9.8	3.8	-2.9	-1.5	1.8	5.7	3.4	3.1	4.1	5.8	8.6	9.4
Italy	12.4	2.7	9.8	9.3	2.2	-12.6	14.1	1.7	4.8	11.7	2.9	-3.7	-0.7	-1.8	11.3	4.6	4.6	10.1	6.9	9.6	5.5
United Kingdom	4.9	5.3	9.8	12.0	0.9	-7.0	4.7	1.5	3.9	9.7	-3.4	-3.0	4.9	6.5	9.9	2.6	6.9	7.9	12.8	7.0	2.5
Total 4 countries	9.8	6.7	9.3	9.5	1.5	-6.4	11.5	1.7	4.6	10.2	1.7	-2.9	1.1	1.1	7.0	3.7	5.2	7.0	8.4	8.3	6.1
Austria	16.9	5.8	11.1	6.2	6.9	-4.6	17.4	6.2	0.1	11.7	6.2	-0.8	-3.3	5.5	9.9	6.2	-1.2	4.7	10.2	9.4	9.3
Belgium	7.1	5.3	8.4	19.4	7.5	-9.8	11.0	15.4	3.7	9.1	0.3	-2.7	0.9	-1.1	6.0	1.0	7.4	9.3	8.5	8.7	7.8
Denmark	9.3	-0.7	1.5	12.8	-3.8	-4.8	15.6	-	0.1	5.0	-6.8	-1.7	3.8	1.8	5.5	8.1	6.8	-2.0	1.4	4.2	2.1
Finland	20.3	-0.6	4.2	13.0	6.7	0.6	-2.0	-1.5	-3.7	18.4	8.3	-4.7	2.5	3.0	1.0	6.8	3.1	9.0	11.1	8.8	-1.7
Ireland	2.3	4.7	5.1	19.0	-2.3	-10.2	14.7	13.3	15.7	13.9	-4.5	1.7	-3.1	4.7	9.9	3.2	5.6	5.0	3.9	10.9	7.7
Netherlands	14.7	6.1	4.8	11.0	-0.8	-4.1	10.1	2.9	6.3	6.0	-0.4	-5.9	1.1	3.9	5.0	6.5	3.6	5.0	6.8	6.0	7.7
Norway	13.6	6.4	-1.0	14.5	4.7	7.0	12.3	3.4	-13.5	-0.7	3.3	1.5	3.7	-	9.5	6.5	9.9	-7.3	-1.7	0.9	6.0
Sweden	10.4	-3.3	4.0	6.9	9.9	-3.5	9.0	-3.8	-5.5	11.6	0.4	-5.8	3.4	0.8	5.4	7.8	4.7	7.2	4.7	7.1	2.2
Switzerland	13.9	6.2	7.3	6.5	-1.0	-15.4	13.1	9.3	10.9	6.9	7.2	-1.3	-2.6	4.4	7.1	5.1	7.1	5.5	5.3	5.5	4.0
Total 9 countries	12.1	3.7	5.3	11.8	3.1	-5.5	11.0	5.1	2.0	8.1	1.3	-3.1	0.8	2.2	6.2	5.3	5.2	4.8	6.2	6.8	5.1
Total western Europe	10.6	5.6	7.8	10.3	2.1	-6.1	11.3	2.9	3.7	9.4	1.5	-3.0	1.0	1.5	6.7	4.3	5.2	6.2	7.6	7.8	5.8
Greece	6.2	7.6	15.4	32.2	-16.3	6.3	6.1	8.0	7.2	7.2	-8.0	3.6	7.0	6.6	0.2	12.8	3.8	16.6	8.1	9.8	7.5
Portugal	0.9	14.5	12.0	12.7	4.8	-25.2	3.4	12.0	0.2	12.6	6.9	2.3	3.9	-6.1	-4.4	1.4	16.9	20.0	16.1	10.5	13.2
Spain	7.0	0.6	24.7	16.4	7.7	-1.1	10.1	-4.7	-0.7	11.5	3.8	-4.2	3.9	-0.6	-1.0	6.2	16.5	20.4	18.9	16.0	9.0
Turkey	22.0	9.7	17.4	0.6	18.3	26.1	32.1	-3.4	-31.8	-14.1	-0.4	12.5	13.0	18.6	14.9	6.9	14.5	15.6	3.5	10.0	11.0
Yugoslavia	27.8	9.2	-6.5	16.4	14.4	-5.6	-3.2	12.5	4.5	18.7	-7.2	-1.5	-16.7	-14.8	2.5	2.6	6.0	-6.9	-0.9	13.1	21.9
Total southern Europe	11.4	6.1	14.2	15.8	6.5	-1.3	9.8	1.3	-4.1	9.3	-0.0	-0.4	1.3	-0.4	1.5	6.2	13.0	15.6	12.6	13.4	10.8
Total Europe	10.7	5.7	8.3	10.8	2.5	-5.6	11.2	2.8	2.9	9.4	1.4	-2.7	1.0	1.4	6.2	4.4	5.9	7.1	8.1	8.4	6.3
United States	4.2	6.8	12.1	10.9	-3.5	-10.5	19.7	12.0	5.7	1.3	-8.2	2.1	-2.4	12.1	23.0	5.2	12.5	6.8	5.5	5.5	4.2
Canada	-1.7	7.2	13.8	14.7	11.1	-3.3	8.6	1.7	7.4	11.4	4.9	8.5	-15.2	9.0	17.1	8.7	7.6	6.7	12.9	5.1	1.4
North America	3.2	6.9	12.4	11.5	-1.1	-9.1	17.5	10.2	6.0	3.0	-5.8	3.4	-5.1	11.5	21.9	5.8	11.6	6.8	6.8	5.4	3.7
Total above	8.4	6.0	9.6	11.0	1.4	-6.7	13.0	5.0	3.9	7.3	-0.9	-0.9	-0.9	4.4	11.2	4.9	7.9	7.0	7.6	7.3	5.4

Sources: National statistics.

APPENDIX TABLE A.7

Current account balances
(Billion US dollars)

	1970	1971	1972	1973	1974	1975	1976	1977	1978	1979	1980	1981	1982	1983	1984	1985	1986	1987	1988	1989	1990
France	-0.2	0.2	-0.1	1.4	-3.9	2.7	-3.4	-0.4	7.1	5.1	-4.2	-4.8	-12.1	-5.2	-0.9	-	2.4	-4.4	-3.5	-3.8	-7.7
Germany, Fed.Rep, of	0.8	1.0	1.2	5.2	10.6	4.4	3.7	4.0	9.1	-5.6	-13.9	-3.3	5.0	5.4	9.8	17.0	40.1	46.1	50.5	55.4	44.0
Italy	0.8	1.6	2.1	-2.5	-8.0	-0.5	-2.8	2.5	6.3	5.5	-10.0	-9.7	-6.4	1.4	-2.5	-3.5	2.9	-1.7	-6.2	-10.6	-13.1
United Kingdom	2.0	2.7	0.5	-2.4	-7.5	-3.4	-1.7	-0.2	1.9	-0.9	7.5	14.5	8.0	5.8	2.6	4.8	0.2	-7.4	-27.3	-32.1	-28.7
Total 4 countries	3.4	5.5	3.7	1.8	-8.7	3.2	-4.2	5.9	24.3	4.2	-20.6	-3.3	-5.4	7.4	9.0	18.2	45.6	32.6	13.5	8.8	-5.5
Austria	-0.1	-0.1	-0.2	-0.3	-0.2	-0.2	-1.1	-2.2	-0.7	-1.1	-1.7	-1.5	0.6	0.2	-0.3	-0.3	0.1	-0.4	-0.5	0.1	0.3
Belgium	0.7	0.6	1.3	1.4	0.8	0.2	0.4	-0.6	-0.8	-3.1	-4.9	-4.2	-2.6	-0.5	-0.1	0.7	3.1	2.8	3.6	3.2	4.3
Denmark	-0.5	-0.4	-0.1	-0.5	-1.0	-0.5	-1.9	-1.7	-1.5	-3.0	-2.5	-1.9	-2.3	-1.2	-1.6	-2.7	-4.5	-3.0	-1.8	-1.4	0.5
Finland	-0.2	-0.3	-0.1	-0.4	-1.2	-2.1	-1.1	-0.1	0.7	-0.2	-1.4	-0.4	-0.8	-0.9	-	-0.7	-0.7	-1.8	-2.8	-5.1	-6.7
Ireland	-0.2	-0.2	-0.1	-0.3	-0.7	-0.1	-0.4	-0.5	-0.8	-2.1	-2.1	-2.6	-1.9	-1.2	-1.0	-0.7	-0.7	0.4	0.7	0.5	0.4
Netherlands	-0.6	-0.2	1.2	2.4	3.0	2.4	3.4	1.2	-1.2	0.2	-1.0	3.7	4.5	5.0	6.6	4.0	3.6	3.7	5.4	8.0	9.3
Norway	-0.2	-0.5	-0.1	-0.4	-1.1	-2.5	-3.7	-5.0	-2.1	-1.0	1.1	2.2	0.7	2.0	2.9	3.1	-4.5	-4.1	-3.7	0.2	3.2
Sweden	-0.3	0.4	0.6	1.4	-0.6	-0.3	-1.6	-2.2	-0.3	-2.4	-4.4	-2.8	-3.4	-1.0	0.2	-1.6	0.1	-1.2	-2.5	-5.2	-5.4
Switzerland	0.2	0.3	0.5	-0.9	-2.8	0.8	2.3	1.9	2.1	-0.2	-0.2	3.4	2.5	1.2	6.1	6.0	4.7	6.3	8.8	8.5	8.5
Total 9 countries	-1.3	-0.5	3.0	2.6	-3.6	-2.5	-3.7	-9.2	-4.7	-12.9	-17.2	-4.0	-2.7	3.6	12.9	7.7	1.0	2.5	7.2	8.7	14.4
Total western Europe	2.2	5.0	6.7	4.4	-12.3	0.7	-7.9	-3.3	19.6	-8.8	-37.8	-7.3	-8.1	11.0	21.9	25.9	46.6	35.2	20.7	17.6	8.9
Greece	-0.4	-0.3	-0.4	-1.2	-1.1	-0.9	-0.9	-1.1	-1.0	-1.9	-2.2	-2.4	-1.9	-1.9	-2.1	-3.3	-1.7	-1.2	-1.0	-2.6	-3.6
Portugal	0.1	0.3	0.4	0.3	-0.8	-0.8	-1.3	-1.0	-0.5	-0.1	-1.1	-2.6	-3.3	-1.0	-0.5	0.4	1.1	0.6	-0.6	-0.6	-1.2
Spain	0.1	0.9	0.6	0.6	-3.2	-3.5	-4.3	-2.1	1.6	1.1	-5.2	-5.0	-4.2	-2.7	2.0	2.9	4.0	-0.2	-3.8	-10.9	-15.7
Turkey	-	-	0.2	0.7	-0.6	-1.6	-2.0	-3.1	-1.3	-1.4	-3.4	-1.9	-1.0	-1.9	-1.4	-1.0	-1.5	-0.8	1.6	1.0	-2.4
Yugoslavia	-0.4	-0.4	0.4	0.5	-1.0	-0.6	0.2	-1.3	-1.3	-3.7	-2.3	-1.0	-0.5	0.3	0.5	0.8	1.1	1.2	2.5	2.4	-
Total southern Europe	-0.7	0.4	1.2	0.9	-6.7	-7.4	-8.3	-8.6	-2.3	-5.9	-14.2	-12.9	-10.8	-7.3	-1.6	-0.2	3.1	-0.4	-1.3	-10.7	-22.9
Total Europe	1.5	5.4	7.9	5.3	-19.1	-6.7	-16.3	-11.9	17.3	-14.7	-51.9	-20.2	-18.9	3.7	20.3	25.7	49.7	34.8	19.4	6.9	-14.0
United States	2.3	-1.4	-5.8	7.1	1.9	18.1	4.2	-14.5	-15.4	0.2	1.2	7.3	-5.9	-40.2	-99.0	-122.3	-145.4	-162.2	-129.0	-110.0	-13.7
Canada	1.0	0.4	-0.3	0.3	-1.3	-4.6	4.2	-4.1	-4.3	-4.1	-1.0	-5.1	2.2	2.5	2.0	-1.5	-7.3	-6.9	-8.2	-14.1	-95.0
North America	3.3	-1.1	-6.1	7.4	0.6	13.5	-	-18.6	-19.7	-3.9	0.2	2.1	-3.6	-37.7	-97.0	-123.7	-152.7	-169.1	-137.2	-124.1	-108.7
Total above	4.8	4.3	1.8	12.7	-18.5	6.8	-16.2	-30.5	-2.4	-18.6	-51.7	-18.1	-22.5	-34.0	-76.7	-98.0	-103.0	-134.4	-117.8	-117.2	-122.7
Japan	2.0	5.8	6.6	-0.1	-4.7	-0.7	3.7	10.9	16.5	-8.7	-10.8	4.8	6.8	20.8	35.0	49.2	85.8	87.0	79.6	57.0	35.8
Total above	6.8	10.1	8.4	12.5	-23.2	6.1	-12.5	-19.6	14.2	-27.3	-62.5	-13.3	-15.7	-13.2	-41.7	-48.8	-17.2	-47.3	-38.2	-60.2	-86.9

Source: IMF, *International Financial Statistics*, February 1991; national statistics (Portugal 1970, 1971, 1989; Italy 1990; Belgium 1990; Switzerland 1990).

APPENDIX TABLE A.8

Industrial production

(Annual percentage change)

	1970	1971	1972	1973	1974	1975	1976	1977	1978	1979	1980	1981	1982	1983	1984	1985	1986	1987	1988	1989	1990 a
France	5.6	6.5	5.5	6.8	2.4	-7.3	8.9	1.4	2.4	4.4	-0.1	-1.5	-0.2	-0.1	0.4	0.5	0.9	1.9	4.7	4.2	1.5
Germany, Fed.Rep. of	5.9	0.9	3.7	6.3	-1.7	-6.2	6.9	2.6	1.9	5.1	..	-1.9	-3.2	0.7	3.0	4.5	2.0	0.4	3.6	4.9	5.5
Italy	6.6	-0.5	4.9	9.8	3.9	-8.8	11.6	..	2.0	6.6	5.2	-2.2	-3.1	-2.4	3.4	1.3	4.1	2.6	6.9	3.9	-1.0
United Kingdom	0.4	-0.5	1.8	9.0	-2.0	-5.4	3.4	5.1	2.9	3.9	-6.7	-3.2	1.7	4.1	0.1	5.5	2.4	3.3	3.6	0.4	-0.5
Total 4 countries	4.6	1.5	3.9	7.6	0.2	-6.8	7.4	2.4	2.3	5.0	-0.5	-2.1	-1.5	0.6	1.8	3.2	2.3	1.8	4.5	3.5	2.0
Austria	8.6	5.9	8.1	3.7	5.5	-6.3	6.6	3.8	2.1	7.7	2.7	-1.6	-0.8	1.0	5.3	4.5	1.1	1.0	4.4	5.9	8.5
Belgium	2.9	1.7	7.7	6.0	4.0	-9.8	7.7	0.4	2.4	4.5	-1.2	-2.7	..	1.9	2.4	2.6	0.8	2.2	5.7	3.5	4.5
Denmark	..	..	..	..	..	..	..	..	..	..	..	..	..	..	..	..	..	..	..	..	..
Finland	10.2	5.6	8.8	6.5	4.5	-1.4	..	1.5	4.3	11.1	7.5	2.3	1.1	3.4	4.3	4.2	1.7	5.1	3.7	2.6	-1.5
Ireland	3.4	3.9	4.5	10.6	1.6	-4.0	..	8.0	7.8	7.8	-4.8	5.4	-0.7	7.9	9.9	3.5	3.2	9.8	10.9	12.4	4.5
Netherlands	9.2	5.6	5.3	6.3	6.0	-5.6	8.8	..	1.1	3.3	..	-2.1	-4.3	2.2	4.4	5.3	..	1.2	0.1	5.1	2.5
Norway	4.3	4.2	8.0	5.6	3.5	5.1	8.3	..	10.6	6.8	5.1	..	8.5	8.5	6.7	5.3	3.5	7.5	5.1	16.3	3.5
Sweden b	5.1	1.2	2.4	7.1	4.4	-2.1	6.5	-5.5	-1.2	7.1	-1.1	-1.1	-2.2	4.6	6.6	3.1	..	2.2	1.1	2.8	3.0
Switzerland	8.7	2.3	2.2	5.5	1.0	-12.4	-2.2	5.9	..	2.2	5.4	-1.0	-3.1	-1.1	3.3	5.3	4.0	1.0	6.7	1.8	3.5
Total 9 countries c	6.9	3.5	5.3	6.0	4.0	-5.8	4.0	0.9	2.2	5.4	1.9	-1.0	-1.8	2.8	4.8	4.3	1.5	2.8	3.8	5.6	2.7
Total western Europe d	5.1	1.9	4.1	7.3	1.0	-6.6	6.7	2.1	2.2	5.1	-	-1.9	-1.6	1.0	2.5	3.4	2.1	2.0	4.4	4.0	2.1
Greece	10.3	11.2	14.3	15.3	-1.6	4.4	10.5	2.0	7.6	6.0	1.0	0.9	0.9	-0.3	2.3	4.2	-1.0	-1.5	5.1	1.9	-2.0
Portugal	6.4	7.7	12.9	11.8	2.8	-4.9	3.3	13.2	6.8	7.2	5.5	2.4	7.7	3.5	2.5	0.7	6.1	2.4	6.2	5.0	7.5
Spain	10.5	2.9	16.1	15.1	9.3	-8.8	5.1	5.3	2.3	0.7	1.3	-1.0	-1.1	2.7	0.9	1.9	3.1	4.6	3.1	4.5	-
Turkey	..	..	..	..	..	..	..	..	..	..	..	..	..	..	..	..	..	..	..	..	..
Yugoslavia	7.5	9.3	8.5	5.9	11.1	5.0	3.2	10.8	8.3	9.0	3.5	3.4	..	1.1	5.4	3.1	4.0	1.0	-1.0	1.0	-10.5
Total southern Europe d	9.5	5.3	13.9	12.8	8.3	-4.7	5.0	6.8	4.5	3.7	2.1	0.5	..	2.1	2.4	2.3	3.3	2.9	2.4	3.4	-2.2
Total Europe e	5.4	2.1	4.9	7.8	1.6	-6.4	6.6	2.5	2.4	4.9	0.2	-1.7	-1.4	1.1	2.5	3.3	2.2	2.1	4.2	3.9	1.7
United States	-3.4	1.4	9.8	8.1	-1.4	-8.8	9.2	7.9	6.6	3.9	-1.9	2.2	-7.1	6.0	11.1	1.9	0.9	5.0	5.5	2.5	1.0
Canada	-1.6	5.7	8.8	11.9	1.9	-7.3	6.7	3.4	3.4	4.8	-3.4	2.1	-9.9	6.5	12.2	5.4	-0.8	4.5	4.9	0.1	-3.0
North America	-3.2	1.7	9.7	8.3	-1.2	-8.7	9.0	7.5	6.3	4.0	-2.0	2.2	-7.3	6.0	11.2	2.2	0.8	4.9	5.4	2.3	0.7
Total above e	0.7	1.9	7.4	8.1	0.1	-7.6	7.8	5.2	4.6	4.4	-1.0	0.4	-4.7	3.8	7.2	2.7	1.4	3.7	4.9	3.0	1.1

Sources: OECD, *Main Economic Indicators,* Paris (monthly), and national statistics.

Note: Data for France, Finland, Norway and Sweden for 1970-1984, as well as for the Netherlands, Switzerland and Yugoslavia for 1970-1990 are calculated from rounded index numbers (1985 = 100). National data are aggregated by means of weights derived from GDP originating in industry, expressed at 1985 US dollar exchange rates.

a Country data rounded to the nearest 0.5 percentage point.
b Refers to mining and manufacturing only.
c Excluding Denmark.
d Excluding Turkey.
e Excluding Denmark and Turkey.

APPENDIX TABLE A.9

Consumer prices [a]

(Annual percentage change)

	1970	1971	1972	1973	1974	1975	1976	1977	1978	1979	1980	1981	1982	1983	1984	1985	1986	1987	1988	1989	1990
France	5.2	5.5	6.2	7.3	13.7	11.8	9.6	9.4	9.1	10.8	13.6	13.4	11.8	9.6	7.4	5.8	2.5	3.3	2.8	3.6	3.3
Germany, Fed.Rep. of	3.3	5.4	5.5	7.0	7.0	5.9	4.3	3.7	2.7	4.1	5.5	6.3	5.2	3.3	2.4	2.0	-0.1	0.2	1.3	2.8	2.7
Italy	4.9	4.8	5.8	10.8	19.1	17.0	16.8	17.0	12.1	14.8	21.2	17.8	16.5	14.6	10.8	9.2	5.9	4.7	5.0	6.3	6.3
United Kingdom	6.4	9.4	7.1	9.1	16.0	24.2	16.5	15.8	8.3	13.4	18.0	11.9	8.6	4.6	5.0	6.1	3.4	4.1	4.9	7.8	9.5
Total 4 countries	4.8	6.2	6.1	8.4	13.5	14.0	11.2	10.8	7.7	10.3	13.9	11.9	10.2	7.7	6.1	5.5	2.7	2.9	3.3	4.9	5.2
Austria	4.4	4.7	6.3	7.6	9.5	8.4	7.3	5.5	3.6	3.7	6.3	6.8	5.4	3.3	5.7	3.2	1.7	1.4	2.0	2.5	3.2
Belgium	3.9	4.3	5.4	6.9	12.7	12.8	9.2	7.1	4.5	4.5	6.6	8.2	8.2	7.7	6.3	4.9	1.3	1.6	1.1	3.2	3.4
Denmark	6.5	5.8	6.6	9.3	15.2	9.6	9.0	11.1	10.1	9.6	12.3	6.8	5.4	3.3	5.6	3.2	1.7	4.0	4.6	4.8	2.7
Finland	2.7	6.1	7.4	11.4	17.8	17.4	14.4	12.5	7.7	7.1	11.7	12.2	9.6	8.3	7.1	5.9	2.9	4.1	5.1	6.6	6.2
Ireland	8.2	9.0	8.6	11.4	17.0	20.9	18.0	13.6	7.6	13.1	18.2	20.4	17.1	10.5	8.6	5.4	3.8	3.2	2.1	4.0	3.4
Netherlands	3.6	7.5	7.8	8.0	9.6	10.2	8.8	6.7	4.1	4.2	6.5	6.7	5.7	2.8	3.2	2.3	0.3	-0.2	0.7	1.1	2.4
Norway	10.7	6.0	7.2	7.6	9.4	11.6	9.2	9.0	8.2	4.8	10.9	13.6	11.3	8.4	6.3	5.7	7.2	8.7	6.7	4.6	4.1
Sweden	7.0	7.4	6.0	6.8	9.9	9.8	10.3	11.4	10.0	7.2	13.7	12.1	8.6	9.0	8.0	7.4	4.2	4.2	5.8	6.4	10.5
Switzerland	3.6	6.6	6.7	8.7	9.8	6.7	1.7	1.3	1.0	3.6	4.1	6.5	5.6	3.0	3.0	3.4	0.7	1.5	1.8	3.2	5.4
Total 9 countries	5.0	6.3	6.7	8.2	11.4	10.7	8.6	7.7	5.6	5.5	8.7	9.0	7.4	5.5	5.4	4.3	2.1	2.5	2.9	3.7	4.7
Total western Europe	4.9	6.2	6.2	8.3	13.0	13.3	10.6	10.1	7.2	9.2	12.6	11.2	9.5	7.2	6.0	5.2	2.5	2.8	3.2	4.6	5.1
Greece	2.9	3.0	4.3	15.5	26.9	13.4	13.3	12.1	12.6	19.0	24.9	24.5	21.0	20.2	18.5	19.3	23.0	16.4	13.5	13.7	20.5
Portugal [b,c]	6.4	11.9	10.7	12.9	25.1	15.3	21.0	27.4	22.0	24.2	16.6	20.0	22.4	25.5	29.3	19.2	11.8	10.2	9.6	12.7	13.5 d
Spain	5.6	8.3	8.3	11.4	15.7	16.9	14.9	24.5	19.8	15.7	15.5	14.5	14.4	12.2	11.3	8.8	8.7	5.3	4.8	6.8	6.7
Turkey [e]	8.1	16.3	12.9	16.6	18.7	20.1	15.3	28.4	49.5	56.5	116.6	35.9	27.1	31.4	48.4	44.9	34.6	38.9	73.7	63.3	60.3 d
Yugoslavia	10.6	15.6	16.6	19.7	21.1	24.3	11.7	14.9	14.3	20.6	30.2	40.9	32.3	42.9	50.0	60.0	87.5	126.7	194.1	1252.0	580.0
Total southern Europe	5.8	9.7	9.0	13.1	18.4	17.1	15.3	24.1	25.4	25.4	38.3	20.7	18.5	18.3	21.5	18.6	16.2	14.2	20.9	20.1	20.3
Total Europe	5.0	6.6	6.5	8.8	13.5	13.6	11.0	11.5	9.1	10.8	15.3	12.2	10.4	8.3	7.5	6.6	3.9	4.0	5.0	6.2	6.6
United States [f]	5.9	4.3	3.3	6.2	11.0	9.1	5.8	6.4	7.6	11.3	13.5	10.3	6.2	3.2	4.3	3.6	1.9	3.7	4.1	4.8	5.4
Canada	3.3	2.9	4.7	7.8	10.8	10.8	7.5	8.0	9.0	9.1	10.2	12.3	10.9	5.7	4.4	3.9	4.2	4.4	4.0	5.0	4.8
North America	5.7	4.2	3.4	6.3	11.0	9.3	5.9	6.6	7.7	11.2	13.3	10.5	6.5	3.4	4.3	3.6	2.0	3.7	4.1	4.8	5.4
Total above	5.4	5.1	4.6	7.3	11.9	10.9	7.9	8.5	8.2	11.0	14.1	11.1	8.0	5.3	5.6	4.8	2.8	3.8	4.5	5.4	5.8

Source: National statistics. Regional aggregates were obtained from time series in annual percentage change form, with weights taken from OECD *National Accounts.* (Private final consumption expenditure in US dollars for 1985 at current prices and exchange rates.) All aggregates *exclude* Yugoslavia.

a Cost-of-living index for the Federal Republic of Germany and Yugoslavia, retail price index for the United Kingdom.
b 1970-1976, Lisbon.
c Break in series after 1975.
d 11-month averages.
e 1970-1982, Ankara; 1983 and thereafter, total urban areas.
f 1970-1978, urban wage earners and clerical workers; 1979 and thereafter, all urban consumers.

APPENDIX TABLE A.10

Average hourly earnings in manufacturing
(Annual percentage change)

	1970	1971	1972	1973	1974	1975	1976	1977	1978	1979	1980	1981	1982	1983	1984	1985	1986	1987	1988	1989
France [a]	10.8	11.2	11.1	14.5	19.6	17.3	14.0	12.7	12.9	13.0	15.1	14.5	15.2	11.2	7.7	5.8	4.3	3.2	3.2	3.9
Germany, Fed.Rep. of	13.8	10.8	8.9	10.7	10.6	8.0	6.4	7.6	5.0	5.5	6.3	5.3	4.9	3.4	2.3	4.5	3.5	4.2	4.3	4.2
Italy [a]	22.4	13.4	10.2	24.4	22.4	26.6	20.8	27.9	16.2	19.0	18.5	23.1	17.1	19.6	11.4	10.9	4.8	6.4	6.1	6.2
United Kingdom [b]	13.1	10.9	12.9	13.0	16.8	26.3	16.6	10.3	14.4	15.7	17.4	13.4	11.2	8.9	8.8	9.1	7.7	8.0	8.5	8.7
Total 4 countries	13.8	11.1	10.0	12.8	14.1	14.4	11.1	11.3	9.7	10.8	12.1	11.6	10.4	9.2	6.7	7.1	4.9	5.4	5.5	5.7
Austria [c]	9.4	13.7	11.6	12.7	15.9	13.3	9.1	8.5	5.7	5.8	7.9	6.2	6.1	4.5	5.0	6.1	4.5	3.1	3.8	4.4
Belgium [d]	15.0	13.0	11.5	17.2	20.6	19.5	12.2	9.1	6.7	7.8	8.7	10.7	6.0	4.5	5.4	3.1	2.4	2.0	0.8	5.6
Denmark [e]	12.4	14.1	12.3	14.1	19.6	22.4	11.5	9.1	10.8	11.1	11.1	9.0	10.1	6.7	5.0	4.9	4.8	9.3	6.6	5.1
Finland	11.1	15.6	14.1	16.6	22.4	21.3	14.8	8.8	7.5	11.4	12.8	12.8	15.1	9.6	10.3	7.6	6.1	6.8	8.7	8.8
Ireland	11.1	20.0	16.7	14.3	25.0	25.0	16.0	20.7	14.3	15.0	21.7	16.1	15.1	11.5	10.4	8.6	7.5	5.9	5.4	4.8
Netherlands [a]	8.3	10.3	14.0	14.3	17.9	12.1	9.5	7.4	5.7	4.3	4.2	3.0	6.8	2.7	0.9	5.3	1.7	1.5	1.3	1.3
Norway [f]	10.0	13.6	11.1	16.7	20.0	14.3	14.3	12.5	7.4	3.4	8.3	10.8	9.7	8.9	8.1	7.5	10.0	16.4	5.5	5.2
Sweden [e]	15.6	5.3	15.6	8.8	10.2	14.9	19.3	6.8	7.7	8.2	8.7	11.1	7.1	8.4	9.3	7.5	7.4	6.4	8.0	10.0
Switzerland [g]	6.2	9.7	9.0	9.2	13.9	7.4	1.6	1.7	3.4	2.1	5.2	5.1	6.2	6.8	1.8	3.6	4.1	2.8	3.6	3.7
Total 9 countries	10.1	11.0	12.0	12.4	16.4	14.2	10.2	7.3	6.4	6.3	7.9	7.9	7.5	6.2	5.3	5.6	4.7	4.9	4.6	5.5
Total western Europe	12.9	11.1	10.5	12.7	14.7	14.4	10.9	10.3	8.9	9.7	11.1	10.8	9.8	8.5	6.4	6.8	4.9	5.3	5.3	5.7
Greece	6.1	8.7	9.3	16.0	26.8	24.4	27.3	21.4	23.5	23.8	26.9	24.2	34.1	20.0	25.8	20.5	13.0	9.7	17.7	19.9
Portugal [h]	29.4	13.6	18.0	16.9	50.7	51.0	22.9	19.2	15.2	21.1	26.2	20.0	20.6	18.6	18.8	21.1	16.8	14.0	11.3	14.9
Spain [i]	13.2	15.0	15.9	20.0	27.1	31.1	30.0	29.3	27.5	23.9	15.3	24.7	15.9	15.0	11.7	10.0	10.9	7.6	8.3	7.3
Turkey [i]																				
Yugoslavia	16.3	22.3	16.1	19.3	27.8	22.4	14.2	17.9	19.1	20.7	24.2	37.0	27.7	27.5	45.3	76.9	105.4	105.0	171.2	1580.6
Total southern Europe [j]	15.0	13.8	15.4	18.8	31.9	34.9	27.8	25.8	24.1	23.3	19.0	23.6	19.2	16.5	15.3	14.3	12.7	9.6	10.7	11.6
Total Europe [j]	12.9	11.1	10.7	12.9	15.3	15.2	11.7	11.1	9.9	10.7	11.7	11.9	10.6	9.3	7.4	7.7	5.9	5.8	6.0	6.5
United States	5.1	6.6	7.0	7.3	7.9	9.3	8.1	8.8	8.7	8.5	8.5	10.0	6.2	4.0	4.0	3.8	2.0	1.9	2.7	2.8
Canada	9.2	8.0	7.4	9.2	12.7	17.2	12.8	11.4	7.8	8.3	9.8	12.1	11.5	4.0	4.7	4.4	3.1	2.4	4.9	5.4
North America	5.4	6.7	7.0	7.4	8.3	9.8	8.5	9.0	8.7	8.5	8.6	10.1	6.6	4.0	4.1	3.9	2.1	1.9	2.9	3.0
Total above [j]	8.8	8.8	8.8	10.1	11.8	12.6	10.2	10.1	9.3	9.7	10.3	11.1	8.9	7.1	6.0	6.1	4.3	4.3	4.8	5.2

Sources: National statistics; OECD, *Economic Outlook - Historical Statistics, 1960-1988*, Paris; OECD, *Main economic indicators*, No. 2, 1991, Paris. National data in annual percentage change form are aggregated by means of weights derived from manufacturing employment in 1985.

a Wage rates.
b Weekly earnings of all employees in Great Britain.
c Monthly earnings in mining and manufacturing.
d Includes transport.
e Includes mining.
f Males only.
g Data refers to workers who had accidents during the relevant period.
h Daily earnings; for 1970-1973, wage bill for all activities.
i Refers to all activities.
j Excluding Turkey and Yugoslavia.

APPENDIX TABLE A.11

Total employment

(Annual percentage change)

	1970	1971	1972	1973	1974	1975	1976	1977	1978	1979	1980	1981	1982	1983	1984	1985	1986	1987	1988	1989	1990
France	0.9	0.4	0.6	1.4	0.9	-0.9	0.8	0.8	0.4	0.1	0.1	-0.6	0.2	-0.4	-0.9	-0.3	0.1	0.3	0.7	1.2	1.2
Germany, Fed.Rep. of	1.3	0.4	0.4	1.1	-1.2	-2.7	-0.5	0.1	0.8	1.7	1.6	-0.1	-1.2	-1.4	0.2	0.7	1.4	0.7	0.8	1.4	2.8
Italy [a]	0.2	-0.1	-0.6	2.2	2.0	0.1	1.5	1.0	0.5	1.5	1.9	-0.0	0.6	0.6	0.4	0.9	0.8	0.4	0.9	0.2	0.7
United Kingdom [b]	-0.4	-0.9	-0.1	2.3	0.3	-0.4	-0.8	0.1	0.6	1.5	-0.3	-3.9	-1.8	-1.2	2.6	1.2	0.1	2.1	3.4	3.2	2.2
Total 4 countries	0.5	-0.0	0.1	1.7	0.4	-1.0	0.1	0.5	0.6	1.2	0.8	-1.2	-0.6	-0.6	0.6	0.7	0.6	0.9	1.5	1.5	1.8
Austria	0.4	1.1	0.7	1.7	0.9	-0.4	0.5	0.9	0.2	0.7	0.4	0.1	-1.2	-0.8	0.1	0.2	0.4	-0.0	0.6	1.4	1.8
Belgium [b]	1.8	1.0	-0.1	1.3	1.4	-1.4	-0.7	-0.2	0.1	1.2	-0.1	-1.9	-1.3	-1.0	-0.2	0.6	0.6	0.5	1.5	1.3	1.0
Denmark	0.7	0.6	2.1	1.2	-0.3	-1.3	1.8	0.8	1.0	1.2	-0.4	-1.3	0.5	0.3	1.7	2.5	2.6	-0.1	..	-0.7	-0.5
Finland	2.1	-0.6	1.0	2.0	0.4	-0.4	-1.3	-2.5	-1.1	2.2	2.9	1.0	0.7	0.4	0.3	-0.2	-0.5	0.2	0.2	-0.2	-0.3
Ireland [c]	-1.2	-0.4	0.3	0.1	1.4	-0.8	-0.8	1.8	2.5	3.2	1.0	-0.9	..	-1.9	-1.9	-2.2	0.2	-0.1	1.1	-0.2	2.8
Netherlands [d]	1.1	0.5	-0.9	0.1	0.2	-0.7	-0.0	0.2	0.7	1.3	0.7	-1.5	-2.5	-1.9	-0.1	1.5	2.0	1.4	1.4	1.6	1.7
Norway [d,e]	1.5	0.9	1.1	0.7	1.3	1.9	3.3	2.6	1.8	1.5	2.3	1.0	0.1	-0.3	0.6	2.7	3.0	2.1	-0.8	-3.1	-0.6
Sweden	2.0	-0.2	0.3	0.4	2.0	2.0	0.4	0.2	0.4	1.5	1.1	0.2	-0.2	0.2	0.8	1.0	0.6	0.8	1.4	1.6	0.9
Switzerland	1.5	1.8	1.4	1.0	-0.1	-4.8	-3.0	0.4	1.0	1.1	2.3	1.3	-0.7	-1.3	4.4	1.9	1.4	1.2	1.2	1.2	1.3
Total 9 countries	1.3	0.6	0.5	1.0	0.8	-0.7	-0.1	0.3	0.6	1.4	1.0	-0.3	-0.8	-0.7	0.8	1.1	1.2	0.7	0.9	0.7	0.9
Total western Europe	0.7	0.1	0.2	1.5	0.4	-1.0	0.1	0.4	0.6	1.3	0.9	-1.0	-0.7	-0.7	0.6	0.8	0.7	0.9	1.3	1.4	1.6
Greece	-0.1	0.3	0.5	1.0	0.1	0.1	2.3	-5.0	6.6	0.6	1.3	4.9	-0.8	1.0	0.3	1.0	0.3	-0.1	1.1	0.7	0.3
Portugal	-0.7	-0.3	-0.6	-0.8	-0.8	-1.4	0.2	-0.1	-0.3	2.2	2.5	-0.3	-0.0	4.8	-2.6	-0.5	0.2	2.6	2.6	2.2	1.2
Spain	1.0	0.9	0.3	2.5	0.5	-1.8	-1.1	-0.8	-2.7	-1.6	-3.0	-2.8	-1.0	-0.6	-2.7	-0.9	2.3	4.5	3.4	4.0	2.4
Turkey	-0.3	2.1	2.3	1.7	1.6	1.7	2.3	1.9	1.0	0.1	-0.1	0.9	2.0	1.8	2.5	2.3	3.1	3.0	1.4	1.1	0.3
Yugoslavia [f]	3.9	4.8	4.3	2.4	5.0	5.5	3.6	4.5	4.5	4.3	3.2	2.9	2.3	2.0	2.1	2.5	2.9	2.1	0.2	-0.3	-2.0
Total southern Europe	0.6	1.5	1.3	1.7	1.2	0.5	1.1	0.5	0.6	0.4	-0.1	0.3	0.7	1.4	0.2	1.0	2.3	2.9	1.8	1.8	0.6
Total Europe	0.6	0.4	0.5	1.6	0.6	-0.6	0.3	0.4	0.6	1.0	0.6	-0.7	-0.3	-0.2	0.5	0.8	1.1	1.4	1.5	1.5	1.4
United States [a]	-0.8	-0.4	2.5	4.3	1.6	-2.1	2.8	3.5	5.0	3.2	0.2	0.9	-1.6	1.0	4.9	2.4	1.7	2.9	2.8	2.3	0.6
Canada	1.0	2.3	2.9	4.9	4.1	1.7	2.0	1.8	3.5	4.0	3.0	2.7	-3.4	0.5	2.4	2.6	2.7	2.9	3.2	2.0	0.8
North America	-0.6	-0.2	2.5	4.4	1.8	-1.7	2.7	3.3	4.9	3.3	0.5	1.1	-1.8	1.0	4.6	2.4	1.8	2.9	2.9	2.3	0.6
Total above	0.2	0.2	1.2	2.6	1.1	-1.0	1.2	1.5	2.2	1.9	0.6	..	-0.9	0.3	2.2	1.5	1.4	2.0	2.1	1.8	1.0

Sources: National statistics: OECD, *National accounts*, detailed tables, vol.II., 1975-1988, Paris; OECD, *Labour force statistics 1968-1988*, Paris.; *Quarterly labour force statistics*, No. 4. 1990. Paris.; ECE secretariat estimates. National data are aggregated by adding the annual data on persons engaged taken from the national accounts statistics, where available. Otherwise the data refer to annual labour force surveys.

a Refers to full-time equivalent data.
b June of each year.
c April of each year.
d Man-years.
e Civilian employment.
f Socialist sector.

APPENDIX TABLE A.12

Annual unemployment rates [a]
(Percentage of total labour force)

	1970	1971	1972	1973	1974	1975	1976	1977	1978	1979	1980	1981	1982	1983	1984	1985	1986	1987	1988	1989	1990
France	2.5	2.7	2.8	2.7	2.8	4.0	4.4	4.9	5.2	5.9	6.3	7.4	8.1	8.3	9.7	10.2	10.4	10.5	10.0	9.4	8.9
Germany, Fed.Rep. of	0.8	0.9	0.8	0.8	1.6	3.6	3.7	3.6	3.5	3.2	2.9	4.2	5.9	7.7	7.1	7.2	6.4	6.2	6.2	5.6	5.1
Italy	5.3	5.3	6.3	6.2	5.3	5.8	6.6	7.0	7.1	7.6	7.5	7.8	8.4	8.8	9.4	9.6	10.5	10.9	11.0	10.9	9.9
United Kingdom	3.0	3.6	4.0	3.0	2.9	4.3	5.6	6.0	5.9	5.0	6.4	9.8	11.3	12.4	11.7	11.2	11.2	10.3	8.5	6.9	6.4
Total 4 countries	2.8	3.0	3.4	3.1	3.1	4.4	5.0	5.3	5.4	5.3	5.7	7.3	8.4	9.4	9.5	9.5	9.5	9.4	8.8	8.0	7.4
Austria	1.1	1.0	1.0	0.9	1.1	1.5	1.5	1.4	1.7	1.7	1.5	2.1	3.1	3.7	3.8	3.6	3.1	3.8	3.6	3.1	3.6
Belgium	2.1	2.1	2.7	2.7	3.0	5.0	6.4	7.4	7.9	8.2	8.8	10.8	12.6	12.1	12.1	11.3	11.2	11.0	9.7	8.1	7.9
Denmark	1.3	1.6	1.6	1.0	2.3	5.3	5.3	6.4	7.3	6.2	7.0	9.2	9.8	10.4	10.1	9.0	7.8	7.8	8.6	9.3	9.6
Finland	1.9	2.2	2.5	2.3	1.7	2.2	3.8	5.8	7.2	5.9	4.6	4.8	5.3	5.4	5.2	5.0	5.3	5.0	4.5	3.4	3.4
Ireland	5.8	5.5	6.2	5.7	5.3	8.3	9.2	9.0	8.2	7.3	8.1	10.0	12.1	13.7	15.4	16.8	17.1	16.9	16.3	15.0	14.6
Netherlands	1.0	1.3	2.2	2.2	2.7	5.2	5.5	5.3	5.3	5.4	6.0	8.5	11.4	12.0	11.8	10.6	9.9	9.6	9.2	8.3	7.3
Norway	1.6	1.5	1.6	1.5	1.5	2.3	1.7	1.4	1.8	2.0	1.6	2.0	2.6	3.4	3.1	2.6	2.0	2.1	3.2	4.9	5.2
Sweden	1.2	2.1	2.2	2.0	1.6	1.3	1.3	1.4	1.8	1.7	1.6	2.1	2.6	2.9	2.6	2.4	2.2	1.9	1.6	1.4	1.5
Switzerland	..	..	..	..	..	0.3	0.7	0.4	0.3	0.3	0.2	0.2	0.4	0.8	1.0	0.8	0.8	0.8	0.7	0.6	0.6
Total 9 countries	1.4	1.7	2.0	1.9	2.0	3.3	3.7	4.1	4.4	4.2	4.3	5.6	6.8	7.2	7.2	6.7	6.3	6.2	6.0	5.5	5.4
Total western Europe	2.5	2.7	3.1	2.8	2.8	4.1	4.7	5.0	5.1	5.1	5.4	6.9	8.1	8.9	9.0	8.9	8.8	8.7	8.2	7.5	7.0
Greece	4.2	3.1	2.1	2.0	2.1	2.3	1.9	1.7	1.8	1.9	2.8	4.0	5.8	7.8	8.1	7.8	7.4	7.4	7.7	7.9	8.3
Portugal	2.2	2.1	2.1	2.2	1.8	3.5	5.8	7.1	7.9	8.2	8.0	7.7	7.5	7.9	8.4	8.5	8.5	7.0	5.7	5.0	4.7
Spain	0.9	1.2	3.1	2.5	2.6	3.6	4.5	5.1	6.8	8.4	11.1	13.8	15.6	17.0	19.7	21.1	20.8	20.1	19.1	16.9	16.0
Turkey	7.8	7.8	7.6	7.9	8.4	8.7	7.9	7.5	7.8	9.7	11.6	11.6	12.3	12.1	11.8	11.3	10.5	9.5	9.8	10.2	16.0
Yugoslavia	7.7	6.7	7.0	8.1	9.0	10.2	11.4	11.9	12.0	11.9	11.9	11.9	12.4	12.8	13.3	13.8	14.1	13.6	14.1	14.9	15.9
Total southern Europe	4.5	4.5	5.0	4.9	5.2	5.9	6.0	6.2	7.0	8.5	10.4	11.4	12.5	13.1	14.0	14.3	13.7	12.9	12.5	11.9	11.6
Total Europe	3.0	3.1	3.5	3.3	3.4	4.5	5.0	5.3	5.6	5.8	6.5	7.9	9.1	9.8	10.1	10.1	9.9	9.6	9.1	8.5	8.0
United States	4.8	5.8	5.5	4.8	5.5	8.3	7.6	6.9	6.0	5.8	7.0	7.5	9.5	9.5	7.4	7.1	6.9	6.1	5.4	5.2	5.5
Canada	5.6	6.1	6.2	5.5	5.3	6.9	7.1	8.0	8.3	7.4	7.4	7.5	10.9	11.8	11.2	10.4	9.5	8.8	7.7	7.5	8.1
North America	4.9	5.8	5.6	4.9	5.5	8.2	7.6	7.0	6.2	6.0	7.0	7.5	9.6	9.7	7.8	7.4	7.2	6.4	5.6	5.4	5.8
Total above	3.8	4.3	4.4	3.9	4.2	6.0	6.1	6.0	5.8	5.9	6.7	7.7	9.3	9.8	9.1	9.0	8.8	8.3	7.7	7.2	7.1

Sources: OECD, *Labour force statistics 1966-1986*, OECD, *Quarterly labour force statistics*, No. 4, 1990. *Main economic indicators*, No. 2, 1990, Yugoslavia: ILO *Yearbook of Labour Statistics 1989-1990*, ECE secretariat estimates. National data are aggregated from annual figures on the number of unemployed and total labour force, and the rates have been calculated as percentages of the total labour force.

Note: Comparisons with previous years are limited due to changes in methodology in the Federal Republic of Germany (1984), United Kingdom (1984), Belgium (1983), Ireland (1983), Netherlands (1983, 1988), Portugal (1983), Finland (1982), Norway (1980), Sweden (1987).

a Adjusted for comparability between countries, except for Denmark, Switzerland, Greece, Turkey and Yugoslavia.

Appendix B. Eastern Europe and the Soviet Union

Data for this section were compiled from national and international [2] statistical sources, as indicated in the notes to individual tables. Volume figures underlying the data in tables B.1-B.2, B.8-B.9, B.11 and B.14 reflect data at constant prices of the following years: Bulgaria, 1982; Czechoslovakia, 1984; German Democratic Republic, 1985; Hungary, 1981; Poland, 1982; Romania, 1977; Soviet Union, 1973.

---

[2] CMEA, UN, IMF.

APPENDIX TABLE B.1

Net material product
(Annual percentage change)

	1970	1971	1972	1973	1974	1975	1976	1977	1978	1979	1980	1981	1982	1983	1984	1985	1986	1987	1988	1989	1990
Bulgaria...............	7.1	6.9	7.7	8.1	7.6	8.8	6.5	6.3	5.6	6.6	5.7	5.0	4.2	3.0	4.6	1.8	5.3	5.0	2.4	-0.4	-13.6
Czechoslovakia.......	5.7	5.5	5.7	5.2	5.9	6.2	4.1	4.2	4.1	3.1	2.9	-0.1	0.2	2.3	3.5	3.0	2.6	2.1	2.4	1.3	-3.1
German Dem. Rep....	5.6	4.4	5.7	5.6	6.5	4.9	3.5	5.1	3.7	4.0	4.4	4.8	2.6	4.6	5.5	5.2	4.3	3.3	2.8	2.1	-19.5
Hungary.............	4.9	5.9	6.2	7.0	5.9	6.1	3.0	7.1	4.0	1.2	-0.9	2.5	2.6	0.3	2.5	-1.4	0.9	4.1	-0.5	-1.1	-5.5*
Poland...............	5.2	8.1	10.6	10.8	10.5	9.0	6.8	5.0	3.0	-2.3	-6.0	-12.0	-5.5	6.0	5.6	3.4	4.9	1.9	4.9	-0.2	-13.0 a
Romania.............	6.8	13.5	9.8	10.7	12.3	9.8	11.3	8.7	7.2	6.5	4.2	-0.4	4.0	6.0	6.5	-1.1	3.0	0.7	-2.0	-7.9	-10.5
Eastern Europe......	5.7	7.3	8.0	8.3	8.6	7.6	6.1	5.8	4.2	2.0	0.3	-2.3	0.3	4.3	5.1	2.7	3.7	3.2	3.1	0.5	-12.0
Soviet Union.........	9.0	5.6	3.9	8.9	5.5	4.4	5.9	4.5	5.1	2.2	3.9	3.3	3.9	4.2	2.9	1.6	2.3	1.6	4.4	2.4	-4.0
Eastern Europe and the Soviet Union	8.0	6.1	5.1	8.7	6.5	5.4	5.9	4.9	4.9	2.1	2.7	1.7	2.8	4.1	3.6	2.2	3.0	2.1	4.0	1.8	-6.3

Sources: ECE secretariat Common Data Base, derived from national or CMEA statistics. National data are aggregated by means of 1981 weights based on CMEA investigations.

a Gross material product.

APPENDIX TABLE B.2

Net material product used for domestic consumption and accumulation
(Annual percentage change)

	1970	1971	1972	1973	1974	1975	1976	1977	1978	1979	1980	1981	1982	1983	1984	1985	1986	1987	1988	1989	1990
Bulgaria [a]																					
Total	3.7	1.6	9.8	9.0	11.8	11.1	0.3	5.2	0.2	3.5	5.1	7.7	1.9	1.2	5.2	2.3	8.4	0.4	3.7	-5.5	..
Consumption	5.6	7.4	6.3	6.6	7.1	7.7	6.0	4.0	3.6	3.0	3.6	5.3	3.7	2.9	4.9	3.3	3.6	4.6	2.2	1.7	..
Accumulation	-0.6	-11.5	21.0	16.0	24.2	18.7	-11.5	8.9	-9.3	5.0	9.5	14.8	-3.3	-3.6	6.2	-0.8	23.8	-10.7	8.3	-26.9	..
Czechoslovakia																					
Total	5.0	4.9	5.7	7.3	8.1	4.5	3.1	1.6	2.7	1.1	2.7	-3.4	-1.6	0.6	1.2	3.2	4.9	2.8	2.0	3.4	1.4
Consumption	1.9	6.6	5.2	5.8	6.1	3.0	3.3	3.7	3.7	0.9	1.0	2.6	-1.1	2.8	3.0	2.8	3.4	3.6	4.5	3.7	1.1
Accumulation	16.7	-0.6	7.7	12.2	14.3	9.2	2.5	-4.5	-0.5	1.8	8.2	-21.7	-3.6	-8.0	-6.6	5.4	12.2	-1.1	-10.2	2.0	3.0
German Dem. Rep.																					
Total [b]	8.4	3.4	5.8	6.3	6.5	2.6	6.3	5.1	0.8	1.1	5.1	1.1	-3.4	-	3.4	4.8	4.2	4.5	5.1	1.6	..
Consumption [c]	4.4	5.0	6.1	5.1	6.7	5.4	5.1	4.6	3.2	3.3	3.0	2.3	1.4	0.1	3.8	4.5	4.3	4.0	3.7	2.8	..
Accumulation [c]	17.3	-2.0	2.5	10.3	5.3	-1.9	9.5	6.2	-5.3	-5.0	11.4	-2.4	-17.6	-0.5	2.0	5.8	3.7	6.2	10.2	-2.7	..
Hungary																					
Total	11.8	11.3	-3.7	2.0	12.7	6.4	1.2	6.0	9.2	-5.8	-1.7	0.7	-1.1	-2.8	-0.6	-0.6	3.9	3.0	-4.3	-1.3	-7.5*
Consumption	8.4	5.4	3.1	3.7	6.9	4.7	2.1	5.0	4.3	3.3	0.3	2.9	1.4	0.5	0.9	1.2	2.0	3.1	-2.9	-0.5	..
Accumulation	23.6	30.4	-21.4	-3.8	34.2	11.5	-1.4	9.3	24.0	-29.0	-8.9	-8.3	-12.4	-20.4	-11.3	-15.0	21.4	2.7	-15.0	-8.5	..
Poland																					
Total	5.0	9.8	12.5	14.3	12.0	9.5	6.5	2.2	0.5	-3.7	-6.0	-10.5	-10.5	5.6	5.0	3.8	5.0	1.8	4.7	0.1	-17.0
Consumption	4.1	7.7	9.1	8.1	7.4	11.1	8.8	6.8	1.7	3.1	2.1	-4.6	-11.5	5.8	4.4	2.9	4.8	2.8	2.9	-1.7	..
Accumulation	7.4	15.2	20.9	27.8	20.5	7.0	2.4	-6.5	-2.0	-19.2	-29.6	-27.6	-6.6	4.9	7.3	7.2	5.4	-2.4	12.8	7.1	..
Romania																					
Total	..	..	..	..	..	..	12.3	6.8	9.6	5.5	0.8	-6.5	-1.5	2.2	2.8	4.8	..	..	..	..	..
Consumption [c]	..	..	..	..	..	..	8.8	7.8	9.4	6.3	3.4	3.0	-1.3	0.7	5.9	7.4	..	..	..	..	..
Accumulation [c]	..	..	..	..	..	..	18.9	5.1	10.1	3.9	-3.7	-24.5	-2.0	6.0	-4.7	-0.2	..	..	..	..	..
Eastern Europe [d]																					
Total	6.5	6.7	7.3	9.2	10.0	6.8	6.0	3.9	3.2	-0.2	-0.3	-4.2	-4.2	1.8	3.2	3.6	5.0	2.6	3.3	0.4	..
Consumption	4.3	6.5	6.7	6.3	6.9	-2.3	6.4	5.7	3.8	3.3	2.2	0.4	-3.4	2.6	4.0	3.9	4.0	3.4	2.7	0.9	..
Accumulation	13.5	6.8	5.8	15.0	17.1	6.8	5.7	1.1	2.8	-7.8	-4.7	-15.8	-7.8	-1.3	-1.2	2.1	10.2	-0.4	3.9	-3.5	..
Soviet Union																					
Total	11.2 [e]	5.1 [e]	3.5 [e]	7.7 [e]	4.1	4.2	5.0	3.5	4.5 [e]	2.0	3.9	3.2	3.5	3.6	2.0	2.1	1.6	0.7	4.6	3.2	..
Consumption	7.5 [e]	5.8 [e]	5.8 [e]	5.1 [e]	4.8	5.5	4.3	4.0	4.6	4.5	6.0	4.0	1.2	3.2	..	2.3	1.2	2.4	4.2	5.3	..
Accumulation	21.3	3.4	-2.1	14.4	0.5	-1.4	6.6	3.3	5.2	-2.9	-0.6	0.9	11.0	5.0	..	1.8	3.0	-4.2	5.6	-3.2	..
Eastern Europe and Soviet Union [d]																					
Total	9.9	5.6	4.6	8.1	5.8	5.0	5.3	3.6	4.0	1.3	2.5	0.8	1.2	3.1	2.3	2.3	2.5	1.2	4.3	2.5	..
Consumption	6.6	6.0	6.1	5.5	5.4	-2.2	5.0	4.5	4.3	4.1	4.7	2.8	-0.3	3.0	..	..	1.9	2.6	3.8	4.2	..
Accumulation	19.5	4.2	-0.3	14.6	4.6	0.8	6.3	2.6	4.4	-4.5	-1.9	-4.3	5.9	3.5	..	..	4.5	-3.7	5.3	-3.2	..

Sources: ECE secretariat Common Data Base, derived from national or CMEA statistics. National data are aggregated by means of 1981 weights based on CMEA investigations.

a Calculated from absolute volume figures at 1962 prices.
b Calculated from rounded index numbers (1950 = 100).
c Calculated from rounded index numbers (1970 = 100).
d Excluding Romania.
e Nominal.

APPENDIX TABLE B.3

Monthly nominal wages [a]
(In national currencies)

	1970	1971	1972	1973	1974	1975	1976	1977	1978	1979	1980	1981	1982	1983	1984	1985	1986	1987	1988	1989	1990
Bulgaria [b]	124	127	131	139	142	146	148	151	157	165	182	192	197	199	207	214	225	234	252	267	...
Czechoslovakia	1937	2009	2091	2161	2232	2304	2369	2444	2517	2579	2637	2677	2738	2789	2837	2883	2927	2985	3054	3123	3380
German Dem. Rep. [c]	750	779	808	835	860	889	920	947	977	1006	1021	1046	1066	1080	1102	1130	1170	1233	1269	1300	...
Hungary [d]	2139	2239	2342	2512	2682	2881	3042	3288	3567	3785	4014	4267	4542	4761	5342	5866	6291	6808	8817	10018	12500*
Poland [e]	2235	2358	2509	2798	3185	3913	4281	4596	4887	5327	6040	7689f	11631f	14475f	16838f	20005f	24095f	29184f	53090	206758	1029637
Romania [g]	1289	1308	1332	1389	1478	1595	1712	1818	2011	2108	2238	2340	2525	2601	2773	2827	2855	2872	2946	3064	3615
Soviet Union [b]	122	126	130	135	141	146	151	155	160	163	169	173	177	181	185	190	196	203	220	240	270

Source: National statistics.

[a] Gross remuneration of full-time workers and employees in the socialist sector (excluding co-operative farmers).
[b] Before deductions for taxation.
[c] In six sectors of the material sphere.
[d] State sector only; excluding bonuses and compensation for price rises. 1988-1990: gross wages.
[e] Excluding bonuses.
[f] Including compensations for price rises.
[g] Total economy; net remuneration, including bonuses.

APPENDIX TABLE B.4

Money incomes of population and volume of retail trade [a]

(*Annual percentage change*)

	1970	1971	1972	1973	1974	1975	1976	1977	1978	1979	1980	1981	1982	1983	1984	1985	1986	1987	1988	1989	1990
Bulgaria																					
Money incomes (nominal)	..	..	..	..	..	..	..	..	..	..	..	..	..	..	..	..	..	..	..	..	..
Retail trade turnover (real) [b]	7.8	6.6	6.5	8.8	9.1	7.9	7.2	3.1	3.1	2.4	2.9	4.6	4.6	2.4	2.8	3.2	4.3	1.4	0.8	3.2	-8.3
Czechoslovakia																					
Money incomes (nominal)	4.6	5.5	6.0	6.4	4.6	3.7	4.9	4.5	3.5	3.6	4.0	2.6	4.3	3.1	2.6	3.2	3.2	3.3	4.3	3.3	8.7
Retail trade turnover (real)	1.3	5.5	5.2	5.9	6.8	2.6	2.7	2.2	3.7	-0.3	-0.7	1.4	-1.7	2.2	2.1	2.3	1.7	2.9.	4.7	2.3	1.3
German Dem. Rep.																					
Money incomes (nominal)	3.1	3.4	6.2	6.3	5.1	3.8	3.7	5.5	3.6	3.0	2.5	3.1	2.8	2.3	3.9	4.0	5.6	4.7	3.9	3.0	..
Retail trade turnover (real) [c]	4.6	3.5	6.6	6.6	6.5	3.5	4.6	4.6	3.4	3.2	4.0	2.3	1.0	0.7	4.2	4.0	4.1	3.6	3.9	1.4	..
Hungary																					
Money incomes (nominal)	10.2	7.8	7.2	9.6	10.1	9.7	6.1	9.8	7.9	8.6	9.2	8.1	7.3	8.5	9.2	9.2	8.1	8.4	13.6	20.4	29.3
Retail trade turnover (real)	12.3	7.4	3.2	5.8	9.7	5.2	1.4	6.2	3.9	1.8	0.1	3.5	1.2	0.3	0.2	2.0	4.5	5.9	-5.3	-0.3	-6.0
Poland																					
Money incomes (nominal)	..	10.4	13.6	14.2	14.8	13.5	12.1	12.3	8.9	9.9	12.1	31.1	64.9	23.0	18.3	23.3	19.2	26.0	83.9	280.4	434.3
Retail trade turnover (real)	3.7	9.3	13.1	8.9	8.8	11.8	8.6	8.4	0.2	1.6	-0.4	-4.4	-15.0	7.3	5.0	3.1	5.7	5.0	5.2	-7.1	..
Romania																					
Money incomes (nominal) [d]	..	8.9	6.1	7.1	9.4	8.4	9.8	8.5	12.1	5.9	8.4	6.4	9.5	5.1	5.5	4.0	3.6	0.5	..	..	..
Retail trade turnover (real)	..	..	..	..	..	..	5.5	6.3	10.1	5.0	5.4	2.7	-3.9	-2.0	4.0	2.2	2.3	2.8	..	-1.7	13.2
Soviet Union																					
Money incomes (nominal)	7.6	7.0	6.8	5.6	7.4	7.4	4.9	5.0	5.1	4.6	5.2	4.3	4.2	4.8	3.8	3.7	3.5	3.9	9.2	12.9	16.9
Retail trade turnover (real) [b]	7.5	6.7	6.5	5.2	5.9	7.0	4.6	4.8	3.9	3.8	5.8	4.3	-0.1	2.8	4.7	1.8	0.5	0.9	4.9	8.3	9.6

Sources: National statistics and ECE secretariat estimates.

a Calculated from sales turnover figures (including public catering) by means of deflation with official retail price indices.
b State and co-operative sector only.
c Excluding sales in canteens of enterprises and institutions.
d Socialist sector only.

APPENDIX TABLE B.5

Real wages and per capita real incomes
(*Annual percentage change*)

	1970	1971	1972	1973	1974	1975	1976	1977	1978	1979	1980	1981	1982	1983	1984	1985	1986	1987	1988	1989	1990
Bulgaria																					
Real wages	6.1	2.2	3.5	6.1	1.5	2.8	0.9	1.8	2.3	0.4	-3.2	4.8	2.5	-0.1	3.2	1.4	1.6	4.3	3.7	-1.2	..
Real incomes	4.9	4.3	7.0	8.7	3.3	5.3	4.5	0.7	1.2	2.8	3.5	5.8	4.2	2.6	3.0	2.9	2.8	4.0	3.4	-2.4	..
Czechoslovakia																					
Real wages	1.3	4.1	4.5	3.2	2.9	2.6	1.9	1.8	1.4	-0.5	-1.1	0.6	-2.3	0.7	0.8	0.3	1.1	1.9	2.1	0.8	-5.6
Real incomes	..	6.2	6.5	5.2	3.1	2.8	3.9	2.4	0.7	-0.2	0.1	1.7	-	1.5	2.5	2.3	2.6	3.6	3.3 [a]	-2.4 [a]	-1.3
German Dem. Rep.																					
Real wages	4.7	3.6	4.2	3.9	3.4	3.4	3.5	3.0	3.3	2.7	1.1	2.2	1.9	1.3	2.0	-4.1	3.7	4.9	0.7	0.2	..
Real incomes	..	..	..	..	..	..	..	..	..	..	..	..	..	..	..	..	..	..	..	..	..
Hungary																					
Real wages	4.9	2.6	1.7	3.8	4.8	3.5	0.6	4.0	3.7	-2.5	-2.8	1.7	-0.4	-2.3	3.6	2.6	1.9	-0.4 ‖	12.1 [b]	-4.3	-3.8
Real incomes	7.0	4.2	3.4	4.6	6.2	4.3	0.9	4.8	2.9	-0.1	0.4	2.9	0.9	1.1	1.0	1.9	2.4	0.7	-1.3	2.4	..
Poland																					
Real wages	1.6	5.7	6.4	8.7	6.6	19.3	4.5	2.4	-2.2	2.2	3.9	2.4	-24.9	1.2	0.5	3.8	2.7	-3.5	14.4	8.3	-27.3
Real incomes	4.0	8.7	11.8	9.7	5.0	9.0	5.6	6.2	-0.5	2.5	0.8	3.3	-18.0	0.3	1.8	6.0	1.7	0.8	13.2	6.2	..
Romania																					
Real wages	7.9	0.9	1.8	3.6	5.3	7.7	6.6	5.6	8.8	2.8	3.1	2.6	-7.7	-2.2	5.5	1.5	0.7	0.2	0.9	3.1	11.6
Real incomes	..	11.8	5.8	4.8	6.1	5.8	8.5	3.5	8.0	2.9	2.8	1.5	-4.8	-2.4	4.3	2.0	3.0	-2.4	9.0	2.3	..
Soviet Union																					
Real wages	4.4	3.2	3.4	3.6	4.6	3.3	3.8	2.5	2.3	0.7	2.7	0.7	-0.6	1.1	3.8	2.2	0.9	1.8	5.9	7.3	6.6
Real incomes [c]	5.6	4.5	3.8	5.1	4.0	4.4	3.7	3.5	3.0	2.9	3.7	3.3	0.2	2.0	2.8	2.4	2.6	2.0	3.2	4.3	..

Sources: Appendix tables B.3 and B.6 (real wages); national statistics (per capita real incomes).

Note: Substantial discontinuities in the value series are indicated by ' ‖ '.

a Real money incomes.
b Not comparable with previous years, due to changes in personal incomes taxation.
c Material consumption of the population.

APPENDIX TABLE B.6

Consumer prices
(Annual percentage change)

	1970	1971	1972	1973	1974	1975	1976	1977	1978	1979	1980	1981	1982	1983	1984	1985	1986	1987	1988	1989	1990
Bulgaria [a]	-0.4	-0.1	-	0.2	0.5	0.3	0.3	0.4	1.5	4.5	14.0	0.4	0.3	1.4	0.7	1.7	2.7	2.7	2.4	6.2	19.3
Czechoslovakia [b]	1.7	-0.4	-0.4	0.2	0.4	0.6	0.9	1.4	1.5	3.0	3.4	0.9	4.7	1.1	0.9	1.3	0.4	0.1	0.2	1.5	9.9
German Dem. Rep. [c]	-0.1	0.4	-0.5	-0.6	-0.4	-	-	-0.1	-0.1	0.3	0.4	0.2	-	-	-	..	-0.2	0.5	2.2	2.3	-2.5*
Hungary [d]	1.3	2.0	2.8	3.3	1.8	3.8	5.0	3.9	4.6	8.9	9.1	4.6	6.9	7.3	8.3	7.0	5.3	8.6	15.5	18.8	28.9
Poland [d]	1.2	-0.2	-	2.6	6.8	3.0	4.7	4.9	8.7	6.7	9.1	24.4	101.5	23.0	15.8	14.4	17.3	25.5	59.0	259.5	584.7
Romania [a]	0.1	0.6	-	0.7	1.1	0.2	0.7	0.5	1.6	2.0	3.0	1.9	16.9	5.3	1.1	0.4	0.3	0.4	1.7	0.9	5.7
Soviet Union [a,e]	-	-	-	-	-	-	-	-	0.7	1.4	0.7	1.4	3.4	0.7	-1.3	0.8	1.9	1.9	2.3	1.9	5.3

Sources: National statistics.

[a] Retail prices in the state sector.
[b] Cost of living index for workers and employees.
[c] Including fees and charges of various kinds (1985 weights).
[d] Cost of living index for workers and employees in the socialist sector.
[e] Including public catering; based on rounded index numbers; 1970-1987: approved "list price" changes only.

APPENDIX TABLE B.7

Dwellings constructed
(Thousands)

	1970	1971	1972	1973	1974	1975	1976	1977	1978	1979	1980	1981	1982	1983	1984	1985	1986	1987	1988	1989	1990
Bulgaria	45.7	48.9	46.5	54.2	44.1	57.2	67.6	75.9	67.8	66.2	74.3	71.4	68.2	69.7	68.9	64.9	56.0	63.6	62.8	40.2	22.1
Czechoslovakia	112.1	107.4	115.6	118.6	129.0	144.7	132.5	134.8	129.3	122.7	128.9	95.4	101.8	95.7	91.9	104.5	78.7	79.6	82.9	88.5	69.4
German Dem. Rep.	65.8	65.0	69.6	80.7	88.3	96.0	103.1	106.8	111.9	117.4	120.2	125.7	122.4	122.6	121.7	99.0	101.0	91.0	93.5	83.4	57.0*
Hungary	80.3	75.3	90.2	85.2	87.8	99.6	93.9	93.4	88.2	88.2	89.1	77.0	75.6	74.2	70.4	72.5	69.4	57.2	50.6	51.5	43.8
Poland	194.2	190.6	205.5	227.1	249.8	248.1	263.5	266.1	283.6	278.0	217.1	187.0	186.1	195.8	195.9	189.6	185.0	191.4	189.6	150.2	132.5
Romania	159.2	147.0	136.0	149.1	154.3	165.4	139.4	145.0	166.8	191.6	197.8	161.4	161.2	146.6	131.9	105.6	108.1	110.4	103.3	60.4	48.5
Eastern Europe	657.2	634.2	663.3	715.0	753.4	810.9	800.0	822.1	847.5	864.1	827.4	717.9	715.3	704.7	680.7	636.1	598.2	593.3	582.6	474.1	373.3
Soviet Union	2266.0	2256.0	2233.0	2276.0	2231.0	2228.0	2113.0	2111.0	2080.0	1932.0	2004.0	1997.0	2002.0	2030.0	2008.0	1991.0	2100.0	2265.0	2230.0	2119.0	1800.0
Eastern Europe and the Soviet Union	2923.2	2890.2	2896.3	2991.0	2984.4	3038.9	2913.0	2933.1	2927.5	2796.1	2831.4	2714.9	2717.3	2734.7	2688.7	2627.1	2698.2	2858.3	2812.6	2593.1	2173.3

Sources: National statistics.

APPENDIX TABLE B.8

Total gross investment
(Annual percentage change)

	1970	1971	1972	1973	1974	1975	1976	1977	1978	1979	1980	1981	1982	1983	1984	1985	1986	1987	1988	1989	1990
Bulgaria [a]																					
Total	10.6	1.7	10.0	6.9	7.8	17.3	0.6	14.2	0.6	-2.2	7.5	10.5	3.6	0.7	0.3	8.6	8.0	7.2	2.4	-7.7	-13.5
Material sphere	7.0	0.4	8.7	6.7	7.8	19.8	-1.3	16.0	0.4	-1.6	5.4	12.2	2.8	-0.9	2.0	10.6	5.6	11.3	3.3	..	..
Non-material sphere	24.0	6.7	13.2	7.2	7.8	10.2	6.6	8.9	1.3	-4.0	14.3	5.3	6.1	5.3	-3.7	3.8	13.6	-2.5	-1.4	..	..
Czechoslovakia																					
Total	5.8	5.7	8.9	9.0	9.1	8.3	4.4	5.7	4.1	1.8	1.4	-4.6	-2.3	0.6	-4.2	5.4	1.4	4.4	4.1	1.6	3.0*
Material sphere	-	4.9	6.2	14.4	9.0	7.7	5.8	6.7	4.8	3.8	2.5	-2.1	-2.1	0.6	-3.9	6.0	2.2	5.7	4.2	0.4	..
Non-material sphere	20.0	7.0	13.2	0.9	9.2	9.2	2.1	3.9	2.9	-2.0	-0.5	-9.5	-2.6	0.4	-5.0	4.1	-0.2	1.5	3.8	4.4	..
German Democratic Republic																					
Total	6.8	1.7	5.0	8.4	5.4	4.6	7.3	5.3	2.8	1.2	0.1	2.4	-5.1	-0.3	-4.9	3.4	5.3	8.0	7.3	0.9	-9.0*
Material sphere	9.0	0.5	3.6	8.1	4.7	4.4	7.8	4.4	1.7	1.3	0.7	1.9	-5.1	0.1	-5.8	3.3	6.9	9.3	8.4	1.6	..
Non-material sphere	-1.0	6.8	11.1	9.6	8.1	5.4	5.5	8.8	6.8	0.9	-1.8	4.3	-5.1	-1.8	-1.7	3.5	0.1	3.3	2.9	-2.0	..
Hungary																					
Total	16.9	10.6	-1.1	3.2	10.9	11.5	-	12.2	4.8	0.8	-5.5	-4.7	-1.6	-3.4	-3.7	-3.0	6.5	9.8	-9.1	0.5	-7.0*
Material sphere	15.0	8.6	-3.6	1.6	9.1	15.1	1.1	14.3	6.4	-	-7.8	-5.0	-2.6	-4.9	-5.4	-2.4	0.6	10.2	-7.6	5.8	..
Non-material sphere	29.0	16.4	6.8	10.0	8.6	8.0	-2.1	9.1	0.9	3.9	-0.3	-5.4	-1.1	2.7	1.5	-2.2	5.8	2.2	-8.0	2.1	..
Poland																					
Total	4.0	7.4	23.0	25.4	22.3	10.7	1.0	3.1	2.1	-7.9	-12.3	-22.3	-12.1	9.4	11.4	6.0	5.1	4.2	5.4	-2.4	-8.0*
Material sphere	3.0	9.6	26.0	26.5	23.3	16.1	0.2	1.6	-0.1	-11.2	-12.8	-23.5	-15.3	8.2	13.8	6.7	5.8	4.2	5.6	-1.8	..
Non-material sphere	8.0	1.4	16.0	19.9	19.8	7.4	4.1	8.6	9.7	2.3	-11.0	-19.9	-5.7	11.4	7.2	4.6	3.7	4.3	5.1	-3.6	..
Romania																					
Total	11.6	10.5	10.4	8.2	13.4	15.1	8.5	11.7	16.0	4.1	3.0	-7.1	-3.1	2.4	6.0	1.6	1.1	-1.4	-2.2	-1.6	-35.0 [c]
Material sphere	10.0	12.2	10.4	8.2	12.0	13.8	9.3	13.4	17.0	3.9	3.4	-6.6	-3.2	4.8	7.5	1.7	0.3	-4.0	-2.1	-5.1	..
Non-material sphere	20.0	2.1	9.3	8.1	19.3	21.2	5.2	4.4	11.0	5.2	1.1	-9.4	-2.6	-8.6	-2.3	1.4	5.9	12.9	-2.4	14.8	..
Eastern Europe																					
Total	8.0	6.4	11.1	12.5	13.4	10.8	3.9	7.3	5.7	-1.0	-2.2	-7.2	-4.4	2.3	2.2	3.9	3.9	4.1	2.1	-1.5	-13.7
Material sphere	7.0	6.5	10.4	13.3	13.0	12.6	4.0	7.5	5.4	-1.6	-2.0	-6.6	-4.9	2.4	2.8	4.4	3.3	4.1	2.6	..	..
Non-material sphere	13.0	5.1	12.3	10.7	14.1	10.2	4.0	7.1	7.1	1.7	-2.8	-8.9	-2.9	1.7	0.4	3.1	4.3	4.4	1.3	..	..
Soviet Union [b]																					
Total	11.4	7.2	7.0	4.6	7.0	8.6	4.3	3.5	5.8	0.7	2.2	3.7	3.5	5.6	1.9	3.0	8.3	5.7	6.2	4.7	-4.3
Material sphere	13.0	8.5	8.6	6.5	7.8	9.3	5.0	3.5	7.1	0.7	2.5	3.5	3.3	5.3	1.3	2.6	7.5	4.0	6.2	4.6	..
Non-material sphere	8.0	4.4	3.7	0.1	5.4	6.7	3.0	4.1	3.1	1.0	1.8	4.6	4.6	6.9	3.6	4.0	10.6	9.5	6.3	4.8	..
Eastern Europe and the Soviet Union																					
Total	10.4	6.9	8.2	6.9	8.9	9.3	4.2	4.7	5.7	0.1	0.8	0.3	1.2	4.7	2.0	3.2	7.1	5.2	5.3	3.1	-6.6
Material sphere	11.0	7.9	9.1	8.5	9.4	10.3	4.7	4.8	6.5	-0.1	1.0	0.4	0.9	4.5	1.7	3.1	6.4	4.0	5.3	..	..
Non-material sphere	10.0	4.6	5.9	3.1	8.0	7.8	3.3	5.1	4.5	1.2	0.2	0.1	2.4	5.4	2.7	3.8	8.9	8.2	5.0	..	..

Sources: ECE secretariat Common Data Base, derived from national or CMEA statistics; *Statisticheskii ezhegodnik stran-chlenov SEV 1972* (CMEA statistical yearbook 1972), p.137; and plan fulfilment reports. National data are aggregated by means of 1975 weights based on CMEA investigations.

a   At current prices in 1984-1989.
b   Calculated from absolute volume figures at 1984 prices.
c   At current prices.

APPENDIX TABLE B.9

Total gross fixed assets [a]
(Annual percentage change)

	1970	1971	1972	1973	1974	1975	1976	1977	1978	1979	1980	1981	1982	1983	1984	1985	1986	1987	1988	1989
Bulgaria [b]																				
Total	8.6	7.3	7.6	7.4	8.7	8.6	7.8	20.8	7.2	6.9	7.1	5.4	7.9	7.4	5.4	6.4	5.4	7.4	5.6	4.3
Material sphere	10.5	8.3	8.2	7.8	11.0	9.4	7.6	8.5	7.6	7.3	8.2	7.3	8.3	7.2	5.2	6.2	5.2	7.8	5.5	..
Non-material sphere	5.8	5.5	6.5	6.6	4.1	6.9	8.0	8.1	6.3	6.0	5.8	7.4	6.9	8.0	5.9	6.9	5.9	6.5	4.9	..
Czechoslovakia																				
Total	5.2	4.9	4.9	5.5	5.6	6.1	6.2	5.4	5.6	5.3	5.4	5.6	4.7	4.5	4.7	4.7	4.4	3.7	3.8	3.7
Material sphere	4.7	5.4	5.2	6.0	5.8	6.6	6.7	6.1	6.1	6.0	5.9	6.5	5.0	4.7	5.2	5.5	4.7	4.2	4.3	4.0
Non-material sphere	3.9	4.4	4.5	4.9	5.5	5.5	5.5	4.4	5.1	4.5	4.6	4.4	4.3	4.1	4.1	3.6	4.0	3.0	3.3	3.4
German Democratic Republic [c]																				
Total	4.7	5.1	4.8	5.2	5.4	6.5	5.3	4.9	4.9	4.7	5.0	4.5	4.8	4.6	4.1	4.3	4.0	3.5	3.6	3.6
Material sphere	5.6	5.8	5.2	5.5	5.5	6.8	5.2	4.9	5.0	4.8	5.3	4.5	4.8	4.3	3.9	4.4	4.2	3.8	4.0	4.1
Non-material sphere	1.7	3.5	3.8	4.6	5.1	5.7	5.6	4.7	4.7	4.3	4.2	4.6	4.8	5.2	4.4	3.9	3.4	2.7	2.8	2.5
Hungary																				
Total	5.9	5.8	6.0	5.7	5.5	6.6	6.0	5.3	5.5	5.5	5.1	3.8	4.3	4.3	3.2	3.3	3.8	3.3	3.4	..
Material sphere	5.0	6.9	6.7	6.6	6.1	7.3	6.4	5.6	6.0	5.9	5.1	3.8	4.2	4.3	2.7	3.0	3.7	3.1	3.0	..
Non-material sphere	..	..	..	..	..	..	5.5	4.7	4.6	4.9	5.2	3.9	4.4	4.4	3.6	4.0	4.0	3.6	4.1	..
Poland																				
Total	5.0	2.9	5.2	5.8	7.8	7.6	7.3	7.5	6.7	6.2	4.4	3.3	1.9	2.5	2.4	2.7	2.5	3.8	2.5	2.8
Material sphere	6.9	4.5	7.2	7.9	10.6	9.7	9.8	9.8	8.6	6.4	5.1	3.5	1.8	2.6	2.8	3.0	2.1	3.2	2.6	4.8
Non-material sphere	3.1	0.9	2.5	2.9	3.6	4.3	3.5	4.2	4.2	4.4	3.1	3.1	2.1	2.4	2.0	2.3	1.6	4.7	2.4	..
Romania [b]																				
Total	9.1	9.2	8.2	8.8	10.4	11.7	10.1	9.7	8.7	8.7	8.5	8.3	8.6	8.5	9.0	7.0	7.0	6.4	..	..
Material sphere	10.9	12.0	9.8	10.6	12.5	14.4	12.0	10.7	10.1	9.2	9.2	8.8	9.4	9.1	10.1	7.7	7.7	7.0	6.0	..
Non-material sphere	5.2	4.0	4.8	4.6	5.3	5.8	5.5	6.7	5.6	6.6	6.2	6.4	6.6	6.2	6.3	4.7	4.8	4.2	3.9	..
Soviet Union																				
Total	8.2	7.9	8.1	8.0	7.8	7.6	7.1	6.8	7.0	6.5	6.4	6.3	6.3	6.2	5.8	5.5	5.2	4.9	4.7	..
Material sphere	8.8	8.7	8.0	8.3	9.8	8.6	7.8	7.4	7.7	7.0	7.1	6.9	6.8	6.6	6.1	5.6	5.2	4.8	4.5	4.1
Non-material sphere	6.7	7.9	7.0	7.1	4.2	6.4	5.8	5.9	5.5	5.6	5.2	5.1	5.3	5.5	5.2	5.1	5.5	5.1	5.2	5.1

Sources: ECE secretariat Common Data Base, derived from national and CMEA statistics.

a On a replacement values in constant prices; end-year basis.
b On an prices of time of installation.
c On an annual averages basis.

APPENDIX TABLE B.10

Employment [a]
(Annual percentage change)

	1970	1971	1972	1973	1974	1975	1976	1977	1978	1979	1980	1981	1982	1983	1984	1985	1986	1987	1988	1989	1990
Bulgaria																					
Total*	0.9	0.9	1.3	-	1.0	0.4	0.2	-0.6	0.2	0.9	0.7	1.3	0.7	0.1	-	-0.1	0.5	-	..	-2.8	..
Material sphere	0.3	0.9	0.7	-0.7	0.4	-0.5	-0.5	-0.6	0.1	0.8	0.1	1.2	0.6	0.1	-0.5	-0.3	0.2	-0.1	..	..	..
Non-material sphere	5.4	0.9	5.1	4.3	4.5	5.3	3.8	-0.4	1.1	1.4	3.3	2.1	1.3	0.1	2.3	1.1	1.6	0.6	..	..	..
Czechoslovakia																					
Total	1.1	0.3	0.1	0.5	1.0	0.8	0.5	0.8	0.9	1.0	1.0	0.7	0.4	0.4	0.9	1.0	1.3	0.6	0.6	0.3	-6.2 [b]
Material sphere	1.1	0.4	-0.4	0.4	0.7	0.4	-	0.3	0.6	0.6	0.4	0.3	0.1	0.4	0.7	0.6	1.0	0.5	0.1	-0.2	..
Non-material sphere	1.0	-	1.9	1.0	2.2	1.9	2.0	2.4	2.1	2.4	3.0	1.7	1.3	0.5	1.7	2.0	2.3	1.0	2.4	..	..
German Dem. Rep. [c,d,e]																					
Total	0.2	0.5	0.1	0.5	0.6	0.5	1.0	0.8	0.8	0.7	0.4	0.5	0.6	0.7	0.5	0.2	-	0.2	0.3	-1.0	..
Material sphere	-0.1	0.1	-0.3	0.1	0.3	0.3	0.8	0.6	0.6	0.4	0.2	0.2	0.2	0.4	0.3	0.1	-0.2	-0.1	*	-0.8	..
Non-material sphere	1.7	2.6	1.6	2.4	1.8	1.6	1.8	1.7	1.7	2.1	1.2	1.7	2.0	1.9	1.3	0.9	0.8	1.2	0.7	-0.1	..
Hungary [c,f]																					
Total	1.2	0.6	0.5	0.3	0.2	0.2	-	-0.2	-	-	-0.7	-0.7	-0.4	-0.6	-0.6	-0.5	-0.3	-0.5	0.6	*	-1.0*
Material sphere	1.1	0.3	0.2	-0.1	-0.3	-0.3	-0.6	-0.7	-0.3	-0.5	-1.2	-1.1	-0.8	0.4	-0.5	-1.2	-1.4	..	-1.0*	-2.0*	..
Non-material sphere	2.3	2.3	2.4	2.7	3.0	2.9	2.8	1.8	1.4	2.5	1.9	1.1	0.9	-1.4	-0.1	2.7	4.0	2.8	2.8	1.0*	-1.0*
Poland																					
Total	1.2	2.0	2.6	2.3	2.0	1.7	0.3	1.3	0.4	0.8	0.3	0.8	-2.9	-0.3	0.3	1.0	0.6	0.2	-0.6	-0.7	-3.2
Material sphere	2.0	1.4	2.3	1.9	1.7	1.9	-	1.2	0.1	0.5	-0.1	0.2	-3.1	-0.8	-0.3	0.5	0.3	-	-1.1	..	..
Non-material sphere	-3.1	5.7	4.5	4.5	3.4	0.4	1.9	2.0	2.0	2.5	2.3	4.0	-2.1	2.4	3.0	3.0	1.7	-1.1	1.4	..	..
Romania																					
Total	-0.4	0.3	-	-0.1	0.4	0.8	0.4	0.2	0.6	0.4	0.1	-0.3	0.7	0.6	0.1	0.7	-	..	..	..	..
Material sphere	-0.4	-0.1	-0.4	-0.2	-	0.4	-0.2	0.2	0.3	-0.2	0.3	-0.6	0.5	0.7	-	0.5	-0.2	-0.1	..	..	..
Non-material sphere	-0.9	2.9	3.0	0.1	3.1	3.6	5.0	0.7	2.5	3.8	-1.3	2.0	1.7	-0.2	0.8	1.6	0.8	1.2	..	..	..
Eastern Europe																					
Total	0.7	1.0	1.0	0.9	1.1	1.0	0.4	0.6	0.5	0.7	0.3	0.5	-0.7	0.1	0.3	0.6	..	..	..	..	..
Material sphere	0.8	0.6	0.6	0.6	0.7	0.8	-	0.5	0.2	0.3	-	-	-0.9	-0.1	-	0.2	..	..	..	..	..
Non-material sphere	-	2.9	3.1	2.7	2.9	2.0	2.6	1.6	1.9	2.5	1.7	2.5	0.3	1.0	1.7	2.1	..	..	..	..	..
Soviet Union [g]																					
Total	1.7	2.0	2.0	1.9	1.9	1.6	1.4	1.5	1.6	1.3	1.2	0.9	0.9	0.6	0.6	0.6	0.5	-0.2	-1.6	-1.5	-0.7
Material sphere	1.3	1.6	1.5	1.5	1.6	1.2	1.5	1.2	1.3	0.8	0.8	0.7	0.7	0.5	0.4	0.3	0.5	-0.3	-2.7	-2.2	..
Non-material sphere	3.4	3.5	3.5	3.4	3.0	3.0	1.1	2.5	2.7	2.9	2.6	1.8	1.3	1.1	1.3	1.5	0.5	0.2	2.0	0.8	..
Eastern Europe																					
and the Soviet Union																					
Total	1.4	1.7	1.7	1.6	1.6	1.4	1.1	1.2	1.3	1.1	0.9	0.8	0.4	0.5	0.5	0.6	..	..	..	..	..
Material sphere	1.1	1.3	1.2	1.2	1.3	1.1	1.0	1.0	0.9	0.6	0.6	0.5	0.2	0.3	0.2	0.3	..	..	..	..	..
Non-material sphere	2.5	3.4	3.4	3.2	3.0	2.7	1.5	2.3	2.5	2.8	2.4	2.0	1.0	1.1	1.4	1.7	..	..	..	..	..

Sources: ECE secretariat Common Data Base, derived from national statistics.

a   Annual averages.
b   State and corporative sector only.
c   Economically active population.
d   30 September of each year.
e   Including apprentices.
f   Mid-year estimates.
g   1970-1989: Workers and *kolkhoz* members engaged in the collective sector.

APPENDIX TABLE B.11

Gross industrial production
(*Annual percentage change*)

	1970	1971	1972	1973	1974	1975	1976	1977	1978	1979	1980	1981	1982	1983	1984	1985	1986	1987	1988	1989	1990
Bulgaria [a]	9.6	9.1	9.1	9.0	8.1	9.6	6.8	6.8	6.9	5.4	4.2	5.4	4.6	4.3	4.2	3.2	4.0	4.2	5.1	2.2	-14.1
Czechoslovakia	8.5	6.9	6.6	6.8	6.2	7.0	5.5	5.6	5.0	3.7	3.5	2.1	1.1	2.8	4.0	3.5	3.2	2.5	2.1	0.8	-3.7
German Dem. Rep.	6.7	5.7	6.0	6.7	7.2	6.4	5.9	4.8	4.8	4.6	4.7	4.7	3.1	4.1	4.2	4.4	3.7	3.1	3.2	2.3	-28.1
Hungary	7.9	6.7	5.2	7.0	8.4	4.7	4.5	5.7	5.4	3.1	-1.7	2.4	2.5	1.2	3.2	0.7	1.9	3.5	-0.3	-2.5	-4.5
Poland	8.1	7.9	10.7	11.2	11.4	10.9	9.3	6.9	4.9	2.7	-	-10.8	-2.1	6.4	5.2	4.5	4.7	3.4	5.3	-0.5	-23.3
Romania	12.1	11.6	11.6	14.4	14.7	12.2	11.4	12.2	9.1	8.0	6.6	2.8	1.0	4.7	6.7	3.9	7.3	2.4	3.1	-2.1	-19.8
Eastern Europe	8.4	7.6	8.3	9.3	9.5	8.8	7.7	7.0	5.8	4.5	3.1	-0.5	1.1	4.4	4.9	3.9	4.5	3.1	3.5	0.1	-19.0
Soviet Union [b]	8.5	7.7	6.5	7.5	8.0	7.6	4.8	5.7	4.8	3.4	3.6	3.4	2.9	4.2	4.1	3.4	4.4	3.8	3.9	1.7	-1.2
Eastern Europe and the Soviet Union	8.5	7.7	7.0	8.0	8.4	7.9	5.6	6.1	5.1	3.7	3.4	2.3	2.4	4.3	4.3	3.5	4.4	3.6	3.8	1.3	-6.2

Sources: ECE secretariat Common Data Base, derived from national or CMEA statistics. National data are aggregated by means of 1965 weights based on CMEA investigations.

a   Based on rounded index numbers (1956 = 100).
b   Based on rounded index numbers (1940 = 100).

APPENDIX TABLE B.12

Industry: Gross investments, gross fixed assets and employment [a]
(Annual percentage change)

	1970	1971	1972	1973	1974	1975	1976	1977	1978	1979	1980	1981	1982	1983	1984	1985	1986	1987	1988	1989
Bulgaria																				
Investment [a]	5.0	-0.9	2.7	7.8	1.1	18.5	1.7	17.8	1.2	-0.2	9.0	10.6	10.1	-2.8	4.3	12.2	11.7	8.6	4.0	..
Gross fixed assets	..	6.8	9.3	9.2	12.9	8.9	6.7	9.7	8.6	8.2	10.2	8.1	9.8	7.5	5.7	7.1	6.1	10.4	6.5	..
Employment	1.1	3.8	2.6	1.8	2.9	2.3	1.3	0.6	1.4	1.8	1.5	2.8	2.4	1.4	0.8	0.5	1.3	1.3	..	..
Czechoslovakia																				
Investment	5.0	4.7	3.2	15.5	7.8	5.0	8.4	7.3	3.2	6.6	3.6	-1.4	-4.4	-3.0	-4.8	6.5	1.6	10.1	6.7	1.4
Gross fixed assets	..	5.3	5.0	5.7	5.7	6.3	6.9	6.2	5.6	5.9	5.9	6.7	5.2	4.6	5.2	5.8	4.8	4.3	4.3	3.5
Employment	1.2	0.2	0.8	0.9	0.4	0.7	0.1	0.5	0.8	0.6	0.5	0.6	0.4	0.5	0.4	0.5	1.4	0.6	0.4	0.1
German Democratic Republic																				
Investment	13.0	3.6	7.6	10.1	-1.0	1.3	8.3	6.5	5.5	3.2	4.0	2.7	-1.4	3.6	-7.4	2.4	5.5	12.8	8.3	1.2
Gross fixed assets	..	5.8	5.6	5.9	6.2	8.0	5.1	4.8	5.1	4.7	5.6	4.6	5.4	4.8	4.3	5.2	4.9	4.1	4.4	4.4
Employment	0.1	0.4	0.7	0.8	0.1	-	0.9	0.7	0.7	0.6	0.1	0.5	0.3	0.3	0.4	0.2	-0.5	-0.3	0.1	-1.4
Hungary																				
Investment	9.0	11.3	0.6	-0.2	9.3	10.8	8.0	23.3	3.3	-1.8	-11.5	-8.1	0.2	-2.5	-2.2	-0.2	-6.3	5.4	-7.0	9.6
Gross fixed assets	..	8.4	8.1	7.4	7.2	9.9	6.6	7.3	9.1	8.1	6.4	4.3	4.9	5.7	4.7	3.3	5.7	3.7	3.6	..
Employment	0.1	-0.4	0.6	1.1	0.4	-0.8	-1.3	-1.0	-0.9	-1.6	-2.3	-2.3	-2.1	-2.2	-1.2	-0.3	-0.4	-1.3	-2.0	..
Poland																				
Investment	1.0	10.4	34.6	26.7	22.2	17.0	2.3	-2.4	-4.7	-15.4	-13.9	-27.2	-12.9	6.2	13.7	9.9	6.8	4.8	4.5	9.0
Gross fixed assets	..	6.3	8.9	9.4	13.8	11.1	10.6	12.3	9.6	6.2	4.6	3.4	2.4	2.8	3.0	3.4	2.3	4.1	2.6	3.3
Employment	1.9	3.0	3.9	2.9	2.4	2.6	0.2	1.0	-0.2	-0.1	0.1	-0.2	-4.7	-0.1	0.7	0.3	-2.0	0.2	-0.3	-1
Romania																				
Investment	4.0	12.9	15.0	13.8	9.4	10.7	4.9	16.3	20.4	7.4	2.6	-5.8	-9.6	5.5	11.1	-2.8	4.7	-6.9	-1.3	-10.5
Gross fixed assets	..	13.0	10.6	12.0	14.3	15.6	11.9	10.6	10.0	9.5	9.8	9.2	9.7	9.1	9.6	7.6	8.7	7.2	7.1	6.1
Employment	4.3	6.6	5.6	6.9	7.1	5.3	3.8	4.1	2.6	3.9	3.2	2.0	2.1	1.7	-0.2	1.7	..	..	..	..
Eastern Europe																				
Employment	1.4	2.1	2.5	2.4	2.1	1.8	0.8	1.1	0.7	0.8	0.6	0.5	-0.9	0.4	0.3	0.6	..	..	..	..
Soviet Union																				
Investment [b]	13.0	5.2	7.1	5.5	7.1	9.3	4.7	4.5	4.9	0.2	4.3	4.0	2.8	5.5	3.7	4.4	8.4	5.7	5.9	7.8
Gross fixed assets	..	9.4	7.5	8.7	8.3	9.1	8.1	7.0	7.9	7.1	7.8	7.0	6.9	6.8	6.6	6.0	5.5	4.3	4.9	4.3
Employment	1.4	1.4	1.3	1.3	1.7	1.9	2.2	1.7	1.7	1.3	1.1	0.9	1.0	0.6	0.3	0.4	0.3	-0.2	-2.0	-2.6
Eastern Europe and the Soviet Union																				
Employment	1.4	1.6	1.7	1.7	1.8	1.8	1.8	1.5	1.3	1.2	0.9	0.8	0.4	0.5	0.3	0.4	..	..	..	..

Sources: ECE secretariat Common Data Base, derived from national or CMEA statistics; *Statisticheskii ezhegodnik stran-chlenov SEV 1972* (CMEA statistical yearbook 1972), p.143; and plan fulfilment reports.

a At current prices in 1984-1988.
b Calculated from absolute volume figures at 1984 prices.

APPENDIX TABLE B.13

Gross agricultural output
(Annual percentage change)

	1970	1971	1972	1973	1974	1975	1976	1977	1978	1979	1980	1981	1982	1983	1984	1985	1986	1987	1988	1989	1990
Bulgaria [a]																					
Total	3.9	1.9	5.6	1.3	-1.5	7.5	4.1	-4.7	4.3	6.1	-4.6	5.9	5.2	-7.2	7.0	-12.3	11.7	-5.1	-0.1	0.4	-8.8
Crop	2.3	-0.3	8.5	0.2	-7.5	7.8	5.6	-9.5	4.5	5.6	-8.7	10.2	7.9	-17.4	14.4	-22.5	22.7	-8.8	-0.3	4.1	-14.0
Animal	6.9	6.1	1.4	3.1	7.4	7.3	2.0	2.0	4.0	6.5	0.3	2.2	2.6	3.0	1.1	-2.9	3.7	-1.9	0.4	-2.6	-3.7
Czechoslovakia																					
Total	1.3	2.0	4.3	3.8	2.2	-1.0	-3.2	9.4	2.1	-3.3	4.8	-2.5	4.4	4.2	4.4	-1.6	0.6	0.9	2.9	1.8	-3.7
Crop	-4.5	0.4	4.5	4.0	1.5	-2.6	-8.2	16.8	1.7	-7.2	6.2	-5.3	13.9	2.8	6.1	-4.1	-2.5	1.8	4.0	1.7	-5.2
Animal	6.3	3.3	4.1	3.6	2.7	0.2	0.5	4.3	2.4	-0.3	3.9	-0.5	-2.0	5.4	3.1	0.4	2.9	0.3	2.1	2.0	-2.6
German Dem. Rep.																					
Total	3.8	-0.3	9.3	-0.3	7.2	-2.0	-5.0	6.2	1.1	3.0	1.3	1.5	-4.1	3.9	6.6	3.9	-	-0.3	-2.1	1.6	-
Crop	10.8	-5.9	18.3	-7.8	8.8	-9.6	-12.5	20.9	-	5.3	-3.2	2.3	1.5	0.9	11.5	5.3	-3.7	-0.3	-6.6	1.4	..
Animal	-	4.0	4.4	5.3	6.1	2.2	-0.6	-0.1	1.7	1.8	3.8	1.5	-7.0	5.5	4.1	3.1	2.2	-0.3	0.3	1.7	..
Hungary																					
Total	-5.7	7.6	2.6	6.3	3.2	3.7	-2.7	10.9	1.1	-1.5	4.6	2.0	7.3	-2.7	2.9	-5.5	2.4	-2.0	4.3	-1.3	-6.5
Crop	-16.4	9.5	5.8	7.8	0.5	4.7	-7.1	12.3	-1.5	-3.2	7.6	1.6	9.4	-7.5	4.9	-5.4	3.7	-5.5	7.5	0.1	-10.5
Animal	10.4	5.5	-1.0	4.5	6.4	2.5	2.7	9.6	3.7	0.1	1.9	2.4	5.3	2.2	1.0	-5.6	1.1	1.5	1.5	-2.7	-2.0
Poland																					
Total	2.2	3.6	8.4	7.3	1.6	-2.1	-1.1	1.4	4.1	-1.5	-10.7	3.8	-2.8	3.3	5.7	0.7	5.0	-2.3	1.2	1.5	-1.4
Crop	4.3	1.1	7.8	6.5	-0.7	-3.0	5.0	-7.2	5.4	-3.7	-15.2	18.9	-2.5	5.9	7.4	-2.0	6.3	-2.0	-0.3	2.7	-
Animal	-1.1	6.6	9.0	8.2	4.2	-1.0	-8.7	13.7	2.6	1.3	-5.6	-8.9	-3.2	0.4	3.7	4.0	3.2	-2.7	3.2	-0.1	-3.2
Romania																					
Total	-4.9	18.9	9.7	1.0	1.1	2.9	17.3	-0.8	-1.2	5.7	-5.0	-0.4	6.9	-	13.3	0.7	-5.5	-8.9	5.7	-5.1	-3.0
Crop	-11.8	26.3	7.6	-3.2	0.6	0.6	21.5	-5.0	-4.3	6.5	-6.1	-1.0	15.2	-3.5	19.1	1.1	-8.8	-14.0	8.4	-1.7	..
Animal	5.4	8.9	12.5	7.7	1.5	6.7	11.5	5.6	2.7	3.7	-3.1	-0.6	-3.7	5.0	6.2	0.5	-1.4	-2.6	3.0	-8.9	..
Eastern Europe																					
Total	0.5	5.1	7.3	4.1	2.3	0.2	1.2	3.2	2.1	0.8	-3.7	1.9	1.5	1.2	6.8	-0.9	1.8	-2.9	1.9	-	-
Crop	-1.1	3.9	8.7	2.0	0.7	-1.8	1.8	1.4	1.5	-0.4	-5.9	6.5	5.3	-0.7	10.0	-2.5	1.4	-4.2	1.5	1.4	..
Animal	2.8	5.9	6.4	6.3	4.4	1.9	-0.8	7.4	2.7	1.9	-1.3	-2.3	-2.2	3.1	3.6	0.9	1.9	-1.4	2.1	-1.8	..
Soviet Union																					
Total	10.3	1.1	-4.1	16.1	-2.7	-5.3	6.5	4.0	2.7	-3.1	-1.9	-1.0	5.5	6.2	-0.1	0.1	5.3	-0.6	1.7	0.8	-2.3
Crop	11.8	-1.3	-7.7	27.1	-10.0	-10.5	18.4	-1.8	5.0	-5.9	-2.3	-2.4	9.2	6.0	-1.9	-1.0	6.1	-2.7	-1.4	1.0	-4.3
Animal	8.7	3.5	-0.6	6.1	5.2	-2.5	-2.4	9.4	0.8	-0.7	-1.6	0.1	2.6	6.3	1.4	1.0	4.7	1.2	4.1	1.6	-0.8
Eastern Europe and the Soviet Union																					
Total	7.0	2.4	-0.4	12.0	-1.1	-3.5	4.6	3.7	2.5	-1.8	-2.5	-0.1	4.1	4.5	2.1	-0.2	4.1	-1.4	1.8	0.5	-
Crop	7.6	0.3	-2.5	18.3	-6.7	-7.6	12.7	-0.8	3.9	-4.2	-3.5	0.4	7.9	3.8	1.8	-1.5	4.5	-3.2	-0.4	1.1	..
Animal	6.7	4.3	1.7	6.2	4.9	-0.9	-1.8	8.7	1.5	0.3	-1.5	0.9	0.9	5.2	2.1	1.0	3.7	0.4	3.4	0.5	..

Sources: ECE secretariat Common Data Base, derived from national or CMEA statistics. National data are aggregated by means of 1965 weights for total agricultural output based on CMEA investigations.

a Based on index numbers (1939 = 100).

APPENDIX TABLE B.14

Agriculture: Gross investments, gross fixed assets and employment

(Annual percentage change)

	1970	1971	1972	1973	1974	1975	1976	1977	1978	1979	1980	1981	1982	1983	1984	1985	1986	1987	1988	1989
Bulgaria																				
Investment [a]	6.0	3.7	11.5	3.8	17.1	5.1	1.4	10.9	-9.8	-1.7	6.9	10.7	-18.6	1.6	2.6	8.0	-12.1	13.0	25.8	..
Gross fixed assets	..	6.6	6.3	6.4	-0.4	14.5	7.3	6.6	4.7	4.5	5.3	5.3	5.0	5.1	2.6	3.5	4.4	3.8	-	..
Employment	-4.1	-4.2	-2.0	-4.1	-3.5	-6.3	-4.9	-4.0	-2.6	-0.1	-1.8	-1.5	-2.8	-3.1	-3.2	-2.5	-2.0	-3.5	..	..
Czechoslovakia																				
Investment	-5.0	5.8	9.0	18.5	10.0	13.1	-0.5	6.3	8.0	-6.6	-3.2	5.0	4.6	12.7	1.6	7.8	3.0	-1.5	0.4	-3.9
Gross fixed assets	..	5.4	5.4	5.5	6.3	6.8	7.2	6.4	6.8	6.3	6.0	6.1	5.3	5.6	5.8	6.4	5.4	5.2	4.9	4.8
Employment	-0.9	-1.5	-6.2	-3.0	-0.8	-2.2	-2.1	-2.3	-1.9	-0.7	-0.2	-0.0	-0.8	-1.4	0.9	0.5	-0.5	-0.9	-1.6	-3.3
German Democratic Republic																				
Investment	-1.0	2.3	-2.6	4.8	9.1	0.8	2.8	3.5	-3.2	-3.9	-1.1	2.6	-7.5	-9.4	-10.8	-5.7	5.8	8.6	9.1	6.1
Gross fixed assets	..	5.6	4.8	5.6	4.3	4.2	4.8	5.1	5.0	5.4	4.9	4.9	4.3	4.0	3.6	3.2	2.9	3.0	3.4	3.3
Employment	-3.3	-2.4	-3.7	-1.9	-1.4	-0.8	-1.4	-0.5	0.5	-0.2	0.3	0.4	0.6	1.5	2.3	0.7	0.5	0.1	0.1	-1.0
Hungary																				
Investment	26.0	-	-13.3	-	7.7	14.3	-5.7	8.8	9.5	-2.0	-11.2	8.0	-1.0	-15.4	-7.2	-7.0	6.9	21.4	-22.5	-7.3
Gross fixed assets	..	9.3	8.6	8.6	6.9	7.0	5.8	5.9	5.8	5.6	4.3	4.3	4.3	3.4	0.5	2.1	1.7	2.5	1.7	..
Employment	-1.7	-2.3	-2.5	-3.4	-3.7	-2.6	-1.9	-1.5	-0.5	0.6	0.2	-0.5	-0.0	-0.3	-2.2	-4.1	-4.6	-3.9	-3.0	..
Poland																				
Investment	3.0	4.7	14.9	17.1	18.0	16.1	2.0	12.9	5.9	-3.6	-17.2	-12.5	-15.3	5.6	4.6	-1.9	0.4	3.6	3.5	-9.5
Gross fixed assets	..	2.9	4.2	5.2	6.1	6.4	7.0	7.2	7.0	6.5	5.7	4.0	1.9	2.0	2.6	2.4	1.6	2.1	2.1	1.5
Employment	-0.3	-0.3	-1.4	-1.8	-1.6	1.4	-0.4	1.4	-0.2	1.7	0.2	1.1	-0.5	-2.2	-1.9	-0.1	-1.2	-0.7	-2.6	..
Romania																				
Investment [a]	25.0	10.9	2.4	0.4	8.9	13.9	12.2	12.1	11.4	-1.7	4.4	10.0	-1.8	8.6	9.2	10.7	-3.4	-3.6	-5.0	3.2
Gross fixed assets	..	10.0	9.1	9.2	9.2	10.5	7.6	10.6	6.9	7.0	5.6	8.8	10.1	9.9	9.2	8.6	7.5	7.1	5.1	3.1
Employment	-3.6	-4.4	-4.9	-4.4	-4.3	-4.5	-4.7	-4.1	-4.1	-5.2	-4.6	-2.7	-1.0	0.3	0.8	-	-0.2	..	..	..
Eastern Europe																				
Employment	-2.1	-2.4	-3.2	-3.1	-2.7	-1.9	-2.4	-1.3	-1.6	-0.8	-1.7	-0.4	-0.7	-1.2	-0.9	-0.6	-1.1	..	..	..
Soviet Union																				
Investment [b]	12.0	14.4	9.2	10.1	8.5	9.1	4.2	2.6	4.6	1.6	1.6	2.6	1.6	3.5	-2.8	1.3	6.4	2.3	6.3	5.8
Gross fixed assets	..	7.5	10.5	8.7	11.7	9.2	7.8	7.8	7.7	6.7	6.7	6.7	7.1	5.9	5.2	4.3	4.4	4.2	2.9	2.5
Employment	-1.5	-0.7	-0.6	0.5	0.1	-1.3	0.4	-0.7	-0.2	-1.1	-0.5	-0.5	0.4	0.2	0.2	-0.7	-1.0	-1.5	-4.2	-2.6
Eastern Europe and the Soviet Union																				
Employment	-1.7	-1.3	-1.5	-0.8	-0.9	-1.5	-0.6	-0.9	-0.6	-1.0	-0.9	-0.5	-	-0.3	-0.2	-0.6	-1.0	..	..	..

Sources: ECE secretariat Common Data Base, derived from national or CMEA statistics; *Statisticheskii ezhegodnik stran-chlenov SEV 1972* (CMEA statistical yearbook 1972), p.143.

a At current prices in 1984-1988.
b Calculated from absolute volume figures at 1984 prices.

APPENDIX TABLE B.15

Export and import volumes

(Annual percentage change)

	1970	1971	1972	1973	1974	1975	1976	1977	1978	1979	1980	1981	1982	1983	1984	1985	1986	1987	1988	1989	1990
Bulgaria																					
Exports	8.7	8.0	11.6	9.6	8.3	12.4	13.4	14.3	10.7	13.7	12.2	8.3	11.4	4.5	4.7	7.4	-3.7	1.8	2.4	-3.4	-26.0*
Imports	4.7	13.3	13.3	10.7	21.9	12.6	-2.3	5.3	7.1	2.1	4.1	9.3	3.1	5.2	2.2	10.5	3.9	-1.4	5.3	-6.5	-20.0*
Czechoslovakia																					
Exports	20.7	8.4	7.7	3.5	5.0	6.8	7.5	8.9	7.5	2.9	4.9	0.3	6.1	5.7	9.5	2.6	1.2	3.4	3.2	-2.0	-13.0*
Imports	15.9	5.9	4.1	9.8	10.9	1.9	3.4	7.1	3.6	2.2	-1.6	-6.9	2.9	2.1	0.3	4.6	2.7	4.3	2.9	2.7	-.*
German Dem. Rep.																					
Exports	8.8	10.1	11.6	7.3	8.2	7.0	6.1	4.3	7.7	8.9	3.7	9.8	6.2	12.0	2.3	2.3	-4.5	-0.1	-0.2	0.5	-.*
Imports	15.9	2.0	7.5	12.9	8.6	4.9	11.0	4.5	-0.2	6.5	5.0	-1.7	-6.2	7.2	4.8	4.1	2.9	9.0	4.7	2.4	15.0
Hungary																					
Exports	7.6	7.6	19.3	12.5	3.5	4.8	8.2	12.6	1.5	12.5	1.0	2.6	7.3	9.4	5.8	-0.3	-2.2	4.0	5.1	-	-4.3
Imports	27.1	17.3	-5.1	2.9	17.5	5.7	3.9	8.5	12.5	-3.3	-1.1	0.1	-0.1	3.9	0.1	1.1	2.1	3.3	-2.0	1.0	-3.4
Poland																					
Exports	10.1	6.5	15.2	11.0	12.8	8.3	5.3	7.0	5.7	6.8	-4.2	-19.0	8.7	10.3	9.5	1.3	4.9	4.8	9.1	0.2	14.9
Imports	10.4	13.8	22.1	22.7	14.1	5.0	10.2	0.2	1.6	-1.2	-1.9	-16.9	-13.7	5.2	8.6	7.9	4.9	4.5	9.4	1.5	-15.6
Romania [a]																					
Exports	3.9	9.8	4.7	18.8	2.2	3.5	11.1	7.3	5.2	5.7	1.2	11.3	-8.3	3.2	15.9	0.3	0.2	-4.3	7.4	-10.8	-46.0*
Imports	8.2	3.1	10.5	10.7	13.4	-3.7	11.5	8.4	17.2	6.8	2.0	-7.2	-22.4	-3.8	10.5	8.5	18.3	-6.3	-5.8	3.7	4.0*
Eastern Europe																					
Exports	10.7	8.6	11.0	9.3	7.0	7.0	7.9	8.0	6.7	7.9	3.1	2.7	5.3	8.0	7.0	2.5	-1.2	1.4	3.7	-2.1	-9.8
Imports	14.0	7.6	8.0	11.9	13.2	4.8	6.2	5.3	4.9	2.7	1.6	-3.4	-4.4	4.2	3.6	5.9	4.4	3.4	3.5	0.5	-0.9
Soviet Union																					
Exports	6.1	3.2	2.7	14.4	2.6	2.5	8.6	10.6	3.4	0.6	1.6	1.9	4.5	3.3	2.5	-4.3	10.0	3.3	4.8	-	-14.0
Imports	7.8	5.9	17.2	14.6	1.0	14.8	7.0	0.9	13.3	1.1	7.5	6.4	9.7	4.0	4.4	4.7	-6.0	-1.6	4.0	9.3	-5.0
Eastern Europe and the Soviet Union																					
Exports	7.8	5.3	6.1	12.3	4.4	4.4	8.3	9.5	4.8	3.8	2.3	2.3	4.9	5.5	4.6	-1.0	4.4	2.4	4.3	-1.0	-12.1
Imports	11.0	6.8	12.2	13.2	7.3	9.4	6.6	3.2	8.9	1.9	4.4	11.5	3.0	4.1	5.2	-1.4	0.8	3.8	5.1		-3.1

Sources: ECE secretariat Common Data Base, derived from national or CMEA statistics. National data are aggregated by means of weights calculated from 1985 US dollar trade shares.

a ECE secretariat estimates.

APPENDIX TABLE B.16

Energy production: Electricity, coal and crude oil
(Billion kWh, million tons)

	1970	1971	1972	1973	1974	1975	1976	1977	1978	1979	1980	1981	1982	1983	1984	1985	1986	1987	1988	1989	1990
Bulgaria																					
Electricity	19.5	21.0	22.3	22.0	22.8	25.2	27.7	29.7	31.5	32.5	34.8	37.0	40.5	42.6	44.7	41.6	41.8	43.5	45.0	44.3	44.0
Coal	29.3	27.0	27.3	26.8	24.3	27.8	25.5	25.2	25.8	28.2	30.2	29.2	32.2	32.4	32.4	30.9	35.2	36.8	34.1	34.3	31.5
Oil	0.3	0.3	0.2	0.2	0.1	0.1	0.1	..	..	..	..	..	..	..	..	0.1	0.1	0.1	..	..	..
Czechoslovakia																					
Electricity	45.2	47.2	51.4	53.5	56.0	59.3	62.7	66.5	69.1	68.1	72.7	73.5	74.7	76.3	78.4	80.6	84.8	85.8	87.4	89.3	86.8
Coal	109.5	113.0	112.9	109.0	110.1	114.4	117.7	121.2	123.2	124.7	123.1	122.8	124.6	127.4	129.3	126.6	126.4	126.1	123.5	117.4	105.0
Oil	0.2	0.2	0.2	0.2	0.1	0.1	0.1	0.1	0.1	0.1	0.1	0.1	0.1	0.1	0.1	0.1	0.1	0.1	0.1	0.1	0.1
German Dem. Rep.																					
Electricity	67.6	69.4	72.8	76.9	80.3	84.5	89.1	92.0	96.0	96.8	98.8	100.7	102.9	104.9	110.1	113.8	115.3	114.2	118.3	119.0	..
Coal	261.6	263.7	249.2	247.0	244.1	247.2	247.4	254.1	253.3	256.1	258.1	266.7	276.0	278.0	296.3	312.2	311.3	309.0	310.3	301.0	..
Oil	0.1	0.1	0.1	0.1	0.1	0.1	0.1	0.1	0.1	0.1	0.1	-	-	..	..	..	..	..	..	..	..
Hungary																					
Electricity	14.5	15.0	16.3	17.6	19.0	20.5	22.0	23.4	25.6	24.5	23.9	24.3	24.7	25.7	26.2	26.7	28.0	29.7	29.2	29.7	29.6
Coal	27.8	27.4	25.8	26.8	25.8	24.9	25.3	25.5	25.7	25.7	25.7	25.9	26.1	25.2	25.0	24.0	23.1	22.8	20.9	20.0	20.1
Oil [a]	1.9	2.0	2.0	2.0	2.0	2.0	2.1	2.2	2.2	2.0	2.0	2.0	2.0	2.0	2.0	2.0	2.0	1.9	1.9	2.0	1.9
Poland																					
Electricity	64.5	69.9	76.5	84.3	91.6	97.2	104.1	109.4	115.6	117.5	121.9	115.0	117.6	125.8	134.8	137.7	140.3	145.8	144.3	145.0	136.0
Coal	172.9	180.0	188.9	195.8	201.8	211.5	218.6	226.9	233.6	239.0	230.0	198.6	227.0	233.6	242.0	249.4	259.3	266.2	266.5	249.4	215.6
Oil	0.4	0.4	0.3	0.4	0.5	0.6	0.5	0.4	0.4	0.3	0.3	0.3	0.2	0.2	0.2	0.2	0.2	0.2	0.2	0.2	0.1
Romania																					
Electricity	35.1	39.5	43.4	46.8	49.1	53.7	58.3	59.9	64.3	64.9	67.5	70.1	68.9	70.3	71.6	71.8	75.5	74.1	75.3	75.9	64.2
Coal	20.5	20.6	23.2	24.9	26.9	27.1	25.8	26.8	29.3	32.8	35.2	36.9	37.9	44.5	44.3	46.6	47.5	51.5	58.8	61.3	38.2
Oil	13.4	13.8	14.1	14.3	14.5	14.6	14.7	14.6	13.7	12.3	11.5	11.6	11.7	11.6	11.5	10.7	10.1	9.5	9.4	9.2	8.0
Eastern Europe																					
Electricity	246.5	262.0	282.7	301.1	318.8	340.4	364.1	380.8	401.9	404.3	419.6	420.6	429.3	445.7	465.8	472.3	485.7	493.1	499.6	503.6	..
Coal	621.6	631.7	627.3	630.3	633.0	652.9	660.3	679.5	690.9	706.4	702.3	680.3	723.7	741.1	769.3	789.7	802.9	812.5	814.1	783.5	..
Oil	16.4	16.7	17.0	17.1	17.4	17.5	17.6	17.4	16.5	14.9	14.0	14.1	14.1	13.9	13.7	13.0	12.4	11.7	11.7	11.5	
Soviet Union																					
Electricity	740.9	800.4	857.4	914.6	975.8	1038.6	1111.4	1150.1	1202.0	1238.2	1293.9	1326.0	1367.1	1418.1	1492.6	1544.0	1599.0	1665.0	1705.1	1721.7	1728.0
Coal	577.5	591.5	603.6	614.7	630.6	644.9	654.4	663.3	664.4	657.6	652.9	637.8	647.3	641.6	634.6	647.8	672.7	680.3	691.5	662.7	628.5
Oil	353.0	371.8	393.8	421.4	450.6	490.8	519.7	545.8	571.5	585.6	603.2	608.8	612.6	616.3	612.7	595.3	614.8	624.2	624.3	607.3	570.0
Eastern Europe and Soviet Union																					
Electricity	987.4	1062.4	1140.2	1215.7	1294.5	1379.0	1475.5	1530.9	1603.9	1642.5	1713.5	1746.6	1796.4	1863.8	1958.4	2016.4	2084.7	2158.1	2204.7	2224.4	..
Coal	1199.1	1223.2	1230.9	1245.0	1263.5	1297.8	1314.7	1342.8	1355.3	1364.0	1355.1	1318.1	1371.1	1382.7	1403.9	1437.4	1475.6	1492.8	1505.6	1445.3	..
Oil	369.4	388.5	410.8	438.5	468.0	508.3	537.3	563.2	588.0	600.4	617.2	622.9	626.7	630.2	626.5	627.2	635.9	636.0	618.7	..	..

Source: Statisticheskii ezhegodnik stran-chlenov SEV (CMEA statistical yearbook), various issues, and ECE secretariat estimates.

a   Excluding gas condensate.

APPENDIX TABLE B.17

Steel production
(Million tons)

	1970	1971	1972	1973	1974	1975	1976	1977	1978	1979	1980	1981	1982	1983	1984	1985	1986	1987	1988	1989	1990
Bulgaria................	1.8	1.9	2.1	2.2	2.2	2.3	2.5	2.6	2.5	2.5	2.6	2.5	2.6	2.8	2.9	2.9	3.0	3.0	2.9	2.9	2.4
Czechoslovakia........	11.5	12.1	12.7	13.2	13.6	14.3	14.7	15.1	15.3	14.8	15.2	15.3	15.0	15.0	14.8	15.0	15.1	15.4	15.4	15.5	15.0
German Dem. Rep.......	5.1	5.4	5.7	5.9	6.2	6.5	6.7	6.8	7.0	7.0	7.3	7.5	7.2	7.2	7.6	7.9	8.0	8.2	8.1	7.8	5.6
Hungary................	3.1	3.1	3.3	3.3	3.5	3.7	3.7	3.7	3.9	3.9	3.8	3.6	3.7	3.6	3.8	3.6	3.7	3.6	3.6	3.4	2.8
Poland.................	11.8	12.7	13.4	14.1	14.6	15.0	15.6	17.8	19.3	19.2	19.5	15.7	14.7	16.2	16.5	16.1	17.1	17.1	16.9	15.1	13.6
Romania................	6.5	6.8	7.4	8.2	8.8	9.5	10.7	11.5	11.8	12.9	13.2	13.0	13.1	12.6	14.4	13.8	14.3	13.9	14.3	14.9	9.7
Eastern Europe.......	39.7	42.0	44.6	46.8	48.9	51.3	53.9	57.5	59.7	60.4	61.5	57.6	56.2	57.5	60.0	59.4	61.2	61.3	61.2	59.1	49.2
Soviet Union..........	115.9	120.7	125.6	131.5	136.2	141.3	144.8	146.7	151.5	149.1	147.9	148.4	147.2	152.5	154.2	154.7	160.5	161.9	163.0	160.1	154.0
Eastern Europe and the Soviet Union	155.6	162.6	170.3	178.3	185.1	192.6	198.7	204.2	211.1	209.5	209.5	206.0	203.4	210.0	214.2	214.1	221.7	223.2	224.2	219.2	203.2

Source: National statistics.

APPENDIX TABLE B.18

Grain production [a]
(Million tons)

	1970	1971	1972	1973	1974	1975	1976	1977	1978	1979	1980	1981	1982	1983	1984	1985	1986	1987	1988	1989	1990
Bulgaria																					
Total	6.9	7.2	8.2	7.4	6.7	7.8	8.6	7.7	7.6	8.4	7.7	8.5	10.1	8.0	9.3	5.5	8.6	7.4	7.9	9.6	8.0
Wheat	3.0	3.1	3.6	3.3	2.9	2.8	3.5	3.4	3.5	3.4	3.8	4.4	4.9	3.6	4.8	3.1	4.3	4.1	4.7	5.4	5.1
Maize	2.4	2.5	3.0	2.6	1.6	2.8	3.0	2.5	2.2	3.2	2.3	2.4	3.4	3.1	3.0	1.3	2.8	1.9	1.6	2.3	1.2
Czechoslovakia																					
Total	7.3	8.9	8.7	9.7	10.5	9.4	9.2	10.5	11.1	9.3	10.9	9.5	10.4	11.2	12.2	12.0	11.0	12.0	12.2	12.3	12.6
Wheat	3.2	3.9	4.0	4.6	5.1	4.2	4.8	5.2	5.6	3.7	5.4	4.3	4.6	5.8	6.2	6.0	5.3	6.2	6.5	6.4	..
Maize	0.5	0.5	0.6	0.6	0.6	0.8	0.5	0.8	0.6	0.9	0.7	0.7	0.9	0.7	0.9	1.0	1.0	1.2	1.0	1.0	..
German Democratic Republic																					
Total	6.5	7.8	8.6	8.6	9.8	9.0	8.2	8.8	9.9	9.0	9.7	8.9	10.1	10.2	11.4	11.7	11.8	11.3	9.9	10.9	..
Wheat	2.1	2.5	2.7	2.9	3.2	2.7	2.7	2.9	3.1	3.1	3.1	2.9	2.7	3.5	3.9	3.9	4.2	4.0	3.7	3.5	..
Maize	-	-	-	-	-	-	-	-	-	-	-	-	-	-	-	-	-	-	-	-	..
Hungary																					
Total	7.8	10.0	10.9	11.8	12.6	12.4	11.5	12.4	13.5	12.2	14.2	13.0	15.1	13.9	15.9	15.0	14.5	14.4	15.4	15.9	12.2
Wheat	2.7	3.9	4.1	4.5	5.0	4.0	5.1	5.3	5.7	3.7	6.1	4.6	5.8	6.0	7.4	6.6	5.8	5.7	7.0	6.5	6.2
Maize	4.1	4.7	5.6	6.0	6.2	7.2	5.1	6.0	6.7	7.4	6.7	7.0	8.0	6.4	6.7	6.8	7.3	7.2	6.3	7.0	4.5
Poland																					
Total	16.6	20.2	20.7	22.2	23.3	19.8	21.1	19.6	21.8	17.6	18.5	19.9	21.4	22.4	24.8	24.2	25.5	26.6	25.1	27.6	28.0
Wheat	4.6	5.5	5.1	5.8	6.4	5.2	5.7	5.3	6.0	4.2	4.2	4.2	4.5	5.2	6.0	6.5	7.5	7.9	7.6	8.5	9.0
Maize	-	-	-	-	-	0.1	0.2	0.2	0.1	0.2	0.1	0.1	0.1	0.1	0.1	0.1	0.1	0.1	0.2	0.2	..
Romania																					
Total	10.9	14.8	17.1	14.0	13.7	15.4	19.9	18.7	19.1	19.4	20.3	20.1	22.5	19.8	23.9	19.8	20.0	17.1	19.5	18.6	17.2
Wheat	3.4	5.6	6.0	5.5	5.0	4.9	6.8	6.5	6.3	4.7	6.5	5.3	6.5	5.3	7.6	5.6	6.4	6.7	8.6	7.5	7.4
Maize	6.5	7.8	9.8	7.4	7.4	9.2	11.6	10.1	10.2	12.4	11.2	11.9	12.6	12.0	13.3	11.9	10.9	7.5	7.2	6.8	6.8
Eastern Europe																					
Total	56.0	68.8	74.3	73.6	76.5	73.8	78.5	77.6	83.0	75.8	81.3	80.1	89.6	85.5	97.6	88.2	91.4	88.8	90.0	94.9	..
Wheat	19.0	24.4	25.6	26.6	27.6	23.8	28.7	28.7	30.2	22.8	29.1	25.9	29.0	29.4	35.9	31.7	33.5	34.7	38.2	38.2	..
Maize	13.5	15.6	19.0	16.6	15.9	20.2	20.5	19.7	19.8	24.2	20.9	22.1	25.0	22.3	24.0	21.2	22.1	17.9	16.2	17.3	..
Soviet Union																					
Total	186.8	181.2	168.2	222.5	195.7	140.1	223.8	195.7	237.4	179.3	189.1	158.3	186.8	192.2	172.6	191.7	210.1	211.4	195.1	211.1	..
Wheat	99.7	98.8	86.0	109.8	83.9	66.2	96.9	92.2	120.9	90.3	98.2	81.1	84.3	77.5	68.6	78.1	92.3	83.3	84.4	92.3	..
Maize	9.4	8.6	9.8	13.2	12.1	7.3	10.1	11.0	8.9	8.4	9.5	9.4	14.7	13.3	13.6	14.4	12.5	14.8	16.0	15.3	..
Eastern Europe and the Soviet Union																					
Total	242.8	250.0	242.5	296.1	272.2	213.9	302.3	273.4	320.4	255.1	270.4	238.3	276.4	277.7	270.2	279.8	301.5	300.2	285.0	305.9	..
Wheat	118.8	123.2	111.6	136.4	111.5	90.1	125.6	120.8	151.2	113.1	127.2	107.0	113.3	106.9	104.6	109.7	125.8	118.1	122.7	130.5	..
Maize	23.0	24.2	28.9	29.8	28.0	27.5	30.6	30.6	28.7	32.6	30.3	31.5	39.7	35.6	37.5	35.6	34.6	32.8	32.2	32.6	..

Sources: ECE secretariat Common Data Base, derived from national and CMEA statistics.

a Including pulses.

APPENDIX TABLE B.19

Saving deposits of the population
(Billions of national currency units)

	1970	1971	1972	1973	1974	1975	1976	1977	1978	1979	1980	1981	1982	1983	1984	1985	1986	1987	1988	1989	1990
Bulgaria	4	5	5	6	7	8	8	9	9	10	10	11	12	13	14	16	16	17	18	19	..
Czechoslovakia	64	74	85	98	107	116	126	137	143	148	156	165	178	191	204	219	235	252	266	278	..
German Dem.Rep.	52	56	60	65	70	75	80	86	92	97	100	103	108	113	119	125	132	142	152	160	..
Hungary [a]	42	48	54	62	71	81	93	107	124	135	144	159	174	191	211	233	261	253	264	261	315
Poland [b]	115	134	167	210	261	303	334	371	409	457	500	665	867	1058	1237	1709	2148	2554	3831	8629	41293
Romania	..	..	..	36	41	47	55	64	80	90	101	115	118	128	139	153	167	177	186	202	247
Soviet Union	47	53	61	69	79	91	103	117	131	146	157	166	174	187	202	221	243	267	297	338	381

Sources: National statistics (CSSR, GDR, Hungary, Poland); IMF, *International Financial Statistics* (Romania); *Statisticheskii ezhegodnik stran-chlenov SEV* (CMEA statistical yearbook) various years (Bulgaria, USSR).

[a] Forint saving deposits only. Since 1987 current accounts of private entrepreneurs are excluded.
[b] For 1980, and 1985-date increased coverage.

Appendix C. International trade and payments

Data for this section were compiled from international [3] and national statistical sources, as indicated in the notes to individual tables. Regional aggregates for tables C.2-C.3 were obtained by means of weights representing 1985 shares in the US dollar value of trade.

---

[3] United Nations COMTRADE data base, IMF, IBRD, OECD, BIS.

APPENDIX TABLE C.1

World trade: Value, by region
(*Billion US dollars*)

	1970	1971	1972	1973	1974	1975	1976	1977	1978	1979	1980	1981	1982	1983	1984	1985	1986	1987	1988	1989	1990 a
Exports																					
Developed market economies	216.8	242.6	288.9	393.0	528.9	564.2	628.0	712.9	854.8	1048.7	1237.7	1221.0	1156.2	1142.9	1219.1	1261.8	1474.0	1722.0	1966.6	2101.1	1752.7
North America	59.4	61.9	70.4	97.3	133.9	142.9	157.4	166.7	194.3	244.7	293.3	311.4	287.7	282.4	314.2	309.8	317.5	352.2	449.0	484.1	389.7
Western Europe b	131.9	149.4	180.3	246.0	322.7	348.0	383.4	443.1	535.4	667.4	771.5	713.7	685.1	669.1	684.3	721.8	887.8	1066.7	1182.6	1255.6	1080.0
Southern Europe	6.2	7.2	9.1	12.7	16.7	17.4	19.9	22.0	26.9	34.3	42.4	44.4	45.0	44.4	50.9	53.1	57.9	71.7	81.1	87.5	76.2
Japan	19.3	24.1	29.1	37.0	55.5	55.8	67.3	81.1	98.2	102.3	130.4	151.5	138.4	147.0	169.7	177.2	210.8	231.3	264.9	273.9	206.7
Developing market economies	53.9	62.8	74.6	110.5	232.4	216.9	262.7	296.3	312.9	442.2	567.7	558.5	467.9	458.3	471.5	449.5	414.8	510.4	580.4	645.5	580.2
Oil-exporting countries c	17.6	23.1	27.5	40.5	131.5	120.8	146.8	159.5	155.6	237.6	303.4	280.8	210.6	180.3	166.1	153.6	112.3	127.3	128.6	144.0	112.2
Non-oil developing countries	36.4	39.7	47.1	69.9	100.9	96.1	115.9	136.8	157.3	204.6	264.3	277.7	257.3	278.0	305.4	295.9	302.5	383.1	451.8	501.5	468.0
Eastern Europe and Soviet Union	31.0	33.8	40.2	52.6	65.6	78.5	85.4	99.5	113.8	136.8	157.4	158.9	166.8	175.1	177.8	166.1	179.7	198.0	208.2	203.7	139.1
Eastern Europe	18.2	20.0	24.7	31.4	38.2	45.2	48.2	54.3	61.4	72.1	80.9	79.5	79.8	83.7	86.6	79.3	82.8	90.4	97.7	94.6	63.0
Soviet Union	12.8	13.8	15.5	21.3	27.4	33.3	37.2	45.2	52.4	64.7	76.5	79.4	87.0	91.4	91.2	86.8	96.9	107.6	110.5	109.1	76.1
Total above	301.7	339.3	403.6	556.1	826.9	859.5	976.1	1108.6	1281.5	1627.8	1962.8	1938.4	1790.9	1776.2	1868.3	1877.4	2068.5	2430.4	2754.7	2950.3	2472.0
Memorandum item																					
ECE region	228.5	252.3	299.9	408.6	539.0	586.8	646.1	731.3	870.4	1083.2	1264.7	1228.4	1184.6	1171.0	1227.2	1250.7	1443.0	1688.7	1909.9	2030.9	1685.1
Imports																					
Developed market economies	227.5	252.8	302.3	414.6	593.1	596.7	687.0	779.7	898.6	1153.2	1384.0	1311.7	1228.9	1211.5	1322.4	1356.9	1535.1	1817.6	2051.1	2212.4	1843.0
North America	56.6	64.8	78.9	97.9	145.1	142.0	172.7	202.5	232.3	278.9	319.5	343.4	313.0	334.7	424.2	433.1	467.8	517.0	572.3	612.7	470.4
Western Europe b	139.8	154.8	183.3	255.5	350.4	359.0	409.2	461.0	540.0	705.0	846.3	750.1	711.0	682.1	693.2	722.1	860.9	1046.5	1173.2	1254.5	1083.4
Southern Europe	12.1	13.3	16.2	22.8	35.6	37.9	40.3	44.9	46.4	59.5	76.8	75.4	73.3	68.3	68.9	71.2	78.8	103.0	118.2	135.4	124.1
Japan	18.9	19.8	23.9	38.4	61.9	57.9	64.9	71.3	79.9	109.8	141.3	142.9	131.5	126.4	136.2	130.5	127.6	151.0	187.4	209.7	165.1
Developing market economies	53.8	61.0	66.0	92.3	151.7	175.0	190.6	229.0	275.8	326.6	436.7	498.0	461.5	436.6	434.6	408.8	398.4	458.4	541.2	575.2	571.2
Oil-exporting countries c	9.6	11.1	13.8	19.9	32.1	50.9	63.1	83.8	94.6	98.0	131.4	158.0	160.3	144.5	125.8	105.2	92.0	91.4	104.1	95.0	74.0
Non-oil developing countries	44.2	49.8	52.2	72.4	119.5	124.2	127.5	145.2	181.2	228.5	305.3	340.0	301.2	292.1	308.8	303.6	306.4	367.0	437.0	480.2	497.2
Eastern Europe and Soviet Union	30.3	32.8	40.6	53.3	67.8	88.2	92.6	101.5	118.9	135.0	155.2	155.2	153.1	157.9	159.7	155.9	170.5	182.7	197.1	201.4	161.0
Eastern Europe	18.5	20.3	24.4	32.4	43.0	51.2	54.4	60.6	68.2	77.3	86.6	82.1	75.4	77.7	79.6	73.0	81.6	86.8	90.0	86.9	71.7
Soviet Union	11.7	12.5	16.2	20.9	24.8	36.9	38.1	40.9	50.7	57.8	68.5	73.2	77.7	80.2	80.1	82.9	88.9	95.9	107.1	114.5	89.3
Total above	311.5	346.6	408.8	560.2	812.6	859.9	970.2	1110.2	1293.4	1614.8	1975.9	1965.0	1843.5	1806.0	1916.7	1921.6	2103.9	2458.7	2789.3	2989.0	2575.2
Memorandum item																					
ECE region	238.8	265.8	319.0	429.6	599.0	627.0	714.7	809.9	937.6	1178.4	1397.9	1324.1	1250.4	1243.0	1346.0	1382.3	1578.0	1849.3	2060.8	2204.0	1838.9

Sources: IMF, *International Financial Statistics*, February 1991 and ECE secretariat calculations, based on national publications for eastern Europe and the Soviet Union.

a January-September.
b Austria, Belgium-Luxembourg, Denmark, Finland, France, the Federal Republic of Germany, Ireland, Italy, the Netherlands, Norway, Sweden, Switzerland and the United Kingdom.
b OPEC members, plus Bahrain, the Congo, Mexico, Syrian Arab Republic, Trinidad and Tobago and Tunisia.

APPENDIX TABLE C.2

World trade: Volume change, by region
(Annual percentage change)

	1970	1971	1972	1973	1974	1975	1976	1977	1978	1979	1980	1981	1982	1983	1984	1985	1986	1987	1988	1989	1990
Exports																					
Developed market economies	10.4	5.6	8.8	13.5	8.2	-4.3	11.3	4.5	6.6	6.2	4.6	2.4	-2.1	2.4	9.6	3.8	1.4	5.4	7.7	7.5	5.5
North America	8.8	0.4	9.2	20.4	5.6	-3.2	5.3	1.8	11.4	7.2	7.5	-2.0	-9.2	-2.4	9.9	-0.2	1.7	10.5	15.5	9.1	7.6
Western Europe	10.4	6.2	8.5	11.2	8.0	-5.7	12.6	5.1	5.4	6.7	0.7	2.8	1.0	3.0	7.6	5.2	2.2	4.3	5.4	7.2	4.5
Southern Europe a	12.3	8.4	16.9	11.9	3.0	-2.1	14.0	3.5	8.1	7.1	8.7	6.8	7.2	5.7	15.2	6.9	-3.1	8.4	4.7	10.8	8.6
Japan	15.8	18.3	6.4	6.8	20.5	-0.2	21.1	8.6	0.7	0.2	17.1	10.7	-2.3	8.7	15.8	4.9	-0.6	0.4	4.4	5.0	4.9
Developing economies b	9.6	7.0	12.1	8.3	1.5	-8.7	13.9	2.6	0.6	5.1	-9.0	-5.5	-6.9	1.5	5.8	-1.0	8.3	-12.1	10.5	6.7	5.0
Oil-exporting countries c	18.1	10.2	4.6	8.9	2.1	-14.0	13.4	0.4	-4.2	2.8	-15.8	-13.9	-14.1	-5.0	-	-4.8	13.6	2.2	12.1	7.6	1.7
Non-oil developing countries	5.0	4.9	17.0	8.0	0.3	0.0	14.6	5.1	6.3	9.3	2.1	4.7	0.2	6.5	9.8	1.4	6.6	15.9	10.0	6.4	6.1
Eastern Europe and Soviet Union	7.8	5.3	6.1	12.3	4.4	4.4	8.3	9.5	4.8	3.8	2.3	2.3	4.9	5.5	4.6	-1.0	4.4	2.4	4.3	-1.0	-12.1
Eastern Europe	10.7	8.6	11.0	9.3	7.0	7.0	7.9	8.0	6.7	7.9	3.1	2.7	5.3	8.1	7.0	2.3	-1.2	1.4	3.7	-2.1	-9.8
Soviet Union	6.1	3.2	2.7	14.4	2.6	2.5	8.6	10.6	3.4	0.6	1.6	1.9	4.5	3.3	2.5	-4.3	10.0	3.3	4.8	-0.0	-14.0
Total above	10.0	5.9	9.3	12.1	6.2	-4.6	11.7	4.5	5.0	5.7	1.1	0.5	-2.7	2.4	8.2	2.3	3.4	6.8	8.0	6.6	3.9
Memorandum item																					
ECE region	9.7	4.8	8.7	13.7	6.7	-3.6	10.3	4.8	6.9	6.5	2.9	1.7	-0.8	2.1	8.1	3.1	2.1	5.7	7.7	6.7	3.2
Imports																					
Developed market economies	9.7	5.6	10.7	12.0	0.9	-7.6	14.4	4.1	6.1	7.4	-1.8	-2.1	-1.2	4.7	12.0	5.7	7.7	7.2	6.8	7.4	5.2
North America	2.0	9.0	14.1	7.0	1.1	-10.4	18.3	8.4	8.8	2.3	-6.8	2.7	-7.9	10.5	22.9	8.3	11.1	3.8	5.9	6.1	3.1
Western Europe	12.1	4.7	8.2	11.1	0.7	-5.8	14.3	1.8	5.1	9.4	1.1	-4.7	2.0	2.6	6.5	5.2	5.8	6.8	6.8	7.2	6.2
Southern Europe a	11.2	10.7	7.3	12.2	5.9	-0.6	6.7	10.3	0.7	8.5	2.8	1.7	1.8	4.3	14.6	6.0	0.7	29.7	7.1	15.8	9.2
Japan	18.7	-0.4	13.9	30.6	-0.7	-12.2	8.9	2.5	6.6	11.4	-5.1	-2.2	-0.6	1.2	10.5	0.0	10.5	9.0	16.6	8.3	5.2
Developing economies b	8.8	8.8	3.9	14.0	18.4	6.5	5.7	10.9	6.3	2.0	9.3	8.0	-4.3	-3.1	1.6	-1.4	-3.0	7.2	10.6	8.6	4.1
Oil-exporting countries c	6.6	11.5	13.4	18.5	26.8	45.2	23.6	22.4	0.3	-10.2	17.2	22.7	-1.8	-12.6	-8.0	-10.8	-19.8	-7.4	6.1	5.4	6.5
Non-oil developing countries	9.2	8.4	2.3	13.0	16.8	-1.6	0.7	6.9	8.8	6.4	6.8	2.2	-5.0	1.8	5.7	2.1	3.1	11.4	11.7	9.3	3.6
Eastern Europe and Soviet Union	11.4	6.8	12.2	13.2	7.3	9.4	6.6	3.2	8.9	1.9	4.4	1.5	3.0	4.1	4.1	5.2	-1.4	0.8	3.8	5.1	-3.1
Eastern Europe	14.0	7.6	8.0	11.9	13.2	4.8	6.2	5.3	4.9	2.7	1.6	-3.4	-4.4	4.2	3.6	5.9	4.4	3.4	3.5	0.5	-0.9
Soviet Union	7.8	5.9	17.2	14.6	1.0	14.8	7.0	0.9	13.3	1.1	7.5	6.4	9.7	4.0	4.4	4.7	-6.0	-1.6	4.0	9.3	-5.0
Total above	9.7	6.4	9.2	12.5	5.1	-3.2	11.9	5.5	6.4	5.8	1.1	0.4	-1.5	3.0	9.1	4.2	4.7	6.6	7.4	7.4	4.5
Memorandum item																					
ECE region	8.8	6.6	10.5	10.2	1.8	-5.3	14.3	4.5	6.4	6.3	-0.9	-1.3	-1.0	5.3	11.8	6.2	6.4	6.4	6.3	7.1	4.3

Sources: IMF, *International Financial Statistics*, February 1991 for the developed market economies; IMF, *IFS Supplement on Trade Statistics* (Supplement Series No.15.) and *World Economic Outlook*, October 1990 for developing countries); ECE secretariat calculations, based on national sources for eastern Europe and the Soviet Union. For market economies and eastern Europe, weights for aggregations are US dollar trade shares in 1985.

a Includes ECE, OECD or World Bank estimates for certain sub-periods for Portugal, Turkey and Yugoslavia.
b IMF definitions for developing countries.
c OPEC members, plus Cameroon, Congo, Mexico, Oman, Trinidad and Tobago.

APPENDIX TABLE C.3

Western Europe and North America: Trade volume change
(Annual percentage change [a])

	1970	1971	1972	1973	1974	1975	1976	1977	1978	1979	1980	1981	1982	1983	1984	1985	1986	1987	1988	1989	1990
Exports																					
France	15.9	8.4	14.1	10.2	9.6	-4.2	9.1	6.5	6.1	10.0	2.1	2.9	-2.9	3.4	5.4	2.7	0.5	3.7	8.7	7.8	4.9
Germany, Fed.Rep. of	14.7	4.1	6.4	13.9	11.0	-11.2	18.6	3.9	3.2	4.9	1.7	6.6	3.3	-0.3	9.1	5.9	1.3	3.0	7.4	7.3	1.6
Italy	8.0	7.9	12.5	1.1	7.7	3.7	11.7	7.6	10.8	7.8	-7.9	4.2	0.5	3.6	6.5	7.5	1.8	2.0	6.0	8.6	4.1
United Kingdom	2.5	7.0	1.2	12.8	5.3	-2.2	8.6	8.4	2.8	3.7	0.8	-1.3	3.3	2.2	8.4	5.8	3.8	5.2	1.1	6.6	6.8
Total 4 countries	10.7	6.3	7.7	10.7	8.9	-5.3	13.0	6.1	5.0	6.3	-0.1	3.6	1.4	1.7	7.7	5.4	1.8	3.5	6.0	7.5	3.9
Austria	7.7	3.2	11.8	8.7	11.6	-7.0	15.7	3.2	10.1	12.9	2.9	5.1	1.1	4.4	9.3	10.1	0.8	2.5	12.1	13.6	8.5
Belgium	11.4	10.2	13.0	13.1	1.4	-7.1	13.8	5.4	2.6	6.3	2.4	-	2.5	4.5	4.3	4.2	8.0	8.3	5.8	8.0	6.5
Denmark	6.7	4.2	8.0	7.4	5.2	-3.3	3.4	4.9	6.3	10.3	8.0	2.5	2.4	4.7	6.7	5.3	-	4.0	4.8	7.3	5.8
Finland	8.0	-3.7	13.5	8.5	-	-17.2	17.0	9.7	7.4	9.6	8.7	3.4	-2.2	3.4	9.9	-	1.0	3.0	-1.0	1.9	3.2
Ireland	8.4	7.1	5.0	5.7	11.9	7.3	3.8	17.7	12.0	8.1	5.4	2.3	6.2	12.3	17.9	5.3	4.0	14.2	7.0	11.3	7.7
Netherlands	11.9	8.5	9.8	12.5	14.3	-5.6	13.2	-1.3	3.9	8.9	5.4	1.2	-1.1	4.7	7.8	3.1	3.0	5.8	8.3	4.2	5.7
Norway	2.5	4.9	11.6	10.4	-1.9	3.8	16.7	-3.2	23.0	5.3	5.1	-1.2	1.2	7.2	9.0	3.1	-4.0	8.3	-1.9	14.7	9.3
Sweden	13.3	3.9	7.5	17.5	6.0	-9.9	4.7	1.5	7.4	8.2	-2.5	1.3	2.6	12.5	7.8	3.1	3.0	3.9	2.8	1.8	1.1
Switzerland	6.1	3.8	5.6	12.3	3.1	-9.1	13.3	11.8	3.9	2.5	2.5	3.6	-3.5	-	7.2	12.4	2.0	1.0	-2.9	5.0	4.5
Total 9 countries	9.7	6.1	9.9	12.2	6.4	-6.5	12.0	3.4	6.2	7.6	2.2	1.5	0.2	5.4	7.6	4.7	3.0	5.7	4.7	6.6	5.7
Total western Europe	10.3	6.2	8.5	11.2	8.0	-5.7	12.6	5.1	5.4	6.7	0.7	2.8	1.0	3.0	7.6	5.2	2.2	4.3	5.5	7.2	4.5
United States	8.5	-1.2	9.1	23.9	8.6	-2.1	3.5	-0.2	11.8	8.9	10.0	-3.2	-11.7	-5.5	6.8	-2.0	-0.5	13.1	18.0	12.5	8.6
Canada	9.9	5.3	9.6	10.6	-3.8	-7.2	12.0	8.9	10.0	1.8	-1.2	2.7	0.1	7.7	18.5	4.2	6.9	4.8	9.4	0.8	5.2
Total above	9.8	4.3	8.7	14.3	7.2	-4.9	10.1	4.0	7.3	6.9	3.0	1.1	-2.5	1.3	8.3	3.5	2.0	6.1	8.6	7.9	5.6
Imports																					
France	6.6	7.5	14.0	13.7	4.3	-7.1	20.8	0.8	5.2	11.7	6.2	-3.3	3.6	-1.9	2.3	4.1	3.3	7.1	6.5	8.7	6.0
Germany, Fed.Rep. of	18.4	8.3	6.4	5.5	-3.9	-0.3	17.8	2.3	6.8	7.5	2.8	-5.0	1.4	3.9	5.3	4.2	6.1	5.5	6.6	7.0	12.0
Italy	15.6	0.3	11.0	11.2	-5.5	-10.7	15.6	-0.4	7.5	13.1	-6.6	-6.6	-	8.6	9.0	8.8	4.5	9.5	6.9	8.3	5.1
United Kingdom	4.8	3.8	9.8	13.7	0.4	-8.7	6.6	1.7	6.8	8.5	-3.9	5.9	-	8.6	10.7	3.6	6.9	6.9	13.6	8.8	2.6
Total 4 countries	11.9	5.4	9.6	10.3	-1.4	-5.9	15.4	1.3	6.5	9.7	1.2	-4.7	2.6	2.7	6.5	4.9	5.3	6.9	8.3	8.1	7.0
Austria	18.1	8.6	14.6	10.5	2.7	-6.8	23.0	9.9	-1.6	10.5	5.0	-4.1	-2.1	7.1	8.7	4.8	5.2	5.2	8.2	10.9	9.9
Belgium	10.0	9.1	8.3	16.9	1.3	-5.2	13.7	3.6	3.5	6.7	1.1	-4.2	1.1	-1.1	5.4	3.1	11.0	7.2	3.2	7.4	7.6
Denmark	9.7	-2.9	3.0	20.6	-6.1	-6.5	19.4	-2.3	4.8	5.7	-8.6	-5.9	3.7	4.8	6.9	7.5	-1.0	6.1	-1.0	1.9	1.9
Finland	21.1	-1.4	4.4	12.7	7.5	-6.5	-3.5	-8.4	-5.3	19.4	11.6	-6.3	1.1	3.3	-	6.4	6.0	13.2	-0.8	15.1	1.9
Ireland	3.6	5.1	3.3	13.7	1.0	-10.1	15.3	12.6	17.0	13.8	-4.9	1.2	-4.0	3.4	9.5	3.3	3.0	6.2	4.7	12.9	-4.2
Netherlands	13.2	1.9	-	10.9	8.5	-5.2	12.3	1.2	6.0	6.8	-2.1	-7.6	1.2	2.3	6.8	6.4	4.0	6.7	7.2	2.5	8.3
Norway	12.8	-3.4	5.4	8.5	15.6	2.7	10.6	8.2	-11.4	5.7	10.8	3.8	3.8	-3.7	12.7	12.4	15.0	-1.7	-9.7	-5.9	5.0
Sweden	11.5	3.3	13.0	16.9	2.7	-18.2	16.7	9.5	8.7	9.3	3.7	2.4	6.3	-7.0	3.5	8.7	4.0	7.7	5.4	6.8	2.7
Switzerland	14.3	5.4	6.8	6.3	-1.5	-8.2	6.7	9.5	8.7	9.3	3.7	2.4	6.0	6.0	8.0	6.6	9.0	6.4	7.9	5.0	2.7
Total 9 countries	12.5	3.5	5.8	12.5	4.5	-5.5	12.4	2.6	2.6	8.9	1.0	-4.6	0.8	2.4	6.6	5.9	6.6	6.5	4.2	5.7	5.0
Total western Europe	12.1	4.7	8.2	11.1	0.7	-5.8	14.3	1.8	5.1	9.4	1.1	-4.7	2.0	2.6	6.5	5.2	5.8	6.8	6.8	7.2	6.3
United States	3.2	8.8	13.4	4.7	-1.4	-12.0	21.8	10.7	10.3	0.1	-7.1	2.6	-5.1	10.4	24.0	8.7	10.5	2.6	3.8	6.4	3.8
Canada	-3.1	9.9	16.9	16.1	10.1	-5.4	7.8	0.5	3.2	11.2	-5.7	2.8	-18.1	11.1	18.6	6.6	13.7	8.9	15.0	4.8	-0.2
Total above	8.6	6.1	10.2	9.7	0.8	-7.4	15.6	4.0	6.4	6.9	-1.6	-2.3	-1.4	5.1	12.0	6.4	7.8	5.6	6.5	6.8	5.0

Source: IMF, *International Financial Statistics*, February 1991. 1990 data for Canada and the US are from national sources. National data are aggregated by means of weights derived from 1985 US dollar trade shares.

[a] Calculated from rounded index numbers (1985 = 100) for Belgium, Denmark, Finland, Netherlands, Norway, Sweden and Switzerland. Comparisons with the previous year are limited due to changes in methodology in France (1973, 1975, 1986), Italy (1970, 1981), UK (1970, 1973), Austria (1979,1988), Belgium (1974, 1985), Denmark (1971, 1974, 1985), Finland (1970, 1977), Greece (1977), Ireland (1975, 1985), Norway (1970, 1980), Sweden (1975, 1983), Netherlands (1985), US (1989), Switzerland (1979 imports only, 1988) and Canada (1981).

APPENDIX TABLE C.4

Eastern Europe and the Soviet Union: Exports by main directions, 1970-1990

(Value, billion US dollars)

	1970	1971	1972	1973	1974	1975	1976	1977	1978	1979	1980	1981	1982	1983	1984	1985	1986	1987	1988	1989	1990
Bulgaria																					
World	2.00	2.18	2.63	3.24	3.84	4.69	5.38	6.35	7.45	8.86	10.39	10.70	11.44	12.14	12.86	13.31	14.14	15.86	17.29	16.22	13.32
ECE-East	1.51	1.64	2.01	2.46	2.73	3.50	4.10	4.81	5.51	6.18	6.90	6.95	7.75	8.87	9.30	9.82	11.26	12.64	13.92	13.35	10.58
ECE-West	0.32	0.34	0.39	0.48	0.55	0.55	0.69	0.75	0.87	1.54	1.92	1.70	1.53	1.48	1.49	1.39	1.10	1.18	1.25	1.47	1.27
Other	0.17	0.20	0.22	0.30	0.55	0.64	0.59	0.79	1.07	1.14	1.57	2.05	2.16	1.78	2.08	2.11	1.78	2.03	2.12	1.40	1.47
Czechoslovakia																					
World	3.79	4.18	4.92	5.99	7.03	8.36	9.03	10.27	11.75	13.19	14.93	14.91	15.64	16.50	17.20	10.66	12.24	13.63	14.88	14.45	12.04
ECE-East	2.43	2.66	3.26	3.89	4.27	5.47	6.18	6.95	7.95	8.69	9.46	9.60	10.42	11.19	11.85	5.69	6.74	7.81	8.51	7.76	5.10
ECE-West	0.92	1.00	1.12	1.51	1.98	1.97	1.98	2.30	2.57	3.15	3.82	3.53	3.51	3.53	3.57	3.35	3.75	4.13	4.58	4.97	5.61
Other	0.43	0.52	0.54	0.60	0.78	0.92	0.87	1.02	1.23	1.35	1.64	1.77	1.71	1.78	1.78	1.62	1.75	1.70	1.79	1.72	1.33
German Democratic Republic																					
World	4.65	5.18	6.32	7.74	9.05	10.44	11.75	12.55	14.04	16.17	18.59	20.67	22.53	24.53	25.41	18.21	16.35	16.40	16.62	17.33	..
ECE-East	3.13	3.50	4.39	5.20	5.60	6.84	7.46	8.29	9.21	10.30	11.05	12.20	12.90	14.27	15.09	7.26	7.02	7.21	7.26	7.23	..
ECE-West	1.16	1.30	1.56	2.09	2.89	2.86	3.41	3.33	3.71	4.58	5.86	6.68	7.49	8.27	8.43	9.09	7.66	7.52	7.92	8.68	..
Other	0.36	0.37	0.37	0.45	0.56	0.74	0.87	0.93	1.12	1.29	1.68	1.79	2.14	1.99	1.89	1.87	1.67	1.67	1.43	1.42	..
Hungary																					
World	2.32	2.50	3.29	4.37	5.13	6.06	4.93	5.82	6.35	7.93	8.61	8.73	8.86	8.77	8.62	8.47	9.17	9.58	10.00	9.67	9.55
ECE-East	1.44	1.62	2.15	2.80	3.22	4.10	2.73	3.25	3.45	4.14	4.33	4.65	4.62	4.32	4.17	4.43	4.95	4.79	4.46	3.96	2.98
ECE-West	0.69	0.68	0.89	1.26	1.49	1.45	1.68	1.97	2.22	2.91	3.27	2.90	2.93	3.19	3.28	2.90	3.19	3.74	4.31	4.64	5.57
Other	0.19	0.20	0.24	0.31	0.42	0.52	0.52	0.60	0.68	0.88	1.01	1.18	1.31	1.25	1.17	1.13	1.04	1.05	1.23	1.07	1.00
Poland																					
World	3.55	3.87	4.93	6.35	8.32	10.29	11.02	12.27	13.77	16.22	17.02	13.29	11.22	11.58	11.76	11.49	12.07	12.21	13.83	12.91	14.31
ECE-East	2.13	2.29	2.97	3.67	4.38	5.82	6.25	6.99	7.90	9.25	8.90	7.41	5.51	5.84	5.68	5.53	5.56	5.03	5.63	4.49	3.60
ECE-West	1.09	1.24	1.60	2.28	3.17	3.49	3.76	4.13	4.66	5.42	6.21	4.22	3.99	4.17	4.54	4.50	4.55	5.51	6.48	6.80	9.20
Other	0.33	0.34	0.35	0.40	0.77	0.98	1.01	1.15	1.21	1.54	1.91	1.66	1.71	1.57	1.54	1.46	1.96	1.67	1.72	1.62	1.51
Romania																					
World	1.85	2.10	2.60	3.67	4.87	5.34	6.14	7.02	8.05	9.72	11.40	11.18	10.12	10.16	10.72	10.99	9.76	10.49	11.39	10.49	5.33
ECE-East	0.92	1.00	1.23	1.65	1.75	2.04	2.33	2.92	3.29	3.48	4.24	3.35	3.24	3.42	3.08	3.94	4.04	4.08	4.29	4.04	1.6*
ECE-West	0.66	0.79	0.97	1.42	2.22	2.03	2.40	2.37	2.95	3.93	4.39	4.16	3.48	3.77	4.20	3.92	3.43	4.14	4.37	4.32	2.6*
Other	0.27	0.31	0.40	0.60	0.90	1.27	1.40	1.73	1.81	2.31	2.77	3.67	3.40	2.98	3.44	3.13	2.29	2.26	2.73	2.12	1.1*
Eastern Europe																					
World	18.16	20.02	24.70	31.35	38.24	45.18	48.25	54.28	61.42	72.10	80.94	79.47	79.81	83.68	86.58	73.13	74.74	78.17	84.02	81.07	54.55 a
ECE-East	11.56	12.71	16.02	19.66	21.96	27.77	29.05	33.21	37.31	42.05	44.89	44.16	44.43	47.92	49.17	36.66	39.57	41.57	44.00	40.82	23.9 a
ECE-West	4.84	5.35	6.55	9.05	12.30	12.34	13.93	14.85	16.98	21.53	25.47	23.20	22.93	24.41	25.50	25.16	23.67	26.22	28.91	30.95	24.2 a
Other	1.75	1.95	2.13	2.65	3.98	5.07	5.27	6.22	7.13	8.52	10.57	12.12	12.44	11.35	11.90	11.31	10.69	10.51	11.36	9.45	6.4 a
Soviet Union																					
World	12.80	13.81	15.47	21.26	27.36	33.29	37.17	45.18	52.38	64.71	76.50	79.39	86.97	91.38	91.20	86.78	96.94	107.62	110.50	109.12	103.57
ECE-East	6.76	7.24	8.17	9.93	11.48	16.44	17.38	20.74	24.88	28.29	32.24	33.78	36.21	39.24	39.72	40.63	50.97	54.28	54.00	50.37	42.9*
ECE-West	2.78	3.16	3.44	5.62	9.24	9.63	11.68	13.55	14.47	21.78	28.13	27.49	29.55	30.20	30.06	25.61	21.23	25.69	27.25	29.58	33.1*
Other	3.26	3.41	3.86	5.71	6.64	7.22	8.11	10.89	13.03	14.64	16.13	18.12	21.21	21.94	21.42	20.53	24.75	27.65	29.25	29.18	27.6*
Eastern Europe and the Soviet Union																					
World	30.96	33.82	40.16	52.62	65.60	78.47	85.41	99.47	113.79	136.81	157.44	158.86	166.78	175.06	177.77	159.90	170.68	185.79	194.52	190.19	158.12 a
ECE-East	18.32	19.95	24.19	29.59	33.44	44.21	46.43	53.96	62.19	70.34	77.13	77.94	80.64	87.16	88.89	77.28	90.54	95.85	98.50	91.19	66.8 a
ECE-West	7.62	8.51	9.98	14.67	21.54	21.98	25.61	28.41	31.45	43.31	53.60	50.69	52.49	54.61	55.56	50.77	44.90	51.92	56.17	60.53	57.4 a
Other	5.01	5.36	5.99	8.36	10.62	12.28	13.37	17.11	20.16	23.16	26.70	30.23	33.65	33.30	35.33	31.85	35.24	38.02	39.85	38.47	34.0 a

Source: Secretariat of the United Nations Economic Commission for Europe, based on national foreign trade statistics. Partner country groupings: ECE-East – east European member countries of CMEA and the Soviet Union; ECE-West – ECE market economies and Japan; Other – all remaining countries.

Note: Substantial discontinuities in the value series are indicated by ‖. These usually relate to large changes in the rouble/dollar cross rate (reductions in the relative valuation of rouble exports). Such changes were introduced by Hungary in 1976, Romania in 1981, Poland in 1982, and Czechoslovakia and the German Democratic Republic (together with other data revisions) in 1989 with application to the trade data from 1985.

a Excluding the German Democratic Republic.

APPENDIX TABLE C.5

Eastern Europe and the Soviet Union: Imports by main directions, 1970-1990

(Value, billion US dollars)

	1970	1971	1972	1973	1974	1975	1976	1977	1978	1979	1980	1981	1982	1983	1984	1985	1986	1987	1988	1989	1990
Bulgaria																					
World	1.83	2.12	2.57	3.21	4.33	5.40	5.63	6.39	7.62	8.51	9.67	10.80	11.54	12.29	12.72	13.63	15.20	16.16	16.71	15.18	12.90
ECE-East	1.33	1.57	1.97	2.40	2.83	3.71	4.13	4.91	5.96	6.59	7.29	7.76	8.56	9.41	9.72	10.04	11.27	12.43	12.32	10.86	9.67
ECE-West	0.38	0.39	0.43	0.56	1.07	1.35	1.12	1.08	1.20	1.42	1.79	2.29	2.04	1.86	1.91	2.20	2.49	2.59	2.72	2.74	2.02
Other	0.13	0.16	0.17	0.24	0.43	0.34	0.37	0.41	0.47	0.50	0.59	0.75	0.95	1.02	1.09	1.39	1.44	1.14	1.66	1.57	1.21
Czechoslovakia																					
World	3.70	4.01	4.67	6.07	7.51	9.09	9.70	11.15	12.57	14.25	15.18	14.67	15.45	16.37	17.13	10.32	12.36	13.78	14.58	14.26	13.32
ECE-East	2.33	2.54	3.04	3.81	4.41	5.85	6.30	7.31	8.43	9.39	9.83	9.79	10.82	11.92	12.82	6.06	7.20	7.96	8.22	7.82	5.81
ECE-West	1.01	1.12	1.22	1.69	2.34	2.52	2.68	2.87	3.23	3.84	4.21	3.80	3.59	3.39	3.14	3.19	3.87	4.56	4.94	4.87	6.05
Other	0.35	0.34	0.41	0.57	0.76	0.71	0.72	0.97	0.91	1.02	1.14	1.08	1.04	1.06	1.16	1.08	1.29	1.26	1.42	1.57	1.46
German Democratic Republic																					
World	4.92	5.09	6.07	8.07	9.94	11.71	13.62	14.92	15.48	17.35	20.29	20.93	20.95	22.27	23.42	15.76	16.13	16.71	17.41	17.78	..
ECE-East	3.19	3.23	3.71	4.81	5.40	7.09	7.97	9.28	9.52	9.82	11.27	12.60	12.97	13.38	14.25	7.60	7.58	7.19	7.05	6.78	..
ECE-West	1.43	1.55	2.09	2.88	3.75	3.91	4.86	4.64	4.92	6.48	7.49	7.14	6.72	7.42	7.56	6.65	7.09	8.27	9.20	9.75	..
Other	0.30	0.30	0.27	0.38	0.79	0.70	0.79	1.01	1.04	1.06	1.54	1.20	1.27	1.47	1.61	1.51	1.46	1.25	1.17	1.24	..
Hungary																					
World	2.51	2.99	3.15	3.88	5.58	7.15	5.53	6.52	7.94	8.68	9.19	9.16	8.87	8.55	8.13	8.18	9.59	9.86	9.37	8.86	8.62
ECE-East	1.56	1.88	1.98	2.33	3.00	4.48	2.81	3.23	3.86	4.33	4.31	4.30	4.33	4.12	3.91	4.04	4.87	4.66	4.10	3.47	2.91
ECE-West	0.72	0.89	0.93	1.21	2.05	2.03	2.09	2.52	3.20	3.46	3.88	3.93	3.48	3.23	3.12	3.41	3.87	4.23	4.34	4.69	4.75
Other	0.22	0.22	0.25	0.34	0.53	0.64	0.64	0.77	0.88	0.89	1.01	0.93	1.06	1.21	1.10	0.73	0.85	0.96	0.93	0.69	0.97
Poland																					
World	3.61	4.04	5.33	7.76	10.49	12.55	13.88	14.63	15.70	17.55	19.12	15.53	10.25	10.60	10.65	10.84	11.21	10.85	12.24	11.34	9.54
ECE-East	2.36	2.58	3.08	3.81	4.40	5.45	6.20	7.25	8.06	8.99	10.09	9.59	5.98	6.25	6.11	5.87	6.09	4.93	4.95	3.64	2.77
ECE-West	0.98	1.18	1.89	3.49	5.41	6.31	6.92	6.44	6.52	6.87	6.92	4.72	3.35	3.29	3.42	3.82	4.08	4.62	5.90	6.41	5.86
Other	0.27	0.28	0.35	0.46	0.68	0.78	0.75	0.94	1.12	1.68	2.11	1.22	0.92	1.06	1.12	1.14	1.04	1.30	1.39	1.29	0.92
Romania																					
World	1.96	2.10	2.62	3.44	5.14	5.34	6.10	7.02	8.88	10.92	13.20	10.98	8.32	7.64	7.56	8.48	8.08	8.31	7.64	8.44	8.15
ECE-East	0.94	0.97	1.17	1.37	1.64	1.97	2.42	2.92	3.27	3.69	4.05	3.44	3.08	3.28	2.89	3.63	4.44	4.27	4.20	4.42	2.5*
ECE-West	0.81	0.89	1.14	1.57	2.64	2.39	2.32	2.65	3.56	4.07	4.35	3.63	2.05	1.48	1.62	1.61	1.61	1.17	1.10	1.10	3.4*
Other	0.21	0.25	0.31	0.50	0.87	0.99	1.36	1.45	2.06	3.15	4.79	3.91	3.20	2.88	3.05	3.24	2.03	2.87	2.35	2.91	2.4*
Eastern Europe																					
World	18.52	20.34	24.41	32.42	42.98	51.24	54.45	60.62	68.20	77.26	86.65	82.06	75.38	77.72	79.60	67.21	72.58	75.67	77.94	75.85	52.53 a
ECE-East	11.71	12.77	14.95	18.53	21.67	28.56	29.82	34.88	39.10	42.82	46.83	47.48	45.73	48.35	49.70	37.24	41.45	41.45	40.76	37.00	23.7 a
ECE-West	5.33	6.03	7.70	11.40	17.26	18.51	20.00	20.20	22.63	26.14	28.64	25.51	21.22	20.67	20.77	20.88	23.01	25.46	28.20	29.56	22.1 a
Other	1.48	1.55	1.76	2.49	4.05	4.17	4.63	5.54	6.46	8.31	11.18	9.08	8.43	8.70	9.12	9.09	8.11	8.76	8.99	9.29	7.0 a
Soviet Union																					
World	11.73	12.48	16.16	20.91	24.85	36.94	38.11	40.89	50.74	57.78	68.53	73.16	77.67	80.21	80.15	82.91	88.85	95.93	107.09	114.51	120.66
ECE-East	6.63	7.26	9.34	10.89	11.35	15.67	16.22	18.82	24.63	26.67	29.43	29.40	33.49	37.05	37.41	39.50	47.26	54.19	57.96	56.84	59.7*
ECE-West	3.02	3.11	4.46	6.37	8.61	14.10	14.98	14.26	17.33	21.23	25.70	28.24	28.98	27.65	25.60	26.51	25.60	24.70	29.96	36.01	38.2*
Other	2.08	2.12	2.36	3.66	4.89	7.17	6.91	7.80	8.78	9.89	13.40	15.52	15.21	15.50	15.85	16.91	15.99	17.04	19.18	21.67	22.7*
Eastern Europe and the Soviet Union																					
World	30.25	32.82	40.57	53.34	67.83	88.18	92.56	101.51	118.94	135.05	155.18	155.23	153.06	157.93	159.75	150.12	161.43	171.60	185.03	190.36	173.19 a
ECE-East	18.35	20.03	24.29	29.42	33.02	44.23	46.04	53.70	63.74	69.49	76.26	76.88	79.22	85.40	87.11	76.74	88.72	95.63	98.71	93.84	83.86 a
ECE-West	8.35	9.13	12.15	17.77	25.87	32.60	34.98	34.46	39.96	47.36	54.34	53.74	50.20	48.32	47.66	47.38	48.61	50.16	58.16	65.57	60.3 a
Other	3.56	3.66	4.13	6.15	8.94	11.34	11.54	13.34	15.24	18.19	24.58	24.61	23.64	24.20	24.98	26.00	24.10	25.80	28.17	30.96	29.7 a

Source: Secretariat of the United Nations Economic Commission for Europe, based on national foreign trade statistics. Partner country groupings: ECE-East — east European member countries of CMEA and the Soviet Union; ECE-West — ECE market economies and Japan; Other — all remaining countries.

Note: Substantial discontinuities in the value series are indicated by ‖. These usually relate to large changes in the rouble/dollar cross rate (reductions in the relative valuation of rouble imports). Such changes were introduced by Hungary in 1976, Romania in 1981, Poland in 1982, and Czechoslovakia and the German Democratic Republic (together with other data revisions) in 1989 with application to the trade data from 1985.

a Excluding the German Democratic Republic.

APPENDIX TABLE C.6

East-west trade: Value of western exports, by country of origin

(Billion US dollars)

	1970	1971	1972	1973	1974	1975	1976	1977	1978	1979	1980	1981	1982	1983	1984	1985	1986	1987	1988	1989	1990 [a]
Austria	0.37	0.39	0.46	0.63	1.08	1.28	1.29	1.42	1.67	2.00	2.11	1.81	1.74	1.87	1.91	1.88	2.17	2.45	2.83	2.92	3.35
Belgium-Luxembourg	0.17	0.18	0.27	0.50	0.82	0.85	0.79	0.76	0.85	1.06	1.31	1.11	0.91	1.09	0.93	1.06	1.03	1.07	1.03	1.26	1.18
Denmark	0.11	0.14	0.14	0.19	0.27	0.29	0.27	0.27	0.32	0.35	0.37	0.27	0.21	0.21	0.26	0.29	0.39	0.34	0.48	0.63	0.85
Finland	0.36	0.33	0.45	0.53	0.90	1.31	1.50	1.71	1.75	1.81	2.81	3.71	3.76	3.46	2.77	3.16	3.54	3.37	3.48	3.70	3.66
France	0.65	0.73	0.95	1.31	1.60	2.60	2.73	2.78	2.92	4.03	4.64	3.91	2.81	3.33	2.96	2.91	2.75	3.09	3.35	3.51	3.14
Germany, Fed. Rep., of [b]	1.30	1.53	2.20	3.75	5.56	6.46	6.25	6.65	7.71	8.69	9.44	7.59	7.53	7.72	7.10	7.32	9.03	9.90	11.18	13.02	14.98
Greece	0.11	0.09	0.12	0.17	0.24	0.26	0.29	0.34	0.39	0.36	0.52	0.34	0.33	0.32	0.28	0.32	0.27	0.28	0.22	0.37	0.55
Iceland	0.01	0.02	0.01	0.02	0.04	0.04	0.04	0.06	0.05	0.06	0.08	0.07	0.06	0.06	0.07	0.06	0.06	0.07	0.08	0.07	0.04
Ireland	0.01	0.01	0.01	0.01	0.03	0.03	0.02	0.03	0.04	0.07	0.11	0.08	0.06	0.08	0.05	0.07	0.11	0.09	0.09	0.12	0.48
Italy	0.70	0.74	0.78	0.98	1.65	2.17	1.96	2.27	2.41	2.64	2.73	2.47	2.45	2.71	2.48	2.63	2.88	3.59	3.57	4.36	5.21
Netherlands	0.21	0.25	0.35	0.50	0.75	0.79	0.76	0.82	0.94	1.15	1.42	1.39	0.99	1.08	0.84	0.91	1.06	1.30	1.25	1.52	1.64
Norway	0.06	0.06	0.09	0.14	0.20	0.25	0.27	0.28	0.32	0.27	0.27	0.26	0.21	0.22	0.16	0.16	0.17	0.22	0.29	0.32	0.41
Portugal	0.01	0.01	0.01	0.01	0.02	0.04	0.08	0.08	0.07	0.10	0.09	0.08	0.09	0.08	0.08	0.09	0.08	0.09	0.10	0.15	0.14
Spain	0.07	0.06	0.12	0.12	0.20	0.26	0.30	0.28	0.35	0.55	0.55	0.79	0.43	0.52	0.58	0.73	0.50	0.54	0.52	0.68	0.67
Sweden	0.34	0.31	0.33	0.52	0.79	1.09	1.03	0.94	0.98	1.18	1.20	1.04	0.81	0.70	0.75	0.78	0.82	0.91	1.03	1.14	1.21
Switzerland	0.21	0.21	0.29	0.43	0.60	0.74	0.79	0.89	1.07	1.07	1.06	0.85	0.81	0.77	0.75	0.86	1.13	1.49	1.69	1.66	1.80
Turkey	0.08	0.08	0.09	0.10	0.15	0.12	0.17	0.17	0.32	0.30	0.48	0.32	0.31	0.23	0.26	0.30	0.28	0.31	0.54	0.94	1.06
United Kingdom	0.60	0.59	0.65	0.76	0.99	1.29	1.18	1.46	1.87	2.05	2.63	2.03	1.51	1.43	1.75	1.53	1.71	1.71	2.13	2.22	2.42
Yugoslavia	0.54	0.67	0.79	0.97	1.45	1.87	2.03	1.90	2.33	2.66	3.98	5.35	5.35	4.55	4.67	5.21	4.88	3.87	4.21	4.60	4.81
Western Europe [c]	6.56	7.12	9.03	12.76	18.76	23.36	23.46	25.01	28.67	32.95	38.71	35.91	33.00	33.15	30.91	32.98	36.31	38.84	42.19	47.53	47.61
Canada	0.13	0.17	0.35	0.37	0.16	0.60	0.79	0.55	0.74	0.99	1.77	1.89	2.04	1.68	1.88	1.37	1.13	0.75	1.10	0.76	1.22
United States	0.35	0.38	0.82	1.80	1.43	2.78	3.50	2.53	3.66	5.66	3.84	4.26	3.59	2.88	4.17	3.21	1.96	2.19	3.63	5.27	4.64
North America	0.49	0.55	1.17	2.17	1.59	3.38	4.28	3.08	4.41	6.65	5.62	6.15	5.62	4.56	6.05	4.57	3.09	2.94	4.73	6.03	5.86
Japan	0.45	0.54	0.74	0.81	1.67	2.20	2.80	2.67	3.20	3.26	3.58	4.01	4.47	3.56	3.01	3.31	3.83	3.28	3.91	3.75	3.14
Developed market economies [c]	7.49	8.20	10.93	15.74	22.02	28.94	30.54	30.75	36.27	42.87	47.91	46.07	43.09	41.27	39.97	40.87	43.23	45.06	50.83	57.31	56.62

Sources: United Nations commodity trade data (COMTRADE); OECD, *Monthly Statistics of Foreign Trade*, Series A, Paris, January 1991; IMF, *Direction of Trade Statistics*, Washington, D.C., January 1991. Data cover reported balances (f.o.b.-f.o.b) with six east European countries (Bulgaria, Czechoslovakia, German Democratic Republic, Hungary, Poland, Romania) and the Soviet Union.

[a] Extrapolations based on data for January-September.
[b] Excluding trade between the Federal Republic of Germany and the German Democratic Republic.
[c] Including trade between the Federal Republic of Germany and the German Democratic Republic.

APPENDIX TABLE C.7

East-west trade: Value of western imports, by country of destination

(Billion US dollars)

	1970	1971	1972	1973	1974	1975	1976	1977	1978	1979	1980	1981	1982	1983	1984	1985	1986	1987	1988	1989	1990 [a]
Austria	0.32	0.37	0.43	0.58	0.84	0.92	1.05	1.21	1.35	1.71	2.29	2.40	2.09	1.94	2.17	2.11	2.13	2.11	2.21	2.24	2.72
Belgium-Luxembourg	0.17	0.21	0.26	0.38	0.54	0.58	0.56	0.68	0.79	1.01	1.57	1.42	1.80	1.49	2.18	1.63	1.50	1.80	1.82	1.76	2.25
Denmark	0.14	0.13	0.15	0.26	0.40	0.49	0.54	0.46	0.53	0.71	0.79	0.57	0.63	0.58	0.67	0.64	0.61	0.60	0.58	0.64	0.78
Finland	0.40	0.47	0.47	0.62	1.41	1.47	1.50	1.67	1.68	2.46	3.64	3.59	3.54	3.50	3.11	2.98	2.65	3.13	2.81	3.20	3.16
France	0.42	0.54	0.67	0.94	1.25	1.62	1.90	2.12	2.45	3.14	5.08	4.84	3.99	3.85	3.66	3.61	4.17	4.29	4.58	4.51	5.42
Germany, Fed. Rep., of [b]	1.03	1.19	1.44	2.18	2.86	3.08	3.88	4.33	5.43	7.72	8.27	7.31	7.48	7.34	8.03	7.80	8.09	8.52	8.65	9.76	12.78
Greece	0.09	0.09	0.11	0.16	0.17	0.24	0.36	0.34	0.58	0.52	0.54	0.52	0.47	0.42	0.72	0.69	0.47	0.59	0.56	0.62	1.03
Iceland	0.01	0.02	0.02	0.03	0.07	0.06	0.06	0.07	0.06	0.09	0.10	0.09	0.09	0.08	0.09	0.07	0.07	0.08	0.08	0.08	0.10
Ireland	0.03	0.03	0.04	0.05	0.09	0.09	0.09	0.11	0.13	0.18	0.14	0.11	0.12	0.13	0.14	0.14	0.17	0.18	0.17	0.19	0.21
Italy	0.73	0.80	1.01	1.35	1.77	1.78	2.30	2.42	2.61	3.45	4.89	4.40	4.82	4.88	5.67	4.55	4.43	4.74	4.29	5.82	6.07
Netherlands	0.20	0.24	0.29	0.42	0.61	0.75	0.89	0.99	1.15	1.71	2.17	2.50	3.10	3.16	2.75	2.93	1.76	2.15	1.94	2.27	2.63
Norway	0.08	0.16	0.13	0.17	0.22	0.24	0.33	0.39	0.31	0.39	0.36	0.39	0.56	0.47	0.49	0.39	0.35	0.43	0.52	0.55	0.65
Portugal	0.01	0.02	0.02	0.03	0.03	0.08	0.15	0.15	0.12	0.19	0.20	0.25	0.12	0.11	0.09	0.09	0.09	0.10	0.10	0.11	0.11
Spain	0.06	0.06	0.12	0.18	0.31	0.43	0.40	0.32	0.35	0.52	0.72	0.81	0.81	0.82	0.85	0.67	0.58	1.20	1.46	1.70	1.81
Sweden	0.31	0.31	0.33	0.47	0.78	1.02	1.06	1.06	1.01	1.65	1.60	1.26	1.51	1.68	1.46	1.45	1.18	1.61	1.64	1.67	1.62
Switzerland	0.13	0.14	0.15	0.24	0.35	0.33	0.48	0.58	0.82	1.10	1.37	1.19	1.12	0.97	0.91	0.85	0.80	0.71	0.66	0.71	0.76
Turkey	0.10	0.10	0.15	0.16	0.23	0.22	0.28	0.30	0.34	0.54	0.71	0.76	0.38	0.70	0.83	0.51	0.71	0.74	0.82	1.08	1.22
United Kingdom	0.55	0.56	0.62	0.81	1.05	1.39	1.76	2.06	2.14	2.78	2.75	1.57	1.86	1.86	2.25	1.94	2.15	2.58	2.73	2.76	2.84
Yugoslavia	0.54	0.72	0.73	1.06	1.55	1.69	1.97	2.32	2.58	3.17	4.05	4.44	4.38	4.05	3.54	3.54	3.44	3.37	3.27	3.92	4.20
Western Europe [c]	5.88	6.82	7.88	11.07	15.80	173.4	21.11	23.30	26.36	35.55	44.29	41.07	41.61	40.72	42.29	39.21	38.51	42.64	42.75	47.43	50.36
Canada	0.06	0.08	0.10	0.13	0.18	0.15	0.18	0.18	0.19	0.25	0.22	0.23	0.16	0.16	0.20	0.18	0.21	0.24	0.41	0.40	0.40
United States	0.23	0.22	0.32	0.53	0.89	0.73	0.86	0.92	1.25	1.35	1.41	1.60	1.11	1.40	2.24	2.01	1.98	2.02	2.38	2.27	2.32
North America	0.29	0.30	0.42	0.66	1.07	0.88	1.05	1.09	1.44	1.61	1.64	1.82	1.26	1.57	2.44	2.19	2.19	2.26	2.80	2.67	2.72
Japan	0.49	0.49	0.59	1.06	1.49	1.21	1.22	1.47	1.48	1.98	1.90	1.59	1.40	1.52	1.62	1.46	1.77	2.33	2.54	3.22	3.68
Developed market economies [c]	6.66	7.61	8.89	12.79	18.36	19.93	23.37	25.86	29.28	39.14	47.83	44.48	44.27	43.81	46.36	42.87	42.46	47.23	48.09	53.32	56.77

Sources: As for Appendix table C.6. Data cover reported balances (f.o.b.-f.o.b) with six east European countries (Bulgaria, Czechoslovakia, German Democratic Republic, Hungary, Poland, Romania) and the Soviet Union.

a Extrapolations based on data for January-September.
b Excluding trade between the Federal Republic of Germany and the German Democratic Republic.
c Including trade between the Federal Republic of Germany and the German Democratic Republic.

APPENDIX TABLE C.8

East-west trade: Western trade balances by western country

(Billion US dollars)

	1970	1971	1972	1973	1974	1975	1976	1977	1978	1979	1980	1981	1982	1983	1984	1985	1986	1987	1988	1989	1990 [a]
Austria	0.05	0.02	0.03	0.05	0.23	0.36	0.23	0.21	0.33	0.29	-0.19	-0.59	-0.35	-0.07	-0.27	-0.23	0.03	0.33	0.62	0.68	0.63
Belgium-Luxembourg	–	-0.02	0.01	0.12	0.28	0.27	0.23	0.08	0.07	0.05	-0.26	-0.31	-0.89	-0.40	-1.24	-0.57	-0.47	-0.73	-0.79	-0.50	-1.07
Denmark	-0.02	0.01	-0.01	-0.07	-0.13	-0.20	-0.27	-0.19	-0.21	-0.36	-0.42	-0.30	-0.42	-0.36	-0.40	-0.35	-0.21	-0.26	-0.11	-0.01	0.07
Finland	-0.04	-0.14	-0.02	-0.09	-0.52	-0.16	–	0.03	0.08	-0.65	-0.82	0.12	0.21	-0.04	-0.34	0.18	0.89	0.24	0.67	0.50	0.50
France	0.22	0.20	0.28	0.37	0.35	0.99	0.83	0.66	0.47	0.89	-0.43	-0.93	-1.18	-0.52	-0.70	-0.70	-1.42	-1.20	-1.23	-1.00	-2.28
Germany, Fed. Rep. of [b]	0.26	0.34	0.76	1.57	2.70	3.37	2.37	2.32	2.28	0.97	1.18	0.27	0.04	0.38	-0.92	-0.49	0.95	1.38	2.53	3.27	2.20
Greece	0.02	-0.01	0.01	–	0.06	0.02	-0.07	-0.01	-0.20	-0.16	-0.02	-0.18	-0.14	-0.10	-0.44	-0.37	-0.20	-0.31	-0.34	-0.25	-0.49
Iceland	–	–	–	–	-0.02	-0.01	-0.02	-0.01	-0.01	-0.03	-0.02	-0.02	-0.03	-0.02	-0.01	-0.01	-0.01	-0.02	–	-0.01	-0.06
Ireland	-0.02	-0.03	-0.03	-0.04	-0.06	-0.05	-0.07	-0.08	-0.09	-0.11	-0.03	-0.03	-0.06	-0.05	-0.09	-0.08	-0.07	-0.09	-0.07	-0.07	0.27
Italy	-0.03	-0.06	-0.22	-0.37	-0.12	0.39	-0.34	-0.15	-0.19	-0.81	-2.16	-1.93	-2.37	-2.17	-3.19	-1.92	-1.55	-1.15	-0.72	-1.45	-0.86
Netherlands	0.01	0.01	0.06	0.08	0.14	0.04	-0.13	-0.17	-0.21	-0.57	-0.75	-1.12	-2.10	-2.08	-1.91	-2.02	-0.70	-0.85	-0.69	-0.75	-0.98
Norway	-0.02	-0.10	-0.04	-0.03	-0.02	0.01	-0.06	-0.11	0.01	-0.14	-0.10	-0.13	-0.35	-0.25	-0.33	-0.23	-0.18	-0.21	-0.22	-0.23	-0.24
Portugal		-0.01	-0.01	-0.01	-0.01	-0.03	-0.07	-0.07	-0.05	-0.09	-0.11	-0.17	-0.03	-0.04	-0.01	-0.02	-0.02	-0.21	-0.22	0.03	0.03
Spain	0.01	0.01	–	-0.06	-0.10	-0.17	-0.09	-0.04	–	0.03	-0.18	-0.02	-0.39	-0.30	-0.26	0.06	-0.09	-0.65	-0.94	-1.01	-1.14
Sweden	0.03	–	-0.01	0.05	0.01	0.08	-0.02	-0.12	-0.02	-0.47	-0.40	-0.22	-0.69	-0.98	-0.71	-0.67	-0.36	-0.70	-0.61	-0.53	-0.40
Switzerland	0.08	0.08	0.13	0.19	0.25	0.41	0.31	0.30	0.25	-0.03	-0.31	-0.34	-0.30	-0.20	-0.16	0.01	0.33	0.78	1.03	0.94	1.04
Turkey	-0.02	-0.02	-0.06	-0.06	-0.08	-0.10	-0.12	-0.12	-0.01	-0.24	-0.23	-0.44	-0.07	-0.47	-0.57	-0.21	-0.43	-0.42	-0.28	-0.14	-0.17
United Kingdom	0.05	0.03	0.03	-0.05	-0.06	-0.10	-0.58	-0.60	-0.27	-0.73	-0.12	0.46	-0.35	-0.43	-0.50	-0.42	-0.44	-0.86	-0.60	-0.54	-0.42
Yugoslavia	–	-0.05	0.06	-0.09	-0.10	0.18	0.06	-0.42	-0.25	-0.51	-0.07	0.91	0.97	0.50	1.14	1.67	1.44	0.50	0.94	0.67	0.61
Western Europe [c]	0.68	0.30	1.15	1.69	2.96	5.52	2.35	1.71	2.30	-2.60	-5.58	-5.16	-8.61	-7.58	-11.38	-6.23	-2.20	-3.80	-0.57	0.10	-2.75
Canada	0.07	0.09	0.25	0.24	-0.02	0.45	0.60	0.37	0.55	0.74	1.55	1.67	1.88	1.52	1.68	1.19	0.93	0.51	0.69	0.36	0.83
United States	0.13	0.16	0.50	1.27	0.54	2.05	2.63	1.62	2.41	4.31	2.43	2.66	2.48	1.47	1.92	1.19	-0.02	0.17	1.25	3.00	2.32
North America	0.19	0.25	0.75	1.51	0.52	2.50	3.24	1.99	2.96	5.05	3.98	4.32	4.36	2.99	3.61	2.38	0.90	0.68	1.94	3.36	3.14
Japan	-0.05	0.05	0.15	-0.25	0.18	0.98	1.58	1.20	1.72	1.28	1.68	2.43	3.07	2.04	1.39	1.85	2.07	0.94	1.37	0.54	-0.54
Developed market economies [c]	0.83	0.60	2.04	2.95	3.66	9.00	7.17	4.90	6.99	3.72	0.08	1.59	-1.17	-2.55	-6.39	-2.00	0.77	-2.17	2.74	3.99	-0.15

Sources: As for Appendix table C.6. Data cover reported balances (f.o.b.-f.o.b) with six east European countries (Bulgaria, Czechoslovakia, German Democratic Republic, Hungary, Poland, Romania) and the Soviet Union.

[a] Extrapolations based on data for January-September.
[b] Excluding trade between the Federal Republic of Germany and the German Democratic Republic.
[c] Including trade between the Federal Republic of Germany and the German Democratic Republic.

APPENDIX TABLE C.9

East-west trade: Western exports, imports and balances by eastern country

(Billion US dollars)

	1970	1971	1972	1973	1974	1975	1976	1977	1978	1979	1980	1981	1982	1983	1984	1985	1986	1987	1988	1989	1990[a]
Western exports to:																					
Bulgaria	0.35	0.35	0.38	0.54	0.91	1.15	1.00	0.94	1.15	1.31	1.71	1.97	1.64	1.68	1.57	1.98	2.32	2.47	2.51	2.54	1.79
Czechoslovakia	0.87	1.03	1.12	1.46	1.91	2.10	2.30	2.25	2.57	3.07	3.38	2.85	2.77	2.56	2.42	2.62	3.12	3.70	4.01	3.97	5.34
German Dem. Rep.	1.14	1.27	1.63	1.96	2.54	2.91	3.18	3.28	4.00	5.23	5.72	5.27	4.69	5.04	4.42	4.50	5.69	7.00	7.32	7.70	2.77
Hungary	0.67	0.80	0.88	1.16	1.88	1.91	1.90	2.41	3.10	3.13	3.47	3.46	3.14	2.86	2.78	3.08	3.71	4.11	4.16	4.87	5.50
Poland	0.92	1.11	1.75	3.23	4.67	5.59	5.63	5.14	5.73	6.21	6.67	4.47	3.39	3.12	3.23	3.45	3.68	4.25	5.21	6.43	7.10
Romania	0.73	0.79	1.04	1.43	2.16	2.09	2.10	2.39	3.08	3.88	4.02	3.11	1.77	1.37	1.45	1.51	1.76	1.31	1.27	1.26	2.77
Eastern Europe	4.68	5.35	6.80	9.78	14.07	15.76	16.12	16.42	19.63	22.83	24.96	21.13	17.40	16.62	15.88	17.14	20.28	22.85	24.52	26.76	25.27
Soviet Union	2.81	2.85	4.13	5.95	7.95	13.17	14.42	14.33	16.64	20.04	22.95	24.94	25.69	24.65	24.09	23.73	22.95	22.21	26.31	30.55	31.34
Total	7.49	8.20	10.93	15.74	22.02	28.94	30.54	30.75	36.27	42.87	47.91	46.07	43.09	41.27	39.97	40.87	43.23	45.06	50.83	57.31	56.62
Western imports (f.o.b.) from:																					
Bulgaria	0.25	0.27	0.29	0.39	0.46	0.43	0.52	0.56	0.63	0.97	1.08	0.95	0.89	0.78	0.80	0.79	0.81	0.83	0.82	0.92	1.12
Czechoslovakia	0.81	0.91	1.02	1.37	1.70	1.83	1.90	2.08	2.39	3.04	3.55	3.18	3.11	3.11	3.19	3.04	3.50	3.84	4.04	4.39	5.02
German Dem. Rep.	0.99	1.14	1.31	1.75	2.30	2.53	2.75	3.05	3.51	4.35	5.38	5.19	5.40	5.39	5.30	5.17	5.87	6.51	6.80	6.98	3.14
Hungary	0.54	0.60	0.81	1.12	1.38	1.29	1.48	1.79	2.07	2.64	2.92	2.63	2.43	2.51	2.72	2.77	3.14	3.80	4.22	4.70	5.86
Poland	1.03	1.20	1.49	2.12	2.82	3.18	3.61	3.85	4.33	5.04	5.47	3.64	3.40	3.40	4.03	4.08	4.36	5.06	5.87	6.34	8.74
Romania	0.54	0.62	0.80	1.14	1.62	1.68	2.06	1.98	2.40	3.26	3.47	3.52	2.58	2.75	3.69	3.45	3.65	4.06	4.05	3.86	2.68
Eastern Europe	4.16	4.75	5.73	7.88	10.28	10.93	12.33	13.30	15.33	19.30	21.87	19.10	17.81	17.95	19.73	19.29	21.33	24.10	25.82	27.18	26.56
Soviet Union	2.50	2.86	3.16	4.90	8.08	9.00	11.04	12.55	13.95	19.85	25.96	25.38	26.46	25.86	26.62	23.57	21.13	23.13	22.76	26.14	30.21
Total	6.66	7.61	8.89	12.79	18.36	19.93	23.37	25.86	29.28	39.14	47.83	44.48	44.27	43.81	46.36	42.87	42.46	47.23	48.09	53.32	56.77
Western trade balances with:																					
Bulgaria	0.10	0.08	0.09	0.15	0.45	0.73	0.48	0.39	0.51	0.33	0.63	1.02	0.75	0.90	0.77	1.20	1.51	1.64	1.69	1.63	0.67
Czechoslovakia	0.06	0.12	0.09	0.09	0.21	0.28	0.40	0.17	0.17	0.03	-0.17	-0.33	-0.34	-0.55	-0.77	-0.42	-0.38	-0.14	-0.04	-0.42	0.33
German Dem. Rep.	0.16	0.13	0.31	0.21	0.24	0.38	0.43	0.24	0.49	0.87	0.34	0.09	-0.71	-0.35	-0.88	-0.67	-0.19	0.49	0.52	0.72	-0.37
Hungary	0.13	0.20	0.07	0.04	0.50	0.63	0.42	0.61	1.04	0.50	0.55	0.83	0.71	0.35	0.06	0.31	0.58	0.31	-0.03	0.17	-0.36
Poland	-0.11	-0.08	0.26	1.12	1.85	2.41	2.02	1.29	1.40	1.17	1.20	0.83	-0.01	-0.29	-0.81	-0.62	-0.68	-0.81	-0.66	0.08	-1.64
Romania	0.18	0.16	0.24	0.30	0.54	0.41	0.04	0.42	0.68	0.62	0.55	-0.41	-0.81	-1.39	-2.23	-1.94	-1.89	-2.75	-2.78	-2.60	0.09
Eastern Europe	0.52	0.61	1.07	1.90	3.79	4.83	3.79	3.12	4.29	3.53	3.09	2.03	-0.41	-1.33	-3.85	-2.15	-1.05	-1.25	-1.30	-0.42	-1.29
Soviet Union	0.31	-0.01	0.97	1.05	-0.13	4.17	3.38	1.78	2.69	0.19	-3.01	-0.44	-0.77	-1.21	-2.54	0.16	1.82	-0.92	4.04	4.42	1.14
Total	0.83	0.60	2.04	2.95	3.66	9.00	7.17	4.90	6.99	3.72	0.08	1.59	-1.17	-2.55	-6.39	-2.00	0.77	-2.17	2.74	3.99	-0.15

Sources: As for Appendix tables C.6-C.8.

[a] Extrapolations based on data for January-September.

APPENDIX TABLE C.10

Eastern Europe and the Soviet Union: Balance of payments in convertible currencies

(Billion US dollars)

	1970	1971	1972	1973	1974	1975	1976	1977	1978	1979	1980	1981	1982	1983	1984	1985	1986	1987	1988	1989	1990
Bulgaria [a]																					
Merchandise export	0.5	0.5	0.5	0.7	0.9	1.0	1.1	1.2	1.5	2.4	3.3	3.4	3.1	2.7	3.3	3.3	2.7	3.3	3.5	3.1	2.5
Merchandise import	0.5	0.5	0.6	0.8	1.1	1.8	1.5	1.5	1.5	1.8	2.5	3.1	2.6	2.7	3.0	3.7	3.5	4.2	4.5	4.3	3.3
Balance	-	-	-	-0.1	-0.2	-0.8	-0.4	-0.3	0.1	0.5	0.8	0.3	0.5	0.1	0.3	-0.4	-0.8	-1.0	-1.0	-1.2	-0.8
Invisibles	-	-	-	-	-	-0.1	-	0.1	0.1	0.1	0.1	0.3	0.3	0.2	0.4	0.3	0.1	0.2	0.1	-0.1	-0.3
Current account	-	-0.1	-	-0.1	-0.2	-0.9	-0.4	-0.3	0.1	0.6	0.9	0.6	0.8	0.3	0.7	-0.1	-0.7	-0.8	-0.8	-1.3	-1.1
Czechoslovakia [a]																					
Merchandise export	0.8	1.0	1.2	1.6	2.2	2.1	2.1	2.5	2.9	3.5	4.4	4.2	4.1	4.0	4.0	3.9	4.3	4.5	5.0	5.4	5.9
Merchandise import	0.9	1.0	1.2	1.7	2.4	2.5	2.8	3.1	3.3	4.1	4.4	3.9	3.4	3.2	3.1	3.2	4.1	4.7	5.1	5.0	6.1
Balance	-0.1	-0.1	-	-0.2	-0.2	-0.4	-0.7	-0.6	-0.4	-0.5	-	0.3	0.7	0.8	0.9	0.7	0.2	-0.1	-0.1	0.4	-0.2
Invisibles	0.1	0.1	0.1	0.2	0.1	0.1	0.2	-	-	0.1	-0.3	-0.3	-0.1	0.1	0.2	0.1	0.2	0.2	0.2	-0.1	-
Current account	-	-	0.1	-	-0.1	-0.3	-0.6	-0.6	-0.4	-0.6	-0.3	-0.3	0.4	0.9	1.1	0.7	0.4	0.2	0.1	0.3	-0.2
German Democratic Republic [a]																					
Merchandise export	1.3	1.4	1.6	2.2	3.0	2.9	3.5	3.4	3.7	4.3	5.7	7.1	8.3	9.0	9.1	10.6	9.0	8.8	8.9	9.6	-
Merchandise import	1.5	1.6	2.1	2.9	4.0	4.0	5.1	4.8	4.7	6.1	7.4	7.1	6.8	7.7	8.1	7.9	8.2	9.1	9.9	10.5	-
Balance	-0.3	-0.2	-0.4	-0.7	-1.0	-1.0	-1.5	-1.4	-1.0	-1.8	-1.7	-	1.5	1.3	1.0	2.7	0.8	-0.4	-1.1	-0.9	-
Invisibles	0.2	0.2	0.2	0.3	0.1	0.2	0.3	0.3	0.3	0.5	0.1	-0.4	-0.4	-0.1	-0.1	0.1	0.3	0.6	0.5	-0.9	-
Current account	-0.1	-	-0.2	-0.5	-0.9	-0.8	-1.3	-1.1	-0.7	-1.3	-1.6	-0.4	1.1	1.2	0.9	2.8	1.1	0.2	-0.6	-0.8	-
Hungary																					
Merchandise export	0.6	0.6	0.9	1.5	2.1	2.2	2.3	2.7	3.2	4.1	4.9	4.9	4.8	4.8	4.9	4.2	4.2	5.0	5.5	6.4	6.3
Merchandise import	0.7	0.8	0.9	1.4	2.5	2.5	2.5	3.0	4.0	4.2	4.6	4.4	4.2	4.1	4.0	4.1	4.7	5.0	5.0	5.9	6.0
Balance	-0.1	-0.2	-	0.1	-0.4	-0.3	-0.2	-0.4	-0.8	-0.2	0.3	0.4	0.7	0.8	0.9	0.1	-0.5	-	0.5	0.5	0.3
Invisibles	-	-	-	-0.1	-0.1	-0.2	-0.2	-0.4	-0.5	-0.7	-0.6	-1.2	-1.0	-0.7	-0.8	-1.0	-1.0	-0.9	-1.3	-2.0	-0.2
Current account	-0.1	-0.3	-0.1	-	-0.5	-0.5	-0.4	-0.8	-1.2	-0.8	-0.4	-0.7	-0.3	0.1	0.1	-0.8	-1.5	-0.9	-0.8	-1.4	0.1
Poland																					
Merchandise export	1.1	1.3	1.6	2.3	3.5	4.1	4.3	4.7	5.3	5.9	7.2	5.5	5.0	5.4	5.8	5.8	6.2	6.9	7.0	8.1	10.9
Merchandise import	1.0	1.1	1.8	3.6	5.6	6.9	7.0	6.6	7.4	8.0	8.1	6.2	4.6	4.3	4.4	4.6	5.1	5.9	7.0	8.0	8.6
Balance	0.1	0.2	-0.2	-1.3	-2.1	-2.8	-2.7	-1.9	-2.1	-2.1	-0.9	-0.8	0.4	1.1	1.5	1.2	1.1	1.0	0.9	0.1	2.2
Invisibles	0.1	0.1	0.1	0.2	-0.2	-0.2	-0.1	-0.3	-0.4	-1.0	-1.7	-2.4	-2.6	-2.3	-2.2	-1.7	-1.7	-1.4	-1.5	-2.0	-1.5
Current account	0.1	0.3	-0.2	-1.1	-2.1	-3.0	-2.8	-2.1	-2.4	-3.1	-2.7	-3.1	-2.2	-1.2	-0.7	-0.5	-0.6	-0.4	-0.6	-1.9	0.7
Romania																					
Merchandise export	0.7	0.8	1.1	1.7	2.6	2.8	3.4	3.7	4.0	5.4	6.5	7.2	6.2	6.2	6.9	6.3	5.1	5.9	6.5	6.0	3.5
Merchandise import	0.8	0.9	1.1	1.7	2.9	2.9	3.3	3.8	4.6	6.5	8.0	7.0	4.7	4.6	4.7	4.8	3.2	3.4	2.9	3.5	5.1
Balance	-0.1	-0.1	-0.1	-0.1	-0.3	-0.1	0.1	-0.1	-0.6	-1.2	-1.5	0.2	1.5	1.7	2.2	1.4	1.9	2.4	3.6	2.6	-1.6
Invisibles	-0.1	-0.1	-0.1	-0.1	-0.2	-0.1	-0.1	-0.2	-0.2	-0.5	-0.9	-1.0	-0.9	-0.8	-0.6	-0.4	-0.4	-0.2	-	0.3	0.1
Current account	-0.2	-0.1	-0.2	-0.2	-0.5	-0.3	-0.1	-0.3	-0.8	-1.7	-2.4	-0.8	0.7	0.9	1.5	0.9	1.5	2.2	3.6	2.9	-1.5
Eastern Europe																					
Merchandise export	5.0	5.6	7.0	9.8	14.2	15.2	16.7	18.2	20.6	25.6	31.9	32.3	31.5	32.2	34.0	34.0	31.5	34.4	37.3	38.7	29.1
Merchandise import	5.4	6.0	7.7	12.1	18.4	20.7	22.2	22.8	25.4	30.7	35.0	31.7	26.3	26.5	27.3	28.2	28.7	32.4	34.5	37.3	29.1
Balance	-0.4	-0.4	-0.8	-2.3	-4.2	-5.4	-5.5	-4.6	-4.8	-5.2	-3.1	0.5	5.1	5.7	6.7	5.8	2.7	2.1	2.9	1.5	-
Invisibles	0.1	0.3	0.4	0.5	0.3	-0.3	0.1	-0.5	-0.7	-1.7	-3.3	-5.0	-4.5	-3.5	-3.0	-2.8	-2.4	-1.6	-1.9	-3.7	-2.1
Current account	-0.3	-0.1	-0.3	-1.8	-4.2	-5.7	-5.5	-5.2	-5.5	-6.9	-6.4	-4.5	0.7	2.2	3.7	3.0	0.3	0.5	0.9	-2.2	-2.1
Soviet Union [a]																					
Merchandise export	4.8	5.1	5.7	9.5	13.6	14.2	16.6	20.7	22.8	30.9	38.2	39.1	43.4	44.2	43.3	36.9	34.6	40.8	42.7	45.1	48.8
Merchandise import	4.3	4.6	6.2	9.0	12.0	18.7	19.3	18.8	21.8	26.7	34.8	39.9	39.1	38.0	36.6	36.2	33.3	32.7	39.2	47.4	50.2
Balance	0.4	0.5	-0.4	0.5	1.6	-4.5	-2.7	1.9	0.9	4.2	3.4	-0.7	4.3	6.2	6.7	0.7	1.4	8.1	3.5	-2.3	-1.4
Invisibles	0.5	0.3	0.3	0.6	0.7	0.3	0.1	-	0.1	0.1	-0.4	-0.9	-0.7	-0.4	-	-0.6	-1.0	-1.0	-1.2	-1.7	-3.1
Current account	0.9	0.8	-0.2	1.1	2.4	-4.2	-2.6	1.9	1.0	4.3	3.0	-1.6	3.6	5.8	6.7	0.1	0.4	7.1	2.3	-4.0	-4.3
Eastern Europe and the Soviet Union																					
Merchandise export	9.7	10.7	12.7	19.3	27.8	29.4	33.3	38.9	43.4	56.5	70.2	71.4	74.9	76.4	77.4	70.9	66.1	75.2	80.0	83.9	77.8
Merchandise import	9.8	10.6	13.9	21.0	30.4	39.3	41.4	41.7	47.3	57.5	69.8	71.6	65.4	64.5	64.0	64.4	62.0	65.0	73.7	84.7	79.3
Balance	0.1	0.1	-1.2	-1.8	-2.6	-9.9	-8.1	-2.8	-3.9	-0.9	0.3	-0.2	9.4	11.9	13.4	6.5	4.1	10.2	6.3	-0.8	-1.5
Invisibles	0.6	0.6	-0.2	1.1	0.7	-	0.1	-0.5	-1.6	-1.6	-3.7	-5.9	-5.2	-3.9	-3.0	-3.4	-3.4	-2.6	-3.2	-5.4	-5.1
Current account	0.6	0.7	-0.5	-0.7	-1.9	-9.9	-8.1	-3.3	-4.5	-2.6	-3.4	-6.1	4.2	8.0	10.4	3.1	0.8	7.6	3.2	-6.1	-6.6

Sources: ECE secretariat Common Data Base. National statistics for Bulgaria, *Czechoslovakia,* Hungary (revised data for 1982-1990; IMF, *Balance of Payment Statistics* for 1971-1981), Poland and Romania. ECE estimates for GDR and the Soviet Union. For these two countries trade balances reflect trade with all developed and developing market economies (non-socialist countries *plus* Yugoslavia) based upon national foreign trade statistics.

Note: Substantial discontinuities in the value series are indicated by ‖.

[a] Trade with all developed and developing market economies (non-socialist countries *plus* Yugoslavia) based upon national foreign trade statistics.

APPENDIX TABLE C.11

Eastern Europe and the Soviet Union: Gross debt, foreign currency reserves and debt in convertible currencies

(Billion US dollars)

	1970	1971	1972	1973	1974	1975	1976	1977	1978	1979	1980	1981	1982	1983	1984	1985	1986	1987	1988	1989	1990
Gross debt																					
Bulgaria	0.7	0.8	1.0	1.1	1.8	2.7	3.3	3.8	4.4	4.6	4.9	4.1	3.5	3.1	2.9	4.1	5.5	7.4	9.1	10.7	11.1
Czechoslovakia	0.3	0.4	0.6	0.7	1.0	1.0	1.7	2.4	3.0	3.8	6.8	6.3	5.8	5.2	4.7	4.6	5.6	6.7	7.3	7.9	8.1
German Democratic Republic	1.1	1.4	1.5	2.2	3.2	5.2	6.0	7.5	9.3	11.1	13.6	14.4	12.6	12.1	11.6	13.6	16.1	19.1	20.2	33.0 [a]	..
Hungary	1.0	1.5	1.9	2.3	3.1	3.9	4.5	5.2	7.6	8.3	9.1	8.7	10.2	10.7	11.0	14.0	16.9	19.6	19.6	20.6	21.3
Poland	1.2	1.1	1.2	2.6	5.2	8.4	12.1	14.9	18.6	23.7	24.1	25.9	26.3	26.4	26.9	29.3	33.5	39.2	39.2	40.8	48.5
Romania	1.0	1.2	1.2	1.6	2.9	2.9	2.8	3.6	5.1	7.2	9.6	10.2	8.9	8.9	7.2	6.6	6.4	5.7	1.9	0.7	1.2
Eastern Europe	5.1	6.4	7.5	10.4	16.9	24.2	30.6	37.5	48.0	58.7	68.1	69.6	68.1	66.3	64.4	72.2	84.0	97.6	97.3	113.7	90.2
Soviet Union	1.6	2.6	4.2	6.0	8.1	15.4	20.9	22.7	24.4	26.1	25.2	29.0	28.4	26.9	25.6	31.4	37.4	40.2	49.4	58.5	62.5
Eastern Europe and the Soviet Union	6.7	9.0	11.7	16.4	25.0	39.5	51.5	60.2	72.4	84.8	93.3	98.6	96.5	93.2	89.9	103.6	121.3	137.9	146.7	172.2	152.7
Foreign currency reserves [b]																					
Bulgaria	-	-	0.1	-	0.3	0.4	0.4	0.5	0.6	0.7	0.8	0.8	1.0	1.2	1.4	2.1	1.4	1.1	1.8	1.2	0.6 [c]
Czechoslovakia	0.3	0.3	0.5	0.5	0.4	0.3	0.4	0.5	0.7	1.0	1.3	1.1	0.7	0.9	1.0	1.0	1.2	1.6	1.7	2.2	1.3
German Democratic Republic	0.2	0.2	0.3	0.3	0.5	1.6	0.8	0.9	1.3	2.0	2.0	2.2	1.9	3.4	4.5	6.2	7.5	9.0	9.5	9.5	..
Hungary	0.2	0.2	0.3	0.3	0.6	0.9	1.2	1.1	0.9	1.2	1.4	0.9	0.7	1.3	1.5	2.3	2.1	1.5	1.4	1.2	1.2
Poland	0.3	0.4	0.4	0.6	0.5	0.7	0.8	0.4	0.8	1.2	0.7	0.8	1.0	1.2	1.5	1.6	1.7	3.0	3.6	2.3	5.2
Romania	-	-	-	0.1	0.5	1.5	0.4	0.2	0.3	0.3	0.3	0.3	0.6	0.5	0.6	0.3	0.6	1.4	0.8	1.8	0.3
Eastern Europe	1.1	1.2	1.7	1.8	2.6	5.4	4.1	3.6	4.6	6.4	6.4	6.0	5.5	8.5	10.8	13.6	14.8	17.6	18.8	18.2	8.6 [c]
Soviet Union	1.0	1.2	1.9	2.6	3.5	3.1	4.7	4.4	6.1	8.8	8.6	8.5	10.0	10.9	11.3	13.1	14.8	14.1	15.3	14.7	7.8 [c]
Eastern Europe and the Soviet Union	2.1	2.4	3.5	4.4	6.1	8.5	8.8	8.0	10.7	15.2	14.9	14.4	15.6	19.5	22.1	26.7	29.4	31.7	34.1	32.8	16.4
Total convertible currency assets [d]																					
Hungary	0.6	0.8	1.0	1.5	1.7	2.0	2.3	2.4	3.1	3.3	3.7	3.2	2.9	3.8	4.4	5.9	6.2	5.9	5.6	5.5	5.2
Romania	..	..	..	..	..	..	..	..	..	2.0	1.7	1.9	2.3	2.9	3.6	3.0	3.1	3.2	3.3	3.1	3.2
Net debt (reflecting foreign currency reserves)																					
Bulgaria	0.6	0.7	0.9	1.0	1.4	2.3	2.9	3.3	3.8	3.9	4.1	3.3	2.5	1.9	1.5	2.0	4.1	6.3	7.3	9.5	10.5
Czechoslovakia	-	0.1	0.1	0.2	0.6	0.7	1.3	1.9	2.3	2.8	5.6	5.3	5.0	4.2	3.7	3.6	4.4	5.1	5.6	5.7	6.8
German Democratic Republic	0.9	1.2	1.2	1.9	2.6	3.6	5.2	6.6	8.0	9.2	11.6	12.3	10.7	8.7	7.1	7.3	8.6	10.1	10.7	23.5	..
Hungary	0.8	1.3	1.5	2.0	2.5	3.0	3.3	4.1	6.7	7.1	7.7	7.8	9.5	9.4	9.4	11.7	14.8	18.1	18.2	19.4	20.1
Poland	0.9	0.7	0.8	2.0	4.7	7.7	11.3	14.5	17.7	22.6	23.5	25.1	25.3	25.2	25.4	27.7	31.8	36.2	35.6	38.5	43.3
Romania	1.0	1.2	1.2	1.5	2.4	1.4	2.4	3.4	4.8	6.9	9.3	9.9	9.5	8.4	6.6	6.3	5.8	4.3	1.1	-1.1	0.9
Eastern Europe	4.0	5.2	5.8	8.6	14.3	18.8	26.5	33.9	43.4	52.3	61.7	63.6	62.6	57.8	53.6	58.6	69.4	80.1	78.5	95.5	81.6
Soviet Union	0.6	1.4	2.3	3.4	4.6	12.2	16.1	18.3	18.3	17.3	16.6	20.5	18.4	16.0	14.2	18.3	22.5	26.1	34.1	43.8	54.7
Eastern Europe and the Soviet Union	4.6	6.6	8.2	12.0	18.8	31.0	42.7	52.2	61.7	69.6	78.3	84.1	81.0	73.8	67.9	76.9	91.9	106.1	112.6	139.3	136.3
Net debt (reflecting total convertible currency assets)																					
Hungary	0.4	0.7	0.9	0.8	1.4	1.9	2.3	2.9	4.5	5.0	5.4	5.5	7.3	7.0	6.5	8.0	10.7	13.7	14.0	15.1	16.1
Romania	..	..	..	..	..	..	..	..	..	5.2	7.8	8.2	7.5	6.0	3.6	3.6	3.3	2.5	-1.4	-2.4	-2.0

Sources: ECE secretariat Common Data Base. National statistics for Bulgaria (1980-1990), the German Democratic Republic (1989), Hungary (revised data 1982-1990), Poland, Romania (1970-1990) and Soviet Union (1988, 1990). For the German Democratic Republic (1980-1988) and the Soviet Union (1980-1987) (including CMEA banks): BIS/OECD *Statistics on External Indebtedness: Bank and trade Related Non-Bank External Claims on Individual Borrowing Countries and Territories*, Paris and Basle (various years). BIS/OECD figures are adjusted here to include gross claims of the Federal Republic of Germany *vis-à-vis* the German Democratic Republic arising from clearing exchanges). For these three countries data reflect convertible currency debt *vis-à-vis* reporting institutions only and thus exclude any claims of developing countries. Secretariat estimates for Bulgaria, Czechoslovakia, the German Democratic Republic and the Soviet Union prior to first discontinuity. IMF, *International Financial Statistics*, March 1991; BIS, *International Banking and Financial Market Developments*, various issues.

Note: Substantial discontinuities in the series are indicated by `·║·`.

[a] End-May 1990.
[b] For Bulgaria, the German Democratic Republic and Soviet Union, assets with BIS reporting banks; also for other countries prior to discontinuity in series.
[c] End-September.
[d] International reserves *plus* other assets (mainly trade credits). Hungarian gold reserves at national valuation: $275/oz (1982-1985); $320/oz (1986-1990).) Romania's gold reserves valued at SDR 35/oz.

SPECIAL STUDIES PUBLISHED IN THE *ECONOMIC SURVEY OF EUROPE* AND THE *ECONOMIC BULLETIN FOR EUROPE* IN THE PERIOD 1981-1990

1. Region-wide and global studies

"Structural changes in north-south trade, with emphasis on the trade of the ECE region, 1965-1983", *Economic Bulletin for Europe*, vol.36, No.4, Published by Pergamon Press for the United Nations, December 1984, chapter 3

"World imports of engineering goods, 1961-1985", *Economic Bulletin for Europe,* vol.39, No.4, Published by Pergamon Press for the United Nations, December 1987

"Long-term prospects in ECE countries: National and international aspects", *Economic Bulletin for Europe,* vol.40, No.4, Published by Pergamon Press for the United Nations, 1988

"Europe's trade in engineering goods: Specialization and technology", *Economic Survey of Europe in 1989-1990,* New York, 1989, Sales No. E.90.II.E.1

2. Market economies of Europe and North America

"Changing trends in productivity growth", *Economic Survey of Europe in 1981*, New York, 1982, Sales No. E.82.II.E.1

"Recent changes in the structure of output and employment in the manufacturing sector of southern Europe", *ibid.*

"The decline in productivity growth after 1973: A further look at explanatory factors", *Economic Survey of Europe in 1982*, New York, 1983, Sales No. E.83.II.E.1

"Aspects of labour market and population developments in western Europe and North America", *Economic Bulletin for Europe*, vol.35, No.3, Published by Pergamon Press for the United Nations, September 1983

"The demand for capital, labour and energy in manufacturing industry before and after the oil shocks", *Economic Survey of Europe in 1983*, New York, 1984, Sales No. E.84.II.E.1

"Monetary policy in the 1980s in the larger market economies", *Economic Survey of Europe in 1985-1986*, New York, 1986, Sales No. E.86.II.E.1

"Alternative measures of productivity growth in the manufacturing sectors of the market economies", *ibid.*

"Early retirement schemes and unemployment", *ibid.*

"Aspects of capital formation in manufacturing industry", *Economic Survey of Europe in 1986-1987*, New York, 1987, Sales No. E.87.II.E.1

"Demographic change and public expenditure", *ibid.*

"Wage rigidity in western Europe and North America" *Economic Survey of Europe in 1987-1988,* New York, 1988, Sales No. E.88.II.E.1

"German economic and monetary union", *The ECE economies in mid-1990*, Geneva, 1990

"The unification of Germany", *Economic Bulletin for Europe*, vol.42, New York, 1990, Sales No. E.90.II.E.37

3. Eastern Europe and the Soviet Union

"Recent economic developments and five-year plans in eastern Europe and the Soviet Union", *Economic Survey of Europe in 1981*, New York, 1982, Sales No. E.82.II.E.1

"Changes in the rate of growth of labour productivity in the centrally-planned economies during the 1970s: Preliminary analysis", *Economic Survey of Europe in 1982*, New York, 1983, Sales No. E.83.II.E.1

"Changes in management and planning of agriculture during the 1970s" (in the centrally planned economies), *Economic Survey of Europe in 1983*, New York, 1984, Sales No. E.84.II.E.1

"Recent developments in the non-material sphere" (of eastern Europe and the Soviet Union), *Economic Survey of Europe in 1984-1985*, New York, 1985, Sales No. E.85.II.E.1

"The commodity structure of east European and Soviet trade at constant prices, 1960-1984: A statistical note", *Economic Bulletin for Europe*, vol.37, No.4, Published by Pergamon Press for the United Nations, December 1985

"Productivity trends in eastern Europe and the Soviet Union, 1970-1983", *Economic Survey of Europe in 1985-1986*, New York, 1986, Sales No. E.86.II.E.1

"Agricultural inputs and efficiency 1970-1985" (in the centrally planned economies), *Economic Survey of Europe in 1986-1987*, New York, 1987, Sales No. E.87.II.E.1

"Energy production, consumption and trade" (in the centrally planned economies), *ibid.*

"Five-year plans 1986-1990 in eastern Europe and the Soviet Union", *ibid.*, chapter 4

"Agricultural country profiles for eastern Europe and the Soviet Union, 1981-1985", *Economic Survey of Europe in 1987-1988*, New York, 1988, Sales No. E.88.II.E.1

"Structural changes in industry of eastern Europe and the Soviet Union, 1971-1990", *ibid.*

"East-west agricultural and food trade: development and prospects", *Economic Bulletin for Europe*, vol.40, No.3, Published by Pergamon Press for the United Nations, 1988, chapter 3

"Retail trade in eastern Europe and the Soviet Union," *Economic Survey of Europe in 1988-1989*, New York, 1989, Sales No. E.89.II.E.1

"Note on the accuracy of the Soviet output statistics", *ibid.*

"Developments in the service sector" (of eastern Europe and the Soviet Union), *Economic Survey of Europe in 1989-1990*, New York, 1990, Sales No. E.90.II.E.1

4. International trade and payments

"Changing comparative advantages in manufactured exports from southern Europe, 1965-1978", *Economic Bulletin for Europe*, vol.33, No.4, Published by Pergamon Press for the United Nations, December 1981

"The relative performance of south European exports of manufactures to OECD countries in the 1970s: An analysis of demand factors and competitiveness", *Economic Bulletin for Europe*, vol.34, No.4, Published by Pergamon Press for the United Nations, December 1982

"Determinants of the export performance of south European countries", *Economic Survey of Europe in 1983*, New York, 1984, Sales No. E.84.II.E.1

"Aspects of intra-west European trade in manufactures, 1962-1985", *Economic Survey of Europe in 1987-1988*, New York, 1988, Sales No. E.88.II.E.1

"The effects of west European integration on imports of manufactures from eastern and southern Europe", *Economic Survey of Europe in 1988-1989*, New York, 1989, Sales No. E.89.II.E.1

"Economic integration and the export performance of west European countries outside the EC", *Economic Survey of Europe in 1989-1990*, New York, 1990, Sales No. E.90.II.E.1

"The free trade agreement between Canada and the United States", *Economic Bulletin for Europe*, vol.42, New York, 1990 Sales No. E.90.II.E.37

5. East-west trade and payments

"The determinants of east-west trade", *Economic Bulletin for Europe*, vol.33, No.4, Published by Pergamon Press for the United Nations, December 1981

"Exports of manufactures from eastern Europe and the Soviet Union to the developed market economies, 1965-1981", *Economic Bulletin for Europe*, vol.35, No.4, Published by Pergamon Press for the United Nations, December 1983

"The changing intensity of east-west trade", *Economic Bulletin for Europe*, vol.37, No.4, Published by Pergamon Press for the United Nations, December 1985

"Investment goods trade of the east European countries and the Soviet Union, 1975-1983", *Economic Survey of Europe in 1985-1986*, New York, 1986, Sales No. E.86.II.E.1

"Eastern imports of machinery and equipment, 1960-1985", *Economic Bulletin for Europe*, vol.38, No.4, Published by Pergamon Press for the United Nations, December 1986

"Eastern consumer goods imports from market economies, 1962-1986", *Economic Survey of Europe in 1987-1988*, New York, 1988, Sales No. E.88.II.E.1

"A note on recent developments in east-west trade in services", *Economic Bulletin for Europe*, vol.41, New York, 1989, Sales No. E.89.II.E.26

"East-west trade in investment goods, 1970-1987", *ibid.*

6. Economic reforms in eastern Europe and the Soviet Union

"Review of current and prospective economic reforms", *Economic Survey of Europe in 1987-1988,* New York, 1988, Sales No. E.88.II.E.1

"Economic reform in the east: a framework for western support", *Economic Survey of Europe in 1989-1990,* New York, 1990, Sales No. E.90.II.E.1

"International initiative in support of eastern reforms", *ibid.*

"Overview" (of economic reforms at the beginning of 1990), *ibid.*

"Economic reform in Poland", *ibid.*

"Economic reform in Hungary", *ibid.*

"Economic reform in the Soviet Union", *ibid.*

"Economic reform in Yugoslavia", *ibid.*

Monographs published by ECE in 1986-1990

1. *Overall economic perspective to the year 2000,* United Nations, New York, 1988 (Sales No. E.88.II.E.4)

2. *Economic reforms in the European centrally planned economies,* United Nations, New York, 1989 (Sales No. GV.E.89.0.3)

3. *Economic reforms and their significance for all-European economic co-operation,* United Nations, New York, 1990 (A transcript of the Round-table organized under the auspices of the Senior Economic Advisers to the ECE Governments in May 1990.)

The publications listed above may be obtained from bookstores and distributors throughout the world. Consult your bookstore or write to: United Nations, Sales Section, Palais des Nations, CH-1211 Geneva 10

ECONOMIC BULLETIN FOR EUROPE

The *Bulletin* has been published regularly since 1948. Between 1981 and 1988 volumes 33 to 40 were published by Pergamon Press for the United Nations. In 1989 publication was resumed by the United Nations. The *Bulletin* now appears once a year in December and contains a review of recent economic developments in Europe and North America, with special emphasis on the trade of the eastern economies in transition, as well as occasional research papers on international trade.

Sales No. E.90.II.E.37   *US$ 55.00*

***

REFORMS IN THE FOREIGN ECONOMIC RELATIONS OF EASTERN EUROPE AND THE SOVIET UNION
(UN/ECE Economic Studies, No.2)

This volume presents the results of an international symposium organized by the ECE in association with Osteuropa Institut and Südost-Institut of Munich, Germany. Three subjects are dealt with in detail:

- institutional framework for foreign economic relations

- economic relations with market economies

- economic relations with CMEA member countries

In addition to country reports, written by national experts and containing an analysis of latest developments, legislation and prospects, there are also comments by western experts on each of the reports, and summaries of the discussion.

Sales No. E.91.II.E.5   *US$ 60.00*

***

ADVANCED POPULATION AGING IN EUROPE AND NORTH AMERICA – DEMOGRAPHIC AND ECONOMIC ASPECTS
(UN/ECE Economic Studies, No.3)

The essays contained in this volume were prepared under a research project of the Economic Commission for Europe on the economic and social consequences of aging in Europe and North America. They include country case studies, as well as cross-country studies. Some essays focus on the demographic aspects of population aging, including the effects of changing vital rates on aging. Others are concerned with the impact of aging on the economy, public expenditure and the labour market.

Forthcoming

***

EAST-WEST JOINT VENTURES NEWS

East-West Joint Ventures News provides information and analysis of new legislation affecting joint ventures in central and eastern Europe, and describes the growth and spread of these firms' operations, drawing on the Economic Commission for Europe's Data Base on East-West Joint Ventures. This Newsletter, which is published every quarter, also contains reviews of recent publications and information on relevant forthcoming conferences.

Those interested in receiving this publication may write to:

Trade Division
Economic Commission for Europe
Palais des Nations
8-10, aveune de la Paix
CH-1211 Geneva 10

***

Further details of these and other ECE publications (except the Joint Ventures News) can be obtained from:

United Nations Bookshop/Sales Section
Palais des Nations
8-10 avenue de la Paix
CH-1211 Geneva 10